3 I

1

August 2007

MW01613734

Ronald T. Borchardt   Edward H. Kerns
Michael J. Hageman   Dhiren R. Thakker
James L. Stevens
Editors

Optimizing the "Drug-Like" Properties of Leads in Drug Discovery

 Springer

Ronald T. Borchardt
University of Kansas
Lawrence, KS 66045
USA
rborchardt@ku.edu

Michael J. Hageman
Pfizer, Inc.
Kalamazoo, MI 49007
USA
Michael.hagemant@bms.com

James L. Stevens
Eli Lilly Research Laboratory
Greenfield, IN 46285
USA

Edward H. Kerns
Wyeth Research
Monmouth Junction, NJ 08852
USA
kernse@wyeth.com

Dhiren R. Thakker
University of North Carolina
Chapel Hill, NC 27599
USA
dhiren_thakker@unc.edu

Library of Congress Control Number: 2006927190

ISBN-10: 0-387-34056-4
ISBN-13: 978-0387-34056-2

Printed on acid-free paper.

Printed in the United States of America.   (IBT)

9 8 7 6 5 4 3 2 1

springer.com

Preface

Drug discovery and development is a very complex, costly, and time-consuming process. Because of the uncertainties associated with predicting the pharmacological effects and the toxicity characteristics of new chemical entities in man, their clinical development is quite prone to failure. In recent years, pharmaceutical companies have come under increasing pressure to introduce new blockbuster drugs into the marketplace more rapidly. Companies have responded to these pressures by introducing new technologies and new strategies to expedite drug discovery and development.

Drug discovery and development have traditionally been divided into three separate processes (i.e., discovery research, preclinical development, and clinical development) that ideally should be integrated both organizationally and functionally. Instead, separate and distinct discovery research, preclinical development, and clinical development divisions were created within many companies during the 1980s and 1990s, Because of their isolation, scientists in the discovery research divisions often were advancing drug candidates into preclinical development that had marginal drug-like properties. For the purpose of this presentation, "drug-like" properties refer to the molecule's physicochemical, absorption-distribution-metabolism-excretion (ADME), and toxicological properties. Lacking optimal drug-like properties often caused these drug candidates to fail in preclinical or clinical development. The increase in the number of drug candidates being advanced into development with marginal drug-like properties arose in part because: (i) discovery scientists did not fully appreciate the complete portfolio of characteristics that a drug candidate must have to succeed in preclinical and clinical development; and (ii) a paradigm shift occurred in discovery research in the late 1980s and early 1990s. This drug discovery paradigm shift involved a transition from whole animal, disease-based screens to biochemical-based screens, which use isolated and purified macromolecules (e.g. receptors, enzymes) assayed *in vitro*. The whole animal, disease-based screens had the advantage that they afforded information about a molecule's pharmacological as well as drug-like properties. For the purposes of this presentation, "pharmacological properties" refers to the molecule's physiological (e.g. decrease blood pressure) or behavioral (e.g. antidepressant) effects in animals and man. In contrast, the biochemical-based screens afforded only information about a molecule's affinity and specificity for the macromolecule(s) thought to mediate its pharmacological effects in animals and man.

Unfortunately, the drug design paradigm that developed in the late 1980's and early 1990's often involved only the interactions of medicinal chemists with biologists (biochemists, cell biologists, molecular biologists, and pharmacologists) in the discovery research division within a company. Input from preclinical development scientists, who have the knowledge and expertise in areas such as physicochemical properties, ADME properties, and toxicological properties, was not sought by the medicinal chemists during this phase of drug design. The result was that scientists in discovery research were advancing what they thought were high quality drug candidates into preclinical development. However, in reality, these compounds were simply high affinity ligands. For the purpose of this presentation, high affinity ligands refer to molecules that bind with high affinity and specificity to a macromolecular target but lack one or more optimal drug-like property.

Retrospective analysis data from the 1980s and 1990s has shown that these high affinity ligands failed in preclinical and clinical development for various scientific reasons including lack of efficacy and/or lack of optimal drug-like properties. The failures arising from the lack of drug-like properties could be due to the paradigm shift in drug discovery described above and/or the availability of new knowledge and more precise and selective assays for characterizing a molecule's physicochemical, ADME, and toxicological properties. Even if these marginal drug candidates succeeded in preclinical and clinical development, they would cost more in time and money to develop into commercial products.

Traditionally, incorporating optimal drug-like properties into a structural lead was not considered by medicinal chemists to be their responsibility. Instead, medicinal chemists felt that the undesirable drug-like properties in their drug candidates would be fixed by preclinical development scientists. However, that view has changed in the past 5–10 years, resulting in another significant paradigm shift in drug discovery. The most significant aspect of this latest paradigm shift is the recognition by medicinal chemists that the drug-like properties of structural hits, structural leads, and drug candidates are intrinsic properties of the molecules and that it is the responsibility of the medicinal chemist to optimize not only the pharmacological properties but also the drug-like properties of these molecules. Therefore, assessment of these drug-like properties is now done early in the drug discovery process on structural hits and structural leads as well as the design of screening libraries. Optimization of these drug-like properties is done through an iterative process in close collaboration with preclinical development scientists. This process is analogous to the process used by the medicinal chemist to characterize and optimize the pharmacological activity of their structural hits, leads and drug candidates.

Recognizing these changes in the paradigm by which drugs are discovered, the American Association of Pharmaceutical Scientists (AAPS) has recently organized and sponsored two focused workshops in the area of profiling drug-like properties during drug discovery.

The first workshop, entitled "Pharmaceutical Profiling in Drug Discovery for Lead Selection", took place in Whippany, NJ on May 19-21, 2003. This workshop, which was co-sponsored by the American Chemical Society-Medicinal Chemistry Division and the Society for Biomolecular Screening, was focused on prediction, measurement, and utilization of drug-like properties during lead selection. From this workshop arose the book entitled **Pharmaceutical Profiling in Drug Discovery for Lead Selection**, which was edited by Ronald T. Borchardt, Edward H. Kerns, Christopher A. Lipinski, Dhiren R. Thakker and Binghe Wang and published by AAPS Press (Arlington, VA) in 2004.

The second workshop entitled "Optimizing the Drug-Like Properties of Leads in Drug Discovery" took place in Parsippany, NJ on September 19-22, 2004. This workshop, which was co-sponsored by the American Chemical Society-Medicinal Chemistry Division, American Chemical Society-North Jersey Section, American Society for Clinical Pharmacology and Therapeutics, European Federation for Pharmaceutical Sciences, International Society for the study of Xenobiotics, and the Society of Toxicology, was focused on the optimization of the drug-like properties of leads in drug discovery. If the strategies and the methodologies presented at this workshop were to be adopted by pharmaceutical and biotechnology companies, it is the belief of the workshop's organizers that more higher quality drug candidates would be advancing into preclinical and clinical development resulting in more efficacious and safer drugs.

To insure that these strategies and methodologies for the optimization of the drug-like properties of leads in drug discovery are disseminated to the broadest audience possible, the workshop's organizing committee decided to edit the workshop proceedings in the form of this book entitled **Optimizing the Drug-Like Properties of Leads in Drug Discovery**. This book was edited by Ronald T. Borchardt, Edward H. Kerns, Michael J. Hageman, Dhiren R. Thakker and James L. Stevens and published by Springer/AAPS Press in 2006.

Ronald T. Borchardt, *The University of Kansas at Lawrence*
Edward H. Kerns, *Wyeth Research*
Michael J. Hageman, *Pfizer, Inc.*
Dhiren R. Thakker, *The University of North Carolina at Chapel Hill*
James L. Stevens, *Eli Lilly and Company*

Contents

1

Strategic Use of Preclinical Pharmacokinetic Studies and *In Vitro* Models in Optimizing ADME Properties of Lead Compounds

Dhiren R. Thakker

Division of Drug Molecular Pharmaceutics
School of Pharmacy
The University of North Carolina at Chapel Hill
Chapel Hill, NC 27599-7360

Table of Contents

List of Abbreviations

ADME......................absorption, distribution, metabolism, and excretion
PK..pharmacokinetic or pharmacokinetics
P-gp ....P-glycoprotein
CYP..cytochrome P450
Papp ....apparent permeability coefficient
AP...apical
BL...basolateral
P_{PD} ....permeability due to passive diffusion
AQ ....absorptive quotient
RT-PCR ....reverse transcriptase polymerase chain reaction

Key words

ADME, absorption, metabolism, distribution, excretion, *in vitro* ADME models, ADME deficiencies in drug candidates, P-glycoprotein, cytochrome P450, intestinal transport

Introduction

The discovery of novel therapies for a disease often begins with identifying the cellular and biochemical target whose malfunction is implicated in the initiation or progression of the disease. Because abnormally high or low activity of proteins (receptors, enzymes, or transporters) or of the genes that code for these proteins is the underlying cause of most diseases, therapeutic intervention requires modulation of the target protein or gene activity by chemical agents. Identifying the chemical agents that can modulate activities of specific proteins or genes with a high degree of selectivity and potency through rational design or high throughput screening with combinatorial libraries has become a less daunting task in the past two decades. This is because most proteins can be readily expressed, isolated, and structurally characterized, their functional activity can be assessed using *in vitro* systems, and vast numbers of compounds can be synthesized using combinatorial approaches as potential modulators of their expression or functional activity. However, it is important to recognize that the therapeutic efficacy of these agents in humans can only by achieved if sufficiently high concentration of these compounds can be attained and maintained at the target site. This requires that the compound has appropriate physicochemical properties so that (i) it can be absorbed effectively from the site of administration (e.g. gastrointestinal tract for orally administered compounds), (ii) it escapes extensive metabolism in the liver and other extrahepatic tissues, (iii) it is distributed sufficiently in the target tissue, and (iv) it is not excreted too rapidly via the renal or the hepatobiliary clearance mechanisms. Thus, the physiological processes involved in the absorption, distribution, metabolism, and excretion (ADME) of a compound are important determinants of its therapeutic efficacy. Therefore, physicochemical properties of compounds should be optimized not only with respect to their potency and selectivity for modulating the target protein or gene, but also with respect to their ability to overcome barriers posed by the ADME processes in achieving optimum concentration at the target within the human body. Thus it is not surprising that studies designed to assess and optimize the ADME properties have become an integral part of the drug discovery process in most pharmaceutical companies. As a result, clinical failure of lead compounds due to adverse ADME properties (Caldwell et al., 2001; Kerns and Li, 2003) has declined from 30-40% (Kennedy, 1997) to ~10% in recent years (Biller, personal communication at AAPS workshop on Pharmaceutical Profiling in Drug Discovery for Lead Selection, 2003). However, it is important to note that the approaches used to assess and optimize the ADME properties of compounds and the extent to which these approaches are integrated in the lead optimization process vary significantly among companies in the pharmaceutical industry. In this chapter, tools and strategies for assessing and optimizing ADME properties of lead compounds are discussed. The goal of this review is not to provide a comprehensive catalog of all the *in vitro* and *in vivo* ADME models, but rather to focus the discussion on how best to use the contemporary ADME models to assess and optimize the ADME properties for the purpose of identifying or designing discovery leads that would perform well in the clinic.

Assessing the ADME Properties:
Role of *In Vitro* and *In Vivo* Models

In order to ensure that the lead candidate will have optimum ADME properties in humans prior to any clinical testing, it is important to have model systems that can serve as surrogates for human ADME processes. Historically, ADME properties have been evaluated in preclinical species such as rodents, dogs, primates, etc. by conducting pharmacokinetic (PK) studies, and extrapolated to humans based on the PK parameters obtained in several preclinical species (reviewed in Rowland, 1985; Obach et al., 1997). This approach suffers from two major pitfalls as it pertains to lead optimization. Firstly, these studies are laborious and time-consuming, and therefore they do not allow evaluation of sufficiently large number of compounds. Second, the prediction of ADME properties in humans is often wrong because the selectivity and activity of transporters and enzymes associated with the ADME processes can be quite different across different species. Over the past several years, advances in molecular biology techniques have made it possible to clone and express drug metabolizing enzymes and transporters of human origin. These proteins and cells of human origin are employed as *in vitro* systems to assess ADME properties of drug candidates (reviewed in Maurel, 1996; Iwatsubo et al, 1996; Obach et al., 1997) with the anticipation that such models will be more predictive of ADME processes in humans. However, it is important to recognize that these *in vitro* systems measure ADME properties of compounds in a relatively simple environment that is very different from the complex *in vivo* environment where several different enzymes, transporters, and physiological processes compete with each other. Hence, these *in vitro* systems often fail to predict ADME properties (e.g. metabolic clearance) of compounds in humans despite the fact that they employ enzymes and transporters of human origin.

A preferred strategy for predicting ADME behavior of compounds in humans is to combine the use of *in vitro* models and targeted PK studies in preclinical species. A well designed set of PK studies in a preclinical species can identify specific ADME processes that are responsible for inadequate systemic or target organ exposure to the drug candidate under investigation. Based on this information, appropriate *in vitro* models can be employed to assess specific ADME properties of the lead compound and its structural analogs so as to identify compounds that exhibit poor, moderate, and good behavior with respect to the ADME property being investigated. The *in vivo* behavior of these compounds is evaluated to determine if the *in vitro* model predicts the correct rank order of compounds with respect to the ADME property under investigation. If this is not so, then further PK and *in vitro* studies should be conducted iteratively to determine the source of the "disconnect" between the *in vitro* model and the *in vivo* ADME behavior of the compounds. Such studies often allow refinement of the *in vitro* system with respect to modeling the *in vivo* ADME behavior that is being optimized. Such refinements in the *in vitro* model derived from the

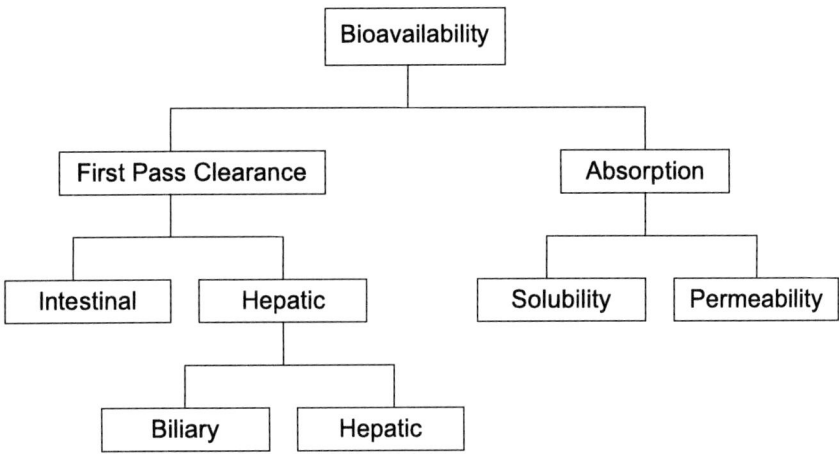

Figure 1. Determinants of oral bioavailability and a decision-tree to assess their role.

preclinical species can be applied to the *in vitro* models of human origin, leading to better prediction of the ADME behavior of the drug candidates in humans.

The initial PK studies in preclinical species with a small number of compounds within a lead series yield parameters, such as oral bioavailability and clearance, which allow overall assessment of the ADME-related problems associated with the lead compounds. Thus, if compounds in a lead series yield low oral bioavailability (e.g. <10%) or short half-life (e.g. < 30 min), it is obvious that physico-chemical properties of these compounds need to be refined to improve these PK parameters. However, before attempting any refinement of the chemical structure of these compounds, the underlying causes for inadequate oral bioavailability or short half-life should be identified. Thus, poor oral bioavailability of a compound could result from poor absorption or pre-systemic (first-pass) removal of the compound by metabolism in the intestine or by metabolism and/or biliary excretion in the liver (Figure 1). Poor absorption could result from poor solubility of the compound or from poor intrinsic permeability across intestinal epithelium (Figure 1). Similarly, the short half-life (or high clearance) of the compound may suggest that the compound is either cleared rapidly via metabolism or excretion via the biliary or the renal route. Teasing out the underlying factors for poor oral bioavailability or short half-life often requires iterative use of PK studies and *in vitro* models. The following examples will illustrate this point. If an acidic compound is orally administered as a soluble salt and yields low oral bioavailability, it is likely that the compound precipitates in the acidic environment of the stomach and does not re-dissolve easily even as the pH of the medium rises during intestinal transit. This solubility behavior can be reproduced using *in vitro* approaches, thus providing credence to the hypothesis that poor solubility is contributing to the low oral bioavailability of the test compound. However, it would be important to confirm this by comparing the bioavailability of the test compound upon oral administration and intraduodenal administration. Since the latter route of administration does not allow the drug to precipitate in the stomach, the bioavailability should increase in comparison with the bioavailability after oral administration. In another example, let us assume that poor bioavailability of a drug candidate is suspected to be due to first pass clearance. This should trigger a follow-up *in vivo* study in which the oral bioavailability of the compound is tested after oral (or intraduodenal) and portal vein dosing. The portal vein receives venous blood supply from the mesentery and thus the entire does of a drug absorbed from the intestine will end up in the portal vein before entering the liver. If the bioavailability is similar (low) upon oral (or intraduodenal) dosing and portal vein dosing, then it can be surmised that liver must be the site of clearance that led to poor bioavailability. However, if the bioavailability increases upon portal vein dosing (in relation to intraduodenal dosing) then it can be concluded that intestinal epithelium must be the site of clearance. Depending on the site (organ) of clearance postulated based on these studies, appropriate *in vitro* models (e.g. microsomes, cell homogenates, cells) derived from either intestinal or hepatic tissue can be employed to confirm the underlying mechanism that is responsible for the low oral bioavailability of the drug. Once these factors are identified, then appropriate *in vitro* models can be implemented to screen for compounds for specific ADME properties (i.e. metabolic stability, permeability across intestinal epithelium, biliary excretion). Such screens not only help identify compounds with "good" ADME properties and weed out poor performers, but they also yield structure-activity relationships with respect to the specific ADME property that is being screened. Such relationships are extremely valuable in refining chemical structure and physico-chemical properties of compounds for optimum ADME behavior.

While the *in vitro* models are valuable for screening large numbers of compounds against specific ADME properties and for developing structure-activity relationships, it must be recognized that the refinement achieved in these ADME properties using the *in vitro* models may not always translate into improved ADME behavior *in vivo*. Hence, it is important to confirm that the *in vitro* model chosen is predictive of the *in vivo* ADME behavior before committing to an extensive screening effort.

In the following sections, discussion will focus on the use of *in vitro* models to address ADME-related problems that have been identified using preclinical PK studies.

In Vitro Studies to Address ADME-related Deficiencies in Drug Candidates

Absorption

When experimental evidence suggests that poor absorption of lead compounds is due to poor intrinsic permeability across intestinal epithelium, the *in vitro* models for drug transport can serve as an excellent screening tool for identifying compounds with improved intestinal permeability. However, studies must be performed to understand the physicochemical and cellular/biochemical

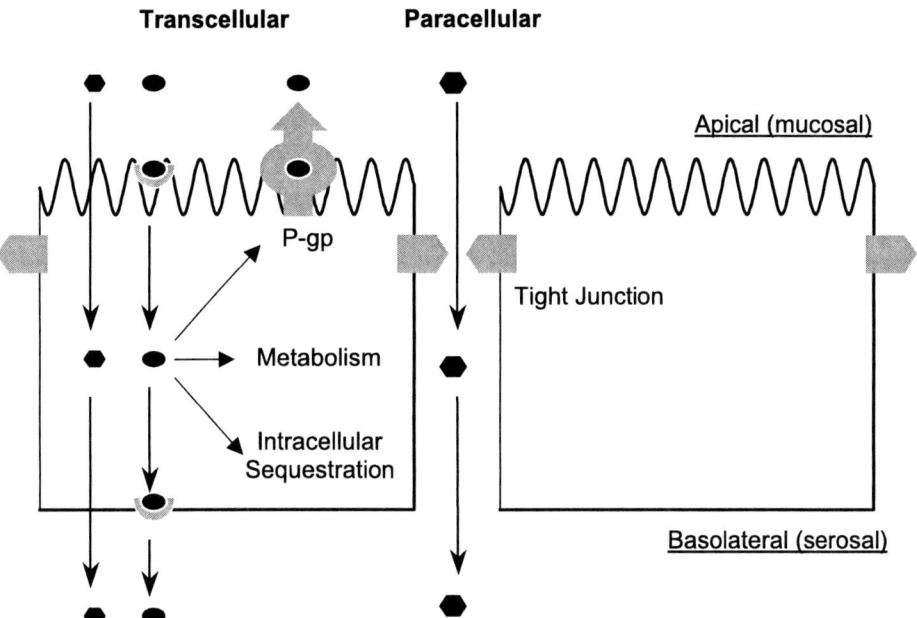

Figure 2. A depiction of (i) the absorptive transport routes across intestinal epithelium and (ii) the physical and biochemical barriers to drug absorption.

basis for poor permeability across the intestinal epithelium prior to setting up a screen. The intestinal epithelium, which comprises a single layer of cells, constitutes a formidable barrier to oral absorption of drugs. Although the epithelium contains several different cell types, the polarized columnar cells, known as enterocytes, play a crucial role both in the absorption of nutrients and xenobiotics and in serving as a barrier to their absorption. The barrier role of the enterocytes is two-fold; the cell membrane and the intercellular junctions, known as tight junctions, constitute a physical barrier to entry of hydrophilic compounds into systemic circulation, whereas the efflux transporters present in the apical membrane (e.g. P-glycoprotein (P-gp)) and metabolic enzymes present in cellular compartments (e.g. esterases, peptidases, cytochrome P450 (CYP), sulfotransferases) constitute a biochemical barrier to lipophilic compounds that are capable of traversing the cell membrane and cross the epithelium via the transcellular route (Figure 2). Thus, an *in vitro* model for intestinal epithelium should mimic the physical and biochemical barrier properties of intestinal epithelium.

Caco-2 cell monolayer, grown on a porous polycarbonate membrane, was initially introduced as an *in vitro* model for intestinal absorption/transport studies in late 1980's and early 1990's (Hidalgo et al., 1989; Artursson, 1991); subsequently, several cell culture-based *in vitro* models have been introduced (reviewed in Borchardt et al., 1996; Weinstein et al., 2003). These *in vitro* models are used extensively in the pharmaceutical industry and academic groups as screening and investigative tools for drug absorption studies. The cells, grown on a porous membrane, differentiate into enterocyte-like cells upon reaching confluence. Absorptive transport across these cell monolayers is typically investigated in a Transwell™ set-up by adding the test compound on the apical

(AP), i.e. lumenal, side and analyzing the compound appearing in the basolateral (BL), i.e. serosal, compartment as a function of time; secretory transport can be studied by reversing the donor and receiver compartments. In addition to the cell culture models, *in vitro* systems employing intestinal tissue from preclinical species (e.g. everted sac) are also employed with the rationale that such models may mimic the intestinal transport more closely than the cell-based models employing immortalized cell lines. *In vitro* models to study absorption across intestinal epithelium have been reviewed previously (Borchardt et al., 1996; and Smith 1997), and will not be elaborated here.

Relatively simple experiments can be devised to answer the following questions regarding the transport mechanism of the lead series of compounds: (1) are the compounds traversing the cell monolayers predominantly via the transcellular or the paracellular route? (2) Is the transport mediated by a transporter? (3) Is an efflux transporter affecting the absorptive transport of the compounds? The information derived from these experiments can provide a rational basis for screening the compounds for optimum transport properties.

Paracellular vs. transcellular transport

Typically, neutral lipophilic molecules traverse the intestinal epithelium via the transcellular route by partitioning into the cell membrane and diffusing through the membrane and/or the cytosolic compartment (Figure 2). In contrast, compounds that are very hydrophilic or that have a net charge cannot effectively partition into the cell membrane, and are often translocated across the intestinal epithelium via the paracellular route (Figure 2) unless they are substrates for one of the transporters that carry hydrophilic nutrient molecules across the intestinal epithelium. The paracellular transport is not very efficient due to the relatively small surface area available to compounds for entry into the intercellular space as compared to rather large surface area presented by the apical membrane of the enterocytes with its microvilli. In addition, the paracellular transport of compounds is further restricted by the presence of the tight junction (reviewed in Powell, 1981, Anderson and Van Itallie, 1995, Ward et al., 2000).

The *in vitro* cell culture models (e.g. Caco-2 cell monolayers) are well suited to determine the primary route by which a compound is translocated across the intestinal epithelium. The experimental approach that is most commonly employed for this purpose involves measuring the flux (permeability) of a compound across the intact cell monolayer and comparing it with the flux across monolayers in which tight junctions are compromised by removal of extracellular Ca^{2+} ions, either by using a Ca^{2+}-free buffer or including a Ca^{2+} chelator such as ethylenediaminetetraacetic acid (EDTA). It is assumed that the compound whose flux increases by several fold when extracellular Ca^{2+} is removed from the transport buffer must be traversing the cell monolayers predominantly via the paracellular route; conversely, the flux of a transcellularly transported compound does not change significantly when Ca^{2+} ions are depleted from the transport medium. This approach is criticized by some because it requires extrapolating results obtained from a perturbed cell monolayer system to explain the transport behavior of compounds in the intact system. Furthermore, it is argued that removal of extracellular Ca^{2+} ions may damage the cell membrane and confound the transport data acquired in the absence of extracellular Ca^{2+} ions. However, no other simple *in vitro* method is available currently to assess relative contribution of paracellular vs. transcellular transport of compounds across intestinal epithelium or the cell culture models of intestinal epithelium.

Carrier-mediated transport

A hydrophilic compound often crosses the intestinal epithelium via a carrier-mediated mechanism when it can mimic a physiologic substrate. For hydrophilic compounds which are not able to effectively cross the cell monolayer via the transcellular diffusion process, a transporter-based mechanism may contribute significantly to its absorptive transport (transporters for drug absorption are reviewed in Amidon and Sadee; 1999). A simple experimental approach, in which the flux of the test compound across cell monolayers is measured as a function of concentration, can provide valuable information regarding the likely involvement of a transporter in the absorptive transport of the compound. A hyperbolic relationship between flux and concentration, in which the flux plateaus at high concentrations, suggests involvement of a transporter, provided that the plateau at high concentrations is not reached by exceeding the solubility of the compounds. Often, a diffusive component contributes significantly to the overall transport of a compound. In such a case, the plot of flux vs. concentration does not reach a plateau; instead, it continues to increase in a non-linear fashion even at concentrations that would saturate the transporter. For a compound exhibiting such a behavior, sometime it may be difficult to determine if a transporter is involved as is the case for transport of ranitidine across Caco-2 cells (Lee and Thakker, 1999). However, analyzing the data in terms of permeability (Papp, flux normalized to concentration and area) as opposed to flux can often reveal the involvement of a saturable mechanism much more clearly. If the compound is a substrate for a transporter, the Papp value often exhibits large changes with changes in the concentration of the compound, particularly over the low concentration range where the transporter mechanism is likely to be dominant. This is diagnostic of a transporter-mediated transport mechanism; in contrast, the Papp value remains unchanged over the entire concentration range for a purely diffusive transport mechanism. Thus, determining the Papp at two widely separated concentrations may be sufficient to get an indication of the involvement of a transporter mechanism for the test compound.

Attenuation of absorptive transport by an efflux transporter

Efflux transporters in the apical membrane of intestinal epithelium represent a significant barrier to intestinal absorption of many compounds that are transcellularly transported across the epithelium (reviewed in Fromm, 2000; Lin and

Chapter 1: Strategic Use of Preclinical Pharmacokinetic Studies
and In Vitro Models in Optimizing ADME Properties of Lead Compounds

10

Yamazaki, 2003). P-gp is one of the most important and widely studied efflux transporters, and most drug discovery programs employ a screen to assess its effect on intestinal drug absorption (reviewed in Polli and Serabjit-Singh, 2004). These screens involve determination of Papp across cell monolayers such as Caco-2 cells or MDCK cells transfected with the MDR1 gene (MDR-MDCK) in the AP to BL and BL to AP directions. A ratio of Papp in BL to AP and AP to BL direction (efflux ratio) is often used as a parameter to assess the extent of interaction between the test compound and P-gp, and a large efflux ratio is considered a liability with respect to the compound's oral absorption (Polli and Serabjit-Singh, 2004). However, we have observed that attenuation of the absorptive transport (AP to BL) by P-gp and enhancement of their secretory transport (BL to AP) are not equal in magnitude for many compounds (Troutman and Thakker, 2003a). Hence, it is conceivable that absorptive transport of a compound with a high efflux ratio may not be affected much by P-gp and that the large efflux ratio is a consequence of a large effect of P-gp on its secretory transport as is the case with rhodamine 123 and doxorubicin (Troutman and Thakker, 2003b). In such cases, the efflux ratio would over-predict the attenuation of absorptive transport by P-gp. This is evident from the comparison of digoxin and rhodamine 123 transport across Caco-2 cells as shown in Figure 3. Both digoxin and rhodamine 123 are substrates for P-gp, and exhibit large efflux ratios in the Caco-2 cell culture model. However, a comparison of absorptive transport of these compounds in the presence and absence of the P-gp inhibitor, GW918, reveals that P-gp has no effect on the absorptive transport of rhodamine 123, whereas it affects both absorptive and secretory transport of digoxin in a much more symmetrical manner.

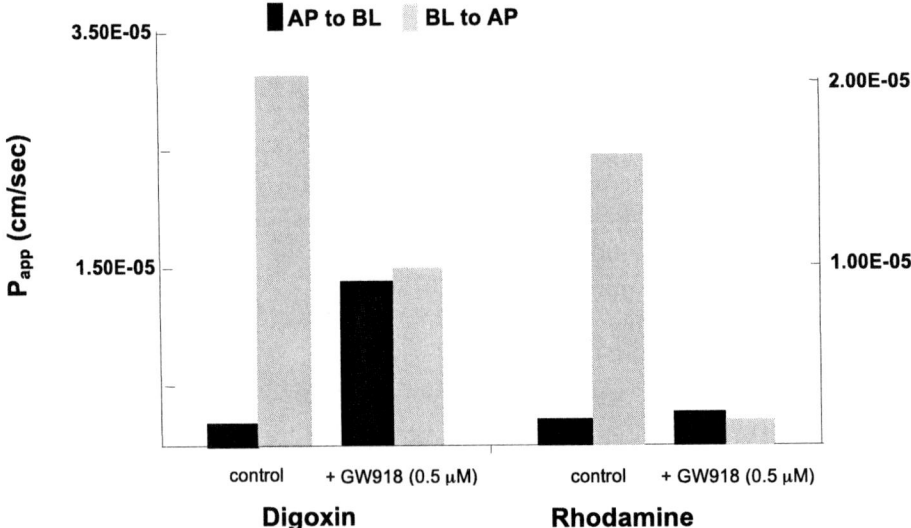

Figure 3. AP to BL and BL to AP transport of digoxin and rhodamine 123 in the absence and presence of the P-gp inhibitor GW918. The experimental design clearly highlights the fact that P-gp affects both absorptive (AP to BL) and secretory (BL to AP) transport of digoxin, but affects only the secretory (BL to AP) transport of rhodamine 123 (adapted from Troutman and Thakker, 2003b).

Based on these observations, we have proposed an alternative approach to screen compounds for P-gp-mediated attenuation of absorptive transport (Troutman and Thakker, 2003c). This approach involves determination of the absorptive permeability (Papp) of compounds and comparing it with the absorptive permeability determined in the presence of sufficiently high concentration of a non-competitive P-gp inhibitor (e.g. GW918) so as to completely inhibit its efflux activity. The permeability value determined in the absence of the P-gp efflux activity would be equivalent to the permeability of the compound due to passive diffusion (P_{PD}) across the cell monolayer, and the difference between P_{PD} and Papp would be equivalent to the attenuation of the absorptive transport by P-gp. This P-gp-mediated attenuation of the absorptive transport (P_{PD} – Papp) can be conveniently expressed by a number between 0 and 1 by normalizing it with respect to P_{PD}. Thus, (P_{PD} – Papp)/P_{PD}, which we refer to as absorptive quotient (AQ), will have the value of 0 when P-gp has no effect on the absorptive permeability of a compound (i.e. P_{PD} = Papp), and the value of 1 when P-gp completely attenuates the absorptive transport of a compound (i.e. Papp = 0). Thus for any P-gp substrates, the AQ value (0 < AQ < 1) will give an indication of the extent to which P-gp is attenuating the absorptive transport of these compounds. Since in a transport screen, one is interested in assessing the effect of P-gp on the intestinal absorption of drug candidates, and not so much the influence of P-gp on secretion, the measurement of AQ is recommended over the measurement of efflux ratio. Recently, Thiel-Demby et al. (2004) have shown that AQ measurement also can correctly identify compounds as P-gp substrates/non-substrates relative to the efflux ratio measurement with 80% accuracy while affording two-fold increase in throughput.

Metabolism

Most of the compounds administered as therapeutic agents are transformed by one or more metabolic enzymes into products that are often more hydrophilic and more amenable to excretion. Metabolic transformation can have profound influence on the therapeutic efficacy and toxicity of drugs.

Rapid metabolism can limit the ability of a drug to attain the efficacious concentrations in the blood (with the exception of iv administration) or in the target tissue and to maintain these concentrations for sufficiently long periods of time to be therapeutically useful. For orally administered drugs, extensive metabolic clearance of the drug can occur in the intestine or in liver prior to reaching systemic circulation. This, so called "first pass effect" can contribute significantly to limit the oral bioavailability of a drug. In addition, repeated administration of a drug can lead to induction of certain drug metabolizing enzymes including those involved in the biotransformation of the administered drug (reviewed in Lin and Liu, 2001; Savas et al., 1999). This, in turn, could lead to greater metabolic clearance and less exposure of the drug than initially anticipated at the time of fixing the dose. Induction could also similarly affect

*Chapter 1: Strategic Use of Preclinical Pharmacokinetic Studies
and In Vitro Models in Optimizing ADME Properties of Lead Compounds*

12

Metabolic Reaction	Functional Group	Metabolic Product
Oxidation	C-H (aliphatic)	Alcohol
	C=C (olephenic)	Epoxide
	C=C (aromatic)	Phenol (isomerization of arene oxide)
	C-H $\propto$ to N (O, S)	Amine + Aldehyde or Ketone
	C-OH	Aldehyde or Ketone
	Ar-NH$_2$	Hydroxyl amine, Nitroso, Nitro, N-oxide
	R-NH$_2$	Aldehyde (monoamine oxidase catalyzed)
	R-S-R	Sulfoxide, Sulfone
Reduction	R-CHO, R-CO-R	Alcohol
	Quinone	Hydroquinone
	R-NO$_2$ (or Ar-NO$_2$)	Nitroso, hydroxylamine, amine
	R-N=N-R'	Hydrazine, amine
	R-S-S-R'	Sulfhydryl
Hydrolysis	C=O(OR)	Carboxylic acid
	C=O(SR)	Carboxylic acid
	C=O(NH$_2$)	Carboxylic acid
	O-C=O(OR)	Carboxylic acid
	O-C=O(NR)	Carboxylic acid
	Ar-O-SO$_3$	Phenol
	R-O-PO$_3$	Alcohol
	Epoxide	*trans*-Dihydrodiol
Conjugation	-OH, -COOH, -NH$_2$	Glucuronide
	Ar-OH	Sulfate
	Epoxide, Ar-Cl	Glutathione conjugate, Mercapturic acid
	Ar-C=O(OH)	Amino acid conjugate
	-NH$_2$	N-acyl derivative

Table 1. Metabolic Reactions, target functional groups, and metabolic products

Oxidation	Hydrolysis
Cytochrome P450 (CYP)	Esterases
Flavin monooxygenase (FMO)	Proteases
Peroxidase	Peptidases
Monoamine oxidase	Glucuronidase
Xanthine oxidase	Sulfatase
Dehydrogenases	Phosphatases
Aldehyde oxidase	
Reduction	**Conjugation**
Keto reductase	Glucuronosyl transferases
DT diaphorase	Sulfotransferases
Azo reductase	Glutathione transferases
Dehydrogenases	Acetyl transferases
Cytochrome P450 (CYP)	Kinases

Table 2. Drug Metabolizing Enzymes

other co-administered drugs that are predominantly cleared by the induced enzyme(s).

Metabolism of drugs can lead to adverse effects under the following circumstances: (i) when a metabolite of the drug exhibits undesirable pharmacological activity, (ii) when a chemically reactive metabolite(s) covalently modifies cellular macromolecules, and (iii) when the drug or its metabolite inhibits a metabolic enzyme(s) which plays a key role in the clearance of a co-administered drug, resulting in reduced clearance of the co-administered drug and overexposure to it.

Clearly, *in vitro* models to assess metabolic stability, induction and inhibition of metabolic enzymes, and formation of reactive metabolites are necessary in order to reduce or eliminate any metabolism-related liability of drug candidates. These *in vitro* models are discussed in the following sections with an emphasis on their use in making decisions for selection/de-selection or re-design of compounds.

Metabolic stability

In designing an appropriate *in vitro* screen for metabolic stability, the obvious question that needs to be addressed is: how does one know which enzyme(s) is involved in the metabolic transformation of the drug candidates? The first step toward addressing this question is to recognize that despite rather wide chemical space covered by drug candidates, their metabolic transformation can be grouped under one of four chemical reaction types: (1) oxidation, (2) reduction, (3) hydrolysis, and (4) conjugation. The *in vitro* model for metabolic stability should be selected based on the most likely metabolic transformations that might occur for the test compounds. The functionalities that can undergo each class of metabolic transformation are shown in Table 1. This Table does not provide an exhaustive list of all functionalities and their respective metabolic transformation(s); instead, it provides frequently encountered metabolic transformations associated with most common functionalities (see reviews by Parkinson, 1996, and Low, 1998 for metabolic transformations and enzymes). Table 2 shows the metabolic enzymes that catalyze each of these four major chemical transformations. Among these, CYP represent the largest group of enzymes coded by a superfamily of genes, affecting metabolism of a large number of endogenous and xenobiotic compounds representing diverse chemical classes. Liver is the predominant source of these enzymes; however, intestinal epithelium, which was considered to be a source of mostly hydrolytic and certain conjugative enzymes, is now proven to be an important source of the oxidative enzymes including CYP.

Tissue slices represent the most complex *in vitro* system with intact cellular and intercellular architecture, thus yielding highest probability that most metabolic transformations that are likely to occur *in vivo* will be reproduced *in vitro* (reviewed in Ekins, 1996). However, this model is technically most challenging to implement and requires consideration of many factors including cell/tissue viability, uniformity and reproducibility of the tissue preparation, and recovery of entrapped drugs/metabolites. Furthermore, it is not as amenable to high throughput screening for metabolic stability as some of the simpler metabolic systems. Suspended or cultured hepatocytes are often used as sources of (hepatic) metabolic enzymes (see Maurel, 1996; LeCluyse et al., 1996; Houston and Carlile, 1997; LeCluyse, 2001). Like tissue slices, they provide intact cellular architecture and full complement of metabolic enzymes as well as co-factors; however, it is important to recognize that many enzyme activities, including CYP activity, decline rapidly subsequent to harvesting the cells. Much effort has been devoted to develop culture conditions (medium composition, extracellular matrix, and co-cultures) that would maintain enzyme activities for long periods of time to make this system more useful for metabolism studies (Maurel, 1996; LeCluyse et al., 1996; LeCluyse, 2001). It is recognized now that often the rate-limiting step in the metabolic transformation of a compound may be its entry into the cell and that transporters may play an important role as determinants of metabolic transformation of compounds by regulating their traffic into and out of cells. Only the cell-based systems can assess the overall impact of both the transporters and enzymes on the metabolic stability of a compound. Cell-free systems including S-9 fraction (supernatant from 9000 x g centrifugation of cell homogenates), microsomes (endoplasmic reticulum), and expressed enzymes provide simpler systems that are more rugged with respect to enzyme stability and more amenable to high throughput platforms (reviewed in Ansede and Thakker, 2004). Selection of a cell-free system to screen for metabolic stability should be made with a recognition that these systems often lack some of the metabolic enzymes (lost during fractionation or denatured during preparation) and/or co-factors. Conjugation reactions are often difficult to reproduce *in vitro* with cell-free systems because each conjugation reaction requires a specific co-factor, requiring multiple enzymes for its biosynthesis. Augmenting the incubation medium by addition of a co-factor may not always lead to an "active" enzyme system because it may not reach the appropriate sub-cellular compartment. Hence, preliminary studies should be done with a more complete system to ensure that the cell-free system will provide adequate complement of enzymes and co-factors. The expressed enzymes can provide insights regarding the role of specific enzymes on the metabolism of test compounds; however, the information on the contribution of individual enzymes toward the overall metabolism is not obtained from studies involving expressed enzymes. Thus it is important to understand the advantages and limitations of various *in vitro* systems so that an optimum system can be chosen for answering specific questions on metabolic stability or setting up an appropriate screen.

CYP inhibition and induction

Screens for metabolic inhibition that are currently being employed are to assess inhibitory potential of drug candidates toward major human CYP enzymes. Typically, these assays involve testing drug candidates at a fixed concentration (% inhibition) or at a range of concentrations (IC_{50} or Ki) as inhibitors of individually expressed CYP enzymes against a known substrate for each enzyme. There are commercially available fluorogenic substrates for each CYP enzyme that, upon oxidation, are converted to fluorescent products. High throughput assays have been implemented using these fluorogenic substrates (reviewed in Ansede and Thakker, 2004). However, it is important to note that the substrates employed in these assays are often "non-drug like" in their properties. Thus inhibition measured against these substrates often shows poor correlation to the inhibitory potency measured against more classical "drug-like" substrates (Cohen et al., 2003). Because of such experiences, several companies have resorted to more resource-intensive LC/MS methods to screen drug candidates as inhibitors of CYP enzymes against "drug-like" substrates (reviewed in Ansede and Thakker, 2004).

Inhibitory potency of drug candidates provide important information regarding their drug interaction potential. However, it must be recognized that clinical implications in terms of seriousness and scope of drug interactions resulting from inhibition of different CYP enzymes is considerably varied. For example, a potent inhibitor of CYP3A4, an enzyme that accounts for (i) metabolism of over 50% of all the pharmaceutical agents (Rendic and Di Carlo, 1997) and (ii) over 30% of all CYP enzymes present in human liver ((Shimada et al., 1994), should be considered unsuitable for further development because it is likely to cause drug interactions with a wide range of co-administered drugs. In contrast, inhibitors of CYP enzymes such as 1A1, 2A6, and 2B6 may affect only a few co-administered drugs because each of these CYP enzymes account for metabolism of <1% of all the pharmaceutical agents (Rendic and Di Carlo, 1997), and together constitute less than 5% of total CYP enzymes in human liver

(Shimada et al., 1994). A potent inhibitor of one of these CYP enzymes can be developed provided that a profile of drug interactions is defined by conducting targeted clinical studies and included in the label. A factor that should be considered in assessing the implications of CYP inhibition by likely co-administered drugs on the exposure/plasma level of a test compound is the number of different CYP enzymes that metabolize the test compound. Thus, disposition of a compound that is metabolized by multiple CYP enzymes is not likely to be affected much due to inhibition of one of the CYP enzymes by a co-administered drug. Finally, as is the case with most *in vitro* parameters, before any decision is made about selection of drug candidates based on their inhibitory potency toward a CYP enzyme, it is important to determine if the *in vitro* potency corresponds to a similar inhibitory potency *in vivo*.

Several human CYP enzymes such as CYP1A1/CYP1A2, and CYP2B6, CYP2C9/CYP2C19, CYP2E1, and CYP3A4, are induced in response to repeat administration of certain agents (reviewed in Lin and Liu, 2001; Savas et al., 1999). Significant induction of CYPs can lead to increased clearance of the drug that induces the CYP, or other co-administered drugs that are substrates for the induced CYP. When this increased clearance leads to sufficient decrease in plasma concentrations such that the efficacy of a therapeutic agent is diminished, it can lead to sub-optimal therapeutic response – e.g. loss of efficacy of contraceptive steroids or HIV protease inhibitors due to CYP3A4 induction. Hence, the potential to induce CYPs is evaluated as a part of the candidate selection process. The *in vitro* model most often used is the one in which primary hepatocytes are cultured with extracellular matrix elements in sandwich-culture configuration (Maurel, 1996; LeCluyse et al., 1996; LeCluyse, 2001; Silva and Nicoll-Griffith, 2002). The cells are exposed to potential inducers for a period of time, after which induction of an enzyme (e.g. CYP3A) is assessed by measuring its activity or by quantifying the corresponding mRNA using quantitative real-time reverse transcriptase polymerase chain reaction (RT-PCR). With improved understanding of the molecular mechanism involving the role of nuclear receptors such as PXR and CAR in the induction of CYP enzymes (Savas et al., 1999, Honkakoksi and Negishi, 2000; Wang and LeCluyse, 2003), efforts are being made to develop and implement high throughput assays based on reporter gene constructs (Moore and Kliewer, 2000). Since there are significant species differences in the induction profile of CYP enzymes, induction potential of test compounds in different species should be evaluated using hepatocytes from the respective species. Better understanding of subtle differences in the regulatory mechanisms for expression of inducible CYP enzymes in different species will provide tools for development of species-specific high throughput assays for CYP induction.

Metabolism-based toxicity

Clinical failure due to toxicity remains a significant risk factor in drug development (Walsh, 2005). Often the toxicity exhibited by a test compound is not due to the parent compound; instead it is caused by a metabolite. The metabolite-induced toxicity is likely to escape detection during preclinical safety assessment since metabolite profiles and metabolite disposition may be different in different species. An important mechanism of metabolite-mediated toxicity is via covalent modification of critical macromolecules by reactive metabolites. It is generally accepted that covalent modification of macromolecules by reactive metabolites is a risk factor with respect to serious toxicity. However, not all covalent modifications lead to toxicity. This lack of well-defined and consistent link between the formation of metabolite-macromolecule adduct and toxicity makes it difficult to use covalent binding of metabolites to macromolecules as a decision tool for selection/de-selection of a drug candidate. However, certain companies, specifically Merck, minimize the risk of reactive metabolite-mediated toxicity by screening for the propensity of lead compounds to form reactive metabolites and "designing it out" by appropriate structural modifications (Evans et al., 2004). Such a screen typically involves incubating test compounds with liver microsomes, trapping any reactive metabolites produced with a nucleophile such as glutathione, and characterizing and quantifying the adduct with LC/MS. Often, a threshold is set (<50 pmol equivalent/mg microsomal protein at Merck) for the formation of glutathione adducts, below which the compound is advanced without further testing (Evans et al., 2004). When the adduct level is above the threshold, further studies are triggered to characterize the reactive metabolite so that medicinal chemistry can design it out of the drug candidate, and to assess covalent binding *in vitro* and *in vivo* using a radiolabeled drug. It is clear from Evans et al. (2004) that a compound is not automatically rejected if it produces protein adducts upon metabolism above the 50 pmol equivalent/mg protein; instead, several decision factors are brought to bear in deciding whether to advance such a compound for further development. While such an approach is an important first step toward reducing the risk of toxicity due to reactive metabolites, much remains to be done to elucidate the events after the initial formation of protein adducts that lead to toxic manifestation.

Excretion

The clearance of drugs and/or metabolites from the body occurs via one or both of the two major excretory mechanisms; i.e. biliary and renal excretion. As depicted in Figure 4, biliary excretion involves uptake of compounds across the sinusoidal membrane of hepatocytes via a diffusive or a carrier-mediated mechanism, intracellular disposition which may involve metabolism and/or sequestration, and subsequent efflux or the parent drug and/or metabolites across the canalicular membrane via an active transport process (Zamek-Gliszczynski and Brouwer, 2004). Depending on whether the compound (and/or metabolites) is removed from hepatocytes via efflux across the canalicular or the sinusoidal membrane, it is excreted via the biliary route or the renal route, respectively. Until recently, the biliary excretion potential of compounds could be evaluated only

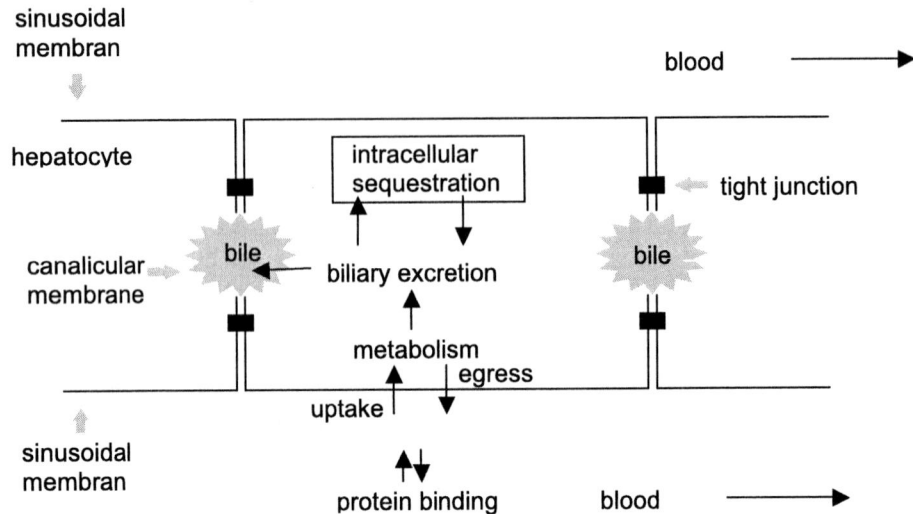

Figure 4. A depiction of the biliary excretion process involving uptake, cellular disposition, and efflux of a compound in hepatocytes (reproduced from Zamek-Gliszczynski and Brouwer, 2004).

using *in vivo* preclinical models or in the perfused liver system. Besides being slow for screening purposes, the information obtained in the preclinical species could not be linked easily to biliary excretion in humans. The first *in vitro* model to assess biliary excretion was developed based on the observation by Liu et al. (1998, 1999a, 1999b), which showed that when hepatocytes are cultured in a sandwich configuration, they develop the architecture that is a two-dimensional representation of the three-dimensional architecture of the liver. The *in vitro* biliary excretion model can be constructed with hepatocytes from different preclinical species and from humans, thus enabling the assessment of biliary clearance in different species (reviewed in Zamek-Gliszczynski and Brouwer, 2004). This is an important development because *in vivo* measurement of biliary clearance in preclinical species would not allow prediction of biliary clearance in humans due to interspecies differences in transporter specificities.

Renal clearance of drugs and metabolites involves filtration, secretion, and re-uptake in different segments of the renal tubule. The secretion and uptake processes are mediated by a variety of transporters. Thus far, an *in vitro* system that can incorporate all the processes involved in renal excretion has not been developed. While *in vitro* cell culture based systems to assess the role of individual transporters in renal excretion have been reported, none of these systems have been implemented as a screen to assess and predict renal excretion as a part of the lead selection process.

Distribution

Upon entering the systemic circulation, compounds leave the blood stream by traversing across the capillary endothelium and distribute into various tissues. Of course, the compound distributed into tissues can re-enter the bloodstream as the plasma concentration of the compound changes over time. At steady-state, each compound is distributed into tissues with a distinct and unique equilibrium constant. The distribution of compounds into tissues at steady state is often measured in terms of volume of distribution (at steady state), which is defined in the simplest term as the total volume of plasma that would be necessary to contain the entire dose of the compound at a plasma concentration achieved after distribution. The distribution of compounds into the tissue space often involves multiple processes, including passive diffusion across the endothelial cells, leakage of solution through the intercellular space in the capillary endothelium, diffusion through the intercellular matrix and across the cell membrane, transporter-mediated translocation across the cell membrane into and out of the cell etc. Thus, the extent of distribution of a compound depends on its physicochemical properties and its ability to serve as a substrate for one or more influx and efflux transporters. To date, *in vitro* models to assess and predict distribution of drug candidates are not well developed although some attempts toward this goal have been made (Ballard et al., 2003a, 2003b, Leahy and Rowland, 2003). *In vitro* models for distribution into specific organ or tissue have also been attempted, e.g. *in vitro* measurement of brain and plasma unbound fraction to assess CNS distribution (Kalvass and Maurer, 2002). The brain-to-plasma ratio (Kp_{brain}) is the most commonly used parameter in drug discovery and development to characterize CNS disposition of a compound. The differences in nonspecific binding between brain and plasma is one possible mechanism underlying different brain-to-plasma ratios among compounds (Rowland, 1985; Waterbeemd et al., 2001a; Waterbeemd et al., 2001b). Since in the absence of distributional impairment, Kp_{brain} is related to the degree of binding to brain tissue and plasma, it is possible to evaluate *in vivo* CNS distribution by measuring brain and plasma unbound fraction *in vitro*. This approach has been used successfully in evaluating the CNS distribution of discovery compounds (Kalvass and Maurer, 2002). Since, distribution of compounds may significantly affect their disposition, and in turn, their efficacy and toxicity, developing good predictive *in vitro* models to assess distribution should be considered a high priority.

References

Amidon and Sadee 1999. *Membrane Transporters as Drug Targets*. New York, NY: Kluver Academic/Plenum Publishers, 1999

Anderson JM and Van Itallie CM. Tight Junctions and the Molecular Basis for Regulation of Paracellular Permeability. *Am J Physiol* 269; 1995:G467-G475

Ansede JH and Thakker DR. In Vitro High Throughput Screening for Inhibition and Metabolic Stability of Compounds Towards Cytochrome P450-mediated Oxidative Metabolism. *J. Pharm.* Sci 93; 2004:239-255

Artursson P. Correlation Between Oral Drug Absorption in Humans and Apparent Drug Permeability Coefficients in Human Intestinal Epithelial (Caco-2) Cells. Biochem Biophys *Res Commun* 1991; 175:880-885

Ballard P, Arundel PA, Leahy DE, and Rowland M. Prediction of *In Vivo* Tissue Distribution from *In Vitro* Data. 2. Influence of Albumin Diffusion from Tissue Pieces During an *In Vitro* Incubation on Estimated Tissue-to-unbound Plasma Partition Coefficients (kpu). Pharm Res 2003a; 20:857-863

Ballard P, Leahy DE, and Rowland M. Prediction of *In Vivo* Tissue Distribution from *In Vitro* Data. 3. Correlation between *In Vitro* and *In Vivo* Tissue Distribution of a Homologous Series of Nine 5-n-Alkyl-5-ethyl Barbituric Acids. Pharm Res 2003b; 20:864-872

Borchardt RT, Smith PL, and Wilson G. *Models for Assessing Drug Absorption and Metabolism*. New York, NY: Plenum Press; 1996

Caldwell GW, Ritchie DM, Masucci JA, Hageman W, and Yan Z. The New Preclinical Paradigm: Compound Optimization in Early and Late Phase Drug Discovery. *Curr Top Med Chem* 2001; 1:353-366

Cohen LH, Remley MJ, Raunig D, and Vaz AD. *In Vitro* Drug Interactions of Cytochrome P450: An Evaluation of Fluorogenic to Conventional Substrates. *Drug Metab Dispos* 2003; 31: 1005-1015

Ekins S. Past, Present, and Future Applications of Precision-cut Liver Slices for *In Vitro* Xenobiotic Metabolism. *Drug Metab Rev.* 1996; 28:591-623

Evans DC, Watt AP, Nicoll-Griffith DA, and Bailie TA. Drug Protein Adducts: An Industry Perspective on Minimizing the Potential for Drug Bioactivation in Drug Discovery and Development. *Chem Res Toxicol* 2004; 17:3-16

Fromm MF. P-glycoprotein: A Defense Mechanism Limiting Oral Bioavailability and CNS Accumulation of Drugs. *Int J Clin Pharmacol Ther* 2000; 38:69-74

Hidalgo IJ, Raub TJ, and Borchardt RT. Characterization of the Human Colon Carcinoma Cell Line (Caco-2) as a Model System for Intestinal Epithelial Permeability. *Gatroenterology* 1989; 96:736-749

Honkakoski P and Negishi M. Regulation of Cytochrome P450 (CYP) Genes by Nuclear Receptors. *Biochem J* 2000; 347:321-337

Houston JB and Calile DJ. Prediction of Hepatic Clearance from Microsomes, Hepatocytes, and Liver Slices. *Drug Met Rev* 1997; 29:891-922

Iwatsubo T, Hirota N, Ooie T, Suzuki H, and Sugiyama Y. Prediction of *In Vivo* Drug Disposition from *In Vitro* Data Based on Physiological Pharmacokinetics. *Biopharm and Drug Disp* 1996; 17:273-310

Kalvass JC and Maurer. TS. Influence of Nonspecific Brain and Plasma Binding on CNS Exposure: Implications for Rational Drug Discovery. *Biopharm Drug Dispos* 2002; 23: 327-338.

Kennedy T. Managing the Drug Discovery/Development Interface. *Drug Discov Today* 1997; 2:436-444

Kerns EH and Li D. Pharmaceutical Profiling in Drug Discovery. *Drug Discov Today* 2003; 8:316-323

Leahy DE and Rowland M. Prediction of *In Vivo* Tissue Distribution from *In Vitro* Data 1. Experiments with Markers of Aqueous Spaces. *Pharm Res* 2000; 17:660-663

LeCluyse EL. Human Hepatocyte Culture Systems for the *In Vitro* Evaluation of Cytochrome P450 Expression and Regulation. *Eur J Pharm* Sci 2001; 13:343-368

LeCluyse EL, Bullock PL, Parkinson A, and Hochman JH. Cultured Rat Hepatocytes. In: Borchardt RT, Smith PL, and Wilson G. *Model for Assessing Drug Absorption and Metabolism*. New York, NY: Plenum Press; 1996. 121-159

Lin JH and Lu AYH. Interindividual Variability in Inhibition and Induction of Cytochrome P450 Enzymes. *Ann Rev Pharmacol Toxicol* 2001; 41:535-567

Lin JH and Yamazaki M. Role of P-glycoprotein in Pharmacokinetics: Clinical Implications. *Clin Pharmacokinet* 2003; 42:59-98

Lee K and Thakker DR. Saturable Transport of H2-Antagonists Ranitidine and Famotidine across Caco-2 Cell Monolayers. *J Pharm Sci*; 1999:88:680-687

Liu X, Brouwer, KL, Gan LS, Brouwer KR, Stieger B, Meier PJ, Audus KL, and LeCluyse EL. Partial Maintenance of Taurocholate Uptake by Adult Rat Hepatocytes Cultured in a Collagen Sandwich Configuration. *Pharm Res* 1998; 15:1533-1539

Liu X, LeCluyse EL, Brouwer KR, Gan LS, LeMasters JJ, Stieger B, Meier PJ, and Brouwer KL. Biliary Excretion in Primary Rat Hepatocytes Cultured in a Collagen-Sandwich Configuration. *Am J Physiol* 1999a; 277:G12-G21

Liu X, Chism JP, LeCluyse EL, Brouwer KR, and Brouwer KL. Correlation of Biliary Excretion in Sandwich-Cultured Rat Hepatocytes and *In Vivo* in Rats. *Drug Metab Dispos* 1999b; 27:637-644

Low LK. Metabolic Changes of Drugs and Related Organic Compounds. In:Delgado JN and Remers WA. *Wilson and Gisvold's Textbook of Organic Medicinal and Pharmaceutical Chemistry* (Tenth Edition). Philadelphia, PA: Lippincott Co.; 1998. 43-122

Maurel P. The Use of Human Hepatocytes in Primary Culture and Other *In Vitro* Systems to Investigate Drug Metabolism in Man. *Adv Drug Delivery* Rev 1996; 22:105-132

Moore JT and Kliewer SA. Use of the Nuclear Receptor PXR to Predict Drug Interactions. Toxicology 2000; 153:1-10

Obach RC, Baxter JG, Liston TE, Silber BM, Jones BC, MacIntyre, F, Rance DJ, and Wastall P. The Prediction of Human Pharmacokinetic Parameters from Preclinical and *In Vitro* Metabolism Data. *J Pharmacol Exp Ther* 1997; 283:46-58

Parkinson A. Biotransformation of Xenobiotics. In: Klaassen CD. *Casarett & Doull's Toxicology* (Fifth Edition) New York, NY:McGraw-Hill; 1996. 113-186

Polli JW and Serabjit-Singh CJ. *In Vitro* Cell-based Assays for Estimating the Effects of Efflux Transporters on Cell Permeation. In: Borchardt RT, Kerns EH, Lipinski, CA, Thakker, DR, and Wang B. *Pharmaceutical Profiling in Drug Discovery for Lead Selection*. Arlington, VA:AAPS Press; 2004. 235-256

Powell DW. Barrier Function of Epithelia. *Am J Physiol* 241; 1981: G275-G288.

Rendic S and Di Carlo FJ. Human Cytochrome P450 Enzymes: A Status Report Summarizing Their Reactions, Substrates, Inducers, and Inhibitors. *Drug Metab Rev* 1997; 29:413-580

Rowland M. Physiological Pharmacokinetic Models and Ineranimal Species Scaling. *Pharmacol Ther* 1985; 29:49-68

Savas U, Griffin KJ, and Johnson EF. Molecular Mechanisms of Cytochrome P450 Induction by Xenobiotics: An Expanded Role of Nuclear Hormone Receptors. *Mol Pharmacol* 1999; 56:851-857

Shimada T, Yamazaki H, Mimura M, Inui Y, and Guengerich FP. Interindividual Variations in Human Liver Cytochrome P-450 Enzymes Involved in the Oxidation of Drugs, Carcinogens and Toxic Chemicals: Studies with Liver Microsomes of 30 Japanese and 30 Caucasians. *J Pharmacol Exp Ther* 1994; 270:414-423

Silva JM and Nicoll-Griffith DA. *In Vitro* Models for Studying Induction of Cytochrome P450 Enzymes. In: Rodrigues AD. *Drug – Drug Interaction*. New York, NY:Marcel Dekker; 2002. 189-216

Smith P. *In Vitro Models for Selection of Development Candidate: Advanced Drug Delivery Reviews*. 1997; 23 (No. 1-3).

Thiel-Demby VE, Tippin TK, Humphreys JE, Serabjit-Singh CJ, and Polli, JW. *In Vitro* Absorption and Secretory Quotients: Practical Criteria Derived from a Study of 331 Compounds to Assess for the Impact of P-glycoprotein-mediated Efflux on Drug Candidates. *J Pharm Sci* 2004; 93:2567-2572

Troutman MD and Thakker DR. The Efflux Ratio Cannot Assess P-glycoprotein-mediated Attenuation of Absorptive and Secretory Transport Across Caco-2 Cell Monolayers. *Pharm Res* 2003a; 20:1200-1209

Troutman MD and Thakker DR. Rhodamine 123 Requires Carrier-Mediated Influx for its Activity as a P-glycoprotein Substrate in Caco-2 Cells. *Pharm Res* 2003b; 20:1192-1199

Troutman MD and Thakker DR. Novel Experimental Parameters to Quantify the Modulation of Absorptive and Secretory Transport of Compounds by P-glycoprotein in Cell Culture Models of Intestinal Epithelium. *Pharm Res* 2003c; 20:1210-1226

Walsh J. Metabolic Activation – Role in Toxicity and Idiosyncratic Reactions. In: Borchardt RT, Kerns EH, Hegeman J, Thakker DR, and Stevens JL. *Optimization of Drug-Like Properties During Lead Optimization*. Arlington, VA:Springer/AAPS Press; 2005. 49-80.

Wang H and LeCluyse EL. Role of Orphan Nuclear Receptors in the Regulation of Drug Metabolizing Enzymes. *Clin Pharmacokinet* 2003; 42:1331-1357

Ward PD, Tippin TK, and Thakker DR. Enhancing Paracellular Permeability by Modulating Epithelial Tight Junctions. *Pharm Sci Tech Today* 2000; 3:346-358

Waterbeemd HVD, Smith DA, Beaumont K, and Walker DK. Property-based Design: Optimization of Drug Absorption and Pharmacokinetics. *J Med Chem* 2001a; 15:1313-1333

Waterbeemd HVD, Smith DA, and Jones BC. Lipophilicity in PK design: Methyl, Ethyl, Futile. *J Comput Aid Mol Design* 2001b; 15:273-286.

Weinstein K, Kardos, P, Strab R, and Hidalgo, IJ. Cultured Epithelial Cell Assays Used to Estimate Intestinal Absorption Potential. In: Borchardt RT, Kerns EH, Lipinski, CA, Thakker, DR, and Wang B. *Pharmaceutical Profiling in Drug Discovery for Lead Selection*. Arlington, VA:AAPS Press; 2004. 217-234

Zamek-Gliszczynski MJ and Brouwer KLR. *In Vitro* Models for Estimating Hepatobiliary Clearance. In: Borchardt RT, Kerns EH, Lipinski, CA, Thakker, DR, and Wang B. *Pharmaceutical Profiling in Drug Discovery for Lead Selection*. Arlington, VA:AAPS Press; 2004. 259-292

24

*Chapter 1: Strategic Use of Preclinical Pharmacokinetic Studies
and In Vitro Models in Optimizing ADME Properties of Lead Compounds*

2

Role of Mechanistic Transport Studies in Lead Optimization

Jerome Hochman[1], Qin Mei[1], Masayo Yamazaki[1], Cuyue Tang[1], Thomayant Prueksaritanont[1], Mark Bock[2], Sookhee Ha[2], Jiunn Lin[1]

Departments of Drug Metabolism[1]
Medicinal Chemistry[2]
Merck and Company
West Point, PA 19486

Table of Contents

Abbreviations

Pgp ....P-glycoprotein

CNS..central nervous system

BBB ....lood brain barrier

NBD...nucleotide binding domain

TMD ....transmembrane domain

TM..transmembrane sequence

SAR..structure activity relationships

Keywords

P-glycoprotein, blood-brain barrier, transporters, structure transport relationships, SAR, drug discovery.

Introduction

During the drug discovery process an average of five to ten thousand compounds are evaluated to identify the small subset of structures with appropriate properties to become a drug. A potential drug is distinguished from a potent agonist /antagonist based on multiple factors affecting safety, exposure and marketability including target selectivity, chemical stability, physical chemical properties, and drug metabolism properties. From the drug metabolism standpoint unfavorable pharmacokinetics is one of the primary barriers to overcome in drug discovery. In the case of most CNS drugs, this is further complicated by the requirement for the compound to traverse the blood-brain barrier in order for it to be efficacious. Thus, for CNS drugs, a compound must balance chemical properties conferring good CNS penetration, favorable metabolic characteristics, and good oral absorption in addition to high potency against the target activity.

Historically the properties defining pharmacokinetic parameters were largely attributed to passive processes defined by the physical chemical properties of drugs and susceptibility of drugs to phase I and II metabolism enzymes. More recently drug uptake and efflux transporters have been shown to mediate transport of a large variety of drugs raising interest in the role of drug transporters in the distribution, elimination and metabolism of drugs and their metabolites. Numerous transporters have been identified with potential to mediate uptake and elimination processes in the intestine, liver, kidney and at the blood-brain barrier. While it is clear that transporters can influence major pathways regulating drug disposition, our current understanding of roles of specific transporters in drug disposition is limited to examples with isolated compounds. This is in part due to the overlapping substrate specificity for different transporters, and scarcity of specific substrates, inhibitors and biological models for studying the roles of specific transporters in vivo. One exception to this is the multi-drug resistance transporter P-glycoprotein (Pgp) which has been shown to influence the pharma-cokinetics and pharmacodynamics of several drugs. This is particularly true in the case of CNS drugs in which Pgp has been shown to attenuate transport across the BBB, thus limiting CNS exposure.

Biology and biochemistry of Pgp:

Much of the current understanding of Pgp has been fueled by the initial observation that overexpression of Pgp in tumor cells was associated with the development of multidrug resistance in tumors. In this mode, Pgp was identified as an efflux pump capable of transporting a wide variety of chemotherapeutic agents out of the cytosilic compartment of cells into the extracellular space. Initially Pgp was viewed solely in view of the consequences of its aberrant expression in tumor cells (Juliano and Ling, 1976; Roninson et al., 1986) but has since been shown to be constitutively expressed on normal cells in the intestine, kidney, liver, brain microvascular endothelia, placenta, adrenal cortex, testis, uterus, lymphocytes and hematopoietic cells (Cordon-Cardo et al., 1990; Thiebaut et al., 1989) where it is believed to afford protection from xenobiotics. The protective role of Pgp was most dramatically highlighted by the studies comparing Pgp-deficient mice with Pgp competent mice (Jonker et al., 1999; Lankas et al., 1997; Lankas et al., 1998; Schinkel et al., 1994; Schinkel et al., 1995; Schinkel et al., 1996; Smit et al., 1999). Pgp-deficient mice survived and appeared normal in a controlled environment, but were found to be hypersensitive to the neurotoxic effects of the Pgp substrate Ivermectin. This hypersensitivity was found to correspond to increased penetration of Ivermectin from the blood into the brains of the Pgp-deficient mice. Similarly, Pgp deficient mice are more sensitive to teratogenic effects of some Pgp substrates and show increased bioavailability and decreased clearance of some Pgp substrates. Thus, Pgp does not appear to play an essential role for survival and development of the mice in an unchallenged environment, but can dramatically influence the pharmacokinetics and pharmacodynamics of exogenous chemical agents.

Pgp is a large (170 Kd) cell surface glycoprotein which like other members of the ABC family of transporters is organized into two transmembrane regions, each containing 6 membrane spanning α-helices (transmemebrane domains (TMDs)) , and two nucleotide binding domains (NBDs) (Ambudkar et al., 1999; Gatmaitan and Arias, 1993). The binding and transport of Pgp substrates is mediated by the TMDs using energy derived from hydrolysis of ATP which is catalyzed by the NBDs. The mechanism by which ATP hydrolysis is linked to transport of Pgp substrates is not well resolved but entails large conformational changes throughout the protein. These conformational changes have been detected using FTIR spectroscopy (Sonveaux et al., 1999), changes in immunoreactivity of Pgp (Mechetner et al., 1997), and susceptibility of Pgp to limited proteolysis (Wang et al., 1997; Wang et al., 1998). Four discrete conformation states have been detected which appear to correspond to different states of ATP binding and hydrolysis. Recently cryoelectron microscopy of two dimensional Pgp crystals has demonstrated major restructuring of the TMDs of Pgp upon binding of ATP (Rosenberg et al., 2001; Rosenberg et al., 2003). Although the large conformational changes would suggest a tight association between ATP hydrolysis and drug transport, comparison of functional transport across cell monolayers and stimulation of Pgp-mediated ATP hydrolysis show significant disparity. In particular some compounds which are subject to significant transport by Pgp do not stimulate Pgp ATPase activity above its basal level, while other compounds which do not show significant Pgp-mediated transport, stimulate high rates of ATP hydrolysis (Polli et al., 2001; Scala et al., 1997).

The initial site of substrate interaction with Pgp is not well resolved. The prevalent models for how Pgp transports substrates entail drugs partitioning into the inner (cytosolic) leaflet of the plasma membrane followed by binding of the substrate by Pgp in the plane of the membrane. Fluorescence resonance energy transfer studies on Pgp containing inside out plasma membrane vesicles demonstrated that the fluorescent Pgp substrate Hoechst 33342 is extracted from the inner leaflet of the bilayer (Shapiro and Ling, 1997). Since Hoechst 33342 fluorescence is low in an aqueous environment, the kinetics of the changes in Hoechst fluorescence further indicated that Hoechst was released directly into an aqueous compartment followed by a slow passive re-association with the outer leaflet of the bilayer. Taken together these results indicate that Pgp can extract compounds from the cytoplasmic leaflet of the bilayer and transport the compounds directly into the extracellular aqueous medium. Low resolution cryoelectron microscopy analysis of structure of Pgp is consistent with substrate interactions occuring within the plane of the membrane (Rosenberg, Velarde, Ford, Martin, Berridge, Kerr, Callaghan, Schmidlin, Wooding, Linton, and Higgins, 2001; Rosenberg, Kamis, Callaghan, Higgins, and Ford, 2003). In the state equivalent to the ATP bound form of the protein, Pgp shows a transient cleft within the plane of the membrane from which drugs can enter a pore to the extracellular space. Images of Pgp equivalent to the nucleotide-free or the ADP-bound state suggest that the cleft closes after hydrolysis of ATP leaving the substrate in a channel that is open to the extracellular fluid. It is worth noting that the cleft in Pgp appears to extend through the length of the lipid bilayer up to the membrane cytosol interface. Consequently interactions with ampiphilic compounds could occur at the membrane-cytosol-interface, but it is unlikely that drugs would enter Pgp directly from the cytosol. Such interactions could account for Pgp efflux of relatively polar compounds such as cimetidine and polar metabolites which show poor transmembrane permeability (Hochman et al., 2001; Lentz et al., 2000). The site of interactions of Pgp with substrates has significant bearing on the chemical nature driving Pgp substrate interactions. Seelig (Seelig and Landwojtowicz, 2000) pointed out that given the hydrophobic nature of the environment surrounding the membrane partitioned drug, polar interactions may dominate recognition of substrates by Pgp since polar Pgp-substrate interactions would be distinct from the hydrophobic interactions occurring in the immediate lipid environment. Consistent with this premise Seelig and others have found hydrogen bonds, in particular hydrogen bond acceptors, to be important determinants for Pgp substrate interactions (Chiba et al., 1998; Ecker et al., 1999; Gombar et al., 2004; Osterberg and Norinder, 2000; Seelig, 1998).

While our understanding of the mechanisms underlying substrate interactions and transport of substrates by Pgp is still in early stages, it is clear that these mechanisms are more elaborate than conventional models for enzyme substrate interactions. Attempts to derive meaningful interpretation of in vitro transport data must take into account these complexities including the involvement of membrane partitioning, a potentially large drug binding site, and potential for non-stoichiometric conformational link between ATP hydrolysis and drug transport. An understanding of these factors is essential in choosing and recognizing the limitations of model systems to evaluate Pgp mediated transport, and in establishing structural guidance to aid chemistry efforts to overcome Pgp as a barrier.

In vivo impact of Pgp

The expression of Pgp in the intestine, liver, kidney and at the blood brain barrier is polarized in a manner consistent with a role in limiting absorption, and facilitating elimination of xenobiotics or in protecting sensitive CNS tissue from potentially toxic xenobiotics. In the intestine, liver and kidney Pgp acts to restrict or facilitate transport across a concentration gradient. In the intestine, Pgp activity transports drugs counter-current to the absorptive transport of drugs, thus posing a barrier to absorption of exogenous compounds (Gan et al., 1996; Hochman et al., 2000; Lown et al., 1997; Wacher et al., 1998). Pgp expression in the liver and kidneys is thought to function in aiding the elimination of drugs from the blood (Smit et al., 1998; Speeg et al., 1992). Studies in bile duct cannulated rats suggest that intestinal Pgp may also contribute to the systemic drug elimination (Mayer et al., 1996; Sparreboom et al., 1997). In absorption Pgp functions in a unidirectional manner restricting drug transport from the lumen of the intestine to the blood. Similarly, unidirectional transport by Pgp may predominate in drug elimination. Thus bidirectional transport ratios (basolateral to apical/ apical to basolateral transport) do not predict the impact of Pgp on these processes (Troutman and Thakker, 2003b; Troutman and Thakker, 2003a) because the effect in the absorptive and secretory direction is not always symmetrical.

Pgp functions in the blood-brain barrier to restrict the distribution of compounds from the blood to the CNS (Lankas, Cartwright, and Umbenhauer, 1997; Schinkel, Smit, van Tellingen, Beijnen, Wagenaar, van Deemter, Mol, Van Der Valk, Robanus-Maandag, te Riele, and ., 1994; Schinkel, Wagenaar, Mol, and van Deemter, 1996). As apposed to unidirectional Pgp mediated transport being important in absorption and elimination, bidirectional transport by Pgp is important in restricting CNS distribution. Thus, lower steady state free drug concentrations in the brain result both from restricting the rate of transport of substrates from the blood to the brain, and efflux of drug from the CNS compartment into the blood. The influence of Pgp activity on minimizing brain exposure to drugs is much more pronounced than its influence on systemic drug exposure. Studies in Pgp deficient mice indicate that Pgp activity can reduce CNS exposure to a drug 10-100 fold, while having little influence on systemic drug exposure. This is illustrated in Tables 1 and 2 in which the impact of Pgp, as determined by comparing disposition of substrates in Pgp deficient and competent mice, is summarized for systemic and CNS exposure of orally and IV administered Pgp substrates. In contrast to the impact that Pgp has on the brain concentrations of substrates, plasma concentrations of Pgp substrates are for the most part relatively unaffected by the expression of Pgp. This would suggest that for many compounds Pgp has dramatic impact on CNS exposure of drugs, but has a very limited if any impact on their clearance or on the extent of intestinal absorption. Indeed many of our discovery compounds which show high Pgp transport have good oral bioavailability (Table 2), and show no significant differences in plasma clearance in Pgp deficient and competent mice (figure 1).

a)

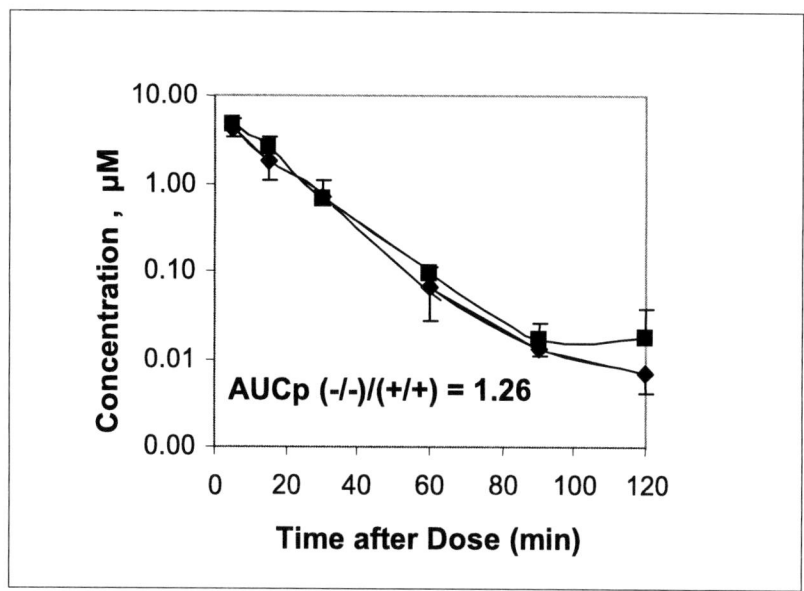

b)

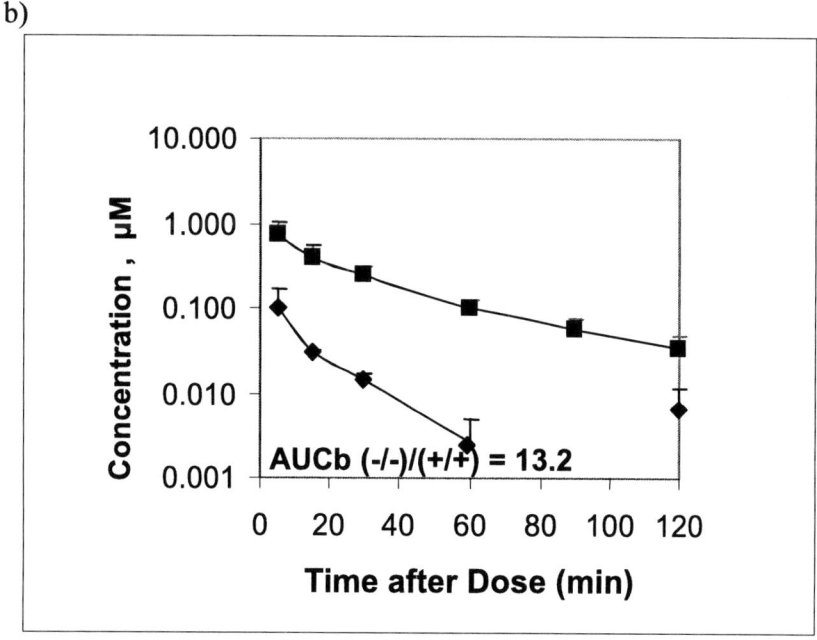

Figure 1. Impact of Pgp on the (a) plasma and (b) brain concentrations of a Pgp substrate in mdr1a deficient (-/-) (■)and mdr1a competent (+/+) (♦) CF-1 mice following iv adminis-tration to the tail vein (3 mg/kg). Pgp had no impact on clearance of the drug as indicated by identical plasma AUCs, but resulted in 13 fold lower AUCs in the brains in Pgp competent mice. The compound administered in this study is a good substrate for mouse Pgp as indicated by high B to A/ A to B transport ratios in LLC-PK1 cells expressing mouse mdr1a.

Drug	Ratio of tissue concentrations in Pgp deficient to Pgp competant mice following oral administration[1]	
	Plasma	Brain
Saqinavir	1.5	3.6
	4	7
Compound I	2	10
Loperamide	2	13.5
Ivermectin	1.5	20
Indinavir	2.03	10.6
Neflinavir	4.8	36

Table 1. Influence of Pgp on plasma and brain drug levels following oral administration. [1]Data summarized from Kim et. al. J Clin. Invest. (1998) 101: 289-294; Schinkel et. al. J Clin. Invest. (1996) 97: 2517-2524; Mol Pharmacol (2001) 59: 806-813; Lankas et. al. Toxicol appl. pharmacol. (1997) 143: 357-365; Prueksaritanont et. al. (2002) Xenobiotica 32:207-20.

Compound	Papp	transport ratio (B to A/ A to B)		Pgp impact on CNS penetration in mice	PK in Rats		
		Human MDR1	mouse mdr1a		CL	%F	% oral absorption[1]
compound 1	3.1	1.4	0.6	1.9	2.5	5	6
compound 2	2.7	1.1	1.1	2.0	12.0	25	29
compound 3	4.1	1.5	1.2	7.1	22.0	17	23
compound 4	18.5	1.6	1.9	3.3	41.0	7	15
compound 5	3.6	**13.0**	**3.7**	**15.3**	22.0	**75**	**103**
compound 6	25.0	**2.5**	**4.3**	**4.0**	13.0	**36**	**43**
compound 7	23.5	**3.9**	**7.8**	**16.6**	24.0	**43**	**61**
compound 8	22.0	2.0	7.9	3.4	31.0	11	18
compound 9	33.0	**4.6**	**8.7**	**14.3**	11.0	**50**	**58**
compound 10	23.0	3.7	8.9	9.3	27.0	16	24
compound 11	14.0	**10.7**	**15.6**	**9.0**	12.0	**77**	**91**
compound 12	11.4	16.2	12.6	19.5	2.0	22	23
compound 13	30.0	**3.1**	**13.5**	**24.7**	7.0	**62**	**68**
compound 14	20.2	**10.4**	**17.3**	**2.9**	5.0	**53**	**57**
compound 15	26.0	15.0	19.0	30.2	34.0	13	23
compound 16	27.0	2.3	21.8	4.8	42.0	21	44
compound 17	35.0	**8.9**	**22.7**	**6.8**	31.0	**66**	**108**

Table 2. Influence of Pgp on oral absorption and brain drug levels following oral administration of a series of discovery compounds. [1]% oral absorption = %F/(1-CL/Q) where the hepatic blood flow (Q)= 80 ml/min/kg and assumes blood/plasma drug levels =1

Given the clear implications for CNS exposure but not systemic exposure, our Pgp studies in drug discovery tend to focus on improving CNS exposure.

Application of in vitro models: In vitro/ in vivo relationships with Pgp transport

A model for the distribution of drug between the blood and the CNS is illustrated in figure 2. In the absence of active transport the unbound drug in the blood is equilibrated with unbound drug in the CNS tissue. Efflux by Pgp reduces the free drug concentration in the CNS relative to that in the blood. The total drug in each compartment is comprised of unbound drug and drug bound to plasma protein in the case of the blood, and drug bound to CNS tissue in the brain. Thus the ratio of the total drug concentrations in the brain and plasma can be significantly influenced by differences in the unbound fractions in the blood and CNS compartments. In addition to tissue/plasma protein binding and Pgp, drug concentrations in the brain can be influenced by the passive permeability of the drug, other efflux and uptake transporters, and ECF/CSF turnover. Given these complicating factors, interpretation of Pgp transport studies are focused on the impact of Pgp on CNS levels as apposed to predicting the absolute CNS drug concentrations.

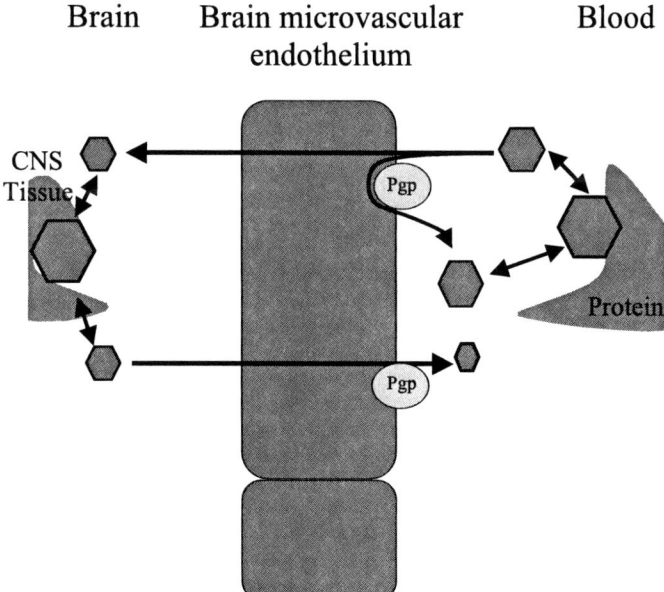

Figure 2. Representation of drug partitioning between the CNS and blood highlighting various components that can influence the distribution of drugs in both components. Drug (hexagon) is present in equilibrium between free and protein or tissue bound states. Free drug can diffuse by transcellular transport across the microvascular endothelial cells. Passive diffusion between endothelial cells is restricted by tight junctions. Pgp mediates transport of compounds from the brain to the blood and attenuates transport of compounds from the blood into the brain.

To assess the role of Pgp in restricting CNS distribution, we integrate in vivo studies in Pgp deficient and competent mice with results from in vitro directional transport studies in LLC-PK1 cells expressing mouse and human Pgp. Through integrating the in vitro and in vivo assays we are able to establish quantitative correlations to predict the consequences of Pgp activity in man. Yamazaki et al. (Yamazaki et al., 2001) demonstrated that under controlled experimental conditions, in vitro transport ratios in mouse Pgp expressing LLC-PK1 cells could quantitatively predict the impact of Pgp on CNS distribution. Further evaluation with discovery and development compounds indicates that the impact of Pgp on CNS exposure can be predicted from in vitro transport studies within a factor of 3 for over 85% of discovery compounds (Figure 3). Most of the compounds falling outside the ability to predict Pgp's impact tend to be low permeability compounds, where a low proportion of transcellular transport relative to Pgp insensitive paracellular transport pathway result in underestimating Pgp efflux in the Pgp expressing LLC-PK1 cells. Thus with the exception of low permeability compounds, predictions of the impact of Pgp on CNS distribution in mice can be made from directional transport studies.

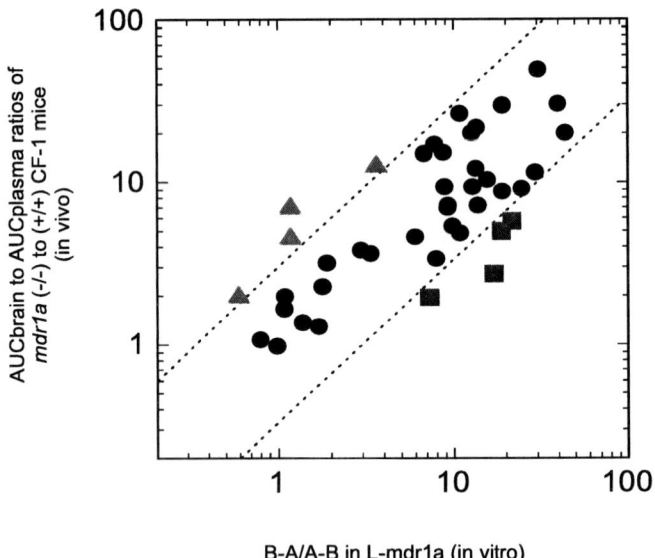

B-A/A-B in L-mdr1a (in vitro)

Figure 3. Comparison of in vitro transport of drugs by mdr1a expressed in LLC-PK1 cells with the impact of mdr1a encoded Pgp on brain penetration in vivo. The in vivo impact of Pgp was determined from the ratio of the brain to plasma AUC values in mdr1a -/- and +/+ CF-1 mice. In vitro transport by mdr1a was determined as the ratio of permeability coefficients for drugs in the B to A direction relative to the A to B direction in LLC-PK1 cells expressing mouse mdr1a (L-mdr1a cells). Parallel directional transport studies were performed in parental LLC-PK1 cells to ensure that observed transport ratios are not due to intrinsic transporters in the PK1 cells. Compounds showing three-fold higher impact of Pgp on CNS penetration in vivo than predicted from the in vitro transport are indicated by the closed triangles (▲), three fold higher impact in vitro than in vivo are indicated by closed squares (■), and comparable in vitro and in vivo values by closed circles (●).

Although in vitro mouse Pgp can predict the contribution of Pgp to restricting brain penetration in mice, we would not expect mouse Pgp to extrapolate well to the impact on human brain penetration. Site-directed mutagenesis studies revealed that amino acid changes, particularly in TM 5, 6, 11, and 12 , produce functional Pgp with altered substrate specificity (Ambudkar, Dey, Hrycyna, Ramachandra, Pastan, and Gottesman, 1999; Ambudkar et al., 2003; Gatmaitan and Arias, 1993) . Comparison of sequences for mouse and human Pgp indicate 13% disparity in the two sequences including modification at residues in all the TMDs including those implicated in substrate interactions. Thus it would not be surprising to find species-specific differences in Pgp transport. Indeed transport ratios in human Pgp transfected cells do not correlate well with the contribution of Pgp to the blood-brain barrier in mice. Comparison of transport ratios from human MDR1 and mouse mdr1a transfected cells is shown in figure 4a. While the majority of compounds show a linear correlation between mouse and human Pgp transport ratios, the ratios from the human and mouse Pgp differ by more than three–fold for approximately 20% of the compounds. This species difference is seen to a various degrees in different structural classes of compounds and is influenced by very subtle chemical changes. In one structural series, modification to a single amide resulted in compounds which had very low human Pgp mediated transport, but retained extensive transport by mouse Pgp (Figure 4b). Thus very subtle structural changes can produce not only quantitative species difference in Pgp efflux but also qualitative differences in which compounds can be substrates in one species but not in others. Similar, species differences have also been observed over a wide range of chemical structures including prototypical Pgp substrates, and diverse compounds from a variety of discovery and development programs. Since our primary interest is predicting the impact of Pgp in man, the paradigm we apply to account for species differences is to establish the in vitro/ in vivo correlations in a chemical series with transport studies in mouse Pgp expressing LLC-PK1 cells combined with brain penetration studies in Pgp deficient and competent mice, and correct for species differences based on ratios observed in directional transport studies with human and mouse expressing Pgp LLC-PK1 cells (figure 5).

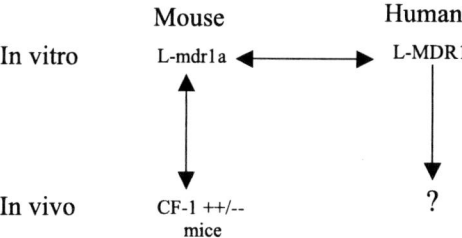

Figure 5. Paradigm for predicting the impact of Pgp on CNS penetration of drugs in man. In vitro directional transport studies using mouse mdr1a and human MDR1 expressing LLC-PK1 cells are used to assess species differences in Pgp transport. In vivo studies in CF-1 mice are used to establish the validity of extrapolating the in vivo impact of Pgp from the vitro transport results.

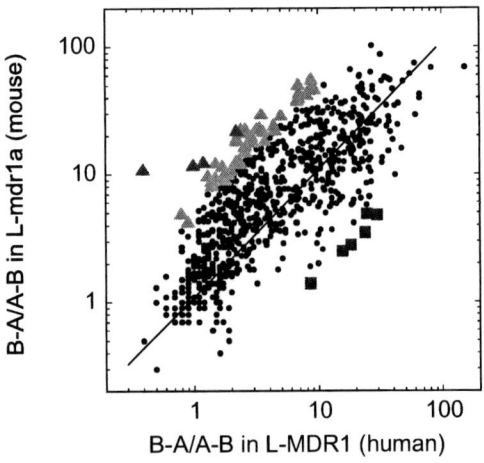

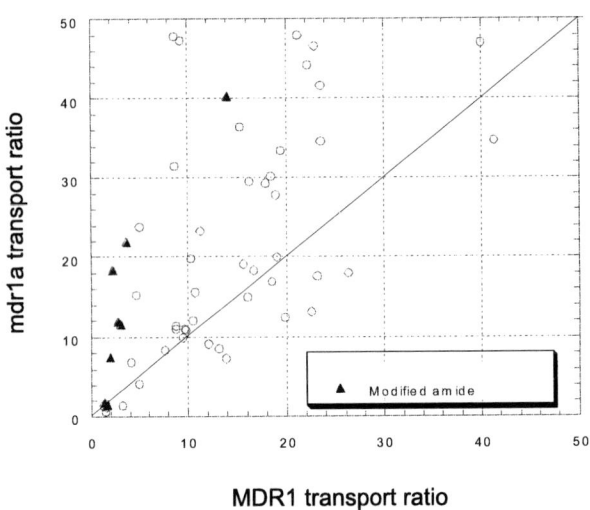

Figure 4. Comparison of in vitro transport of drugs by mouse mdr1a and human MDR1 expressed in LLC-PK1 cells. a) In vitro transport by mdr1a and MDR1 encoded Pgp were determined as the ratio of permeability coefficients for drugs in the B to A direction relative to the A to B direction in LLC-PK1 cells expressing mouse mdr1a or human MDR1. Parallel directional transport studies were performed in parental LLC-PK1 cells to ensure that observed transport ratios are not due to intrinsic transporters in the PK1 cells. Compounds where the transport ratios are in general agreement (within a factor of five) are represented as circles. Compounds in which human MDR1 transport ratios are greater than 5 time the mdr1a transport ratios are represented as squares. Compounds with mouse mdr-1a transport ratios 5-10 or exceding 10 times the transport ratios for human MDR1 are represented as light and dark triangles respectively. b) Comparison of in vitro transport by mouse mdr1a and human MDR1 encoded Pgp for a chemical series. Modification of a single amide (▲) (see figure 8) resulted in loss of directional transport by human Pgp transport but not by mouse Pgp.

Case study: establishment of Structure-activity relationships (SAR) to minimize Pgp efflux.

One of the primary values to the in vitro LLC-PK1 transwell bidirectional transport assay is the potential to generate sufficient information within a structural series to establish chemical strategies to overcome Pgp efflux. The demonstration of a quantitative relationship between in vitro Pgp transport ratios and the impact of Pgp on blood –brain barrier permeability of drugs indicates that the potential exists to establish meaningful SAR in vitro for overcoming Pgp efflux at the BBB. Three approaches to establishing a structural basis for overcoming Pgp are:

1) To identify structural templates with the lowest probability for Pgp transport when multiple structural classes of compounds are available.

2) To identify specific substituents in compounds which confer susceptibility to Pgp efflux, and determine structural modifications which reduce Pgp efflux while maintaining pharmacological potency.

3) Identify global physical chemical properties which confer susceptibility to Pgp efflux, and direct structural modifications to optimize these properties to reduce susceptibility to Pgp efflux.

We have found that all three approaches have proven valuable in overcoming Pgp efflux when they are applied in context with other factors influencing drug-like properties. Our experience in one CNS program provides an example of the judicial use of structural relationships to develop CNS permeable compounds. In this program information from the Pgp susceptibility conferred by specific substituents (approach 2) was combined with evaluation of the global chemical properties (approach 3) to establish strategies to effectively overcome Pgp transport. It is important to note that although CNS penetration is an essential feature for a drug candidate in this program, good CNS permeability is only one feature to optimize, and structural changes to improve CNS penetration are of little value if they come at the expense of acceptable potency, selectivity, pharmacokinetics, metabolism and safety.

At the point that Pgp studies were initiated in this program, compounds were identified with good potency and moderate pharmacokinetic properties. However every potent membrane permeable compound was subject to extensive Pgp efflux resulting in poor CNS penetration. In order to establish meaningful structure transport relationships for Pgp we increased the range of directional transport ratios, and the structural diversity of the compound series by examining selected compounds irrespective of their pharmacological potencies. By comparisons of analogous compounds differing at only one position we were able to discriminate substituents into groups according to their potential to increase susceptibility to Pgp efflux (figure 6). From this comparison specific functional groups were identified which were compatible with pharmacological activity and low Pgp transport. Moreover, a general trend was resolved showing increasing numbers potential hydrogen bond acceptors associated with sub groups that conferred high potential for Pgp efflux. A histogram comparing the number of heteroatoms (O and N) with the proportion of compounds with transport ratios greater than 2 indicated that the probability a compound will be a Pgp substrate increases with increasing heteroatoms (figure 7). Analysis of structural features determining susceptibility to Pgp efflux was complemented with KNN and QSAR molecular modeling approaches (Kauffman and Jurs, 2001) to evaluate all the pgp transport data within this series. The KNN approach predicts whether a compound will be a susceptible to Pgp efflux (transport ratio greater than 2 or 3) based on the efflux properties of the most closely related structural analogues. The consesus efflux properties of the five nearest neighbors was then used to predict the properties of a novel compound. This analysis provided accurate predictions for 85% of novel compounds within this chemical series with no bias

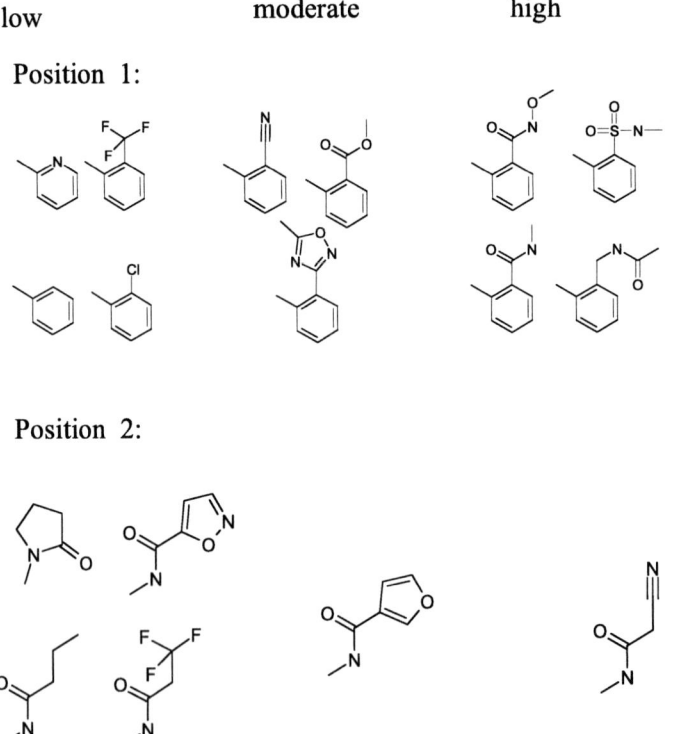

Figure 6. Influence of substituents on Pgp mediated transport. The influence of different functional groups was evaluated by comparing structural analogues which differ at a single position as described in the text. Although the absolute transport ratios for compounds were also dependent on other structural features in the molecules, comparisons between structural analogues showed that specific functional groups consistently conferred little or no influence on human PGP mediated efflux (low), showed a mild increase in Pgp efflux (moderate), or conferred a significant PGP mediated efflux (high). For example one structural series of compounds containing functional groups classified as low, moderate or high had transport ratios less than 2, 2-5, or >5 respectively.

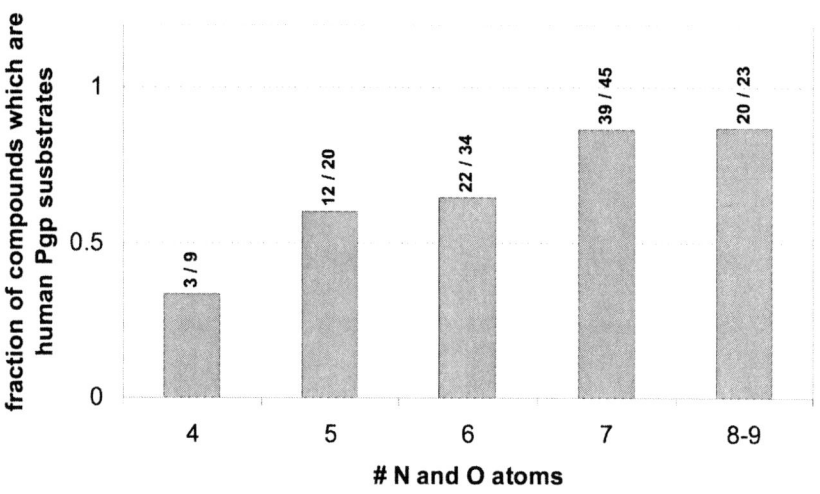

Figure 7. The influence of potential hydrogen bond acceptors as estimated by the number of O and N atoms on susceptibility of compounds to Pgp efflux. A compound is determined to be a Pgp substrate in this study if it has directional transport greater than 2 in transport studies with L-MDR1 cells. The number of compounds showing directional transport greater than 2 over the total number of compounds in each category is presented above the bar.

toward false positive or false negative results. The majority of incorrect predictions had transport ratios between two and three. The second modeling approach determined the probability that a compound would be subject to Pgp efflux based on calculated physical chemical parameters. This approach yeilded similar predictive potential to the KNN approach. Although both of these models could be useful for virtual screening, the greatest value came from the potential to resolve out of the model structural features conferring Pgp susceptibility. In the case of the KNN model specific functional groups could be identified which conferred susceptibility to Pgp. The functional groups identified were consistent with those identified through manual comparison of structures, and tended to show groups with greater number of hydrogen bond acceptors as liabilities which increased Pgp efflux. QSAR analysis using molecular operating environment (MOE) resolved 7 physical chemical descriptors which were most influential in determining susceptibility to Pgp. These descriptors were heavily weighted toward polarity (cLogP; sLog P) and hydrogen bond acceptors (number of nitrogen atoms, surface area of hydrogen bond acceptors, etc). This trend toward increasing hydrogen bond acceptors in compounds which are Pgp substrates is consistent with reported predicitive models for identifying Pgp substrates. Seelig et. al. (Seelig, 1998; Seelig and Landwojtowicz, 2000) evaluated the chemical properties of 100 Pgp substrates, inhibitors, inducers and non-substrates revealing a pattern where two hydrogen bond acceptors separated by 4.6 Å or three acceptors positioned 2.5 Å from each other were consistent motifs in compounds interacting with Pgp. Other predicitive models have also implicated hydrogen bonding as a determinant for Pgp substrate recognition, and studies on a homologous series suggest a correlation between hydrogen bond acceptor potency and potential to interact with Pgp (Gombar, Polli, Humphreys, Wring, and Serabjit-Singh, 2004; Osterberg and Norinder, 2000; Xue et al., 2004). Collectively these results suggest that one approach to reducing Pgp efflux of the compounds is to lower the hydrogen bond acceptor potency.

Applying the strategy of reducing hydrogen bond acceptors combined with the empirical SAR proved successful eventually resulting in over 70% of the new discovery compounds having good pharmacological activity and low Pgp transport. However due to metabolism related liabilities in the core structure, a new structural template had to be pursued which presented new challenges.

In contrast to the initial series in which Pgp susceptibility could be controlled by altering the substituents at two positions, Pgp liability was intrinsic to the core structure of the new series. The effects of specific substituents on Pgp transport did not transfer from the first structural series to the second. Instead, modification which increased the log P of compounds resulted in increased Pgp efflux. As noted previously Pgp-substrate interactions appear to entail partitioning of the drug into the membrane followed by interactions of the substrate with the protein. Increasing Pgp efflux with increasing Log P would be consistent with membrane partitioning being the primary limitation to transport for this series suggesting that determinants that confer high potential for recognition and transport by Pgp are intrinsic to the core structural template. In this series an amide bond was added to the core structure in place of a secondary amine. Addition of an amide bond in the first chemical series had previously been shown to dramatically increase susceptibility of compounds to Pgp. Initial attempts to replaced the amide, to introduce direct modifications to the amide bond, or to introduce steric hindrance to the amide bond reduced Pgp transport, but at the expense of pharmacological potency (figure 8a and b). Consequently, the structural features which conferred susceptibility to Pgp could not be separated from features required for pharmacological activity. The solution to this problem came through modification of the hydrogen bond acceptor potential of the amide bond. As noted previously, SAR from the initial series indicated that minimizing hydrogen bond acceptor potential could reduce susceptibility to Pgp efflux. Placing an electron withdrawing substituent (CF_3) immediately adjacent to the amide bond reduces its electron density, making it a weaker hydrogen bond acceptor. Incorporating this modification into this series resulted in compounds which were not Pgp substrates and maintained high affinity to the biochemical target. Using this approach as well as other approaches to decrease the electron density of the amide bond, several compounds were prepared which maintained nanomolar potency and were not Pgp substrates. Thus, by combining empirically derived SAR with our current functional understanding of Pgp-substrate interactions strategies were developed for making potent compounds with high potential for CNS penetration such that 80-90% of compounds being prepared in this series were not substrates for human Pgp.

While in vitro studies indicated low susceptibility to human Pgp efflux and good passive permeability for these compounds, several of the compounds

a)

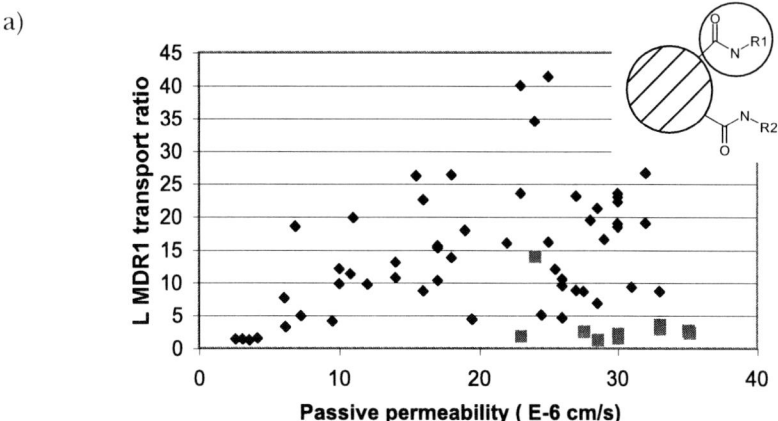

b)

R	MDR1 transport ratio (B to A/ A to B)	Papp LLC PK1 (cm/s E-6)	Potent
	8.6	28	Y
	8.6	24	Y
	3	12	N
	2.7	35	N
	2.2	18	N
	2.6	32	N
	2.8	22	Y
	2.2	33	Y

Figure 8. : Influence of amide modifications on human Pgp mediated directional transport of new structural series. a) Pgp transport versus passive permeability for compounds containing an unmodified amide bond adjacent to R1 (♦) and compounds with modified amide bonds (■). b) Influence of amide associated substituents and modifications on Pgp transport, passive permeability, and pharmacological potency of compounds in the new structural series. Modifications which reduced Pgp efflux included replacement of the amide, methylation of the amide N, steric hindrance to the amide, and incorporation of electron withdrawing groups adjacent to the amide. Only incorporation of electron withdrawing groups retained potency while reducing Pgp efflux.

maintained significant transport by rodent Pgp and showed low brain penetration in rats. Therefore the decision to pursue clinical studies in man requires considerable confidence that the in vitro human Pgp results will extrapolate to brain penetration in man. Some confidence that the low Pgp transport would extrapolate to better brain penetration in man was obtained from analysis of brain tissue and plasma drug levels in monkeys used for receptor occupancy studies. Monkey MDR1 shares 96% homology with human Pgp in which most of the amino acid substitutions are in positions which are not anticipated to significantly alter substrate interaction. With few exceptions compounds which show Pgp B to A/ A to B transport ratios lower than 3 have brain tissue drug levels between 40% and 140% of the plasma drug levels. In contrast drug levels of compounds with transport ratios greater than 3 are all below 20% of the plasma drug concentrations. Although species differences between human and monkey CNS penetration may exist for some compounds, the general trend observed suggests that in spite of the species difference in rodent, the low Pgp efflux observed for human Pgp transport in vitro will translate to high CNS penetration in vivo.

Conclusions

The case study presented in this chapter illustrates the potential value of using in vitro transport models to establish structure based approaches to overcome Pgp efflux. The successful application of this approach requires that the in vitro model used has direct relevance to the barrier to CNS transport, and that development of SAR take into account mechanistic aspects of Pgp transport. In addition to this case study, we have found that establishment of structure transport relationships for Pgp have proven valuable in several CNS programs in which Pgp efflux has been an issue. Although specific SAR from one chemical series may not directly translate to other programs, general principles and strategies can be applied across different programs. This has allowed us to identify sites conferring Pgp susceptibility more rapidly and has yielded an assortment of approaches to overcome the liabilities in new structural series. With increased knowledge of Pgp-drug interactions and the establishment of better global SAR for Pgp transport, a broader array of strategies for limiting Pgp efflux should become available. However, it should be recognized that even with extensive SAR, identifying structural modifications to limit Pgp efflux which are compatible with maintenance of pharmacological potency, target specificity, and good drug metabolism and pharmacokinetic properties will remain a major challenge. The blood-brain barrier is an added complication to the already difficult task of transforming a pharmacologically active agent into a drug. Overcoming the numerous hurdles to discovery and development of a safe effective drug requires the coordinated efforts of medicinal chemists, biologist, pharmacologists, and drug metabolism scientist. In this regard effective communication is the most effective tool in the strategic development of CNS drugs.

Acknowledgements

The authors would like to thank Sergey Krymgold, Xiadong Shen Scott Fauty, Todd Killino and William Neway for technical assistance on portions of this work. The authors would also like to thank Chris Culberson, Rebecca Ann Perlow-Poehnelt, Georgia B. McGaughey, , Chris Tong, Ken Korzekwa, Neville Anthony, Raymond Evers and Tomoyuke Ohe for valuable discussions and suggestions.

References

Ambudkar SV, Dey S, Hrycyna CA, Ramachandra M, Pastan I, and Gottesman MM. Biochemical, cellular, and pharmacological aspects of the multidrug transporter. *Annu Rev Pharmacol Toxicol* 1999; 39:361-398.

Ambudkar SV, Kimchi-Sarfaty C, Sauna ZE, and Gottesman MM. P-glycoprotein: from genomics to mechanism. *Oncogene* 2003; 22:7468-7485.

Chiba P, Holzer W, Landau M, Bechmann G, Lorenz K, Plagens B, Hitzler M, Richter E, and Ecker G. Substituted 4-acylpyrazoles and 4-acylpyrazolones: synthesis and multidrug resistance-modulating activity. *J Med Chem* 1998; 41:4001-4011.

Cordon-Cardo C, O'Brien JP, Boccia J, Casals D, Bertino JR, and Melamed MR. Expression of the multidrug resistance gene product (P-glycoprotein) in human normal and tumor tissues. *J Histochem. Cytochem.* 1990; 38:1277-1287.

Ecker G, Huber M, Schmid D, and Chiba P. The importance of a nitrogen atom in modulators of multidrug resistance. *Mol Pharmacol* 1999; 56:791-796.

Gan LS, Moseley MA, Khosla B, Augustijns PF, Bradshaw TP, Hendren RW, and Thakker DR. CYP3A-like cytochrome P450-mediated metabolism and polarized efflux of cyclosporin A in Caco-2 cells. *Drug Metab Dispos* 1996; 24:344-349.

Gatmaitan ZC and Arias IM. Structure and function of P-glycoprotein in normal liver and small intestine. *Adv.Pharmacol* 1993; 24:77-97.

Gombar VK, Polli JW, Humphreys JE, Wring SA, and Serabjit-Singh CS. Predicting P-glycoprotein substrates by a quantitative structure-activity relationship model. *J Pharm Sci* 2004; 93:957-968.

Hochman JH, Chiba M, Nishime J, Yamazaki M, and Lin JH. Influence of P-glycoprotein on the transport and metabolism of indinavir in Caco-2 cells expressing cytochrome P-450 3A4. *J Pharmacol Exp Ther* 2000; 292:310-318.

Hochman JH, Chiba M, Yamazaki M, Tang C, and Lin JH. P-glycoprotein-mediated efflux of indinavir metabolites in Caco-2 cells expressing cytochrome P450 3A4. *J Pharmacol Exp Ther* 2001; 298:323-330.

Jonker JW, Wagenaar E, van Deemter L, Gottschlich R, Bender HM, Dasenbrock J, and Schinkel AH. Role of blood-brain barrier P-glycoprotein in limiting brain accumulation and sedative side-effects of asimadoline, a peripherally acting analgaesic drug. *Br J Pharmacol* 1999; 127:43-50.

Juliano RL and Ling V. A surface glycoprotein modulating drug permeability in Chinese hamster ovary cell mutants. *Biochim Biophys Acta* 1976; 455:152-162.

Kauffman, GW and Jurs PC. QSAR and k-nearest neighbor classification analysis of selective cyclooxygenase-2 inhibitors using topological based numerical descriptors. *J Chem Inf Comput Sci* 2001; 41:1553-1560.

Kim RB, Fromm MF, Wandel C, Leake B, Wood AJJ, Roden DM, Wilkinson GR. The drug transporter P-glycoprotein limits oral absorption and brain entry of HIV-1 protease inhibitors. *J Clin Invest* 1998; 101:289-294.

Lankas GR, Cartwright ME, and Umbenhauer D. P-glycoprotein deficiency in a subpopulation of CF-1 mice enhances avermectin-induced neurotoxicity. *Toxicol Appl Pharmacol* 1996; 143:357-365.

Lankas GR, Wise LD, Cartwright ME, Pippert T, and Umbenhauer DR. Placental P-glycoprotein deficiency enhances susceptibility to chemically induced birth defects in mice. *Reprod.Toxicol* 1998; 12:457-463.

Lentz KA, Polli JW, Wring SA, Humphreys JE, and Polli JE. Influence of passive permeability on apparent P-glycoprotein kinetics. *Pharm Res* 2000; 17:1456-1460.

Lown KS, Mayo RR, Leichtman AB, Hsiao HL, Turgeon DK, Schmiedlin-Ren P, Brown MB, Guo W, Rossi SJ, Benet LZ, and Watkins PB. Role of intestinal P-glycoprotein (mdr1) in interpatient variation in the oral bioavailability of cyclosporine. *Clin Pharmacol Ther* 1997; 62:248-260.

Mayer U, Wagenaar E, Beijnen JH, Smit JW, Meijer DK, van Asperen J, Borst P, and Schinkel AH. Substantial excretion of digoxin via the intestinal mucosa and prevention of long-term digoxin accumulation in the brain by the mdr 1a P-glycoprotein. *Br J Pharmacol* 1996; 119:1038-1044.

Mechetner EB, Schott B, Morse BS, Stein WD, Druley T, Davis KA, Tsuruo T, and Roninson IB. P-glycoprotein function involves conformational transitions detectable by differential immunoreactivity. *Proc Natl Acad Sci U S A* 1997; 94:12908-12913.

Osterberg T and Norinder U. Theoretical calculation and prediction of P-glycoprotein-interacting drugs using MolSurf parametrization and PLS statistics. *Eur J Pharm Sci* 2000; 10:295-303.

Polli JW, Wring SA, Humphreys JE, Huang L, Morgan JB, Webster LO, and Serabjit-Singh CS. Rational use of in vitro P-glycoprotein assays in drug discovery. *J Pharmacol Exp Ther* 2001; 299:620-628.

Prueksaritanont, T., Meng, Y., Ma, B., Leppert, P., Hochman, J., Tang, C., Perkins, J., Zrada, M., Meissner, R., Duggan, M.E. and Lin, J.H. Differences in the absorption, metabolism and biliary excretion of a diastereomeric pair of alpha(upsilon)beta(3)-antagonists in rat: Limited role of P glycoprotein. Xenobiotica, 2002; 32: 207-220.

Roninson IB, Chin JE, Choi KG, Gros P, Housman DE, Fojo A, Shen DW, Gottesman MM, and Pastan I. Isolation of human mdr DNA sequences amplified in multidrug-resistant KB carcinoma cells. *Proc Natl Acad Sci U S A* 1986; 83:4538-4542.

Rosenberg MF, Kamis AB, Callaghan R, Higgins CF, and Ford RC. Three-dimensional structures of the mammalian multidrug resistance P-glycoprotein demonstrate major conformational changes in the transmembrane domains upon nucleotide binding. *J Biol Chem* 2003; 278:8294-8299.

Rosenberg MF, Velarde G, Ford RC, Martin C, Berridge G, Kerr ID, Callaghan R, Schmidlin A, Wooding C, Linton KJ, and Higgins CF. Repacking of the transmembrane domains of P-glycoprotein during the transport ATPase cycle. *EMBO J* 2001; 20:5615-5625.

Scala S, Akhmed N, Rao US, Paull K, Lan LB, Dickstein B, Lee JS, Elgemeie GH, Stein WD, and Bates SE. P-glycoprotein substrates and antagonists cluster into two distinct groups. *Mol Pharmacol* 1997; 51:1024-1033.

Schinkel AH, Smit JJ, van Tellingen O, Beijnen JH, Wagenaar E, van Deemter L, Mol CA, Van Der Valk MA, Robanus-Maandag EC, te Riele HP, et.al. Disruption of the mouse mdr1a P-glycoprotein gene leads to a deficiency in the blood-brain barrier and to increased sensitivity to drugs. *Cell* 1994; 77:491-502.

Schinkel AH, Wagenaar E, Mol CA, and van Deemter L. P-glycoprotein in the blood-brain barrier of mice influences the brain penetration and pharmacological activity of many drugs. *J Clin Invest* 1996; 97:2517-2524.

Schinkel AH, Wagenaar E, van Deemter L, Mol CA, and Borst P. Absence of the mdr1a P-Glycoprotein in mice affects tissue distribution and pharmacokinetics of dexamethasone, digoxin, and cyclosporin A. *J Clin Invest* 1995; 96:1698-1705.

Seelig A. A general pattern for substrate recognition by P-glycoprotein. *Eur J Biochem* 1998; 251:252-261.

Seelig A and Landwojtowicz E. Structure-activity relationship of P-glycoprotein substrates and modifiers. *Eur J Pharm Sci* 2000; 12:31-40.

Shapiro AB and Ling V. Extraction of Hoechst 33342 from the cytoplasmic leaflet of the plasma membrane by P-glycoprotein. *Eur J Biochem* 1997; 250:122-129.

Smit JW, Huisman MT, van Tellingen O, Wiltshire HR, and Schinkel AH. Absence or pharmacological blocking of placental P-glycoprotein profoundly increases fetal drug exposure. *J Clin Invest* 1999; 104:1441-1447.

Smit JW, Schinkel AH, Weert B, and Meijer DK. Hepatobiliary and intestinal clearance of amphiphilic cationic drugs in mice in which both mdr1a and mdr1b genes have been disrupted. *Br J Pharmacol* 1998; 124:416-424.

Sonveaux N, Vigano C, Shapiro AB, Ling V, and Ruysschaert JM. Ligand-mediated tertiary structure changes of reconstituted P-glycoprotein. A tryptophan fluorescence quenching analysis. *J Biol Chem* 1999; 274:17649-17654.

Sparreboom A, van Asperen J, Mayer U, Schinkel AH, Smit JW, Meijer DK, Borst P, Nooijen WJ, Beijnen JH, and van Tellingen O. Limited oral bioavailability and active epithelial excretion of paclitaxel (Taxol) caused by P-glycoprotein in the intestine. *Proc Natl Acad Sci U S A* 1997; 94:2031-2035.

Speeg KV, Maldonado AL, Liaci J, and Muirhead D. Effect of cyclosporine on colchicine secretion by a liver canalicular transporter studied in vivo. *Hepatology* 1992; 15:899-903.

Thiebaut F, Tsuruo T, Hamada H, Gottesman MM, Pastan I, and Willingham MC. Immunohistochemical localization in normal tissues of different epitopes in the multidrug transport protein P170: evidence for localization in brain capillaries and crossreactivity of one antibody with a muscle protein. *J Histochem.Cytochem.* 19889; 37:159-164.

Troutman MD and Thakker DR (2003a) Efflux ratio cannot assess P-glycoprotein-mediated attenuation of absorptive transport: asymmetric effect of P-glycoprotein on absorptive and secretory transport across Caco-2 cell monolayers. *Pharm Res* 2003a; 20:1200-1209.

Troutman MD and Thakker DR. Novel experimental parameters to quantify the modulation of absorptive and secretory transport of compounds by P-glycoprotein in cell culture models of intestinal epithelium. *Pharm Res* 2003b; 20:1210-1224.

Wacher VJ, Silverman JA, Zhang Y, and Benet LZ. Role of P-glycoprotein and cytochrome P450 3A in limiting oral absorption of peptides and peptidomimetics. *J Pharm Sci* 1998; 87:1322-1330.

Wang G, Pincheira R, and Zhang JT. Dissection of drug-binding-induced conformational changes in P-glycoprotein. *Eur J Biochem* 1998; 255:383-390.

Wang G, Pincheira R, Zhang M, and Zhang JT. Conformational changes of P-glycoprotein by nucleotide binding. *Biochem J* 1997; 328 (Pt 3):897-904.

Xue Y, Yap CW, Sun LZ, Cao ZW, Wang JF, and Chen YZ.　Prediction of P-glycoprotein substrates by a support vector machine approach. *J Chem Inf Comput Sci* 2004;　44:1497-1505.

Yamazaki M, Neway WE, Ohe T, Chen I, Rowe JF, Hochman JH, Chiba M, and Lin JH.　In vitro substrate identification studies for p-glycoprotein-mediated transport: species difference and predictability of in vivo results. *J Pharmacol Exp Ther* 2001;　296:723-735.

3

Metabolic Activation-Role in Toxicity and Idiosyncratic Reactions

John S. Walsh

Dept of Drug Metabolism
Metabolic and Viral Center for Excellence in Drug Discovery
GlaxoSmithKline
Research Triangle Park
North Carolina 27709

Table of Contents

List of Abbreviations:

CYP...Cytochrome P450
MAO ....Monoamine oxidase
FMO ....Flavin monooxygenase.

Key Words:

Electrophile, Radical, Idiosyncratic reactions, Hepatotoxicity, Reactive metabolite, Acylators, Activated double bonds, Redox cycling, Nucleophiles

Introduction

Adverse drug reactions continue to pose a major impediment to drug development, and the clinical management of marketed products. These are typically divided into acute, dose dependent reactions (Type A), and reactions that may occur in only a small percentage of patients, where the frequency of occurrence in the population is not dependent on dose (Type B), although more complex classifications have also been proposed, (Park *et al*, 2000). According to a recent PhRMA review, the most frequently encountered toxicities in pre clinical drug development are hepatotoxicity and dermal reactions (Olson *et al*. 2000). Hepatotoxicity may take many forms (Ward and Daly 2001), so implying drug metabolism generally would be presumptive, but as the major organ responsible for the metabolism of drugs it seems clear that metabolism is important in many cases. Type A reactions generally may be mediated through parent compound or metabolites, and the role of chemically reactive metabolites has been well recognized (Hinson *et al*. 1994). Type B reactions, also referred to as idiosyncratic or hypersensitivity reactions, have been the subject of extensive reviews in recent years (Uetrecht 2000, Ju and Uetrecht, 2002). These are generally believed to be immune mediated, and are not predictable from pre clinical animal studies, thus they may not be identified until late clinical stages, or post marketing. Type B reactions have been reported to constitute 25% of all clinical adverse events (Lazarou et al, 1998). While direct T cell stimulation has been proposed as a possible mechanism (Zanni *et al*. 1998), bioactivation to reactive metabolites that covalently bind to proteins is still believed to be a key event in the origin of most Type B reactions, and is the basis of the Hapten hypothesis (Uetrecht 2003). Much has been written on the role of covalent binding for both type A and Type B reactions (Knowles *et al*. 2003), and clearly protein binding can be dissociated from toxicity (Goldlin and Boelsterli 1994). The dilemma of the significance of protein binding in type B reactions can be addressed in part by the Danger Hypothesis, where by the immune system requires a second signal to trigger a response (Matzinger, 1994). This may be cellular damage or an infection (Pirmohamed *et al*. 2002). Thus in general covalent protein binding is still considered a key factor in most Type B reactions.

Drug metabolism therefore, is implicated in the most problematical toxicities in drug development and clinical practice. This raises the question whether such properties can be rationally designed out at an early stage of development, based on knowledge of metabolic pathways or simply structure, and such consideration have been widely discussed (Uetrecht 2000). The ability to do this effectively remains elusive, but it seems clear that an understanding of how functional groups can be metabolized to reactive metabolites is likely to reduce the prevalence of both type A and B reactions. This review will survey the more extensively studied reactive metabolites which have been encountered in drug molecules.

Types of Reactive Metabolites

Up to 30 different types of functional groups have been shown or implicated to undergo some type of metabolic activation, (personal observation). However, those most frequently encountered in drug development may be only about one third of this. Reactive metabolites can be broadly grouped into either electrophiles or radicals. Carbenes would not fall into either group, and while well recognized as a species involved in CYP (Cytochrome P450) inactivation (Murray *et al.* 1985) they have not been significantly implicated in toxicities. To some degree, the different biological effects of electrophiles and radicals can be rationalized based on their chemistry. Thus the closed shell electrophiles will react readily with biological nucleophiles, such as proteins to give covalent adducts, where as radicals are more likely to abstract a hydrogen radical from the protein (Sorani *et al.* 1994). However, oxygen existing in the triplet state, is ideally set up to react with unpaired electron species, and so this tends to be the more prevalent reaction course for many radicals. Consequently, free radical formation is more frequently associated with oxidative stress, and electrophiles with covalent binding. While radicals may be implicated in some idiosyncratic reactions, for most drugs showing this form of toxicity where a bioactivation mechanism has been proposed, most appear to involve electrophiles (Li 2002). This statement is something of a generalization however, and as more work is done specifically looking for radical formation more examples may be found.

Reactive metabolites may be derived from a wide range of metabolic reactions including oxidation (CYP, peroxidases, MAO (Monoamine oxidase)), reduction (CYP, CYP reductase), and conjugation (glucuronyl transferases, sulfotransferases, glutathione transferase, Acyl Co-A synthase). While oxidative CYP mediated reactions predominate, peroxidases present in blood cells may play a major role in agranulocytosis and other blood toxicities.

There are a number of recent reviews of metabolic activation covering the ranges of structures which have been shown to have bioactivation potential (Uetrecht, 2003 Nelson, 2001). This review will focus more on the commonality of reactivity patterns for reactive metabolites derived from these widely different structural features. This may help to simplify the mechanistic aspects of this undesirable drug development property.

Electrophiles

Regardless of the structure from which they are metabolically derived, electrophiles may be grouped as either: 1. Acylators, 2. Activated double bonds, 3. Other electrophilc carbon centers, or 4. Electrophiles based on nitrogen or sulfur, or derived from sulfur oxidation. An important and quite common observation is that metabolism of a particular functional group may give rise to more than one type of electrophile, as shown in some of the examples below.

Acylators

These may be defined as electrophiles which result in the biological nucleophile being bonded to an sp2 hybridized carbon, usually double bonded to oxygen. Examples of functional groups which may produce acylating electrophiles are: carboxylic acids, acetylenes, formamides, halogenated hydrocarbons, and thiazolidinediones.

Carboxylic acids may act as acylators either via glucuronidation or acyl CoA ester formation (Figure 1).

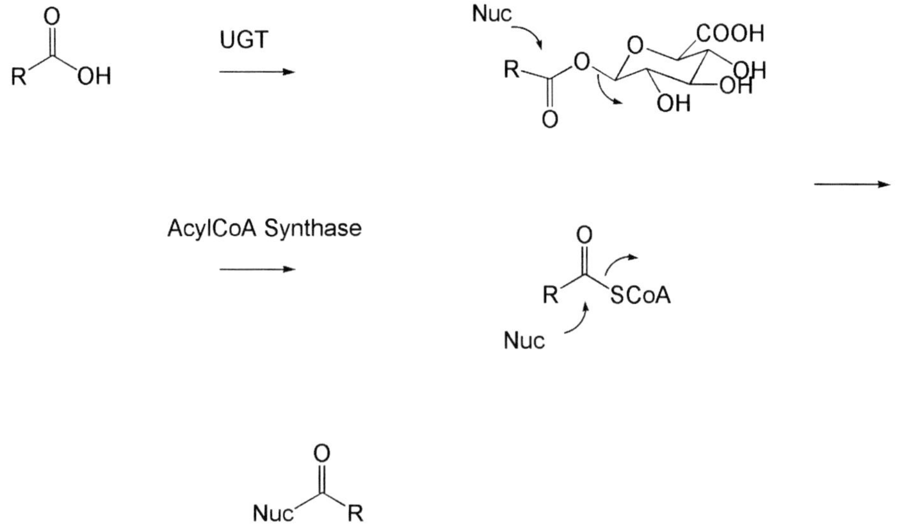

Figure 1. Acylating metabolites derived from conjugation of carboxylic acids : acylglucuronide and acyl CoA esters.

Acyl glucuronides are perhaps the most widely studied of reactive metabolites, and there are many good reviews on this subject (Spahn-Langguth and Benet 1992, Sallustio *et al.* 2000). A large number of carboxylic acid containing drugs known to be metabolized by acyl glucuronidation, have been marketed. This level of clinical experience makes this functionality some what unique as regards the potential for an empirical risk assessment. Of note are the number of drugs metabolized via acyl glucuronidation which have been withdrawn from the market for safety reasons, (Table 1). Between 1974-1993, there were a total of 29 drug withdrawals for safety reasons from the U.S., U.K and Spanish markets (Bakke 1995), and seven of these are reported to be metabolized by acyl glucuronidation. While no causative link has been found between acyl glucuronidation and the limiting toxicities for these compounds, it is a pathway of metabolism observed in a significant percentage of compounds which have been withdrawn from the market due to safety factors.

In addition to acting as acylating agents, acyl glucuronides can undergo an intramolecular rearrangement to generate an aldehyde which can bind to proteins, (Figure 2). This mechanism is distinct from the acylating mechanism, thus the acyl glucuronidation pathway can give rise to two distinct types of reactive species.

Drug	Status	Toxicity	Evidence for Anaphylaxis/HSR
Alclofenac	Withdrawn	Skin rash	Yes
Benozaprofen	Withdrawn	Hepatotoxicity	Questionable
Fenclofinac	Withdrawn	Skin rash	+
Grepafloxicin	Withdrawn	QT prolongation	None
Ibufenac	Withdrawn	Pulmonary. Drug induced meningitis	+
Indoprofen	Withdrawn	Aplastic anaemia	+
Pirprofen	Withdrawn	Hepatoxicity, GI Toxicity	None
Suprofen	Withdrawn	Renal Toxicity	+
Trovafloxicin	Restricted	Hepatotoxicity	+
Temafloxicin	Withdrawn	Severe anaphylaxis	Yes
Tycrinafen	Withdrawn	Hepatotoxicity	Yes
Zomepirac	Withdrawn	Pulmonary toxicity	Yes

Table 1. Drugs that form acyl glucuronides which have been withdrawn from the market for safety reasons, or have restricted labeling.

+ : Not pronounced , but at least one report

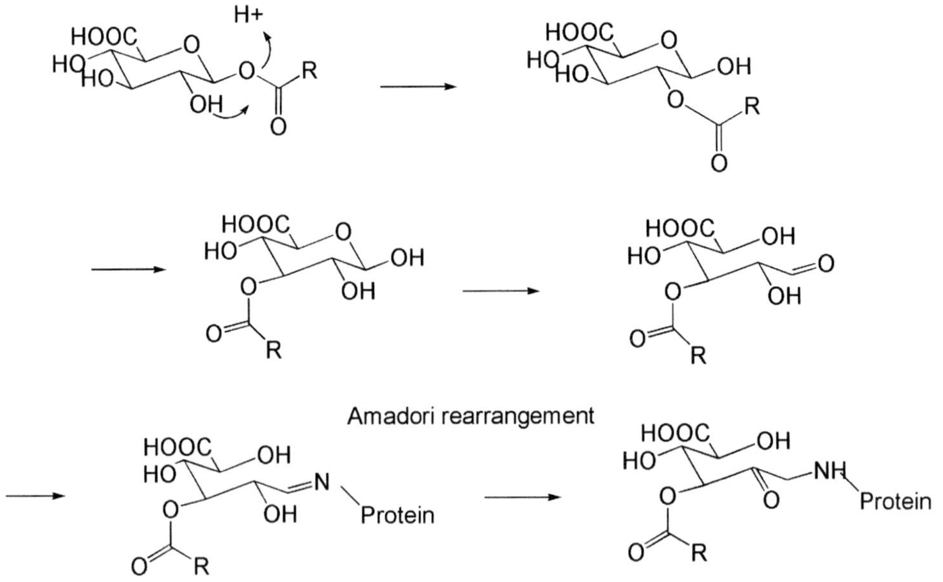

Figure 2. Migration of acylglucuronides to generate an electrophilic carbon center (aldehyde), reaction with nitrogen nucleophile of proteins, and rearrangement to a stable product.

Carboxylic acids may also be metabolized to acylating agents via formation of acyl CoA esters, which can lead to covalent binding, and this constitutes an alternative bioactivation pathway which has been proposed to lead to toxicity, (Li *et al.* 2003a, Li *et al.* 2003b).

Acetylenes may form ketenes during CYP450 mediated oxidation, and these also function as an acylators, most particularly as mechanism based inhibitors of CYP (Fan *et al.* 2003, Johnson et al, 1991). (Figure 3)

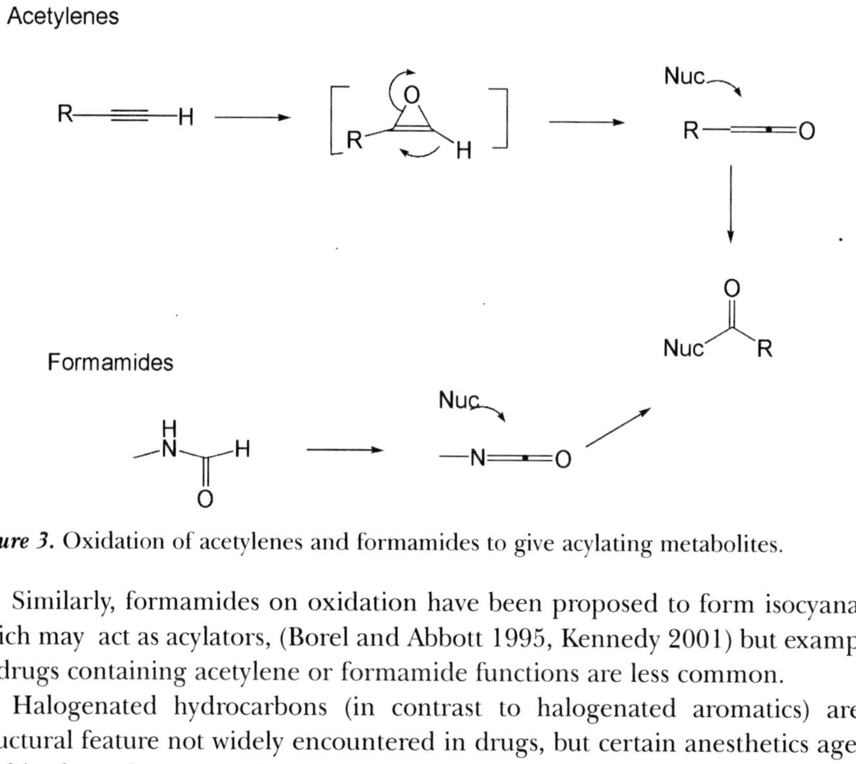

Acetylenes

Formamides

Figure 3. Oxidation of acetylenes and formamides to give acylating metabolites.

Similarly, formamides on oxidation have been proposed to form isocyanates which may act as acylators, (Borel and Abbott 1995, Kennedy 2001) but examples of drugs containing acetylene or formamide functions are less common.

Halogenated hydrocarbons (in contrast to halogenated aromatics) are a structural feature not widely encountered in drugs, but certain anesthetics agents in this class of compounds are among the most mechanistically well studied in regard to metabolic activation and idiosyncratic reactions. The best example is halothane (Figure 4) which undergoes oxidation to generate an acyl halide, a very effective acylating agent, (White and Matteis 2001). The protein targets for the acyl halides, and their implication in the immune response have also been studied (Pumford et. al. 1993, Martin *et al.* 1993). Halogenated hydrocarbons can also be bioactivated by glutathione conjugation, followed by a series of steps to generate thioacyl halides (Figure 5). Nephrotoxicity has been a common observation for compounds showing this pathway, but impairment of mitochondrial function and other toxicities have also been noted (Cooper *et al.* 2002).

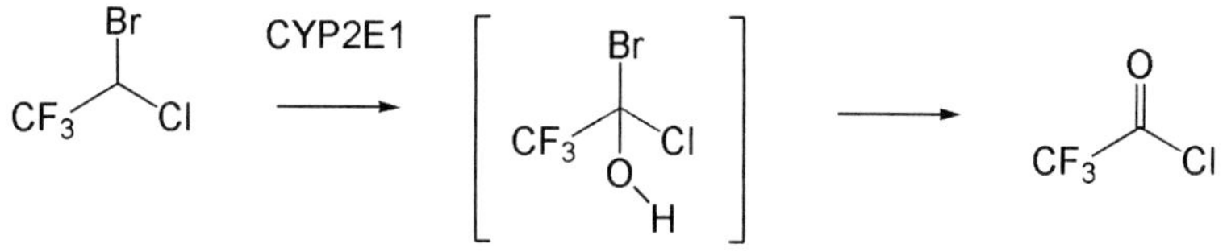

Figure 4. Oxidation of halothane to an acyl chloride.

Trfluoroacetyl chloride

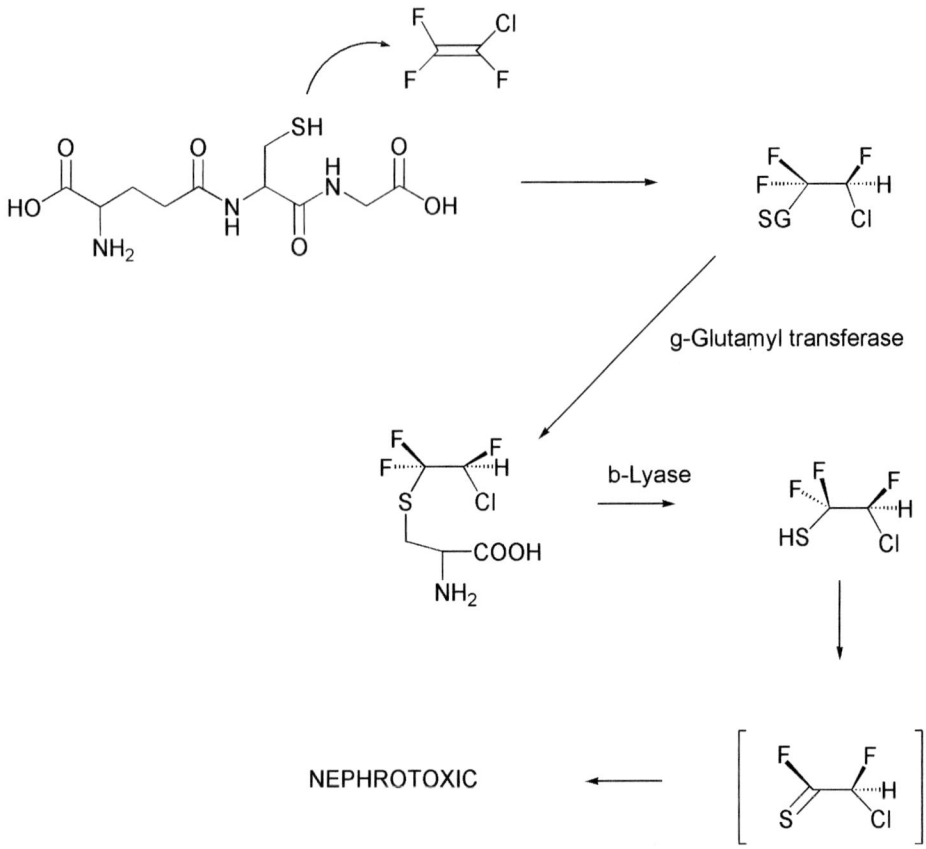

Figure 5. Generation of an acylating thioacyl metabolite via conjugation with glutathione.

A third bioactivation pathway for halogenated hydrocarbons involves reductive metabolism to form radicals which will be discussed below. Thiazolidinediones may undergo oxidation as shown in Figure 6 to produce both an isocyanate (acylator) and a sulfenic acid, a sulfur based electrophile, (Kassahun *et al.* 2001). This was first noted for troglitazone, which has been withdrawn from the market due to idiosyncratic hepatic toxicity. Other thiazolidinedione

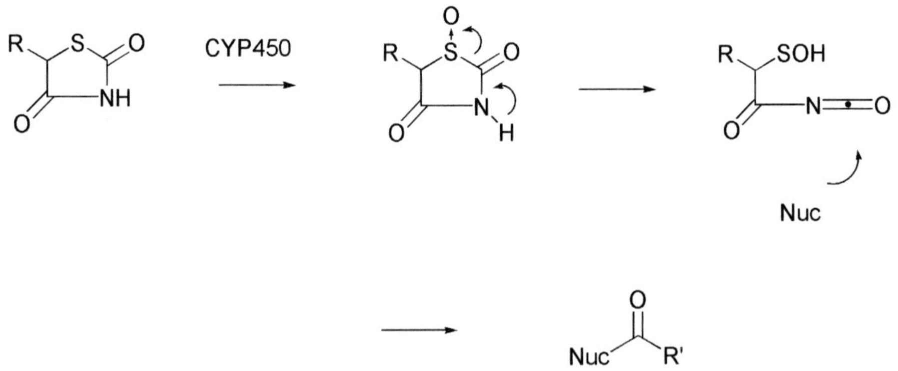

Figure 6. Oxidation of the thiazolidinedione ring system to give a thiocyanate which may act as an acylator, and a sulfenic acid (electrophilic sulfur center).

containing drugs such as pioglitazone and rosiglitazone, are also likely to have this oxidative pathway, however these drugs are considered to be essentially non hepatotoxic, (Figure 7). This is most likely due to the much lower doses at which these drugs are used (Cox *et al.* 2000, Gillies and Dunn 2000).

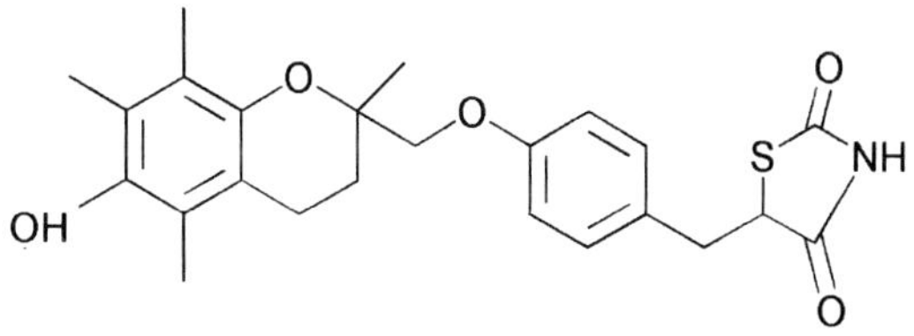

TROGLITAZONE   Hepatotoxic. Withdrawn From Market

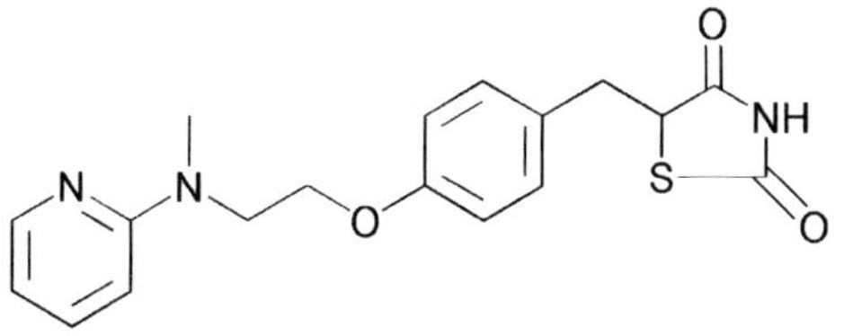

ROSIGLITAZONE

Less toxic. Lower Doses

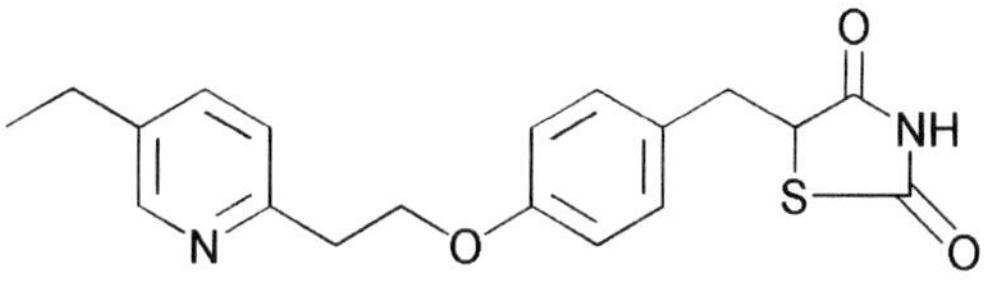

PIOGLITAZONE

Figure 7. Examples of thiazolidindione containing drugs.

Activated Double bonds

A wide range of functionalities can be metabolized to electrophiles which are capable of reacting with nucleophiles by a 1,4 addition process. These function-alities include: nitrogen or oxygen substituted benzenoids, allylic alcohols (or precursors or derivatives), furans, thiophenes, and some indoles. Among the most important type of electrophiles associated with toxicities are quinone type structures (Figure 8). These are typically derived from aromatic systems activated by nitrogen or oxygen substituents, and is one of the more commonly encountered bioactivation pathways, due to the prevalence of these types of aromatic systems in drugs. In many cases, it is probably not possible to differentiate between toxicities arising due to an alkylation process as opposed to redox cycling and oxidative stress (see below). Some examples are indicated in Table 2, and the structures of

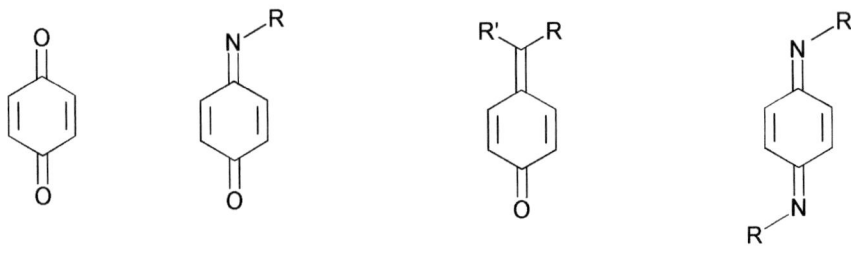

QUINONE   QUINONE IMINE   QUINONE METHIDE

Figure 8. Quinone type structures which may be formed metabolically, which may act as Michael type acceptors.

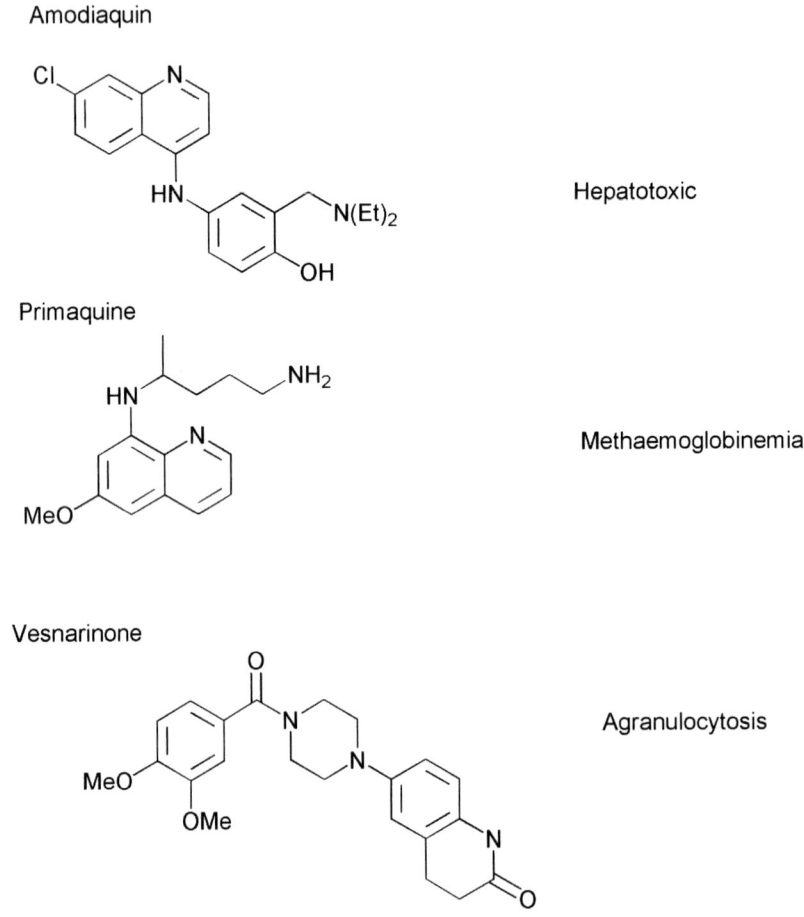

Figure 9. Examples of drugs metabolized to quinone type activated double bond electrophiles.

Compound	Toxicity	Reference
Acetaminophen	Hepatotoxicity	Holme *et. al.* 1984
Amodiaquine	Hepatotoxicity	Maggs *et. al.* 1987
5,6 Dihydroxytryptamine[1]	Neurotoxicity	Singh and Dryhurst 1991
Vesnarinone	Agranulocytosis	Uetrecht *et. al.* 1994
p-Phenetidine	Haemolytic anaemia	Lindqvist *et. al.* 1991
Carbamazepine[2]	Hepatotoxicity	Ju and Uetrecht 1999
Tacrine	Hepatotoxicity	Madden *et. al.* 1995
p-Trifluoromethyl phenol	Hepatotoxicity (in vitro)	Thompson *et. al.* 2000
Diclofenac	Hepatotoxicity	Miyamoto *et. al.* 1997
Isaxonine[3]	Immunoallergic hepatitis	Martinat *et. al.* 1992
Estrogens	Mutagenic	Cao *et. al.* 1998
Primaquine	Methaemaglobinemia	Vasquez-Vivar & Augusto 1994

Table 2. Examples of drugs which may form quinone like metabolites.

1. Redox cycling has also been implicated.

2. Other reactive metabolites such as an epoxide are also formed.

3. A quinone imine metabolite has not been officially proposed, but is likely candidate for the reactive metabolite based on reported metabolic information.

three of these drugs are shown in Figure 9, where by the structural features that lead to these types of reactive metabolites are apparent.

Of novel interest is p-trifluoromethylphenol, which can form a quinone methide non enzymatically with loss of HF (Figure 10). This ultimately leads to formation of a carboxylic acid group, but the intermediate quinone methide has been trapped with glutathione, and p-trifluoromethylphenol is hepatotoxic in vitro (Thompson *et al.* 2000). Aryl trifluoromethyl groups are not normally considered to have metabolic risk, but where relevant structural features exist, this may not always be the case.

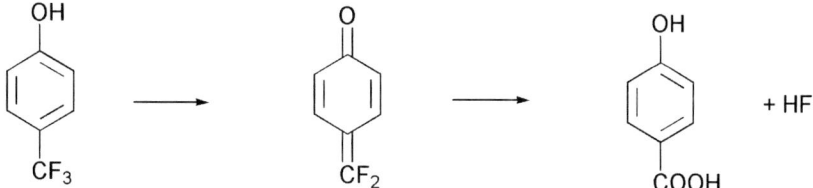

Figure 10. Hydrolysis of p-trifluoromethylphenol to from an electrophilic quinone methide.

Leflunomide (Figure 11) shows a high enough incidence of hepatotoxicity that public interest groups have lobbied for it's withdrawal. The FDA has subsequently ruled in it's favor, and more recent studies suggest that the hepato-toxicity is manageable (Van Roon *et al.* 2004) . Imino methide formation would seem to be feasible here, either directly or after amide hydrolysis. However, no such mechanism has yet been demonstrated. The major metabolite observed is the ring opened structure shown which is a malononitrile, isomeric with the isooxazole ring, (Kalgutkar *et al.* 2003).

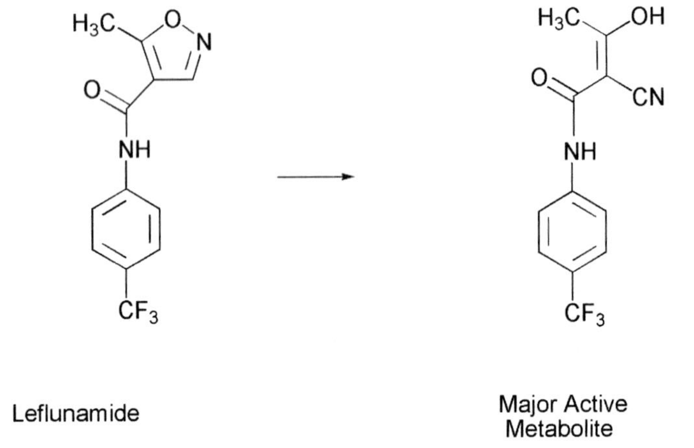

Leflunamide   Major Active
                                     Metabolite

Figure 11. The Metabolism of Leflunomide.

Mechanistically distinct from the above aromatic systems is the case of the antiepileptic agent felbamate, which also produces a metabolite with an activated double bond. While not toxic in rats, Felbamate showed idiosyncratic toxicities in humans, chiefly hepatotoxicity and aplastic anemia which resulted in a Black Box warning for the drug. This may be rationalized based on differences in metabolism (Dieckhaus *et al.* 2000). Felbamate is a bis-carbamate of a propane 1,3 diol (Figure 12), and following hydrolysis and oxidation, carbamic acid can be eliminated to give an αβ unsaturated aldehyde (designated as ATPAL by the authors). This will form glutathione conjugates in vivo confirming it's electrophilicity, and this pathway appears to be more prominent in human. Rats metabolize the drug predominantly by direct oxidation of parent. The reverse transcriptase inhibitor Abacavir marketed for the treatment of HIV infection shows hypersensitivity reactions in a small percentage of patients. The drug is metabolized by alcohol dehydrogenase isozymes to produce an aldehyde intermediate that binds to proteins and this is likely to involve a 1,4 addition mechanism, (Walsh *et al.* 2002).

Drugs may also indirectly produce activated double bond electrophiles from endogenous compounds via lipid peroxidation. This is associated primarily with drugs that form free radicals (see below). For example, 4-hydroxynonenal, a known product derived from radical mediated lipid oxidation, is believed to be toxic due to its inherent electrophilicity and protein binding potential (Laurent *et al.* 2000). Thus for idiosyncratic immune based reactions, this provides an alternative mechanism by which haptenized proteins may be generated, involving an electrophilic process but, initiated by free radicals. This mechanism however, remains hypothetical.

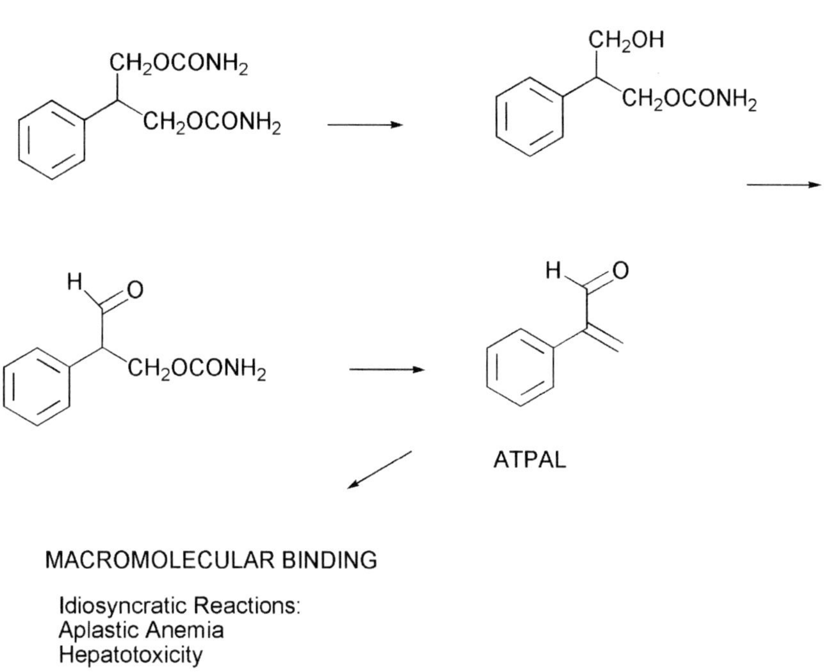

MACROMOLECULAR BINDING

Idiosyncratic Reactions:
Aplastic Anemia
Hepatotoxicity

Figure 12. The metabolism of Felbamate to a reactive metabolite containing an activated double bond.

The π excessive heterocycles furan and thiophene are present in a wide array of drugs and their electron rich state makes them prime sites for oxidative metabolism. In both cases, oxidation leads to structures whose chemical reactivity is basically that of activated double bonds. Menthofuran is a hepatotoxic terpenoid present in mint plants, which contains a furan that is bioactivated via oxidation to a ring opened γ ketoenal, (Figure 13) a reactive Michael type acceptor (Thomasson *et al.* 1991). Thiophene can be oxidized to S-oxides which have activated double bond character (Figure 14), but in this case the ring system stays intact (Dansette *et al.* 1992). Tienilic acid, a thiophene containing diuretic, was withdrawn from the US market in 1980 due to immunoallergic hepatitis. The metabolism of this drug has been extensively studied, and toxicity is believed to be due to this type of S-oxidation pathway (although an arene oxide type mechanism has also been proposed). Mechanistic aspects leading to the immune mediated hepatitis, have been reported (Bonierbale *et al.* 1999).

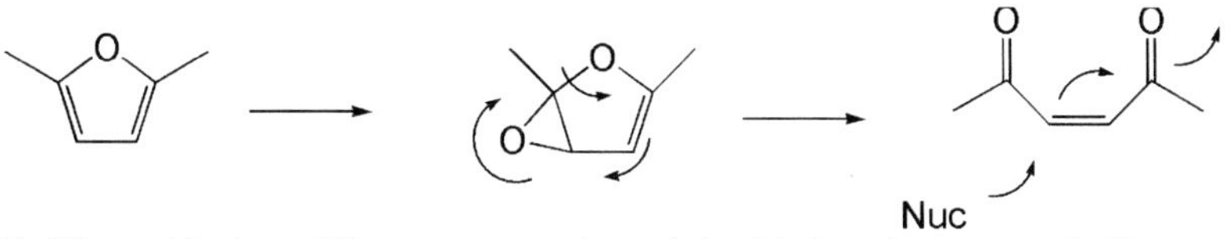

Figure 13. The oxidation of furan to an activated double bond type metabolite.

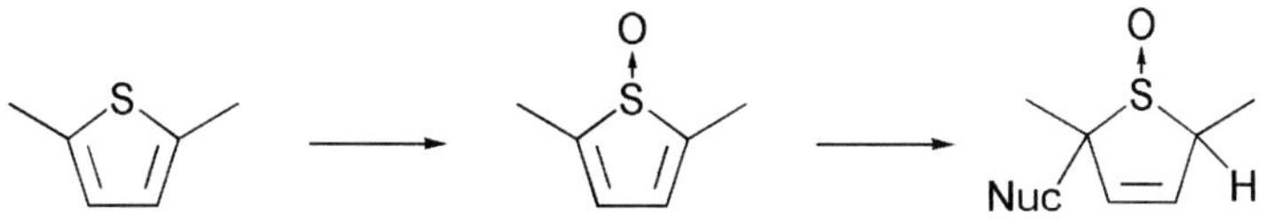

Figure 14. The oxidation of thiophene to a thiophene -S- oxide, reactive by virtue of an activated double bond character.

Another heterocyclic ring system capable of bioactivation is the indole ring which has appropriate 3-substitution. 3-Methyl indole is a pulmonary toxin that undergoes dehydrogenation of the methyl group by CYP2F1 to produce a methylene imine (Figure 15) which can covalently bind to proteins (Lanza *et al.*1999).

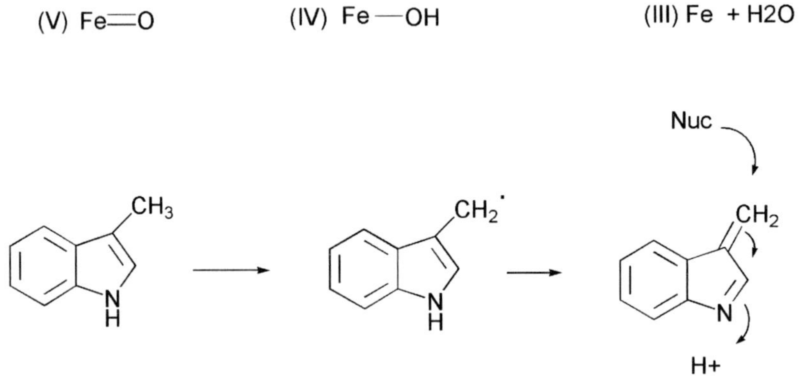

Figure 15. Activated double bond metabolite derived from oxidation of 3-methylindole.

The above indicated reactions for these five membered heterocycles constitute only a portion of the types of transformations possible for these structures, yet represent the most probable bioactivation pathways. The metabolism of five membered heterocycles has been recently reviewed, (Dalvie *et al.* 2002).

Other Electrophilic Carbon Centers

There are a number of other carbon centered electrophiles that can be distin-guished from acylators or activated double bonds. These include epoxides, arene oxides, imines and some carbonyl compounds. The most important example of the latter is the aldehyde /Amadori mechanism for covalent binding of acyl glucuronides to proteins mentioned above (Figure 2). It is important to note that a large number enzymes have evolved specifically for the metabolism of the carbonyl group (Rosemond and Walsh 2004). This is likely due to two reasons: 1. The low reactivity towards one electron oxidative or reductive processes, making them poor substrates for CYP mediated transformations, and 2. Their inherent electrophilicity. Thus the diversity of enzyme systems and isozymes that have evolved to process aldehydes and ketones speaks to their biological significance. Aldehydes are initial products of O-and N-dealkylation reactions, although these are not frequently associated with adverse events. The aldose reductase inhibitor, Sorbinil, shows hypersensitivity reactions manifested by rash and fever, and in rare cases more severe dermal reactions. Bioactivation has been proposed to be due to an O-dealkylation process with subsequent covalent binding of the aldehyde to form a Schiff base (Maggs and Park 1988). One mechanism for ethanol induced hepatitis has been proposed to involve oxidation to acetaldehyde and Schiff base formation with N-terminal amino groups on proteins. These can be subsequently stabilized by a cyclization process to form imidazolidindiones. (Sillanaukee *et al.* 1996). These mechanisms are outlined in Figure 16.

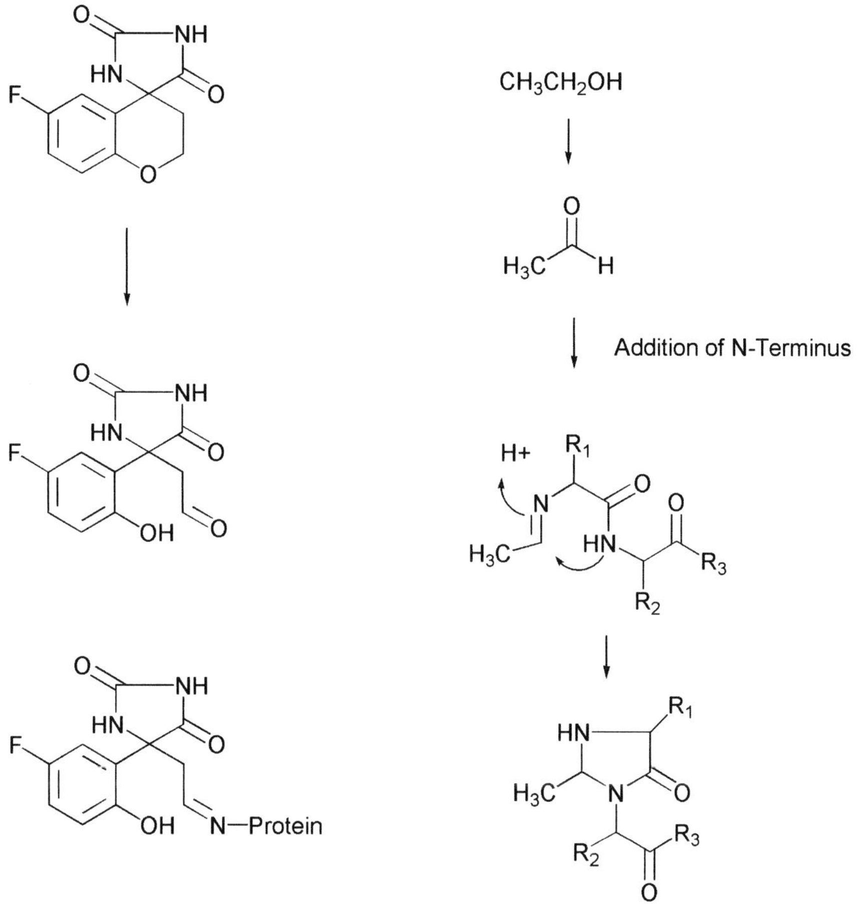

Figure 16. Sorbinil and Ethanol : Examples of compounds where toxicity has been proposed derive from aldehyde formation, showing their proposed reaction with nitrogen protein nucleophiles.

Aliphatic epoxides (as distinct from arene oxides), are probably of more toxicological importance for industrial chemicals than for drugs (Melnick 2002). The toxicity of mycotoxins, such as aflatoxin is believed to be mediated through epoxide formation (Galtier 1999, Guengerich and Johnson 1999). Arene oxides are more widely implicated in drug toxicities, even though much earlier work on these electrophiles was done to elucidate the mechanism of carcinogenicity for polycyclic aromatic hydrocarbons (Jerina, 2000). Cabamazepine is an anticonvulsant associated with various hypersensitivity reactions. Metabolism is complex, and an arene oxide has been suggested as a metabolite that might be associated with the idiosyncratic reaction, but an epoxide, and quinone imines have also been proposed (Figure 17) (Madden *et al.* 1996). Lamotrigine (Figure 18) is used as adjunct therapy in epilepsy, but shows a rare incidence of a severe dermal reaction, (Stevens Johnson Syndrome). Presumed to be immunologically based, bioactivation pathways have been investigated, and evidence for arene oxide formation in rats has been demonstrated (Maggs *et al.* 2000). While this pathway has not yet been demonstrated in humans, it does constitute the most likely metabolic activation pathway associated with the idiosyncratic reaction.

Imines form another class of electrophiles in this group, and are formed from oxidation of alicyclic amines. These functionalities are very common in drugs, but to date there appear to be few cases where their formation has been associated with toxicity, (Gorrod and Aislaitner 1994).

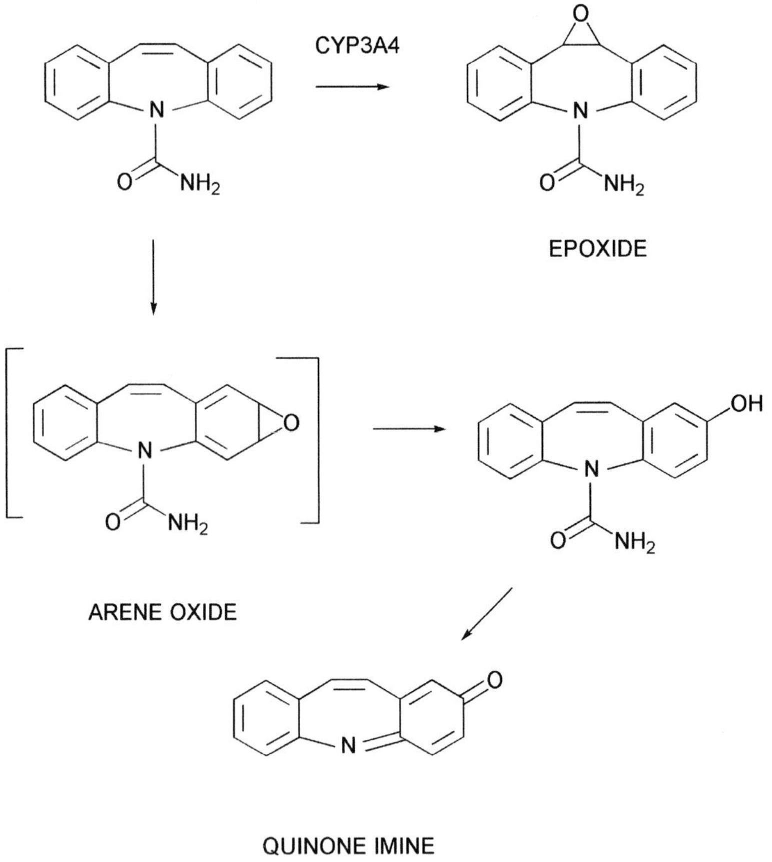

Figure 17. The metabolism of Carbamazepine to reactive carbon centered electrophiles : epoxide and arene oxide. A quinone imine (activated double bond) has also been proposed.

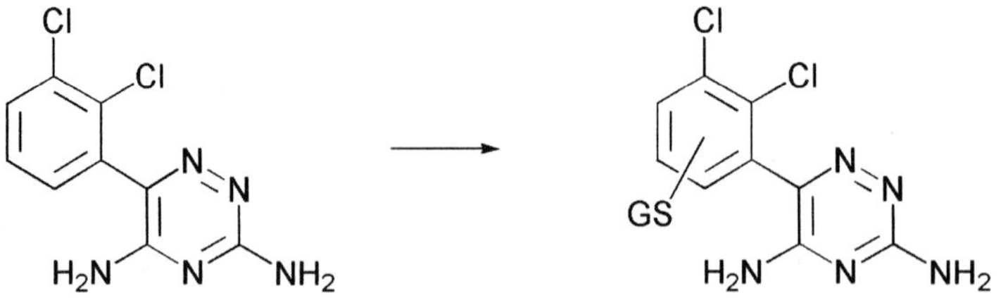

Figure 18. The metabolism of Lamotrigine to a glutathione adduct, consistent with an arene oxide intermediate.

Electrophiles Localized on Nitrogen or Sulfur, or Derived from Oxidation of Sulfur.

Functional groups that are capable of generating this type of electrophile include : nitroaromatics, aromatic amines and hydroxylamines, thioureas, and thiazolidinediones. Nitoaromatics may undergo reduction usually mediated by CYP or CYP reductase. The initial one electron reduced product is the nitro radical anion, which may undergo redox cycling generating active oxygen species (see below). Further reduction generates nitroso and hydroxylamine species, both of which posses electrophilic nitrogen centers. While nitro aromatic groups are generally avoided in drug development for this reason, this metabolic pathway may be encountered inadvertently in natural products. An example is the procarcinogen aristolochic acid, a component of certain Chinese herbs. The herbal product had been taken as a dietary supplement and weight loss agent in some European countries, and has been associated with carcinogenicity and renal nephropathy. Aristolochic acid is an aromatic nitro derivative, and has been shown to undergo CYP mediated reduction to an electrophilic nitroso derivative which subsequently forms DNA adducts, the presumed mechanism for the observed toxicity (Stiborova *et al.* 2001), (Figure 19).

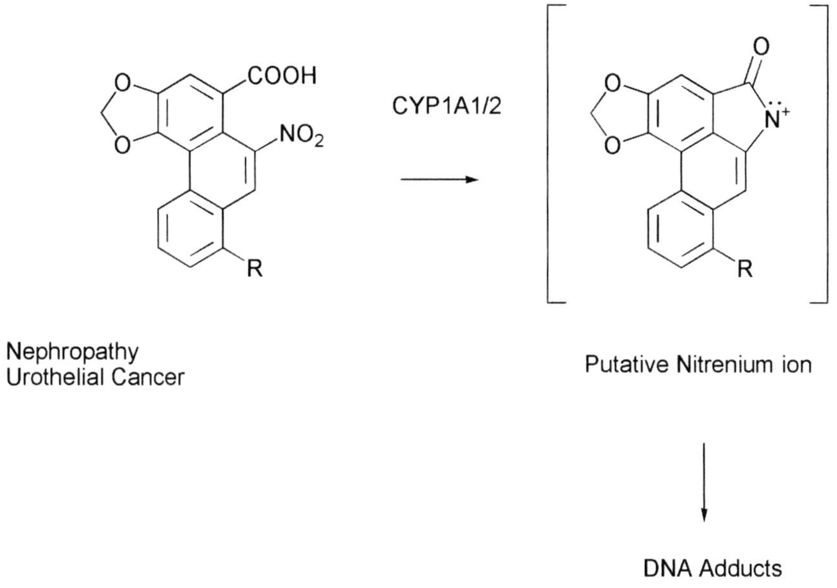

Nephropathy
Urothelial Cancer

Putative Nitrenium ion

DNA Adducts

Figure 19. The reduction of the nitro group of Aristolochic acid to generate an electrophilic nitrogen center, and its reaction with nucleosides.

Aromatic amines may be oxidized to these same intermediates, and Sulphamethoxazole is probably one of the most studied compounds in this respect. This aromatic amine containing sulphonamide is associated with a range of idiosyncratic reactions (e.g. fever and rash) in 2-3% of the population. Metabolism is known to involve oxidation of the aromatic amine function to hydroxylamine and nitroso derivatives. These have been shown to react with biological nucleophiles (Naisbitt *et al.* 1996), and haptenize lymphocytes and neutrophils (Naisbitt *et al.* 1999), (Figure 20). Other aromatic amines such as acetylaminofluorene and 4-dimethylaminobenzene, have well recognized carcinogenic properties. This appears to derive from the formation of hydroxy-lamines which subsequently undergo sulfation followed by nitrogen/oxygen bond cleavage to form electrophilic nitrogen species, most likely nitrenes (Chou *et al.* 1995, Glatt 2000).

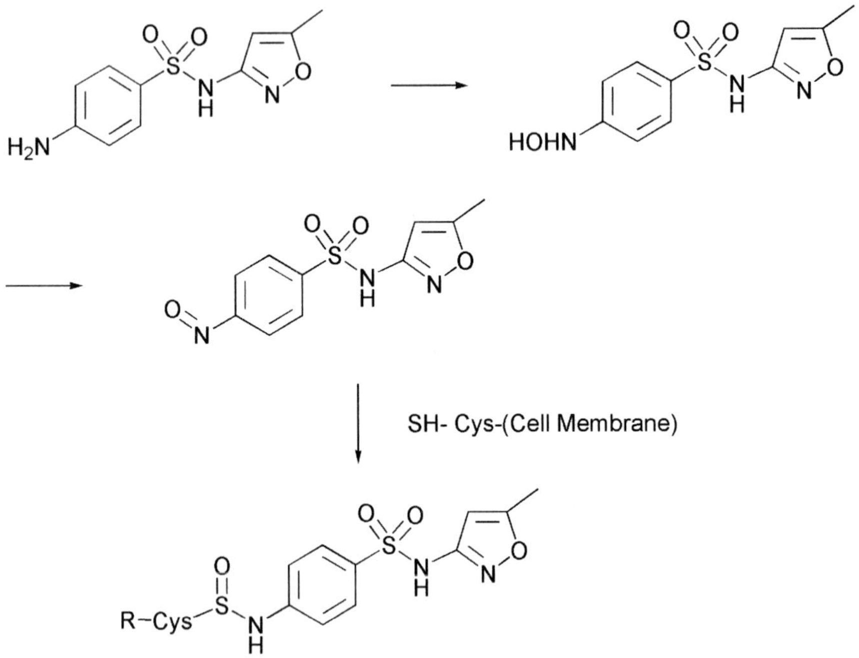

Figure 20. The oxidation of sulfamethoxazole to an electrophilic nitroso metabolite and its reaction with cell surface thiols.

Simple thiourea containing compounds may show hepatic or pulmonary toxicities believed to be associated with bioactivation, and covalent binding of sulfur (Hanzlik *et al.* 1978, Scott *et al.* 1990), although the mechanism has not been clearly defined. Both CYP and FMO mediated metabolism has been implicated. Thioamides will also inhibit thyroid functions, and have been used in the treatment of hyperthyroidism. The major adverse reactions for these drugs are hematological dysfunctions and immunosuppression (Bandyopadhyay *et al.* 2002). The thyrostatic agent propyl thiouracil is associated with idiosyncratic agranulo-cytosis, and metabolism has been shown to involve oxidation of sulfur to a sulfonate derivative (Waldhauser and Uetrecht 1991). This is likely to involve the formation of the intermediate oxidation states corresponding to sulfenates and sulfinates. Sulfenyl chloride formation via myeloperoxidases and hypochlorite was also proposed, and both this, and the sulfenate possess electrophilic sulfur centers, (Figure 21). However, the sulfonate metabolite of propylthiouracil itself also appears to be chemically reactive, and has been shown to cause T-cell sensiti-zation, (Von Schmiederberg *et al.* 1996). Sulfonates are not usually considered good leaving groups, but in the case of those derived from thioamides their displacement by nucleophiles is precedented, (Bartke and Pfleiderer 1989). Therefore, reaction of propylthiouracil sulfonate with sulfhydryl groups of proteins, is likely to be the means by which this drug covalently binds to proteins.

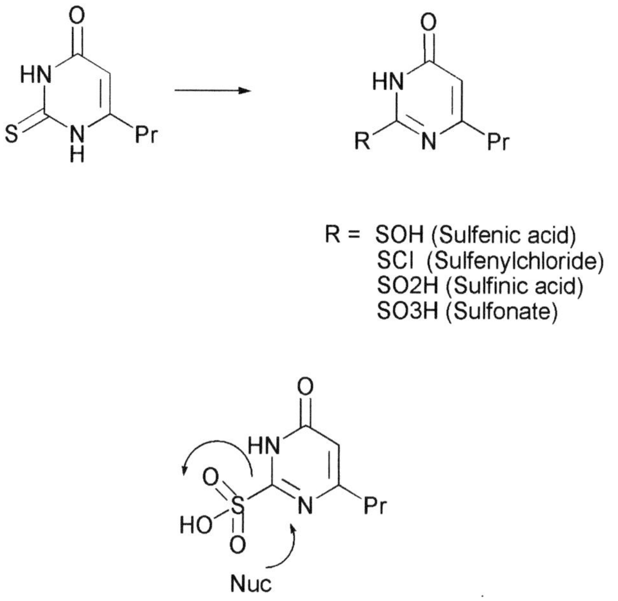

R = SOH (Sulfenic acid)
SCl (Sulfenylchloride)
SO2H (Sulfinic acid)
SO3H (Sulfonate)

Figure 21. The sulfur oxidation of propylthiouracil to generate electrophilic metabolites.

Thiazolidinediones as discussed above, may undergo oxidative ring opening to form sulfenic acid derivatives (Figure 6), and a glutathione adduct, consistent with the formation of such a metabolite, has been isolated (Kassahun *et al.* 2001). More recently a different glutathione adduct of troglitazone has been identified, which has also been proposed to derive from sulfur oxidation, but via sulfonium ion formation, (He *et al.* 2004).

Radicals

While radicals have been widely implicated in many toxicities, the chemical details of the mechanisms associated with these toxicities are less well defined. This is complicated in part by the fact that many radical forming drugs also generate electrophiles, and due to the difficulty in studying radicals in general. Radicals contain one or more unpaired electrons, and may participate in nucleophilc or electrophilic type reactions, but these are mechanistically distinct from the electrophilic processes discussed above. Reactivity can be markedly influenced by orbital symmetry, which in turn is effected by substituents (Mile 2000). The reactions of relevance to biological systems involve: 1. Direct reaction with cellular constituents to form a covalent adduct (and a resulting more stable radical). 2. Hydrogen radical abstraction to form a radical based on an endogenous cellular constituent or 3. Direct reaction with a second unpaired electron species, most importantly, molecular oxygen, generating reactive oxygen species and oxidative stress. It is likely that this last process has the most important toxicological consequences. It should be noted that the first two processes result in the formation of new radicals which potentially could also react with oxygen, and it is perhaps for this reason that the literature frequently does not address this level of mechanistic detail when oxidative stress is observed. Some of these points, together with a discussion of pathologies believed to be associated with radical formation, have been recently reviewed (Sorg 2004).

Examples of free radicals directly forming covalent adducts with biological molecules include certain compounds noted as mechanism based inhibitors of CYP (Ortiz De Montellano 1990). Thus the free radical formed during oxidation reacts with the heme group to form a covalent bonds. The particular function-alities capable of this type of mechanism based inhibition is in part a reflection the combination of their capacity for one electron oxidation chemistry mediated by CYP, and the highly delocalized nature of the heme prosthetic group, where a more stable radical localized on the heme can be formed, (although a number of different reactions are possible). Functionalities which can cause mechanism based inactivation of CYP by this mechanism include halocarbons, hydrazines, olefins, sydnones, cylopropylamines, and some dihydropyridines and dihydro-quinolines. The cyclopropylamine group is encountered in a number of drugs, and may be bioactivated to form a distonic radical cation as shown in Figure 22. The direct relevance of cyclopropylamines oxidation to toxicity seems to be predominantly associated with a higher risk for drug interactions, since to date there seems to be little evidence that this property is the causative event for other forms of toxicity, idiosyncratic or otherwise.

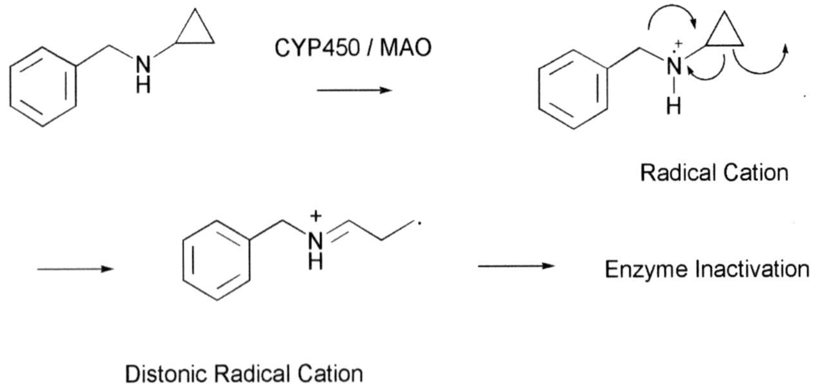

CYP450 / MAO

Radical Cation

Enzyme Inactivation

Distonic Radical Cation

Figure 22. The oxidative metabolism of cyclopropylamines to distonic radical cations.

Radicals may react with proteins to abstract a hydrogen radical, (Sorani *et al.* 1994), and sulfhydryl and tyrosyl groups may be likely sites for this to occur (Ostdal *et al.* 1999, Kolberg *et al.* 2002). Subsequent molecular events associated with this reaction and their possible toxicological significance have not been significantly studied, but it seems a likely initial event which may lead to covalent adduct formation, in that reaction with a second drug radical could form a closed shell species. Thus the mechanism by which radicals may form a covalent adduct to proteins is likely to be a two step process, (in contrast to electrophiles). Perhaps for this reason covalent binding of radicals to proteins with subsequent toxicological significance has been significantly less well demonstrated than for electrophiles. Among the few examples are ethanol, halogenated hydrocarbons, and possibly hydrazines. α Hydroxyl ethyl radicals have been shown to be formed during microsomal incubations with ethanol, and to subsequently covalently bind to proteins. These adducts have also been shown to be immunogenic, and therefore provide an alternative mechanism from acetaldehyde covalent binding, for ethanol induced immune mediated hepatitis (Moncada *et al.* 1994). In addition to the oxidative pathways discussed earlier, low molecular weight halocarbons can undergo reductive metabolism to form carbon or chlorine centered radicals and these have been considered as possible alternative mediators of observed hepatotoxicity. For chloroform, the reductive pathway leading to dichloromethyl radical formation is now thought to have less toxicological relevance than oxidative pathways, since the former pathway requires very high concentrations and anaerobic conditions (Gemma *et al.* 2003). Isoniazid is a drug used to treat tuberculosis, and is associated with idiosyncratic toxicities such as Lupus. It is a hydrazine derivative, and hydrazine itself has been shown to form acetyl radicals following metabolic acetylation in perfused rat livers (Sinha 1987). Iproniazid was an MAO inhibitor used for depression and was withdrawn from the market due to hepatotoxicity. Isoniazid and iproniazid have been shown to generate free radicals in vitro (Sipe *et al.* 2004, Johnsson and Schultz 1994), (Figure 23). Both macromolecular binding and oxidative stress have been

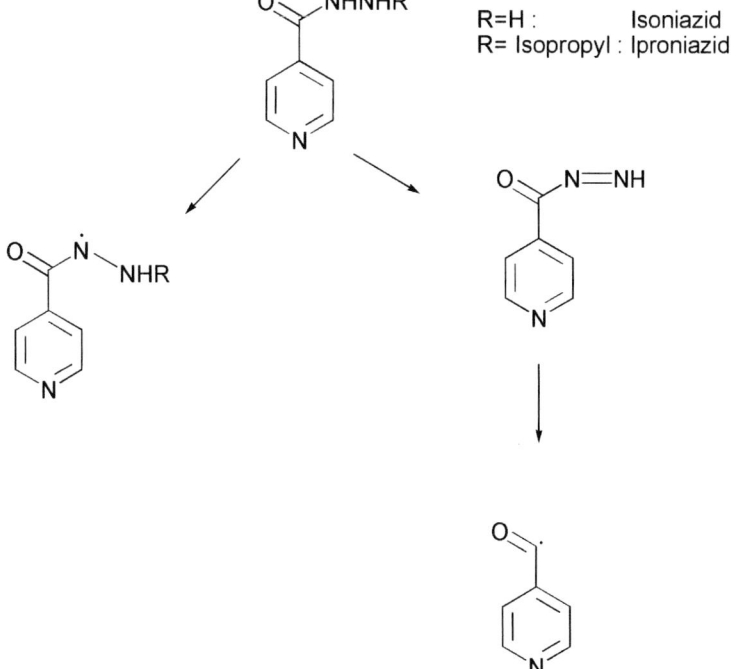

Figure 23. Proposed radicals produced by metabolic oxidation of Isoniazid and Iproniazid.

proposed as biological consequences (Albano and Tomassi 1987). Isoniazid acetyl radicals also appear to form covalent adducts with NAD(H), (Nguyen *et al.* 2001).

The reaction of radicals with oxygen to produce reactive oxygen species and their subsequent biological significance has been well reviewed (Cohen and Doherty 1987, Sorg 2004, Stoh 1995). The formation of superoxide anion and hydrogen peroxide by this process may lead to glutathione depletion and oxidation of cellular components such as lipids (oxidative stress). While any radical in principle may potentially react with molecular oxygen, compounds that can reversibly form radical anions are likely to cause greater effect, since the formation of the reduced oxygen species will be in excess of the stoichiometric

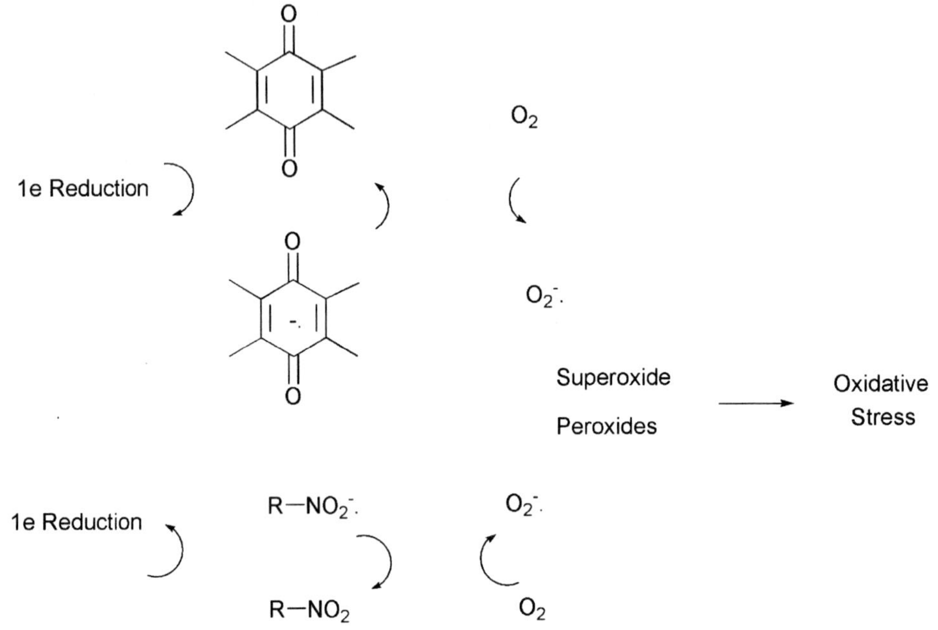

Figure 24. Redox cycling by one electron oxidation of quinones and nitro aromatics, to produce reduced, active oxygen species.

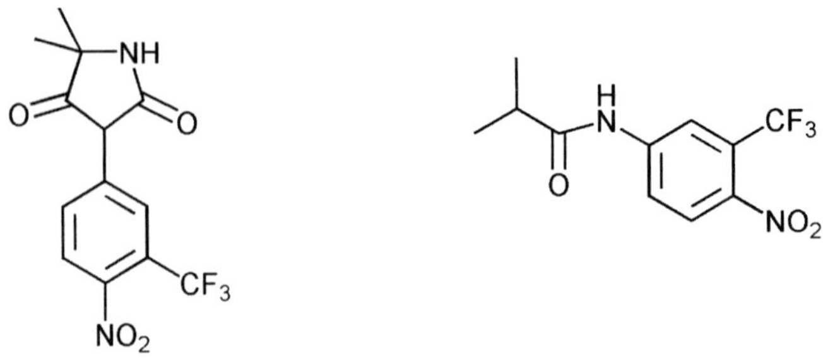

Nilutamide

Therapeutic use: Prostate Cancer
Toxicity: Acute Hepatitis
Mechanism: CYP450 Reductase
mediated Nitro reduction

Flutamide

Therapeutic use: Prostate Cancer
Toxicity: Hepatoxicity
Mechanism: Nitro reduction
Oxidative stress

Figure 25. The structures of Nilutamide and Flutamide.

amount of drug (Figure 24). From a drug development standpoint however, this is mitigated by the fact that a rather limited number of functionalities so far have been noted that are capable of redox cycling by this mechanism: quinones, nitroaromatics, some quaternary ammonium compounds and transition metal complexes. Quinone redox cycling has been most extensively studied with the anthraquinone antineoplastic agents such as Doxorubicin. Long term use of Doxorubicin is associated with cardiomyopathy due to mitochondrial toxicity, and despite continued investigations, reversible quinone reduction leading to oxidative stress remains the most likely mechanism (Wallace 2003). The reduction of aromatic nitro compounds may lead to nitrogen centered electrophiles as discussed above, but the initial one electron reduction product is the nitroradical anion which may undergo redox cycling. The antiandrogen Nilutamide is used to treat prostate cancer, is hepatotoxic, and to a lesser extent also a pulmonary toxin. This appears to be due to redox cycling (Fau *et al.* 1992), but the free radical can also undergo further reduction to nitroso and hydroxylamine intermediates (Berson *et al.* 1994). Flutamide is another nitro aromatic antiandrogen associated with hepatotoxicty, and redox cycling via nitro reduction is implicated (Nunez-Vergara *et al.* 2001). The structures of these drugs are shown in Figure 25.

Conclusion

Reactive intermediates may be grouped according to their reactivity patterns, and reactive metabolites with similar reaction properties may derive from quite different functional groups. Reactive metabolites may be broadly classified as either electrophiles or radicals. At present, electrophiles constitute the more important group due to the wide diversity of structures that can produce these, and are hence more likely to be encountered in drug development. However, as more work focuses on searching for radical intermediates, their implication in toxicity mechanisms is likely to increase. In all but a few cases, proposed reactive metabolites have not been proven to be the cause of the toxicities to which they are associated, and in many cases a particular compound, or even a particular functional group, is capable of forming more than one type of reactive metabolite. This makes application of this type of information to drug development problematical. Never the less, approaches have been proposed by which this type of information might be applied to minimize safety risk in drug development (Evans *et al.* 2004).

The emphasis on bioactivation or covalent binding frequently remains a point of contention in selecting candidates for drug development. Bioactivation must be put in context with other properties of the compound, (most particularly anticipated dose level), to gauge the level of concern, and in the future is more likely to find value in combination with other types of data. The use of genomic and proteomic information to gauge safety risk in preclinical toxicology will increase significantly in coming years (Cohen 2004, Lord 2004, Selkirk and Tennat 2003, Walgren and Thompson 2004). Thus if changes in the expression of genes associated with the processing of electrophilic metabolites or oxidative stress are observed, knowing if such mechanisms are operating for a particular compound will help significantly in interpreting these findings. Also, if such properties are identified in a lead candidate, it is only by an understanding of the underlying chemistry behind them that such properties can be rationally designed out of follow up compounds.

While risk can potentially be minimized by these approaches, managing the consequences of idiosyncratic toxicities will remain a clinical issue for the foreseeable future. Here, genomics may also have significant potential. The feasibility of identifying genetic risk factors for individuals towards a particular idiosyncratic reaction has now been demonstrated (Martin *et al.* 2004), and if this approach is found to be general, may have significant impact in managing these important metabolically mediated toxicities.

References

Albano E and Tomassi A. Spin Trapping of Free Radical Intermediates Produced During the Metabolism of Isoniazid and Iproniazid in Isolated Hepatocytes. *Biochem Pharmacol* 1987; 36(18): 2913-20

Bakke O.M. Drug Safety Discontinuations in the United Kingdom, the United States, and Spain from 1974-1993: A Regulatory Perspective. *Clinical Pharmacology and Therapeutics* 1995; 58(1): 108-117

Bandyopadhyay U, Biswas K, and Banerjee RK. Extrathyroidal Actions of Anithyroid Thionamides. *Toxicology Letters* 2002; 128: 117-127

Bartke M and Pfleiderer W. Pteridines. LXXXVII. Oxidations and Reactions of 2- and 4-Thiolumazine Derivatives. Synthesis and Properties of Pteridinesulfinates and –Sulfonates. *Pteridines.* 1989; 1(1): 45-56

Berson A, Wolf C, Chachaty C, Fau D, and Pessayre D. Interest of ESR in Determining the Mechanisms of Drug Toxicity: Application to the Antiandrogen Nilutamide. *Journal de Chimie Physique et de Physico-Chimie Biologique* 1994; 91(11/12): 1809-19

Bonierbale E, Valadon P, Pons C, Desfosses B, and Dansette PM. Opposite Behaviors of Reactive Metabolites of Tienilic acid and It's Isomer Towards Liver Proteins; Use of specific Anti-Tienilic Acid –Protein Adduct Antibodies and the Possible Relationship with different Hepatotoxic Effects of the Two Compounds. *Chem Res Toxicol* 1999; 12(3):286-296

Borel AG, and Abbot FS. Characterization of Novel Isocyanate- derived Metabolites of the Formamide N-Formylamphetamine with Combined Use of Electrospray Mass spectrometry and Stable Isotope Methodology. *Chem Res Toxicol* 1995; 8(6): 891-9

Cao K, Stack DE, Ramaanathan R, Gross ML, Rogan EG, and Cavalieri EL. Synthesis and Structure Elucidation of Estrogen quinones conjugated with Cysteine, N-Acetylcysteine, and Glutathione. *Chem Res Toxicol* 1998; 11: 909-916

Chou HC, Lang NP, and Kadlubar FF. Metabolic Activation of N-Hydroxy Heterocyclic Amines by Human Sulfotransferases. *Cancer Research* 1995; 55(3): 525-9

Cohen SM. Risk Assessment in the Genomic Era. *Toxicologic Pathology* 2004; 32(Suppl. 1): 3-8

Cohen GM and Doherty MD. Free Radical Mediated Cell Toxicity by Redox Cycling Chemicals. *Br J Cancer* 1987; 55 (Suppl VIII): 46-52

Cooper AJL, Bruschi SA, and Anders MW. Toxic Halogenated Cysteine S-conjugates and Targeting of Mitochondrial Enzymes of Energy Metabolism. *Biochemical Pharmacology* 2002; 64: 553-564

Cox PJ, Ryan DA, Holis FJ, Harris AM, Miller AK,Vousden M, and Cowley H. Absorption, Disposition and Metabolism of Rosiglitazone, a Potent Thiazolidinone Insulin Sensitizer in Humans. *Drug Metab Dispos* 2000; 28(7): 772-780

Dalvie DK, Kalgutkar AS, Khojasteh-Bakht SC, Obach RS, and O'Donnell JP. Biotransformation Reactions of Five - Membered Aromatic Heterocyclic Rings. *Chem. Res Toxicol* 2002; 15(3): 269-299

Dansette PM, Thang DC, El Amiri H, and Mansuy D. Evidence for Thiophene S-oxide as a Primary Reactive Metabolite of Thoiphene in vivo: Formation of a Dihydrothiophene Sulfoxide Mercapturic Acid. *Biochem Biophys Res Commun* 1992; 186(3): 1624-1630

Dieckhaus CM, Miller TA, Sofia RD, and MacDonald TL. A Mechanistic Approach to Understanding Species Differences in Felbamate Bioactivation: Relevance to Drug- Induced Idiosyncratic Reactions. *Drug Metab Dispos* 2000; 28(7): 814-822

Evans DC, Watt AP, Nicoll-Griffith DA, and Baillie TA. Drug-Protein Adducts: An Industry Perspective on Minimizing the Potential for Drug Bioactivation in Drug Discovery and Development. *Chem Res Toxicol* 2004; 17: 3-16

Fan PW, Gu C, Marsh SA, Stevens JC. Mechanism Based Inactivation of Cytochrome P450 2B6 by a Novel Terminal Acetylene Inhibitor. *Drug Metab Dispos* 2003; 31(1): 28-36

Fau D, Berson A, Eugene D, Fromenty B, Fisch C, and Pessayre D. Mechanism for the Hepatotoxicity of the Antiandrogen Nilutamide. Evidence Suggesting that Redox Cycling of this Nitroaromatic Drug Leads to Oxidative Stress in Isolated Hepatocytes. *J Pharmacol. Exp Ther* 1992; 263(1): 69-77

Galtier P. Biotransformation and Fate of Mycotoxins. *J. Toxicology Toxin Reviews* 1999; (18 3&4): 295-312

Gemma S, Vittozzi L, Testai E. Metabolism of Chloroform in the Human Liver and Identification of the Competent P450's. *Drug Metab Dispos* 2003; 31(3): 266-274

Gillies PS and Dunn CJ. Pioglitazone. *Drugs* 2000; 60(2): 333-343

Glatt H. Sulfotransferases in the Bioactivation of Xenobiotics. *Chemico-Biological Interactions* 2000; 129(1-2): 141-170

Goldin C, and Boelsterli UA. Dissociation of Covalent Protein Adduct Formation from Oxidative Injury in Cultured Hepatocytes Exposed to Cocaine. *Xenobiotica.* 1994; 24(3): 251-264

Gorrod JW and Aislaitner G. The Metabolism of Alicyclic Amines to Reactive Iminium Ion Intermediates. *Eur J of Drug Metabolism and Pharmacokinetics.* 1994; 19(3): 209-217

Guengerich FP and Johnson WW. Kinetics of Hydrolysis and Reaction of Aflatoxin B1 Exo-8,9-Epoxide and Relevance to Toxicity and Deactivation. *Drug Metab Rev* 1999; 31(1): 141-158

Hanzlik RP, Vyas KP, and Traiger GJ. Substituent Effects on the Hepatotoxicity of Thiobenzamide Derivatives in the Rat. *Toxicol and Appl Pharmacol* 1978; 46(3): 685-94.

He K, Talaat RE, Pool WF, Reily MD, Reed JE, Bridges AJ, and Woolf TF. Metabolic Activation of Troglitazone : Identification of A Reactive Metabolite and Mechanisms Involved. *Drug Metab Dispos* 2004; 32(6): 639-646

Hinson JA, Pumford NR, and Nelson SD. The Role of Metabolic Activation in Drug Toxicity. *Drug Metab Rev.* 1994; 261(1&2): 395-412

Holme JA, Dahlin DC, Nelson SD, and Dybing E. Cytotoxic Effects of N-Acetyl-p-Benzoquinone Imine, a Common Arylating Intermediate of Paracetamol and N-Hydroxyparacetamol. *Biochem Pharmacol* 1984; 33: 401-406

Jerina DM. From Arene Oxides to Diol Epoxides and DNA. *Polycyclic Aromatic Hydrocarbons* 2000; 19(1-4): 5-36

Johnston JN, Wright CL, Leeson GA. Regioselectivity of Metabolic Activation of Acetylenic Steroids by Hepatic Cytochrome P450 Enzymes. *Steroids* 1991; 56(4): 180-184

John K, and Scultz PG. Mechanistic Studies of the Oxidation of Isoniazid by Catalase Peroxidase from Mycobacterium tuberculosis. *J Amer Chem Soc* 1994; 116: 7425-7426

Ju C, and Uetrecht JP. Detection of 2-Hydroxyiminostilbene in the Urine of Patients Taking Carbamazepine and Its Oxidation to a Reactive Iminoquinone Intermediate. *J Pharmacol Exp Ther* 1999; 288: 51-56

Ju C and Uetrecht JP. Mechanism of Idiosyncratic Drug Reactions:Reactive Metabolite Formations, Protein Binding, and the Regulation of the Immune System. *Current Drug Metabolism* 2002; 3:367-377

Kassahun K, Pearson P, Tang W, McIntosh I, Leung K, Elmore C, Dean D, Wang R, Doss G, and Baillie TA. Studies on the Metabolism of Troglitazone to a Reactive Intermediate *in vitro* and *in vivo*. Evidence for novel Biotransformation Pathways Involving Quinone Methide Formation and Thiazolidinedione Ring Scission. *Chem Res Toxicol* 2001; 14: 62-70

Kalgutkar AS, Nguyen HT, Vaz ADN, Doan A, Dalvie DK, McLeod DG, and Murray JC. In vitro Metabolism Studies on the Isoxazole Ring Scission in the Anti-Inflammatory Agent Leflunomide to its Active alpha-Cyanoenol Metabolite A771726: Mechanistic Similarities with the Cytochrome P450- Catalysed Dehydration of Aldoximes. *Drug Metab Dispos* 2003; 31(10):1240-1250

Kennedy GL. Biological effects of Acetamide, Formamide, and their Mono and Dimethyl Derivatives: An Update. *Critical Reviews in Toxicology* 2001; 31(2): 139-222

White INH, and Matteis FD. The role of CYP Forms in the Metabolism and Metabolic activation of HCFC's and other Halocarbons. *Toxicology Letters* 2001; 124: 121-128

Knowles SR, Shapiro LE, and Shear NH. Reactive Metabolites and Adverse Drug Reactions. *Clinical Reviews in Allergy and Immunology* 2003; 24: 229-238

Kolberg M, Bleifuss G, Grslund A, Sjberg BM, Lubitz W, Lendzian F, and Lassmann G. Protein Thiyl Radicals Observed by EPR Spectroscopy. *Archives of Biochemistry and Biophysics* 2002; 403(1): 141-144

Lanza DL, Code E, Crespi CL, Gonzalez FJ, and Yost GS. Specific Dehydrogenation of 3-Methylindole and epoxidation of naphthalene by recombinant human CYP2F1 expressed in lymphoblastoid cells. *Drug Metab Dispos* 1999; 27(7):798-803

Laurent A, Perdu-Durand E, alary J, Debrauwer L, and Cravedi JP. Metabolism of 4-Hydroxynonenal, a Cytotoxic Product of Lipid Peroxidation, in Rat Precision-Cut Liver Slices. *Toxicol Lett* 2000; 114(1-3): 203-214

Lazarou J, Pomeranz BH, and Corey PN. Incidence of Adverse Drug Reactions in Hospitalized Patients. *JAMA* 1998; 279(15): 1200-1205

Li AP. A Review of the Common Properties of Drugs with Idiosyncratic Hepatotoxicity and the "Multiple Determinant Hypothesis" for the Manifestation of Idiosyncratic Drug Toxicity. *Chemico-Biological Interactions* 2002; 142: 7-23

Li C, Olurinde MO, Hodges LM, Grillo MP and Benet LZ. Covalent Binding of 2-Phenylpropionyl-S-Acyl-CoA Thioester to Tissue Proteins in vitro. *Drug Metab Dispos* 2003; 31(6): 727-730

Li C, Grillo MP, and Benet LZ. In vitro Studies on the Chemical Reactivity of 2,4-Dichlorophenoxyacetyl-S-Acyl CoA Thioester. *Toxicology and Applied Pharmacology* 2003; 187(2): 101-109

Lindqvist T, Kenne L, and Lindeke B. On the chemistry of the Reaction between N-Acetylcysteine and 4-[(4-Ethoxyphenyl)imino]-2,5-Cyclohexadien-1-one, an Ethoxyaniline Metabolite formed during Peroxidase Reactions. *Chem Res Toxicol* 1991; 494: 489-496

Lord PG. Progress in Applying Genomics in Drug Development. *Toxicology Letters* 2004; 149(1-3): 371-375

Madden S, Maggs JL, and Park BK. Bioactivation of Carbamazepine in the Rat in vivo. Evidence for the Formation of Reactive Arene Oxides. *Drug Metab Dispos* 1996; 24(4): 469-479

Madden S, Spaldin V, Hayes RN, Woolf TF, Pool WF, and Park BK. Species Variation in the Bioactivation of Tacrine by Hepatic Microsomes. *Xenobiotica* 1995; 25(1): 103-106

Maggs JL, Naisbitt DJ, Tettey JNA, Pirmohamed M, and Park BK. Metabolism of Lamotrigine to a Reactive Arene Oxide Intermediate. *Chem Res Toxicol* 2000; 13(11): 1075-1081

Maggs JL and Park BK. Drug Protein Conjugates XVI. Studies of Sorbinil Metabolism: Formation of 2-Hydroxysorbinil and Unstable Protein Conjugates. *Biochem Pharmacol* 1988; 37(4): 743-748

Maggs JL, Kitteringham NR, Breckenridge AM, and Park BK. Autoxidative Formation of a Chemically Reactive Intermediate from Amodiaquine, a Myelotoxin and Hepatotoxin in Man. *Biochem Pharmacol* 1987; 36(13): 2061-2062

Martin AM, Nolan D, Gaudieri S, Almedia CA, Nolan R, James I, Carvalho F, Philips E, Christiansen FT, Purcell AW, McClusky J, and Mallal S. Predisposition to Abacavir Hypersensitivity Conferred by HLA-B 5701 and Haplotypic Hsp-Hom Variant. *Proceedings of the National Academy of Sciences* 2004; 101(12): 4180-4185

Martin JL, Kenna JG, Martin BM, Thomassen D, Reed GF, and Pohl LR. Halothane Hepatitis Patients have Serum Antibodies that React with Protein Disulfide Isomerase. *Hepatology* 1993; 18(4): 858-863

Martinat C, Amar C, Dansette PM, Leclaire J, Lopez Garcia P, Do Cao T, Nguyen HN, Mansuy D. In vitro Metabolism of Isaxonine Phosphate: Formation of Two metabolites, 5-Hydroxyisoaxonine and 2-Aminopyrimidine, and Covalent Binding to Microsomal Proteins. *Eur J of Pharmacology* 1992; 228(1): 63-71

Matzinger P. Tolerance Danger, and the Extended Family. *Ann Rev Immunol* 1994;12: 991-1045

Melnick RL. Carcinogenicity and Mechanistic Insights on the Behavior of Epoxides and Epoxide Forming Chemicals. *Annals of NY Acad Sci* 2002; 982: 177-189

Mile B. Free Radical Participation in Organic Chemistry: Electron Spin Resonance (ESR) Studies of Their Structures and Reactions. *Current Organic Chemistry* 2000; 4: 55-83

Moncada C, Torres V, Vargese G, Albano E, and Israel Y. Ethanol-Derived Immunoreactive Species Formed by Free Radical Mechanisms. *Molecular Pharmacology* 1994; 46(4): 786-91

Miyamoto G, Zahid N, and Uetrecht JP. Oxidation of Diclofenac to Reactive Intermediates by Neutrophils, Myeloperoxidase, and Hypochlorous acid. *Chem Res Toxicol* 1997; 10: 414-419

Murray M, Hetnarski K, and Wilkinson CF. Selective Inhibitory Interactions of Alkoxymethylenedioxybenzenes towards Mono-Oxygenase Activity in Rat Hepatic Microsomes. *Xenobiotica* 1985; 15(3): 369-379

Naisbitt DJ, Hough SJ, Gill HJ, Pirmohamed M, Kitteringham NR, and Park BK. Cellular Disposition of Sulphamethoxazole and its Metabolites: Implications for Hypersensitivity. *Br J Pharmacology* 1999; 126: 1393-1407

Naisbitt DJ, O'Neill P, Pirmohamed M, and Park BK. Synthesis and Reactions of Nitroso Sulphamethoxazole with Biological Nucleophiles: Implications for Immune Mediated Toxicity. *Bioorganic & Medicinal Chemistry Letters* 1996; 6(13): 1511-1516

Nelson SD. Molecular Mechanisms of Adverse Drug Reactions. *Current Therapeutic Research* 2001; 62(12): 885-899

Nguyen M, Claparols C, Bernadou J, and Meunier B. A Fast Efficient Metal-Mediated Oxidation of Isoniazid and Identification of Isoniazid –NAD(H) Adducts. *CHEMBIOCHEM* 2001; 2: 877-883

Nunez-Vergara LJ, Farais D, Bollo S, and Sequella JA. An Electrochemical Evidence of Free Radicals Formation from Flutamide and its Reactivity with Endo/Xenobiotics of Pharmacological Relevance. *Bioelectrochemistry* 2001; 53(1):103-110

Olson H, Betton G, Robinson D, Thomas K, Monro Akolaja G, Lilly P, Sanders J, Sipes G, Bracken W, Dorato M, Van Deun K, Smith P, Berger B, and Heller A. Concordance of the Toxicity of Pharmaceuticals in Humans and Animals. *Regulatory Toxicology and Pharmacology* 2000; 32: 56-67

Ortiz De Montellano PR. Free Radical Modification of Prosthetic Heme Groups. *Pharmac Ther* 1990; 48: 95-120

Ostdal H, Anderson HJ, Davies MJ. Formation of Long Lived Radicals on Proteins by Radical Transfer from Heme Enzymes-A Common Process? *Archives of Biochemistry and Biophysics* 1999; 362(1): 105-112

Park BK, Kitteringham NR, Powell H, and Pirmohamed M. Advances in Molecular Toxicology-Towards Understanding Idiosyncratic Drug Reactions. *Toxicology* 2000; 153: 39-60

Pirmohamed M, Naisbitt DJ, Gordon F, and Park BK. The Danger Hypothesis-Potential Role in Idiosyncratic Drug Reactions. *Toxicology* 2002;181-182: 55-63

Pumford NR, Martin BM, Thomassen D, Burris JA, Kenna JG, Martin JL, and Pohl LR. Serum Antibodies from Halothane Hepatitis Patients React with the Rat Endoplasmic Reticulum Protein ERp72. *Chem Res Toxicol* 1993; 6: 609-615

Rosemond MJC, and Walsh JS. Human Carbonyl Reduction Pathways and a Strategy for their Study In vitro. *Drug Metab Rev* 2004; 36(2): 335-361

Salustio BC, Sabordo L, Evans AM, and Nation RL. Hepatic Dispositon of Electrophilic Acyl Glucuronide Conjugates. *Current Drug Metabolism* 2000; 1: 163-180

Scott AM, Powell GM, Upshall DG, and Curtis CG. Pulmonary Toxicity of Thioureas in the Rat. *Environmental Health Perspectives* 1990; 85: 43-50

Selkirk JK, and Tennant RW. Toxicogenomics: Impact on Human Health. *Pure and Applied Chemistry* 2003; 75(11-12): 2413-2414

Sillanaukee P, Hurme L, Tuominen J, Ranta E, Nikkari S, and Seppa K. Structural Characterization of Acetaldehyde adducts formed by a Synthetic Peptide Mimicking the N-terminus of Hemoglobin β-Chain under Reducing and Nonreducing Conditions. *Eur J Biochem* 1996; 249: 30-36

Singh S, and Dryhurst G. Interactions between 5,6-Dihydroxytryptamine and Cysteine. *Bioorganic Chemistry* 1993; 19(3): 274-82

Sinha BK. Activation of Hydrazine Derivatives to Free Radicals in the Perfused Rat Liver: A Spin Trapping Study. *Biochimica et Biophysica Acta* 1987; 924(2): 261-9

Sipe HJ, Jaszewski AR, and Mason RP. Fast Flow EPR Spectroscopic Observation of the Isoniazid, Iproniazid, and Phenylhydrazine Hydrazyl Radicals. *Chem Res Toxicol* 2004; 17: 226-233

Sorg O. Oxidative Stress: Theoretical Model or a Biological Reality ? *Comptes Rendus Biologies* 2004; 327: 649-662

Soriani M, Pietraforte D, Minetti M. Antioxidant Potential of Anaerobic Human Plasma: Role of Serum Albumin and Thiols as Scavengers of Carbon Radicals. *Archives of Biochemistry and Biophysics* 1994; 312(1): 180-188

Spah-Langguth H, and Benet LZ. Acyl Glucuronides Revisited: Is the Glucuronidation Process a Toxification as well as a Detoxification Mechanism ?. *Drug Metab Rev* 1992; 24(1): 5-48

Stiborova M, Frei E, Weissler M, and Schmeiser HH. Human Enzymes Involved in the Metabolic Activation of Carcinogenic Aristolochic Acids: Evidence for Reductive Activation by Cytochromes P450 1A1 and 1A2. *Chem Res Toxicol* 2001; 14:1128-1137

Stohs SJ. The Role of Free Radicals in Toxicity and Disease. *Journal of Basic & Clinical Physiology & Pharmacology* 1995; 6(3-4): 205-228

Thomassen D, Knebel N, Slattery JT, McClanahan RH and Nelson S. Reactive Intermediates in the Oxidation of Menthofuran by Cyochromes P-450. *Chem Res Toxicol* 1992: 5: 123-130

Thompson DC, Perera K, and London R. Spontaneous Hydrolysis of 4-Trifluoromethylphenol to a Quinone Methide and Subsequent Protein Alkylation. *Chemico- Biological Interactions* 2000; 126: 1-14

Uetrecht JP. Bioactivation In: Lee JS, Obach RS, and Fisher MB. *Drug Metabolizing Enzymes. Cytochrome P450 and Other Enzymes in Drug Discovery and Development.* : New York: Marcel Decker; 2003: 87-145

Uetrecht JP. Is it Possible to More Accurately Predict which Drug Candidates will cause Idiosyncratic Reactions ?. *Current Drug Metabolism* 2000;1:133-141

Uetrecht JP, Zahid N, and Whitefield D. metabolism of Vesnarinone by Activated Neutrophils: Implications for Vesnarinone-Induced Agranulocytosis. *J Pharmacol Exp Ther* 1994; 270(3): 865-872

Van Roon EN, Jansen TLTA, Houtman NM, Spoelstra P, Brouwers JRBJ. Leflunomide for the Treatment of Rheumatoid Arthritis in Clinical Practice: Incidence and Severity of Hepatotoxicity. *Drug Safety* 2004; 27(5): 345-352

Vasquez-Vivar J and Augusto O. Oxidative Activity of Primaquine Metabolites on Rat Ethrocytes *In vitro* and *In vivo*. *Biochemical Pharmacology* 1994; 47(2): 309-316

Waldhauser L, and Uetrecht J. Oxidation of Propylthiouracil to Reactive Metabolites by Activated Neutrophils. Implications for Agranulocytosis. *Drug Metab Dispos* 1991; 19(2): 354-9

Walgren JL and Thompson DC. Application of Proteomic Technology in the Drug Development Process. *Toxicology Letters* 2004; 149(1-3): 377-385

Wallace KB. Doxorubicin - Induced Cardiac Mitochondrionopathy. *Pharmacology & Toxicology.* 2003; 93(3): 105-115

Walsh JS, Reese M, and Thurmond LM. The Metabolic Activation of Abacavir by human Liver Cytosol and Expressed Human Alcohol Dehydrogenase Isozymes. *Chemico-Biological Interactions* 2002; 142(1-2): 135-154

Ward F, and Daly M. Hepatic Disorders. In: Lee A. *Adverse Drug Reactions* Pharmaceuticl Press 2001: 77-97.

Zanni MP, von Greyerz S, Schnyder B, Brander KA, Frutig K, Hari Y, Valitutti S, and Pichler WJ. HLA Restricted Processing-and Metabolism –Independent Pathway of Drug Recognition by Human ·, T Lymphocytes. *J Clin Invest* 1998; 102(8): 1591-1598

4

Case History – Use of ADME Studies for Optimization of Drug Candidates

**Liang-Shang Gan, Frank W. Lee,
Nelamangala Nagaraja, Ping Li,
Jason Labutti, Wei Yin,
Cindy Xia, Hua Yang,
Vinita Uttamsingh, Chuang Lu,
Sandeepraj Pusalkar, J. Scott Daniels,
Ron Huang, Mark Qian,
Jing-Tao Wu, Kym Cardoza,
Suresh K. Balani, and Gerald T. Miwa**

Drug Metabolism and Pharmacokinetics
Drug Safety and Disposition,
Millennium Pharmaceuticals, Inc.
40 Landsdowne Street
Cambridge, MA 02139, USA

Table of Contents

List of Abbreviations

ABT 1-aminobenzotriazole
ADME........................absorption, distribution, metabolism and excretion
AUC..area under the concentration curve
CLhep...hepatic clearance
CLp ....plasma clearance
CLr ....renal clearance
Cmax...maximum plasma concentration
CNS ....central nerve system
CRTH2 ....chemoattractant receptor-homologous
                        molecule expressed on Th2 lymphocytes
CYP...cytochrome P-450
DC...development candidate
DMPK.......................................drug metabolism and pharmacokinetics
DABS...discovery assays by stage
DC...development candidate
DDI..drug drug interaction
EC_{50}...................................concentration gives 50% of maximum effect
HTS ....high throughput screen
HTL...hit-to-lead
IC_{50} ....concentration causes 50% of maximum inhibition
IP ....intraperitoneally
IV..intravenously
IVIVC...*in vitro in vivo* correlation
ka..absorption rate constant

LO ....lead optimization
MEC ....minimum effective concentration
MTD ....maximum tolerable dose
MOA...mode of action
NOAEL ....no adverse effect level
NOEL..no effect level
pADME ....predictive ADME
Pgp ....P-glycoprotein
PPB ....plasma protein binding
Papp ....apparent permeability coefficient
POC ....proof of concept
RBC...red blood cell
$t_{1/2}$ ....half-life
TK..toxicokinetics
Vd ....volume of distribution
Vss ....volume of distribution at steady state.

Keywords

discovery assays by stage (DABS); absorption, distribution, metabolism and excretion (ADME); drug metabolism and pharmacokinetics (DMPK); hit to lead (HTL); lead optimization (LO); Drug Drug Interaction (DDI), maximum tolerable dose (MTD); no adverse effect level (NOAEL); no effect level (NOEL), therapeutic index, and safety window.

Introduction

Efficacy and safety are the two key elements in the drug discovery and development processes. The primary goal for pharmaceutical research companies is to identify and manufacture therapeutic agents that are safe and efficacious for patients. In principle, benefits versus risks have to be considered for target patient populations. The risks are relatively high in life threatening diseases, e.g. cancer, compared to general areas, e.g. inflammation. Pharmacology, medicinal chemistry, pharmaceutical sciences, safety assessment, drug metabolism and pharmacokinetics (DMPK), clinical research, etc. are the essential multidisciplinary R&D functions assembled within the pharmaceutical R&D engine to accomplish the aforementioned mission. Pharmacokinetics (PK) is generally viewed as the universal biomarker which reflects the processes of how a drug molecule is absorbed (e.g. ka), distributed (e.g. Vd) in the body, and cleared from the body through metabolism and excretion. The area under the drug plasma concentration versus time curve (AUC) provides an indirect assessment of the exposure level and duration of action of the therapeutic agent at the site of action (e.g. synovial fluid, tumor, brain). An ideal drug candidate should possess a plasma drug level which is above the therapeutic concentration (i.e. efficacious) and below the toxic concentration (i.e. safe). In general, the therapeutic index is calculated by dividing the plasma exposure at the NO (toxic) Effect Level (NOEL), or NO Adverse Effect Level (NOAEL), by the minimum plasma concentration required for efficacy (e.g. EC50) and the safety margin is calculated by dividing NOEL (or NOAEL) plasma concentration by the maximum plasma drug concentration (Cmax) achieved at an efficacious dose. The wider the safety margin, the safer the therapeutic agent, the lower the need for drug concentration monitoring. The definition of therapeutic index changes a bit for cytotoxic molecules in the oncology area where it can be considered as a ratio of exposure at MTD to that associated with efficacy. In the preclinical setting, the therapeutic index naturally is calculated based on the available data (e.g., pathophysiologic data, animal safety data, and projected human PK data).

Pharmacogenetic expression and polymorphisms of drug metabolizing enzymes and transporters (i.e. drug disposition proteins, collectively) as well as interactions of concomitant therapeutic agents with drug disposition proteins are the main causes for inter-individual variations of drug exposure. The so-called "drug-drug interactions" (DDI) are characterized, in part, as an increase in the plasma drug exposure due to "inhibition" of drug disposition proteins (Figure 1). In some cases, increased plasma exposure is accompanied by an increase of plasma half-life, as a result of inhibition or "inactivation" (i.e. mechanism-based inhibition) of the clearance of the therapeutic agent. DDI due to inhibition of the metabolic clearance can be a safety concern as the plasma exposure of a drug can potentially exceed the NOEL or NOAEL. DDI can also be seen with a decrease in the plasma drug exposure when drug disposition proteins are induced by the concomitant drug(s), which renders the therapeutic agent inefficacious (Figure 2). Induction of drug disposition proteins can also be triggered by the therapeutic agent itself (i.e. auto-induction), which often is accompanied by a decreased plasma half-life.

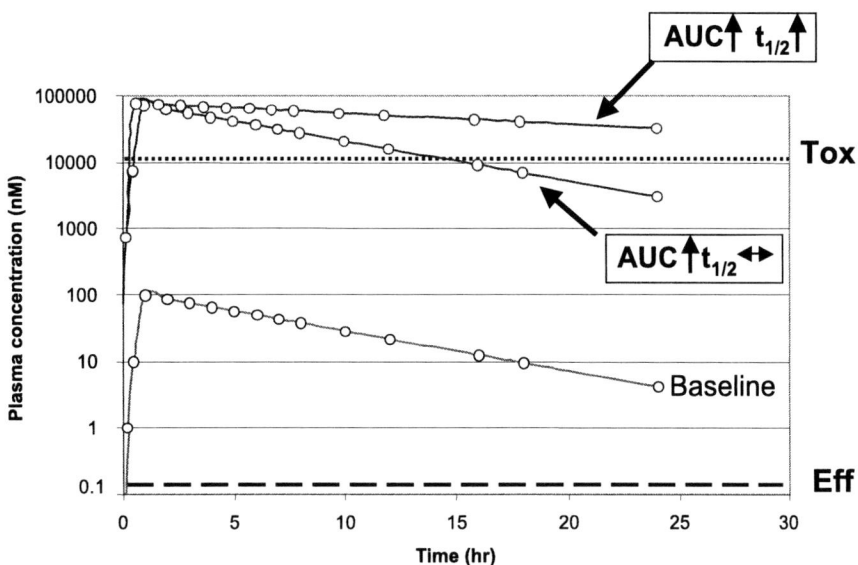

Figure 1. Hypothetical plot of a plasma drug concentration vs. time curve in the absence and presence of an inhibitor for drug transporter(s) (with no effect on clearance) resulted in an increased AUC with no change in $t_{1/2}$. Inhibition of drug metabolizing enzyme(s) by concomitant drug(s) or auto-inactivation of drug metabolizing enzyme(s) by the therapeutic agent itself resulted in an increase of both AUC and $t_{1/2}$.

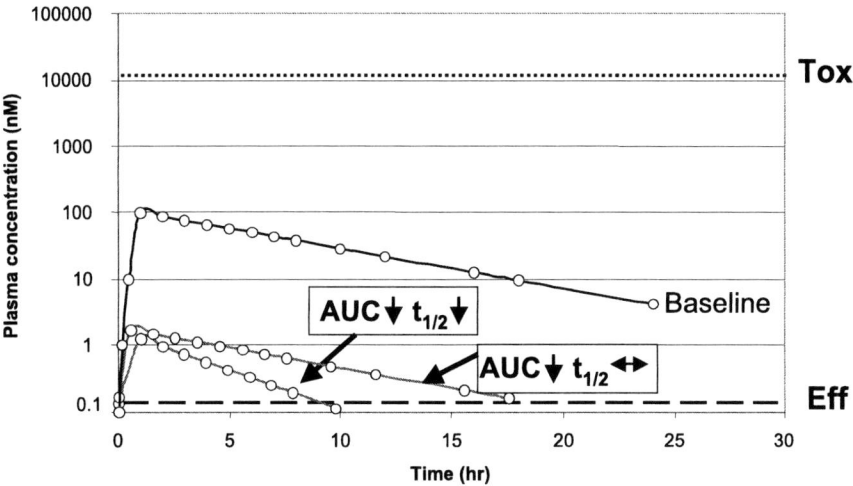

Figure 2. Hypothetical plot of a plasma drug concentration vs. time curve in the absence and presence of an inducer for drug transporter(s) (with no effect on clearance) resulted in a decreased AUC with no change in $t_{1/2}$. Auto-induction of drug metabolizing enzyme(s) by the therapeutic agent itself resulted in a decrease of both AUC and $t_{1/2}$.

Discovery Assays by Stage (DABS)

The primary task of DMPK during the discovery support phase is to project the plasma exposure of potential therapeutic agents in humans by conducting appropriate studies in preclinical species or with human and animal *in vitro* systems. The ultimate mission for the DMPK group is to: (1) eliminate drug attrition in clinical development due to exposure-based failures, (2) eliminate metabolism based toxicities, and (3) minimize the potential for drug-drug interactions. In 2002, a new discovery paradigm "Discovery Assays by Stage (DABS)" was initiated at Millennium Pharmaceuticals, Inc. The discovery process is divided into four stages: (1) High Throughput Screen (HTS), (2) Hit to Lead (HTL), (3) Lead Optimization (LO), and (4) Development Candidate (DC) selection. The main emphasis of the HTS stage, for both medicinal chemistry and pharmacology, is to identify pharmacophore series / chemical scaffolds (i.e. Hits). The involvement of DMPK at this stage is predictive ADME (i.e. pADME). Metabolism scientists use databases (i.e. *in silico*) or personal experience/knowledge (i.e. *in cerebro*) to identify structural alerts related to "hits" and to predict potential metabolic liabilities. *In vitro* evaluation of CYP inhibition and reactive metabolite formation can be carried out at this stage to confirm/address potential metabolic liabilities of chemical scaffolds. The official support of DMPK starts at the "Hit to Lead" stage where both *in vivo* PK and *in vitro* ADME screens commence. Experience has taught us that an effective way to improve the DMPK properties of drug molecules is working on drug potency/efficacy and DMPK properties in parallel at the HTL stage, after DMPK issues have been identified for the lead series. Figure 3 illustrates DMPK's deliverables at HTL and LO stages.

HTL	Early LO	Late LO
• ID any PK issues	• Optimization of animal PK profiles for DC candidates	• Projected human effective dose, dose frequency and therapeutic window
• ID relevant in vitro or in vivo tools for LO	• ADME profiles and potential drug/drug interactions for DC candidates	• Anticipated human drug/drug interactions
• POC in pharmacology model	• PK/PD relationship in pharmacology model	• ID suitable tox species based on relevance of metabolites to humans
		• Calculation of preliminary safety margin

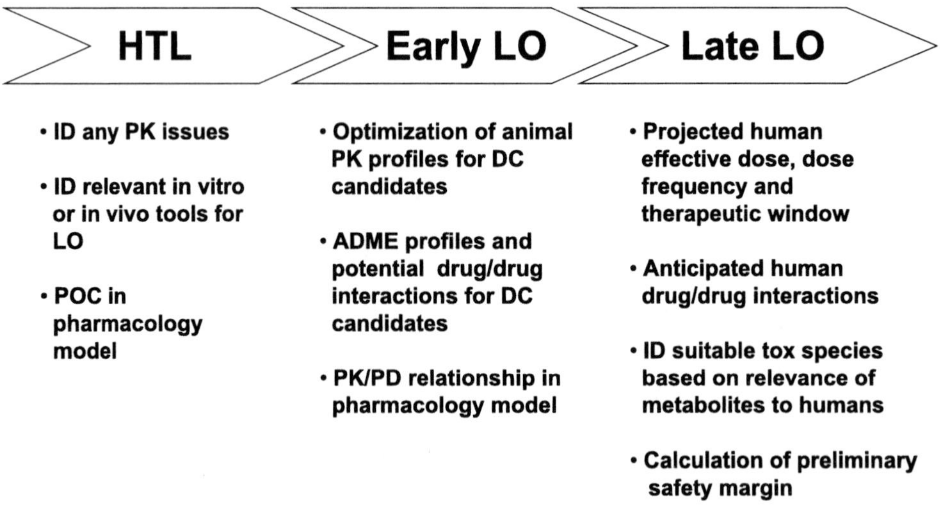

Figure 3. DMPK's deliverables at HTL and LO stages

Pharmacokinetic Optimization from "Hit-to-Lead" (HTL) to "Lead Optimization" (LO)

Clearance (CL)
A. Hepatic clearance

Once the chemical series (pharmacophores with low micromolar *in vitro* IC_{50} potency) are selected from the HTS and there is confidence that a predictable SAR relationship can be established, the project is advanced to the HTL stage. Both *in vitro* ADME experiments and *in vivo* PK studies will be conducted for at least five compounds per series in parallel to identify DMPK issues and to select appropriate *in vitro* tools for screening new molecules. *In vitro* parameters such as projected hepatic clearance CLhep (e.g. derived from the measured intrinsic clearance CLint in microsomes), Caco-2 permeability (Papp), and competitive CYP inhibition (e.g. IC_{50} values) are collected. PK parameters such as CLp, Vss, CLr, $t_{1/2}$, Tmax, Cmax, and AUC in rats (a commonly used preclinical PK species) are also determined. Equations 1 and 2 illustrate the calculation of intrinsic clearance (CLint) and predicted "hepatic" clearance (CLhep) using human liver microsomes without considering the unbound fraction:

$$\text{CLint} = (0.693 \,/\, \text{in vitro } t_{1/2}) \text{ x (incubation volume/mg of microsome) x (20}$$
$$\text{mg microsome/gram of liver) x (45 gm of liver / kg body weight)}.........(1)$$
$$\text{CLhep} = Qh \text{ x CLint } / \text{ (Qh + CLint)} ....(2)$$

where Qh is the human hepatic blood flow. The major contributing factors for the lower plasma exposure or shorter $t_{1/2}$ (e.g. hepatic and extra-hepatic metabolism, renal and biliary excretion and volume of distribution) will be first determined. If the rat CLp values agree well with the rat CLhep values and the SAR of rat CLhep correlates well with the human CLhep, hepatic metabolism is then regarded as the primary route of elimination and the rat liver microsomal stability experiment will be implemented as the screening tool. If direct conjugations (e.g. glucuronidation and sulfation) are possible, due to the structural features of drug molecules, S9 or hepatocyte stability experiments are carried out instead (Lu, 2004). Other animal models (i.e. mouse, dog, guinea pig and monkey) will be evaluated if rat is not the suitable species for the human PK optimization. For example, if the dog microsomal clearance correlates well with both human microsomal and dog plasma clearance, the dog microsomal assay can then be used as a human clearance model in rank ordering compounds. Biliary excretion may be examined if CLp is less than hepatic blood flow but greater than the predicted CLhep (using microsomes, S9, or hepatocytes) and the renal clearance CLr is low (Qh > CLp > CLhep >> CLr). Extrahepatic metabolism will be investigated if CLp is greater than the Qh and the CLr is low. Caco-2 permeability data can be used to assist in the oral bioavailability assessment, and in some reported cases (Lohmann et al., 2002), brain penetration. An *in vivo* cassette dosing PK scheme is generally used as the screening tool when renal or biliary excretions are the major routes of clearance.

B. Extrahepatic clearance

In general, extrahepatic clearance is evaluated when the CLp is greater than the hepatic blood flow (e.g. >3.3 L/hr/kg for rats). However, surprises do arise sometimes. For example, a series of arylalkyl primary amine compounds were evaluated as potential therapeutic agents in one of our discovery programs. Pharmacokinetic studies at the HTL stage revealed high CLp values for these primary amines in rodents. The *in vitro* CLhep values (measured in both microsomes and S9 fractions) were much lower than the *in vivo* CLp values. This poor *in vitro/in vivo* correlation (IVIVC) was observed in rats, dogs, and monkeys. The CLp value in rats was much higher than the rat liver blood flow (Qh) with less than 20% urinary excretion and less than 2% biliary excretion, suggesting the possibility of extrahepatic metabolic clearance. There was no obvious CYP-mediated metabolism when these alkyl amines were incubated with microsomes from various species. The blood to plasma ratio was close to unity, thus blood clearance was similar to that in plasma. Metabolism of these amines by monoamine oxidases (MAOs) was not observed. Schiff's base formation between these amines and endogenous sugars was also not observed, nor was there any significant *in vivo* lung first-pass effect. Surprisingly, an N-acetylated metabolite was identified in rat bile. This uncommon (though precedented) N-acetylated metabolite was subsequently observed in rat blood, plasma, urine, hepatocytes, as well as liver subcellular fractions when incubated with acetyl CoA indicating N-acetylation as a primary route of metabolism for the alkyl primary amines in this program. Acetylation may also be the general mechanism of clearance in the rat as N-acetylated ML106 (the lead compound) was detected in rat liver, kidney, and lung S9 incubations. Species specificity was observed with the degree of the N-acetylation much greater in rat S9, followed by monkey and human S9 fractions,

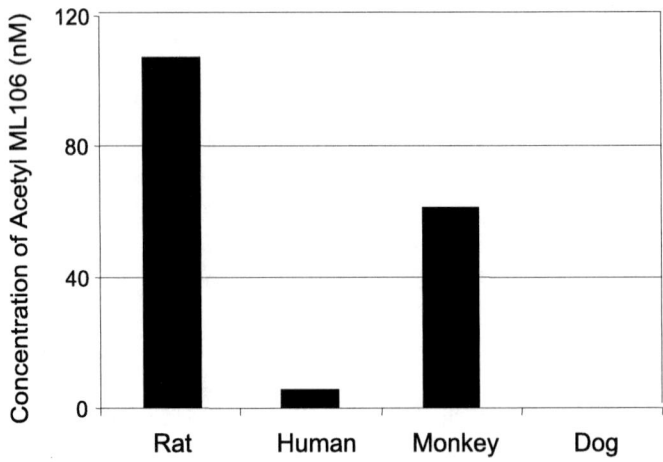

Figure 4. Species specific N-acetylation of ML106 in rat, human, monkey, and dog liver S9 fractions.

and absence in the dog S9 (Figure 4) (Li *et al.*, 2004). While the identification of the enzyme(s) responsible for the N-acetylation of these arylalkyl amines is in progress, the dog is a species known to lack N-acetyl transferases (NAT1 and NAT2), the enzymes that catalyze the N-acetylation of "aromatic" amines. The high clearance of these primary amines in rats precluded the potential to rank order compounds in this species. The absence of N-acetylation in dogs led the DMPK team to select monkeys as the appropriate animal surrogate for humans to screen new compounds.

Volume of Distribution (Vd)

A high volume of distribution (Vd) can be advantageous for targets where efficacy correlates with the ability of compounds to penetrate tissues, for instance, high tumor concentrations for oncology targets and high brain uptake for CNS targets. In addition, for compounds with comparable clearance, a high Vd translates into longer half-life ($t_{1/2}$) values and better durations of action. In contrast, high volumes may also result in pharmacology based toxicities due to potentially ubiquitously higher tissue exposures.

While volume of distribution is mostly determined via the conventional plasma pharmacokinetics, prediction of Vd has been attempted by a number of laboratories using tissue/ plasma drug concentration ratio, plasma protein binding, lipophilicity (e.g. logD), etc. (Poulin and Theil, 2002; Lombardo et al., 2002 and 2004).

A. Brain uptake

A number of imidazole-based small molecules were identified as antagonists for the melanocortin 4 (MC4) receptor, a CNS target responsible for body weight regulation and energy homeostasis (Vos et al., 2004 and Marsilje et al., 2004). Permeability studies in Caco-2 cells suggested that these molecules are not substrates for efflux pumps (e.g. Pgp). Uptake of these molecules into brain was

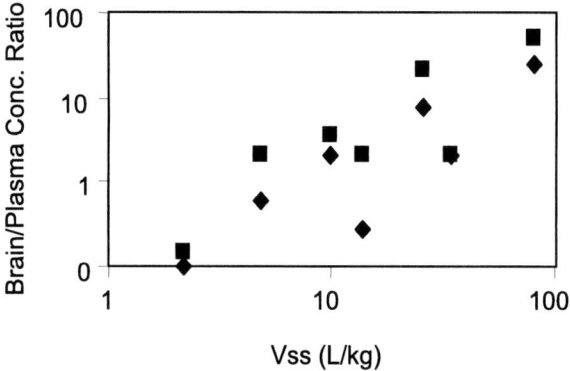

Figure 5. Correlation between the brain plasma ratios vs. volume of distributions at steady state (Vss) ($R^2 = 0.8$) for a group of seven MC4 antagonists (♦ one-hour samples, ■ four-hour samples).

evaluated in rats. Compounds were dosed intravenously (IV) to rats (1mg/kg) and the PK parameters CLp, Vd, $t_{1/2}$, and AUC were calculated. Oral studies at the doses of 10 mg/kg were also conducted and brain tissues were collected. Brain concentrations of drug molecules were measured and brain to plasma ratios were calculated. A good correlation (R^2 = 0.8) between the brain to plasma ratios vs. Vd was observed (Figure 5) (Yin et al., 2004). This result led the DMPK team to use Vd values in screening compounds for selective brain uptake studies, which expedited compound advancement to oral efficacy evaluations.

B. RBC partition

PK parameters (e.g. CLp, $t_{1/2}$, Vd, etc.) of drug molecules are conventionally derived from plasma exposure measurements. This practice can sometimes give rise to misinterpretation of the disposition profiles of drug molecules. ML-X was a lead compound in one of our discovery programs and served as an example of an incorrect conclusion being made from only the plasma PK parameters. ML-X possesses high plasma CLp (8.7 L/hr/kg) and Vd (8.2 L/kg) in rats. However, the rat liver microsomal CLhep was relatively low (~2 L/h/kg) and the renal excretion was insignificant, suggesting that the high CLp may be due to a) the extra-hepatic metabolism, b) plasma instability, or c) high red blood cell (RBC) uptake. ML-X was found to be stable in the rat plasma. The ML-X RBC/plasma partitioning experiment was then conducted and the RBC/plasma ratios of ML-X in rats, mice, and humans were determined to be 28, 9, and 3, respectively. In addition, the whole blood CL (0.13 L/hr/kg) and Vd (0.58 L/kg) of ML-X in rats were determined and shown to be much lower than the plasma CLp and Vd (Figure 6). The RBC binding of ML-X was determined to be tight, concentration dependent, but reversible. Further studies in the blood of xenograft mice suggested that ML-X binds to the carbonic anhydrase present in the RBCs (Wong et al., 1994). ML-X bound to RBC can be displaced by its structural analog and by chlorthalidone (Johnston et al., 1981), a sulfonamide diuretic known to strongly bind to carbonic

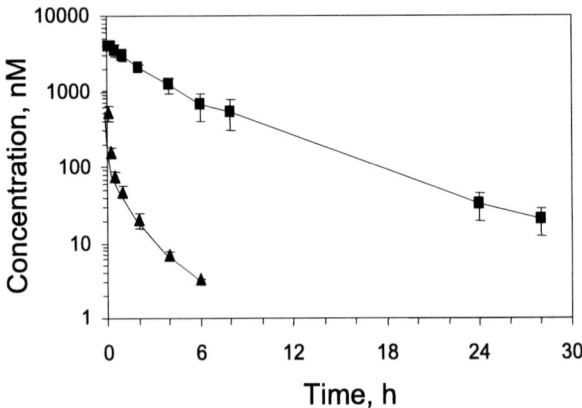

Figure 6. Whole blood and plasma concentration-time profiles of ML-X in male Sprague-Dawley rats following 1 mg/kg IV bolus dose (■ whole blood concentrations, ▲ plasma concentrations).

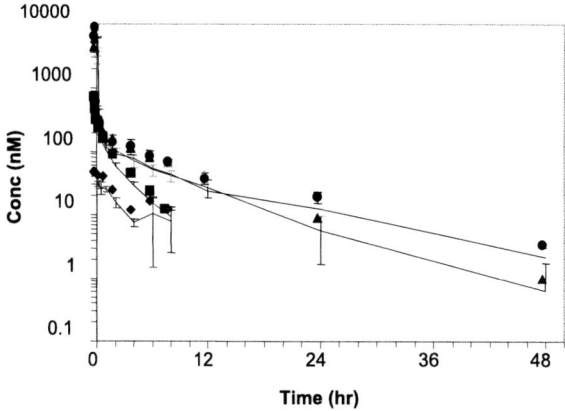

Figure 7. Plasma concentration-time profiles of ML106 in mice (♦), Sprague-Dawley rats (■), dogs (▲), and monkeys (●) following 1 mg/kg IV bolus dose (rats and mice) or 5 min infusion (dogs and monkeys).

anhydrases in the cytosol of RBC (Lettieri and Portelli 1983; Xia et al., 2004). Nova screen results also indicate that ML-X binds to carbonic anhydrases I and II with the IC50 value of 0.63 μM and < 0.16 μM, respectively.

The above results suggest that the high plasma CL and Vd of ML-X was a reflection of high RBC/plasma partitioning and tight binding to carbonic anhydrases. The DMPK team decided to screen compounds from this discovery project using whole blood PK parameters.

Human Pharmacokinetics (PK) and Dose Projections

Human dose projection is used at the drug discovery stage to guide the selection of potential development candidate (DC). More objective projections of the potential clinical efficacy and safety/toxicity are possible from the projected PK in humans for a compound relative to the clinical target product profile. Allometric scaling based on the preclinical PK data is the routine way to project the PK parameters in humans. Human PK projections from CLhep have also been used when there is evidence that metabolic clearance is the basis for plasma clearance. In addition, PK projections from animal models of human drug disposition have been employed when there was confidence that the animal model was predictive of humans with related sentinel molecules with known human PK.

The primary amines mentioned earlier (see extrahepatic section) showed a very high CLp (greater than the liver blood flow) and high Vd in rodent species. The project team was skeptical of suitability of the chemical series for human dosing (i.e. due to a concern that the short half-life will make it impossible to meet the target product profile). To address this issue, IV PK studies were conducted for the lead compound ML106 in higher species dogs and monkeys (Figure 7) and the results indicated that clearance was substantially lower in these non-rodent species (Figure 8). Several *in vitro* studies were also conducted. Which demonstrated that the high CLp of ML106 and other lead compounds was rodent

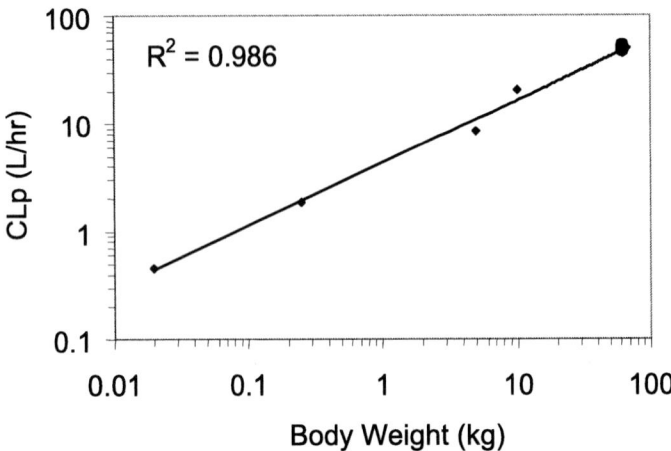

Figure 8. Allometric scaling of ML106 clearance in humans (R^2 = 0.986). CLp human = 4.3 x (body weight)$^{0.5831}$. Projected human blood clearance is 0.51 L/hr/kg.

specific. A combination of monkey PK parameters and allometrically scaled clearance was used to project the human dose to maintain a minimum effective plasma concentration for longer than one and a half days, while keeping the Cmax below the NOEL established in rats and dogs. The projected narrow safety margin prompted the project team to continue screening more compounds for better PK, safety, and efficacy.

Proof of Concept (POC) in Pharmacology

Pharmacology often uses the mouse or the rat as a disease model to test for drug efficacy. Obtaining the required plasma drug exposure for efficacy is critical in translating a preferred target to proof of disease modification. The role of DMPK in drug discovery POC studies includes, but is not limited to a) selecting right compounds for POC/MOA studies, based on pharmacokinetic properties and b) addressing potential *in vitro* and *in vivo* discrepancies in pharmacological activity. In most cases, plasma protein binding is measured to compare free drug concentration with the IC_{50} to determine whether and how long the free drug concentrations are maintained above an *in vitro* effect target (e.g. IC_{50} and IC_{90}). Multiple dosing, alternative dosing routes, infusion and broad CYP inhibition by co-administration of 1-aminobenzotriazole (ABT) are common techniques used to elevate the exposure of metabolically unstable but potent drug molecules. Similarly, specific Pgp, MRP and BCRP transporter inhibitors are tried to enhance the target organ concentrations where compounds are identified as a susbtrate of the transporter. The relationship between plasma concentration and target organ site concentration (e.g., tumor, brain, and synovial fluid) are compared to assess the relevance of plasma $t_{1/2}$ to effect and to determine the PK/PD relationship.

A. Discrete vs. cassette PK studies

When selecting compounds to establish animal models for efficacy, MOA, biomarker identification or validation, and other pharmacology studies, compounds at the HTL or early LO stage are screened *via* PK studies in the intended animal disease model. This exercise, in fact, helps the selection of optimal dose and dosing scheme for validation of the efficacy model. The screening PK can be done in the discrete or cassette mode. An example of discrete PK studies on the CRTH2 antagonists in mice (the pharmacological model) is shown in Figure 9 and the molecule ML5 with better PK profile was selected for further evaluation.

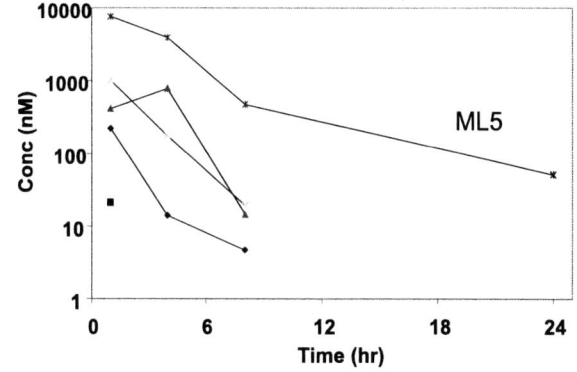

Figure 9. Plasma concentration-time profiles of potent CRTH2 compounds in mice after 10 mg/kg discrete PO dose. Lower limit of detection is 0.3 nM.

An example using cassette studies to rank order compounds based on their tumor exposures is provided by compounds in one of our discovery programs which showed high clearance (CLp) and high volume of distribution (Vd) in rodents. It was difficult to rank order compounds based on the plasma PK. In order to reduce the number of sequential PK studies to select compounds with good tumor uptake, cassette dosing studies were conducted in tumor bearing mice to directly measure the tumor uptake of compounds so that the lead compound with the best tumor PK profile could be identified for an in vivo efficacy study in a solid tumor xenograft model (Figure 10). A reference compound (e.g. ML101) is included in all cassette studies to provide assurance that DDIs have not affected either the PK or the tumor distribution of the cassette. Based on PK properties, as well as the tumor to plasma ratio, ML107 was selected to establish POC for this class of compounds following a discrete PK study to confirm the cassette data (data not shown).

Sometimes in drug discovery even unfavorable experimental results (when good results were expected) are analyzed thoroughly for knowledge that can be used to guide further compound design. For example, in one of the oncology projects, primary *in vitro* screening involved enzyme-based and cell-based assays. ML110 was more potent than ML111 in an enzyme assay. In the cell-based assay, however, ML110 did not show any cytotoxic activity whereas ML111 showed

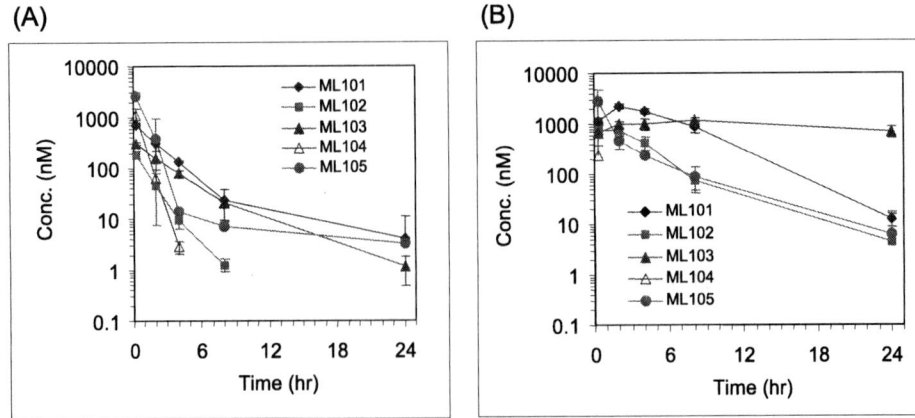

Figure 10. (A) Plasma concentration-time profiles and (B) tumor concentration-time profile of five anticancer agents from a cassette PK study (2 mg/kg per compound given IP) in tumor bearing mice.

excellent activity. A logical reason for this discrepancy was that ML110 could not permeate the cell membrane. However, permeability experiments in Caco-2 cells did not indicate substantial differences between these two molecules. Stability of the compounds was then assessed in the cell-based assay containing buffer and tumor cells (cytotoxicity end-point was measured using the water soluble tetrazolium (WST)). ML111 was stable for 24 hours. In contrast, ML110 concentration showed a significant decline in the system. Although the mechanism of ML110 disappearance (e.g. degradation, nonspecific binding, etc.) is still under investigation, the results established the reason for the discrepancy between enzyme and cell based activity profiles of these two interesting compounds. The results also demonstrated one potential reason for *in vitro- in vivo* discrepancies when evaluating compounds in pharmacological models.

B. Inhibition of CYP activities by ABT

1-Aminobenzotriazole (ABT) is a nonspecific inhibitor of CYPs (Constan et al., 1999; Huijzer et al., 1989). The dosing regimen to effectively inhibit CYPs and hence decrease the plasma clearance and increase the exposure of a non-specific CYP substrate antipyrine (AP) (Sharer and Wrighton, 1996) in rats, dogs and monkeys has been established (Balani *et al.*, 2002) and extended to mice and guinea pigs which are also routinely used for PK, safety evaluation and pharmacology studies (Balani *et al.*, 2004). Pretreatment of animals with ABT significantly inhibits the oxidative metabolism of test compounds. This provides a useful means to evaluate the role of metabolism in compound-based toxicities, or for assessing systemic level of a compound available for a target enzyme or receptor. This approach was applied to the compound ML123 in one of our discovery projects. ML123 possesses good *in vitro* pharmacological activity but no *in vivo* efficacy in the rat disease model. ML123 has a high plasma clearance CLp (6.6 L/hr/kg) which is greater than hepatic blood flow, Q_h, indicating potential extrahepatic metabolism and/or renal excretion.   In order to conduct a proof of concept study in the rat disease model it was necessary to boost the systemic concentrations of ML123.   Accordingly, ML123 was administered to rats 2 hr after oral administration of ABT (100 mg/kg).   Clearance of ML123 decreased by 60% and AUC increased 3-fold when ML123 was given by IV.   The effect of ABT was even more pronounced when ML123 was given orally to rats.   There was a 10-fold increase of ML123 AUC when animals were pretreated with ABT (Figure 11).   This intentional DDI helped achieve establishment of MOA which had been elusive otherwise due to poor systemic exposure to molecules.

Toxicokinetics (TK) are also determined for single rising dose and repeat dose drug safety evaluation studies (to identify the maximum tolerable dose, MTD) before development candidate selection.   The TK data provide valuable information such as plasma exposure associated with NOEL and NOAEL.   The NOEL (or NOAEL), Cmax (or AUC), and EC_{50} (or AUC at EC_{50} dose) are used to estimate the initial safety and therapeutic index.   The selection of a development candidate is based, in part, on its potency, PK profile, potential for DDI, major metabolic clearance by polymorphic CYPs, and safety and therapeutic index.

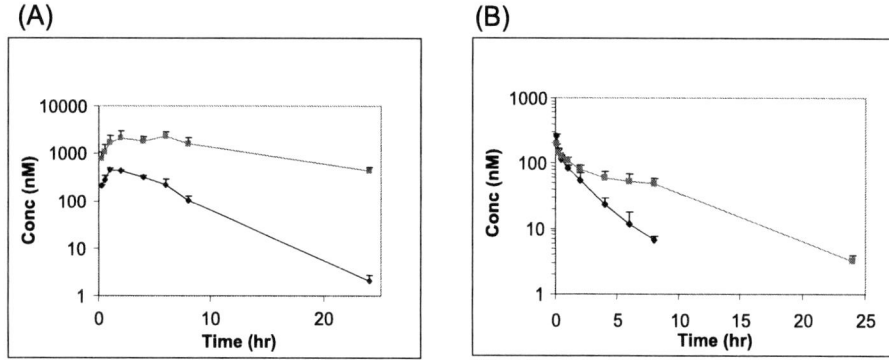

(A)   **(B)**

Figure 11. Plasma concentration-time profiles of ML123 in rats after (A) 10 mg/kg oral dose and (B) 1 mg/kg IV dose in the absence (◆) and presence (■) of ABT given orally 2 hour prior to the administration of ML123.

Acknowledgments

The authors would like to thank Dr. Jing-Tao Wu's Bio-analytical team for the excellent analytical support. The authors also thank Ms. Miao Guan, Ms. Myrtha Durena, and Mr. Jackson Kalanzi of the Comparative Medicine for assisting with in vivo studies. The authors wish to thank Mr. Richard Gallegos, Ms. Ning Liu, Ms. BeiChing Chuang, Ms. Shelley Li, and Mr. Dun-Xue Mu for their technical support. Special thanks to colleagues in Drug Safety Evaluation, Medicinal Chemistry, and Pharmacology departments.

References

Balani SK, Zhu T, Yang TJ, Liu Z, He B, and Lee FW. Effective Dosing Regimen of 1-Aminobenzotriazole for Inhibition of Antipyrine Clearance in Rats, Dogs and Monkeys. *Drug Metab Dispos* 2002; 30:1059-1062.

Balani S, Li P, Nguyen J, Cardoza K, Zeng H, Mu DX, Wu JT, Gan LS, Lee FW. Effective Dosing Regimen of 1-aminobenzotriazole for Inhibition of Antipyrine Clearance in Guinea Pigs and Mice using Serial Sampling. *Drug Metab Dispos* 2004; 32, 1092-1095.

Constan AA, Sprankle CS, Peters JM, Kedderis GL, Everitt JI, Gonzalez FL, and Butterworth BE. Metabolism of Chloroform by CYP 2E1 is Required for Induction of Toxicity in the Liver, Kidney and Nose of Male Mice. *Toxicol Appl Pharmacol* 1999; 160:120-126.

Huijzer JC, Adams JD, Jaw JY, and Yost GS. Inhibition of 3-Methylindole Bioactivation by Cytochrome P450 Suicide Substrate 1-Aminobenzotriazole and ·-Methylbenzylamino-benzotriazole. *Drug Metab Dispos* 1989; 17:37-42.

Johnston MM, Rosenberg M, Dorsey TE, Doyle RF. Automated Analysis of Chlorthalidone Based on the Inhibition of Carbonic Anhydrase. *Methodological Surveys* 1981; 10:253-8.

Li P, Labutti J, Lu C, Daniels JS, Nagaraja N, Huang R, Gallegos R, Uttamsingh V, Balani SK, Lee FW, Miwa G, and Gan LS. N-Acetylation of a Primary Alkylamine as a Major Metabolic Clearance Route in Rats. *Drug Metabolism Rev* 2004; 36 (S1):327.

Lettieri JT, Portelli ST. Effects of Competitive Red Blood Cells Binding and Reduced Hematocrit on the Blood and Plasma Levels of [14C]Indapamide in the Rat. *Journal of Pharmacology and Experimental Therapeutics* 1983; 224:269-72.

Lohmann C, Huwel S, Galla HJ. Predicting Blood-Brain Barrier Permeability of Drugs: Evaluation of Different In Vitro Assays. *Journal of Drug Targeting* 2002; 10:263-276.

Lombardo F, Obach RS, Shalaeva MY, Gao F. Prediction of Human Volume of Distribution Values for Neutral and Basic Drugs. 2. Extended Data Set and Leave-Class-Out Statistics. *Journal of Medicinal Chemistry* 2004; 47:1242-1250.

Lombardo F, Obach RS, Shalaeva MY, Gao F. Prediction of Volume of Distribution Values in Humans for Neutral and Basic Drugs Using Physicochemical Measurements and Plasma Protein Binding Data. *Journal of Medicinal Chemistry* 2002; 45:2867-2876.

Lu C, Li P, Gallegos R, Xia C, Uttamsingh V, Miwa G, and Gan LS. Comparison of Intrinsic Clearance in Liver Microsomes, S9, and Hepatocytes from Rats and Humans. *Drug Metabolism Rev* 2004; 36 (S1), 429.

Marsilje TH, Roses JB, Calderwood EF, Stroud SG, Forsyth NE, Blackburn C, Yowe DL, Miao W, Drabic SV, Bohane MD, Daniels JS, Li P, Wu L, Patane MA, Claiborne CF. Synthesis and Biological Evaluation of Imidazole-based Small Molecule Antagonists of the Melanocortin 4 Receptor (MC4-R). *Bioorganic & Medicinal Chemistry Letters* 2004; 14:3721-3725.

Poulin P, Theil FP. Prediction of pharmacokinetics prior to in vivo studies. 1. Mechanism-based prediction of volume of distribution. *Journal of Pharmaceutical Sciences* 2002; 91:129-156.

Sharer JE, and Wrighton SA, "Identification of the Human Hepatic Cytochromes P450 Involved in the In Vitro Oxidation of Antipyrine", *Dug Metab Dispos* 1996; 24:487-494.

Vos TJ, Caracoti A, Che JL, Dai M, Farrer CA, Forsyth NE, Drabic SV, Horlick RA, Lamppu D, Yowe DL, Balani S, Li P, Zeng H, Joseph IBJK, Rodriguez LE, Maguire MP, Patane MA, Claiborne CF. Identification of 2-{2-[2-(5-Bromo-2-methoxyphenyl)-ethyl]-3-fluorophenyl}-4,5-dihydro-1H-imidazole (ML00253764), a Small Molecule Melanocortin 4 Receptor Antagonist that Effectively Reduces Tumor-Induced Weight Loss in a Mouse Model. *Journal of Medicinal Chemistry* 2004; 47:1602-1604.

Wong BK, Bruhin PJ, Lin JH. Dos-dependent Pharmacokinetics of L-693,612, a Carbonic Anhydrase Inhibitor, Following Oral Administration n Rats. *Pharmaceutical Research* 1994; 11:438-441.

Yin W, Li P, Gan LS, Lodenquai P, Wu JT, Cardoza K, Yang H, Lee FW and Miwa G. Pharmacokinetics and Brian Uptake of Substituted 1,2-Diaryl-Ethane Melanocortin 4 (MC4) Receptor Antagonists in Rats. *Drug Metabolism Rev* 2004; 36(S1): 167.

5

Solubility, Solubilization and Dissolution in Drug Delivery During Lead Optimization

Michael J. Hageman

Pharmaceutical Sciences
Pfizer Inc.
Kalamazoo, MI 49001 USA

Table of Contents

List of Abbreviations

ADME ....Absorption, distribution, metabolism and excretion
AUC...Area under the curve (drug in plasma)
CD...Cyclodextrin
Cmax ....Maximum concentration (drug in plasma)
CMC...Critical micelle concentration
Cs...Saturation solubility
DMSO ....Dimethyl sulfoxide
FCS...Fetal calf serum
GI ....Gastrointestinal
HP-β-CD ....Hydroxypropyl-β-cyclodextrin
HSA...Human serum albumin
HTS...High throughput screening
IV ....Intravenous
Ka ....Ionization constant
Ksp.....................................Solubility product (equilibrium constant)
MAD..Maximum absorbable dose
MSA..Methane sulfonic acid
MTS ....Medium throughput screening
μ..Chemical potential
NCE ....New chemical entity
PBS ....Phosphate buffered saline
Pe ....Permeability
PK...Pharmacokinetics
PO...Oral dosing

SAR ....Structure activity relationship
SPR ....Structure property relationship
SBE-β-CD ....Sulfobutyl ether-β-cyclodextrin

Keywords

Bioavailability, Dissolution, Drug Delivery, Formulation, Permeability, Precipitation, Solubility, Supersaturation

Introduction

At this symposium, as in much of the literature over the last 5-10 years, there has been continued discussion regarding ways to reduce drug candidate attrition during the more costly drug development phases. Much of this discussion has revolved around the recognized importance of selecting drug candidates that have "drug-like" properties, i.e. physical, chemical and structural properties that appear to differentiate nondrug and drug molecules (Kennedy, 1997; Lipinski *et al.*, 2001; Kola and Landis, 2004). As a result, there has been a conscious effort made to move from highly potent ligands toward a molecule that has "drug-like" properties, presumably with a lower risk to attrit during development. In an effort to address these properties sooner, preclinical groups such as pharmaceutics, metabolism and toxicology have been brought into the drug candidate selection process.

In an earlier symposium in this series, significant discussion occurred around the process of moving from hit to lead selection and the potential role of "drug-like" properties even at such an early stage (Borchardt *et al.*, 2004). The key driver for pursuing drug-likeness at the lead selection stage is to avoid templates where inherent properties of the template may be difficult, if not impossible, to overcome with synthetic modification during the property optimization phases. There continues to be a lot of discussion regarding "lead-likeness" versus "drug-likeness" and what is important to have in a lead molecule (Oprea *et al.*, 2001; Oprea, 2002; Rishton, 2003; Hann and Oprea, 2004; Borchardt *et al.*, 2004). Irrespective of the definition, the process of lead optimization is intended to move a lead compound toward a drug candidate containing "drug-like" properties in addition to high potency.

The process most often implemented to reduce attrition at later phases usually involves introduction of a set of "drug-like" criteria that must met for a lead to be considered as a drug candidate, i.e. the "gate-keeper" strategy. While this approach is likely to minimize the attrition of compounds in later phases or at the very least, reduce downstream surprises, it does not necessarily follow that there will be an equal number of strong drug candidates coming forward. In fact, a reduction in number of candidates often will occur, but those accepted will be of much higher quality. The real proliferation of more "drug-like" molecules will be better realized as the role of the preclinical groups evolves from that of a "gate-keeper" to that of becoming a full partner in the discovery process. Simply making measurements on molecules and relaying a meets or doesn't meet decision back to the discovery organization is inefficient. While such criteria will induce the discovery teams to think about the drug-like criteria during optimization, which is obviously advantageous, the team will need to take on the added burden of learning and incorporating preclinical sciences into the selection process. The more efficient utilization of resources at a corporate level requires partnership in the drug discovery process between pre-existing preclinical science areas and the discovery teams. This "partnership" mentality will move the teams from discerning a drug candidates potential, to applying multidisciplinary scientific expertise to the design of the screening funnels and data interpretation, facilitating design of drug-like properties into what was a lead template.

Depending on particular organizational constructs, the ability of preclinical groups to work with discovery teams can range from expected and appreciated to difficult. It becomes critical that the preclinical groups of drug metabolism, pharmaceutics and toxicology all work with one another in order to effectively influence lead optimization. The absorption, distribution, metabolism and elimination (ADME) components described in the first session of this book begin to address the behavior of a drug-lead *in vivo*. However, the effective design of improved ADME behavior requires an understanding of the inherent physicochemical properties of a lead and how they impact ADME behavior. This is where the interactions of the ADME and Pharmaceutics groups become critical. These groups need to think in terms of property optimization in a rapidly moving, quick decision making environment, where experimental data and compound availability are limited.

Pharmaceutics has traditionally been regarded as the scientific discipline focusing on the development of a dosage form for marketing and easy administration to the target species. It has become increasingly recognized that the physical chemistry and engineering components leading to quality design of a dosage form is only part of the role they should play. The inability to deliver the drug to the target site, at a concentration sufficient to illicit a pharmacological response, will make the most elegant formulation designs useless. It is critical for the pharmaceutical scientist to be prepared to apply their knowledge of physicochemical properties to molecular level behavior at the biological interface in the discovery environment. While the same science still applies in this environment, the way it is employed and how decisions must be made quickly, often with less than adequate data, will be very different than the highly regulated environment a pharmaceutical chemist typically operates in. An understanding of how the inherent physicochemical properties of a molecule are reflected in the ability of that molecule to be delivered to the intended target can have a crucial impact on the iterative process of lead optimization. Progressing through lead optimization with drug delivery issues in mind will ultimately result in potential drug candidates that have a drug delivery facet designed into them and meeting the preordained "drug-like" criteria set forth will be a natural consequence.

This chapter will discuss potential roles that the pharmaceutics scientist can play in helping with drug delivery attributes of leads during lead optimization. The physicochemical properties that the pharmaceutical chemist is trained to measure and assess include things like solubility, partitioning, ionization, dissolution, supersaturation, complexation, binding, association, surface activity, physical state, material properties, and diffusional transport. The influence of these physicochemical properties on design and readout of screening funnels will be discussed, wherein these properties play a critical role on the exposure of the molecule to the target of interest, whether that target is *in vitro* or *in vivo*.

Delivering Drug to the Test System

During the hit identification phase and the hit-to-lead selection process, the chemical diversity of the compound libraries evaluated can be very large, hence dictating the need for a generic vehicle to deliver compounds into the test system of interest. Polar aprotic solvents such as dimethyl sulfoxide (DMSO) have become the mainstay for delivering compounds into high throughput screening (HTS) assays of all types and in some cases actually storage of compound libraries. The value of these solvents derives from their ability to solubilize a very diverse set of chemical structures and yet be completely miscible with aqueous media, thus acting as a transfer agent for delivery of compound to the aqueous based assays.

The potential impact of these diluted aprotic solvents on the readout of the assay is generally built into validation of the assays, wherein tolerances and ranges of acceptable solvent levels are defined. However, it is not really possible to account for the highly variable propensity for compound precipitation upon dilution of the aprotic solvent into aqueous media. This problem continues to plague HTS and is generally accepted as part of the noise affiliated with HTS at the hit-to-lead stage, the tradeoff being the exceedingly large number of compounds screened and a general feeling that if the compound is too insoluble upon dilution it is good that it is discarded anyway. This thinking is fine when the number of hits is high and leads plentiful, but becomes more of a concern when the target is such that the number of hits and leads are very low, and any sort of false negative is undesirable.

The probability of precipitation of the compound is particularly high upon dilution of an aprotoic solvent into aqueous media, especially if the drug is near saturation solubility in the solvent itself. The solubility of the compound decreases

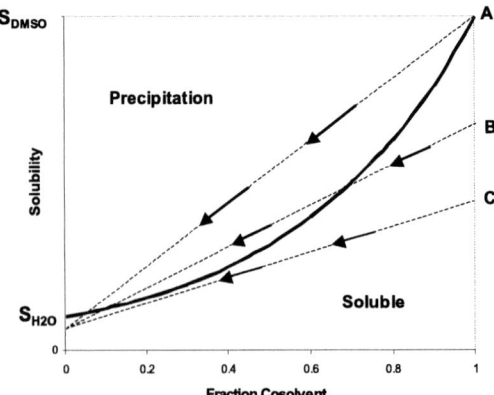

Figure 1. Typical compound solubilization curve in a cosolvent system such as DMSO / water (solid line). Samples below the curve would be soluble, while those above the curve would be prone to precipitation. Upon linear dilution from Point A (where compound is near saturation solubility in the DMSO) the probability for precipitation is high. Dilution from B may or may not result in precipitation depending on the dynamics of the dilution and exactly what the final dilution is. Dilution from point C should not precipitate. S_{DMSO} and S_{H2O} are saturation solubilities in neat solutions of DMSO and water, respectively.

exponentially as a function of decreasing cosolvent concentration, whereas the concentration of the drug and the aprotic solvent both decrease linearly upon dilution (Figure 1). Therefore, as shown in Figure 1, depending on the concentration initially in the DMSO solution (A vs B vs C on Figure 1) and the degree of dilution, the potential exists to be at concentrations exceeding the solubility of compound in that cosolvent mixture (curved bold line). In some cases, the final concentration may be at a point where it was soluble, but it was necessary to go through a region of coslovent composition where the compound could precipitate, but continue to a point where it would be soluble, leading to variable results depending on timing of transfers and readouts associated with the assay. The propensity for precipitation of a drug is governed by several processes; the actual concentration of the drug being a driver with respect to the statistical probability of molecules to come together for nucleation, the level of supersaturation, i.e. how high the concentration is above the thermodynamic saturation solubility, the inherent tendency for the solid to nucleate and then demonstrate crystal growth as dictated by solid energetics, and finally the factors which influence the diffusional rates of the molecules in the media.

As HTS or moderate throughput screening (MTS) assays are employed in the lead optimization stage, the level of chemical diversity is diminished, but the use of polar aprotic solvents often continues in this phase as well. However, since the goal is now one of optimization of structural properties, a readout free of ambiguity and false negatives becomes much more important to avoid miss-directing structural modification strategies. Unfortunately, once the optimization screening assays move toward *in vivo* evaluations, there is often a continued use of these aprotic solvents because they are known to solubilize the compound in previous *in vitro* studies. Continued use of DMSO often results from a lack of compound, resources or time to evaluate other vehicles or consider alternative delivery systems at this stage.

Lead optimization relies on a combination of HTS and MTS, along with a limited number of lower throughput assays, which often includes *in vivo* evaluation in animals. Irrespective of whether the assay involves ligand binding, ligand displacement, receptor occupation, or enzyme inhibition, the response is monitored as a function of the amount of compound added. However, the real driving force for a molecule to interact with a receptor is related to "free compound" in solution, or more correctly the chemical potential (μ) of the compound in the respective media. The μ of the compound is a thermodynamic measure of the molecules escaping tendency from the solvating media surrounding it, hence the greater the μ, the greater will be the tendency of the molecule to diffuse to a point of lower μ or interact with another molecule or receptor, which in effect reduces it's μ. Similarly, the rate at which a molecule traverses a membrane (d(mass)/d(time)) of given surface area (A) is the rate of flux per unit area (J).

$$\frac{d(mass)}{d(time)} \cdot \frac{1}{A} = J \qquad \text{Eqn. 1}$$

Flux, J, is dictated by the effective permeability (Pe) and the concentration gradient of the compound from the apical (C_{apical}) to the basolateral ($C_{basolateral}$) side of the membrane, or more correctly, the difference in chemical potential between the two sides of the membrane, μ_{apical} and $\mu_{basolateral}$ (Hilgers et al., 1990; Camenisch et al., 1996; Bohets et al., 2001).

$$J = Pe \cdot (\mu_{apical} - \mu_{basolateral}) \approx Pe \cdot \mu_{apical} \qquad \textbf{Eqn. 2}$$

In most cases where transport across a membrane is considered, removal and systemic distribution of the compound will result in sink conditions, making the flux dependent on the Pe and the μ at the membrane surface. Pe is then directly proportional to the diffusion coefficient of the molecule through the membrane and the partition coefficient, P, between the membrane and the media (Pe $\propto$ P = (μmembrane / μmedia)) and inversely proportional to the thickness of the membrane. As reviewed by Camenisch et al., (1996), the form of the relationship between P and Pe can take many shapes depending on the data set chosen. Depending on the *in vitro* cell based assay, there may actually be an equilibrium reached if sink conditions are not present, wherein the transport rates will decrease with time until the μ on both sides of the membrane is equal. In such situations, the final distribution of the compound will be related to the relative partitioning between two compartments and any binding or association that may occur in those compartments. In any event, it is clear that the actual flux across a membrane, or the equilibrium distribution, is related to the chemical potential of the compound in solution and not necessarily the concentration (Raub et al., 1993; Koeplinger et al., 1999).

Determination of drug concentration in solution is a simple concept, but is highly dependent on how separation and analytical methodology is employed to obtain the measurement. The analytical measurement of how much drug is "in solution" is often dependent on the intended use of the information. The two extremes range from the total amount of compound in solution, irrespective of the state of the drug (i.e. two phase dispersions, associated complexes, etc.) to the actual μ of the drug in solution (indicative of the level of solvation at a molecular level.) The intended application of the "solubility" number will play a significant role in what type of number should be determined. If neither solubility nor dissolution are limiting, the total compound dispersed in the system is probably of greatest interest, as it all behaves as if were in solution. If a process is dissolution rate limited then the μ and the total solubilized drug are important, whereas if solubility is limiting, the "free compound" or μ is the primary measurement of interest. If the *in vitro* system involves receptor binding or occupation, the chemical potential is of greatest interest. It is important to always consider what is to be done with the solubility number to help define how to generate it.

Drug Delivery for *In vitro* Screening in Funnels

Drug delivery is often confined to consideration of formulation and *in vivo* delivery. The definition of drug delivery during template/lead selection and optimization should be considered to encompass a number of situations within the screening funnel (Figure 2). "Drug delivery" can relate to 1° activity assays typically run as part of a HTS platform, wherein "delivery" relates to the accessibility of the compound to interact with the corresponding target. Obviously, the compound has to be in solution and "free" for interaction with the intended target, i.e. the ability to interact is dictated by the μ of the compound.

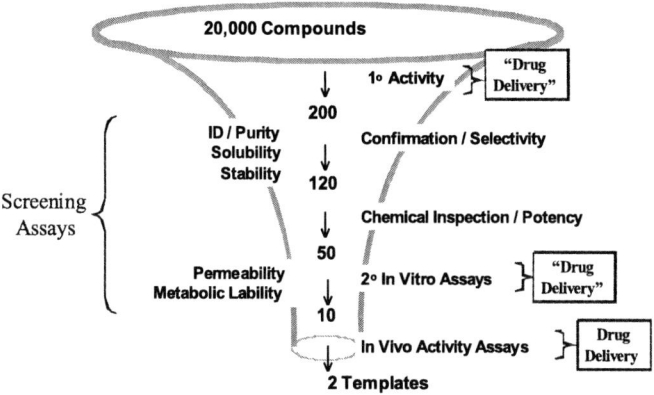

Figure 2. Example of a lead selection funnel and the role of both *in vitro* and *in vivo* "drug delivery" in the funnel.

One of the more common problems encountered during optimization screening can be related to high variability between repeat assays and inconsistency in potency numbers between different assays (Figure 3). Different *in vitro* assays are often developed in different labs. Generally, assay development is based on certain past experiences and ways to avoid common problems that have been encountered in the past. This, coupled with the fact that the assays can have very different criteria for the media selected to maintain ligands, proteins or cells,

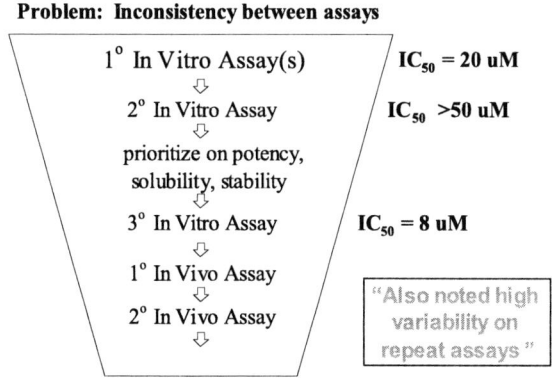

Figure 3. Potential ramifications of "drug delivery" problems in the screening funnel and the impact on potency readouts.

can result in very different dilution sequences between assays and types of media exposures through the dilutions (Figure 4). It is generally perceived that this should be irrelevant with respect to the final readouts, but these different dilution sequences and media manipulations can lead to convoluted results wherein structure activity relationship (SAR) becomes difficult to interpret. Taken to the extreme, the SAR can reflect physicochemical properties such as solubility, propensity to precipitate or propensity to undergo protein binding, yielding a structure property relationship (SPR) as much as it does SAR.

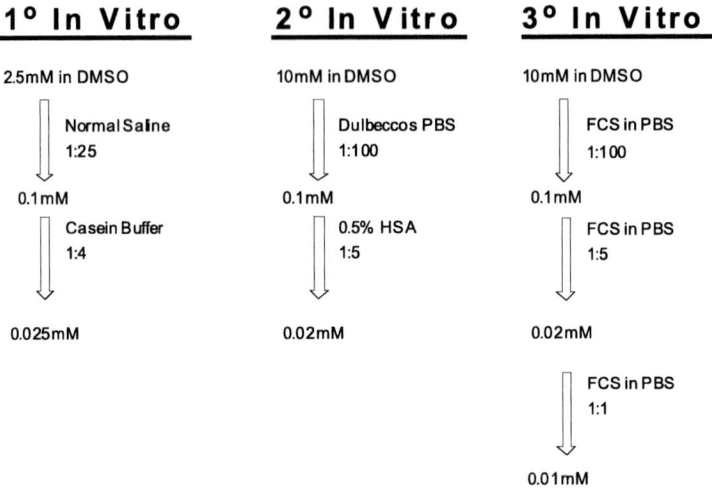

Figure 4. Examples of dilution sequences used for *in vitro* assays during lead optimization screening. Dilutions of more than 100 fold are difficult with most liquid handling equipment, hence sequential dilutions are often used.

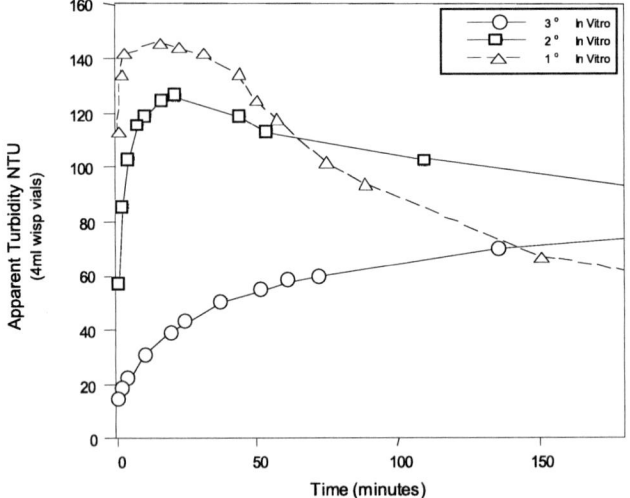

Figure 5. Example where a poorly soluble lead results in precipitation (monitored by turbidity) when making the first dilution from DMSO into various media for each of three different *in vitro* assays (see Figure 4 for dilution schemes).

As observed in Figure 5, precipitation of compound (observed as turbidity) can occur very rapidly upon dilution of both the 2.5 or 10 mM DMSO solutions of compound. In some cases, the turbidity decreases with time due to aggregation of precipitated primary particles into larger aggregates, which can then settle from solution. In the case of the 3° assay, the presence of the fetal calf serum (FCS) apparently retards the rate of precipitation and even limits the extent of precipitation. Within the HTS platform the timing of aliquots and dilutions can play a role in the precise amount of compound that gets transferred into the next well or dilution sequence. Depending on the situation, there may be redissolution of the resulting precipitate upon the next dilution, again a highly time dependent process which only adds to potential for variability. In some cases, simple modifications of an assay or dilution sequence can provide improvements; for example, by replacing the normal saline in the first dilution with the same casein containing buffer used for the second dilution, it is possible to obtain the same final conditions, but the presence of the casein is shown to reduce the turbidity by almost 7 fold and the subsequent tendency to aggregate and settle. Similarly, including human serum albumin (HSA) in the phosphate buffered saline (PBS) almost completely eliminated any evidence of precipitation for many of the compounds following the first dilution. The physical chemistry background of pharmaceutical chemists can be advantageous when working with the biologist designing the assays, ultimately leading to improved assays with less variability and ambiguity in the readout.

Even though the presence of the these different proteins can be very valuable with respect to preventing precipitation and increasing apparent solubility, they can also act to sequester the drug and decrease the "free drug" concentration. In the above example, Raub and coworkers (1999) were able to demonstrate that the free drug concentration for the compound in question was very different in each of the media and dependent on the amount and type of protein in those media (Figure 6). Such protein binding can completely mask the actual potency of the molecule (Figure 7). Through a reduction in the amount of albumin present, improved readouts on activity, for what appeared to be an inactive compound at the 0.5% albumin level, can be obtained. It is obvious that the optimized lead will have to be highly potent and active in the presence of albumin to be a viable drug candidate, but the ability to unambiguously assign structural modifications, during lead optimization, to alterations in receptor binding versus protein binding is critical for rational drug design. While it is impractical to determine binding constants for all potential leads during the optimization phase, it can be very helpful to develop the screening assays in a such a way that they can be run at more than one concentration of albumin or other potential binding protein.

In vitro assays that are cellular based, with intracellular targets, can also have an additional permeability component that can confound results from those assays. Depending on the molecule and type of cellular therapeutic model, various active transport systems, including efflux pump systems can also play a role. During the lead optimization phases it becomes particularly important to understand the impact of structural modifications relative to the individual

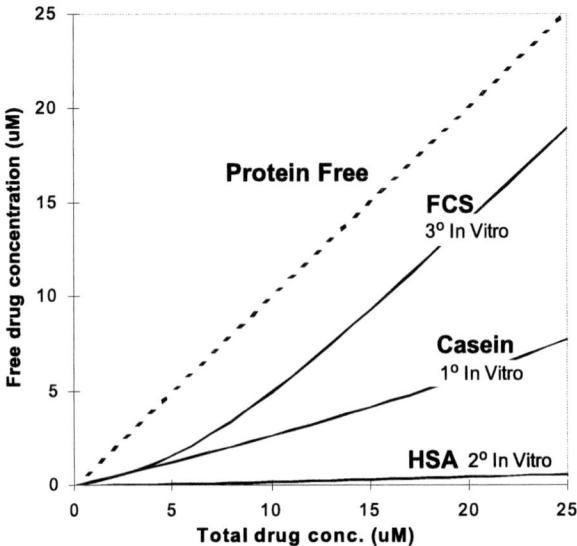

Figure 6. The effect of protein binding and free drug in various screening assays which each employ different media components and proteins. Curves were determined using appropriate binding constants determined by independent experiments.

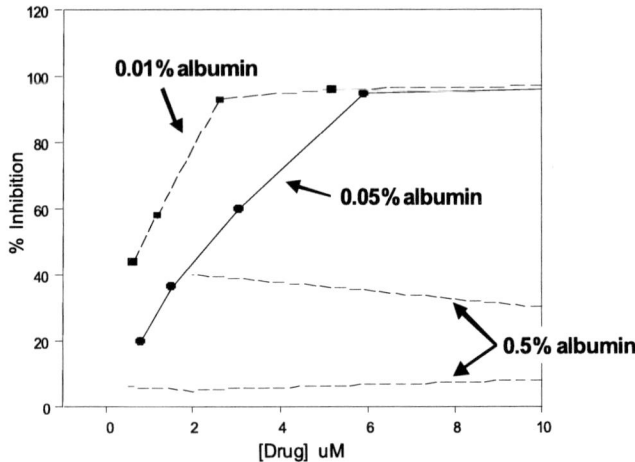

Figure 7. The presence of serum albumin protein can mask the actual interaction with the desired target and greatly impact efforts to generate SAR around target binding. The value of using several protein concentrations to help deconvolute the data is demonstrated.

components of the assay or model and be able to recognize when SPR versus SAR is actually being probed. While the deconvolution of data may take time up front, it can avoid generating erroneous SAR. Systematic and logical drug design, with analog synthesis driven by computational models, make it even more imperative that the output of screening assays is representative of only the intended target binding and not convoluted factors which will derail the value of the computational model. Therefore, while the involvement of pharmaceutical scientists to help the search for more druggable compounds is valuable, it is equally important that they also provide greater clarity to the funnel and assist in eliminating or selecting data to feed into the computational models.

It is often assumed that poor solubility, high protein binding or poor permeability, all leading to inadequate exposure to drug, will all tend to eliminate compounds which are minimally acceptable, anyway. What is very difficult to sort out, is the impact of lost opportunity due to chasing SAR on a convoluted target, or the probability for false positives as well as false negatives. It is generally assumed that these physicochemical limitations will result in false negatives, but in our experience, poor physicochemical properties can also lead to false positives in the screening assays. The occurrence of a false negative or positive is highly dependent on the assay and how the readout or reporting system will be influenced by aggregates and particulates, or the potential for coprecipitation of compound and reagents in the assay. Often overlooked is the potential of compounds to have intrinsic surface activity or detergency leading to self-micellar-ization (leading to a disconnect with concentration added and the μ) which can lead to sequestration of reagents in the micelle or nonspecific membrane pertur-bation in cellular based assays (McGovern et al., 2002). While many of these types of interferences cannot be avoided when screening, the potential ambiguity they create needs to be recognized so it can be dealt with.

Drug Delivery for *In vivo* Screening

Progression to the *in vivo* screen can quickly demonstrate the team's grasp on the separate "druggable" components and their role in the composite phenomena, or as is often the case, provides evidence for our difficulty in constructing the composite from the individual components. Even more so than with the *in vitro* assays, results are highly convoluted, even assuming the molecule can be administered in such a way that only its intrinsic properties are being assessed. Unfortunately, the mode, method, dose and composition of the administered delivery vehicle can be intertwined to impact the results. Excipient acceptability for safety and toxicology studies is obvious, but the potential vehicle interferences in pharmacology models can be problematic in certain cases. Similarly, the choice of delivery vehicle, administration route or dose can influence resulting PK parameters and biodistribution as well. The use of appropriate controls and placebos become critical, but still may not avoid an interaction term that arises from the impact of the delivery vehicle on how the animal responds. For example, an excipient may influence transporters, illicit a localized inflammatory response, alter kidney clearance, influence metabolic enzymes, cause nonspecific changes in membrane integrity, cause diarrhea, induce hemolysis, and other things. In fact, the less drug-like the compound, the more likely is the need for more heroic administration strategies and the more important these administration factors become on the outcome.

Through a combination of the screening assays and the initial *in vivo* studies it is important to identify the limiting factors that result in unfavorable drug delivery. In the case of oral drug delivery, the potential factors of solubility, permeability, clearance and stability need to be sorted out prior to extensive work on trying to structurally optimize and overcome the limitation. Unfortunately, or maybe fortunately, these factors all tend to influence one another to some degree. Fortunately, in the sense that balance can be struck and possible synergies sought. Unfortunately, because structural influences may result in physicochemical property changes that are offsetting.

If clearance issues are evidenced by metabolic *in vitro* screens and rapid plasma clearance following IV administration, the potential role of presystemic and first-pass clearance in limiting oral exposure should be delineated before extensive formulation efforts are undertaken to enhance exposure. Oral formulation approaches to address first pass limitations are pretty much limited to lipid based delivery systems which target lymphatic uptake, although they are generally still very selective with respect to the molecule and capacity (i.e. dose amount to be absorbed) (see chapter by Charman *et al*). More commonly, alternatives other than a formulation strategy are likely to be considered. Prodrug strategies might be viable if the metabolic soft spot can be identified and blocked (see chapter by Stella). Often, alternate administration routes such as subcutaneous, intramuscular, rectal, buccal, transdermal and pulmonary are proposed for high first past clearance drugs. However, all of these routes are either much more invasive or restricted to use of much lower doses (i.e. typically below 20 mg). The co-dosing of metabolic enzyme inhibitors can be undertaken at the concept testing stage to help verify the importance, or lack thereof, for a particular metabolic pathway. Except in the case of a clear unmet medical need, the requirement to use a metabolic inhibitor to get exposure will likely spell termination for candidate.

If chemical instability of the compound under acidic conditions mimicking the gastric conditions is indicated, it may be possible to consider the use of animal models where inhibitors of acid secretion, such as omeprazole, are predosed to the animals. This might allow for a better understanding of whether overcoming the acid instability would likely provide the necessary oral exposure. If necessary, later screening could consider formulation strategies that utilize enteric-coated systems for acid-labile compounds, although engineering of the acid-lability out of the molecule during optimization should be the first choice. Enzymatic lability in GI fluids can sometimes occur and will be a difficult challenge to overcome. While some work has been done with enzymatic inhibitors to inhibit enzymes in the GI fluids, the results are often variable, and hence not regarded as a viable long term strategy to overcome this difficulty; instead, the enzymatic-lability in GI fluids should be optimized out of the molecule.

Even though, solubility and permeability are very closely linked and the interplay between them can often make it difficult to sort out the relative importance of each as limiting factors, it is very valuable to understand the interplay to effectively guide drug design. While many elaborate models have been devised to better understand the relationship between these factors, their complexity and need for numerous input functions, which are not available at the lead optimization stage, make them difficult to use. Simpler models such as the absorption potential model of Dressman and coworkers (1984; 1985) and the maximum absorbed dose (MAD) model outlined by Johnson and Swindell (1996), are more reasonable for application at very early stages. Further discussion of models and their application to understanding the interplay of solubility, dissolution, dose and permeability is discussed in the following chapter by Rohrs.

The typically inverse relationship of most structural modifications on passive permeation and aqueous solubility provide the impetus to use simple models that can describe the net effect of modifications on drug absorption. As pointed out by Curatolo (1998), the application of a model such as MAD at the optimization phase can provide guidance with respect to the level of solubility or permeability enhancement that might be needed for a given template. He makes the point that the absorption rate (related to permeability) can realistically vary over about a 50-fold range, whereas solubility can vary by as much as 100,000-fold, making solubility in many ways an easier target to focus on for the medicinal chemist. However, there is a tendency for potency and permeability to be impacted similarly by structural modifications, hence favoring increases in molecular potency and permeability while sacrificing solubility. One of the additional advantages of the MAD calculation is that it allows one to quickly see the impact that dose might have, in addition to permeability and solubility, on the fraction of dosed compound absorbed.

Although the MAD model was initially developed to provide estimates of drug absorption in man, it can also be used, with appropriate parameterization, to anticipate the solubility and permeability interplay in the commonly used lead optimization model of the rat, which in turn, provides valuable feedback into the lead optimization loop regarding potential exposure issues (Hilgers *et al.*; 2003). The investigators were careful to evaluate the potential role that differences in clearance of the analogs might play in the percent bioavailability (the typical experimental measurement that is made in animal studies). This points out one of the difficult aspects of applying a model such as MAD to a very chemically diverse subset of structures, particularly in a prospective fashion. Hilgers and coworkers (2003) were able to effectively use CACO-2 cell permeability information to convert to absorption rates for the rat model (based on previously determined relationship between a CACO-2 permeability values and rate of absorption in a rat model). Not too surprisingly, they saw a poor correlation between permeability alone and the bioavailability, but when the solubility was included via the MAD model, they were able to generate useful information for prioritization of compounds with respect to their oral absorption potential. It was also observed that in cases where the extent of absorption was underestimated, it was typically for very low water solubility compounds which have higher solubilities in more GI-like media, i.e. easily solubilized by presence of low levels of surfactants. This is a challenge we continue to grapple with; what is the most relevant solubility number or solubility media to use with respect to compound absorption?

There may be many reasons that a compound does not have appropriate permeability properties and it is outside of the scope of this chapter to explore all of those. The reader is directed toward chapters in this book by Burton, Hochman and Thakker for more information on permeability. There are also some good reviews in this area that can provide an overview for this extensively studied area, for which many unanswered questions still exist (Conradi *et al.* 1996; Camenisch *et al.* 1996).

Enabling Formulation Strategies for Drug Delivery

The value of oral exposure enabling formulation strategies at these early phases of lead optimization is very contingent on having a clear understanding of the potential reasons for poor oral exposure of a given lead or template (Amidon *et al.*, 2003). It must be recognized that the decision to use a formulation enabling technology has the potential to begin guiding optimization in favor of delivery by that particular formulation strategy. This potential must be recognized and accepted as a possible outcome of incorporating enabling formulations into the optimization process. Enabling formulations can be very useful for proof of concept testing in which very little is known about the target and adequate blood levels for testing are difficult to obtain. The enabling formulation can allow verification of template activity and establish whether this template warrants further resource investment to engineer in adequate oral exposure without enabling formulations.

The use of enabling formulation strategies is most effective when there is clear evidence that the drug has poor water solubility but has a very high permeability. Solubility limitations can either be due to dissolution rate limitations or actual solubility limitations that govern flux rates across the membrane. (Oh *et al.*, 1995; Rohrs subsequent chapter). To avoid dissolution rate limitations it is desirable for the solid form of the drug to undergo dissolution at a rate approaching that of absorption of the drug from the GI-lumen. The dissolution rate, or the rate at which a certain mass of molecules can "escape" the solid phase and enter the bulk medium, becoming available for absorption, is described by the Noyes-Whitney equation

$$\frac{d(mass)}{d(time)} = k \cdot A \cdot (Cs - C) \qquad \textit{Eqn. 3}$$

where k is a constant that is related to the hydrodynamics of the dissolution medium and conditions, A is the surface area in contact with the medium, Cs is the saturation solubility of the compound in that media, and C is the concentration of "free" compound in the media. Under sink conditions, i.e. where C<<Cs, the dissolution rate becomes directly proportional to the saturation solubility of the compound, Cs (Hamlin *et al.*, 1965). While the dissolution rate can be increased by altering k through the changes in hydrodynamic constraints of the particular situation, (i.e. increases in media agitation or decreases in solution viscosity), the scientist has minimal control over this variable in the GI lumen. More commonly, efforts are undertaken to increase surface area through

particle size reduction, increase Cs through formation of high energy solid forms or minimize C by creating sink, or near sink, conditions in the dissolving media.

Particle Size Reduction

When considering whether particle size reduction will provide added value, a rule of thumb is that the particle size diameter in microns should be less than the solubility in mcg/mL. Therefore, compounds with solubilities < 100 mcg/mL are likely to benefit from some sort of particle size reduction and those with solubilities < 10 mcg/ml will almost certainly benefit from some sort of milling or micronization. If the solubilities are approaching 1 mcg/mL, then micronization will be a must and nanoparticulates are probably preferred. A more careful analysis like the one described by Rohrs in the following chapter (see Figure 6 in Rohrs' chapter), based on the dissolution rate being inversely proportional to the square of the particle radius and a conservative criteria for dissolution time, should be used for a safer and more accurate assessment of the particle size needed. In comparison to the rule of thumb, Rohrs' analysis would require particle size of < 16 um for 50 mcg/mL, < 5 um for 5 mcg/mL and <1.5 um for 0.5 mcg/mL, i.e. providing similar numbers to rule of thumb over this solubility range. However as you begin to approach higher solubilities, the particle size estimates from Rohrs' analysis would indicate a need to have particle sizes no greater than 50 um, even with solubilities of 1 mg/ml. Simple methods such as a milling, mortar and pestle attrition or high shear suspension homogenization can typically yield particle sizes down to 50 um. To get below 15 um, micronization is often required, and to get below 2-3 um, specialized techniques are often necessary, being a challenge during optimization when compound is limited.

The above discussion assumes that the particles are all of one size, monodisperse, when in reality there is generally a distinct distribution of particle sizes. It is generally the small fraction of larger particles present that really limit the composite rate of dissolution. (Rohrs' subsequent chapter, Higuchi and Hiestand, 1963; Johnson and Swindell, 1996) This is primarily due a very large fraction of the total compound mass is in the small number of larger particles and the surface area to mass ratio of these particles is small. Therefore, it is really the minimization of the number of large particles that should be sought.

The characterization of milled or micronized solids can be carried out in abbreviated fashion during lead optimization to make sure that large particles have been eliminated. This can often be assessed by simple microscopy for size ranges greater than a couple of microns. Another common testing method at this stage may be simple filtration using appropriate pore sized membranes and assaying total solution concentrations before and after, then coupling that information with supernatant assessments after centrifugation. More extensive characterization to obtain mean particle size information can be carried out as appropriate. The important point of the characterization during lead optimization is to make sure that you have in fact reduced the particle size below some threshold and that you have some sort of means to compare future formulations of the same material.

The potential for particle size reduction to enhance dissolution and oral absorption has been recognized for some time (Levy, 1963). However, it can also result in other changes in pharmacokinetics and on occasion reductions in exposure if not careful with characterization or formulation of the milled solid. While the enhanced oral exposure is typically measured by the area under the curve (AUC) for plasma concentration versus time curves, it is also possible to significantly impact the shape of the PK profile. The maximum plasma concentration (Cmax) and time at which it is reached (Tmax) can be shifted to higher levels and shorter times with increased rates of dissolution following particle size reduction. Even in cases where the extent of absorption may be relatively high, there may be advantages in altering Cmax or Tmax without significant gains in AUC (Bihanzadeh *et al.*, 1996).

Particle size reduction does not always result in formulation performance consistent with an increase in dissolution rates. With reductions in particle size, increase surface energies are generated and there is an increased driving force for agglomeration of the primary particles to form higher order aggregates. There also can be greater difficulty in wetting the surface of the smaller particles, an obvious prerequisite to dissolution of the solid. If the primary particles are not regenerated through disruption of the aggregates, the advantages of particle size reduction can be lost and actual reductions in exposure can be noted with milling of the solids (Jindal *et al.*, 1995). It is critical that the selection of excipients, typically polymers and surfactants, and their level, are appropriate to facilitate wetting and minimize aggregate formation. During lead optimization, the need for any sort of long term physical stability of the suspension is somewhat obviated by ability to coordinate suspension preparation and dosing. This requires a close communication and coordination between the dosing groups and the pharmaceutical chemistry group.

High Energy Solids

The formation of high-energy solids, such as amorphous solids, also has the potential to enhance the rate of dissolution through increases in Cs. These high-energy solid forms have the potential to also provide effective concentrations of compound exceeding that limited by the saturation solubility of the compound with respect to its crystal form of the drug. These high level supersaturated (with respect to crystal) concentrations are often transitory in nature and result in the precipitation of the more stable crystalline form of the drug with time. These supersaturated concentrations of compound provide not only the potential for faster dissolution, but also provide a higher solution concentration and the potential to enhance the transmembrane flux where permeability is poor and the rate of flux is solubility limited.

While the quasi-stable form of these types of amorphous solids or high-energy dosage forms can provide enhanced performance from an oral exposure perspective, it is this same meta-stable situation that can cause tremendous challenges with regards to reproducibly generating such solids and maintaining them in a high-energy state long enough to take advantage of their properties. The successful use of high-energy solids is generally linked to the use of some sort of stabilizing excipient. Potential pharmaceutical significance of amorphous solids were discussed by Hancock and Zografi (1997) and the advantages of formulating solid dispersions have been outlined by Leuner and Dressman (2000).

The unintentional generation of amorphous or partially amorphous solids during synthesis and isolation of compounds at the lead optimization stage actually generate many challenges for the team, despite the high solubility and dissolution rate it may afford. The meta-stable properties of these materials can make it very difficult to obtain the same results with later preparations or even the same preparation at a later time. This metastable amorphous solid, that is not intentionally stabilized to form solid dispersions, is easily influenced by the mode of preparation of dosing vehicle, level and type of agitation, composition of the dosing vehicle and the time interval between preparation and dosing. This is an example where it becomes important to avoid getting locked into an amorphous form of the drug during the optimization process without it being a conscious decision, with formulation strategies taken to support such an approach. The team must be made aware of the potential ramifications in later development should a compound with amorphous tendencies move forward.

Solubility Enhancement

Another strategy to overcome dissolution rate limitations is to provide the compound in a non-solid form, or most commonly, some type of solubilized formulation, where dissolution isn't necessary. This really amounts to providing the compound in combination with excipients that are able to solubilize the compound prior to introduction to the media of the GI lumen, and then avoid significant precipitation of drug upon dilution into those media. As will be discussed, these systems can often end up providing supersaturated drug levels upon dilution of the solubilizer and compound.

The solubilization of a compound describes the ability to increase the total concentration of drug "in solution". It is important to understand that the only way to increase the apparent solubility is through either increasing the free energy of the solid phase, which was discussed in some examples above, or by providing an alternative media or equilibrium in which the compound becomes "solubilized". In effect, the compound becomes solubilized by decreasing the chemical potential of the compound in the "solvated state" by providing preferential solvation or sequestration in a facile and reversible system. It should also be realized that the chemical potential of a compound in a compound-saturated cosolvent solution is, by definition, no greater than that of a saturated aqueous solution, i.e. both are in equilibrium with and dictated by the chemical potential of the solid state. Therefore, while the total solubility in a cosolvent system may be 5 to 50 fold higher, maybe more, the actual driving force for transport across a membrane will still be similar. This has been demonstrated with respect to transdermal permeations studies (Higuchi, 1960; Pellet *et al.*, 1994; Megrab *et al.*, 1995; Pellet *et al.*, 1997; Iervolino *et al.*, 2001). However, it is very common to see enhanced transport or absorption when dosing with cosolvent types of systems. This is likely to be related to potential for supersaturation or membrane perturbation, which will result in enhanced transport, again demonstrated with membrane permeation studies (Pellet *et al.*, 1994; Pellet *et al.*, 1997).

Cosolvents

One way of increasing the preferential solvation, is through the use of a miscible cosolvent that confers on the mixed media new solvation properties through highly correlated changes in physicochemical properties such as solubility parameter, dielectric constant, hydrogen bonding potential (Yalkowsky, 1999). While the solubilization capability of these solvents is the functional impact desired, it is offset by the limitations of toxicological response following *in vivo* administration. Even during lead optimization stages, care must be taken to insure that the desired compound properties (pharmacology, toxicology, etc.) are not masked by the cosolvent. It is also very difficult to sort out the potential impact of the cosolvent on the membrane barrier itself, which leads further to questions of the degree of reversible or nonreversible change that actually occurs with the membrane barrier. Furthermore there is evidence of potential changes in physiological parameters such as gastric transit times with the use of common cosolvent formulations (Basit *et al.*, 2001; Schulze *et al.*, 2003).

The most common cosolvents are ethanol, glycerin, propylene glycol and polyethylene glycol, with the latter two often being preferred because they usually provide the greatest solubilization relative to the amount of vehicle that can be safely administered. Representative LD50 values can be found in Wade and Weller, 1994. The general relationship between solubilization by coslovents is usually a logarithmic increase in compound solubility with increasing volume fraction of the cosolvent. While this allows for exponential increases in solubility with increasing cosolvent addition, it also results in an increased propensity for precipitation of drug upon linear dilution of the drug concentration in the aqueous mileu upon administration (Figure 1). Precipitate formation can vary from the formation of very large aggregates with low surface area for redissolution (obviously undesirable) to a finely dispersed nanoparticle material with extremely high surface area. Depending on the compound and composition of media, it is often possible to maintain varying levels of supersaturation for extended periods of time prior to precipitation. This type of in situ formation of supersaturated solutions, coupled with potential physiological changes due to the cosolvent and the inherent variability of animals, makes it very difficult to interpret the actual impact of cosolvent solubilization on compound delivery and, more times than not, results in high levels of variability in the resulting exposure. Therefore, while such cosolvent systems may be able to afford exposure during lead optimization studies, they are not really a viable formulation strategy to take forward as part of an overall package for drug candidate selection, i.e. a compounds need for cosolvent solubilization to obtain exposure is not really consistent with a compound which has "drug-like" properties.

Ionization and pH Adjustment

The remaining solubilization methods are oriented around the generation of an alternative equilibrium for "sequestration" or "solubilization" of a drug. The method of first choice is generally pH adjustment, providing the molecule has an appropriate ionization constant. This approach takes advantage of the typically high level of solvation of a charged species and the ionization equilibria to provide a total solubility equivalent to the sum of the intrinsic solubility of the weak base and the solubility of the protonated form of the weak base. Taking into account the ionization constant (pKa), the total solubility for a weak base can be described by the solubility profile shown in Figure 8. The total solubility at the pKa is twice the intrinsic solubility, and then with each pH unit below the pKa, the total solubility will increase by a factor of ten. It is important to note that the total solubility does not increase indefinitely with a decrease in pH, at some point the solubility of salt will become limiting. As shown in Figure 8, the saturation solubility of the salt is dependent upon the counter ion; in this plot, as is often the case; the methane sulfonate salt is more soluble than the hydrochloride salt. The saturation solubility of a salt is typically characterized in terms of the equilibrium solubility product (Ksp) (Morris *et al.*, 1994). It is noted here that the total solubility can actually decrease with the further addition of an acid that contains the counter ion of the precipitating salt, i.e. further addition of hydrochloric acid results in precipitation of the chloride salt.

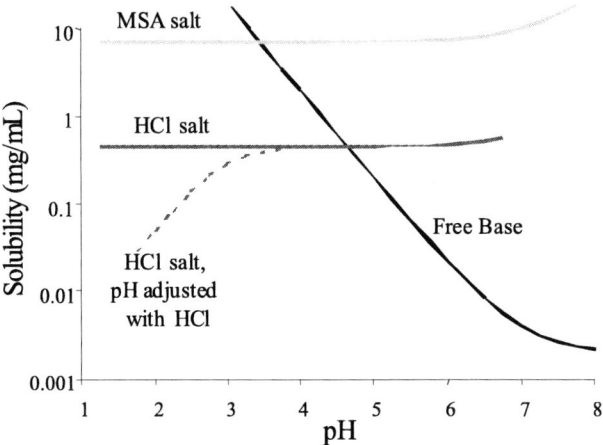

Figure 8. Solubility curve (bold line) for a free base (pKa ~ 7; intrinsic solubility ~ 2 µg/ml) showing limiting solubility of the salt is dependent on counter ion. The methane sulfonic acid (MSA) salt is more soluble than the hydrochloride salt. Additional pH adjustment with hydrochloric acid can actually result in decreased solubility due to the common ion effect.

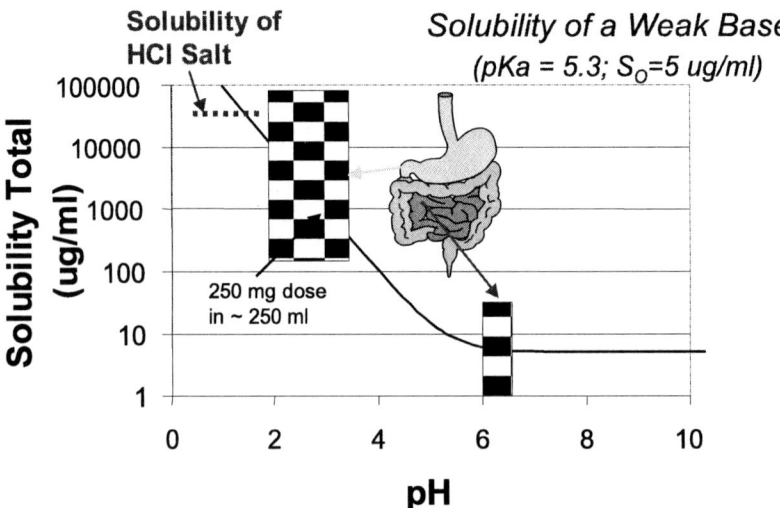

Figure 9. A 250 mg dose of a weak base (pKa ~5.3) is diluted in a total volume of the about 250 ml in the stomach to yield a concentration which is less than the solubility at pH 1.5 – 3. On reaching pH 6-6.5 duodenum, even with some dilution, the concentration will now be significantly greater than the solubility and precipitation is likely to occur.

The ionized form of the compound is generally regarded as being non-available for membrane permeation and as such contributes minimally to the concentration of unionized form driving the flux, however the proton transfer of ionization is very rapid and the ionized form of the drug is able to act as a sink to replace any non-ionized compound absorbed. As with other solubilization methods, an adjustment of pH upon administration or upon transportation down the GI track can result in a rapid shift of the ionization equilibrium and precipitation of the poorly soluble unionized form. Figure 9 provides an example where the drug may be dosed as a solution into a total volume (resting stomach volume plus formulation volume) where it is soluble, but as the compound is emptied into the duodenum where the pH is now closer to six, the total amount of drug in solution now exceeds the solubility by more than 100-fold, resulting in a supersaturated solution leading to precipitation. This pH effect often results in a greatly reduced exposure for weak bases and a highly variable response from animal to animal.

Preparing a pH-adjusted solution for dosing corresponds to preparing a solution of a salt *in situ*. The preparation of such solutions or suspensions of the salt can be used to overcome the dissolution rate limitations that may occur with the free base. It is important to recognize that the formation of salts of a drug really only address dissolution rate-limited exposure and the total solubility will still be dictated by the pH of the media, with the solubility of the unionized form of the drug remaining constant and in equilibrium with the precipitated unionized form. The formation of a salt is not going to increase the solubility of the drug at a given pH in the GI tract, it may impact how rapidly the saturation solubility is obtained, but not what it is. With respect to oral exposure, the value of salts, is to enhance dissolution rates and provide the potential propensity for supersaturation prior to precipitation. The dissolution of salts and the importance of pH and various buffering ions in that dissolution process has been very nicely explained in work by Mooney and coworkers (1981a; 1981b). The selection of counter-ions and appropriate salts for further investigation will generally include many aspects of solid state chemistry besides the biopharmaceutical ramifications. Readers are referred to reviews that also include the importance of the physical and material properties of the salt in further processing, formulation, manipulation and storage (Morris *et al.*, 1994; Ware and Lu, 2004).

Surfactants

The use of surfactants for purposes of solubilizing compounds continues to be a popular approach. Largely due to toxicological reasons, the nonionic surfactants are highly favored and through formation of a micelle, provide the lipophilic poorly soluble compounds a stable "nonaqueous" environment to reside in. The preferential partitioning of compounds into the micelle is often related to the octanol-water partition coefficient (Mithani *et al.*, 1996). The total compound in solution (compound in micelle and free compound) increases linearly with a linear increase in surfactant concentration once the surfactant concentration exceeds the critical micelle concentration (CMC) of the surfactant. While this linear response limits the degree of solubilization somewhat, it minimizes the potential for supersaturation or precipitation upon dilution. Even if there is precipitation of drug, the presence of surfactants in the solutions can facilitate the dissolution solids.

Similar to solubilization by cosolvents or pH adjustment, surfactants can be used to overcome dissolution rate limited absorption. The sequestration of the compound in the micelle provides a continual sink for compound to partition from and become available for absorption. While this sequestration in a micelle can help to overcome dissolution issues, the maximal compound available for membrane transport will still be limited by amount of free drug in solution, or the saturation solubility of the drug.

Solubilization by sequestration in micelles is a good example of where the total amount of drug in solution increases but the "free compound" or effective concentration to drive flux across a membrane is actually reduced. The impact of compound sequestration on caco-2 transport has been addressed in conjunction with potential for inhibition of polarized efflux pumps by surfactants (Nerurkar *et al.*, 1996). Evidence consistent with reduced free drug concentrations has also been demonstrated for perfusion models using rat intestinal segments (Poelma *et al.*, 1990).

Dispersed Lipid Phases

In some cases, compounds have properties that will allow them to be dissolved in neat surfactants or in mixtures of surfactants, lipids and cosolvents, which upon contact with an aqueous media can result in formation of micelles, microemulsions or coarser emulsions, depending on composition of the vehicle. These self-emulsifying drug delivery systems (SEDDS) have been discussed by many and are the subject of the chapter by Charman et al. in this book. The solubilization of compounds in these systems and the mechanism for enhanced absorption from them is discussed in depth in that chapter and other recent review articles (Pouton, 1997; Humberstone and Charman, 1997; Charman, 2000; Bagwe *et al.*, 2001; Gao and Morozowich, 2005). The use of SEDDS-like formulations in early preclinical studies is often limited by the amount of excipients present when conducting high-dose toxicological investigations of the compound. While excipient-induced effects are important in high dose toxicology studies, the more realistic doses encountered in pharmacology models or clinical investigations would likely be much more amenable to SEDDS approaches. Hence, while these types of delivery systems may be invoked during lead optimization, they would be largely limited to preclinical proof of concept and generally would not be carried into toxicology studies, but could be reconsidered at clinical stages of development.

The use of emulsions and liposomes, which unlike the thermodynamically stable microemulsions, are metastable dispersions which typically use phospholipids with and without added lipid components, can provide an opportunity for sequestration of the compound to avoid precipitation and maintain "solubility". Given the appropriate selections of phospholipids, the safety profile permits their us for parenteral delivery of poorly soluble compounds. The utility of these systems has been discussed elsewhere (Collins-Gold *et al.*, 1990; Benita and Levy, 1993; Ranson *et al.*, 1996) and must be used with recognition that the delivery system may influence phrarmacokinetic and distribution properties of the compound. Parenteral emulsions have also been used to minimize the level of drug irritation upon injection of certain poorly soluble compounds, presumably through reductions of free drug at the injection site (Wang *et al.*, 1999). While de novo formulations of macroemulsions and liposomes will often be required, it is often easier, especially at the lead optimization phases, to utilize pre-existing emulsions with extemporaneously added drug (Klang *et al.*, 1998). It should be recognized that characterization and reproducible preparation of these systems can often be very challenging and make it difficult to get consistent data during lead optimization phases where the time and availability of material for characterization is usually at a premium.

Complexation

Solubilization through complexation or association is easily understood in terms of a sequestration of drug in an associated state and free drug concentration. While association with proteins could fall into this category, proteins are seldom used for purposes of formulation, but as discussed in an earlier part of this chapter, they can play a significant role in dictating the amount of free drug available for *in vitro* assays.

The most common formulation strategies using complexation are centered around the use of cyclodextrins, with more emphasis generally placed on derivatized cyclodextrins because of their greater solubility and improved *in vivo* safety margin. Hydroxypropyl-β-cyclodextrin (HP-β-CD) and sulfobutyl ether-β-cyclodextrin (SBE-β-CD) have both been used successfully for solubilization of compounds for parenteral administration (Thompson, 1997). While there still seems to be a lot of concern about the dissociation of compounds from the cyclodextrins upon dilution or administration, the arguments presented by Rajewski and Stella (1986) seem to make it highly unlikely that the compounds remain bound, except in very rare instances where the complexation constants are extremely high. When cyclodextrin solutions are used orally, care must be taken to avoid an excess of cyclodextrin that would have the potential to actually reduce bioavailability due to sequestration, i.e. no more cyclodextrin than is necessary should be added to the formulation. The impact of cyclodextrins on *in vitro* membrane transport has been noted (Cho *et al.*, 1995). More often, the use of cyclodextrins at later stages of development for oral delivery involve the formation and isolation of the solid complexes, which generally will provide greatly enhanced dissolution rates to avoid dissolution rate limitations.

Combinations of solubilizing strategies can be beneficial in some cases, but most generally tend to work with varying levels of success. Often, combinations of cosolvents and surfactants tend to work against one another, as do cosolvents and complexing agents, as do surfactants and complexing agents. The potential use of combined solubilization methods have been described by Yalkowsky (1999) in his chapter on "Overview and Strategy for Solubilization".

Supersaturation

Formulation strategies which can provide the potential for generation of supersaturated solutions relative to the saturation solubility of the most stable solid phase, typically a crystalline phase, can in one sense be very valuable and in another be very problematic. The value in such supersaturated systems comes in that they are one of the few ways that actual driving force, μ, can exceed that of the saturated solution of the crystalline compound and provide the potential to enhance absorption of poorly permeable drugs to a meaningful level. The disadvantage of such formulations is that they are highly prone to catastrophic precipitation and the ability to anticipate or predict when or what type of precipitate is poor at best. Therefore, formulations that rely on supersaturation can often show high variability in performance if not appropriately optimized.

The most common ways to initiate supersaturation is through 1) solids of increased free energy, i.e. solid dispersions, amorphous solids, solvates and high energy polymorphs, 2) use of salts which will rapidly dissolve with dissociation from the counter-ion or 3) use of solubilized formulations of the compound which can then result in supersaturated conditions upon dilution into aqueous media, i.e. pH adjusted solutions, cosolvent systems, self-emulsifying or micellarizing systems, or higher order complexes of compounds.

Through the use of a supersaturated cosolvent solution for oral dosing to dogs, it was possible to demonstrate significant absorption enhancement over a micronized suspension of the compound by almost tripling the AUC obtained (Figure 10). While it is difficult to explicitly ascribe the enhanced exposure to supersaturation, a number of other observations certainly indicated that it was likely to be one of the primary reasons for the observation. The use of the supersaturated cosolvent formulation permitted evaluation of the compound at much higher exposure with a near linear dose response (AUC) obtained (Figure 11). While this formulation could be used for proof of concept studies and even limited toxicology studies, it was not possible to take it into the clinical setting, again pointing out the need for optimizing toward a compound that does not require heroic formulation efforts such as these to get exposure.

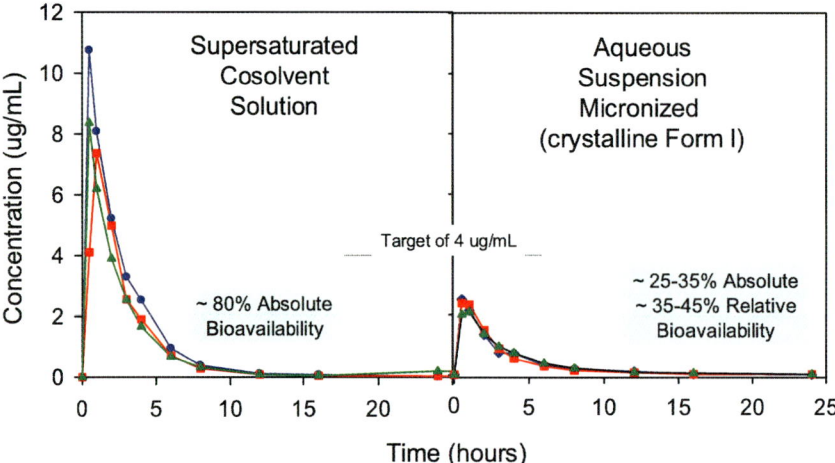

Figure 10. Dog plasma profiles comparing the dosing of a supersaturated cosolvent solution of a lead compound versus an aqueous micronized suspension. Absolute bioavailability is in comparison to AUC after IV dosing (not shown). Relative bioavailability of the suspension is to that of supersaturated cosolvent solution.

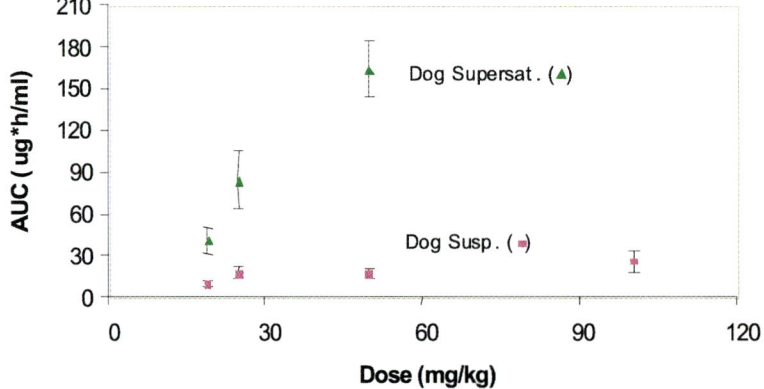

Figure 11. The use of a supersaturated solution of a lead compound gave far superior dose linearity (AUC) for oral exposure relative to the micronized suspension of the same lead compound. (n=3 dogs at each dose)

Ping Gao and coworkers (2003; 2004) were able to prepare and demonstrate the potential utility of a supersaturable self-emulsifying drug delivery system (S-SEDDS) for oral delivery of Paclitaxel and another poorly water soluble drug. This supersaturation was obtained through the addition of hydroxypropyl methylcellulose (HPMC) to the SEDDS formulation as a precipitation inhibitor.

One of the greatest difficulties in obtaining a supersaturated solution resides in obtaining concentrations that are significantly higher than the saturation solubility (> 5-10 fold), but not so high as to induce rapid precipitation. Unless the compound itself has a very high tendency to supersaturate, generally linked to poor propensity to crystallize, it can be very difficult to obtain and maintain levels of supersaturation much beyond that of 10 fold for periods approaching hours, even with precipitation inhibitors. The exponential changes in solubility commonly afforded by pH adjustment of ionizable compounds or cosolvent solubilization of compounds can many times lead to supersaturation levels of 100 or even 1000 times the saturation solubility upon dilution, resulting in very rapid precipitation.

Conclusion

The incorporation of "drug-like" criteria into the drug candidate selection process via a "gate-keeper" approach is certainly a first step in driving lead optimization toward the consideration of "drug-like" properties. However, the efficient integration of "drug-like" principles during the lead optimization process will require an interactive partnership between pharmaceutics, drug metabolism, toxicology and the Discovery team.

The concept of "drug delivery" during lead optimization should be expanded beyond *in vivo* oral exposure assessments to also include exposure of a compound to the intended target in an *in vitro* assay within a screening funnel. An appreciation of how physical chemical properties such as protein binding, solubility, permeability and surface activity may influence the readout of *in vitro* assays provides a perspective that can help to avoid ambiguous interpretation of data.

The enhancement of *in vivo* exposure following oral dosing can often be influenced through the use of various formulation and solubilization technologies. However, it is essential that the potential ramifications of applying these technologies during lead optimization are recognized and accepted by the team. In many cases, to carry these technologies well beyond the preclinical proof of concept studies may not be desirable. Therefore, while solubilization technologies can certainly be applied to overcome poor solubility, the preferred approach is and always will be to engineer out the poor solubility during the lead optimization phases when possible. When it isn't possible, then use of an enabling formulation should become an integral part of the screening process.

References

Amidon GE, He X, and Hageman MJ. Physicochemical Characterization and Principles of Oral Dosage Form Selection. In: Abraham DJ. *Burger's Medicinal Chemistry and Drug Discovery*, 6th Ed. John Wiley & Sons, NY, 2003, Chapt 18

Bagwe RP, Kanicky JR, Palla BJ, Patanjali PK, and Shah DO. Improved Drug Delivery Using Microemulsions: Rationale, Recent Progress, and New Horizons. *Critical Rev Therap Drug Carrier Syst* 2001;18:77-140

Basit AW, Newton JM, Short MD, Waddington WA, Ell PJ, and Lacey LF. The Effect of Polyethylene Glycol 400 on Gastrointestinal Transit: Implications for the Formulation of Poorly-Water Soluble Drugs. *Pharm Res* 2001; 18(8):1146-1150

Benita S, and Levy MY. Submicron Emulsions as Colloidal Carriers for Intravenous Administration: Comprehensive Physicochemical Characterization. *J Pharm Sci* 1993; 82(11):1069-1079

Bihanzadeh M, Mahmoudian M, Zolfaghari ME, Gouya MM, Kazinia T, and Khosravi A. The Influence of Particle Size and Dissolution Rate on Bioavailability of Two Indomethacin Capsules, *J of the School of Pharmacy, Tehran Univ. of Medical Sciences and Health Services* 1996; 5(1&2):14-24

Bohets H, Annaert P, Mannens G, van Beijsterveldt L, Anciaux K, Verboven P, Meuldermans W, and Lavrijsen K. Strategies for Absorption Screening in Drug Dscovery and Development. *Curr Top Med Chem* 2001; 1:367-383

Borchardt RT, Kerns EH, Lipinski CA, Thakker, DR, and Wang B. Pharmaceutical Profiling in Drug Discovery for Lead Selection. (Proceedings of the Workshop held 19-21 May 2003 in Whippany, NJ) [In: Biotechnol Pharm Aspects, 2004, 1]. 2004, 482 p

Caldwell GW. Compound Optimization in Early- and Late-Phase Drug Discovery: Acceptable Pharmacokinetic Properties Utilizing Combined Physicochemical, *In Vitro* and *In Vivo* Screens. *Curr Opin Drug Dis Develop* 2000; 3:30-41

Camenisch G, Folkers G, and van de Waterbeemd H. Review of Theoretical Passive Drug Absorption Models: Historical Background, Recent Developments and Limitations. *Pharm Acta Hel* 1996; 71:309-327

Charman WN. Lipids, Lipophilic Drugs and Oral Drug Delivery – Some emerging concepts. *J Pharm Sci* 2000; 89:967-978

Cho M J, Chen F J, and Huczek DL. Effects of Inclusion Complexation on the Transepithelial Transport of a Lipophilic Substance *In Vitro*. *Pharm Res* 1995; 12(4):560-564

Collins-Gold LC, Lyons RT, and Bartholow LC. Parenteral Emulsions for Drug Delivery. *Adv Drug Delivery Rev* 1990; 5(3):189-208

Conradi RA, Burton PS, and Borchardt RT. Physico-chemical and Biological Factors that Influence a Drug's Cellular Permeability by Passive Diffusion in Methods and Principles in Medicinal Chemistry. In: Pliska V, Testa B, and van de Waterbeemd H. *Lipophilicity in Drug Action and Toxicology* VCH Publishers 1996; 233-252

Curatolo W. Physical Chemical Properties of Oral Drug Candidates in the Discovery and Exploratory Development Settings. *Pharmaceutical Science & Technology Today* 1998; 1(9):387-393

Dressman JB, Fleisher D, and Amidon GL. Physicochemical Model for Dose-Dependent Drug Absorption. *J Pharm Sci* 1984; 73(9):1274-1279

Dressman JB, Amidon GL, and Fleisher D. Absorption Potential: Estimating the Fraction Absorbed for Orally Administered Compounds. *J Pharm Sci* 1985; 74(5):588-589

Gao P, Rush RD, Pfund WP, Huang T, Bauer JM, Morozowich W, Kuo MT, and Hageman MJ. Development of a Supersaturatable SEDDS (S-SEDDS) Formulation of Paclitaxel With Improved Oral Bioavailability. *J Pharm Sci* 2003; 92:2395-2407

Gao P, Guyton ME, Huang T, Bauer JM, Stefanski KJ, and Lu Q. Enhanced Oral Bioavailability of a Poorly Water Soluble Drug PNU-91325 by Supersaturatable Formulations. *Drug Dev Ind Pharm* 2004; 30:221-229

Hamlin WE, Nothram JI, and Wagner JG. Relationship Between *in vitro* Dissolution Rates and Solubilities of Numerous Compounds Representative of Various Chemical Species. *J Pharm Sci* 1965; 54:1651-1653

Hancock BC, and Zografi G. Characteristics and Significance of the Amorphous State in Pharmaceutical Systems, *J Pharm Sci* 1997; 86:1-12

Hann MM, and Oprea TI. Pursuing the Leadlikeness Concept in Pharmaceutical Research. *Current Opinion in Chemical Biology* 2004; 8(3):255-263

Hilgers AR, Conradi RA, and Burton PS. Caco-2 Cell Monolayersas a Model for Drug Transport Across the Intestinal Mucosa. *Pharm Res* 1990; 7:902-909

Hilgers AR, Smith DP, Biermacher JJ, Day JS, Jensen JL, Sims SM, Adams WJ, Friis JM, Palandra J, Hosley JD, Shobe EM, and Burton PS. Predicting Oral Absorption of Drugs: A Case with a Novel Class of Antimicrobial Agents. *Pharm Res* 2003; 20:1149-1155

Higuchi T. Physical Chemical Analysis of the Percutaneous Absorption Process. *J Soc Cosmetic Chemists* 1960; 11:85-97

Higuchi WI, and Hiestand EN. Dissolution Rates of Finely Divided Drug Powders: I. Effect of Distribution of Particle Sizes in a Diffusion-Controlled Process. *J Pharm Sci* 1963; 52:67-71

Humberstone AJ, and Charman WN. Lipid-based Vehicles for Oral Delivery of Poorly Soluble drugs. *Adv Drug Deliv Rev* 1997; 25:103-128

Iervolino M, Raghavan RL, and Hadgraft J. Membrane Penetration Enhancement of Ibuprofen using Supersaturation. *Int J Pharm* 2000; 198:229-238

Jindal KC, Chaudhary RS, Singal AK, Gangwal SS, and Khanna S. Effect of Particle Size on the Bioavailability and Dissolution Rate of Rifampicin. *Indian Drugs* 1995; 32(3):100-107

Johnson KC, and Swindell AC. Guidance in the Setting of Drug Particle Size Specification to Minimize Variability in Absorption. *Pharm Res* 1996; 13:1795-1798

Kennedy T. Managing the Drug Discovery/Development Interface. *Drug Discov Today* 1997; 2:436-444

Klang SH, Parnas M, and Benita S. Emulsions as Drug Carriers. Possibilities, Limitations and Future Perspectives. In: Muller RH, Benita S, and Bohm BHL *Emulsions and Nanosuspensions for the Formulation of Poorly Soluble Drugs*, Medpharm Publ., Stuttgart, Germany, 1998; pp 31-65

Koeplinger KA, Raub TJ, Padbury GE, and Zhao Z. Equilibrium Distribution of HIV Antiviral Drugs into Human Peripheral Blood Mononuclear Cells (PBMC) is Controlled by Free Drug Concentration in the Extracellular Medium. *J. Pharm. Biomed. Anal.* 1999; 19(3-4):399-411

Kola I, and Landis J. Opinion: Can the Pharmaceutical Industry Reduce Attrition Rates? *Nature Reviews Drug Discovery* 2004; 3(8):711-716

Kubinyi H. Opinion: Drug Research: Myths, Hype and Reality. *Nature Reviews Drug Discovery* 2003; 2(8):665-668

Leuner C, and Dressman J. Improving Drug Solubility for Oral Delivery Using Solid Dispersions. *Eur J Pharm Biopharm* 2000; 50:47-60

Levy G. Effect of Particle Size on Dissolution and Gastrointestinal Absorption Rates of Pharmaceuticals. *Am J Pharm* 1963; 135:78-92

Lipinski CA, Lombardo F, Dominy BW, Feeney PJ. Experimental and Computational Approaches to Estimate Solubility and Permeability in Drug Discovery and Development Settings. *Adv Drug Delivery Rev* 2001; 46(1-3):3-26

Megrab NA, Williams AC, and Barry BW. Oestradiol Permeation Through Human Skin Silastic Membrane: Effects of Propylene Glycol and Supersaturation. *J Control Rel* 1995; 36:277-294

McGovern SL, Caselli E, Grigorieff N, and Shoichet BK. A Common Mechanism Underlying Promiscuous Inhibitors from Virtual and High-Throughput Screening. *J Med Chem* 2002; 45(8):1712-1722

Mithani SD, Bakatselou V, TenHoor CN, and Dressman JB. Estimation of the Increase in Solubility of Drugs as a Function of Bile Salt Concentration. *Pharm Res* 1996; 13(1):163-167

Mooney KG, Mintun MA, Himmelstein KJ, and Stella VJ. Dissolution Kinetics of Carboxylic Acids I: Effect of pH Under Unbuffered Conditions. *J Pharm Sci* 1981a; 70(1):13-22

Mooney KG, Mintun MA, Himmelstein KJ, and Stella VJ. Dissolution Kinetics of Carboxylic Acids II: Effect of Buffers. *J Pharm Sci* 1981b; 70(1):22-32

Morris KR, Fakes MG, Thakur AB, Newman AW, Singh AK, Venit JJ, Sagnuolo CJ, and Serajuddin, ATM. An Integrated Approach to the Selection of Optimal Salt Form for a New Drug Candidate. *Int J Pharm* 1994; 105(3):209-217

Nerurkar MM, Burton PS, and Borchardt RT. The Use of Surfactants to Enhance the Permeability of Peptides Through Caco-2 Cells by Inhibition of an Apically Polarized Efflux system. *Pharm Res* 1996; 13(4):528-534

Oh D-M, Curl RL, and Amidon GL. Estimating the Fraction Dose Absorbed from Suspensions of Poorly Soluble Compounds in Humans: A Mathematical Model. *Pharm Res* 1993; 10(2):264-270

Oh D-M, Curl RL, Yong C-S, and Amidon GL. Effect of Micronization on the Extent of Drug Absorption from Suspensions in Humans. *Arch Pharmacal Res* 1995; 18(6):427-433

Olah MM, Bologa CG, and Oprea TI. Strategies for Compound Selection. *Current Drug Discovery Technologies* 2004; 1(3):211-220

Oprea TI. Current trends in lead discovery: Are We Looking for the Appropriate Properties?   *J Computer-Aided Molecular Design* 2002; 16(5/6):325-334

Oprea TI, Davis AM, Teague SJ, and Leeson PD. Is There a Difference Between Leads and Drugs? A Historical Perspective. *J Chemical Info Computer Sciences* 2001; 41(5):1308-1315

Pellet MA, Davis AF, and Hadgraft J. Effect of Supersaturation on Membrane Transport: 2. Piroxicam. *Int J Pharm* 1994; 111:1-6

Pellet MA, Castellano S, Hadgraft J, and Davis AF. The Penetration of Supersaturated Solutions of Piroxicam Across Silicone Membranes and Human Skin *In Vitro*. *J Control Rel* 1997; 46:205-214

Poelma FGJ, Breas R, and Tukker JJ. Intestinal Absorption of Drugs. III. The Influence of Taurocholate on the Disappearance Kinetics of Hydrophilic and Lipophilic Drugs from the Small Intestine of the Rat. *Pharm Res* 1990; 7:392-397

Pouton CW. Formulations of Self-Emulsifying Drug Delivery Systems. *Adv Drug Delev Rev* 1997; 25:47-48

Rajewski RA, and Stella VJ. Pharmaceutical Aplications of Cyclodextrins. 2. In Vivo Drug Delivery. *J Pharm Sci* 1996; 85(11):1142-1169

Ranson M, Howell A, Cheeseman S, and Margison J. Liposomal Drug Delivery. *Cancer Treat Rev* 1996; 22(5):365-379

Raub T J; Barsuhn C L; Williams L R; Decker D E; Sawada G A; and Ho N F Use of a Biophysical-Kinetic Model to Understand the Roles of Protein Binding and Membrane Partitioning on Passive Diffusion of Highly Lipophilic Molecules Across Cellular Barriers. *J Drug Targ* 1993; 1(4):269-286

Raub TJ, Bauer JM, Goodman TG, Hageman MJ, and Bajt-Jaeschke ML unpublished results, Pharmacia & Upjohn 1999

Rishton GM. Nonleadlikeness and Leadlikeness in Biochemical Screening. *Drug Discovery Today* 2002, 2003; 8(2):86-96

Schulze JDR, Waddington WA, Ell PJ, Parsons GE, Coffin MD, and Basit, AW. Concentration-Dependent Effects of Polyethylene Glycol 400 on Gastrointestinal Transit and Drug Absorption. *Pharm Res* 2003; 20(12):1984-1988

Serajuddin ATM. Solid Dispersion of Poorly Water-soluble Drugs: Early Promises, Subsequent Problems, and Recent Breakthroughs. *J Pharm Sci* 1999; 88(10):1058-1066

Thompson DO. Cyclodextrins –Enabling Excipients: Their Present and Future Use in Pharmaceuticals. Crit Rev Therap Drug Carrier Syst 1997; 14:1-104

Tong WQ, and Whitesell G. In situ Salt Screening – A Useful Technique for Discovery Support and Preformulation Studies. *Pharm Dev Tech* 1998; 3(2):215-223

Wade A, and Weller PJ. *Handbook of Pharmaceutical Excipients*, 2nd ed., American Pharmaceutical Association, Washington, DC, 1994

Wang Y, Mesfin GM, Rodriguez CA, Slatter JG, Schuette MR, Cory AL, and Higgins MJ. Venous Irritation, Pharmacokinetics, and Tissue Distribution of Tirilazad in Rats Following Intravenous Administration of a Novel Supersaturated Submicron Lipid Emulsion. *Pharm Res* 1999; 16(6):930-938

Ware EC, and Lu DR. An Automated Approach to Salt Selection for New Unique Trazodone Salts. *Pharm Res* 2004; 21(1):177-184

Yalkowsky SH. *Solubility and Solubilization in Aqueous Media* Oxford Univ Press, New York, 1999

6

Lipid-based Systems, Drug Exposure and Lead Optimization

William N. Charman[1]
Susan A. Charman[1]
and Christopher J. H. Porter[2]

[1]Centre for Drug Candidate Optimization
Victorian College of Pharmacy, Monash University (Parkville campus)
381 Royal Parade
Parkville, Victoria 3052, Australia

[2]Department of Pharmaceutics
Victorian College of Pharmacy, Monash University (Parkville campus)
381 Royal Parade
Parkville, Victoria 3052, Australia

Table of Contents

Enhancing Drug Exposure
and Lipid-based Formulations

Pharmaceutical formulations containing natural and/or synthetic lipids are an accepted strategy for potentially improving the oral bioavailability and systemic exposure of poorly water soluble, highly lipophilic drug candidates. For example, lipid-based formulations are commercially available for various drugs including cyclosporine, saquinavir, ritonavir, dutasteride and amprenavir. Consequently, lipid-based systems are often considered when needing to increase drug exposure during pre-clinical drug development.

When considering lipid-based systems as a potential means for enhancing drug exposure, the particular pre-clinical or clinical context will dictate the available (and acceptable) range of formulation options that can be considered. In a discovery environment where the biology/chemistry focus involves development of a structure activity relationship for a new chemical series/scaffold, the range of acceptable excipients and formulation options are broader and more "accommodating" than when needing to design a commercially relevant formulation for a compound in clinical development. Midway between these two scenarios would be situation of selecting excipients for early stage exploratory toxicology studies where lipid-based systems can provide enhanced drug exposure. Therefore, the flexibility of formulation design and range of excipient choice for lipid-based systems decreases as compounds progress from discovery into clinical development.

Typically, the "pharmaceutics-related" issues relevant to designing formulations to enhance drug exposure are relatively well understood in terms of solubility, dose, stage of development and the biopharmaceutic profile of the compound. However, it is essential that the "non-pharmaceutics" issues are also well understood and addressed as scientists from different disciplines often have different mindsets, expectations and understandings of the issues at hand. A prospective strategy to manage potential "non-pharmaceutics" issues should be considered where lipid-based systems are being explored to enhance drug exposure.

When evaluating strategies to enhance drug exposure during pre-clinical development, it is essential to identify the actual factors limiting drug exposure after oral administration. Unless there is a clear physicochemical basis for the limited exposure of drug after oral administration such as poor aqueous solubility and/or low dissolution rate, then exploration of a lipid-based system to enhance exposure will most likely be unsuccessful. Limiting factors such as hepatic pass clearance will not be attenuated by administration of a compound in a lipid-based system, unless the compound happens to be a candidate for intestinal lymphatic transport (see later section in this chapter for a discussion of intestinal lymphatic transport).

Lipids are believed to assist the absorption of poorly water soluble compounds by reducing the inherent limitations of slow and incomplete dissolution and by facilitating the formation of colloidal species within the intestine that are capable of maintaining poorly water soluble drugs in solution. The formation of these solubilizing species does not necessarily arise directly from the administered lipid, rather it more frequently arises from the intraluminal processing of the formulation-related lipids via digestion and dispersion (Charman, 1992; Humberstone and Charman, 1997; Porter and Charman, 2001a).

The co-administration of drugs with lipids can influence the actual pathway of drug absorption. Whilst most orally administered drugs gain access to the systemic circulation via the portal vein, some highly lipophilic drugs are transported to the systemic circulation via the intestinal lymphatics (thereby avoiding presystemic hepatic metabolism) (Charman, 1992; Porter *et al.*, 2001; Porter and Charman, 2001b; O'Driscoll, 2002). In addition, it has long been understood that certain lipids can delay gastric transit and enhance passive intestinal permeability (Hunt and Knox, 1968; Anderberg *et al.*, 1993; Lindmark *et al.*, 1995; Lindmark *et al.*, 1998). It has been suggested that certain lipids and lipidic excipients may attenuate the activity of cytochrome P-450 enzymes and/or reduce drug efflux processes, thereby leading to possible increases in the apparent permeability of drug across the absorptive barrier (Nerurkar *et al.*, 1996; Nerurkar *et al.*, 1997; Batrakova *et al.*,1998; Cornaire *et al.*, 2000; Hugger *et al.*, 2002; Wacher *et al.*, 2002; Cornaire *et al.*, 2004; Shono *et al.*, 2004), however, definitive clinical evidence demonstrating these effects are not yet available.

This chapter will discuss some of the key issues associated with using lipid-based systems to enhance drug exposure. Firstly, the relevant physiology of lipid digestion will be briefly described as it provides the foundation for then considering lipid-based systems for enhancing drug exposure. Secondly, key formulation design issues associated with the administration of such formulations will be highlighted. Thirdly, as lymphatic transport is a potential absorption pathway for highly lipophilic drugs, recent data and advances in this area will briefly described. Lastly, an approach whereby it may be beneficial to consider more lipophilic drug candidates as part of an overall lead optimisation program will be presented.

Digestion and Absorption of Lipids

The digestion and absorption of lipids has been extensively reviewed in the literature (Nutting *et al.*, 1999; Ros, 2000; Nordskog *et al.*, 2001; Phan and Tso, 2001). Briefly, lipid digestion involves three main sequential steps: (i) dispersion of fat globules into a coarse emulsion (ii) enzymatic hydrolysis of triglyceride (TG) at the oil/water interface and (iii) dispersion of the digestion products into a fine emulsion of high surface area from which absorption can readily occur (Carey *et al.*, 1983). Digestion of dietary lipids, which are predominantly in the form of poorly water soluble neutral TG, begins in the stomach where lingual and gastric lipases secreted by the salivary gland and gastric mucosa, respectively, initiate the hydrolysis of TG to its component diglyceride (DG) and free fatty acid (FA) components. Liberation of these more water soluble lipid digestion products, in combination with the shear force encountered during antral contraction and gastric emptying, facilitates the formation of a coarse emulsion which upon entry into the duodenum, stimulates the secretion of bile salts and biliary lipids from the gall bladder and the release of lipase enzymes from the pancreas (Borgstrom and Hildebrand, 1975; Ladas *et al.*, 1984; Hernell *et al.*, 1990). Biliary-derived phospholipid and cholesterol adsorb to the surface of the oil droplets comprising the crude emulsion, resulting in improved colloidal stability and a reduction in the oil droplet size with an attendant increase in surface area. These changes facilitate lipid hydrolysis, which occurs at the oil/water interface through the combined actions of colipase and pancreatic lipase enzymes, and results in the production of one molecule of 2-monoglyceride (MG) and two molecules of FA for each TG molecule hydrolysed. As lipolysis proceeds, these digestion products collect at the surface of the lipid droplets, typically forming liquid crystalline structures which slough off from the droplet surface and, in conjunction with bile salts and phospholipids, form multilamellar and unilamellar vesicles and ultimately, bile salt-lipid mixed micelles (Hernell *et al.*, 1990; Staggers *et al.*, 1990). While the specific mechanisms controlling the gastrointestinal absorption of lipids have not been fully elucidated, it is known that bile salt mixed micelles are not absorbed intact but must dissociate and release the emulsified lipid digestion products prior to absorption into the enterocyte (Hoffman, 1970; Simmonds, 1972). Dissociation of mixed micelles may be triggered by a microclimate of lower pH associated with the intestinal brush border membrane (Shiau, 1990; Thomson *et al.*, 1993).

In addition to passive diffusion, there is now evidence to suggest that specific membrane bound carrier proteins may facilitate the transport of lipid digestion products across the apical membrane of the enterocyte (Stremmel *et al.*, 1985; Stremmel, 1988; Poirier *et al.*, 1996). Once within the enterocyte, the cytosolic fatty acid binding proteins L-FABP and I-FABP bind to FA and facilitate FA solubilisation and distribution to the cell nucleus and endoplasmic reticulum (Ockner and Manning, 1974; McArthur *et al.*, 1999; Besnard *et al.*, 2002; Huang *et al.*, 2002).

Formulation Design Issues

The design of a lipid-based system, whether for early pre-clinical investigation or later clinical development of a candidate drug, requires careful and prospective assessment of the likelihood of success. For a lipid-based system to be successful in enhancing drug exposure, it is essential the compound is sufficiently lipophilic to be dissolved within the proposed formulation composition. In many cases, poorly water soluble drugs are not sufficiently soluble within the typical excipients used in lipid-based systems (such as triglycerides and mixed mono/diglycerides, formulation-relevant and miscible surfactants and co-solvents) to provide an adequate unit dose of drug. Hence, such compounds are considered hydrophobic and lipophobic *and* formulation approaches other than lipid-based systems need to be explored for enhancing their bioavailability after oral administration. In the clinical formulation design environment, unit doses of 25-100 mg of drug are considered a reasonable "drug load" per unit dose of a lipid-based formulation.

There are various formulation approaches that can explored as a means of formulating lipophilic drug candidates and drugs (Pouton, 2000). Although a description of formulation design strategies is beyond the scope this chapter, the following comments briefly highlight some of the key points of difference between the various lipid-based systems. Broadly, there are three types of common lipidic formulation, comprising simple lipid-based solutions self-emulsifying drug delivery systems (so called SEDDS) or microemulsion pre-concentrate formulations. In terms of lipid, there is a choice between triglyceride lipid, and the correspondingly more polar mono/diglyceride lipid blends and for each of these lipid classes, there is the opportunity of using medium chain (e.g. C_8-C_{12}) or long chain lipids (e.g. C_{18}) with a further consideration being the degree of unsaturation in the long chain lipids. Typically, co-solvents are also used in the self-emulsifying and microemulsion pre-concentrate formulations in order to facilitate formulation dispersion.

In vitro assessment of prototype lipid-based formulations is a significant area of on-going research as it holds the promise of being able to at least rank order the likely performance of such systems. Studies from our laboratories (Porter and Charman, 2001c; Sek *et al.*, 2002; Kaukonen *et al.*, 2004a,b; Porter *et al.*, 2004a,b) and others (Reymond and Sucker, 1998; Zangenberg *et al.*, 2001a, b) have utilised *in vitro* lipid digestion methodologies to examine the potential of drugs of varying physicochemical characteristics to: (i) remain associated with the undigested lipid phase of a formulation; (ii) partition into the colloidal species formed on interaction of the lipid formulation or its digestion products with biliary derived lipids, and (iii) precipitate during intestinal processing of the lipid formulation.

Although detailed discussion of these factors is beyond the scope of this chapter, it is clear that avoidance of drug precipitation *in vivo* and transfer of drug into the colloidal species from which absorption is assumed to occur is paramount for optimal absorption. Depending on the physicochemical characteristics of the particular drug and the formulation excipients, drug precipitation may occur upon initial dispersion of the dosage form in the stomach. This is particularly likely for formulations containing large quantities of water soluble surfactants, co-surfactants and co-solvents (which is most common in the microemulsion pre-concentrate systems) in which dispersion of the water soluble excipients may reduce the overall solubilizing capacity of the formulation. In contrast, formulations containing a larger proportion of poorly water soluble components, such as low HLB surfactants and lipids (e.g. lipid solutions or coarse emulsions) are less likely to be affected by dispersion in the gut contents. However, the performance of these formulations is more susceptible to influence by lipid digestion as demonstrated in our recent studies which highlighted the possibility of drug precipitation following digestion of formulations comprised primarily of medium chain lipids. Since the digestion products of these lipids are considerably more water soluble than those comprised of long chain lipids, digestion may substantially reduce the solubilizing capacity of formulations incorporating medium chain lipid excipients (Porter *et al.*, 2004a,b).

When working in a discovery/early development support area, it is important to consider the extent of formulation "optimization" undertaken in support of the program realising that many of the compounds considered will fail. The authors believe that where possible, minimal formulation optimization work should be undertaken at these early stages as it is important to enable determination of key SAR issues such as potency and selectivity – without the performance of the formulation having too large an effect on the resulting activity profiles. In this regard, DMSO-based solutions have an advantage as a generic 'formulation' during discovery, since the resulting activity data are relatively more uniform as all compounds are administered from the same system and the resulting biological profile of the compounds are less confounded by differences in exposure resulting from different formulations. Whilst this approach has merit, it is important to realise that rapid drug precipitation from a DMSO solution may occur after administration which could limit drug exposure. In this situation, and realising that the biological effects of many highly lipophilic compounds can be beneficially enhanced through the judicious use of a lipid-based system, in our experience, as a second tier approach we have found that relatively robust medium chain lipid or long chain lipid-based systems as described by Khoo *et al.*, (1998) offer a useful starting point once the decision to use a lipid-based system has been made. Although these prototype formulation compositions will not be optimal for all lipophilic drugs, they can be used without any further optimisation assuming that the drug is adequately soluble in the formulation components.

A difficulty working with early stage compounds in pre-clinical species such as mice and rats is the significant limitation regarding the volume of formulation which can be administered. A further issue is the temptation to administer increasingly larger volumes of formulation in the hope that drug exposure may be enhanced – however, in many cases, this will not result as the larger volumes administered are physiologically and pharmaceutically unreasonable thereby confounding the results. For example, in spite of the relatively small sizes of the stomach of the mouse and rat, they are often administered volumes of fluid (including lipid-based systems) as high as 1 mL/kg (excluding any volume used to flush through the oral gavage needle) which equates on a mL/kg basis to approximately 230 mL for a 70 kg human! Hence, these large volumes may swamp the capacity of the stomach to modulate gastric emptying and the capacity of the intestine to digest and absorb the administered lipid. Few studies have formally addressed the effect of increasing liquid (and lipid) volume to rodents and the effects on physiological processing and drug absorption. Consequently, it is difficult to either extrapolate such exposure data to higher species, or to predict whether there would be a "formulation effect" on drug absorption in higher species based on rodent data after administration of physiologically and pharmaceutically unreasonable volumes.

A further issue associated with assessing rat exposure data after administration of lipid-based formulations is that they do not have a gall bladder. Therefore, as bile flow in the rat is essentially constant in contrast to the typical pre-prandial (fasting) and post-prandial (fed) response observed in higher species such as the dog and humans, it is difficult to extrapolate the likely performance of formulations if bile salt solubilisation is an important process in the enhanced absorption. In contrast, dogs have a gall bladder and their pre- and post-prandial state is reasonably representative of that observed in humans in terms of changing biliary and related secretions. Furthermore, the physical size of the dog makes them well suited to ingest a unit dose human-relevant formulation making them well suited for the extrapolation of bioavailability and exposure data to higher species. Although the permeability of hydrophilic low molecular weights drugs in the dog is higher than observed in humans, there is no such issue when assessing poorly water soluble drugs that are absorbed by the transcellular route making them well suited for studying lipid-based systems of such compounds. As the fasting gastric pH of dogs can be variable, it is important to consider the pre-treatment of dogs with penatgastrin in order to normalise their stomach pH values if it is likely to impact on drug stability, formulation performance or absorption.

Intestinal Lymphatic Drug Transport

For the majority of drug candidates, the intestinal lymphatics are unlikely to play a significant role in the transport of drug from the intestine to the systemic circulation. However, for some highly lipophilic compounds, intestinal lymphatic transport may play a role in their absorption. From a development perspective, early information as to the possible role of lymphatic transport and its formulation dependence is important for several reasons. Firstly, drug transport to the systemic circulation via the lymphatics avoids first pass hepatic metabolism and therefore for drugs where first pass hepatic metabolism is high, formulations or prodrug approaches which enhance intestinal lymphatic transport may lead to significant improvements in oral bioavailability. An excellent example of such a prodrug approach is the use of the highly lipophilic undecanoate ester of testosterone to promote intestinal lymphatic transport and to afford delivery of testosterone to the systemic circulation (Shackleford *et al.*, 2003). In this example, whilst the proportion of the testosterone undecanoate dose delivered systemically via the intestinal lymph is low (2-3%), it has been shown that this accounts for greater than 80% of the systemically available testosterone, illustrating that the relatively modest proportion of the dose transported lymphatically was clinically relevant where first pass metabolism is significant (Shackleford *et al.*, 2003). Secondly, if the proposed site of action of a drug candidate is in the lymph, such as an immune system modulator or an anti-cancer agent, specific delivery to the lymphatics and exposure of the lymphatic capillaries to relative high drug concentration may be advantageous. Thirdly, it has been suggested that the clearance of drugs delivered to the systemic circulation via the lymphatics, and in association with lymph chylomicrons, may be different to that of the same drug absorbed systemically (Hauss *et al.*, 1994; Caliph *et al.*, 2000) which has implications for the design and conduct of safety assessment studies -- particularly if the formulation used during chronic toxicology studies results in a different proportion of lymphatic transport compared with the clinical formulation.

Historically, there have been relatively few studies of drugs transported through the intestinal lymphatics because (i) there have been various animal model limitations associated with the study of lymph transport, and (ii) prior to the utilisation of higher throughout screening and *in vitro* technologies in drug discovery, many of the emerging drug candidates were not sufficiently lipophilic to be lymphatic transport candidates.

The intestinal lymphatics are a specialised absorption pathway for lipids and lipidic derivatives as well as a number of highly lipophilic xenobiotics and drugs including DDT (Sieber, 1976; Charman *et al.*, 1986), benzo[a]pyrene (Laher *et al.*, 1984), cyclosporin (Ueda *et al.*, 1983), naftifine (Grimus and Schuster, 1984), probucol (Palin and Wilson, 1984), lipid soluble vitamins (Kuksis, 1987), mepitiostane (Ichihashi *et al.*, 1992a,b), testosterone undecanoate (Shackleford *et al.*, 2003) and halofantrine (Porter *et al.*, 1996 a,b; Khoo *et al.*, 2002; Khoo *et al.*, 2003). Whilst these compounds have widely varying structures, it is possible to identify the relevant features that support lymph transport which include (i) high lipophilicity (e.g. log P > 5 and significant solubility in a triglyceride lipid) to support increased partitioning and association with enterocyte-derived lipoproteins [if the compound is a salt of a highly lipophilic free acid or free base, then the profile of the neutral form should also be considered (Khoo *et al.*, 2002; Taillardat-Bertschinger *et al.*, 2003)], (ii) reasonable molecular weight to provide transcellular permeability, (iii) adequate metabolic stability within the gastrointestinal tract and the enterocyte. In terms of a prodrug approach, it is possible to advantageously incorporate structural features of natural lipids into the prodrug structure to provide a potential mechanism to exploit endogenous absorption and biosynthetic pathway for lipids such as triglycerides and phospholipids (Shackleford *et al.*, 2004).

Biosynthesis of Enterocyte-derived Lipoproteins

The absorption of lipid digestion products by the enterocyte is preceded by transport through the unstirred water layer to the brush-border surface. Hence, the efficiency of transport to the enterocyte depends on lipid diffusion in association with the colloidal structures in which they are solubilised in the gastrointestinal tract (since their intrinsic aqueous solubility is too low to support sufficient mass transport). The uptake mechanism(s) of lipid digestion products across the apical membrane of the enterocyte is not fully understood, although it appears to involve both active and passive processes (Stremmel *et al.*, 1985; Stremmel, 1988; Thomson *et al.*, 1993; Poirier *et al.*, 1996).

Once within the enterocyte, 2-monoglycerides and fatty acids are rapidly and efficiently incorporated into a number of lipid processing pathways (Figure 1). As a rule of thumb, medium chain fatty acids (e.g. C_{12} and below) are transported directly into portal blood, whereas longer chain length fatty acids and 2-monoglygerides (e.g C_{18} and greater) are re-synthesised within the enterocyte to triglyceride primarily via the mono-acyl glycerol pathway involving direct and sequential acylation of 2-monoglyceride by CoA-activated fatty acids. However, the mono-acyl glycerol is not the sole source of TG as the glycero-3-phosphate (G-3-P) pathway produces de novo TG under conditions of low lipid load, and indeed this pathway is inhibited under conditions where MG is readily available such as after post prandial administration (Nordskog et al., 2001).

Irrespective of the biosynthetic pathway from which they are derived, triglycerides are progressively processed through various intracellular organelles where the surface of the developing colloid (lipoprotein) is stabilised by the ordered addition of phospholipids (which are absorbed or synthesised de novo in a series of specific enzymatic processes) and various apoproteins. Under conditions of low lipid load (i.e. fasting conditions), the primary lipoproteins produced by the small intestine incorporating TG synthesised by the G-3-P pathway are very low density lipoproteins (VLDL), whereas under conditions of high lipid load (e.g. after a meal) the predominant lipoproteins produced which incorporate TG synthesised by the mono-acyl glycerol pathway are chylomicrons (CM) (Nordskog et al., 2001). Following their assembly, VLDL and CM fuse with the basolateral membrane of the intestinal cell and are released into the lamina propria where they are preferentially absorbed via the open capillaries of the mesenteric lymphatics rather than into intestinal blood vessels. The exclusive movement of VLDL and CM into mesenteric lymphatic capillaries rather than into blood vessels is due to the fact that lymphatic capillaries lack a basement membrane therefore being "permeable" to the large colloids, whereas blood vessels possess tight inter-endothelial junctions and a continuous basal lamina precluding facile access of colloidal lipoproteins (Swartz, 2001).

Assessment of Intestinal Lymphatic Drug Transport

An early indication of whether lymphatic transport is likely to play a role in drug disposition is important. A number of animal models have been described and reviewed recently (Hauss et al., 1998; Caliph et al., 2000; Edwards et al., 2001; Boyd et al., 2004) for estimating intestinal lymphatic drug transport, with the majority of studies having been conducted in either rats or dogs. As discussed, drugs transported to the systemic circulation via the intestinal lymphatics are typically highly lipophilic and have very low aqueous solubility. Therefore, to assess the likelihood of lymphatic transport, conditions and models should be sought which maximise the quantity of drug that is absorbed into the enterocyte, and enhance the proportion of the absorbed dose transferred into the lymphatics. The co-administration of food can, in many cases, represent a simple method by which the otherwise limiting luminal solubility and dissolution of poorly water soluble drugs can be diminished. Therefore, post-prandial administration of a candidate drug to a lymphatically cannulated dog is an excellent proof-of-concept study as the post-prandial administration can enhance drug absorption while providing a ready supply of lipids to enable chylomicron formation and intestinal lymphatic drug transport. Details of the triple cannulated dog model have been described (Edwards et al., 2001; Khoo et al., 2001) as well as recent drug-related studies (Khoo et al., 2001; Khoo et al., 2003; Shackleford et al., 2003; Shackleford *et al.*, 2004). In this model, if the quantity of lipid (fat) administered in food is known, then it is possible to monitor the efficiency of lipid absorption and lymphatic transport by determining lymph triglyceride levels. This allows indicative transport data to be obtained in a small number of dogs, and in our experience, duplicate experiments are typically sufficient to provide a clear yes/no indication of the role of lymphatic transport for the administered drug. A practical consideration is the relatively high cost per animal associated with the complex surgery and aftercare. Therefore, screening studies examining the impact of formulation approaches on the extent of lymphatic transport may be more readily conducted in smaller species such as rats. There are varied methodologies/protocols used with rat studies encompassing different sites of cannulation and lymph fistulation (Noguchi *et al.*, 1985), extent of hydration, fasting/fed state of the rat after lymph duct cannulation (Charman *et al.*, 1986), whether the experiment is performed in a conscious or anaesthetized animals (Porter *et al.*, 1996a,b) and the site of drug/lipid administration (Porter *et al.*, 1996a). For example, we have previously examined the impact of anaesthesia, degree of formulation dispersion and administration route on the lymphatic transport of halofantrine in rats (Porter *et al.*, 1996a,b). In anaesthetised rats, there was a significant effect of the degree of lipid dispersion in the formulation after intraduodenal administration with the lymphatic transport of halofantrine increasing from 3.9% when administered as a simple lipid solution, to 11.8% after administration as an emulsion to 17.7% when administered as a highly dispersed micellar formulation (Porter *et al.*, 1996b). In all cases the type (2:1 molar mixture of oleic acid:glycerylmonooleate) and the volume of administered lipid (50 µL) was the same. In contrast, when the same formulations were administered orally to conscious rats there was no effect of formulation dispersion on lymphatic transport of halofantrine which was similar for the lipid solution and micellar solution (19.1% and 20.0%, respectively) (Porter *et al.*, 1996a). These data suggest that the inherent reduction in intestinal processing in an anaesthetised rat and the intraduodenal administration led to the differing degree of formulation dispersion impacting the relative extent of drug absorption. In contrast, in the conscious rats that received oral formulations, the improved gastrointestinal processing of the lipid solution led to efficient in situ dispersion thereby removing the likely consequence of differences in the extent of initial formulation dispersion.

Fig1 illustrates how conscious rat data can be used to broadly screen for formulation-related changes in lymphatic transport, and that the rank order data are comparable to data obtained in higher species such as dogs. In this example, the lymphatic transport of halofantrine after oral administration of a simple lipid solution formulation to conscious rats (Fig 1A) was increased after administration as a medium chain lipid solution compared with a lipid free suspension formulation (Caliph *et al.*, 2000). However, significantly more lymphatic transport was observed after administration of halofantrine formulated in a long chain (C_{18}) lipid solution vehicle. These data presumably reflect the increased propensity of long chain lipids for resynthesis back to triglyceride in the enterocyte and assembly into lymph lipoprotein precursors and lymph lipoproteins, thereby providing a lymphatic lipid sink into which the drug may partition. In contrast, medium chain lipids are typically transported through the enterocyte without re-esterification and are absorbed into the portal blood, thereby limiting the possible extent of lymphatic transport. A key issue associated with assessment of prospective formulations to rats is the self-evident realisation that prototypical humans formulations (e.g. tablets, hard or soft gelatin capsules) cannot physically be administered to small animals. However, the data in Fig 1B suggest that the relative patterns of lymphatic transport in conscious rats may reflect the rank

Panel A: Fasted Dogs

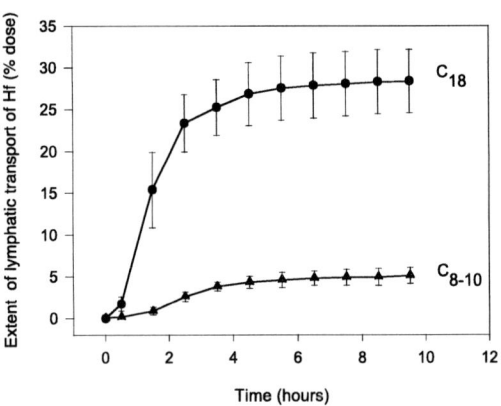

Panel B: Fasted Rats

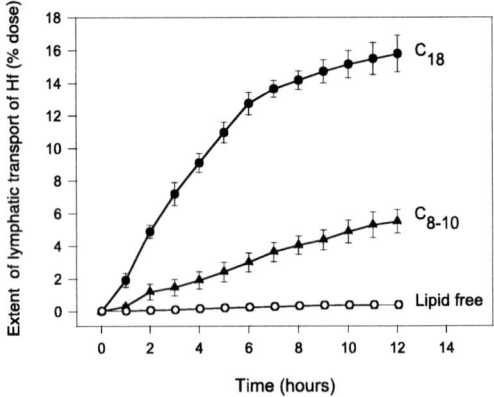

Figure 1. Lymphatic transport of halofantrine (Hf) after administration to fasted dogs or fasted in formulations comprising lipids with different fatty acid chain lengths. **Panel A.** Extent of lymphatic transport of Hf (% dose, mean ± SD, n=3/4) in greyhound thoracic lymph after oral administration of 50 mg Hf in self emulsifying formulations containing cremophor EL and either long chain lipids (●) or medium chain lipids (▲). Figure adapted from Khoo *et al.*, 2003. **Panel B.** Extent of lymphatic transport of Hf (% dose, mean ± SD, n=3/4) in rat mesenteric lymph after oral administration of 2.5 mg Hf dissolved in long chain triglyceride lipid (●), medium chain triglyceride lipid (▲) or as a lipid-free aqueous suspension (○). Figure adapted from Caliph *et al.*, 2000.

order effect after administration of single unit dose formulations (in this case soft gelatin capsule-based, self emulsifying formulations based on medium and long chain lipids) to larger species such as the dog (Khoo *et al.*, 2003).

Recently, our laboratory examined whether the small quantities of lipid present in unit dose microemulsion formulations comprising medium (C_{8-10}) or long chain (C_{18}) glyceride lipids was able to stimulate the intestinal lymphatic transport of halofantrine when administered to thoracic lymph duct cannulated fasted dogs (Khoo *et al.*, 2003). Drug was formulated as a single soft gelatin capsule containing approximately 1 g of a microemulsion preconcentrate based on either medium or long chain glycerides and thoracic lymph was collected and systemic plasma samples taken over 10 hr post dose. The extent of lymphatic transport of Hf after administration of the long chain lipid formulation was high (28.3% of dose), and significantly higher than that seen after administration of the medium chain formulation (5.0% of dose). These data are the first to demonstrate that the small amounts of lipid present within a single lipid-based dose form can support intestinal lymphatic transport in the fasted state, with long chain glycerides appearing to be more effective with respect to lymphatic transport than the equivalent medium chain formulation.

Consideration of Lipophilic Drug Candidates

As part of lead optimisation programs, much consideration has been directed towards the design and development of "more water soluble and readily developable" drug candidates. The advantages of such a strategy are clear as it will often enhance the speed of development and the success of the discovery program. However, in some cases, the biology and chemical characteristics of putative targets/receptors are such that the intrinsic potency of compounds can become rapidly diminished as the hydrophobicity (and possibly lipophilicity) of the compounds is decreased. This realisation, coupled with the understanding that a major limitation in the design of lipid-based formulations is the insufficient lipid solubility of a drug thereby limiting the unit dose that can be achieved, raises the following interesting possibility: that as part of a lead optimisation, it is worthwhile to at least explore more lipophilic (not hydrophobic) candidates as they may confer better potency while making them more amenable to formulation in a lipid-based formulation.

Fig 2 is a simple representation of this concept whereby the exploration of more hydrophilic *and* more lipophilic derivatives is considered while optimising the chemical scaffold and/or lead candidates. When exploring the more lipophilic candidates, the advantages include (i) a more complete exploration of the SAR of relevant scaffolds, (ii) possibly enhanced potency through increased lipophilicity, with a likely formulation approach being a lipid-based system to provide enhanced and reproducible bioavailability, and (iii) better protection of the overall intellectual property base surrounding the discovery program. The negative possibilities of exploring more lipophilic candidates include (i) the potential for increased drug metabolism due to increased lipophilicity of the compounds (although this can be assessed *in vitro*), (ii) the increased reliance on a lipid-based formulation during pre-clinical and possibly clinical development, (iii) the possibility that oral bioavailability then becomes formulation-dependent due to the role of the lipid-based formulations, and (iv) an overall increase in the complexity (perceived or otherwise) of the development program.

Therefore, in situations where exploration of hydrophilic functional groups on a lead scaffold has led to a loss of potency or selectivity, consideration of the advantages of enhanced lipophilicity in the context of a more traditional lead optimisation may offer a means of addressing otherwise intractable developmental issues with the particular target SAR profile.

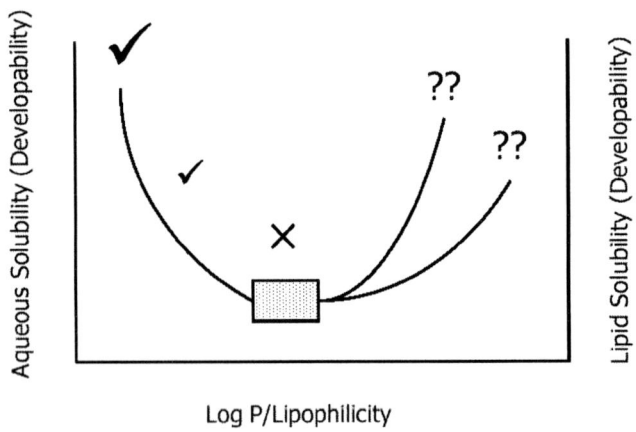

Figure 2. Representation of the changing effects of altering the lipophilicity characteristics of a compound series on its "developability profile" (ignoring the impact on metabolism and toxicology issues). For the purposes of the diagram, it is simplistically assumed that aqueous and lipid solubility are reasonable surrogates for the unit dose that could be formulated in a conventional oral solid dose form or a lipid-based formulation, respectively. The hatched box signifies the difficulties often encountered when formulating poorly water soluble/poorly lipid soluble drugs that have intermediate log P values.

Summary

Formulations containing natural and/or synthetic lipids can be confidently considered as a viable means for potentially enhancing the oral bioavailability and systemic exposure of poorly water soluble, highly lipophilic drug candidates. However, the flexibility of formulation design and the range of excipient choice for lipid-based systems decreases as compounds progress from discovery into clinical development. When evaluating formulation strategies, it is essential that the factors limiting drug exposure are initially identified in order to guide a rational formulation design program. As the co-administration of highly lipophilic drugs with lipids can influence their possible transport via the intestinal lymphatics, it is also prudent to consider whether lymphatic transport may contribute to oral bioavailability of highly lipophilic, poorly water soluble drugs.

References

Anderberg EK, Lindmark T, Artursson P. Sodium caprate elicits dilatations in human intestinal tight junctions and enhances drug absorption by the paracellular route. *Pharm Res* 1993; 10:857-864.

Batrakova EV, Han HY, Alakhov V, Miller DW, Kabanov AV. Effects of pluronic block copolymers on drug absorption in Caco-2 cell monolayers. *Pharm Res* 1998; 15:850-855.

Besnard P, Niot I, Poirier H, Clement L, Bernard A. New insights into the fatty acid-binding protein (FABP) family in the small intestine. *Mol Cell Biochem* 2002; 239:139-147.

Borgstrom B, Hildebrand H. Lipase and co-lipase activities of human small intestinal contents after a liquid test meal. *Scand J Gastroenterol* 1975; 10:585-591.

Boyd M, Risovic V, Jull P, Choo E, Wasan KM. A stepwise surgical procedure to investigate the lymphatic transport of lipid-based oral drug formulations: Cannulation of the mesenteric and thoracic lymph ducts within the rat. *J Pharmacol Toxicol Methods* 2004; 49:115-120.

Caliph SM, Charman WN, Porter CJ. Effect of short-, medium-, and long-chain fatty acid-based vehicles on the absolute oral bioavailability and intestinal lymphatic transport of halofantrine and assessment of mass balance in lymph-cannulated and non-cannulated rats. *J Pharm Sci* 2000; 89:1073-1084.

Carey MC, Small DM, Bliss CM. Lipid digestion and absorption. *Ann Rev Physiol* 1983; 45:651-677.

Charman WN. Lipid vehicle and formulation effects on intestinal lymphatic drug transport. In: Charman WN, Stella VJ, eds. Lymphatic Transport of Drugs. Boca Raton: CRC Press, 1992:113-179

Charman WN, Noguchi T, Stella VJ. An experimental system designed to study the in situ intestinal lymphatic transport of drugs in anaesthetized rats. *Int J Pharm* 1986; 33:155-163.

Cornaire G, Woodley JF, Saivin S, Legendre JY, Decourt S, Cloarec A, Houin G. Effect of polyoxyl 35 castor oil and Polysorbate 80 on the intestinal absorption of digoxin in vitro. *Arzneimittelforschung* 2000; 50:576-579.

Cornaire G, Woodley J, Hermann P, Cloarec A, Arellano C, Houin G. Impact of excipients on the absorption of P-glycoprotein substrates in vitro and in vivo. *Int J Pharm* 2004; 278:119-131.

Edwards GA, Porter CJ, Caliph SM, Khoo SM, Charman WN. Animal models for the study of intestinal lymphatic drug transport. *Adv Drug Deliv Rev* 2001; 50:45-60.

Grimus R C and Schuster I. The role of the lymphatic transport in the enteral absorption of naftifine by the rat. *Xenobiotica* 1984; 14:287-297.

Hauss DJ, Mehta S, Radebaugh GW. Targeted lymphatic transport and modified systemic distribution of CI-976, a lipophilic lipid-regulator drug, via a formulation approach. *Int J Pharm* 1994; 108:85-93.

Hauss DJ, Fogal SE, Ficorilli JV. Chronic collection of mesenteric lymph from conscious, tethered rats. *Contemp Topics Lab Animal Sci* 1998; 37:56-58.

Hernell O, Staggers JE, Carey MC. Physical-chemical behaviour of dietary and biliary lipids during intestinal digestion and absorption. 2. Phase analysis and aggregation states of luminal lipids during duodenal fat digestion in healthy adult human beings. *Biochemistry* 1990; 29:2041-2056.

Hoffman NE. The relationship between uptake in vitro of oleic acid and micellar solubilization. *Biochim Biophys Acta* 1970; 196:193-203.

Huang H, Starodub O, McIntosh A, Kier AB, Schroeder F. Liver fatty acid-binding protein targets fatty acids to the nucleus. Real time confocal and multiphoton fluorescence imaging in living cells. *J Biol Chem* 2002; 277:29139-29151.

Hugger ED, Novak BL, Burton PS, Audus KL, Borchardt RT. A comparison of commonly used polyethoxylated pharmaceutical excipients on their ability to inhibit P-glycoprotein activity in vitro. *J Pharm Sci* 2002; 91:1991-2002.

Humberstone AJ, Charman WN. Lipid based vehicles for the oral delivery of poorly water soluble drugs. *Adv Drug Deliv Rev* 1997; 25:103-128.

Hunt JN, Knox MT. A relation between the chain length of fatty acids and the slowing of gastric emptying. *J Physiol (Lond)* 1968; 194:327-336.

Ichihashi T, Kinoshita H, Takagishi Y and Yamada H. Effect of bile on absorption of mepitiostane by the lymphatic system in rats. *J Pharm Pharmacol* 1992a; 44:565-569.

Ichihashi T, Kinoshita H, Takagishi Y and Yamada H. Effect of oily vehicles on absorption of mepitiostane by the lymphatic system in rats. *J Pharm Pharmacol* 1992b; 44:560-564.

Kaukonen AM, Boyd BJ, Porter CJ, Charman WN. Drug solubilization behavior during in vitro digestion of simple triglyceride lipid solution formulations. *Pharm Res* 2004a; 21:245-253.

Kaukonen AM, Boyd BJ, Charman WN, Porter CJ. Drug solubilization behavior during in vitro digestion of suspension formulations of poorly water-soluble drugs in triglyceride lipids. *Pharm Res* 2004b; 21:254-260.

Khoo SM, Humberstone AJ, Porter CJH, Edwards GA, Charman WN. Formulation design and bioavailability assessment of lipidic self emulsifying formulations of halofantrine. *Int J Pharm* 1998; 167:155-164.

Khoo SM, Edwards GA, Porter CJ, Charman WN. A conscious dog model for assessing the absorption, enterocyte-based metabolism, and intestinal lymphatic transport of halofantrine. *J Pharm Sci* 2001; 90:1599-1607.

Khoo SM, Prankerd RJ, Edwards GA, Porter CJ and Charman WN. A physicochemical basis for the extensive intestinal lymphatic transport of a poorly lipid soluble antimalarial, halofantrine hydrochloride, after postprandial administration to dogs. *J Pharm Sci* 2002; 91:647-659

Khoo SM, Shackleford DM, Porter CJ, Edwards GA, Charman WN. Intestinal lymphatic transport of halofantrine occurs after oral administration of a unit-dose lipid-based formulation to fasted dogs. *Pharm Res* 2003; 20:1460-1465.

Kuksis A. Absorption of fat soluble vitamins. In: Kuksis A. Fat Absorption. Boca Raton: *CRC Press*; 1987:65-86.

Ladas SD, Isaacs PE, Murphy GM, Sladen GE. Comparison of the effects of medium and long chain triglyceride containing liquid meals on gall bladder and small intestinal function in normal man. *Gut* 1984; 25:405-11.

Laher J M, Rigler M W, Vetter R D, Barrowman J A and Patton J S. Similar bioavailability and lymphatic transport of benzo(a)pyrene when administered to rats in different amounts of dietary fat. *J Lipid Res* 1984; 25:1337-1342.

Lindmark T, Nikkila T, Artursson P. Mechanisms of absorption enhancement by medium chain fatty acids in intestinal epithelial Caco-2 cell monolayers. *J Pharmacol Exp Ther* 1995; 275:958-964.

Lindmark T, Schipper N, Lazorova L, de Boer AG, Artursson P. Absorption enhancement in intestinal epithelial Caco-2 monolayers by sodium caprate: assessment of molecular weight dependence and demonstration of transport routes. *J Drug Target* 1998; 5:215-223.

McArthur MJ, Atshaves BP, Frolov A, Foxworth WD, Kier AB, Schroeder F. Cellular uptake and intracellular trafficking of long chain fatty acids. *J Lipid Res* 1999; 40:1371-1383.

Nerurkar MM, Burton PS, Borchardt RT. The use of surfactants to enhance the permeability of peptides through Caco-2 cells by inhibition of an apically polarized efflux system. *Pharm Res* 1996; 13:528-534.

Nerurkar MM, Ho NF, Burton PS, Vidmar TJ, Borchardt RT. Mechanistic roles of neutral surfactants on concurrent polarized and passive membrane transport of a model peptide in Caco-2 cells. *J Pharm Sci* 1997; 86:813-821.

Noguchi T, Charman WN, Stella VJ. Lymphatic appearance of DDT in thoracic or mesenteric lymph duct cannulated rats. *Int J Pharm* 1985; 24:185-192.

Nordskog BK, Phan CT, Nutting DF, Tso P. An examination of the factors affecting intestinal lymphatic transport of dietary lipids. *Adv Drug Deliv Rev* 2001; 50:21-44.

Nutting DF, Kumar NS, St Hilaire RJ, Mansbach CM. Nutrient absorption. *Curr Opin Clin Nutr Metab Care* 1999; 2:413-419.

Ockner RK, Manning JA. Fatty acid-binding protein in small intestine. Identification, isolation, and evidence for its role in cellular fatty acid transport. *J Clin Invest* 1974; 54:326-338.

O'Driscoll CM. Lipid-based formulations for intestinal lymphatic delivery. *Eur J Pharm Sci* 2002; 15:405-415

Palin KJ, Wilson CJ. The effect of different oils on the absorption of probucol in the rat. *J. Pharm. Pharmacol.* 1984; 36:641-643

Phan CT, Tso P. Intestinal lipid absorption and transport. *Front Biosci* 2001; 6:D299-319.

Poirier H, Degrace P, Niot I, Bernard A, Besnard P. Localization and regulation of the putative membrane fatty-acid transporter (FAT) in the small intestine. Comparison with fatty acid-binding proteins (FABP). *Eur J Biochem* 1996; 238:368-373.

Porter CJ, Charman WN. Lipid-based formulations for oral administration: opportunities for bioavailability enhancement and lipoprotein targeting of lipophilic drugs. *J Recept Signal Transduct Res* 2001a; 21:215-257.

Porter CJ, Charman WN. Intestinal lymphatic drug transport: an update. *Adv Drug Deliv Rev* 2001b; 50:61-80.

Porter CJ, Charman WN. In vitro assessment of oral lipid based formulations. *Adv Drug Deliv Rev* 2001c; 50 Suppl 1:S127-47.

Porter CJH, Charman SA, Humberstone AJ, Charman WN. Lymphatic transport of halofantrine in the conscious rat when administered as either the free base or the hydrochloride salt: effect of lipid class and lipid vehicle dispersion. *J Pharm Sci* 1996a; 85:357-361.

Porter CJH, Charman SA, Charman WN. Lymphatic transport of halofantrine in the triple-cannulated anesthetized rat model: effect of lipid vehicle dispersion. *J Pharm Sci* 1996b; 85:351-356.

Porter CJ, Edwards GA, Charman SA. Lymphatic transport of proteins after s.c. injection: implications of animal model selection. *Adv Drug Deliv Rev* 2001; 50:157-171.

Porter CJ, Kaukonen AM, Taillardat-Bertschinger A, Boyd BJ, O'Connor JM, Edwards GA, Charman WN. Use of in vitro lipid digestion data to explain the in vivo performance of triglyceride-based oral lipid formulations of poorly water-soluble drugs: studies with halofantrine. *J Pharm Sci* 2004a; 93:1110-1121.

Porter CJH, Kaukonen AM, Boyd BJ, Edwards GA, Charman WN. Susceptibility to lipase-mediated digestion reduces the oral bioavailability of danazol after oral administration as a medium-chain lipid based microemulsion formulation. *Pharm Res* 2004b; 21:1405-1412.

Pouton CW. Lipid formulations for oral administration of drugs: non-emulsifying, self emulsifying and 'self microemulsifying' drug delivery systems. *Eur J Pharm Sci* 2000; 11 Suppl. 2:S93-S98.

Reymond JP, Sucker H. In vitro model for ciclosporin intestinal absorption in lipid vehicles. *Pharm Res* 1988; 5:673-676.

Ros E. Intestinal absorption of triglyceride and cholesterol. Dietary and pharmacological inhibition to reduce cardiovascular risk. *Atherosclerosis* 2000; 151:357-379.

Schoeller C, Keelan M, Mulvey G, Stremmel W and Thomson AB. Oleic acid uptake into rat and rabbit jejunal brush border membrane. *Biochim Biophys Acta* 1995; 1236:51-64.

Sek L, Porter CJ, Kaukonen AM, Charman WN. Evaluation of the in-vitro digestion profiles of long and medium chain glycerides and the phase behaviour of their lipolytic products. *J Pharm Pharmacol* 2002; 54:29-41.

Shackleford DM, Faassen WA, Houwing N, Lass H, Edwards GA, Porter CJ, Charman WN. Contribution of lymphatically transported testosterone undecanoate to the systemic exposure of testosterone after oral administration of two andriol formulations in conscious lymph duct-cannulated dogs. *J Pharmacol Exp Ther* 2003; 306:925-933.

Shackleford DM, Porter CJH, Charman WN. Lymphatic absorption of orally-administered prodrugs. In Prodrugs: Challenges and Rewards, Eds. V.J. Stella, R.T. Borchardt, M.J. Hageman, R. Oliyai, J.W. Tilley and H. Magg, AAPS Press, Washington DC, in press. 2004.

Shiau YF. Mechanism of intestinal fatty acid uptake in the rat: the role of an acidic microclimate. *J Physiol* 1990; 421:463-474.

Shono Y, Nishihara H, Matsuda Y, Furukawa S, Okada N, Fujita T, Yamamoto A. Modulation of intestinal P-glycoprotein function by cremophor EL and other surfactants by an in vitro diffusion chamber method using the isolated rat intestinal membranes. *J Pharm Sci* 2004; 93:877-885.

Sieber S M. The lymphocytic absorption of p,p'-DDT and some structurally-related compounds in the rat. *Pharmacology* 1976; 14:443-454

Simmonds WJ. The role of micellar solubilization in lipid absorption. *Aust J Exp Biol Med Sci* 1972; 50:403-421.

Staggers JE, Hernell O, Stafford R.J, Carey MC. Physical-chemical behaviour of dietary and biliary lipids during intestinal digestion and absorption. 1. Phase behaviour and aggregation states of model lipid systems patterned after aqueous duodenal contents of healthy adult human beings. *Biochemistry* 1990; 29:2028-2040.

Stremmel W. Uptake of fatty acids by jejunal mucosal cells is mediated by a fatty acid binding membrane protein. *J Clin Invest* 1988; 82:2001-2010.

Stremmel W, Lotz G, Strohmeyer G, Berk PD. Identification isolation and partial characterization of a fatty acid binding protein from rat jejunal microvillus membranes. *J Clin Invest* 1985; 75:1068-1076.

Swartz MA. The physiology of the lymphatic system. *Adv Drug Deliv Rev* 2001; 50, 3-20.

Taillardat-Bertschinger A, Perry CS, Galland A, Prankerd RJ, Charman WN. Partitioning of halofantrine hydrochloride between water, micellar solutions and soybean oil: Effects on its apparent ionisation constant. *J Pharm Sci* 2003; 92, 2217-2228.

Thomson AB, Schoeller C, Keelan M, Smith L, Clandinin MT. Lipid absorption: passing through the unstirred layers, brush-border membrane, and beyond. *Can J Physiol Pharmacol* 1993; 71:531-555.

Ueda C T, Lemaire M, Gsell G and Nussbaumer K. Intestinal lymphatic absorption of cyclosporin A following oral administration in an olive oil solution to rats. *Biopharm Drug Dispos* 1983; 4:113-120.

Wacher VJ, Wong S, Wong HT. Peppermint oil enhances cyclosporine oral bioavailability in rats: comparison with D-alpha-tocopheryl poly(ethylene glycol 1000) succinate (TPGS) and ketoconazole. *J Pharm Sci* 2002; 91:77-90.

Zangenberg NH, Mullertz A, Kristensen HG, Hovgaard L. A dynamic in vitro lipolysis model. I. Controlling the rate of lipolysis by continuous addition of calcium. *Eur J Pharm Sci* 2001a; 14:115-122.

Zangenberg NH, Mullertz A, Kristensen HG, Hovgaard L. A dynamic in vitro lipolysis model. II: Evaluation of the model. *Eur J Pharm Sci* 2001b; 14:237-244.

7

Biopharmaceutics Modeling and the Role of Dose and Formulation on Oral Exposure

Brian R. Rohrs, Ph.D.

Pharmaceutical Sciences
Pfizer
Kalamazoo, MI

Table of Contents

Introduction

Early in the drug development process, *in vivo* studies are often run to help select molecules with appropriate ADME characteristics, generate data in efficacy models, and evaluate toxicity. Poor exposure can lead to highly variable data, and/or ambiguous study results. Use of resource and scarce API for un-interpretable study outcomes is highly inefficient, and based on poor data, a compound may be given an undeservedly low priority. Because exposure is such a critical factor for compound evaluation during lead optimization, the formulation of the compound can be a key component of the drug selection process.

Biopharmaceutical modeling is often used to estimate the fraction absorbed of a given dose delivered (F_{abs}). Models range from a simple algebraic calculation of maximum absorbable dose, or MAD (Johnson and Swindell, 1996), through empirically parameterized models like IDEA™ (LION Bioscience AG) to the highly sophisticated GastroPlus™ (Simulations Plus, Inc.). Each biopharmaceutics model has utility within the drug development process and in capable hands with good inputs, can yield reasonably accurate estimates of bioavailability. While these models are most often used to evaluate the impact of physical and chemical properties of drugs on fraction absorbed, some of these models may also be used to help guide formulation approaches to achieve better bioavailability.

At the lead optimization stage, one needs a simple assessment of where a drug sits in the "biopharmaceutical landscape" so that strategies for formulation options can be assessed. A model developed at the University of Michigan (Oh, *et al.*, 1993) called the microscopic mass balance approach (abbreviated here as MiMBA) meets this criterion. Understanding the model output can help answer questions such as:

"Why am I getting poor exposure?"
"Will a better formulation help me?"
"What formulation technologies should be tried?"

MiMBA

For details of this model, one should consult the original paper. (Oh, *et al.*, 1993) A summary will be presented here so that the reader has the background to understand the subsequent discussion.

Conceptually, MiMBA involves placing a dispersed suspension of drug particles at the beginning of a cylindrical tube representing the intestinal tract. As the particles traverse the intestine, dissolution of the particles occurs, increasing the concentration of drug within the tube. Simultaneously, absorption takes place, effectively decreasing the drug concentration within the tube. This is shown schematically in Figure 1. The trade off between dissolution and absorption dictates the time course of the drug concentration in the intestine. At the end of the intestinal tube, the total fraction absorbed is calculated by subtracting from the initial dose everything remaining inside the intestine, i.e., the fraction remaining as solid particles and the fraction that dissolved but did not get absorbed.

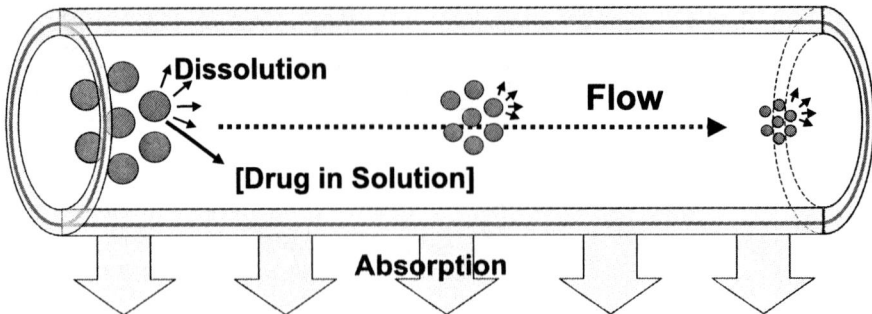

Figure 1. Conceptual model upon which MiMBA is based showing the dissolution and absorption processes as particles transit the intestine.

Mathematically, MiMBA utilizes three dimensionless variables that encompass the physical and chemical properties of the drug as well as the physiological system in which dissolution and absorption takes place. These variables are then incorporated into a system of two differential equations, one describing the fate of the particles' radii, the other describing the concentration along the intestinal tract. The equations can be solved using a mathematical or engineering software package such as MathCad® (Mathsoft, Inc.) or Mathematica® (Wolfram Research, Inc.), and total fraction absorbed calculated.

The three dimensionless variables are described below and deal respectively with the solubilization process, the absorption process, and the dissolution process.

Solubilization

The solubilization process is described by the relative solubility of the dose compared to the capacity of the medium. The calculated variable is termed the dose number, D_o, and is determined by:

$$D_o = \frac{M_o/V_o}{C_s}$$

Where,

M_o is the mass of the dose
V_o is the internal volume into which the dose is dissolved
C_s is the saturation solubility of drug in the intestinal medium

As dose number varies from 0 to 1, the medium is increasingly saturated with solubilized drug until at $D_o = 1$, complete saturation occurs at equilibrium. For $D_o > 1$, there is excess solid present since the dose has exceeded the capacity of the medium to solubilize the drug.

The dose M_o is normally dictated by experimental protocol. The volume V_o is dependent on the physiology and the dosing protocol, and can be estimated from the sum of resting volume in the stomach, the liquid ingested at time of dosing, plus a quantity to account for dilution after gastric emptying occurs.

Determining the relevant value for saturation solubility C_s can be difficult. In reality, there is most likely a range of solubilities that impact the incremental absorption potential as the compound moves down the intestine, especially for ionizable compounds. Simple biopharmaceutic models (e.g., MAD and MiMBA) attempt to capture this in one solubility value, whereas more sophisticated models (e.g., IDEA and GastroPlus) account for this by varying solubility as a function of pH in different regions of the intestine. The tradeoff is complexity. For the discussion here, we are interested in a qualitative or at most semi-quantitative evaluation, so we opt for simplicity.

As a starting point, aqueous solubility at pH 6.5 is often used. This is probably a reasonable estimate for non-ionizable compounds with log D < ~2 to 3. The intestinal milieu is not, however, pH 6.5 phosphate buffer. It is a complex mix of bile salts, lecithin and other solubilizing components. For compounds with a high log D, solubility is greatly enhanced by partitioning into mixed micelles. (Wiedmann and Kamel, 2002)

Ionization also plays a role. The intestinal pH ranges from about 6.6 ± 0.5 in the jejunum to 7.5 ± 0.5 in the ileum. (Evans, *et al.*, 1988) Ionization of a weakly acidic compound could increase the effective solubility by a factor of about ten over this range. Of even greater consequence, weakly basic compounds are protonated at stomach pH, yet deprotonated at intestinal pH. Solubilization occurs within the stomach environment, and upon gastric emptying the intestine is presented with a relatively large fraction of the drug in solution. Precipitation competes kinetically with absorption to remove compound from solution. Depending on the rapidity of the precipitation process, the effective solubility could be several orders of magnitude higher than what would be determined by an equilibrium measurement at pH 6.5.

To mimic *in vivo* solubilization, several artificial or simulated intestinal fluids (SIFs) have been proposed. (Staggers, *et al.*, 1990; Dressman, *et al.*, 1998; Stella, *et al.*, 1998) and these media have been shown to significantly increase the equilibrium solubility of some poorly aqueous-soluble compounds. One or more of these media should be used to evaluate compound solubility, and that value used in the MiMBA calculation. If the compound is ionizable, solubility could be evaluated over a range of pHs, say 4 to 7.5, with the values then used as boundaries for subsequent analysis.

Absorption

The absorption process is described by the ratio of the absorption rate to the GI transit rate. The calculated variable is termed the absorption number A_n and is given by:

$$A_n = \frac{P_{eff} \cdot \pi \cdot R \cdot L}{Q}$$

Chapter 7: Biopharmaceutics Modeling and the Role of Dose
and Formulation on Oral Exposure
156

where

P_{eff} is the effective permeability coefficient in the species of interest (cm/s)

R is the radius of the intestine (cm)

L is the intestinal length (cm)

Q is the volume flow rate down the GI tract (cm^3/min)

In a relative sense, as the absorption rate becomes slower than the transit rate ($A_n < 1$), material passes through the intestine before it can be absorbed.

The variables R, L, and Q are assigned values based on species physiology and estimated intestinal transit time. The more sophisticated biopharmaceutic models account for regional permeability differences, but again, for the sake of simplicity, we assume permeability, P_{eff}, is constant. As a first approximation, one assumes that absorption takes place in the small intestine only. If colonic absorption occurs, the effect is one of increasing A_n by a factor proportional to the relative increase in transit time.

Effective permeability is the variable into which a compound's behavior gets incorporated. An estimate for P_{eff} can be determined by linking a permeability measurement in a cell-based (e.g., Caco2) or an artificial membrane (e.g., PAMPA) assay to a species-specific value through the means of standards. Metoprolol (P_{eff} in human = 1.34e-6 cm/s) is often used as one of the standards since its permeability is the boundary for highly permeable compounds in the biopharmaceutics classification scheme (BCS). (FDA, 2000)

Permeability may be reported as an absorption rate constant 'k' (min^{-1}) as opposed to a P_{eff} value. The conversion between the two is merely geometric surface to volume ratio of the intestine:

$$P_{eff} = k \cdot \frac{Vol}{SA} = k \cdot \frac{\left(\pi \cdot R^2 \cdot L\right)}{\left(2 \cdot \pi \cdot R \cdot L\right)} = k \cdot \frac{R}{2}$$

where

R is the intestinal radius of the species of interest

Dissolution

The dissolution process is described by the ratio of the GI residence time to the time for complete dissolution. The calculated variable is termed the dissolution number D_n and is given by:

$$D_n = \left(\frac{\pi \cdot R^2 \cdot L}{Q}\right) \bigg/ \left(\frac{r_0^2 \cdot \rho}{3 \cdot D \cdot C_s}\right)$$

where

r_0 is the initial particle radius (μm)

D is the diffusivity (diffusion coefficient) of the compound (cm^2/sec)

ρ is the density of the compound solid (g/cm^3)

C_s, Q, R, L are as previously defined

As the residence time exceeds time for complete dissolution ($D_n > 1$), all material is in solution and is available for absorption. If $D_n > 10$, then all drug particles are dissolved in a tenth of the transit time and we can comfortably assume that particle size has a limited influence on the fraction absorbed.

For MiMBA, the approximation is made that all particles are of the same size, i.e., mono-dispersed. While in reality this is not the case since a powder contains a distribution of particle sizes, an upper boundary can be established for the initial radius r_0 from a microscopic image. The eye is naturally drawn to the larger particles, and these can be used to estimate a 'worst case' r_0.

The diffusivity 'D' is a function of molecular size. For a typical small molecule (MW of 300 to 500), D will be about 7 to 8 $\times 10^{-6}$ cm²/sec. The density 'ρ' of an organic solid is typically between 1 to 1.5 g/cm³.

Fraction Absorbed

The calculation of fraction absorbed involves solving a system of two differential equations. (Oh, et al., 1993)

$$\frac{dr^*}{dz^*} = -\frac{D_n}{3} \cdot \frac{1-C^*}{r^*}$$

$$\frac{dC^*}{dz^*} = D_o \cdot D_n \cdot r^* \cdot (1-C^*) - 2 \cdot A_n \cdot C^*$$

The first equation determines the decrease in radius (i.e., dissolution) as the particles transit the intestine. This rate is proportional to the dissolution number (the greater D_n, the faster the dissolution) and the difference between the saturation solubility and concentration in solution (given by $1 - C^*$). The second equation determines the change in concentration down the intestinal tract and is the difference between the amount of drug getting in solution via dissolution and the amount of drug being removed from solution via absorption.

Total fraction absorbed is determined by evaluating these equations at the end of the intestine (mathematically when $z^* = 1$) using the expression

$$F = 1 - \{r^*(1)\}^3 - \frac{C^*(1)}{D_o}$$

Conceptually, this can be considered as the initial dose fraction (by definition = 1) minus what has not dissolved and is left as a solid at the end of the intestine (= $r^*(1)^3$) minus what has dissolved, but has not been absorbed (= $C^*(1)/D_o$).

Chapter 7: Biopharmaceutics Modeling and the Role of Dose
and Formulation on Oral Exposure
158

Biopharmaceutics Landscape

For a given absorption number A_n, if fraction absorbed is calculated over a range of dose numbers D_o and dissolution numbers D_n, one can generate the three-dimensional biopharmaceutics landscape for the compound as shown in Figure 2. This contour plot demonstrates the effect on fraction absorbed of increasing the dose (D_o therefore increases) shown by the vertical arrow on the right-hand side of the plot, and the effect of increasing particle size (D_n decreases) shown by the horizontal arrow. The cross-sections of the contour plot along the arrows are also shown.

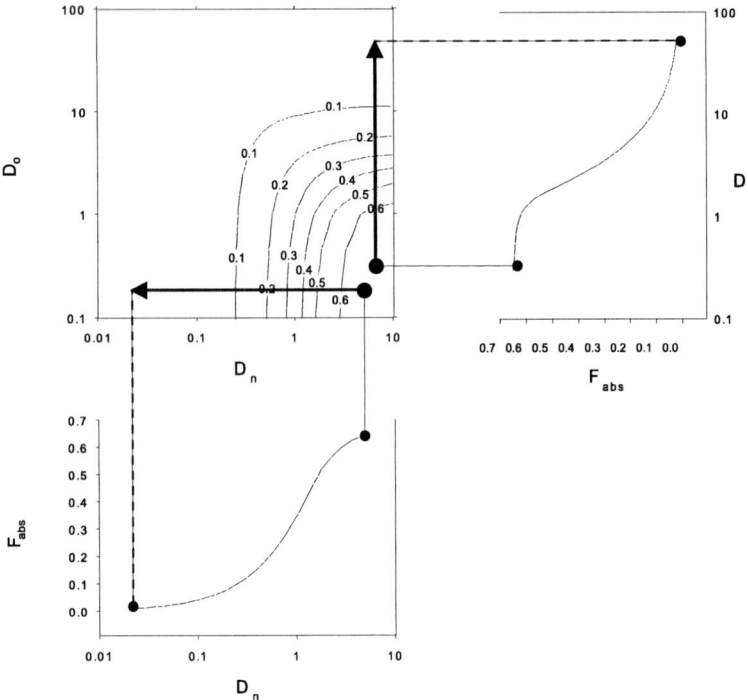

Figure 2. Contour plot of fraction absorbed (F_{abs}) as a function of dose number (D_o) and dissolution number (D_n) for a low permeability compound. As dose increases (D_o increases), F_{abs} decreases. As particle size increases (D_n decreases), F_{abs} decreases.

Role of Dose on Oral Exposure

If we put some real numbers to the dimensionless variables, we can see how increasing the dose effects oral exposure. Figure 3 plots fraction absorbed and the actual amount absorbed for escalating doses of a low permeability, low solubility compound. There is a region of dose linearity, which corresponds to the flat region of the F_{abs} tracing. As the dose increases, linearity is no longer predicted and at high dose, the amount absorbed plateaus such that even though ever more drug is given, no more is absorbed.

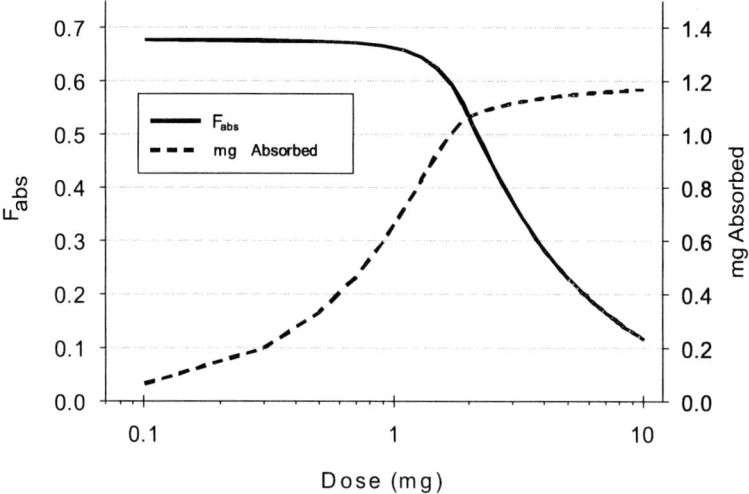

Figure 3. An example of the relationship between fraction absorbed and amount absorbed as dose increases. A plateau in amount absorbed is eventually reached as the intestine becomes saturated with solubilized drug.

The physical explanation for this plateau is that at some dose, the intestinal milieu becomes saturated with drug. As the dose moves down the intestinal tract, the surrounding medium remains saturated throughout the entire absorption region. Above this dose, any more solid material added never dissolves, but just passes through the intestine. This phenomenon is the basis for the MAD (Maximum Absorbable Dose) calculation. (Johnson and Swindell, 1996)

During drug development, this behavior is often observed in toxicity studies when high exposure is desired. If the exposure (AUC or C_{max}) vs. dose curve has flattened, a formulation approach may be employed to help increase the amount absorbed, although there must be a trade-off between the desire for increased exposure and the addition of components that might influence a toxicity outcome.

Regions of Limited Bioavailability

From the contour plot in Figure 4, we can identify three reasons for limited bioavailability. The upper right-hand corner (high D_o, high D_n) is the region of solubility-limited absorption. As explained in the above section, this occurs when saturation solubility in the intestinal medium is reached.

In the lower left-hand corner (low D_o, low D_n) is the region of dissolution-limited absorption. The dissolution rate is slower than the absorption rate and therefore dissolution is the rate-limiting step for bioavailability.

In the lower right-hand corner (low D_o, high D_n) is the region of permeability-limited absorption. Low permeability (low A_n) controls bioavailability and although dose and dissolution rate are optimal, one can only absorb a fraction of the dose – in the example of Figure 4, about 70%. At the lower limit of paracellular permeability, $A_n \approx 0.3$ which results in a maximum $F_{abs} \approx 0.45$ for permeability-limited absorption.

The key premise of this discussion is that where you are located in the biopharmaceutic landscape determines what formulation strategy you should employ to enhance bioavailability.

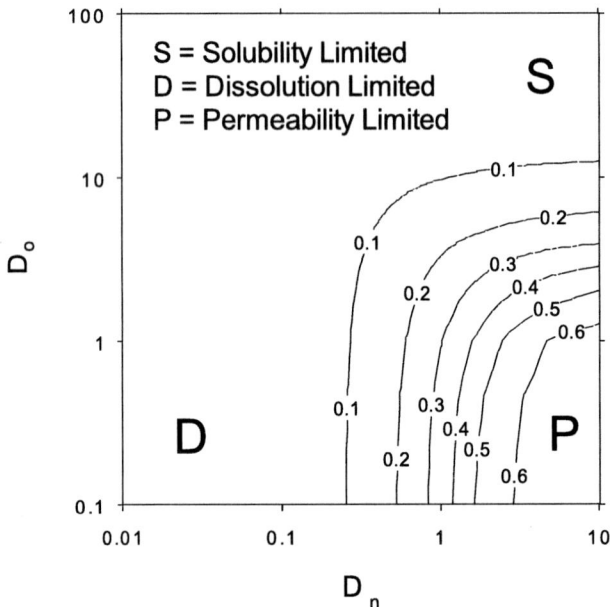

Figure 4. Contour plot of fraction absorbed (F_{abs}) for a low permeability compound showing the different regions of limiting bioavailability.

Estimating A_n, D_n, and D_o Values

To facilitate use of the model, estimates for the Absorption, Dissolution and Dose Numbers are necessary. Many of the variables used to calculate A_n, D_n, and D_o are physiologically based and therefore do not change as new compounds are tested. In addition, the density of the solid and the molecular diffusivity (related to molecular weight) do not vary significantly across typical drug-like organic compounds, and so representative values can be used with reasonable accuracy. Therefore, a simple method for estimating A_n, D_n, and D_o is to combine the relatively constant physiological and physical parameters into single factors which are then multiplied by the compound specific variables. Table 1 contains estimates for those factors for oral dosing into rat, dog, and human. The compound specific variables in the first column are multiplied by the species-specific factor to calculate the dimensionless variable in the last column. For example, solubility (in mg/ml) divided by the square of the estimated particle size (in μm) multiplied by 14850 yields the estimated dissolution number for humans.

The factors in Table 1 are approximations and are meant to be used a starting point. As one gathers data, it may become evident that a different value may be more appropriate. For example, a class of compounds may have regional permeability issues, and so the factor for permeability may have to be adjusted.

Measured Property	× (Estimated Factor) =			Parameter
	Rat	**Dog**	**Human**	
P_{eff} (cm/s)	54260	11781	9920	A_n
Sol/r^2 (mg/ml)/(μm^2)	13500	7200	14850	D_n
Dose/Sol (mg)/(mg/ml)	0.1	0.1	0.004	D_o

Table 1. List of estimated multiplicative factors for converting measured physical properties of a drug into the dimensionless variables of absorption number, dissolution number, and dose number for rat, dog, and human.

Formulation Strategy

To use MiMBA in a practical way, first, estimate the dimensionless variables A_n, D_n, and D_o. Next, choose an absorption contour plot based on the absorption number A_n; Figures 5a-d represent low, moderate, high and very high permeability compounds (A_n = 0.6, 1.3, 8.5 and 20 respectively). As a point of reference, metoprolol, the compound used in the biopharmaceutic classification scheme (BCS) (FDA, 2000) to define the boundary between low and high permeability compounds, has an A_n of 1.33 in humans. Graphically place the calculated D_n and D_o on the contour plot to determine the starting point and the limitation (i.e., dissolution, solubility, or permeability) to bioavailability. Then, choose an appropriate formulation approach as outlined in the following section to enhance bioavailability.

Dissolution Limited

Dissolution rate is proportional to solubility and inversely proportional to the square of the particle radius. To enhance bioavailability, one must either reduce particle size or increase the solubility (note that increasing solubility effects both D_n and D_o). As D_n becomes greater than 10, the enhancement of F_{abs} due to particle size reduction decreases. One can deduce this from the contour plots in Figure 5 as the contour lines begin to run parallel to the D_n-axes at or about D_n = 10. Note that this occurs in each of the plots, and so this phenomenon is independent of the permeability. The physical interpretation of D_n > 10 is that the time to complete dissolution is at least ten-fold less than the intestinal transit time.

From a formulation perspective, it is of benefit for particle size not to be a major determinant of bioavailability in order to get consistent exposure between lots of material. During lead optimization, often one has only one batch of material to evaluate, but dosing decisions for further ADME-Tox studies are often

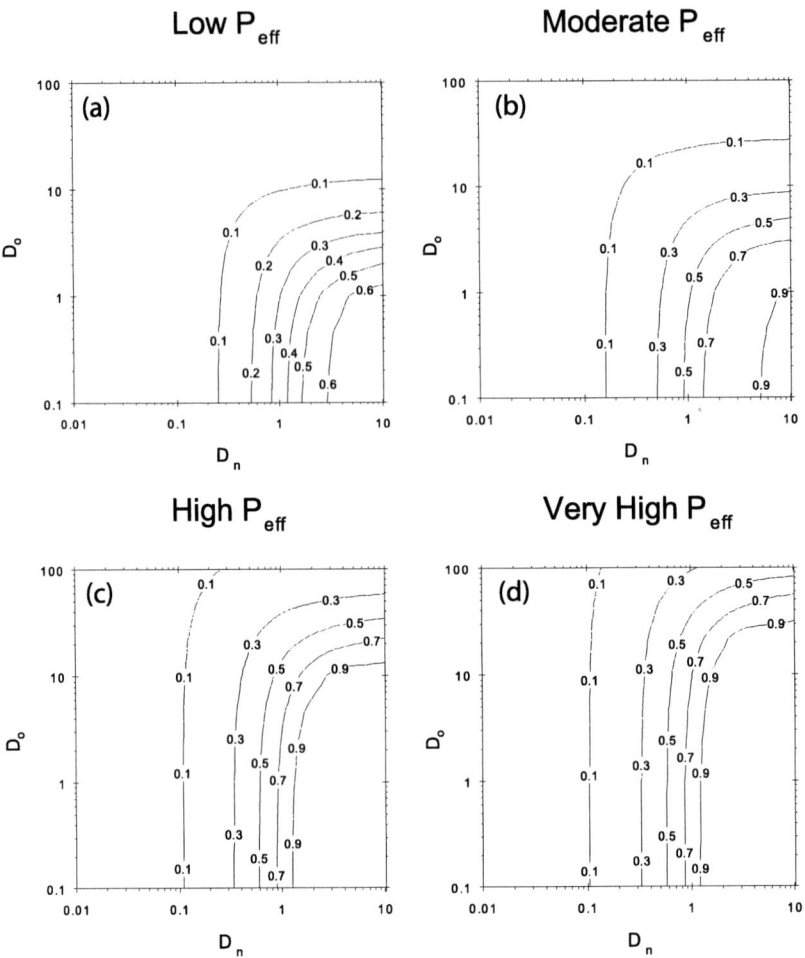

Figure 5. Contour plots of fraction absorbed (F_{abs}) for An equal to (a) 0.6, (b) 1.3, (c) 8.5 and (d) 20 representing low, moderate, high and very high permeability compounds respectively. Plots are to be used to estimate the location of an unknown compound in the biopharmaceutics landscape.

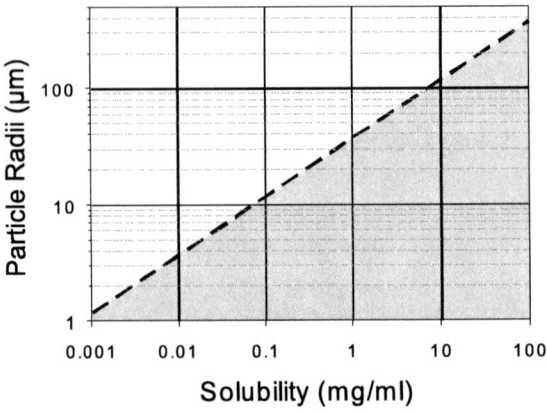

Figure 6. Particle size as a function of solubility for $D_n > 10$ (shaded region) such that dissolution plays a minor role in influencing bioavailability.

made with the assumption that subsequent batches of material will perform equivalently to the initial batch. One way to help assure this is to have particle size small enough such that $D_n > 10$. Figure 6 shows the particle size limit necessary to have $D_n > 10$ as a function of solubility, with the shaded region being desirable.

It is important to note that it is the <u>effective</u> particle size that dictates the dissolution rate. If the primary particles are very small, yet they form large aggregates in suspension, it will be the aggregate size that controls dissolution. In practice, one can sonicate the suspension to help break up aggregates. Also, if dosed as a solid (e.g., powder in a capsule), dispersion of the particles becomes an important step in the dissolution process.

If the effective particle size is small enough that dissolution is not at all rate-limiting, then fraction absorbed may be estimated from the contour plot in Figure 7, where F_{abs} is calculated as a function of dose number D_o and absorption number A_n. The solubility-limited region is the upper portion of the plot where F_{abs} is < 0.9 and the permeability-limited region is the lower left-hand corner where the F_{abs} contours become parallel to the D_o-axis.

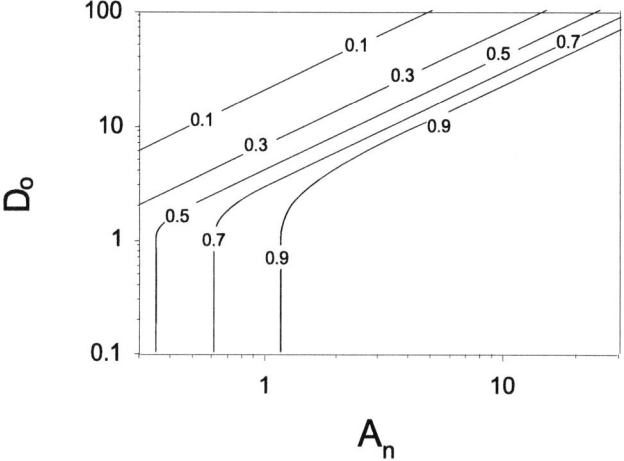

Figure 7. Contour plot of fraction absorbed (F_{abs}) as a function of dose number (D_o) and absorption number (A_n) if dissolution plays no role in influencing bioavailability.

Solubility Limited

The relative solubility (dose number) is proportional to dose and inversely proportional to solubility. Dose is dictated by study design, so lowering it to decrease the dose number is typically not an option. Therefore, increasing solubility becomes the only way to reduce the dose number and increase F_{abs}. Formulation strategies fall into two general categories. The first is solubilization in a medium, which upon dilution by the intestinal mileau, generates a supersaturated solution. Adding pH-modifying agents to enhance solubility through compound ionization and dosing with co-solvents are common examples of this approach. The second category involves modifying the lattice energy of the solid through disorder (low-crystalline or amorphous materials), or changing the inter-molecular bonding network (polymorphs or salts). Other chapters in this section provide more detail on these types of formulations.

Permeability Limited

Permeability influences the flux across the intestinal membrane (Flux $\propto P_{eff}$ ·Concentration), and it is the integrated flux that determines the total amount absorbed. Flux is incorporated into the differential equation describing concentration as the second set of terms (underlined):

$$\frac{dC^*}{dz^*} = D_o \cdot D_n \cdot r^* \cdot \left(1 - C^*\right) - \underline{2 \cdot A_n \cdot C^*}$$

If one is in a permeability-limited region of the biopharmaceutics landscape, then to increase bioavailability, either P_{eff} or solubility needs to be increased.

The most effective way to increase permeability is to change the molecule. This is typically not a practical solution, but a pro-drug strategy might be considered if an overall class of compounds has poor permeability. If the molecule is a P-gp substrate, co-administration of a P-gp inhibitor may reduce efflux and increase the effective permeability. Suggested inhibitors include Cremophor EL, Vitamin E-TGPS, and Polysorbate 80 (Nerurkar, *et al.*, 1996; Yu, *et al.*, 1999). While this approach has been demonstrated *in vitro*, and there is strong evidence that this mechanism can explain certain drug-drug interactions (for example, Boyd, *et al.*, 2000), verification of its utility as a formulation strategy *in vivo* is limited.

The alternative for enhancing flux is to increase solubility via a technology that provides supersaturation compared to the crystalline material at the absorption site, as described in the previous section. The most effective formulation strategies are those that provide the highest degree of supersaturation, yet do not induce precipitation. Materials that inhibit precipitation (typically polymeric) may be added to the formulation.

One must keep in mind that while concentration is the factor used in the flux equation, it is the chemical potential that dictates the true driving force. The chemical potential is modified by the presence of solubilizing agents competing with the membrane for drug. (See the chapter by Hageman in this section for further discussion)

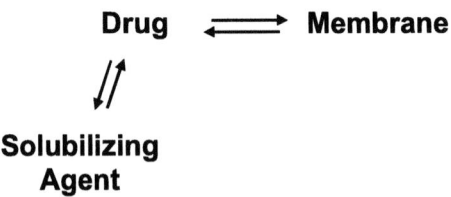

The attenuation of the driving force is most pronounced when there is an excess of the solubilizing agent relative to the amount needed to completely solubilize the drug. The effect has been demonstrated *in vitro* in Caco2 assays as shown in Figure 8 (data re-plotted from Nerurkar, *et al.*, 1996 and Yu, *et al.*, 1999). In both examples surfactant added acted as a P-gp efflux inhibitor. At low concentrations, the AP (apical) to BL (basolateral) flux increased with a corresponding decrease in the BL to AP flux. As the concentration of solubilizing agent further increased, a decrease in the AP to BL flux was observed and was attributed to the competition of the surfactant micelles for drug molecules and therefore a decrease in the chemical potential across the Caco2 membrane.

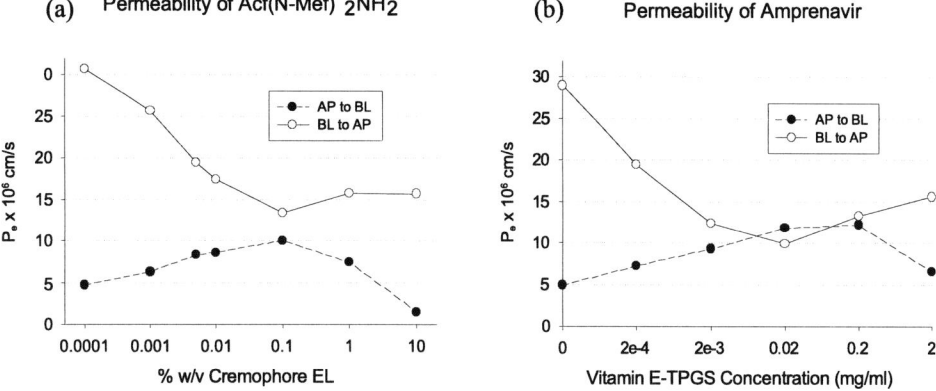

Figure 8. Effect of solubilizing agents on permeability in Caco2 assays demonstrating P-gp efflux inhibition at low surfactant concentrations and decreased chemical potential at higher surfactant concentrations. Data re-plotted from (a) Nerurkar, *et al.*, 1996 and (b) Yu, *et al.*, 1999.

Summary

To enhance bioavailability through formulation technologies, determine where you sit in the biopharmaceutics landscape via the contour plots presented in Figures 5a-d, then select the appropriate formulation technology to move up the slope to higher F_{abs}. This scheme is meant to be qualitative, a starting point to estimate the direction one must take. As *in vivo* data is collected, one should develop a feedback system to adjust the model parameterization (i.e., what factors should be used in Table 1).

To estimate the compound's effective permeability, one must have an established correlation of an *in vitro* or ex vivo method to P_{eff}.

Reducing effective particle size will never hurt bioavailability. If dosed as a suspension, agglomeration of primary particles increases the effective particle size. If dosed as a solid, rapid dispersion of the formulation to primary particles is important for assuring maximum exposure.

If using solubility enhancers, too much can decrease bioavailability via a reduction in chemical potential. This is likely to happen only after complete solubilization of the compound.

References

Boyd RA, Stern RH, Stewart BH, Wu X, Reyner EL, Zegarac EA, Randinitis EJ, and Whitfield L. Atorvastatin Coadministration May Increase Digoxin Concentrations by Inhibition of Intestinal P-Glycoprotein-Mediated Secretion. *J Clinical Pharmacology* 2000; 40(1):91-98

Dressman JB, Amidon GL, Reppas C, and Shah VP. Dissolution Testing as a Prognostic Tool for Oral Drug Absorption: Immediate Release Dosage Forms. *Pharm Res* 1998; 15(1):11-22

Evans DF, Pye G, Bramley R, Clark AG, Dyson TJ, and Hardcastle JD. Measurement of Gastrointestinal pH Profiles in Normal Ambulant Human Subjects. *Gut* 1988; 29:1035 - 1041

FDA, Guidance for Industry. Waiver of *in vivo* Bioavailability and Bioequivalence Studies for Immediate-Release Solid Oral Dosage Forms Based on a Biopharmaceutics Classification System. Posted August 2000. http://www.fda.gov/cder/guidance/3618fnl.htm (accessed September 2004)

Johnson KC, and Swindell AC. Guidance in the Setting of Drug Particle Size Specification to Minimize Variability in Absorption. *Pharm Res* 1996; 13:1795-1798

Nerurkar MM, Burton PS, and Borchardt RT. The Use of Surfactants to Enhance the Permeability of Peptides Through Caco-2 Cells by Inhibition of an Apically Polarized Efflux System. *Pharm Res* 1996; 13(4):528-534

Oh D-M, Curl RL, and Amidon GL. Estimating the Fraction Dose Absorbed from Suspensions of Poorly Soluble Compounds in Humans: A Mathematical Model. *Pharm Res* 1993; 10(2):264-270

Staggers JE, Hernell O, Stafford RJ, and Carey MC. Physical-Chemical Behavior of Dietary and Biliary Lipids During Intestinal Digestion and Absorption. 1. Phase Behavior and Aggregation States of Model Lipid Systems Patterned After Aqueous Duodenal Contents of Healthy Adult Human Beings. *Biochemistry* 1990; 29:2028-2040

Stella VJ, Martodihardjo S, Teradea K, and Rao VM. Some Relationships Between the Physical Properties of Various 3-Acyloxymethyl Prodrugs of Phenytoin to Structure: Potential *in vivo* Performance Implications. *J Pharm Sci* 1998; 87(10):1235-1241

Wiedmann TS, and Kamel L. Examination of the Solubilization of Drugs by Bile Salt Micelles. *J Pharm Sci* 2002; 91(8):1743-1764

Yu L, Bridgers A, Polli J, Vickers A, Long S, Roy A, Winnike R, and Coffin M. Vitamin E-TPGS Increase Absorption Flux of an HIV Protease Inhibitor by Enhancing its Solubility and Permeability. *Pharm Res* 1999; 16(12):1812-1817

8

Application of Physicochemical Data to Support Lead Optimization by Discovery Teams

Li Di and Edward H. Kerns

Wyeth Research
P.O. Box CN 8000
Princeton, NJ 08543-8000

Table of Contents

List of Abbreviations

2D6 ....Cytochrome P450 isozyme 2D6
BBB ....Blood brain barrier
BCEC ....Bovine conjunctival epithelial cells
BCSFB ....Blood CSF barrier
Caco-2 ....Human colon cancer cell line
CNS ....Central nerve system
CNS- ....Low CNS penetration
CNS+ ....High CNS penetration
CSF ....Cerebrospinal fluid
I.M. ....Intra muscular
IC50 ....Concentration of an inhibitor at which 50% inhibition
Ki ....Inhibition constant
LC-MS...............................Liquid Chromatography – Mass Spectroscopy
LC-MS-MS...........Liquid Chromatography – Tandem Mass Spectroscopy
LC-UV..........................Liquid Chromatography-Ultraviolet spectroscopy

LLC-PK1 Renal epithelial cell line originally derived from porcine kidneys
MAD...Maximum Absorbable Dose
MC...Methylcellulose
MDCK ....Madin – Darby Canine Kidney cell line
MDR1-MDCKII ....Multi drug resistant 1 - MDCKII cell line
Mpk ....Milligram per kilogram
MRP ....Multi-drug resistant proteins
PAMPA .... Parallel artificial membrane permeability assay
PAMPA-BBB ....Parallel artificial membrane permeability assay for BBB
PC ....Phosphatidyl Choline
Pe...Effective permeability
PEG...Polyethylene glycol
Pgp ....P-glycoprotein
pKa ....Acidity constant
SGF ....Simulated gastro fluid
SIBLM...Simulated bile salt lecithin mixture
SIF...Simulated intestinal fluid
TM-BBB ....Transgenic mouse - BBB
TR-BBB ....Transgenic rat - BBB
UV ....Ultraviolet

Key Words

Solubility, Permeability, Blood brain Barrier, High throughput, Pgp, PAMPA, Caco-2, Structure-Property Relationship, ADME, Absorption

Introduction

A successful drug must combine both potency and drug-like properties. Traditionally, pharmaceutical companies have focused on activity optimization, based on *in vitro* and *in vivo* biological assays. Nowadays, many of the pharmaceutical property assays are implemented early in drug discovery, so that properties can be optimized in parallel with activity (Smith, 2002; Kerns, 2001; Kerns and Di, 2003; Di and Kerns, 2003).

Physicochemical properties of drug candidates play an important role in drug discovery and development. A solid drug has to dissolve and permeate through the gastro-intestinal membrane in order to be absorbed into systemic circulation. Therefore, solubility and permeability are two important factors that affect oral absorption.

Solubility not only affects *in vivo* oral bioavailability, but also has tremendous impact on *in vitro* assays. Here is an example from a discovery project: a compound was tested in a biological assay, and was not very potent (IC_{50} = 10 µM). However, owing to the faith that the chemist has in his compound, it was retested. When the biologist retested this compound, she found it was not soluble, and used special conditions to dissolve the compound. This time, the IC_{50} was 1 nM. By solublizing the compound, the potency increased 1000 fold!

Solubility also affects property assays. Here is an example from our lab: a compound was tested for CYP450 inhibition. The IC_{50} for 2D6 inhibition, when first tested, was greater than 10 µM. However, when the compound was retested, it was observed to be insoluble in DMSO stock solution. When it was solublized under special conditions, the IC_{50} was 0.6 µM. Because of the poor solubility of the compound, the assay initiallyunderestimated the potential toxicity due to drug-drug interaction.

Solubility is a prerequisite for many assays. An insoluble compound will be undetected in many Pharmaceutical Profiling assays, such as PAMPA, PAMPA-BBB or pKa determination. In biological assays, if a compound is insoluble in the assay buffer, the activity of the compound will be underestimated. Active compounds may be unnoticed due to insolubility, because very little material was in the test solution. Only when the compound is completely in solution, does measured activity reflect true activity. Insoluble compounds tend to have erratic assay results, give artificially low potency and have poor oral bioavailability. Insoluble compounds can also be challenging for drug development. The burden can be transferred to the patient. For example, due to low aqueous solubility and poor metabolic stability of Amprenavir, patients have to take eight capsules twice a day. Early solubility information can help discovery teams optimize the compounds and reduce the burden for drug development and patient use.

A drug must cross many biological barriers before it can reach the therapeutic target. The barriers can be gastro-intestinal membrane, blood-brain barrier and other cell membranes. Good permeability is essential for good oral bioavailability. For example, a project team discovered a very potent compound containing two carboxylic acid groups with a K_i of 7 nM. However, the compound had low permeability, with a P_e of 0.1 x 10^{-6} cm/s in PAMPA. The oral bioavailability of the compound was less than 1%. The compound was later modified through a prodrug approach. The monoester prodrug of the compound was quite permeable, with a P_e of 7.0 x 10^{-6} cm/s in PAMPA. The oral bioavailability of the compound increased to 18%. Unlike solubility, permeability cannot be improved, in general, through formulation. Though, there are several research groups actively studying enhancement of permeability, enhancers are not commonly used in the industry due to potential toxicity (Ward *et al.*, 2000). Improvement of permeability usually requires structural modification.

These examples indicate the major impact that physiochemical properties have. This chapter discusses key physicochemical properties for drug optimization. For each property, methods used to measure the property, applications of the data, strategies for compound improvement, and structure-property relationship are provided.

Solubility

Solubility Methodology

There are two kinds of solubility measurements that are typically obtained in drug discovery: kinetic solubility (i.e., non-thermodynamic solubility) and equilibrium solubility (i.e., thermodynamic solubility). The differences between the two solubilities are summarized in Table 1.

In the kinetic solubility experiment, equilibrium between the solid material and the solution is not necessarily established. Kinetic solubility is typically measured by adding a concentrated DMSO stock solution to aqueous buffer. The excess compound precipitates out of solution. The analytical method used for solubility can be turbidimetry or nephometry to detect the appearance of insoluble particles or UV spectrometry to measure the concentration of dissolved

Comparison	Kinetic Solubility	Thermodynamic Solubility
Initial State	DMSO Stock	Solid Crystals
Mixing Time	Variable	Long mixing
Temperature	Room Temperature	Controlled Temperature
Equilibrium	Not Established	Established
Crystal Form	Meta-Stable Forms	Stable Form
Target Solubility	100 μg/mL	10 mg/mL
Throughput	150 Compounds/day	20 Compounds/day
Material	1.5 mg for 4 pHs	100 mg for 20 solvents

Table 1. Comparison of Kinetic and Equilibrium Solubility

compound using Beer's law. Precipitated solid material can be a mixture of meta-stable crystal forms, such as amorphous material and mixtures of different crystal forms. The crystal form of the precipitate is usually not characterized.

In an equilibrium solubility experiment, the solid material, which is usually in a stable crystal form, is placed in contact with the solution until it reaches equilibrium. An equilibrium solubility measurement is performed by adding buffer to solid material, which is in excess. The solution mixture is shaken gently for 24 to 72 hours to come as close to equilibrium as is practical. At the end of this period, the solution is filtered to remove excess solid and the concentration of the filtrate is determined using LC-UV or LC-MS. There are several commercial integrated systems for solubility measurement (Kerns, 2001).

Recently, in silico methods have become available to predict aqueous solubility (Jorgensen and Duffy, 2002). In silico methods are useful for evaluating screening libraries and for solubility predictions before compounds are made. Solubility is more difficult to predict accurately in silico than Log P or pKa. The two important factors that govern solubility are lipophilicity and melting point (Yalkowsky and Banerjee, 1992). Melting point is related to crystal packing energy, which is not well understood and hard to predict accurately. Reliable solubility data is largely dependent on experimental measurement, especially solubility-pH profile.

Applications of Solubility in Lead Optimization

Since most biological assays in drug discovery use DMSO stock solutions, kinetic solubility most closely mimics biological assay conditions in drug discovery, in terms of DMSO content, meta-stable crystal forms, target concentration, incubation time and throughput. Thus, kinetic solubility is most applicable for hit selection, lead selection and lead optimization. Kinetic solubility has many applications in drug discovery, such as: to provide an early alert for potential *in vivo* absorption issues, to help diagnose erratic bioassay or property assay results, to develop structure-solubility relationships, to select compounds for NMR-binding and X-ray co-crystallization studies. Formulation in drug discovery faces many challenges due to the limited amount of sample, short timelines, high dose, multiple animal species and multiple routes of administration. To assist in developing a compound formulation for *in vivo* dosing during drug discovery, early kinetic solubility information at different pHs can be used as input along with pKa and LogP, using a decision tree approach (Lee *et al.*, 2003).

Equilibrium solubility is very applicable for the later lead optimization and candidate selection phases. Equilibrium solubility provides detailed information to help diagnose *in vivo* results, aid formulation, IND filings and to help develop strategies for drug development. Equilibrium solubility of development candidates is typically determined in a wide range of solvents, including physio-logical buffers, formulary solvents and solvents that measure lipophilicity. An example of different solvents used for solubility determination of development candidates is shown in Table 2.

Physiological Buffers	Formulary Solvents	Lipophilicity
pH 1	Tween 80	Octanol
pH 4.5	PEG 200	Labrasol
pH 6.6	PEG 400	Cyclohexane
pH 7.4	Phosal 53 MCT	
pH 9	Phosal PG	
SGF	Benzyl Alcohol	
SIF	EtOH	
SIBLM	Corn Oil	
Plasma	2% Tween / 0.5% MC	

Table 2. Solvents Commonly Used for Solubility Determination of Development Candidates in Late-Stage Drug Discovery

It is commonly thought in the industry that high fat diet will increase solubility of lipophilic compounds and therefore enhance absorption. Food can affect oral bioavailability in many different ways (Zimmerman, *et al.*, 1999). This is because food can either increase or decrease oral bioavailabity by delaying gastric emptying (prolongs absorption), slowing input into intestine (prolongs absorption), stimulating bile salt secretions (increases solubility of lipophilic compounds), altering the pH of the gastro-intestinal fluid (changes solubility), increasing blood flow (improve sink condition, faster metabolism) and increasing competition for metabolic enzymes (slows down metabolism). Different buffers have been developed to simulate gastric fluid conditions in fasted and fed states (Dressman *et al.*, 1998). It has been found that solubility measured in gastric fluid gave better prediction for oral bioavailability than solubility measured in aqueous buffer alone, when permeability is considered (Aungst *et al.*, 2002).

A question that is commonly asked by discovery teams is: what is the minimum acceptable solubility for a development candidate? This relates to the dose. If all the administered drug is completely absorbed, the dose is the "maximum absorbable dose" (MAD). MAD is a function of solubility and permeability (Johnson and Swindell, 1996; Curatolo, 1998). Assuming that MAD is the same as the target dose, the minimal solubility for maximum human absorption can be calculated using Equation (1) (Johnson and Swindell, 1996; Curatolo, 1998).

Target Solubility (mg/mL) = 0.015 x Target Dose (mg) / Permeability (min⁻¹)
Equation (1)

Figure 1 shows the relationship between solubility, permeability and dose. For a compound with 1 mpk dose and moderate permeability, 60 μg/mL solubility is

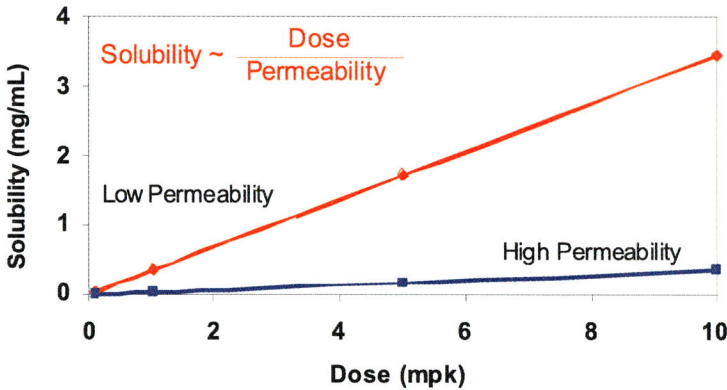

Figure 1. Correlation between Solubility, Permeability and Dose

the minimal acceptable solubility (Lipinski, 2000). However, if the compound is less potent, has a dose of 10 mpk and poor permeability, the minimum solubility needed is 2000 μg/mL, in order to achieve maximum absorption. On the other hand, if the compound is much more potent, with a dose of 0.1 mpk and high permeability, the minimum solubility needed is 1 μg/mL.

Lipinski has classified the solubility ranges (high is > 60 μg/mL, moderate is 10-60 μg/mL, low is < 10 μg/mL) to provide a general guideline for achieving acceptable human absorption for compounds with average potency and permeability. This classification might not be suitable for animal dosing and it is different than the solubility classification ranges in the Biopharmaceutics Classification Systems (BCS). For example, for a 1 mpk I.V. dose in rat with an ideal dosing volume of 1-5 mL/kg, the required concentration is 0.2 – 1 mg/mL. This is much higher than 60 μg/mL. Thus, for animal dosing, a "high" solubility classification for human might not be sufficient for preparing a dosing solution for rat. BCS is typically used for bio-waiver in drug development for *in vitro* and *in vivo* correlations. A "high" solubility requires that: 1) the dose divided by the solubility be less than or equal to 250 mL, and 2) 85% dissolution is achieved at pH 1-8 within 15 minutes. This is very different than the "high" solubility classification used as a guide in drug discovery.

Strategies on Improving Solubility

Structural Modifications to Increase Solubility

There is a pH gradient created throughout the length of the gastrointestinal tract, from acidic pH in the stomach to basic pH at the last portion of the small and large intestine (Dressman *et al.*, 1998). Solubility-pH profiles are very useful for ioniziable drugs. Solubility at different pHs is described by the Henderson-Hasselbalch equation (Equation 2 for acidic compounds), where S_{tot} is total solubility at a particular pH, and S_o is the intrinsic solubility of an acid in its neutral form. Intrinsic solubility is defined as solubility of the neutral species.

$$S_{tot} = S_o \left(1 + 10^{(pH-pKa)}\right)$$
Equation (2)

An example is shown in Figure 2, which illustrates the contributions of intrinsic solubility and pKa. Compound A and B have the same pKa, but a different intrinsic solubility (Figure 2a). Compound A is more soluble than Compound B through the entire pH range, due to higher intrinsic solubility. Ways to increase intrinsic solubility include introduction of polar functional groups, hydrogen bonds and reducing MW and size.

Compound C and D have the same intrinsic solubility, but a different pKa (Figure 2b). Compounds are much more soluble in their ionized state, suggesting that introduction of an ionization center is an effective way to increase solubility. Solubility increases exponentially with the difference in pH and pKa. Ways to increase solubility by introducing ionizable centers will be discussed in the next section.

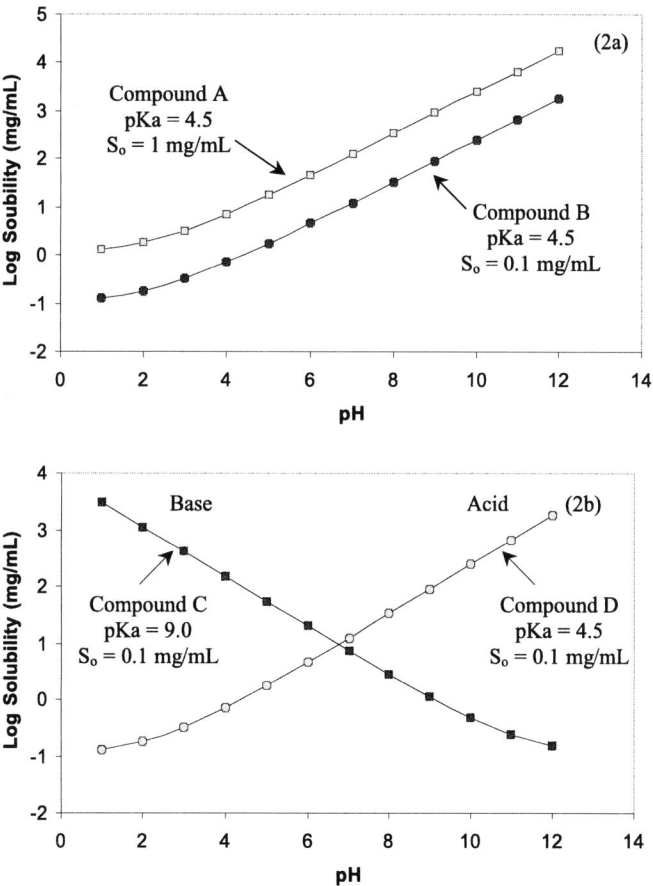

Figure 2. Solubility-pH profile. (2a) Compound A and B have the same pKa, but different intrinsic solubility. Compound A is more soluble than Compound B through the entire pH range, due to higher intrinsic solubility. (2b) Compound C and D have the same intrinsic solubility, but a different pKa. Compounds are more soluble in their ionization state.

Salt Form

Salt forms usually will not change the equilibrium solubility of an acid or a base in pH buffers, but will change the dissolution rate. Salts increase absorption by increasing the dissolution rate. Salts typically have a time window during which their concentration is higher than their equilibrium solubility. This effect increases absorption. This is due to super-saturation and slow precipitation. Any precipitate tends to be amorphous material, which has higher solubility than crystalline material. A classic example is para-amino salicylic acid (PAS) (Wan *et al.*, 1974). The absorption of the free acid is incomplete. Only 77 % is absorbed. The absorption of salts (Na^+, K^+ and Ca^+) reaches completion due to higher dissolution rate and slower precipitation. Therefore, salt form approaches can be applied to discovery compounds that contain ionizable groups, in order to enhance absorption.

Prodrug Approaches

Prodrug strategies to improve solubility are not very common, due to the substantial cost associated with prodrugs, including additional synthetic steps and complex development requirements. Nevertheless, there are some successful examples in the industry of prodrugs that improve solubility (Ettmayer *et al.*, 2004). For example, phenytoin has a solubility of 20-25 µg/mL. The parenteral I.M. formulation is problematic. The phosphate prodrug, Fosphenytoin, has a solubility of 142 mg/mL, which is a 4400-fold increase in solubility. It has been successfully marketed as Cerebyx™ (Stella, 1996).

Structure-Solubility Relationship

Through the years, many state-of-the-art and cutting-edge technologies have been developed to formulate insoluble compounds. In drug discovery, we would like to solve drug delivery problems 'with covalent bonds', as stated very nicely by William Curatolo (1998). Some of the practical approaches to improve solubility through 'covalent bonds' are described in the following sections.

Introduction of Basic Nitrogen

One of the most common approaches to increase solubility is to introduce ionizable centers, such as a basic nitrogen. Indinavir is a potent, orally active protease inhibitor. The early lead compound, L-685434, had good potency in enzyme and cell-base assays (Scheme 1). However, it was inactive orally, due to poor solubility, which made oral absorption nearly impossible. The compound was later modified by introduction of basic amine ionization centers into the molecule. At the same time, potency was maintained. The modified compound is much more soluble than L-685434 and the oral bioavailability in human is 60% (Panchagnula and Thomas, 2000; van de Waterbeemd *et al.*, 2001). This example

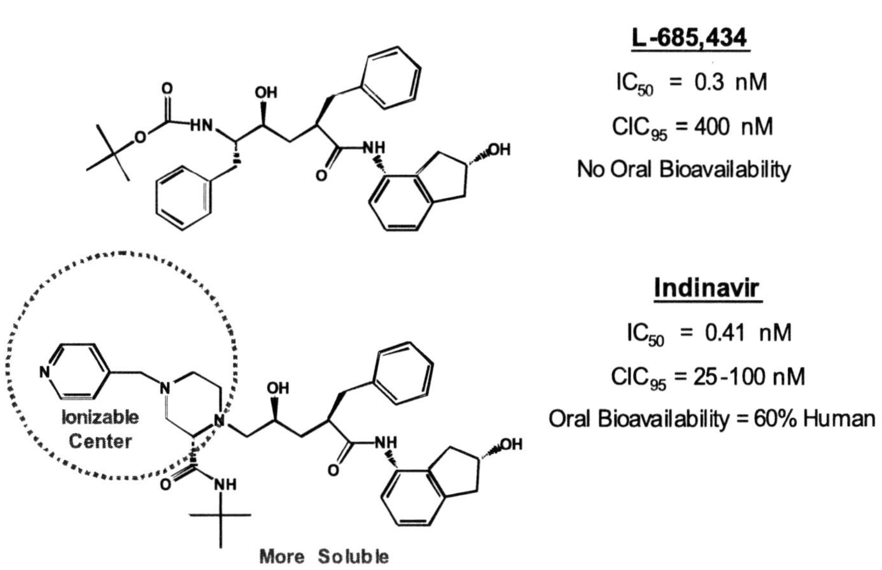
L-685,434
IC50 = 0.3 nM
CIC95 = 400 nM
No Oral Bioavailability
Indinavir
IC50 = 0.41 nM
CIC95 = 25-100 nM
Oral Bioavailability = 60% Human
Ionizable Center
More Soluble

Scheme 1. Indinavir: Improving Solubility of by Introduction of Basic Nitrogen (Panchagnula and Thomas, 2000; van de Waterbeemd *et al.*, 2001)

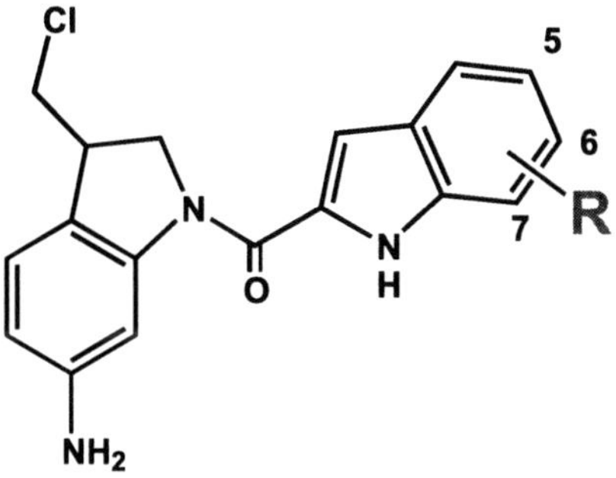

R	Solubility (μM)	IC_{50} (μM) AA8	UV4	EMT6	SKOV3
5,6,7-triOMe	32	0.35	0.055	0.27	0.63
5-OMe	23	0.31	0.047	0.23	0.67
5-$O(CH_2)_2NMe_2$	700	0.16	0.044	0.12	0.26
5-OMe, 6-$O(CH_2)_2NMe_2$	>1200	0.22	0.039	0.11	0.15
5-OMe, 7-$O(CH_2)_2NMe_2$	47	0.14	0.029	0.09	0.16

Scheme 2. Improving Solubility by Introduction of Basic Amines for a Series of Antitumor Agents (Milbank *et al.*, 1999)

showed that by improving properties, medicinal chemists can convert inactive compounds to highly successful drugs.

Scheme 2 shows a series of antitumor agents (Milbank *et al.*, 1999). The compounds with methoxyl substituents show good potency against a panel of tumor cell lines, but low solubility. The compounds were modified by introducing tertiary amines as ionizable centers. The solubility increased dramatically. At the same time, potency was maintained. It is interesting to note that the last two compounds in the table differ only on the position of the substituent (C6 vs. C7). The solubilities of the compounds are very different. This could potentially be due to the differences in crystal packing.

It is a common phenomenon that the most active compound *in vitro* is not necessarily the most active compound *in vivo*. The example Scheme 3 shows that the 1st compound was very potent *in vitro*, but was inactive *in vivo* due to poor solubility (Al-awar *et al.*, 2003). The 2nd compound was 5-fold less potent *in vitro*, but very soluble, due to the presence of the ionizable amines. The compound was very active *in vivo*. It is sometimes advantageous to improve properties at the expense of potency, especially when the compound series is very potent.

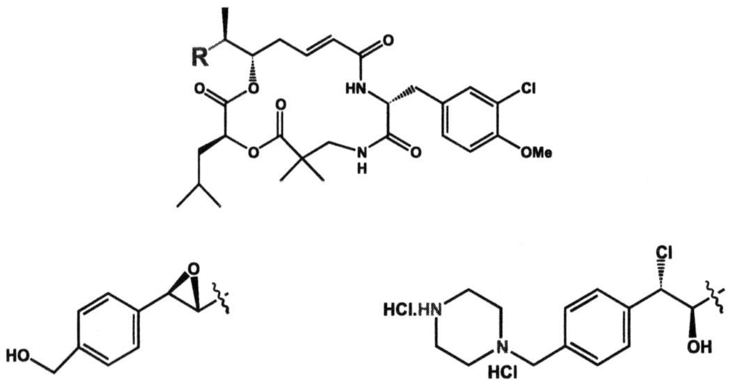

IC$_{50}$ = 0.004 nM, Low solublity

Weak activity *in vivo*

IC$_{50}$ = 0.021 nM, Soluble

Very active *in vivo*

Scheme 3. Introduction of Basic Nitrogen Improves Solubility and In Vivo Activity (Al-awar *et al.*, 2003)

Reduction of Crystal Packing Energy

Crystal packing is another important factor that governs solubility, in addition to lipophilicity. This is because compounds have to overcome the crystal packing force to dissolve in solution. Disruption of tight crystal packing can increase solubility. The example in Scheme 4 illustrates this strategy. By introducing an ethyl group in an area that is less critical for activity, it disrupted the π - stacking of the molecules and reducing crystal packing energy, as indicated by the lower melting point. The compound is much more soluble while retaining high potency (Fray *et al.*, 2001).

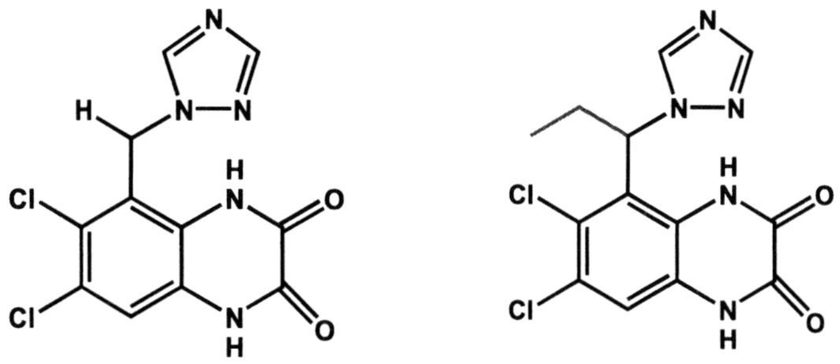

IC$_{50}$ = 25 nM
Sol. < 10 μg/mL

IC$_{50}$ = 4 nM
Sol. ~ 1 mg/mL

Scheme 4. Introduction of Ethyl Group Disrupted π-Stacking, Reduced Crystal Packing Energy and Improved Solubility (Fray *et al.*, 2001)

Permeability

Oral Absorption

Transport Mechanisms for Oral Absorption

There are several transport mechanisms across the gastrointestinal membrane. Most drugs are absorbed through passive diffusion across the lipid bilayer membrane of the epithelial cells into systemic circulation. The process is driven by concentration gradient. The PAMPA assay is designed to measure passive diffusion through a lipid membrane. Paracellular transport requires that the compounds go through the junctions between the cells. The junctions are quite small, 3-10 Å in diameter and negatively charged. The paracellullar pathway is usually limited to polar compounds with MW less than 200. There are also active processes, such as influx transport by amino acid or peptide transporters and efflux transport by Pgp or MRP. Substrates of influx transporters have special structural motifs such as sugars, amino acids and peptides. Efflux substrates are typically determined by using Caco-2 or MDR1-MDCKII assays. Endocytosis transports compounds in a vesicle. An example is the uptake of lipophilic vitamins.

Permeability Methodology

Since most drugs are absorbed by passive diffusion. PAMPA has received a lot of attention in the industry as a screening tool for permeability in drug discovery (Kansy *et al.*, 1998; Wohnsland and Faller, 2001; Avdeef, 2001; Sugano *et al.*, 2001; Zhu *et al.*, 2002; Hwang *et al.*, 2003; Kerns *et al.*, 2004). Here is how the assay

Comparison	PAMPA	Caco-2
Membrane	Phospholipid	Cell Monolayer
Mechanisms	Passive	Passive, Influx, Efflux, Metabolism
Throughput	500 / week	30 / week
Cost	< $1 / sample	~ $30 / sample
Manpower	0.35 FTE	2 FTE

Table 3. Comparison of PAMPA and Caco-2 Assay

works. Compounds are diluted with pH buffer (e.g., pH 7.4) from DMSO stock solution and added to the donor wells. The acceptor is a filter plate, coated with lipid (PC in dodecane) and filled with buffer (pH 7.4). The acceptor plate is placed carefully on the donor plate to form the PAMPA sandwich. Compounds will diffuse through the lipid membrane and enter the acceptor. After a certain period of time, the acceptor plate is removed from the donor plate. The concentration in both the acceptor and the donor is determined using a UV plate reader. From these concentrations the effective permeability (P_e) is derived. There are several variations of the PAMPA assay being used in the industry, including different lipid compositions, different filter membranes and thickness, different buffer pHs, acceptor sink conditions, sink composition, and different quantitation methods (e.g., UV plate reader, LC-UV, LC-MS-MS). The variations are intended to mimic *in vivo* conditions to produce higher correlations. For example, sink conditions trap molecules on the acceptor side, mimicking *in vivo* trapping by protein binding and blood flow away from the intestine.

Before PAMPA came along, the Caco-2 assay was commonly used in the industry for permeability measurement. The comparison of PAMPA and Caco-2 is shown in Table 3. The membrane in PAMPA is composed of phospholipid in alkane, and Caco-2 is composed of a Caco-2 cell monolayer. The transport mechanism of PAMPA is passive diffusion. Caco-2 is a multiple mechanism assay: passive diffusion, active influx and efflux. Compounds can also be metabolized in Caco-2. The throughput of PAMPA is approximately 500 compounds / week and Caco-2 is approximately 30 compounds / week. The cost of PAMPA is less than $1 / sample and Caco-2 is about $30 / sample. It takes 0.35 FTE to run PAMPA assay, but 2 FTE to run Caco-2 assay. Thus, PAMPA is more applicable for early drug discovery and Caco-2 is more applicable for late-stages of drug discovery and development. The combined use of the two assays can help diagnose transport mechanisms. It has been reported that PAMPA has good correlation with cell-based assays, such as Caco-2 and MDCK, for compounds that are passively absorbed (Kerns *et al.*, 2004). For compounds that are actively influxed, Caco-2 gives higher permeability relative to PAMPA. For compounds that are effluxed, Caco-2 or MDR1-MDCKII gives comparatively lower permeability than PAMPA.

Structure-Permeability Relationship

Increasing lipophilicity and decreasing H-bonds are two major approaches to improve permeability. Scheme 5 shows an example from a discovery project. The substituents are for a common core structure. The compounds with methyl or chlorine substituents have high PAMPA permeability, the compounds with methoxyl or fluorine atoms showed low permeability. This is consistent with an increase in permeability that results from a decrease in H-bonding and polarity.

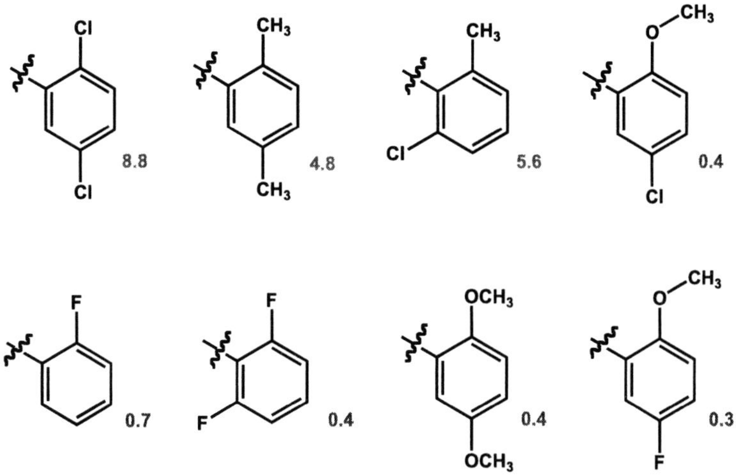

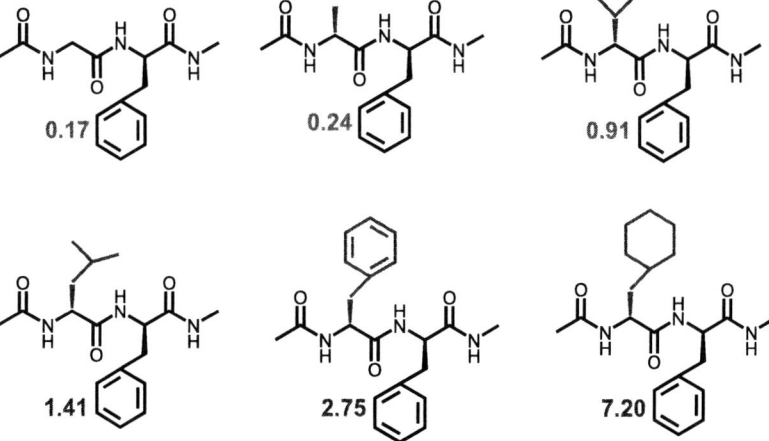

Scheme 5. Examples of Increasing Permeability by Decreasing H-Bonds and Polarity. PAMPA Permeability is in P_e x10^{-6} cm/s.

Scheme 6 shows the effect of lipophilicity on Caco-2 permeability for a series of phenylalanine dipeptides. As the substituents change through the progression H, methyl, i-propanyl, i-butyl, benzyl and cyclohexanylmethyl groups, the lipophilicity increases and results in increasing permeability (Goodwin *et al.*, 2001).

Scheme 6. Effect of lipophilicity on Caco-2 Permeability of Phenylalanine Dipeptide Series. Permeability values shown are P_{eff} (apical to basolateral) x 10^{-6} cm/s (Goodwin *et al.*, 2001)

Scheme 7 shows the effect of different substituents on permeability for benzyl imidazole and benzyl pyrazole core structures. Compounds with CN substitution are more permeable than NH_2 or $CONH_2$. Carboxylic acids are least permeable (Fichert, *et al.*, 2003).

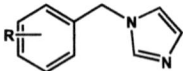

R	P_{Caco-2} X 10^6 (cm/sec)
H	68
m-CN	67
m-CONH$_2$	6.9
p-CH$_2$COOH	0.71
p-CO$_2$H	0.67
m-CO$_2$H	0.65

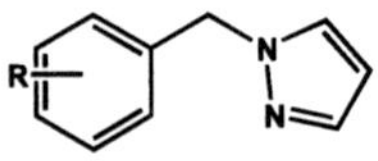

R	P_{Caco-2} X 10^6 (cm/sec)
m-CN	72
m-CONH$_2$	44
m-CH$_2$NH$_2$	28
p-CO$_2$H	3.7
p-CH$_2$CO$_2$H	2.9
m-CO$_2$H	2.9

Permeability: CN > NH$_2$ ~ CONH$_2$ > COOH

Scheme 7. Effects of Different Substituents of Caco-2 Permeability (Fichert *et al.*, 2003)

Enalkiren is a first generation of Renin inhibitor (Scheme 8). It is dosed in an I.V. formulation. The compound has poor oral bioavailability due to poor permeability. It was modified later by reducing H-bonds and replacing the amide group. This, not only improved permeability, but also the metabolic stability of the compound against various enzymes. The oral bioavailability was 53% in dog (Panchagnula and Thomas, 2000).

Scheme 9 shows two Factor Xa inhibitors. They have very similar potency and metabolic profile, but their oral bioavailability is 4-fold different. The tertiary amine was more permeable in the Caco-2 assay, due to fewer H-bonds than the secondary amine, which resulted in higher oral bioavailability (Quan *et al.*, 2004).

Blood-Brain Barrier

Blood Brain Barrier and Transport Mechanisms

CNS is the second largest therapeutic area, right behind cardiovascular diseases (IMS Health, 2005). Five out of the top ten causes for disability are due to CNS disorders. Stroke is the 3rd leading cause of death. Alzheimer's disease affects 15 million people in US alone and it is the 2nd most expensive disease. However, many of the brain diseases still do not have adequate treatment (Pardridge, 2001). A major challenge for CNS therapy is the blood brain barrier (BBB). It has been estimated that only 2% of the CNS discovery compounds can cross the BBB and potentially reach the therapeutic targets.

Enalkiren

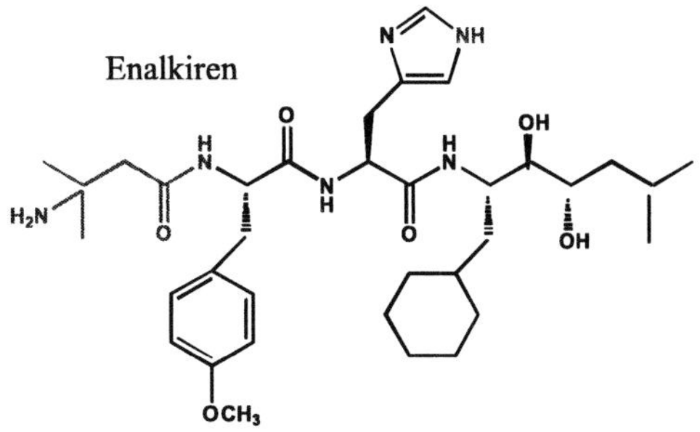

- I.V. dosage form
- No oral bioavailability

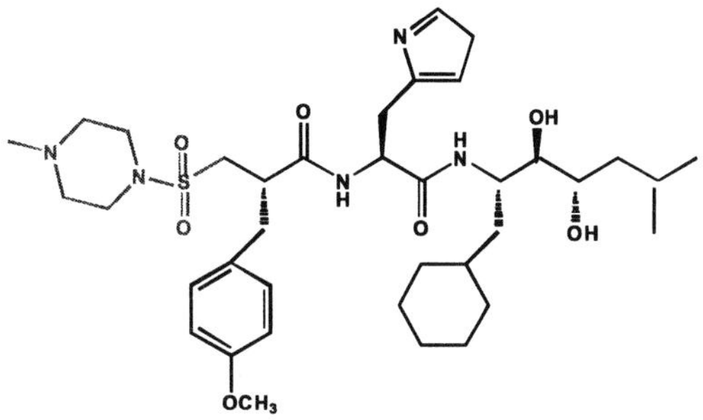

- Reduce H-bonds
- Improve stability
- 53% oral bioavailability (dog)

Scheme 8. For this Renin Inhibitor, Reduction of H-bonds Increased Permeability and Stability, Resulting in Increased Oral Bioavailability (Panchagnula and Thomas, 2000)

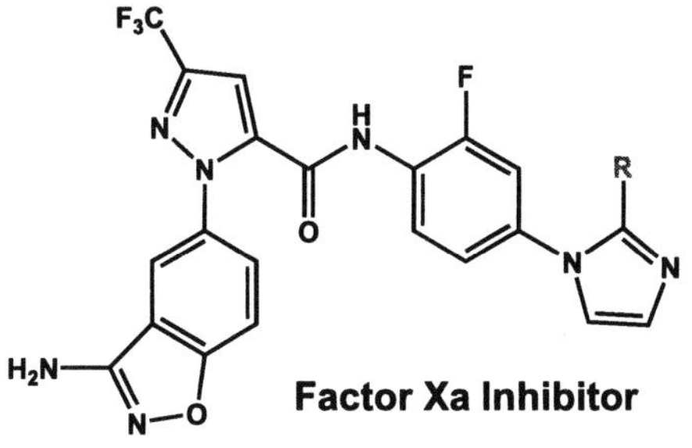

Factor Xa Inhibitor

R	FXa K_i (nM)	Caco-2 P_{app} ($\times 10^{-6}$ cm/s)	CL (L/h/Kg)	$T_{1/2}$ (h)	Vdss (L/Kg)	F (%)
CH_2NHMe	0.12	0.2	1.1	3.7	4.6	24
CH_2NMe_2	0.19	5.6	1.1	3.4	5.3	84

Scheme 9. Effect of Permeability on Oral Bioavailability for Factor Xa Inhibitor (Quan *et al.*, 2004)

The BBB is the membrane that separates the blood from the interstitial fluids of the brain. There are 400 miles of blood capillaries in the brain. The BBB consists of brain endothelial cells that line the capillaries. They have very tight intercellular junctions and strong Pgp efflux activity. The function of the BBB is an interplay among four different cell types: the endoththelial cells, astrocytes, pericytes and neurons. In addition to the BBB, there is a blood-CSF barrier. The surface area of the BBB is 5000 times larger than blood-CSF barrier. The CSF flow through the arachnoid villi back to the blood is too fast to allow any significant absorption into the inner area of the brain where most of the therapeutic targets are located. Therefore, the BBB is the major barrier for CNS penetration.

The BBB has many of the transport mechanisms discussed above for oral absorption. Most CNS drugs used in the clinic pass the BBB by passive diffusion. The BBB also exhibits active processes: influx and efflux transport. There are limited pinocytosis and paracellular processes. Determination of BBB penetration is of great importance, not only for CNS drugs, but also for non-CNS therapeutic targets, where BBB penetration might cause unwanted side effects.

Methodology for BBB Penetration

There are several common approaches to predict BBB penetration, including rules, in silico prediction, physicochemical methods, cell-based models and *in vivo* assays. Rules are very effective for medicinal chemists. Table 4 shows Partridge's Rule of 2 and Clark's rules for predicting BBB penetration. Computational methods have gone a long way to predict BBB penetration. Both classification and QSAR models have good accuracy (Clark, 2001; Lobell *et al.*, 2003). Computational methods are particularly useful to predict BBB penetration prior to synthesis and to guide structural modifications. Many cell-based *in vitro* BBB and blood-CSF barrier (BCSFB) models with different animal species have been developed to predict penetration. These cell lines include MDR1-MDCKII, Caco-2, BCEC, LLC-PK1, TM-BBB, and TR-BBB. The limitations of the cell-based assays are that many of the transporters are down regulated and variable from batch-to-batch and passage-to-passage. Furthermore, transporters are species dependent. Cell-based assays are particularly useful to diagnose Pgp efflux transport (Kerns *et al.*, 2004), which plays a very important role in protecting the brain and is, at the same time, a major challenge for CNS drug candidates.

Pardridge's Rule of 2 (Pardridge, 1995)	Clark's Rules (Clark, 2001)
Total H-bonds < 8-10 MW < 400-500	$N+O \leq 5$ $Clog P - (N+O) > 0$ $PSA \leq 60\text{-}70$ $MW < 450$ $Log D = 1\text{-}3$

Table 4. Rule-Based Methods to Enhance BBB Penetration

At Wyeth Research, we have developed a high throughput PAMPA-BBB assay (Di *et al.*, 2003). The assay predicts a compound's potential for BBB penetration through passive diffusion. Passive diffusion is the major driving force to move the compounds into the brain, but there are other processes trying to prevent or slow down the compounds from entering the brain, such as Pgp efflux, protein binding and metabolism (Figure 3). A useful screening strategy is to use PAMPA-BBB for 1st-tier screening of large numbers of compounds and then validate results with *in vivo* studies of selected compounds. If there is a disconnect between the two assays, secondary assays can be used to diagnose transport mechanisms.

Pgp Efflux

Metabolism   **Protein Binding**

BBB

Passive Diffusion

Figure 3. Complex Mechanism *In Vivo* for BBB Penetration

Structure-BBB Penetration Relationship

CNS drugs tend to be basic and contain basic nitrogens. Scheme 10 shows two compounds having different BBB penetration (Clark, 2001). Trifluoroperazine has a basic pKa of 7.8. It is CNS+. Indomethacin has an acidic pKa of 4.2. It is CNS-. One explanation is that the BBB is negatively charged. Acidic compounds will be negatively charged at pH 7.4 and be repulsed by the BBB. Basic amines will be positively charged at pH 7.4. The charged species will be neutralized by the negatively charged membrane, so that they can cross the BBB. Hydrogen bonds decrease the ability of a molecule to cross the BBB.

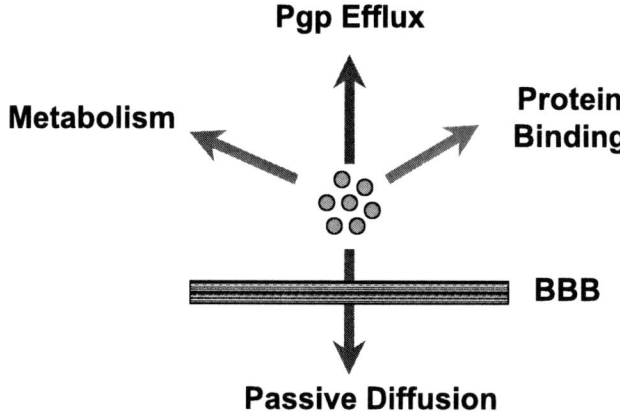

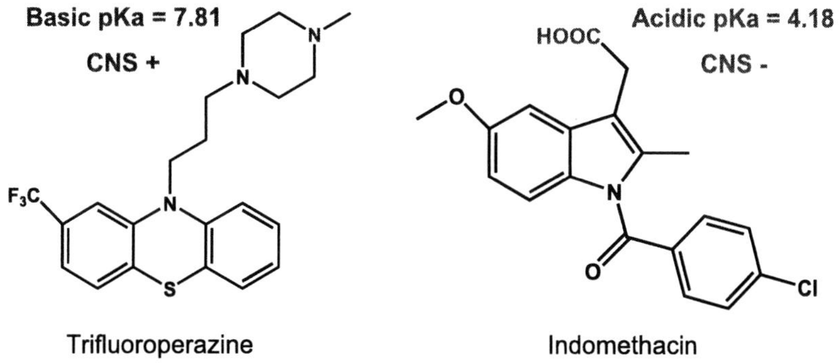

Basic pKa = 7.81
CNS +

Acidic pKa = 4.18
CNS -

Trifluoroperazine   Indomethacin

Scheme 10. CNS Drugs Tend to be Basic (Clark, 2001)

Scheme 11 shows the correlation between *in vivo* brain permeability and H-bonds. Permeability decreased with increasing number of H-bonds for a series of steroids (Pardridge, 1995). BBB penetration also increases with increase in lipophilicity.

Scheme 12 shows how replacement of one hydroxyl group of morphine with a methoxyl group to make codeine increased BBB penetration 10 fold. When both hydroxyl groups were replaced by acetates to make heroin, the BBB penetration increased 100 fold (Pardridge, 1995). This example suggested that BBB penetration improved with decreasing H-bonds and increasing lipophilicity.

Utilization of intra-molecular H-bonding is a very effective way to increase CNS penetration. Scheme 13 shows that, when the first compound was modified by introducing a tertiary amine and an intra-molecular H-bond, not only did the solubility increase dramatically while maintaining potency, but also , more remarkably, the brain to plasma (B/P) ratio increased 10-fold (Ashwood *et al.*, 2001).

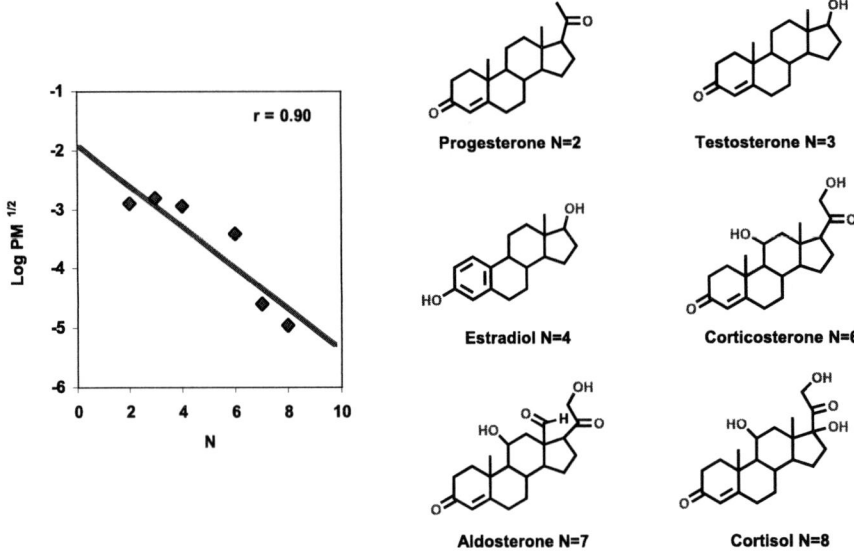

Scheme 11. Effects of H-Bonding on BBB Penetration (Pardridge, 1995)

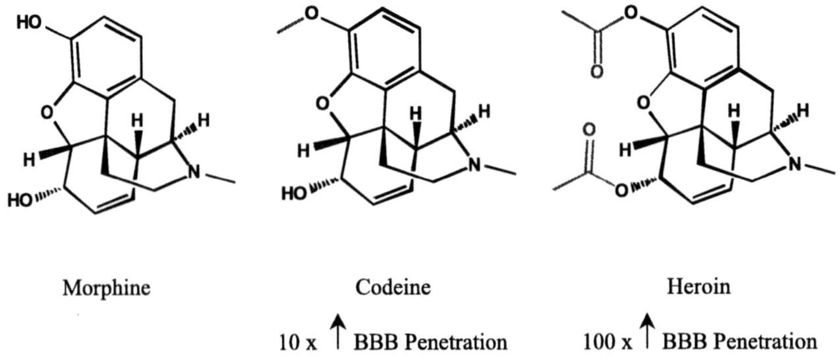

Scheme 12. Effect of Lipophilicity on BBB Penetration (Pardridge, 1995)

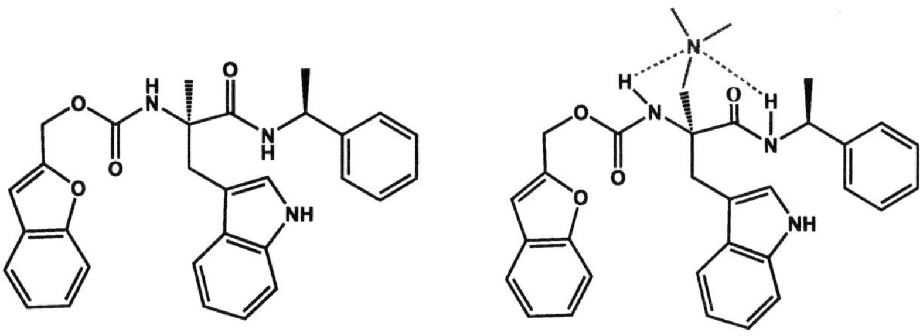

IC$_{50}$ = 5.9 nM

Solubility < 2 µg/mL

Vehicle = 0.76 mg/mL

B/P = 0.6

IC$_{50}$ = 5.5 nM

Solubility = 0.7 mg/mL

Vehicle = 10 mg/mL

B/P = 6.0

Scheme 13. Utilization of Intra-molecular H-bond to Increase CNS Penetration (Ashwood *et al.*,2001)

Cell-based Assays

Permeability plays an important role for cell-based activity assays. If a compound can not permeate through the lipid membrane and enter the cells, it will not be able to interact with the targets inside the cells. Table 5 shows two series of compounds for a particular target. The first series is very potent and the second series have moderate potency in the enzyme assay. However, the first series, with better potency, was inactive in the cell-based assay, while the second series, with weaker potency, was active. Further studies showed that the first series had low permeability in the PAMPA assay and the compounds were Pgp substrates in the Caco-2 assay. The second series showed high PAMPA permeability and no Pgp substrate specificity. Thus, because of the good permeability of the second series, they were much more active in the cell-based assay, even through the activity was weaker in the enzyme assay.

In Scheme 14, Compound A is a dicarboxylic acid and has poor permeability as indicated by Caco-2 data (< 1 x 10^{-7} cm/s) (Liljebris *et al.*, 2002). A bioisoteric replacement of one of the carboxylic groups with tetrazole improved permeability of the compound, while maintaining the same potency. Even through the permeability of the compound is still low (Caco-2 P$_e$ = 1.9 x 10^{-7} cm/s), it was able

Assays	Series I	Series II
Enzyme Assay	Potent	Moderate
Cell-Based Assay	Inactive	Active
PAMPA Permeability	Low	High
Pgp Efflux	Yes	No

Table 5. Correlation Between Permeability and Cell-Based Activity

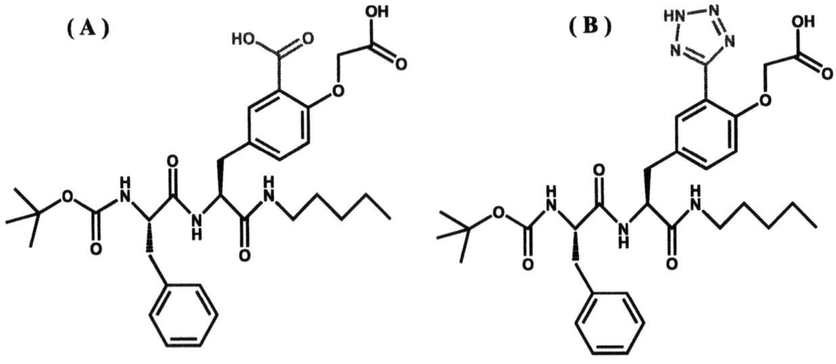

(A)

K_i (PTP1B)= 2 μM
Caco-2 < 1 x 10^{-7} cm/s

(B)

K_i (PTP1B)= 2 μM
Caco-2 = 1.9 x 10^{-7} cm/s
Positive Cellular Activity

Scheme 14. Bioisosteric Replacement of Carboxylic Acid with Tetrazole to Improve Permeability (Liljebris *et al.*, 2002)

to penetrate cell membranes better than Compound A and to show cellular activity.

The compound in Scheme 15 is a potent and selective PTP1b inhibitor (Andersen *et al.*, 2002). The compound has acceptable oral bioavailability, despite the polar dicarboxylic acid functional groups, zwitterions at physiological pHs and low permeability in the MDCK assay. However, disappointingly, the compound was inactive in insulin-stimulated 2-deoxyglucose (2-DOG) uptake into C2C12 cells due to poor cell membrane permeability. The diethyl ester prodrug of the compound has high permeability in the MDCK assay. The insulin-stimulated 2-DOG uptake into C2C12 cells of the di-ester prodrug was 70% of maximum insulin response (Andersen *et al.*, 2002).

These examples demonstrate that good permeability is essential in order to achieve activity in cell-based assays.

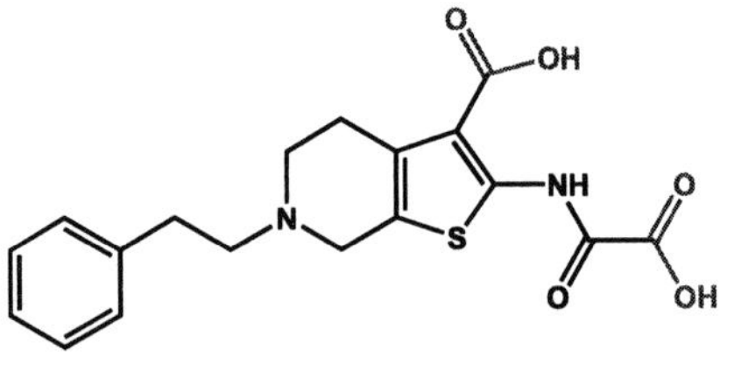

	Diacids	Di-Ethyl Ester Prodrug
In vitro (PTP1B)	Potent & Selective	
Oral Bioavailability (Rat)	13 %	Not Determined
Permeability (MDCK)	Low	High
2-DOG Uptake in C2C12 Cell	Inactive	70%

Scheme 15. Permeability Effects Activity in Cell-Based Assays (Andersen *et al.*, 2002)

Conclusions

Physicochemical properties are fundamental properties to achieve optimal oral bioavailability, reproducible Discovery assay results, BBB penetration and activity in cell-based assays. Table 6 summaries approaches for structural modifications to optimize drug-like properties.

Property	Modification
Solubility	Add ionizable center Increase H-bonds and polarity Decrease lipophilicity Reduce crystal packing
Permeability	Increase lipophilicity Reduce hydrogen bonding Reduce polarity Prodrug approaches
BBB	Introduce basic amines Reduce hydrogen bonding Increase lipophilicity Introduce intra-molecular H-bonding Prodrug approaches

Table 6. Structural Modifications to Optimize Properties

The molecular properties that govern solubility and permeability are: H-bonding capacity, size/MW, lipophilicity and ionization/charge (van de Waterbeemd , 1998). All these properties are inter-related. Changing one can affect several others. For example, an increase in H-bonding capacity and ionization will increase solubility. On the other hand, this will decrease permeability. Increasing lipophilicity and size, to some extent, will increase permeability. However, this will decrease solubility. For optimal oral absorption, the key is to reach a balance between the different physiochemical properties.

The difference in permeability between a highly permeable compound and a poorly permeable compound ranges 50 fold. The difference between a highly soluble compound and a poorly soluble compound can be 1 million fold. If a structural modification increases solubility 1000 fold, but decreases permeability by 10 fold, a 100 fold increase in absorption will be gained (Curatolo, 1998).

A drug discovery program that is focused on activity optimization will lead to a good target ligand. An activity- and property-focused approach is the path for successful drugs.

Acknowledgements

The authors thank Guy Carter and Magid Abou-Gharbia for their support, encouragement, and leadership; thank the pharmaceutical profiling team for their contributions, especially Susan Petusky and Susan Li.

References

Al-awar RS, Ray JE, Schultz RM, Andis SL, Kennedy JH, Moore RE, Golakoti T, Subbaraju GV, Corbett TH. A Convergent Approach to Cryptophycin 52 Analogues: Synthesis and Biological Evaluation of a Novel Series of Fragment A Epoxides and Chlorohydrins. *J Med Chem* 2003; 46:2985 – 3007

Andersen HS, Olsen OH, Iversen LF, S rensen ALP, Mortensen SB, Christensen MS, Branner S, Hansen TK, Lau JF, Jeppesen L, Moran EJ, *et al.* Discovery and SAR of a Novel Selective and Orally Bioavailable Nonpeptide Classical Competitive Inhibitor Class of Protein-Tyrosine Phosphatase 1B. *J Med Chem* 2002; 45:4443 - 4459

Ashwood VA, Field MJ, Horwell DC, Julien-Larose C, Lewthwaite RA, McCleary S, Pritchard MC, Raphy J, Singh L. Utilization of an Intramolecular Hydrogen Bond To Increase the CNS Penetration of an NK1 Receptor Antagonist. *J Med Chem* 2001; 44:2276-2285

Aungst BJ, Nguyen NH, Taylor NJ, Bindra DS. Formulation and Food Effects on the Oral Absorption of a Poorly Water Soluble, Highly Permeable Antiretroviral Agent. *J Pharm Sci* 2002; 91:1390-1395

Avdeef A. Physicochemical Profiling (Solubility, Permeability and Charge state). *Curr Topics Med Chem* 2001; 1:277-351

Clark DE. In Silico Prediction of Blood-Brain Barrier Permeation. *Drug Discovery Today* 2001; 8:927-933

Curatolo W. Physical Chemical Properties of Oral Drug Candidates in the Discovery and Exploratory Development Settings. Pharm *Sci Tech Today* 1998; 1: 387-393

Di L, Kerns EH. Profiling Drug-like Properties in Discovery Research. *Curr Opinion in Chem Biology* 2003; 7: 402-408

Di L, Kerns EH, Fan K, McConnell OJ, Carter G: High Throughput Artificial Membrane Permeability Assay for Blood-Brain Barrier. *Eur J Med Chem* 2003; 38:223-232

Dressman JB, Amidon GL, Reppas C, Shah VP. Dissolution Testing as a Prognostic Tool for Oral Drug Absorption: Immediate Release Dosage Forms. *Pharm Res* 1998; 15:11-22

Ettmayer P, Amidon GL, Clemant B. Testa B. Lessons Learned from Marketed and Investigational Prodrugs. *J Med Chem* 2004; 47:2393-2404

Fichert T, Yazdanian M, Proudfoot JR. A Structure-Permeability Study of Small Drug-like Molecules. *Bioorg Med Chem Lett* 2003; 13:719-722

Fray MJ, Bull DJ, Carr CL, Gautier ECL, Mowbray CE, Stobie A. Structure-Activity Relationships of 1,4-Dihydro-(1H,4H)-quinoxaline-2,3-diones as N-Methyl-D-aspartate (Glycine Site) Receptor Antagonists. 1. Heterocyclic Substituted 5-Alkyl Derivatives. *J Med Chem* 2001; 44:1951 - 1962

Goodwin JT, Conradi RA, Ho MFH, Burton PS. Physicochemical Determinants of Passive Membrane Permeability: Role of Solute Hydrogen-Bonding Potential and Volume. *J Med Chem* 2001; 44:3721-3729

Hwang KK, Martin NE, Jiang L, Zhu C. Permeation Prediction of M100240 Using the Parallel Artificial Membrane Permeability Assay. *J Pharmacy Pharmaceutical Sci* 2003; 6:315-320

IMS Health. Drug Monitor. http://www.ims-global.com/ (Accessed Jan. 2005)

Johnson KC, Swindell AC. Guidance in the Setting of Drug Particle Size Specifications to Minimize Variability in Absorption. *Pharm Res* 1996; 13:1795-1798

Jorgensen WL, Duffy EM. Prediction of Drug Solubility from Structure. *Adv Drug Del Rev* 2002; 54:355-366

Kansy M, Senner F, Gubernator K. Physicochemical High Throughput Screening: Parallel Artificial Membrane Permeation Assay in the Description of Passive Absorption Processes. *J Med Chem* 1998; 41:1007-1010

Kerns EH. High Throughput Physicochemical Profiling for Drug Discovery. *J Pharm Sci* 2001; 90:1838-1858.

Kerns EH, Di L. Pharmaceutical Profiling in Drug Discovery. *Drug Discovery Today* 2003; 8:316-323

Kerns EH, Di L, Petusky S, Farris M, Ley R, Jupp P. Combined application of parallel artificial membrane permeability assay and Caco-2 permeability assays in drug discovery. *J Pharm Sci* 2004, 93:1440-1453

Lee YC, Zocharski PD, Samas B. An Intravenous Formulation Decision Tree for Discovery Compound Formulation Development. *Int J Pharm* 2003; 253:111-119

Liljebris C, Larsen SD, Ogg D, Palazuk BJ, Bleasdale JE. Investigation of Potential Bioisosteric Replacements for the Carboxyl Groups of Peptidomimetic Inhibitors of Protein Tyrosine Phosphatase 1B: Identification of a Tetrazole-Containing Inhibitor with Cellular Activity. *J Med Chem* 2002; 45: 1785 - 1798

Lipinski CA. Drug-like Properties and the Causes of Poor Solubility and Poor Permeability. *J Pharm Tox Methods* 2000; 44:235-249

Lobell M, Molnár L, Keserü GM. Recent Advances in the Prediction of Blood-Brain Partitioning from Molecular Structure. *J Pharm Sci* 2003; 92:360-370

Milbank JBJ, Tercel M, Atwell GJ, Wilson WR, Hogg A, Denny WA. Synthesis of 1-Substituted 3-(Chloromethyl)-6-aminoindoline (6-Amino-seco-CI) DNA Minor Groove Alkylating Agents and Structure-Activity Relationships for Their Cytotoxicity. *J Med Chem* 1999; 42:649 - 658

Panchagnula R, Thomas NS. Biopharmaceutics and Pharmacokinetics in Drug Research. *Int J Pharm* 2000; 201:131-150

Pardridge WM. Transport of Small Molecules Through the Blood-Brain Barrier: Biology and Methodology. *Adv Drug Del Rev* 1995; 15:5-36

Pardridge WM. Crossing the blood-brain barrier: are we getting it right? *Drug Discovery Today* 2001; 6:1-2

Smith DA. High-throughput Screening - Brain Versus Brawn. Ernst Schering *Research Foundation Workshop* 2002; 37:203-212

Quan ML, Lam PYS, Han Q, Pinto DJP, He MY, Li R, Ellis CD, Clark CG, Teleha CA, Sun JH, *et al*. Discovery of 1-(3'-Aminobenzisoxazol-5'-yl)-3-trifluoromethyl-N-[2-fluoro-4- [(2'-dimethylaminomethyl)imidazol-1-yl]phenyl]-1H-pyrazole-5-carboxyamide Hydrochloride (Razaxaban), a Highly Potent, Selective, and Orally Bioavailable Factor Xa Inhibitor. *J Med Chem* 2004; ASAP Article

Stella VJ, A Case for Prodrugs: Fosphenytoin. *Adv Drug Del Rev* 1996; 19:311-330

Sugano K, Hamada H, Machida M, Ushio H, Saitoh K, Terada K. Optimized Conditions of Bio-mimetic Artificial Membrane Permeability Assay. *Int J Pharm* 2001; 228:181-188

van de Waterbeemd H. The Fundamental Variables of the Biopharmaceutics Classification System (BCS): a Commentary. *Eur J Pharm Sci* 1998; 7:1-3

van de Waterbeemd H, Smith DA, Beaumont K, Walker DK. Property-Based Design: Optimization of Drug Absorption and Pharmacokinetics. *J Med Chem* 2001; 44:1313 - 1333

Wan SH, Pentikainen PJ, Azarnoff DL. Bioavailability of Aminosalicylic Acid and its Various Salts in Humans. III. Absorption from Tablets. *J Pharm Sci* 1974; 63:708-11

Ward PD, Tippin TK, Thakker DR. Enhancing Paracellular Permeability by Modulating Epithelial Tight Junctions. *Pharm Sci Tech Today* 2000; 3: 346-358

Wohnsland F, Faller B. High-Throughput Permeability pH Profile and High-Throughput Alkane/Water Log P with Artificial Membranes. *J Med Chem* 2001; 44:923-930

Yalkowsky SH, Banerjee S. Aqueous Solubility: Methods of Estimation for Organic Compounds. New York, NY: Marcel Dekker, Inc; 1992.

Zhu C, Jiang L, Chen TM, Hwang KK. A Comparative Study of Artificial Membrane Permeability Assay for High Throughput Profiling of Drug Absorption Potential. *Eur J Med Chem* 2002; 37: 399-407

Zimmerman JJ, Ferron GM, Lim HK, Parker V. The Effect of a High-Fat Meal on the Oral Bioavailability of the Immunosuppressant Sirolimus (Rapamycin). *J Clin Pharmacol* 1999; 39:1155-1161

9

Computational Models Supporting Lead Optimization in Drug Discovery

**Philip S. Burton[1], Italo Poggesi[2],
Massimiliano Germani[2]
and Jay T. Goodwin[1]**

[1]ADMETRx, Inc.
1477 Campus Drive, Suite 600
Kalamazoo, MI 49008, USA

[2]Pharmacokinetics, Dynamics and Metabolism
Nerviano Medical Sciences
Milan, Italy

Table of Contents

Abbreviations

ADME ....absorption distribution metabolism excretion

AUC..area under the concentration-time curve

CAT ....compartmentalized absorption and transit

CYP ....cytochrome P450

E_T ....extraction ratio

$f_{u,p}$..fraction unbound in plasma

GFR...glomerular filtration rate

NPSA..non-polar surface area

PB-PK...physiology-based pharmacokinetic

PK ....pharmacokinetic

$P_{T:P}$ ....blood to plasma partition coefficient

PSA ....polar surface area

Q_T ....blood flow

RMSPE...root mean squared prediction error

SPR ....structure-property relationships

Keywords:

ADME, Biopharmaceutics, Computational, In Silico, Modeling, Physiology-based, Pharmacokinetic, PB-PK, Prediction, Simulation, Structure-property relationships

Introduction

Design of successful drug development candidates requires balancing a number of different characteristics simultaneously including intrinsic activity, biopharmaceutical properties, synthesis, stability, and many others. Independently, each of these can be considered a barrier to drug performance or development success (Kerns and Di, 2003). Among the most important of these processes determining *in vivo* performance are absorption, distribution, metabolism and excretion, collectively referred to as ADME. The structure and physicochemical characteristics of the drug are important determinants of these processes, as are the characteristics of the physiological mechanisms. Further complicating the issue is the interrelationship of many of these processes, frequently in antagonistic ways. Increasing solute lipophilicity, for example, can decrease aqueous solubility, which frequently compromises oral absorption. Also, it can increase metabolic clearance, thus making difficult sustaining the pharmacologically relevant systemic exposure. In contrast, permeability, in many cases, increases with increasing lipophilicity, favoring absorption (Conradi *et al.*, 1996; Hansch *et al.*, 2004). The actual result will be determined by the relative contributions of these two competing phenomena.

Permeability is also an important determinant of distribution, metabolism and excretion. Given these multiple dependencies upon specific drug structural characteristics, it can be seen that simultaneously optimizing all of these processes can present a formidable challenge.

Occasionally, one specific, clearly dominant problem, can be identified in a particular drug discovery program. In this case, focusing on the specific property can result in successful solution of the problem and identification of a promising drug candidate. The recent interest in development of computational structure property relationships has resulted in the discovery of promising tools to aid in these problem solving and property optimization objectives (Ekins *et al.*, 2000; Lombardo *et al.*, 2003; Wilson *et al.*, 2003).

More generally, the interrelationship of multiple solute properties must be considered simultaneously in order to achieve the desired outcome. A simple example of this is the interrelationship of solute solubility and permeability in determining oral absorption potential (Hilgers *et al.*, 2003). Briefly, bi-directional Caco-2 cell permeability data and aqueous solubility data were measured for a series of relatively homologous antimicrobial agents at Pharmacia. All compounds were dosed both intravenously and orally in rats in order to calculate total clearance and oral bioavailability. The clearance data supported the expectation that these compounds had minimal first pass metabolism such that bioavailability was directly related to the fraction of solute absorbed (Hilgers *et al.*, 2003). In attempting to predict absorption of these compounds, it was found that no significant correlation existed between bioavailability (fraction absorbed) and either solubility or permeability alone.

While high permeability solutes did seem to be well absorbed, so were many of the low permeability solutes. What was common among these poorly permeable, well absorbed compounds was high aqueous solubility, suggesting that this property may help to compensate for the poor *in vitro* permeability.

One simple model for interrelating solubility and permeability quantitative data to predict absorption is the Maximum Absorbable Dose (MAD) model (Johnson and Swindell, 1996; Curatolo, 1998). MAD is a hypothetical value that estimates the amount of an infinite dose that could be absorbed, given a combination of solubility and absorption rate (calculated from permeability coefficient). In the present case, since a finite dose was actually given, the fraction of the dose absorbed can be estimated by dividing the MAD value by that actually dosed. Since MAD calculates a theoretical mass of solute assuming an infinite dose, it is possible to predict masses absorbed greater than than atually dosed. In this case, the predicted fraction absorbed is assigned a value of 1. In general, the correlation between predicted fraction dose absorbed and observed bioavailability was good except for the most highly permeable, lowest solubility compounds (Hilgers *et al.*, 2003). On the assumption that for such solutes aqueous solubility may underestimate the intestinal solubility arising from bile salts and other surfactants present in the lumen, solubility of these compounds were measured in simulated intestinal fluid (SIF) and predicted fraction absorbed recalculated. These results are shown in **Figure 1**. The lesson from this example is that solubility and permeability must be considered together in prioritizing these candidates with respect to absorption potential and, for highly permeable solutes, solubility in biologically relevant media may need to be considered.

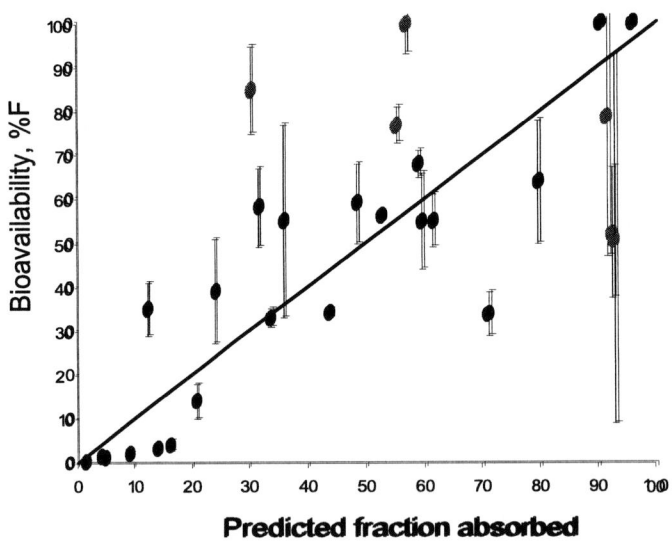

Figure 1. Oral absorption of oxazolidinone antibiotics in the rat. Rats were administered 25 mg/kg suspensions of the compounds as previously described (Hilgers, *et al.*, 2003). Predicted fraction absorbed was calculated from Caco-2 cell absorptive permeability coefficients and solubility in simulated intestinal fluid (SIF) according to the Maximum Absorbable Dose (MAD) model.

Physiology based pharmacokinetic (PB-PK) models to support lead optimization

While the MAD model is a useful strategy for interrelating solubility and permeability in predicting oral absorption, a more general approach to integrating solute structural characteristics into an anatomically and physiologically relevant approach for modeling absorption and disposition of xenobiotics is physiology-based pharmacokinetic (PB-PK) modeling (Bernareggi and Rowland, 1991; Grass and Sinko, 2002; Leahy, 2003; Rowland *et al.*, 2004; Poggesi, 2004). In PB-PK models the body is described as a system of tissue compartments perfused by known blood flows and characterized by their volumes, structures and compositions. Elimination processes are described using physiologically relevant approaches as described by Rowland, *et al.* (1973). Disposition of the drug as a function of time is described by a series of mass balance equations, written as a system of differential equations, and the system is fitted to the available plasma and/or tissue concentrations. Historically, such PB-PK models are used on well characterized drugs or toxicants. They are rarely used on new chemical entities, probably due to the need of individual structural models for tissues (e.g. perfusion vs permeability-rate limitations) and the substantial amount of information required for their parameterization (tissue partition coefficients, tissue clearances, plasma and tissue protein binding, etc.).

In an attempt to extend PB-PK modeling to use in a discovery setting, Poulin and Theil (2000, 2002) described a basic PB-PK model for rat, which was effective in predicting the pharmacokinetics of ethoxybenzamide, propranolol and diazepam, based on a very limited input (log P, pKa, intrinsic CL, protein binding, blood to plasma ratio). Such a model clearly has potential for simulating the outcome of the first-time-in-animal study.

Following Poulin and Theil's lead we developed a rodent PB-PK model to support lead optimization in the discovery setting (Germani *et al.*, 2005). The basic model consisted of differential equations describing 13 tissue compartments: muscle, bone, skin, adipose, brain, heart, lungs, spleen, gut, liver, kidneys and the arterial and venous blood pools. Drug mass balance in a generic tissue compartment is described as:

$$\frac{dC_T}{dt} = C_T \left(\frac{-Q_T}{\frac{P_{t:p}}{B:P} \cdot V_T} \right) + Q_T \cdot C_{input} \left(\frac{1 - E_T}{V_T} \right)$$

where C_T is the drug concentration for the tissue T, C_{input} is drug concentration in input to the tissue T, Q_T is the blood flow, V_T is the tissue volume, $P_{t:p}$ is the tissue to plasma partition coefficient, B:P is the blood to plasma ratio, and E_T is the extraction ratio. The system of differential equations was solved simultaneously for providing tissue and plasma concentration-time curves. Physiological data on blood flows (Q_T) and volumes (V_T) were obtained from the literature (Brown *et al.*, 1997).

Partition into tissue compartments was assumed to be perfusion-rate limited. The partition coefficients (including B:P) were calculated using lipophilicity measurements (logP, logD), protein binding and the tissue composition model described by Poulin and Theil (2000, 2002). Finally, composition data were taken from the literature (Poulin and Theil, 2000; Poulin and Krishnan, 1995).

Elimination was restricted to the liver and kidney compartments. The hepatic extraction ratio E_H was calculated from intrinsic clearance obtained from liver preparations and assuming the well-stirred model for hepatic clearance. Renal clearance was modeled assuming glomerular filtration only, as $GFR \cdot f_{u,p}$, where GFR is the glomerular filtration rate and $f_{u,p}$ is the fraction unbound to plasma proteins.

As an example of this approach, we modeled 45 Pharmacia compounds which had been dosed intravenously to rats (Germani *et al.*, 2004). The results of a representative example are shown in **Figure 2**. The input parameters were logP = 2.78, pKa = 7.3, $f_{u,p}$ = 0.065, CLint (estimated from rat hepatocytes) = 40.4 mL/min/kg. Blood:plasma ratio was estimated according to Poulin and Krishnan (1995). As can be seen from the Figure, good correspondence between predicted and observed plasma levels with time were found. This particular example represents a good prediction from the data and validates the general assumptions and interrelationships of the inputs in the model for this compound.

While such a model, using only computational and/or *in vitro* inputs commonly obtained in a discovery setting, can be useful in prioritizing or ranking compounds prior to the first in animal evaluation, an additional application in helping to focus a lead optimization program can also be envisioned. In this case, the PB-PK model is used to predict blood-level time profiles from the *in vitro* and physicochemical characteristics of the lead. The compound is then dosed to the

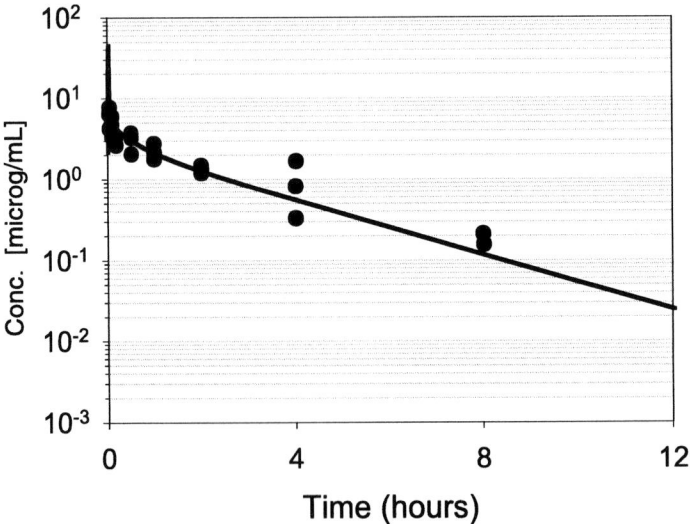

Figure 2. Physiology based pharmacokinetic (PB-PK) model prediction for a model compound. Solid line blood level-time profiles were predicted from solute parameters and rodent physiological parameters as described in the text. The data points were obtained from intravenous dosing of three animals.

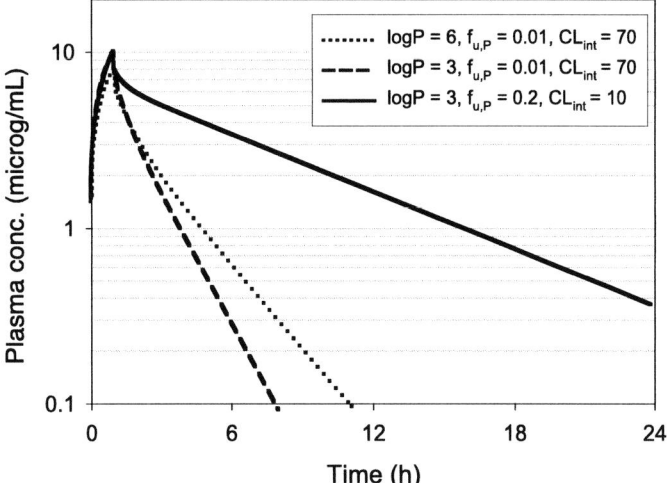

Figure 3. Sensitivity analysis reflecting relative influence of logP, fraction unbound in plasma ($f_{u,p}$) and clearance on predicted blood level time profiles for a prototype lead candidate. Based on this analysis, decreasing logP and clearance will have greater influence on drug levels than plasma protein binding. Such analysis helps to focus optimization program on most important biopharmaceutical properties.

animal in order to validate the model. If the resulting validation is reasonably successful, as in the example shown above, the PB-PK model can be used to identify those properties most important in optimizing the *in vivo* performance by means of a sensitivity analysis. These most sensitive parameters can then be focused on in the refinement program.

Figure 3 illustrates this approach for a potential drug candidate. Consider the lead compound to have logP = 6, $f_{u,p}$ = 0.01 and CLint = 70 mL/min/kg. This combination of properties results in a fairly rapid elimination from the systemic circulation after administration. Decreasing logP to a more favorable value of 3 actually increases clearance, probably resulting from decreased tissue and/or B:P partitioning. On the other hand, decreasing clearance, while retaining the more favorable logP value, significantly increases predicted exposure. In this last example, the unbound fraction ($f_{u,p}$) was also allowed to increase. Based on these considerations, the most important parameter contributing to *in vivo* performance is clearance, and a target value for an improved analog can be identified, helping to focus the chemistry effort (Crivori *et al.*, 2002).

An enhancement to the model to add oral absorption capability has also been explored. Sophisticated compartmentalized absorption and transit (CAT) models have been developed which allow the user to model absorption into portal blood of solutes administered as solutions or solid dosage forms (Yu *et al.*, 1996; Yu and Amidon, 1999). In these models the intestinal tract is segmented into a series of compartments with associated physiological characteristics of the animal species of interest such as lumenal volume, surface area, pH and residence or transit time. The solute parameter inputs are aqueous solubility as a function of pH, intestinal permeability, particle size, if administered as a suspension, and dissolution rate.

The model then calculates time dependent absorption as the solute moves through the sequential compartments based on these permeability/solubility-dissolution characteristics. This profile can then be used as the input venous-blood concentration parameter to the basic PB-PK model.

An example of this application is shown in **Figure 4**. In this figure, blood level time profiles are predicted and then compared to those actually observed for the model compound from Figure 2. The solute parameters used in the CAT model were solubility of 29.4 mg/ml at pH 1.8, 4.4 mg/ml at pH 4.6, 2.8 mg/ml (pH 5.7) and 0.06 mg/ml (pH 7.3). Permeability was measured in Caco-2 cells (26.0 ± 6.1 x 10^{-6} cm/sec in Ap->Bl direction and 18.0 ± 1.0 x 10^{-6} cm/sec in Bl->Ap direction) scaled to the rat intestine, as described previously (Hilgers *et al.*, 2003). These values were then used in GastroPlus™ (www.simulations-plus.com) assuming a solution dosage form. In **Figure 4** is shown the predicted blood-level time profile compared to the experimental results. Again, as in the case of the intravenous model, the agreement is very good for this particular compound, capturing, in general, C_{max}, T_{max} and the overall clearance profile.

Here also, the resulting validated model can be used to perform sensitivity analysis for parameters most important to *in vivo* performance. As shown in **Figure 5**, both permeability and clearance properties contribute to overall blood-level time profiles, with clearance having the most significant impact for this particular biopharmaceutical property profile. On the other hand, if the starting point were a more problematic combination of properties, these tools can give guidance in the direction in which to focus the optimization program and some boundary conditions on the magnitude of improvement necessary to achieve the desired end. In this regard, sensitivity analysis on fraction unbound or logP had little influence on the shape of the curves, except in the case of extreme logP values (**Figure 5**), suggesting these would not be profitable directions to explore synthetically.

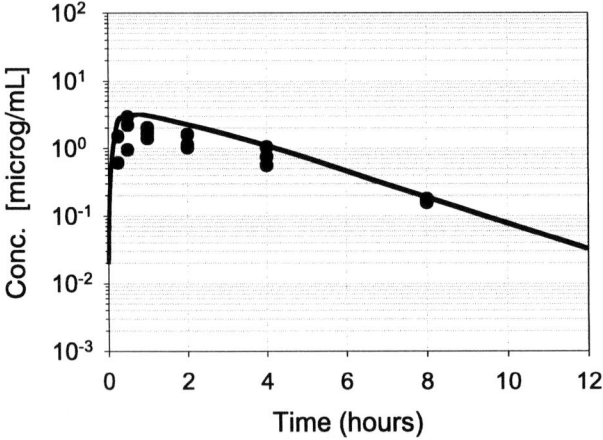

Figure 4. Comparison of predicted (solid line) and measured (symbols) blood level time profiles after oral administration of a prototype lead candidate. The oral absorption parameters were estimated from GastroPlus™ as described in the text and distribution and elimination from Figure 2. Data points were obtained from oral dosing of three animals.

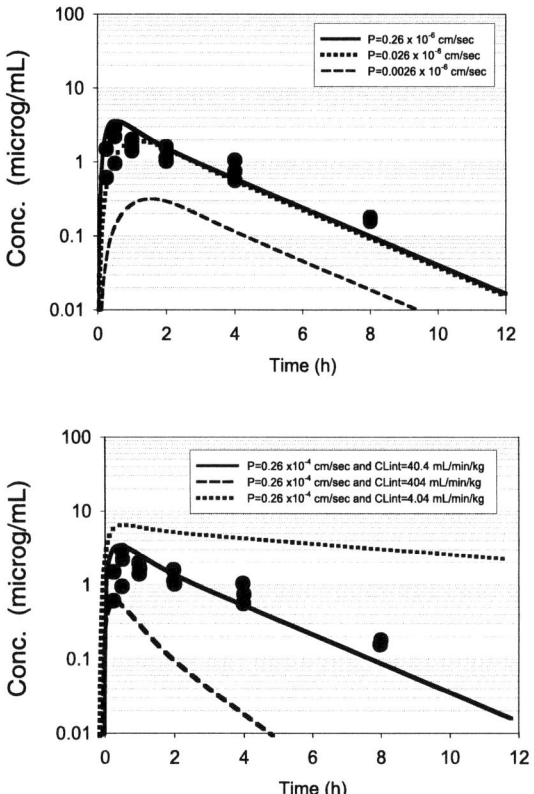

Figure 5. Sensitivity analysis reflecting relative influence of intestinal permeability (panel A) and clearance (panel B) on predicted blood level time profiles for model compound shown in Figure 4. While modest changes in permeability have little influence on the prediction, increasing or decreasing clearance result in significant changes in overall exposure. Such analyses allow the chemist to identify parameters most important to focus on in the optimization program.

Structure-based property models to support lead optimization

There has been significant activity in recent years toward the objective of developing structure-based predictive models of important biopharmaceutical properties for use in designing successful drug candidates (Ekins *et al.*, 2000; Butina *et al.*, 2002; Lombardo *et al.*, 2003; Stouch *et al.*, 2003; Wilson *et al.*, 2003; van de Waterbeembd and Gifford, 2003; Beresford *et al.*, 2004). Such models may be useful in the optimization campaign, helping to identify promising structural analogs improving on the properties found to be most important in the context of the PB-PK model. As shown in **Figure 6**, the major ADME events can be considered in terms of the solute biopharmaceutical processes determining them. These biopharmaceutical processes can in turn be related to solute structural and/or physicochemical parameters of most importance in the specific property.

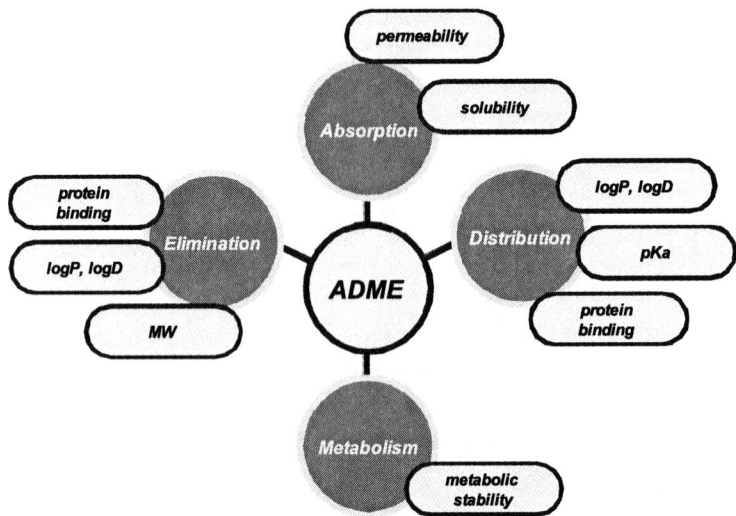

Figure 6. Relationship of biopharmaceutical processes and solute structural properties to ADME events. These dependencies form the basis for predictive structure-property relationships (SPR's) which can be used in the lead optimization program.

This then forms the basis for development of predictive structure property relationships (SPR's) which can be used in lead optimization.

In the next few sections we will review some characteristics of different SPR's in the context of specific lead optimization strategies. The intent is not to comprehensively review the SPR literature, which is fairly extensive, but rather consider general issues which should be addressed in the process of implementing any given property model.

Solubility

Solute solubility, as has been shown, is an important parameter in the oral absorption process. Generally, aqueous solubility is evaluated early in the lead selection process and minimally acceptable limits identified in order to consider taking a compound forward (Lipinski, 2000). However, in the various environments a drug will encounter *in vivo*, purely aqueous buffer is not one of them. Especially in the case of the intestinal lumen, various solubilizing agents are present which, in many cases, may improve the effective solubility of a solute *in vivo* compared to that predicted from the purely aqueous point of view. Similarly, lipids and proteins in blood may serve to increase the circulating solute concentration far beyond that expected for certain "insoluble" compounds. In spite of these caveats, aqueous solubility is an important reference point which needs to be considered and has been the subject of considerable modeling efforts (Abraham and Le, 1999; Jorgensen and Duffy, 2000; Huuskonen, 2000; McElroy and Jurs, 2001; Gao *et al.*, 2002).

Developing structure-based solubility models from a mechanistic perspective requires specific consideration of the solvation process at a molecular level. The forces involved in solubility are solute-solute, solvent-solvent and solute-solvent interactions (Kamlet *et al.*, 1986). These are the same considerations that apply in solute partitioning between two immiscible liquid phases. To a first approximation then, aqueous solubility of a liquid can be modeled as a partitioning of a solute between itself, or an organic solvent surrogate, and water. Consistent with this simple model, it has been possible to correlate aqueous solubility directly with octanol-water partition coefficients for liquid solutes (Hansch *et al.*, 1968; Valvani *et al.*, 1981).

In the case of solids, solute-solute forces existing in the crystal lattice complicate the prediction of solubility. At the present time, no reliable methods are available for estimating the energetics of these solid state, solute-solute interactions which must be overcome in order for the solute to release from the crystal and dissolve in water. An alternative approach to predicting solubility of solids is use of empirical, correlative models derived from collections of experimental data. Numerous examples of such models have been published, differing generally in the composition of the training data set, descriptor representation of the solutes, and statistical method for establishing the correlation (Abraham and Le, 1999; Huuskonen, 2000; Katritzky *et al.*, 2000; McFarland *et al.*, 2001; McElroy and Jurs, 2001; Jorgensen and Duffy, 2002; Gao *et al.*, 2002). Since these are empirical models, they are generally more accurate if the structure of the query molecule is similar to those in the training set. Thus these models strive to employ sufficient structural diversity to be useful in the entire chemistry space of interest to the medicinal chemist. Further, given the correlative nature of the model, the accuracy can be no better than the experimental accuracy of the training set data, which is generally assumed to be about 0.5 log units (Myrdal *et al.*, 1995; Katritzky *et al.*, 1998).

An additional complication in the development and implementation of structure-based models is the influence of solute ionization state of the solute on its apparent solubility at a given pH. Since many drugs are either weakly acidic or basic, this is an important consideration. The solubility of such substances depends upon the intrinsic solubility of the neutral species and relative concentration of neutral and charged species at the pH of interest (Yalkowsky, 1999). These concentrations depend upon the relative values of the pKa(s) of the solute and pH of medium. From a practical perspective this means that in training a model with such solutes, only the intrinsic solubility should be used. If the model is developed from apparent solubility, the relationship of pKa with the pH of data measurement must be taken into consideration, adding considerable complexity to the model. Further, if the model predicts a low intrinsic solubility, this may be somewhat misleading if the solute is expected to be highly charged at physiological pH. In such a situation, it is desirable to incorporate a pKa estimation algorithm with an intrinsic solubility model in order to predict apparent solubility at a relevant pH.

Finally, as with most statistical models, performance is measured by the model's prediction capability and this depends on the space on which the model was trained. With commercial packages, the user generally does not know on which chemical classes the model was trained. When large errors are observed between the predicted and the experimental values it is assumed that the model is not useful. This is one of the main reasons that local solubility models are developed. In this situation, local is defined as representing a relatively focused, homogeneous region of chemical space while global models are developed over much greater structural diversity.

In using such models it is important to understand the limitations of the model in terms of applicability and accuracy in different chemistry and property spaces. Toward that end, a study was undertaken at Pharmacia to compare accuracy and bias in prediction for three commercially available solubility models and a model developed at Pharmacia over different regions of chemistry spaces and three different solubility levels (Crimin, *et al.*, 2004). The four solubility models were: ACD Labs PhysChem v. 6.0, QikProp v. 2.1, Cerius2 and the in-house model (Gao *et al.*, 2002). The in-house solubility model was trained on literature and in-house data. The training sets for the three commercial models were not known.

In the study, six data sets containing a total of 713 compounds were utilized. Four of the sets were local collections of data developed from internal discovery programs. They represent relatively homogeneous structural features generally arising from optimization around a biologically relevant template. One (data set 2) was a structurally diverse collection of Pharmacia data from a variety of discovery program teams and was used for continuous testing of the "in-house" solubility model (Gao *et al.*, 2002). Finally, the last set, data set 5, contained 85% simple, monofunctional organic compounds and the remaining 15% drugs and pesticides.

The experimental solubility was compared to the predicted solubility obtained from each of the four solubility models. **Figure 7** shows the root mean squared prediction error (RMSPE) for all six data sets with the four models. RMSPE represents the accuracy of the prediction model in these specific data sets and is assumed to reflect the similarity of the structures in the training, model, space to the query structure. Only in the case of data sets 4 and 6, were all the compounds predicted by all four models. In the other cases, one or more of the models failed to predict solubility for some of the structures in the sets. From the results presented in the table, the in-house model has the smallest RMSPE in three out of the six data sets (1, 2, 3). This is, in part, due to the fact that the training set of this model includes compounds that are similar, but not identical, to structures in those data sets. Similarly, QikProp and Cerius2 perform comparably to the in-house model for data sets 1 and 3 respectively. None of the models perform particularly well with data set 6 suggesting this is an especially challenging region of chemistry space. The implications of these results is that, while all the models are accurate in specific applications, none of them perform well over all structural diversity present in the test sets. From the perspective of prioritizing structures to synthesize based on predicted solubility properties, the existence of such biases should be taken into consideration.

Root Mean Square Prediction Error

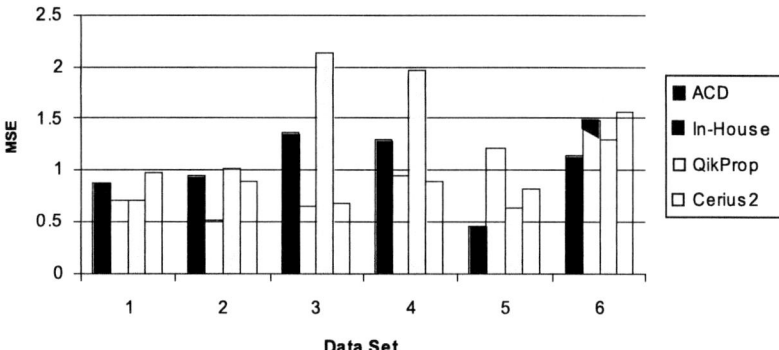

Figure 7. Prediction accuracy of several global aqueous solubility models. ACD. QikProp, Cerius2 and a Pharmacia developed model were used to predict solubility of several collections of homologous structures from Pharmacia discovery programs (Data sets 1, 3,4 and 6) and diverse structures from both the Pharmacia collection and structures taken from the literature (Data sets 2 and 5). It can be clearly seen that the prediction error depends both upon the model and characteristics of the query structures.

The residual plots for data set 5 are shown in **Figure 8**, differentiated by solubility range. Residual is the difference between experimental value and predicted value for each of the models and shows any bias to under or overpredict in the model. ACD and QikProp appear to be unbiased over all solubility ranges while the in-house model is over-predicting at all solubilities and Cerius2 over-predicts for low solubility compounds and under-predicts high solubility structures. Biases were observed in all the data sets, with no consistent trends with respect to the different models. Again, from the objective of using these models prospectively in making synthetic decisions, such biases should be acknowledged and taken into consideration.

With respect to lead optimization programs to overcome potential pharmaco-kinetic problems, accuracy in predicting the impact of subtle structural changes in a fairly homogenous structural space is desired. The results of this analysis clearly show that the performance of the different models is dependent upon the chemistry space and solubility range within that space, both with respect to accuracy and bias. While bias itself does not necessarily preclude the utility of a model, recognition that it exists and in what direction can help the user make more informed decisions with the predictions. At the least, these considerations suggest that the user of any model should characterize and validate the model in an intended application before general use.

Permeability

As shown in Figure 6, permeability is an important determinant of absorption and a number of other ADME processes dictating the *in vivo* performance of a drug. However, permeability itself is a complex process containing contributions

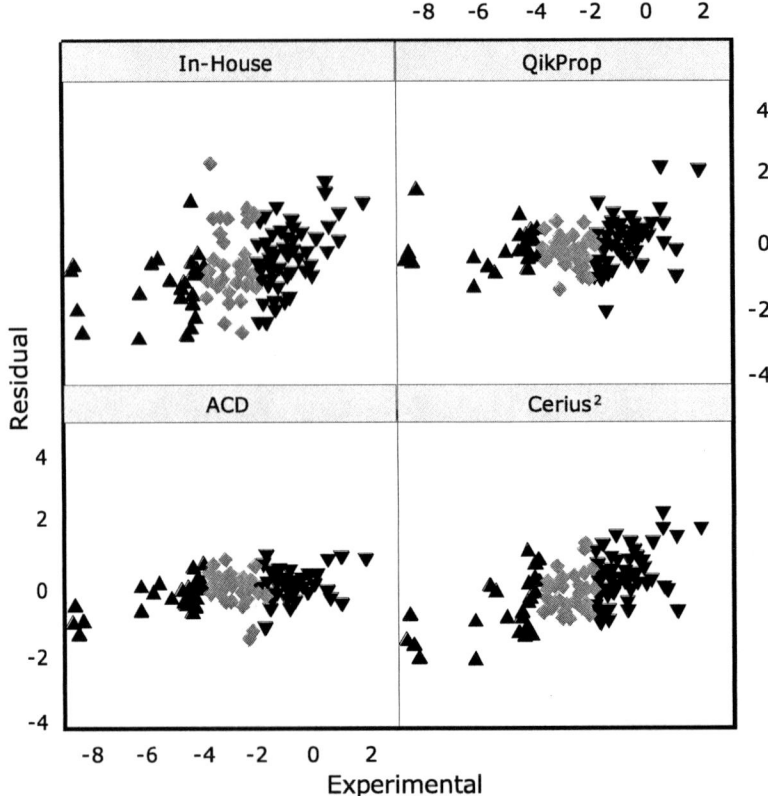

Figure 8. Comparison of prediction bias for ACD, QikProp, Cerius2 and Pharmacia aqueous solubility models. Structures are grouped into low (triangles, solubility $\leq$ 100 μM), moderate (diamonds, solubility between 100 and 10,000 μM) and high (inverted triangles, solubility $\geq$ 10,000 μM) solubility ranges. Residual (y-axis) is the difference between experimental value and predicted value for each of the models. The experimental solubility (log S in μM) is on the x-axis. Considerable bias is seen both in the computational model employed and solubility range for the structural series. Similar, unpredictable biases were observed for the other data sets summarized in **Figure 7** (Crimin, *et al.*, 2005).

from a number of different transport mechanisms, the relative contributions of which depend upon the structural features of the drug. After oral administration, a drug must move from the intestinal lumen through an unstirred water layer and mucus coat adjacent to the epithelial cell surface. Movement across the epithelial layer takes place by two independent routes-transcellular flux, *i.e.* movement across the cell, and paracellular flux, or movement between adjacent epithelial cells, restricted by the presence of tight junctions between the cells (Diamond, 1977; Gumbiner, 1987; Jackson, 1987). The solute then encounters a number of microenvironments including a basement membrane, interstitial space and capillary wall in accessing the mesenteric circulation. Any and all of these microenvironments can be considered a resistance to solute movement with an associated permeability coefficient. Further, the influence of drug structure with permeability in these different domains will be different. For example, unstirred water layer permeability is inversely related to solute size while paracellular permeability is dependent upon both size and charge. In the latter case, the characteristics of the paracellular "pore" result in size restricted diffusion as the size of the solute approaches that of the paracellular space. Further, cations are more permeable than neutral species, which in turn are more permeable than anions, consistent with the negative charge characteristics of the paracellular space (Adson *et al.*, 1995; Kottra and Frömter, 1983).

With respect to transcellular permeability, the relationship of solute structure with permeability again depends upon the mechanism involved. Historically, a passive diffusion pathway has been assumed for most solutes. However, an increasing number of active absorptive and secretory processes in intestinal epithelial cells are being identified for which many common drugs are substrates (Tsuji and Tamai, 1996). These same considerations apply to tissue distribution and excretion (**Figure 6**), both of which are also dependent upon passive and active transport mechanism. With respect to structure/ transport or permeability relationships, while active transport involves specific interactions between solute and transporter, passive diffusion is dependent upon solute partitioning into the cellular plasma membrane and diffusion coefficient within the membrane (Jackson, 1987).

Considerable structure-property relationship (SPR) work has been published over the years to describe the passive transport mechanism, still believed in many cases to be the most significant pathway responsible for intestinal permeability and oral drug absorption. A very successful model for predicting passive permeability is the so called passive/diffusion model in which the cellular barrier is reduced conceptually to a homogenous, single biomembrane. Both partitioning and diffusion are influenced by the physicochemical and structural characteristics of the drug. Factors influencing plasma membrane partitioning are solute size, lipophilicity, hydrogen bonding potential and charge characteristics, while diffusion is dependent upon size or total molecular surface area properties (Conradi *et al.*, 1996). In general, non-polar surface area favors partitioning while polar, hydrogen bonding functionality opposes partitioning. With respect to diffusion, an inverse relationship with size is found, similar to the situation with paracellular permeability.

These multiple influences on permeability are manifested in a number of different ways. If intestinal permeability of a number of homologous, non-actively transported solutes is measured as a function of membrane partitioning, or more commonly, an organic solvent partition coefficient such as octanol as a surrogate, a sigmoidal relationship is frequently observed (Ho *et al.*, 1977; Camenisch *et al.*, 1996). For solutes with little or no membrane affinity, permeability is low, resulting primarily from paracellular diffusion of the solute between cells. As the propensity of the solute to partition into the cell membrane increases, permeability also increases as a result of the significant increase in surface area of the transcellular pathway relative to the paracellular route. This increase in permeability will approach a plateau value beyond which further increases in partition coefficient do not result in increased permeability. This is the so-called aqueous boundary layer limited situation where diffusion across the cell is very rapid relative to diffusion of the solute through the unstirred water/mucus layer adjacent to the cell (Westergaard and Dietschy, 1974). The dimensions, and resistance, of this layer can be modified by perturbing hydrodynamics which shift the plateau to a new, limiting permeability.

In the case of ionizable solutes, permeability is also pH dependent. The neutral, uncharged species is capable of transcellular, passive diffusion while the charged species is restricted to the paracellular pathway. Thus the observed permeability of such molecules is dependent upon the relative concentrations of charged and neutral species. In the case of a weak acid such as salicylic acid for example, at pH less than about 5.5, rat intestinal permeability is aqueous boundary controlled. Increasing pH results in progressively lower permeability coefficients until at pH greater than 9, a limiting, small permeability is achieved which is independent of further pH increases. This limiting permeability represents the paracellular diffusion of the charged anion (Ho *et al.*, 1983). For such ionizable solutes a correlation with permeability and logD, defined as the apparent octanol-water partition coefficient at a specific pH, frequently 6.5 or 7.4, is used to predict permeability. Both ClogP and ClogD algorithms are available to help optimize permeability characteristics of lead structures where this property is not found to be in a favorable range to effect the desired *in vivo* performance.

However, octanol-water partition coefficients are not always useful for predicting permeability of all solutes. In the case of highly functionalized solutes such as peptides, permeability has been found to be better correlated with structural and physicochemical measures of hydrogen bond potential (Conradi *et al.*, 1991, 1992). One such system is the ΔlogP model where ΔlogP is the difference between octanol-water partition coefficient and hydrocarbon-water partition coefficient of the solute (Seiler, 1974; El Tayer *et al.*, 1991). At the present time, no reliable computational models are available for predicting ΔlogP, although recent work in this direction has appeared in the literature (Ruelle, 2000).

Polar surface area (PSA) of a solute, which can be computed from structure, has been proposed as an alternative to octanol-water and/or ClogP for predicting intestinal permeability (Palm *et al.*, 1996,1997). Recent examples of successful correlations using this simple metric have been published (Ertl *et al.*, 2000; Papageorgiou *et al.*, 2001) suggesting this as a useful general tool for optimizing permeability characteristics of a solute. However, failure of PSA to correlate cellular permeability of a series of peptidomimetics has also been reported. In this case, a reasonable correlation could be obtained by taking a weighted average of PSA and NPSA (non-polar surface area) of the solutes (Stenberg *et al.*, 1999). The conclusion from these examples is that, as in the case of computational solubility modeling, application of a specific tool for predicting permeability must be validated by the user as appropriate for the molecular structure of interest.

Clearance

Solute clearance as a PB-PK parameter includes both metabolism and excretion mechanisms. As shown in Figure 6, metabolism and excretion rates are dependent upon biopharmaceutical processes such as active and passive permeability, and physicochemical properties of the solute which influence these processes. With regards to SPR models of these pathways, considerable work has been focused on models for predicting metabolism of potential drug candidates, primarily identifying sites of reactivity in the solute (Jones *et al.*, 2002; Zamora *et al.*, 2003; Harris, 2004; Crivori *et al.*, 2004). These include models for most of the major cytochrome P450 (CYP450) isoforms. Octanol-water partition coefficients have been correlated with CYP450 binding for both substrates and inhibitors and may be considered as a design strategy to decrease association with the enzymes (Lewis *et al.*, 2004). Further, given that lipophilicity also plays a role in passive diffusion, decreasing logP may both decrease binding to CYP's and solute permeability in the liver to the site of metabolism.

Along with passive permeability, a major contribution from active, frequently vectorial transport both to metabolism and excretion pathways is increasingly being recognized (Faber *et al.*, 2003; Hirano *et al.*, 2004). SPR models for these processes is of considerable current interest and some progress has been made towards identifying substrates and/or inhibitors for some of them, most notably P-glycoprotein (Seelig, 1998; Stouch and Gudmundsson, 2002; Gombar *et al.*, 2004). As in the case of metabolism, these models focus on recognition events such as binding and do not generally predict rates of reaction. However, at least in one case, a structure-based predictive model for hepatic clearance rates has been reported, derived from an internal training set of such data (www.lionbiosciences.com). Until such kinetic models are more generally available, *in vitro* data will likely continue to be required for use in PB-PK modeling.

Distribution

As is the situation with permeability, metabolism and clearance, both biopharmaceutical processes and physicochemical solute properties define tissue distribution. Reasonably accurate predictions of blood-level time profiles can be obtained in PB-PK models considering only plasma-tissue partition coefficients derived from unbound plasma solute concentrations and octanol-water partition coefficients, as shown earlier in this review and in other, similar models (Poulin and Theil, 2002). Alternatively, a distribution parameter utilizing octanol-water partition coefficients and fraction unionized at pH 7.4, has been shown to provide good estimates of volume of distribution in humans for neutral and basic compounds (Lombardo *et al.*, 2004). At the present time, these are experimentally determined inputs in contrast to exclusively computed values.

Again, complicating the issue is the role of active transport processes on distribution especially in tissues such as brain and lung. In the case of brain for example, P-glycoprotein plays a significant role in limiting distribution of solutes which are substrates into the brain (Raub, *this volume*). This can be clearly seen in cases where P-glycoprotein inhibitors were administered with the therapeutic agent and significantly greater CNS toxicities were noted which were not observed in the absence of inhibitor (Tsujikawa *et al.*, 2003). The ability to predict these processes from structure alone presently remains an unsolved challenge.

Plasma protein binding

Fraction unbound is an important determinant of both tissue distribution and clearance in the PB-PK model. Computational SPR models of protein binding are focused almost entirely on serum albumin, primarily human serum albumin (Colmenarejo, 2003; Ermondi *et al.*, 2004). Generally, these models use lipophilicity and charge of the solute to estimate association between the solute and protein. A recent review challenged these models and proposed an alternative approach employing a pharmacophore similarity concept and partial least squares as a more generally accurate strategy (Kratochwil *et al.*, 2002). While this and other approaches are useful as a starting point for consideration of protein binding issues, a major weakness is the limitation to albumin as the only relevant potential binding component in blood. Other blood components important for binding certain classes of drugs are lipoprotein particles and α-1-acid glycoprotein (Boffito *et al.*, 2003; Akhlaghi and Trull, 2002; Chung and Wasan, 2004).

Concluding remarks

Biopharmaceutical properties such as solubility, cellular permeability and metabolic stability, among others are important in the successful discovery and development of new drug candidates. Significant progress has been made in recent years towards development and use of computational, structure-based models of these properties and such models are increasingly being used in the lead optimization process. While these biopharmaceutical properties are important individually, the ultimate *in vivo* performance of a drug candidate is a complex function of all the properties. Physiology-based pharmacokinetic (PB-PK) models using *in vitro* and physicochemical data can be useful in defining these functional relationships and identifying the important biopharmaceutical characteristics of a lead candidate, helping focus the optimization strategy. Presently, such models do not easily include non-ideal drug behavior such as active transport, for example. However, this can be an advantage in some cases. Significant deviations of experimental observations from prediction can be an alert that such processes are important for a specific lead candidate and needs to be more closely examined. Further, these early generation PB-PK models do not easily accomodate interdependencies of physicochemical properties on multiple biopharmaceutical processes. Generally, these must be considered individually in carrying out a sensitivity analysis query. However, as the models are evolved, these limitations are likely to be addressed and the use of integrated structure-based property models with PB-PK models will find more general applications in the lead optimization process.

Acknowledgements

The authors would like to acknowledge the large number of Pharmacia colleagues who were involved in various aspects of this work. Kimberly Crimin, Thomas J. Vidmar, Gerald M. Maggiora, Christian Orrenius, Patrizia Crivori, Pieter F. W. Stouten, Allen R. Hilgers, Robert A. Conradi, Norman F.H. Ho and Alan G.E. Wilson all contributed significantly to the structure-based modeling described in this work.

References

Abraham MJ and Le J. The Correlation and Prediction of the Solubility of Compounds in Water Using and Amended Solvation Energy Relationship. *J Pharm Sci* 1999; 88:868-880.

Adson A, Burton PS, Raub TJ, Barsuhn CL, Audus KL and Ho NFH. Passive Diffusion of Weak Organic Electrolytes Across Caco-2 Cell Monolayers: Uncoupling the Contributions of Hydrodynamic, Transcellular and Paracellular Barriers. *J Pharm Sci* 1995; 84:1197-1204.

Akhlaghi F and Trull AK. Distribution of Cyclosporin in Organ Transplant Recipients. *Clin Pharmacokinet* 2002; 41:615-637.

Beresford AP, Segall M and Tarbit MH. In silico Prediction of ADMET Properties: Are we Making Progress? *Curr Opin Drug Discov Devel* 2004; 7:36-42.

Bernareggi A and Rowland M. Physiololgic Modeling of Cyclosporine Kinetics in Rat and Man. *J Pharmacokinet Biopharm* 1991; 19:21-50.

Boffito M, Back DJ, Blaschke TF, Rowland M, Bertz RJ, Gerber JG and Miller V. Protein Binding in Antiretroviral Therapies. *AIDS Res Hum Retroviruses* 2003; 19:825-835.

Brown RP, Delp MD, Lindstedt SL, Rhomberg LR and Beliles RP. Physiological Parameter Values for Physiologically Based Pharmacokinetic Models. *Toxicol Indust Health* 1997; 13:407-484.

Butina D, Segall MD and Frankcombe K. Predicting ADME Properties in silico: Methods and Models. *Drug Discov Today* 2002; 11(Suppl):S83-S88.

Camenisch G, Folkers G and van de Waterbeembd H. Review of Theoretical Passive Drug Absorption Models: Historical, Background, Recent Developments and Limitations. *Pharm Acta Helv* 1996; 71:309-327.

Chung NS and Wasan KM. Potential Role of the Low-density Lipoprotein Receptor Family as Mediators of Cellular Drug Uptake. *Adv Drug Deliv Rev* 2004; 56:1315-1334.

Colmenarejo G. In silico Prediction of Drug-binding Strengths to Human Serum Albumin. *Med Res Rev* 2003; 23:275-301.

Conradi RA, Hilgers AR, Ho NFH and Burton PS. The Influence of Peptide Structure on Transport Across Caco-2 Cells. *Pharm Res* 1991; 8:1453-1460.

Conradi RA, Hilgers AR, Ho NFH and Burton PS. The Influence of Peptide Structure on Transport Across Caco-2 Cells. II. Peptide Bond Modification Which Results in Improved Permeability. *Pharm Res* 1992; 9:435-439.

Conradi RA, Burton PS and Borchrdt RT. Physicochemical and Biological Factors that Influence a Drug's Cellular Permeability by Passive Diffusion. In: V Pliska, B Testa, H van de Waterbeemd, R Mannhold, H Kubinyi and H Timmerman. *Lipophilicity in Drug Action and Toxicoloy*,., VCH Publishers, BRD; 1996.

Crimin KS, Orrenius C, Lee P, Gao H, Catana C, Crivori P, Dearden JC, Vidmar TJ, Goodwin JT, Stouten PFW and Burton PS. Prediction of Aqueous Solubility of Organic Molecules: Evaluation of Accuracy and Bias in Several Models. *J Med Chem* 2005; submitted.

Crivori P, Poggesi I and Rocchetti M. Estimation of Human Drug Clearance from Chemical Structure. 14th European Symposium on Quantitative Structure-Activity Relationships. September 2002; Bournemouth, UK.

Crivori P, Zamora I, Speed B, Orrenius C and Poggesi I. Model Based on GRID-Derived Descriptors for Estimating CYP3A4 Enzyme Stability of Potential Drug Candidates. *J Comput Aided Mol Des* 2004; 18:155-166.

Curatolo W. Physical Chemical Properties of Oral Drug Candidates in the Discovery and Exploratory Development Settings. *Pharm Sci Technol Today* 1998; 1:387-393.

Diamond JM. The Epithelial Junction: Bridge, Gate and Fence. *Physiologist* 1977; 20:10-18.

Ekins S, Waller CL, Swaan PW, Cruciani G, Wrighton SA and Wikel JA. Progress in Predicting Human ADME Parameters in Silico. *J Pharmacol Toxicol Methods* 2000; 44:251-272.

El Tayar N, Tsai R-S, Testa B, Carrupt P-A and Leo A. Partitioning of Solutes in Different Solvent Systems: The Contribution of Hydrogen-bonding Capacity and Polarity. *J Pharm Sci* 1991; 80:590-598.

Ermondi G, Lorenti M and Caron G. Contribution of Ionization and Lipophilicity to Drug Binding to Albumin: A Preliminary Step Toward Biodistribution Prediction. *J Med Chem* 2004; 47:3949-3961.

Ertl P, Rohde B and Selzer P. Fast Calculation of Molecular Polar Surface Area as a Sum of Fragment-based Contributions and its Application to the Prediction of Drug Transport Properties. *J Med Chem* 2000; 43:3714-3717.

Faber KN, Muller M and Jansen PL. Drug Transport Proteins in the Liver. *Adv Drug Deliv Rev* 2003; 55:107-124.

Gao H, Shanmugasundaram V and Lee P. Estimation of Aqueous Solubility of Organic Compounds with QSPR Approach. *Pharm Res* 2002; 19:497-503.

Germani M, Crivori P, Rocchetti M, Burton PS, Wilson AGE, Smith ME and Poggesi I. Evaluation of a Physiologically-based Pharmacokinetic Approach for Simulating the First-time-in-animal Study. *Basic Clin. Pharmacol. Toxicol.* 2005; 96:254-6.

Gombar VK, Polli JW, Humphreys JE, Wring SA and Serabjit-Singh CS. Predicting P-glycoprotein Substrates by a Quantitative Structure-Activity Relationship Model. *J Pharm Sci* 2004; 93:957-968.

Grass GM and Sinko PJ. Physiololgically-based Pharmacokinetic Simulation Modeling. *Adv Drug Deliv Rev* 2002; 54:433-451.

Gumbiner B. Structure, Biochemistry, and Assembly of Epithelial Tight Junctions. *Am J Physiol* 1987; 253:C749-C758.

Hansch C, Quinlan JE and Lawrence GL. The Linear Free Energy Relationship Between Partition Cofficients and the Aqueous Solubility of Organic Liquids. *J Org Chem* 1968; 33:347-350.

Hansch C, Leo A, Mekapati SB and Kurup A. QSAR and ADME. *Bioorg Med Chem* 2004; 12:3391-3400.

Harris DL. In silico Predictive Metabolism: A Structural/electronic Filter Method. *Curr Opin Drug Discov Devel* 2004; 7:43-48.

Hilgers AR, Smith DP, Biermacher JJ, Day JS, Jensen JL, Sims SM, Adams WJ, Friis JM, Palandra J, Hosley JD, Shobe EM and Burton PS. Predicting Oral Absorption of Drugs: A Case Study with a Novel Class of Antimicrobial Agents. *Pharm Res* 2003; 8:1149-1155.

Hirano M, Maeda K, Shitara Y and Sugiyama Y. Contribution of OATP2(OATP1B1) and OATP8 (OATP1B3) to Hepatic Uptake of Pitavastatin in Humans. *J Pharmacol Exp Ther* 2004; 311:139-146.

Ho NFH, Park JY, Morozowich W and Higuchi WI. Physical Model Approach to the Design of Drugs with Improved Intestinal Absorption. In: Roche EB. *Design of Biopharmaceutical Properties Through Prodrugs and Analogs*, American Pharmaceutical Association, Academy of Pharmaceutical Sciences, Washington, DC. 1977:136-227.

Ho NFH, Park JY, Ni PF and Higuchi WI. Advancing Quantitative and Mechanistic Approaches in Interfacing Gastrointestinal Drug Absorption Studies in Animals and Man. In: Crouthamel WG and Sarapu A. *Animal Models for Oral Drug Delivery in Man: In Situ and in vivo Approaches*. AphA/APS, Washington, D.C. 1983: 27-106.

Huuskonen J. Estimation of Aqueous Solubility for a Diverse Set of Organic Compounds Based on Molecular Topology. *J Chem Inf Comput Sci* 2000; 40:773-777.

Kerns, EH and Di L. Pharmaceutical Profiling in Drug Discovery. *Drug Discov Today* 2003; 8:316-323.

Jackson MJ. Drug Transport across Gastrointestinal Epithelia, in *Physiology of the Gastrointestinal Tract, Second Edition* (Johnson LR, ed) 1987; Raven Press, New York, pp 1597-1621.

Johnson KC and Swindell AC. Guidance in the Setting of Drug Particle Size Specifications to Minimize Variability in Absorption. *Pharm Res* 1996; 13:1795-1798.

Jones JP, Mysinger M and Korzekwa KR. Computational Modles for Cytochrome P450: A Predictive Electronic Model for Aromatic Oxidation and Hydrogen Atom Abstraction. *Drug Metab Dispos* 2002; 30:7-12.

Jorgensen WL and Duffy EM. Prediction of Drug Solubility from Monte Carlo Simulations. *Bioorg Med Chem Lett* 2000; 10:1155-1158.

Jorgensen WL and Duffy EM. Prediction of Drug Solubility from Structure. *Adv Drug Deliv Rev* 2002; 54:355-366.

Kamlet MJ, Doherty RM, Abboud JLM, Abraham MW and Taft RW. Linear Solvation Energy Relationships:36. Molecular Properties Governing Solubilities of Organic Nonelectrolytes in Water. *J Pharm Sci* 1886; 75:338-349.

Katritzky AR, Wang Y, Tamm T and Karelson M. QSPR Studies on Vapor Pressure, Aqueous Solubility, and the Prediction of Water-air Partition Coefficients. *J Chem Inf Comput Sci* 1998; 38:720-725.

Katritzky AR, Maran U, Lobanov VS and Karelson M. Structurally Diverse Quantitative Structure-property Relationship Correlations of Technologically Relevant Physical Properties. *J Chem Inf Comput Sci* 2000; 40:1-18.

Kottra G and Frömter E. Functional Properties of the Paracellular Pathway in Some Leaky Epithelia. *J Exp Biol* 1983; 106:217-229.

Kratochwil NA, Huber W, Muller F, Kansy M and Gerber PR. Predicting Plasma Protein Binding of Drugs: A New Approach. *Biochem Pharmacol* 2002; 64:1355-1374.

Leahy DE. Progress in Simulation Modelling for Pharmacokinetics. *Curr Topics Med Chem* 2003; 3:1257-1268.

Lewis FV, Jacobs MN and Dickins M. Compound Lipophilicity for Substrate Binding to Human P450s in Drug Metabolism. *Drug Discov Today* 2004; 9:530-537.

Lipinski CA. Drug-like Properties and the Causes of Poor Solubility and Poor Permeability. *J Pharmacol Toxicol Methods* 2000; 44:235-249.

Lombardo F, Gifford E and Shalaeva MY. In Silico ADME Prediction: Data, Models, Facts and Myths. *Mini Rev Med Chem* 2003; 3:861-875.

Lombardo F, Obach RS, Shalaeva MY and Gao F. Prediction of Human Volume of Distribution Values for Neutral and Basic Drugs.2. Extended Data Set and Leave-class-out Statistics. *J Med Chem* 2004; 47:1242-1250.

McElroy NR and Jurs PC. Prediction of Aqueous Solubilty of Heteroatom-containing Organic Compounds from Molecular Structure. *J Chem Inf Comput Sci* 2001; 45:1237-1247.

McFarland JW, Avdeef A, Berger CM and Raevsky OA. Estimating the Water Solubilities of Crystalline Compounds from Their Chemical Structures Alone. *J Chem Inf Comput Sci* 2001; 41:1355-1359.

Myrdal PB, Manka AM and Yalkowski SH. AQUAFAC 3: Aqueous Functional Group Activity Coefficients: Application to the Estimate of Aqueous Solubility. Chemosphere 1995; 30:1619-1637.

Palm K, Luthman K, Ungell AL, Strandlund G and Artursson P. Correlation of Drug Absorption with Molecular Surface Properties. *J Pharm Sci* 1996; 85:32-39.

Palm D, Stenberg P, Luthman K and Artursson P. Polar Molecular Surface Properties Predict the Intestinal Absorption of Drugs in Humans. *Pharm Res* 1997; 14:568-571.

Papageorgiou C, Camenisch G and Borer X. Cell Permeability as a Parameter for Lead Generation in the Protein Tyrosine Kinase Inhibition Field. *Bioorg Med Chem Lett* 2001; 11:1549-1552.

Poggesi I. Predicting Human Pharmacokinetics from Preclinical Data. *Curr Opinion Drug Discov Develop* 2004; 7:100-111.

Poulin P and Krishnan K. An Algorithm for Predicting Tissue:blood Partition Coefficients of Organic Chemicals from n-Octanol:water Partition Coefficient Data. *J Toxicol Environ Health* 1995; 46:117-129.

Poulin P and Theil FP. A priori Prediction of Tissue:plasma Partition Coefficients of Drugs to Facilitate the use of Physiologically-Based Pharmacokinetic Models in Drug Discovery. *J Pharm Sci* 2000; 89:16-35.

Poulin P and Theil FP. Prediction of Pharmacokinetics prior to *in vivo* Studies. II. Generic Physiologically Based Pharmacokinetic Models of Drug Disposition. *J Pharm Sci* 2002; 91:1358-1370.

Raub TJ. Early Preclinical Evaluation in Support of Hit Identification and Lead Optimization for Brain Exposure. *This volume*, 2004.

Rowland M, Benet L and Graham GC. Clearance Concept in Pharmacokinetics. *J Pharmacokinet Biopharm* 1973; 1:123-136.

Rowland M, Balant L and Peck C. Physiologically Based Pharmacokinetics in Drug Development and Regulatory Science: A Workshop Report (Georgetown University, Washington,DC, May 29-30, 2002). *AAPS PharmSci* 2004; 6:1-12.

Ruelle P. The n-Octanol and n-Hexane/water Partition Coefficient of Environmentally Relevant Chemicals Predicted from the Mobile Order and Disorder (MOD) Thermodynamics. *Chemosphere* 2000; 40:457-512.

Seelig A. A General Pattern for Substrate Recognition by P-glycoprotein. *Eur J Biochem* 1998; 251:252-261.

Seiler P. Interconversion of Lipophilicities from Hydrocarbon/water Systems into the Octanol/water System. *Eur J Med Chem* 1974; 9:473-479.

Stenberg P, Luthman K and Artursson P. Prediction of Membrane Permeability to Peptides from Calculated Dynamic Molecular Surface Properties. *Pharm Res* 1999; 16:205-212.

Stouch TR and Gudmundsson O. Progress in Understanding the Structure-activity Relationships of P-glycoprotein. *Adv Drug Deliv Rev* 2002; 54:314-328.

Stouch TR, Kenyon JR, Johnson SR, Chen X, Doweyko A and Li Y. In silico ADME/Tox: Why Models Fail. *J Comp-Aided Mol Design* 2003; 17:83-92.

Tsuji A and Tamai E. Carrier-mediated Intestinal Transport of Drugs. *Pharm Res* 1996; 13:963-977.

Tsujikawa K, Dan Y, Nogawa K, Sato H, Yamada Y, Murakami H, Ohtani H, Sawada Y and Iga T. Potentiation of Domperidone-induced Catalepsy by a P-glycoprotein Inhibitor, Cyclosporin A. *Biopharm Drug Dispos* 2003; 24:105-114.

Valvani SC, Yalkowsky SH and Roseman TJ. Solubility and Partitioning IV: Aqueous Solubility and Octanol-water Partition Coefficiencts of Liquid Nonelectrolytes. *J Pharm Sci* 1981; 70:502-507.

van de Waterbeembd H and Gifford E. ADMET in silico Modelling: Toward Prediction Paradise? *Nat Rev Drug Discov* 2003; 2:192-204.

Westergaard H and Dietschy JM. Delineation of the Dimensions and Permeability Characteristics of the Two Major Diffusion Barriers to Passive Mucosal Uptake in the Rabbit Intestine. *J Clin Investig* 1974; 54:718-732.

Wilson AGE, White AC and Mueller RA. Role of Predictive Metabolism and Toxicity Modeling in Drug Discovery. *Curr Opinion Drug Discov Devel* 2003; 6:123-128.

Yalkowsky SH. *Solubility and Solubilization in Aqueous Media*. 1999; Oxford University Press, New York.

Yu LX, Lipka E, Crison JR and Amidon GL. Transport Approaches to the Biopharmaceutical Design of Oral Drug Delivery Systems: Prediction of Intestinal Absorption. *Adv Drug Deliv Rev 1996*; 19:359-376.

Yu LX and Amidon GL. A Compartmental Absorption and Transit Model for Estimating Oral Drug Absorption. *Int J Pharm* 1999; 186:119-125.

Zamora I, Afzelius L and Cruciani G. Predicting Drug Metabolism: A Site of Metabolism Prediction Tool Applied to the Cytochrome P450 2C9. *J Med Chem* 2003; 46:3213-2324.

10

Prodrug Strategies for Improving Drug-Like Properties

Valentino J. Stella

Department of Pharmaceutical Chemistry
The University of Kansas
Lawrence, Kansas, 66047 USA

Table of Contents

List of Abbreviations

ADME ....Absorption, distribution, metabolism and execration
CRO...Contract research organizations
GIT ....Gastrointestinal tract
HTS..High throughput screens
IM ....Intramuscular
IOP...Intraocular Pressure
IV ....Intravenous
NCE ....New chemical entity
PD...Pharmacodynamics
PK...Pharmacokinetics

Keywords

Prodrugs, History, Rationale, Patents, Teamwork, Promoiety, Paradigm shift

Introduction

My colleagues in this workshop have commented on what is meant by the terms "drug-like" or "drugable" properties. Clearly, most companies prefer to develop drugs that do not require heroic interventions to achieve drug delivery, pharmacokinetic (PK) and pharmacodynamic (PD) goals. Thus a drug should have adequate water solubility to facilitate dissolution if administered orally and superior solubility if a parenteral solution dosage form is required. The drug should have the ability to cross biological membranes either via passive permeation or via a carrier-mediated process. If it is unable to do so, absorption from the gastrointestinal tract (GIT) may be limited and access to intracellular sites a challenge. For passive permeation, having lipophilic properties is ideal, thus this property can conflict with the goal of adequate water solubility. The drug must have adequate chemical stability in its desired dosage forms, once in solution and adequate metabolic stability so that it does not undergo excessive presystemic clearance and has a reasonable *in vivo* residence time. The drug should have properties such as taste, odor, etc. that allow for ease of formulation and it would be ideal if the drug had greater affinity for the activity receptor site than for sites and receptors that could lead to toxic outcomes.

For the last 100 years, many small molecules have been identified with desirable therapeutic benefits. Most have "drugable" properties, since the ability to deliver and test drugs without these properties has been limited. That is, earlier *in vivo* screening techniques led to a natural selection process of drugs with drugable properties while discarding otherwise efficacious but poorly deliverable molecules. With combinatorial chemistry increasing chemical libraries to mega-numbers, receptor and cell culture based assays and high throughput screening (HTS) assays, and an increase in scientific sophistication, molecules have been identified which should be active, if they are capable of reaching and maintaining adequate concentrations at the appropriate receptor site. Along with this increased sophistication, increased frustration has occurred as receptor or enzyme based assays have not always translated to *in vivo* efficacy. The negative *in vivo* responses and lack of "developability" of many of these molecules have etiologies that include poor "drugable" properties (Horspool and Lipinski, 2003; Lipinski, 2000; Lipinski *et al.*, 1997). On the positive side, these assays and the novel chemistries have helped identify new chemical entities (NCEs) with complex structures, which would have been discarded in earlier times due to apparent lack of apparent *in vivo* efficacy. What if these agents could now be delivered? These "leads" could result in new drug molecules with truly novel structures. However, further analog development of these leads often fall into the category of what has been termed the "high affinity trap" whereby the constraints for receptor activity no longer allow the incorporation of drugable properties through analog modifications. A possible solution to this dilemma is the rational design of prodrugs.

Prodrugs and Drug-Like Properties

Many have used the following scheme (Scheme 1) to describe the prodrug approach to the delivery of problematic molecules.

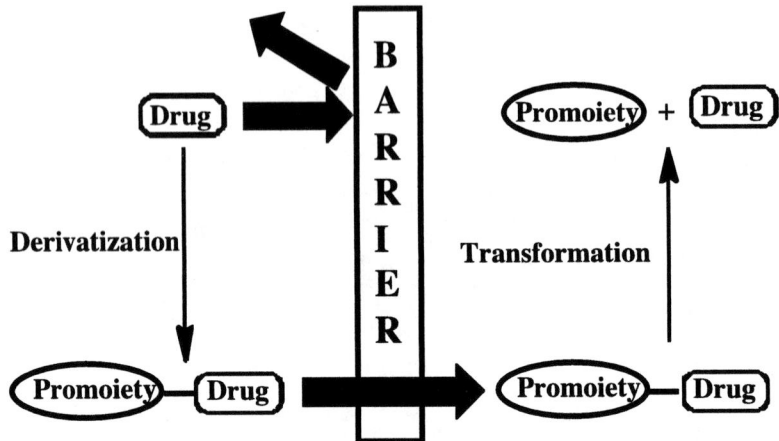

Scheme 1. An illustration of the prodrug concept.

Prodrugs are chemical modifications of drug or potential drug molecules used to overcome barriers to the efficacy, deliverability and utility of problematic molecules. The barrier shown in the scheme can include but is not limited to;

- low water solubility leading to compromised oral, dermal. ophthalmic and parenteral delivery
- high polarity leading to poor cellular permeability
- poor chemical and metabolic stability leading to presystemic metabolism and short biological residence times
- lack of site of action targeting leading to high side effects and compromised pharmacodynamics (PD)
- compromised physicochemical properties leading to patient acceptability and formulability issues
- poor intellectual property right protection leading to the lack of economic incentive

Ferres (1983) has used Scheme 2 to illustrate the possible advantages of the prodrug solution compared to an analog approach

In this scheme, the delivery problems could be overcome without compromising receptor activity since the active species remains with the analog or what has been referred to in the prodrug literature as the parent molecule or parent drug. A significant number of recently marketed molecules are prodrugs (about 14% at small molecule NCEs approved worldwide in 2001and 2002) yet the use of prodrugs to address solutions to the formulation and delivery of problematic drugs was often disdained in both big pharma as well as in emerging companies. This appears to be changing. Having consulted for the pharmaceutical industry for the last 32 years on a number of issues including the use of prodrugs, I have

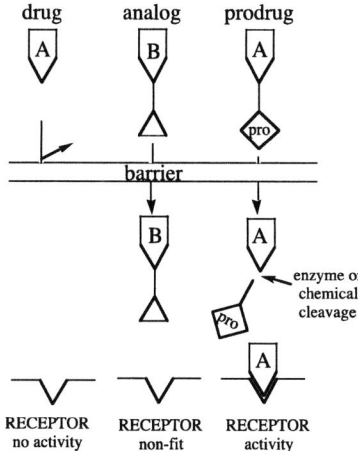

Scheme 2. . Illustration used by Ferres (1983) to show the potential differences between an analog and a prodrug approach to drug receptor activity. Reproduced with permission (Ferres, 1983).

had more requests to give talks and to consult on the possible use of prodrugs as a problem solving technique in the last two to three years than in my previous 30 years. The basis for some of this increased interest is discussed in some recent publications (Krise and Stella, 2003; Stella, 2004). The number of prodrug patents has increased dramatically in the last 10 years (2000% increase over 1993, see Figure 1) and the number of recently approved drugs that are in fact prodrugs strongly suggest that prodrug strategies are becoming an integral part of the drug discovery paradigm (Stella, 2004). Drug discovery teams seem to be raising the idea of the use of prodrugs earlier rather than as an afterthought.

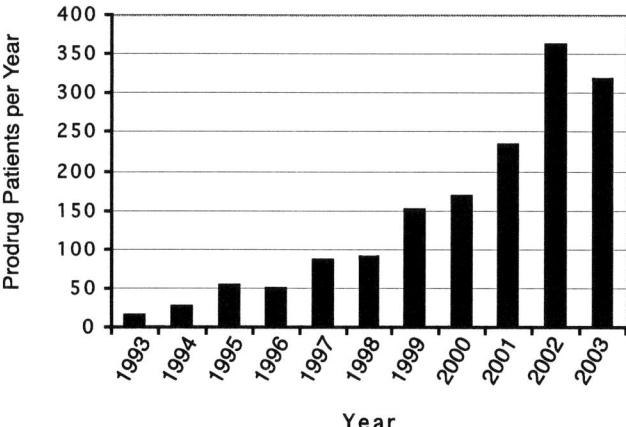

Figure 1. Plot of the number of patents per year over the last 10 years from a search using the terms, prodrugs, drug latentiation, bioreversible derivatives and ADEPT (Stella, 2004). The number of patents for 2003 was only estimated from the numbers collected over approximately the first half of the year.

Professor Adrian Albert, the author of the term pro-drug or pro-agent, spoke eloquently of the topic of this workshop in his book, "Selective Toxicity" in the 1950s (see Albert, 1985). He recognized the often disconnect between receptor binding and receptor access so suggesting the prodrug approach as a means of overcoming the gap. Have we really come a long way since the 1950s?

What Have You Done for Me Recently?

The prodrug concept has been the subject of numerous reviews by Harper, 1959, 1962; Sinkula and Yalkowsky, 1975; Higuchi and Stella, 1975; Sinkula, 1975; Roche, 1977; Bundgaard, 1985; Bundgaard, 1989; Sloan, 1992; Stella, 1996a; Wermuth, 1996. All tell an eloquent tale of the prodrug story while Denny, 2001, 2003; Seddon *et al.*, 2004; and others too numerous to mention discuss how the technique has specific targeting applications in areas such as cancer chemotherapy. The prodrug technique clearly has utility. Of the 43 new drugs approved in 1993, five were prodrugs and an additional two or three had structures indicating the possibility that they might have active metabolites (Stella, 1996b). Bernardelli *et al.* (2002) and Doherty (2003) reported on new approved drugs for 2001 and 2002. In that two-year period there were 49 new chemical entities (non-biologicals) approved, seven, or 14%, of which were clearly prodrugs, one was an acknowledged "soft" drug and one could argue that three other approvals were possibly acting as prodrugs. Table I provides the structures of some of these recently approved prodrugs, the barrier that was overcome and the enzymatic/chemical process likely for the bioreversion of the prodrug to drug. The most well known examples in this table are ones used to overcome GIT permeability and solubility limitations. Also included are a few examples that were approved a few years earlier, as well as an example of a prodrug that is currently in later phase clinical trials. This list is not comprehensive but does illustrate some very successful newer examples.

Some colleagues and I are currently completing an extensive new book on prodrugs to be titled "Prodrugs: Challenges and Rewards" that should be published in 2006 by Springer. Included in the book will be numerous case study chapters that will highlight both old and new examples of commercially successful prodrugs.

The patent literature also provides some insight into the future, since drugs will only be developed if their exclusivity can be protected. The patent literature on prodrugs has recently been reviewed (Stella, 2004). Although the search engine used was not comprehensive (Stella, 2004), the trends were notable. That is, there was an almost exponential increase in prodrug patents over the 10-year period. Many of these patents were described as being defensive patents. Just as in the past when terms such as "and physiologically acceptable salts thereof" began to be used to cover possible future novel salts from competitors, statements such as "and prodrugs thereof" have begun to appear. This was most prevalent in patents originating from Japan but has also begun to appear in patents from American-based multinationals (see Stella, 2004 for a more complete discussion of

Prodrug **clinical use**	*Structure*	*Barrier*	**Bioreversion** *Mechanism*
latanoprost (Xalatan) glaucoma		corneal permeability, tolerance, safety	esterases byproduct is isopropyl alcohol
travoprost (Travatan) glaucoma		corneal permeability, tolerance, safety	esterases byproduct is isopropyl alcohol
unoprostone isopropyl (Rescula) glaucoma		corneal permeability, tolerance, safety	esterases byproduct is isopropyl alcohol
bimatoprost (Lumigan) open-angle glaucoma		corneal permeability, tolerance, safety	amidases byproduct is ethylamine
tenofovir disoproxil fumarate (Viread) antiviral used to treat AIDs		GI permeability	esterases and phosphodiestereases byproducts are carbon dioxide, isopropyl alcohol, formaldehyde
adefovir dipivoxil (Hepsera) hepatitis B antiviral		GI permeability	esterases and phosphodiestereases byproducts are pivalic acid formaldehyde
valacyclovir hydrochloride (Valtrex) antiviral		GI permeability	esterases/ peptidases byproduct is L-valine
valganciclovir hydrochloride (Valcyte) antiviral		GI permeability	esterases/ peptidases byproduct is L-valine
oseltamivir (Tamiflu) anti-influenza (neurominidase inhibitor)		GI permeability	esterases byproduct is ethanol

Table 1. *(Continued on next page.)*

Prodrug clinical use	Structure	Barrier	Bioreversion Mechanism
olmesartan medoxomil (Benicar) anti-hypertensive		GI permeability	esterases byproducts are carbon dioxide and 2,3 butanedione
ximelagatran (Exanta) anticoagulant clot preventive		GI permeability	esterases, and reductive enzymes byproducts ethanol other products
prulifloxicin (Sword, Japan) antibacterial		presumed to be improved oral bioavailability	paraoxonase byproducts are carbon dioxide and 2,3 butanedione
fosamprenavir (Lexiva) HIV protease inhibitor antiviral		ease of formulation for oral dosing patient compliance	phosphatases byproduct is inorganic phosphate
fosphenytoin (Cerebyx) anticonvulsant		greater safety, ease of administration	phosphatases byproducts are formaldehyde and inorganic phosphate
fosfluconazole (Procif, Japan) antifungal		adequate solubility for parenteral dosing	phosphatases byproduct is inorganic phosphate
aquavan (in phase III clinical trials) anesthetic		solubility and lower pain on injection aqueous versus emulsion formulation	phosphatases byproducts is inorganic phosphate and formaldehyde
parecoxib sodium (Dynastat) analgesic		adequate solubility for parenteral dosing	unknown but presumably esterases/ peptidases/ amidases byproduct is proprionic acid

Table 1. Table showing the structures and properties of some prodrugs approved by various regulatory bodies since 1996. This list is not comprehensive.

this topic). A separate search at the US Patent Office site for the period 1976 to the present using just the word prodrug/s resulted in about 6,500 hits. This probably underestimates the real number by at least 50% as many prodrugs are not identified as such. Similar searches in PubMed and SciFinder with the keyword prodrug/s resulted in high publication hit rates confirming the patent trend.

This Paper

Rather than summarize what will be presented in a much more comprehensive book format in the near future, this chapter will review recent examples of approved prodrugs, their structures, the problem overcome, the rationale for the choice of promoiety, byproducts formed, and the enzymes likely responsible for the bioconversion. The emphasis will be on what "non-drugable" property was overcome via the prodrug modification. Table I provides much of this information in a table format.

Recently Approved Prodrugs

Prostaglandin analogs

Latanoprost (Xalatan®), bimatoprost (Lumigan®), travoprost (Travatan®) and unoprostone isopropyl (Resula®) are four recently approved prostaglandin analogs used ophthalmically for the treatment of glaucoma. The use of prostaglandins and their analogs for the treatment of glaucoma derives from the observation in the 1970s that at low doses prostaglandins lowered intraocular pressure (IOP) while at higher doses IOP was raised (Bito *et al.*, 1983, 1987; Lee *et al.*, 1988). Prostaglandins themselves were also shown to cause significant hyperemia and irritation. In an effort to separate the activity from toxicity various prostaglandin analogs were prepared, however, the carboxylic acid forms of these agents proved ophthalmically less clinically effective until converted to either their isopropyl ester form (travoprost, unoprostone isopropyl and latanoprost) or their ethanolamine amide (bimatoprost). The FDA approved Latanoprost in 1996 while the other prodrugs were approved more recently.

The three isopropyl ester derivatives are clearly prodrugs and are readily converted to the parent prostaglandin analog in the cornea by the action of esterases present in corneal tissue to release isopropyl alcohol and the parent drug. For a time it was uncertain whether bimatoprost, as an N-ethyl amide, was behaving as a prodrug but studies by Maxey *et al.* (2002) and Hellberg *et al.* (2003) did show hydrolysis in ocular tissues while Sharif *et al.* (2003) showed that bimatoprost acid was a prostanoid FP receptor agonist. The byproducts of bioconversion are isopropyl alcohol for the three ester prodrugs and ethanolamine for bimatoprost. Both of these byproducts appear to be safe and well tolerated.

Improved corneal permeation and safety were the non-drugable properties addressed by these prodrugs. In their carboxylate form they are both poorly permeable and more irritating than their prodrug forms. Thus the prodrugs offered an improved therapeutic index compared to their parent molecules.

Antivirals with poor GIT permeability

Many antivirals of the nucleoside type are polar and poorly permeate the GIT. Two recent examples are tenofovir and adefovir. As phosphonates, these antivirals are very polar exhibiting oral bioavailabilities of less than 5% in their non-prodrug forms. Tenofovir was first evaluated as its bis-pivaloyloxymethyl ester but found to have some side effects that were felt to be caused by carnitine depletion due to the pivalic acid promoiety (Brass, 2002). A series of carbonate bis-esters (Shaw *et al.* 1997) were found to be superior with tenofovir disoproxil, fumarate salt (Viread®), being chosen as the prodrug of choice for further clinical testing. Cleavage of the prodrug results in the formation of two moles each of carbon dioxide, formaldehyde and isopropyl alcohol. The conventional wisdom is that the first phosphonate protecting-group is cleaved via the action of esterase enzymes at the isopropyl carbonate linkage resulting in the monoester intermediate. Cleavage of the second group is probably via a combination of esterase and phosphodiesterase activity. Animal species differences were seen in tenofovir availability from its prodrugs but human availability appears to be adequate and dose independent (Kearney *et al.* 2004). Tenofovir disoproxil was recently approved and is now one of the top-selling anti-AIDs drugs on the market.

Many relatively non-polar prodrugs of polar parent molecules often result in less than quantitative oral availability. Many ester type prodrugs of which tenofovir disoproxil is one can be subject to premature cleavage in the GIT resulting in the non-absorbable polar intermediate or parent molecule. Often not considered is the role of cleavage in the enterocytes contributing to less than

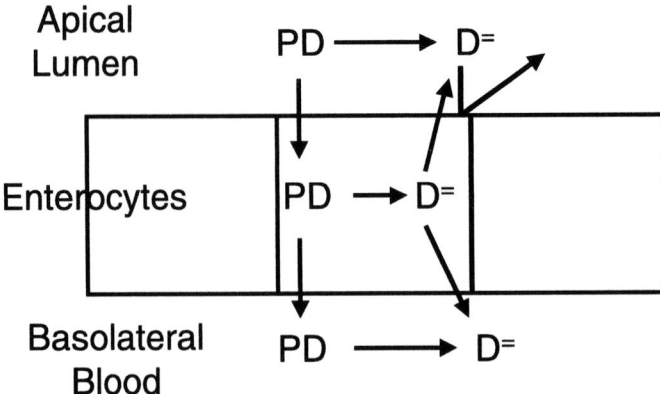

Scheme 3. Illustration showing that a non-polar prodrug (PD) of a polar drug (D=) may show less than complete oral availability due to premature cleavage in the GIT or the enterocytes.

quantitative availability. This is illustrated in Scheme 3. The ideal prodrug of a polar non-absorbable parent is one that is chemically and enzymatically stable in the lumen and the enterocytes but is then quantitatively and selectively cleaved on reaching systemic circulation. If cleavage occurs in the entrocyctes diffusion or efflux of the parent back into the lumen is possible and highly probable since there is just as much driving force for the drug to go in that direction as there is for systemic delivery.

Adefovir dipivoxil was developed and approved as a bis-pivalate for the treatment of hepatitis B after an initial trial for the treatment of AIDs. Because of the lower dose needed to treat the hepatitis B indication, the amount of pivalic acid formed during the prodrug deprotection did not result in sufficient carnitine depletion to be of concern. Like the tenofovir prodrug, oral availability of the prodrug is good and results in effective therapy.

Adefovir dipivoxil and tenofovir disoproxil metabolism results in the production of two moles of formaldehyde. Company toxicologists and regulators often raise concern about formaldehyde production especially since it gives a positive Ames test. There are numerous marketed prodrugs that form formaldehyde, fosphenytoin is a good example (Stella, 1996c). Nevertheless, each time a formaldehyde-producing prodrug is proposed, new concerns are raised.

Taking 300 mg of tenofovir disoproxil per day exposes one to 0.035 grams of formaldehyde. To place this into perspective, two glasses of red wine will expose you to about 0.040 grams of methanol/formaldehyde. Yes, one must be concerned with excessive formaldehyde exposure, but by any reasonable estimate most prodrugs will not add significantly greater methanol/formaldehyde/formate exposure than that seen in normal input from diet and the environment.

Two earlier marketed nucleoside antivirals are acyclovir and gangciclovir. Both are absorbed from the GIT but on a limited basis. Their limited permeability across the GIT mucosa is the result of their high polarity. Numerous efforts to improve oral availability by the innovators and various other research groups focused on the simple mono-esterification of acyclovir or mono- or bis-esters of gangciclovir (Martin *et al.*, 1987). The discovery by Burrows Wellcome scientists that the L-valine ester of acyclovir (valacyclovir, Valtrex®) gave superior performance compared to other esters was surprising and was initially attributed to the combination of solubility and lipophilicity enhancement of the prodrug compared to the parent (Beauchamp *et al.*, 1992). It was not until later that it was discovered that valacyclovir was actively transported across biomembranes by the di- and tripeptide transporter (Balimane *et al.*, 1998, Han *et al.*, 1998). Similar results were observed with the L-valine ester of gangciclovir (valgangciclovir, Valcyte®) (Sugawara *et al.*, 2000). Of note is the better performance of the monoester compared to the bis-ester (Hans Maag, personal communications).

Valacyclovir is an example where "lady luck" plays a role and illustrates the role that serendipity plays in the drug discovery process. Is the choice of L-valine esters one that someone would make from first principles? It is unlikely, but the discovery and development of valgangciclovir was influenced by the observations made with valacyclovir.

Relenza® or zanamivir is a neuraminidase inhibitor useful for the treatment of influenza, but, because of its high polarity, is only available in an inhaler form. No oral form is available. When developing oseltamivir (Tamiflu®, Gilead Pharma), another neuraminidase inhibitor, not only did the product have to compete against zanamivir, but the preferred route of administration of most medications in most of the world is oral delivery. As an ethyl ester, oseltamivir is well absorbed orally in man and readily breaks down to its active form, oseltamivir carboxylate (GS-4071), *in vivo*. GS-4071 only showed an oral availability of 4.3 ± 1.6 % in rats. Significant animal species differences were observed in bioavailability after oral dosing of the prodrug, with 30%, 35%, 11% and 73% bioavailability in mice, rats, ferrets and dogs, respectively (Li *et al.*, 1998). The bioavailability in man is around 40-50%. Breakdown of oseltamivir is due to the action of esterases resulting in production of small quantities of ethanol. As an oral product, oseltamivir appears to have had a greater commercial impact than zanamivir, while the discoverers of zanamivir should be credited with pioneering this novel route of influenza treatment.

Other polar drug examples

Three additional drugs were recently approved for which the use of a prodrug modification resulted in commercially viable products of parent drugs that were polar. Two that use the same promoiety are olmesartan medoxomil (Benicar®), an antihypertensive agent, and prulifloxicin (Sword®), an antibacterial. Both these agents use the (5-methyl-2-oxo-1,3-dioxol)methyl promoiety. In one case, it is used in the form of an ester and, in the second case, it is used in the form of an N-alkylation of a secondary amine group. In the case of olmesartan medoxomil, protection of the acidic carboxyl group allows for acceptable absorption of the deprotected antihypertensive active. The mechanism of deprotection of the (5-methyl-2-oxo-1,3-dioxol)methyl promoiety, first used, to my knowledge, as a promoiety for altering the polarity of penicillins and cephalosporins in the mid-1980s, has been proposed to be first, esterase cleavage of the cyclic carbonate linkage, followed by an elimination reaction (Ikeda *et al.*, 1984, Sakamoto et al, 1984). This results in the formation of the parent drug, carbon dioxide and 2,3-butanedione. When attached to the secondary amine group, as in the case of prulifloxicin, some have suggested a more complex mechanism involving N-oxide formation of the tertiary amine formed by the N-alkylation by the promoiety (Kondo *et al.*, 1989).

Ximelagatran (Exanta®) is an anticoagulant. Although approved in Europe, it recently was turned down for approval in the USA. The innovator was asked to supply additional supporting data. Ximelagatran is a double prodrug, whereby a carboxyl group is protected as an ethyl ester and the benzamidine functionality is in the form of an N-hydroxyl moiety. The parent drug, melagatran, has an oral availability of only 3-7%, while ximelagatran results in an oral bioavailability of melagatran of about 20% (Gustafasson *et al.*, 2001). Melagatran is zwiterionic, with an anionic carboxylate group and cationic benzamidine group, accounting for its poor permeability from the GIT tract. Gustafasson (2003) has shown, on oral dosing, that ximelagatran produces two intermediates. One is ethylmelagatran resulting from the reduction of the -N-OH to $-NH_2$, but with the ethyl ester moiety intact and melagatran-OH, where the ethyl ester group is removed, presumably via esterase action, but the –NH-OH has yet to be reduced. Neither is present in plasma in high concentration.

Water soluble prodrugs of poorly soluble drugs

There are not many commercialized prodrugs that were designed to overcome the poor oral availability of solubility-limited drugs. A good older example is Merck's non-steroidal antiinflammatory drug (NSAID, sulindac. Sulindac is an S-oxide prodrug of its reduced parent sulindac sulfide. As the S-oxide prodrug, sulindac has superior solubility and lower GIT toxicity than the sulfide and was promoted as a less corrosive NSAID (Shen and Winter, 1977).

A more recent example is fosamprenavir, a phosphate ester of the HIV protease inhibitor, amprenavir (Anon. 2003; Hale *et al.*, 2002). Amprenavir is a high dose drug with marginal water solubility. To achieve adequate oral availability, the drug was formulated as a soft gelatin capsule containing 150 mg of drug. Because the dose of amprenavir is 1,200 mg twice a day, eight capsules, taken twice daily, were required for therapy. It can be readily agreed that eight capsules twice a day is not convenient and could lead to patient compliance issues. The innovators synthesized a phosphate ester prodrug, calcium salt, fosamprenavir (see Table I). Fosamprenavir has very good water solubility and is readily formulated as 700 mg tablets (molar equivalent of 600 mg amprenavir). Fosamprenaviir shows an oral biavailability equivalent to the amprenavir capsules. If fosamprenavir is so water soluble, isn't polarity a problem? The dianionic fosamprenavir is not absorbed intact. The surface of the enterocytes lining the small intestines is very rich in alkaline phosphatases. These embedded enzymes are capable of hydrolyzing fosamprenavir to amprenavir right at the intestinal cell surface. Since amprenavir is readily permeable, it is well absorbed. This coupling of metabolism and absorption is readily seen with the absorption of folic acid from food sources (Rosenberg, 1981) and has been proposed much earlier as a prodrug strategy by others (see Fleisher *et al.*, 1985; Heimbach *et al.*, 2003). Phosphate ester prodrugs appear as some of the better examples of the prodrug technique as a means of increasing the oral availability of solubility-limited drug molecules.

The use of water soluble prodrugs of poorly water soluble drugs to effect parenteral dosing has been an accepted solution to solubility limitations since its application in the 1960s to the antibiotic chloramphenicol as chloramphenicol hemisuccinate, sodium salt (Glazko *et al.*, 1973; Nahata and Powell, 1981), and the hemisuccinate and phosphate esters of various steroids (see various earlier reviews for references). In 1996 fosphenytoin was approved as a water soluble and safe injectable form of phenytoin (Stella, 1996c). More recently, two novel prodrugs are parecoxib sodium (Dynastat®), which is the injectable form of valdecoxib (Bextra®), and fosfluconazole (Bentley *et al.*, 2002), a phosphate ester prodrug of fluconazole, both of which were approved for parenteral use (see Table I). Ueda *et al.* (2003) recently described some novel phosphate ester prodrugs of another clinical antifungal drug.

Parenteral formulations of poorly soluble drugs can present some unique challenges to prodrug scientists. First, solubilities greater than 10 mg/ml are often needed, thus for truly poorly soluble parent drugs, orders of magnitude increases in solubility are needed. Consider the phenytoin/fosphenytoin example. Phenytoin has a solubility of about 25 μg/ml while an injectable dose of 50 mg/ml (as sodium phenytoin) or about 47 mg/ml phenytoin equivalent would have to be matched by a prodrug. Fosphenytoin met that goal without the need for co-solvents. Having met the solubility goal, the second problem was aqueous stability. While fosphenytoin showed excellent chemical stability, it, along with all parenteral prodrugs, suffers from the fact that the most likely degradants of these prodrugs are the poorly soluble parent drugs. Thus the shelf-life of the prodrug in aqueous solution is often dictated, not by the time to lose less than 10% of the prodrug, but by possible precipitation of insoluble degradation products. Therefore, some water-soluble prodrugs of insoluble parent molecules must be formulated, not as ready-to-use solutions, but as freeze-dried powders for reconstitution prior administration. Fosphenytoin is sufficiently stable to allow for a ready-to-use solution, but it does require refrigeration. An alternative room temperature stable formulation has been proposed (Narisawa and Stella, 1998).

Aquavan (see Table I) is a water-soluble prodrug of the anesthetic agent, propofol (Stella *et al.*, 2001). The promoiety, in this case, is identical to that used for fosphenytoin, except that the phosphonoxymethyl group is attached to the sterically hindered phenolic group of propofol. The pharmacokinetic properties of aquavan in rats and humans (Schywalsky *et al.*, 2003; Fechner *et al.*, 2003) have been shown to be quite interesting. This drug recently entered phase III clinical trials in the USA. Aquavan was designed to overcome the limitations of the current propofol formulation, where the drug must be administered in a 10% oil/water emulsion. The limitation is low concentration, requiring large volumes of the emulsion to be administered when used to maintain a coma. This can result in lipid overload. Brachial pain on injection, emulsion cracking during long term infusion, and difficulty in maintaining formulation sterility, due to the emulsion being a very good growth media for bacteria, are other limitations. Aquavan is very water-soluble, so no lipids are required and more concentrated solutions are possible. It is rapidly converted to propofol *in vivo*, both in animal models and humans; thus, there is a rapid onset of anesthesia. Since the injection site only sees the inert prodrug, there is no pain on injection. The injection is in the form of a ready-to-use solution and is easy to maintain in a sterile state.

It Takes a Team to Develop a Prodrug Program

Just as it takes a team to efficiently develop analogs, a successful prodrug program depends highly on quick evaluation of prodrug candidates by a team. For big pharma, a prodrug solution to the lack of developability of drug candidates has been an act of last resort, or, when applied to an agent going off patent, an effort to maintain market exclusivity. This was not always the case. In the 1960s, the Parke Davis Company developed a number of very successful prodrugs, as did a concerted effort by the Upjohn Company in the mid-1960s to the mid-1970s.

In most companies, a prodrug program is only initiated when a specific problem is identified and the effort is only maintained while the immediate need presents itself. Because the effort is initiated in response to a specific problem area, after more traditional methods of overcoming the barrier to developability are exhausted, the development of the drug candidate is delayed and made more complex by the need for additional toxicology and ADME studies. Thus, a prodrug solution to a problem is often viewed negatively by management. What if a prodrug solution to a developing problem is proposed early?

Imagine the scenario where a discovery team appears to be going down the path leading directly to a series of leads/candidates having clear drugability issues. Would it not make sense to raise the question in the development team of a prodrug solution in the event that other strategies do not work? If implemented early, would a prodrug solution be any more expensive than normal analog development? The answer is probably no. If a prodrug becomes the NCE, some issues in its development may add some additional burden to the drug metabolism and toxicology staff. However, this approach may be less financially burdensome in the long run than the added expense of a significant time delay in development, if the prodrug strategy is implemented six months after the problem/barrier is identified.

When the need for a prodrug solution presents itself, who should constitute the "prodrug team"? First, it is important to identify the cause or etiology of the drugability problem and to identify the strengths and weaknesses of this team as it relates to the general prevailing knowledge of the prodrug concept. The views expressed here are based on experience as a prodrug researcher and the knowledge gained from being a consultant to big and small pharma over the last 30+ years and is inherently biased by these experiences.

First the etiology of the drugability problem must be identified with some degree of certainty. Is it solubility, permeability (from either the intrinsic properties of the drug candidate or due to the drug being an efflux candidate), presystemic metabolism, or poor pharmacokinetic properties? Or is it a combination of more than one property? Identification of the etiology is not easy and, sometimes, a property such as limited aqueous solubility, can mask other underlying problems and lead to flawed approaches. There is a greater chance that the true cause of the problem is accurately identified if the decision to pursue a prodrug solution is made by a team constituted of medicinal chemists, ADME specialists, toxicologists and pharmaceutical formulation scientists, with input from marketing. If the right experiments are performed and the etiology or causes are identified, the probability of success is greatly enhanced.

Once the problem/cause/s are identified, what prodrug solution should be applied? Precedent easily identifies some solutions, while others require greater creativity.

The medicinal chemist brings to the table the ability to synthesize complex molecules as well as highly developed observation skills. However, they are sometimes put off by the perceived trivial nature of some prodrug chemistry and are often naïve when it comes to issues of the safety and reversibility of possible promoieties.

The pharmacologist and molecular biologist must test prodrugs with the view that they might not be active per se, so it takes a different mindset in reviewing data from various screens. That is, receptor based screens will not tell the whole story, while cell-based and *in vivo* screens are likely to be more meaningful.

The drug metabolism, ADME and early PK specialists often perform *in vitro* metabolism and permeability studies and small animal PK studies on prodrugs. However, they must be conscious of the limitations of the *in vitro* screens and the over-interpretation of studies performed in mice/rats in relation to eventual human studies. Drug metabolism and early PK specialists often help identify the problem/s with the parent molecules and have sufficient knowledge to suggest possible prodrugs, but often do not have the capability to synthesize possible prodrug candidates.

Toxicologists often are not supportive of prodrug programs, because it makes their work more demanding. They not only must be concerned about the active drug, but must also address toxicology questions related to the prodrug and its breakdown products. See earlier questions raised about formaldehyde production and the role of pivalic acid in depleting carnitine levels

The presence of a formulation scientist on the team is critical. Their role is to make sure that any testing of the prodrug uses realistic formulations that can be scaled to human use and that issues, such as chemical stability, are addressed up front. For example, prodrugs proposed and moved into development can be so chemically unstable that they will never be developed as an approvable entity. If properly trained with a strong physical/chemical background, the formulation scientist is critical to the success of a prodrug program.

While bench scientists often do not appreciate the role played by marketing, marketing specialists can play a very important role as part of this team. For example, if an injectable prodrug is needed for a specific product, it is important to know if a reconstitutable lyophilized product would be acceptable or if a ready-to-use solution is required. This may be dictated by the disease being treated or by competitor products. If a ready-to-use solution is needed, then that will dictate what promoiety or chemistry can be applied. Prodrugs, by their very nature, tend to be more or less chemically unstable. This can present a problem for the formulation scientists. Therefore, the type of formulation needed, often dictated by marketing and patient acceptability issues, may require a greater and more creative effort.

The formula for a successful prodrug effort is teamwork. Such a team is difficult to put together on an as-needed basis. Big pharma companies have recently shifted toward a paradigm where specialty prodrug teams have been constituted to work with discovery teams to identify prodrug strategies immediately when the need begins to present itself. That is, prodrug strategies are becoming an integral part of the drug discovery paradigm. There are also small companies whose business plan/strategy is to design prodrug solutions, both as a conduit for new drug candidates and/or as CROs, to help big and small pharma solve drugability problems.

Conclusion

In this chapter and in earlier writings (Stella 1996a, 2004), a case was made for continued prodrug research as a complementary tool in drug design. There are numerous unmet needs in prodrug research, such as novel strategies for overcoming presystemic metabolism (Johnson, 1980; Svensson and Tunek, 1988; Elger *et al.*, 1995, 1998) and prodrug approaches to improve drug targeting. There is no question, supported by the relatively large percentage of recently approved drugs that are prodrugs, that prodrugs are being considered more and earlier as a solution to problems with poorly drugable molecules.

References

Albert A. Chemical aspects of selective toxicity. *Nature* 1958; 182:421–423

Albert A. *Selective Toxicity: The Physico-Chemical Basis of Therapy*. 7th edition. New York, NY: Chapman and Hall; 1985. pp.97–109, pp. 208–214

Anon. Lexiva (fosamprenavir calcium) tablets. Prescribing information. GlaxoSmithKline and Vertex. 2003; 1–36

Balimane, P. V., I. Tamai, A. Guo, T. Nakanishi, H. Kitada, F. H. Leibach, A. Tsuji and P. J. Sinko. Direct evidence for peptide transporter (PepT1)-mediated uptake of a nonpeptide prodrug, valacyclovir. *Biochem. Biophys. Res. Com.* 1998; 250: 246-251

Beauchamp, L. M., G. F. Orr, P. De Miranda, T. Burnette and T. A. Krenitsky. Amino acid ester prodrugs of acyclovir. *Antiviral Chem. Chemother.* 1992; 3: 57-64

Bentley A, Butters M, Green SP, Learmonth WJ, MacRae JA, Morland MC, O'Connor G, and Skuse J. The Discovery and Process Development of a Commercial Route to the Water Soluble Prodrug, Fosfluconazole. *Org. Process Res. Dev.* 2002; 6:109–112

Bernardelli P, Gaudilliere B, and Vergne F: To Market, to Market - 2001. *Ann. Rep. Med. Chem.* 2002; 37: 257–277

Bito LZ, Draga A, Blanco J, and Camras CB. Long-term maintenance of reduced intraocular pressure by daily twice daily topical application of prostaglandins to cat of rhesus monkey eyes. *Invest. Ophthalmol. Vis. Sci.* 1983; 24:312-319

Bito LZ. Prostaglandins, old concepts and new perspectives. *Arch. Ophthalmol.* 1987; 105:1036-1039

Brass EP. Pivalate-generating prodrugs and carnitine homeostasis in man. *Pharmacol Rev.* 2002; 54:589–598

Bundgaard H. *Design of Prodrugs*. Amsterdam: Elsevier; 1985

Bundgaard H. (Ed), Themed issue. *Prodrugs for Improved Drug Delivery. Adv. Drug Del. Rev.* 1989; 3:1–154

Denny WA. Prodrug Strategies in Cancer Therapy. *Eur. J. Med. Chem.* 2001; 36: 577–595

Denny WA. Prodrugs for Gene-Directed Enzyme-Prodrug Therapy (Suicide Gene Therapy). *J. Biomed. Biotech.* 2003:48–70

Doherty AM. To Market, to Market - 2002. *Ann. Rep. Med. Chem.* 2003; 38: 347–374

Elger W, Schwarz S, Hedden A, Reddersen G, and Schneider B. Sulfamates of Various Estrogens are Prodrugs with Increased Systemic and Reduced Hepatic Estrogenicity at Oral Application. *J. Steroid Biochem. Mol. Biol..* 1995; 55:395–403

Elger W, Palme H-H, and Schwarz S. Novel Oestrogen Aulfamates: A New Approach to Oral Hormone Therapy. *Exp. Opin. Invest. Drugs* 1998; 7:575–589

Fechner J, Ihmsen H, Hatterscheid D, Schiessi C, Vornov, JJ, Burak E, Schwilden H, and Schuttler J. Pharmacokinetics and Clinical Pharmacodynamics of the New Propofol Prodrug GPI 15715 in Volunteers. *Anesthesiol.* 2003; 99: 303–313

Ferres H. Pro-Drugs of ,-Lactam Antibiotics. *Drugs of Today* 1983; 19:499–538

Fleisher D, Stewart B, and Amidon GL. Design of prodrugs for Improved Gastrointestinal Absorption by Intestinal Enzyme Targeting. *Methods Enzymol.* 1985; 112:360–381

Glazko AJ, Carnes HE, Kazenk A, Wolf LM, and Reutner TF. Succinic Acid Esters of Chloramphenicol. *Antibiot. Annu.* 1957-58; 792-802

Gustafsson D, Nystrom J, Carlsson S, Bredberg U, Eriksson U, Gyzander E, Elg M, Antonsson T, Hoffmann K, Ungell A, Sorensen H, Nagard S, Abrahamsson A, and Bylund R. The Direct Thrombin Inhibitor Melagatran and Its Oral Prodrug H 376/95: Intestinal Absorption Properties, Biochemical and Pharmacodynamic Effects. *Thromb Res.* 2001; 101:171–181

Gustafsson D. Oral Direct Thrombin Inhibitors in Clinical Development. *J. Intern. Med.* 2003; 254: 322–334

Hale MR, Tung RD, Baker CT, and Spaltenstein A, Prodrugs of Aspartyl Protease Inhibitors. *US patent* #6,436,989, August 20, 2002

Han, H.-K., R. L. A. De Vrueh, J. K. Rhie, K.-M. Y. Covitz, P. L. Smith, C.-P. Lee, D.-M. Oh, W. Sadee and G. L. Amidon. 5'-Amino acid esters of antiviral nucleosides, acyclovir, and AZT are absorbed by the intestinal PEPT1 peptide transporter. *Pharm. Res.* 1998; 15 : 1154-1159

Harper NJ. Drug Latentiation. *J. Med. Pharm. Chem.* 1959; 1:467–500

Harper NJ. Drug Latentiation. *Prog. Drug Res.* 1962; 4:221–294

Heimbach T, Oh DM, Li LY, Forsberg M, Savolainen J, Leppanen J, Matsunaga Y, Flynn G, and Fleischer D. Absorption Rate Limit Considerations for Oral Phosphate Prodrugs. *Pharm. Res.* 2003; 20:848–856

Hellberg MR, Ke TL, Haggard K, Klimko PG, Dean TR, and Graff G. The hydrolysis of the prostaglandin analog prodrug bimatoprost to 17-phenyl-trinor PGF2alpha by human and rabbit ocular tissue. *J. Ocul. Pharmacol. Ther.* 2003; 19:97-103

Higuchi T, and Stella V. *Pro-drugs as Novel Drug Delivery Systems*. Washington DC. ACS Symposium Series #14, American Chemical Society; 1975

Horspool KR, Lipinski CA. Enabling Strategies: Advancing New Drug Delivery Concepts to Gain the Lead. *Drug Del. Tech.* 2003; 3(7): 34–46

Ikeda S, Sakamoto F, Kondo H, Moriyama M and Tsukamoto G. Studies on Prodrugs. III. A Convenient and Practical Preparation of Ampicillin Produgs. *Chem. Pharm. Bull.* 1984; 32:4316-4322

Johnson P. Pro-drugs and First-Pass Effects. *Chem. Ind.* 1980; June 7:443–447

Kearney BP, Flaherty JF, Shah J. Tenofovir disoproxil fumarate: clinical pharmacology and pharmacokinetics. *Clin Pharmacokinet.* 2004; 43:595-612

Kondo A, Sakamoto F, Uno T, Kawahata Y, and Tsukamoto G. Studies on Prodrugs 11. Synthesis and Antimicrobial Activity of N-[4-Methyl-5-methylene-2-oxo-1,3-dioxolan-4-yl)oxy]norfloxacin. *J. Med. Chem.* 1989; 32;671-674

Krise JP, and Stella VJ. Prodrugs: A Year of Renewed Interest in an Old Concept. *AAPS Newsmagazine.* 2003; December:25

Lee P-Y, Shao H, Xu L, and Qu C-K. The effect of prostaglandin F2·? on intraocular pressure in normotensive human subjects. *Invest. Ophthalmol. Vis. Sci.* 1988; 29:1474-1477

Li W, Escarpe PA, Eisenberg EJ, Cundy KC, Sweet C, Jakeman KJ, Merson J, Lew W, Williams M, Zhang L, Kim CU, Bischofberger N, Chen MS, Mendel DB. Identification of GS 4104 as an Orally Bioavailable Prodrug of the Influenza Virus Neuraminidase Inhibitor GS 4071. *Antimicrob Agents Chemother.* 1998; 42:647-53

Lipinski CA. Drug-Like Properties and the Causes of Poor Solubility and Poor Permeability. *J. Pharmacol. Toxicol. Meth.* 2000; 44: 235–249

Lipinski CA, Lombardo F, Dominy BW, and Feeney PJ. Experimental and Computational Approaches to Estimate Solubility and Permeability in Drug Discovery and Development Settings. *Adv. Drug Del. Rev.* 1997; 23: 3–25

Martin JC., Tippie MA, McGee DPC and Verheyden JPH, Synthesis and antiviral activity of various esters of 9-[(1,3-dihydroxy-2-propoxy)methyl]guanine. *J. Pharm. Sci.* 1987; 76; 180-184

Maxey KM, Johnson JL, and LaBrecque J. The hydrolysis of bimatoprost in corneal tissue generates a potent prostanoid FP receptor agonist. *Surv. Ophthalmol.* 2002; 47:S34-40

Nahata MC. and Powell DA. Bioavailability and Clearance of Chloramphenicol after Intravenous Chloramphenicol Succinate. *Clin. Pharmacol. Ther.* 1981; 30:368–372

Narisawa S, and Stella VJ. Increased Shelf-Life of Fosphenytoin: Solubilization of a Degradant, Phenytoin, through Complexation with (SBE)7M-,-CD. *J. Pharm. Sci.* 1998; 87:926–930

Roche EB. *Design of Biopharmaceutical Properties Through Prodrugs and Analogs.* Washington, DC: American Pharmaceutical Association; 1977

Rosenberg IH. Intestinal Absorption of Folate. In: Johnson LR. *Physiology of the Gastrointestinal Tract.* Raven Press, New York, NY 1981; Vol. 2:1221–1230

Sakamoto F, Ikeda S, and Tsukamoto G. Studies on Prodrugs II. Preparation and Characterization of (5-Substituted 2-Oxo-1,3-dioxolen-4-yl)methyl Esters of Ampicilllin. *Chem. Pharm. Bull.* 1984; 32;2241-2248

Schywalsky M, Ihmsen H, Tzabazis A, Fechner J. Burak E. Vornov J, and Schwilden H. Pharmacokinetics and Pharmacodynamics of the New Propofol Prodrug GPI 15715 in Rats. *Eur. J. Anesthesiol.* 2003; 20: 182–190

Seddon B, Kelland LR, and Workman P. Bioreductive Prodrugs for Cancer Therapy. *Methods Mol. Med.* 2004; 90:515–542

Sharif NA, Kelly CR, Crider JY, Williams GW, and Xu SX. Ocular hypotensive FP prostaglandin (PG) analogs: PG receptor subtype binding affinities and selectivities, and agonist potencies at FP and other PG receptors in cultured cells. *J. Ocul. Pharmacol. Ther.* 2003; 19:501-15

Shaw JP, Sueoko CM, Oliyai R, Lee WA, Arimilli MN, Kim CU, and Cundy KC. Metabolism and Pharmacokinetics of Novel Oral Prodrugs of 9-[(R)-2-(phosphonomethoxy)propyl] Adenine (PMPA) in Dogs. *Pharm. Res.* 1997; 14:1824–1829

Shen T-S, and Winter CA. Chemical and Biological Studies on Indomethacin, Sulindac and Their Analogs. *Adv. Drug Res.* 1977; 12;89-246

Sinkula AA. Prodrug Approach in Drug Design. *Ann. Rep. Med. Chem.* 1975; 10:306–316

Sinkula AA, and Yalkowsky SJ. Rationale for the Design of Biologically Reversible Derivatives: Prodrugs. *J. Pharm. Sci.* 1975; 64:181–210

Sloan KB. Prodrugs: Topical and Ocular Drug Delivery. New York, NY: Marcel Dekker Inc; 1992

Stella VJ. Themed issue. Low molecular weight prodrugs. *Adv. Drug Del. Rev.* 1996a; 19:111-330

Stella VJ. Preface. *Adv. Drug Del. Rev.* 1996b; 19:111–114

Stella VJ. A Case for Prodrugs, Fosphenytoin, *Adv. Drug Del. Rev.* 1996c; 19:311–330

Stella VJ. Prodrugs as Therapeutics. *Exp. Opin.* 2004; 14:277—280

Stella VJ, Zygmunt JJ, Georg IG, and Safadi MS. Water Soluble Prodrugs of Hindered Alcohols. *US patent* #6,204,257, March 20, 2001

Sugawara M, Huang W, Fei YJ, Leibach FH, Ganapathy V and Ganapathy ME, Transport of valganciclovir, a ganciclovir prodrug , via peptide transporters PEPT1 and PEPT2. *J. Pharm. Sci.* 2000; 89; 781-789

Svensson LA, and Tunek A. The Design and Bioactivation of Presystemically Stable Prodrugs. *Drug Metab Rev.* 1988; 19:165–194

Ueda Y, Matiskella JD, Golik J, Connolly TP, Hudyma TW, Ventaesh S, Dali M, Kang S-H, Barbour N, Tejwani R, Varia S, Knipe J, Zheng M, Mathew M, Mosure K, Clark J, Lamb L, Medin I, Gao Q, Huang S, Chen C-P, and Bronson JJ. Phosphonooxymethyl Prodrugs of the Broad Spectrum Antifungal Azole, Ravuconazole: Synthesis and Biological Properties. *Bioorg. Med. Chem. Lett.* 2003; 13:3669–3672

Wermuth CG. Designing prodrugs and bioprecursors. In: Wermuth CG. *Practice of Medicinal Chemistry*. Academic Press, London, UK 1996; pp. 697–715. An earlier version of this paper also appeared in 1984 in *Drug Design: Fact or Fantasy* by the same publisher.

11

The Application of Multivariate Data Analysis to Compound Property Optimization

John W. Ellingboe

Exploratory Medicinal Chemistry
Wyeth Research
401 N. Middletown Rd.
Pearl River, NY 10965

Table of Contents

List of Abbreviations

5-HT$_6$...5-hydroxytryptamine-6 receptor
Acp..acyl carrier protein
AcpS ....acyl carrier protein synthase
ADME ....absorption distribution metabolism excretion
BBB PAMPA..blood brain barrier parallel
                                                           artificial membrane permeability assay
COST ....changing one separate factor at a time
CYP...cytochrome P450
DMSO..dimethyl sulfoxide
DoE..Design of Experiments
FAB ....fatty acid biosynthesis
MIC...minimal inhibitory concentration
MVA ....multivariate data analysis
PAMPA............................parallel artificial membrane permeability assay
PCA ....principal component analysis
PLS ....projection to latent structures by means
                                                                of a partial least squares analysis
R$_2$X..goodness of fit
Q$_2$...goodness of prediction
SAR ....structure activity relationship

Keywords

ADME, Profiling (Pharmaceutical Profiling), PAMPA, Permeability, Solubility, 5-HT$_6$, Multivariate (Multivariate Data Analysis), PCA (Principal Component Analysis), DOE (Design of Experiments), AcpS (Acyl Carrier Protein Synthase)

Introduction

Pharmaceutical profiling assays generate much useful data that contributes to the lead optimization process in early drug discovery. The solubility, permeability, and metabolic stability of compounds need to be optimized simultaneously with potency, functional activity, cellular activity, selectivity and other biological parameters. However, the data from all of these assays for the numerous compounds prepared by parallel synthesis makes the interpretation of results challenging. The use of multivariate data analysis and design of experiments software helps in the effective utilization of all data in the optimization process.

Many assays for physical properties related to ADME have been introduced into the research efforts of pharmaceutical companies. Because ADME issues have been responsible for many failures of drug candidates in the development stage, the trend in industry has been to move assays predictive of later ADME issues earlier into the discovery stage. If properties related to ADME can be optimized earlier in the discovery process, it is hoped that there will be fewer failures at the development stage. Assays for physical properties of importance for good levels of oral absorption such as solubility and permeability, as well as assays to assess metabolic stability and interaction with CYP enzymes can now be run in medium or high throughput modes, yielding information on all new compounds synthesized for lead optimization programs. In addition to yielding information related to ADME, these data are also useful for optimizing properties for earlier phases of testing, such as enzyme assays, cellular assays, and *in vivo* models. When run in a high throughput mode, generally only single point data are generated. However, this type of data is useful when looking at trends within series of compounds. Taken together, the data from these assays is termed the pharmaceutical profile of a compound. Five assays make up the standard pharmaceutical profile at Wyeth (Kerns and Di, 2003; Di and Kerns, 2003). These include solubility, permeability, blood brain barrier permeability, microsomal stability, and cytochrome P450 inhibition. Each of these assays will be described in more detail below.

Pharmaceutical Profiling Assays

Kinetic solubility is measured by taking a DMSO stock solution (20 mg/mL) of a compound and adding it to a pH 7.4 buffer, filtering, and measuring the concentration of the resulting solution. The assay is run in a 96-well format. Results are reported in µg/mL and classified as high (>60 µg/mL), moderate (10-60 µg/mL), or low (<10 µg/mL). These solubility ranges correlate with high, moderate, and low oral absorption (Lipinski *et al.*, 1997). However, solubility is also important for the behavior of compounds in *in vitro* and *in vivo* assays in the discovery phase of drug research. The kinetic solubility assay closely resembles the conditions of an *in vitro* bioassay where a DMSO stock solution of a compound is added to a buffer.

Permeability is measured using the Parallel Artificial Membrane Permeability Assay (PAMPA) (Kansy *et al.*, 1998). In this assay, an artificial membrane composed of phosphatidyl choline and dodecane is adhered to a filter plate, which is stacked on top of a receiving plate filled with pH 7.4 buffer. A DMSO stock solution of a compound is added to a pH 7.4 buffer solution that is added to the filter plate. Following an 18 hour incubation, the concentration of compound is measured in the receiving plate and the filter plate. The assay is run in a 96-well format. Results are reported as cm/sec and classified as high (>1 x 10^{-6} cm/sec), moderate ($0.1 - 1$ x 10^{-6} cm/sec), or low (<0.1 x 10^{-6} cm/sec). These ranges also correlate to high, moderate, and low oral absorption for compounds having average to high solubility. A second version of this assay for categorizing blood brain barrier permeability (Di *et al.*, 2003) is also part of the standard profile, so two permeability data points are generated for each compound. Results are reported as cm/sec and classified as CNS+ (>4 x 10^{-6} cm/sec), CNS+/- ($2 - 4$ x 10^{-6} cm/sec), or CNS- (<2 x 10^{-6} cm/sec). Since these assays utilize artificial membranes, they only measure passive diffusion across membranes.

Metabolic stability is measured by incubation of compounds with rat liver microsomes. The stability is measured at a single compound concentration of 3 μM, and results are reported as percent of parent compound remaining after 15 minutes and half life ($t_{1/2}$). Ranges are classified as high ($>80\%$ remaining), moderate ($20 - 80\%$ remaining), and low ($<20\%$ remaining).

Cytochrome P450 (CYP) inhibition is measured for three CYP isozymes: 3A4, 2C9, and 2D6. The inhibition is measured at a single concentration of 3 μM and is reported as percent inhibition at this concentration. The results are classified as high ($>50\%$ inhibition), moderate ($15 - 50\%$ inhibition), and low ($<15\%$ inhibition).

As mentioned above, all of these assays are run in a 96 well format at a single concentration and are intended to quickly indicate potential issues with compounds. As compounds advance in the discovery phase, any issues are followed up with more in depth work, such as determining IC_{50} values for CYP inhibition, looking at other measurements of permeability in Caco-2 cells, and running pharmacokinetic studies. However, the standard pharmaceutical profile is useful for looking at trends in series of compounds, particularly when there are large numbers of compounds in a series where more detailed information such as IC_{50}s may not be available. Pharmaceutical profiling data can be used in a negative sense to rank series and to deprioritize those that have an issue across many members of the series. It can also be used in a more positive sense to highlight properties of a series that need to be optimized in parallel with biological properties such as potency and functional activity. A series of compounds undergoing optimization may range in size from tens of compounds initially to hundreds of compounds as the optimization process progresses. In the early stage of discovery there are generally several types of biological data generated, including binding, functional and or cellular activity, and selectivity. When these data are combined with the pharmaceutical profiling data for tens or hundreds of compounds, interpretation by simple inspection of spreadsheets is not possible, unless one focuses on only one variable. But by focusing on only one variable one may miss correlations that involve multiple variables. Table I illustrates part of a typical data matrix. This table includes twenty-six compounds from a larger set that were synthesized for a serotonin 5-HT$_6$ receptor modulator project (Ellingboe *et al.*, 2004). The twelve variables include eight calculated properties (molecular weight, plogD at pH 4.0, plogD at pH 7.4, plogD at pH 9.0, number of hydrogen bond donors, topological polar surface area, number of hydrogen bond acceptors, and number of rotatable bonds) and the results from four assays (solubility at pH 7.4, PAMPA, blood brain barrier PAMPA, and 5-HT$_6$ binding).

While this data table is relatively small, it is clear that it is not easy to understand all correlations with only visual inspection. The effective utilization of pharmaceutical profiling data to optimize physical properties along with biological properties requires the use of multivariate data analysis tools.

Multivariate Data Analysis

Multivariate Data Analysis (MVA) is a very useful tool for classifying sets of compounds and identifying the primary latent variables that summarize the data through Principal Component Analysis (PCA), and for identifying correlations between variables describing the properties of compounds and the biological effects of these compounds through Projection to Latent Structures by means of a Partial Least Squares analysis (PLS).

PCA is a projection method that allows one to take a multivariate data matrix and represent it in low-dimension space. It then becomes more straightforward to identify dominant patterns and major trends in the data. The relationships between compounds and data, and among the data variables, are uncovered. In PCA we take linear combinations of observations (compounds) and variables. The data matrix is summarized row-wise as scores (t_a) and column-wise as loadings (p_a). The directionality in a scores plot corresponds to that of a loadings plot, so the dominant variables associated with a compound can be identified (Eriksson, 1999).

An example that illustrates the use of PCA is the characterization of a set of 130 aldehydes. Aldehydes are a commonly used reagent class in organic synthesis that are routinely used in lead optimization. When selecting a set of reagents to use in an array synthesis, calculated properties are generally used to aid in the array design process. With the set of 130 aldehydes we conducted a far more extensive characterization including calculation of eighteen properties and measurement of nine physical properties. With twenty-seven variables it is difficult to use all the data to select a smaller subset of the reagents needed for an array synthesis. Using SIMCA P 9.0 (www.umetrics.com) we generated a PCA model with six components (R^2X 0.901, Q^2 0.687). The plot of the first two scores (t_1 and t_2) showed a good spread of observations with no obvious clusters (Figure 1). Lipophilic aldehydes are located in the upper right quadrant and polar aldehydes are found in the upper left. The scores for each aldehyde can be used to select a representative set of the aldehydes when designing an array of compounds.

Compound	MW	Solubility at pH 7.4 (mg/ml)	PAMPA at pH 7.4 (10-6 cm/s)	BBB-PAMPA (10-6 cm/s)	5-HT6 K (nM)	plogD 4.0	plogD 7.4	plogD 9.0	HB donors	TPSA	HB acceptors	Rotatable bonds
1	371.44	25.9	0.02	7.06	1	-1.57	0.5	1.96	2	85	5	3
2	338.43	18.6	4.67	10.35	2	-0.46	1.72	3.03	1	59	3	3
3	373.45	19.6	0.03	11.25	2	-0.78	-0.2	0.98	2	85	5	3
4	353.44	19.0	0.05	4.28	3	-1.74	0.29	1.74	2	85	4	3
5	383.47	25.2	0.02	5.44	3	-1.7	0.35	1.81	2	94	5	4
6	387.89	24.4	0.23	2.79	3	-1.12	1.02	2.48	2	85	4	3
7	368.46	18.8	17.05	11.50	3	-0.4	3.1	3.1	1	68	4	4
8	374.41	21.7	5.57	20.08	3	-0.08	2.18	3.48	1	59	5	3
9	389.91	21.9	0.02	11.52	3	-0.34	0.27	1.5	2	85	4	3
10	432.34	24.4	0.41	4.58	4	-0.94	0.13	1.23	2	85	4	3
11	406.48	6.3	1.91	equilibrated	4	0.86	2.04	3.21	1	59	4	3
12	382.44	21.2	8.69	equilibrated	7	-0.35	1.84	3.15	1	77	5	3
13	340.45	15.7	3.28	14.27	12	0.29	0.54	1.79	1	59	3	3
14	418.49	24.3	1.06	16.05	12	0.58	0.87	2.15	1	77	6	5
15	358.44	16.6	4.33	12.93	20	0.47	0.74	2.01	1	59	4	3
16	418.49	19.5	1.42	14.73	21	0.58	0.87	2.15	1	77	6	5
17	358.44	16.3	4.19	13.19	27	0.47	0.74	2.01	1	59	4	3
18	408.50	18.8	2.24	undetected	31	1.54	1.92	3.28	1	59	4	3
19	408.50	21.4	5.07	equilibrated	31	1.54	1.92	3.28	1	59	4	3
20	521.89	8.7	0.46	0.64	38	2.58	4.46	5.97	1	87	3	3
21	467.39	8.2	1.07	1.32	39	1.52	3.94	5.25	1	59	3	3
22	422.93	31.6	1.35	1.61	165	1.33	3.73	5.04	1	59	3	5
23	463.00	0.6	0.00	0.00	238	3.56	5.94	6.09	0	50	3	3
24	422.93	4.1	1.14	1.76	387	1.33	3.73	5.04	1	59	3	3
25	467.39	25.0	1.31	0.56	1039	1.52	3.94	5.25	1	59	3	3
26	494.61	10.7	0.87	1.14	1123	2.23	4.72	6.03	1	68	4	6

Table 1.

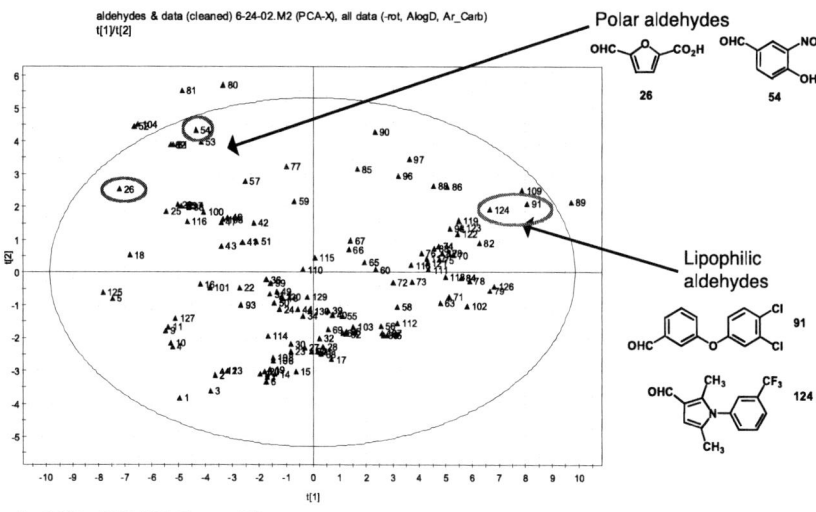

Figure 1. PCA t[1]/t[2] Score Plot

These trends are reflected in the loadings plot (p_1 and p_2) where lipophilicity variables dominate the first component and polarity variables dominate the second (Figure 2). Also, there is an inverse correlation between solubility and the lipophilicity variables.

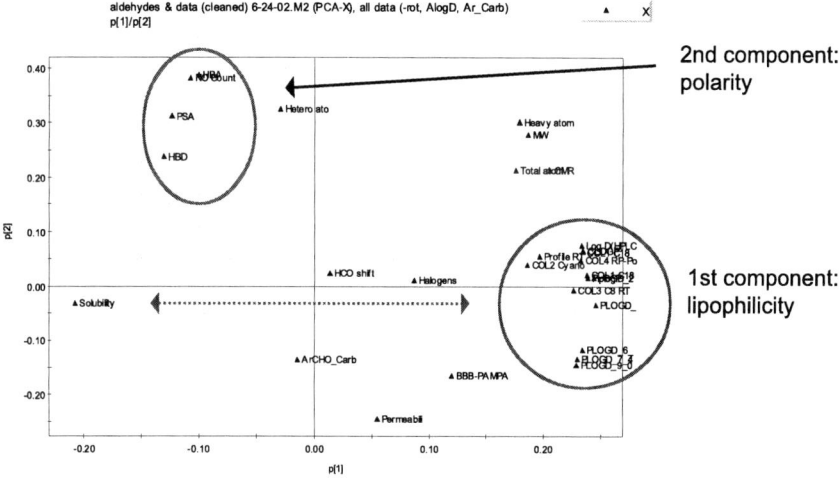

Figure 2. PCA p[1]/p[2] Loadings Plot

This example illustrates how PCA can be used to characterize compound sets. In order to analyze correlations between one data matrix (X) and a second data matrix (Y) it is necessary to use the PLS method. There are many situations in drug discovery where this approach is useful, but one key area is trying to find correlations between calculated or measured physical properties and biological responses. The following example from an early phase drug discovery project illustrates the use of PLS.

Optimization of Acyl Carrier Protein Synthase Inhibitors

Acyl carrier protein synthase (AcpS) is an enzyme that plays a crucial role in the functional activation of acyl carrier protein (Acp) in the fatty acid biosynthesis (FAB) pathway in bacteria. It catalyzes the transfer of the 4'-phosphonopan-tetheinyl moiety of CoA to the side chain of a conserved Ser residue on apo-Acp (inactive) to generate holo-Acp (active). Holo-Acp reacts with acetyl-CoA/malonyl-CoA and carries all intermediates in the fatty acid biosynthesis pathway. AcpS is required for the biosynthesis of important components of membrane lipids and bacterial lipopolysaccharides, so the inhibition of bacterial AcpS is a potentially novel approach to antibacterial therapy (Gilbert *et al.*, 2004). Wyeth ran a high throughput screen against *B. subtilis* AcpS and two of the hits that were identified are furosemide (**1**) and an oxazolone compound (**2**) (Figure 3).

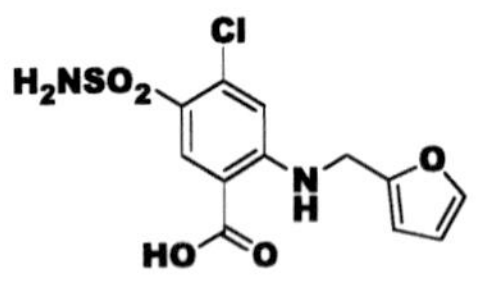

Compound **1**
B. subtilis AcpS IC50: 4.2 µM
B. subtilis MIC: > 200 µM
Aqueous Solubility (pH 7.4): > 100 µg/mL
PAMPA Permeability: 0×10^{-6} cm/s

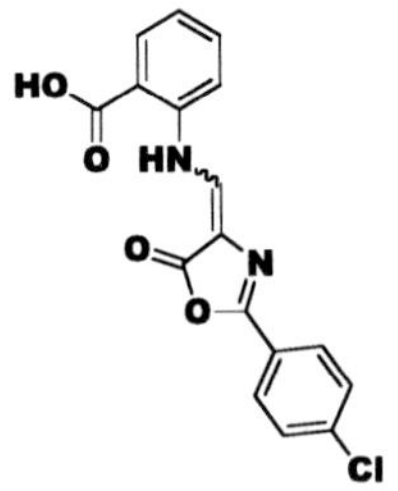

Compound **2**
B. subtilis AcpS IC50: 15 µM
B. subtilis MIC: > 200 µM
Aqueous Solubility (pH 7.4): 4.5 µg/mL
PAMPA Permeability: 0.05×10^{-6} cm/s

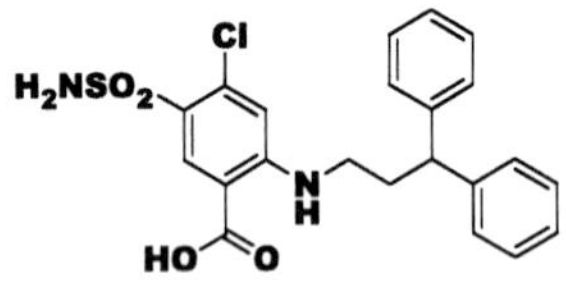

Compound **3**
B. subtilis AcpS IC50: > 20 µM
B. subtilis MIC: 50 µM
Aqueous Solubility (pH 7.4): 26.5 µg/mL
Permeability: 0.15×10^{-6} cm/s

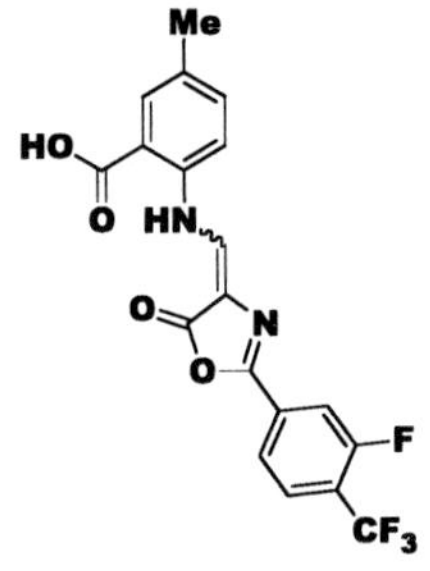

Compound **4**
B. subtilis AcpS IC50: 0.27 µM
B. subtilis MIC: 25 µM
Aqueous Solubility: 2.0 µg/mL
Permeability (pH: 7.4): 0.67×10^{-6} cm/s

Figure 3. Compound Structures

These compounds inhibit AcpS with IC_{50} values of 4.2 µM and 15 µM, respectively. Neither compound exhibits antibacterial activity (*B. subtilis* minimal inhibitory concentration (MIC) >200 µM). Compound **1** has excellent aqueous solubility (>100 µg/mL) while compound **2** has low solubility (4.5 µg/mL). Neither compound demonstrates good permeability in the PAMPA assay (Gilbert, 2003;

Gilbert, 2004). Both compounds were deemed suitable starting points for further synthetic work because X-ray co-crystal structures were available to guide compound design.

The crystal structure of compound **1** with *B. subtilis* AcpS indicated that there was room for larger hydrophobic substituents in the region occupied by the furanylmethyl group. An array of twenty-four compounds was synthesized where the furanylmethyl group was replaced with a variety of substituents derived from a diverse set of aldehydes through reductive amination. An analog (**3**) was identified with weak antibacterial activity (MIC 50 μM) and slightly improved permeability (0.15 x 10^{-6} cm/sec) but with an enzyme IC_{50} >20 μM. The MIC activity of the analogs in this series can be improved by increasing the lipophilicity of the N(2) substituent and this observation was validated by a multicomponent PLS model. However, there is no correlation between enzyme inhibition and antibacterial activity. Additional compounds were synthesized, but again, no correlation was found between enzyme inhibition and antibacterial activity, so the series was dropped from further consideration.

Structural information for compound **2** indicated that several regions of the molecule could accommodate additional substituents. When optimizing a hit with more than one region that can be varied, it is important to not vary only one group at a time while holding the others constant. The strategy of changing one separate factor at a time (COST) does not necessarily lead to the optimal compound. Systems influenced by more than one factor are poorly studied by the COST strategy (Eriksson *et al.*, 2000). To avoid missing an optimal compound without having to synthesize every possible combination of substituents (which could require the synthesis of many thousands of compounds), the use of a Design of Experiments (DoE) approach is both efficient and can lead one towards the optimal combination of substituents. Using DoE, one avoids synthesizing redundant compounds and obtains the maximum amount of structure activity relationship (SAR) information through the synthesis of a relatively small number of representative compounds (Figure 4). Also, a designed set of compounds can give a better PLS model.

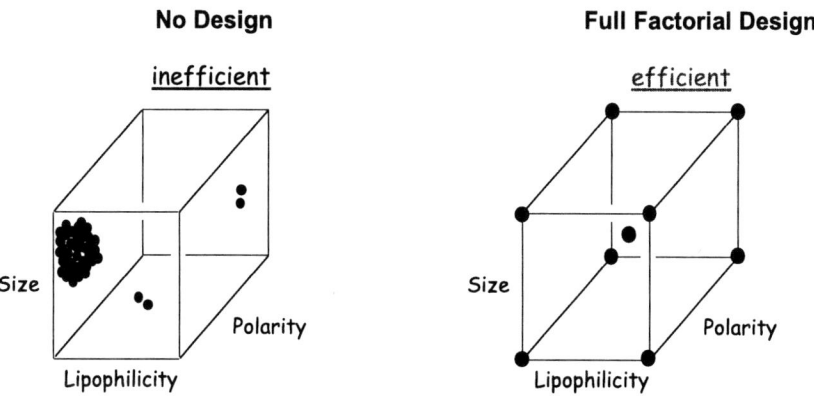

Figure 4. Experimental Design

Using a D-optimal design (Eriksson *et al.*, 2000) generated with MODDE (www.umetrics.com) an initial screening set of forty-two analogs of compound **2** was designed and synthesized, and the biological testing results were analyzed by PLS (Gilbert *et al.*, 2004). A PLS model can be used to correlate the variation in chemical structure as described by a data matrix X to biological responses as described by data matrix Y. Two PLS models were generated for the screening set of forty-two compounds: one that correlates physicochemical properties with AcpS inhibition (two components, R^2X 0.50, R^2Y 0.71, Q^2cum 0.63) and a model that correlates physicochemical properties, AcpS inhibition, and antibacterial activity (two components, R^2X 0.50, R^2Y 0.44, Q^2cum 0.29). These models suggested that the focus for the next array of analogs should be on an overall increase in lipophilicity for the compounds and an increase in the lipophilicity and molecular weight of the substituents on the terminal phenyl ring (occupied by a chlorine in compound **2**). A second optimization set of sixty-nine analogs of compound **2** was designed with a D-optimal design, synthesized, and tested. A number of analogs with improved enzyme inhibition (IC_{50}) and antibacterial activity (MIC) were identified. Compound **4** has the best overall profile with a *B. subtilis* AcpS IC_{50} of 0.27 µM, a *B. subtilis* MIC of 25 µM, and PAMPA permeability of 0.67×10^{-6} cm/sec. However, aqueous solubility remains low. Substituents that improved the permeability of the compounds as measured by PAMPA tended to have improved antibacterial activity.

Summary

Pharmaceutical profiling assays contribute key data that contributes to the lead optimization process in early drug discovery. The use of multivariate data analysis and experimental design helps in the effective utilization of these data in the optimization process. The utility of profiling data, MVA, and DoE has been illustrated with an example taken from an early drug discovery program, AcpS inhibitors. Permeability and solubility data were of particular use for optimizing antibacterial activity in this program.

Acknowledgments

Many people contributed to the work summarized in this paper. In particular I would like to acknowledge Dr. Adam Gilbert for the work on AcpS inhibitors, Dr. David Nunn for developing tools needed for generating compound descriptors, Dr. Mark Tischler and the Wyeth Discovery Analytical Chemistry group for generating the pharmaceutical profiling data and Dr. Svante Wold for training and consultation on the use of SIMCA and MODDE for MVA and DoE.

References

Di L and Kerns EH. Profiling drug-like properties in discovery research. *Current Opinion in Chemical Biology* 2003; 7: 402-408

Di L, Kerns EH, Fan K, McConnell OJ, Carter GT. High throughput artificial membrane permeability assay for blood-brain barrier. *Eur. J. Med. Chem.* 2003; 38: 223-232

Ellingboe JW, Cole DC, Nunn D, Gilbert AM, Stock J, Lennox W, Kelly MF, Lin M, Tischler M, Yaczko D, Sabus C. Library Design: Characterization of Building Block Sets by Principal Component Analysis. Gordon Research Conference on Combinatorial Chemistry, Oxford, UK, July 7-12, 2002

Ellingboe JW, Cole DC, Gilbert AM, Nunn D. The Application of Parallel Synthesis, High Throughput Pharmaceutical Profiling and Multivariate Analysis Tools to Lead Optimization. Advances in Synthetic, Combinatorial, and Medicinal Chemistry, Moscow, RU, May 5-8, 2004

Eriksson L, Johansson E, Kettaneh-Wold N, Wold S. *Introduction to Multi- and Megavariate Data Analysis Using Projection Methods* (PCA & PLS). Umeå, Sweden: Umetrics AB; 1999. 490 p

Eriksson L, Johansson E, Kettaneh-Wold N, Wold S. *Design of Experiments, Principles and Applications*. Umeå, Sweden: Umetrics AB; 2000. 320 p

Gilbert AM. Statistical Molecular Design and Multivariate Analysis of Acyl Carrier Protein Synthase (AcpS) Inhibitors. Gordon Research Conference on Combinatorial Chemistry, Tilton, NH, July 6-10, 2003

Gilbert AM. Physicochemical Compound Profiling/PLS Analysis: Tools to Optimize *In Vitro*/MIC Activity of Acyl-Carrier Protein Synthase (AcpS) Inhibitors. Drug Profiling Strategies: Compound-centric Approaches to Pharmaceutical Characterization and Prioritization Conference, Philadelphia, PA, June 29-30, 2004

Gilbert AM, Kirisits M, Toy P, Failli A, Dushin E, Novikova E, Petersen P, Joseph-McCarthy DM, McFadyan I, Fritz CC. Anthranilate 4H-Oxazol-5-ones: Novel Small Molecule Antibacterial Acyl Carrier Protein Synthase (AcpS) Inhibitors. *Bioorg. Med. Chem. Lett.* 2004; 14: 37-41

Kansy M, Senner F, Gubernator K. Physicochemical High Throughput Screening: Parallel Artificial Membrane Permeation Assay in the Description of Passive Absorption Processes. *J. Med. Chem.* 1998; 41:1007-1010

Kerns EH and Di L. Pharmaceutical profiling in drug discovery. *Drug Discovery Today* 2003; 8: 316-323

Lipinski CA, Lombardo F, Dominy BW, Feeney PJ. Experimental and computational approaches to estimate solubility and permeability in drug discovery and development setting. *Adv. Drug Deliv. Rev.* 1997; 23:3-25

12

Case History: Toxicology Biomarker Development Using Toxicogenomics

David E. Watson
Timothy P. Ryan
James L. Stevens

Investigative Toxicology
Eli Lilly and Company
Greenfield, IN, 46140

Table of Contents

Keywords

toxicogenomics, biomarker, bile duct, hyperplasia, biliary, proliferation, genomics, diagnostic

Overview

Toxicology biomarkers are structural or functional measurements that correlate with an adverse change in the physiology of an organism. A familiar example is elevated serological alanine aminotransferase (ALT) activity as a biomarker of hepatic injury. Toxicology biomarkers such as ALT help us select compounds with desirable margins of safety in the lead optimization (LO) phase of drug development, and allow us to identify target-organ toxicities that should be monitored in patients during clinical drug development. Unfortunately, useful clinical and pre-clinical biomarkers are not available for many compound-induced pathologies. Promising new molecular techniques that can address this gap by finding candidate biomarkers include genomics, proteomics, and metabonomics. Successful application of these technologies to develop toxicology biomarkers could increase the quality and number of clinical candidates selected during LO, and improve our ability to monitor drug safety in patients. In this chapter we present a case history using toxicogenomics in which DMBT1 was developed as a transcriptional biomarker of bile duct hyperplasia induced via oval cell proliferation, a toxicologic pathology for which biomarkers are needed.

Bile Duct Hyperplasia

Bile duct hyperplasia (BDH) is a relatively common toxicologic pathology that occurs in both rodent and non-rodent species. Two distinct processes can lead to chemical-mediated BDH: cholestasis and oval cell proliferation. The pathogenesis involving cholestasis is exemplified by α-naphthylisothiocyanate (ANIT; Lopez and Mazzanti, 1955; Desmet *et al.*, 1968; Kossor *et al.*, 1998). A single oral dose of ANIT leads to a rapid decrease in biliary function within 24 hr, measurable as decreased biliary taurocholate transport and decreased elimination of erythritol from systemic circulation, a compound normally excreted via the bile. Biliary epithelial cell necrosis ensues ~48 hr after exposure to ANIT, leading to sloughing of epithelial cell debris into bile ducts, causing complete obstruction of many ducts. A compensatory proliferative response 4-7 days after treatment with ANIT increases the number of bile ducts and biliary epithelial cells per bile duct, resulting in BDH (Lopez and Mazzanti, 1955; Desmet *et al.*, 1968; Kossor *et al.*, 1998).

BDH pathogenesis involving oval cell proliferation is less clearly defined, in large part because of the complex biology of oval cells. Oval cells are thought to be progenitor cells that can differentiate into both parenchymal (i.e., hepatocytes) and non-parenhymal (i.e., biliary epithelial) hepatic epithelial cell types (Germain *et al.*, 1988; Yasui *et al.*, 1997). Under normal conditions in the mammalian liver oval cells occur at low abundance, but under pathological conditions they can become a prominent feature, particularly following severe liver injury. Oval cells are recognizable by the ovoid shape of their nuclei, a large nuclear:cytoplasm ratio, and basophilia using H&E stain (Dabeva and Shafritz, 1993). Their proliferation can be induced with compounds such as acetylaminofluorene (Park and

Suh, 1999; Bisgaard *et al.*, 2002), in transgenic mice that overexpress SV40 large T antigen (Montag *et al.*, 1993) or ErbB-2 (Kiguchi *et al.*, 2001), and by genetic disruption of genes such as Tg737 (Richards *et al.*, 1996). In each of these models, oval cells proliferate around the portal triad and expand into the periportal region. Under severe conditions basophilic oval cells delineate periportal regions. Concurrent with oval cell proliferation in these models is the proliferation of bile ducts, and proliferation of biliary epithelial cells per bile duct. Progression of these lesions to cholangiocarcinoma can occur in animals that live sufficiently long.

Interpretation of BDH for Drug Development

BDH can progress to cholangiocarcinoma with low margin of safety, a scenario that can lead to costly, late stage compound terminations and increased risk to patient safety. On the other hand, progression of BDH to neoplasia is not a certainty; at least one blockbuster medication (Lipitor®) is taken chronically by patients to reduce cholesterol, in spite of the fact that this compound caused BDH at 3 months or less in both rats and dogs (NDA 20-702). Interpretation of the significance of BDH therefore requires consideration of a number of variables, including duration of exposure, margin of safety, intended patient population, and availability of biomarkers to monitor patient safety.

Many compounds cause BDH after just a few days of once daily dosing. In such instances it is reasonable to expect that with greater duration of exposure BDH will progress in severity and become observable at lower doses, leading to decreased margin of safety in GLP studies that support clinical trials. Because progression of BDH with extended treatment contributes to compound attrition during drug development, methods to identify compounds that do not cause BDH, or with improved margin of safety, are desirable. Ideally this would be an *in vitro* screen that is predictive of the *in vivo* response.

Considerable effort has been made to develop *in vitro* culture techniques for biliary epithelial cells, including their use in screening assays (Gall and Bhathal, 1987; Couchie *et al.*, 2002; Suzuki *et al.*, 2002; Yin *et al.*, 2002; Qin *et al.*, 2004). This work has improved our understanding of oval cells and other hepatic progenitor cell populations, but an *in vitro* assay to screen compounds for their ability to cause BDH has yet to be reported. Several factors are likely operative in limiting the success of *in vitro* BDH assays, including failure of progenitor cells to proliferate and differentiate in culture, and inability of primary cells to metabolize xenobiotics. In addition, since BDH occurs in some instances due to signals emanating from physical obstruction of the bile duct or bile cannaliculi, culture models may not accurately replicate some pathophysiological events that are important in the etiology of BDH.

The desire to identify compounds that do not cause BDH, and the lack of adequate models to screen compounds *in vitro*, requires testing additional compounds *in vivo*. This strategy can be successful when the incidence of BDH in the structural series is reasonably low. If, however, the incidence of BDH in the structural series is high, or the lesion does not appear until prolonged exposure, the need to screen multiple compounds *in vivo* can result in significant delays or even program termination. Thus, drug developers need an alternative strategy, such as a biomarker that predicts outcome of long-term exposures. Such biomarkers would be useful not only for pre-clinical toxicology testing, but also to support clinical drug development.

Currently there is a substantial difference in the availability of *in vivo* biomarkers of BDH for the two mechanisms that lead to compound-induced BDH. Changes in liver function associated with the cholestasis mechanism can be monitored pre-clinically and clinically using serological biomarkers such as total bilirubin concentration, alkaline phosphatase activity, and γ-glutamyl-transpeptidase activity (Smith *et al.*, 2002). Consequently, development of compounds that cause BDH through a cholestatic mechanism is supported by well-validated serological biomarkers. In contrast, BDH induced via oval cell proliferation is a toxicological endpoint for which drug developers do not have biomarkers to support clinical or pre-clinical drug development. Instead, we are limited to histology of biopsy tissue to monitor this pathogenesis. As a result, development of compounds that cause BDH is more challenging for molecules that cause oval cell proliferation than for compounds that cause cholestasis. Biomarkers to monitor or predict oval cell proliferation would therefore be of value to drug developers, both to screen compounds during LO and to minimize risk to patients during clinical development.

BDH Biomarker Identification

Identification of a candidate biomarker

Our objective was to identify a serum-based protein biomarker of oval cell mediated BDH that could be incorporated into a clinical pathology panel. Our execution of this strategy began with gene expression analysis using microarrays to identify transcripts that were induced by compounds that cause BDH via a mechanism involving oval cell proliferation. Bioinformatic analyses were used to identify differentially expressed transcripts that encode a secretable protein. We then evaluated the specificity and sensitivity of these biomarkers by measuring their transcript and/or protein concentrations in livers of animals treated with compounds that cause BDH or other hepatotoxicities.

A number of technical challenges were anticipated. Principal among these was distinguishing gene expression changes occurring in biliary epithelial and oval cells compared with those in other cell types in the liver. Biliary epithelial cells constitute <1% of liver volume in mammals (Gall and Bhatal, 1987), therefore we expected >95% of the RNA isolated from rat liver to be unrelated to the phenomenon of interest. Furthermore, many toxicologic pathologies that alter hepatic gene expression may be coincidental with compound-induced BDH, such as cytotoxicity, hepatocyte regeneration, inflammation, apoptosis, and altered metabolic enzymes. We therefore needed a chemical tool that would maximize

BDH and minimize unrelated toxicological phenomena, combined with a strategy to increase the proportion of transcripts isolated from proliferating bile ducts and oval cells.

Methapyrilene treatment of rats was selected as a model for BDH because it caused a moderate increase in BDH without causing extensive hepatocellular injury or inflammation that would complicate microarray analysis. Chronic treatment of F344 rats with methapyrilene produced marked proliferation of oval cells, severe BDH, and progression to cholangiocarcinoma (Jelinsky *et al.*, 1980). Our goal was to identify early markers of this process. Rats were administered methapyrilene hydrochloride (MP) at 200 mg/kg at 0 and 48 hr and sacrificed at 96 hr. Histological examination showed oval cell proliferation and BDH, with some evidence of hepatocellular apoptosis, necrosis, and inflammation (Fig.1). In order to minimize the contribution of hepatocytes to the gene expression profile, a collagenase perfusion technique was developed to remove the hepatocyte population. The technique is similar to that used to prepare primary cultures of hepatocytes, but instead of harvesting the hepatocytes, we retained the biliary tree for microarray analysis. In this way we enriched for biliary epithelial cells by eliminating ~80% of the wet weight of the liver due to loss of hepatocytes. Importantly, the bile ducts isolated using the collagenase perfusion were largely devoid of hepatocytes and had normal histology.

RNA samples were prepared from the biliary trees of vehicle-treated and MP-treated rats and processed for analysis using Affymetrix U34A microarrays. The transcript levels of hundreds of genes were altered by treatment with MP. Since our goal was to identify a secreted biomarker, the transcript pool was further analyzed

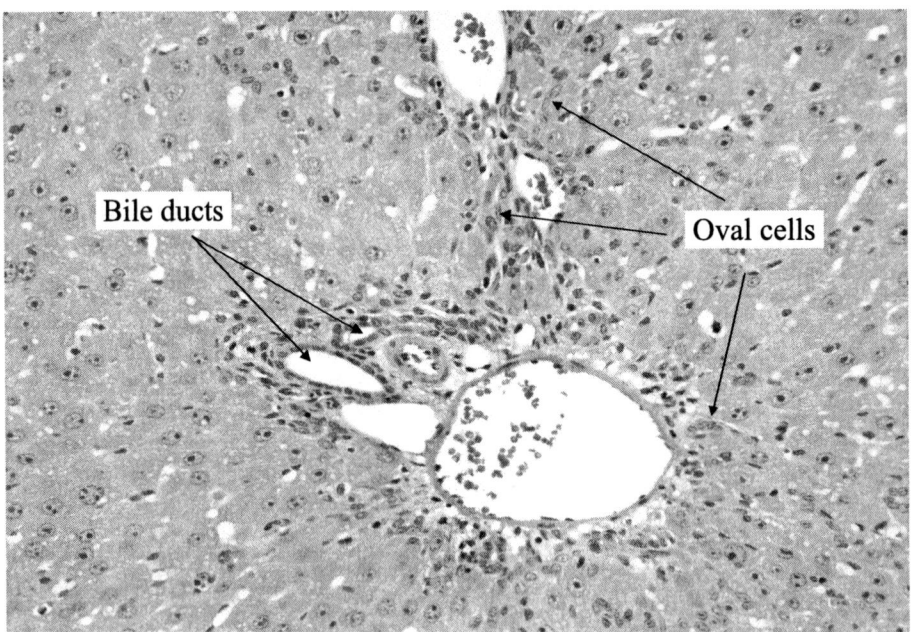

Figure 1. Low magnification image of formalin-fixed, paraffin-embedded, H&E stained F344 rat liver showing proliferating oval cells. Rat was treatment with oral doses of methapyrilene hydrochloride at 200 mg/kg at 0 and 48hr and sacrificed at 96hr.

Treatment	Sample Type	Ebnerin Probe Set #1		Ebnerin Probe Set #2	
		Signal	Call	Signal	Call
Control	Hepatocytes	19	A	2574	P
	Liver	50	A	2827	P
	Portal Tree: untreated animals	5196	P	9837	P
Treated	Portal Tree: Methapyrilene	14617	P	22960	P
	Fold Change (Treated/Control)	2.8x		2.3x	

Figure 2. Affymetrix data for two probe sets attributed to the ebnerin transcript on Affymetrix U34A arrays. RNA was obtained from collagenase-perfused livers of rats treated with vehicle or methapyrilene hydrochloride at 200 mg/kg at 0 and 48hr and sacrificed at 96hr. Data are the average of three hybridizations, one from each of three animals per treatment. Values from rat hepatocytes and whole rat liver are shown for comparison.

to identify the fraction of transcripts that encoded proteins containing motifs typical of secreted proteins, and for which there was evidence for preferential expression in epithelial cells. One such transcript is called ebnerin (Fig.2).

Ebnerin is expressed in secretory duct epithelial cells of the von Ebner gland (VEG) of the rat tongue (Li and Snyder, 1995). It is a large protein (170 – 210 kDa) that contains repeats of two protein domains, SRCR and CUB, with high homology to secreted proteins and transmembrane receptors, respectively. The VEG secretes many proteins and other biological molecules into the lumenal surface along the apical region of taste buds. Of interest to us was the observation that ebnerin was detectable in secretions from VEG (Li and Snyder, 1995), human tear fluid (Schulz *et al.*, 2002), and in the medium of cell cultures (Sasaki *et al.*, 2002).

In earlier studies, ebnerin transcripts were not detected in rat tissues other than tongue, including liver, lung, kidney, colon, testes, brain, and spleen (Li and Snyder, 1995). However, it is common that transcripts and proteins that are first identified under one experimental condition are later discovered to have additional structures and functions in other tissues and other biological processes. We therefore considered it a possibility that ebnerin could be made by, and secreted from, oval and/or biliary epithelial cells, and as such might be detectable in serum and/or GI contents of animals treated with compounds that cause BDH through oval cell proliferation.

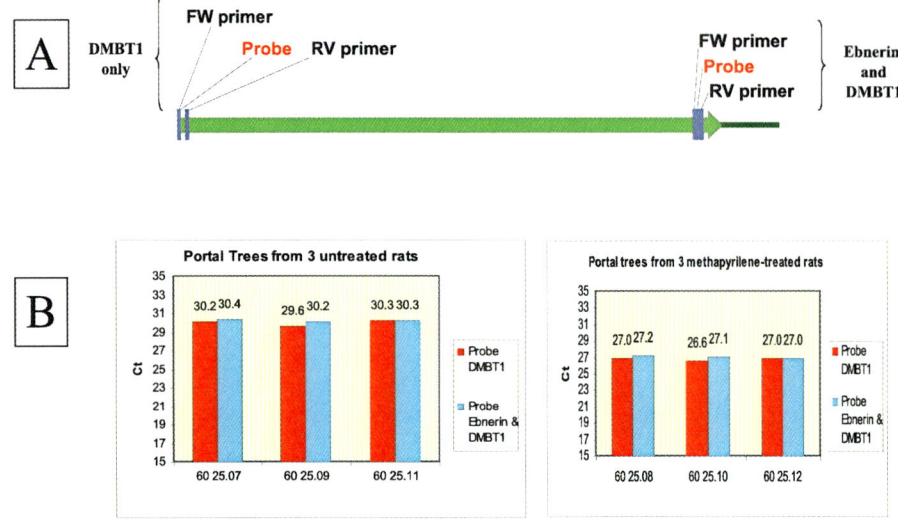

Figure 3A. Location of TaqMan primer/probe sets designed to discriminate between ebnerin and DMBT1 transcripts. The probe set at the 5' end of the gene will detect DMBT1 but not ebnerin. The probe set at the 3' end of the gene will detect both DMBT1 and ebnerin.

Figure 3B. Quantitation of transcript levels for ebnerin and DMBT1 by TaqMan analysis of livers from rats treated with vehicle or methapyrilene hydrochloride, as described in Fig.1A. CT values were comparable between the two primer/probe sets for animals treated with vehicle and methapyrilene hydrochloride.

Biomarker identity and confirmation of induction

Examination of the primary structure of ebnerin transcripts in GenBank and the published literature helped us deduce that a group of transcripts encoded by the same gene had been studied in different species under different names, including ebnerin, gp340, hensin, CRP-ductin, and DMBT1. The transcripts varied significantly in size from 4.5 to 8 kb as a function of species, tissue, and stage of biological development (Mollenhauer *et al.*, 2001). Splice variants lacking exons at the 5' end of the transcript were identified as a distinguishing feature of the ebnerin transcript. QPCR using TaqMan® can be used to distinguish subtle variations in nucleic acid sequence (Li *et al.*, 2004). We therefore designed two sets of TaqMan® primers and probes to quantify two different regions of the transcript: one for an exon toward the 5' end of the transcript and one for an exon toward the 3' end. Of these two exons, only the 3' exon is associated with ebnerin transcripts, whereas both exons are associated with DMBT1 transcripts (Fig.3A). Similar levels of expression were observed for both exons (Fig.3B), demonstrating that the livers of both vehicle and MP-treated rats primarily expressed a transcript that is more properly named deleted in malignant brain tumor 1 (DMBT1), than ebnerin.

DMBT1 transcript induction measured using TaqMan® (~10 fold; Fig.4) was significantly greater than that detected using microarrays (Fig.2; 2.3-fold to 2.8-

fold). This points to tradeoffs related to the use of microarrays. The single hybridization procedure that permits detection of thousands of transcripts requires that we accept decreased accuracy and narrower linear dynamic range for individual transcripts. Complementary techniques, such as TaqMan®, are therefore used in parallel with microarrays to improve qualitative and quantitative assessments of individual transcripts.

Investigation of the kinetics of induction of DMBT1 in livers of rats treated with MP revealed a 2-fold increase 4 hr following treatment, greater than 5-fold after 24 hr, and approximately 10-fold at 96 hr following a second administration (Fig.4). DMBT1 transcript induction was therefore delayed relative to the kinetics of compound exposure. This differential pattern of drug exposure and response suggests that the cause of induction is not a direct effect of methapyrilene; rather,

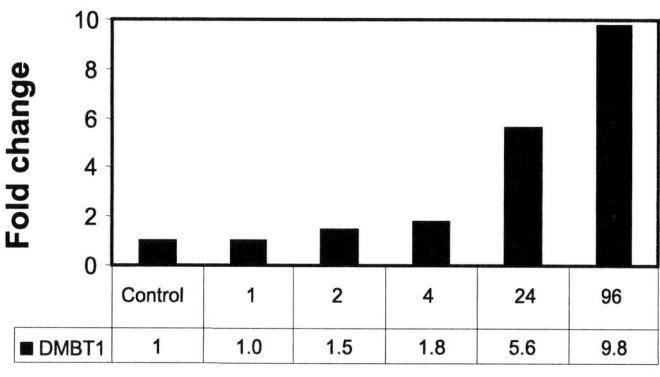

Time (hr)

Figure 4. Quantitation of DMBT1 transcript in livers of rats treated with methapyrilene hydrochloride at 200 mg/kg at 0 and 48hr and sacrificed at 96hr. Data for 96hr came from animals that received methapyrilene hydrochloride at 200 mg/kg at 0 and 48hr and were sacrificed at 96hr. All other animals received a single dose of methapyrilene hydrochloride at 200 mg/kg at 0hr.

it results from a cascade of events initiated by the compound through an as yet unknown mechanism.

DMBT1 protein induction and function

Further confirmation of the induction of DMBT1 by MP was demonstrated by immunoblotting for DMBT1 protein. An immunodetectable band at the appropriate molecular weight was observed in rat liver from MP-treated animals but not from vehicle-treated animals (Fig.5). The band was faint, consistent with the estimate that biliary epithelial cells constitute just 0.14% of the total volume of the liver (Gall and Bhatal, 1987). The apparent molecular weight of DMBT1 in our experiments (164 kDa) was similar to that reported previously for the expressed cDNA for ebnerin, but was smaller than what was detected in VEG of

Western blot data

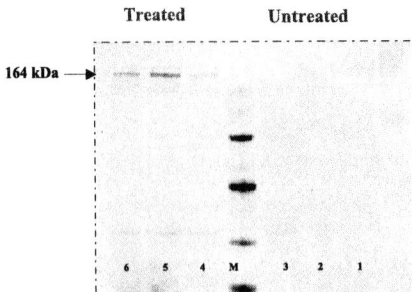

Apparent MW of DMBT1 is 164 kDa,
consistent with theoretical and published

Figure 5. Western blot of liver protein from rats treated with methapyrilene hydrochloride at 200 mg/kg at 0 and 48hr and sacrificed at 96hr. An apparent molecular weight of 165 kDa was determined for the immunodetectable band in animals treated with methapryilene hydrochloride at 200 mg/kg at 0 and 48hr and sacrificed at 96hr.

rat tongue (Li and Snyder, 1995). Splice variants and differences in extent of protein glycosylation are both likely to contribute to the apparent difference in molecular weight of DMBT1 in these different tissues.

DMBT1 protein has been localized by other investigators and ourselves to biliary epithelia and oval cells (Bisgaard *et al.*, 2002; Kadura *et al.*, 2005), as well as epithelial cells in other tissues (Ma *et al.*, 2001; Mollenhauer *et al.*, 2001). The proteins encoded by transcripts of this gene appear to play a significant role in terminal differentiation of epithelial cells of the prostate and vas deferens (Ma *et al.*, 2001) and of kidney epithelial cells cultured *in vitro*, including polarity reversal of the intercalated cells taken from rabbit kidney (van Adelsberg *et al.*, 1994; Takito *et al.*, 1999; Al-Awqati *et al.*, 2000). It is likely that DMBT1 plays a role in oval cell differentiation into biliary epithelial cells, and may involve protein-protein interactions with extracellular matrix proteins such as galectin-3 (Hikita *et al.*, 2000).

Biomarker Evaluation and Development

Specificity and sensitivity

Proper evaluation of biomarkers requires their application by many independent investigators using hundreds of compounds causing a wide range of toxicologic pathologies in the major organs of multiple species. This level of experience reveals the strengths and weaknesses of any biomarker, and builds confidence in our use of the biomarker to make decisions about drug safety. To begin this evaluation process for DMBT1 as a biomarker of BDH, we measured DMBT1 transcript levels in liver tissues from rats treated with compounds that

Compound	Bile duct proliferation (Histology score)	DMBT1 Average Fold-Change (Group)	DMBT1 Std Deviation (Group)	DMBT1 Fold Change (Individual)
Control	0	0.9	0.1	1.0
	0			0.8
	0			1.0
1	2	2.7	0.6	3.0
	1			1.9
	3			3.1
2	1	2.2	0.9	2.0
	1			3.1
	1			1.4
3	0	1.4	0.3	1.1
	0			1.7
	0			1.3
4	0	1.0	0.1	0.9
	0			1.0
	0			1.1
5	2	3.9	0.7	4.8
	2			3.4
	3			3.6
6	0	1.3	0.2	1.5
	0			1.1
	0			1.2

Figure 6. Quantitation of DMBT1 transcript in livers of rats administered agents that cause hepatocellular necrosis and apoptosis. Compounds that also caused bile duct hyperplasia are indicated, along with histological assessment of severity of BDH.

caused a range of hepatotoxicities. Of six compounds from one lead optimization program, three caused hepatocellular necrosis, vacuolation, and bile duct hyperplasia, and three caused only hepatocellular necrosis and vacuolation. The severity of BDH and magnitude of transcriptional induction of DMBT1 after 4 days exposure showed that all compounds causing BDH also caused greater than 2-fold increases in the level of DMBT1 transcript, whereas those compounds that did not cause BDH did not increase transcription of DMBT1 (Fig.6). These data show not only that DMBT1 induction correlates with BDH, but also that DMBT1 is not induced by more common toxicologic pathologies of the liver, including hepatocellular necrosis and vacuolation.

DMBT1 transcript levels were determined for a second set of compounds to assess the effect of phospholipidosis (PL) on DMBT1 transcription. All six of these compounds caused PL in livers of rats exposed *in vivo*. Of these, the development of three of these compounds was terminated in lead optimization because they induced PL at exposures that were too similar to those that cause efficacy in rodent models. None of these compounds was known to cause BDH, and therefore were chosen as "negative controls" that should cause hepatotoxicity in the form of PL but should not induce DMBT1. We were surprised to identify a compound that increased DMBT1 transcription (Fig.7). Upon more focused histologic examination of the livers, it became apparent that of the six compounds, this compound was the only one that caused BDH. Interestingly, this compound has been studied extensively for its ability to induce PL (Rorig, Ruben, and Anderson, 1987), but to our knowledge there are no descriptions in the literature reporting

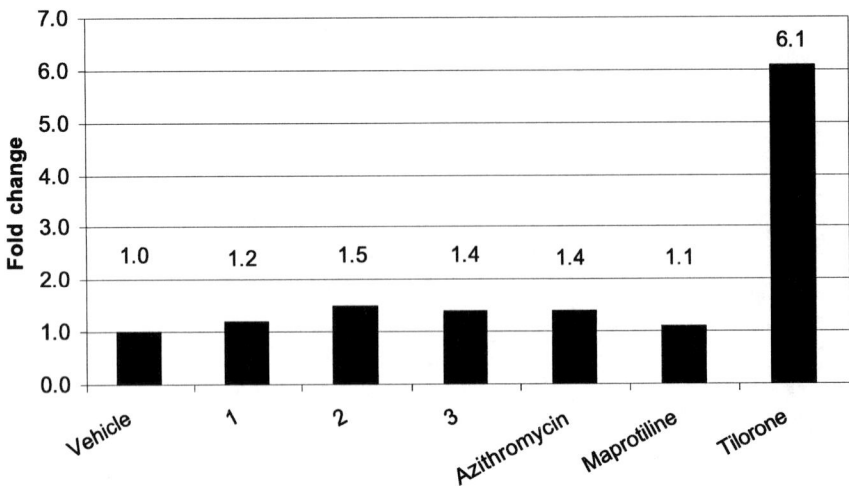

Figure 7. Quantitation of DMBT1 transcript levels in livers of rats administered agents that cause phospholipidosis. Tilorone has not previously been reported to cause bile duct hyperplasia.

its ability to cause BDH. This unexpected event bolstered our confidence in the value of DMBT1 as a biomarker of BDH.

Finally, we examined hepatic DMBT1 transcript levels in rats treated with eight different kinase inhibitors. These compounds have a common pharmacological target, inhibition of which causes a dramatic increase in hepatocyte mitotic index. The key question we asked was whether DMBT1 would be induced in hepatocellular proliferation, or whether there was specificity for cholangiocytes and oval cells. None of the eight compounds caused a significant increase in DMBT1 transcript level (data not shown), consistent with the hypothesis that DMBT1 is specifically involved in proliferation and/or differentiation of biliary epithelial cells.

Streamlining biomarker development

Development of DMBT1 as a biomarker of BDH is a successful case study in the application of toxicogenomics for biomarker discovery. The objective of developing a serum-based biomarker of BDH was not achieved, however, in spite of evidence that DMBT1 is a secreted protein (Sasaki *et al.*, 2002). As occurs in drug development itself, where the majority of candidates selected during lead optimization will ultimately fail, we can expect that the majority of candidate biomarkers will also fail to meet our validation criteria. Biomarker efforts are therefore more likely to be successful if we think in terms of developing biomarker panels, rather than individual biomarkers (Ryan, Watson, and Berridge, 2004), and thus DMBT1 is just one of a set of markers being developed to detect oval cell proliferation.

The ability to move quickly from biomarker discovery to biomarker evaluation is an important attribute of a successful biomarker development strategy. A key resource to support these biomarker evaluations are sera and tissues banked from toxicology studies that are conducted routinely by pharmaceutical companies. In the case of DMBT1, livers of rats treated with greater than 30 compounds that caused hepatotoxicity in lead optimization studies helped us to quickly evaluate the specificity and sensitivity of DMBT1 as a biomarker of BDH. The value of specimens such as the rat livers used in these studies is largely attributable to the data sets associated with them, including pharmacology, clinical pathology, histology, and animal behavior. Convenient access to both the specimens and the associated data sets is therefore a necessary component of a successful biomarker development program.

Summary

Toxicity has historically been a significant cause for compound attrition in drug development. This is unlikely to change in the near future. What can change is the timing of our decisions to terminate compounds due to toxicity, and the amount of time spent searching for compounds with adequate margins of safety. Toxicology biomarkers will play an increasingly important role in each of these opportunities.

Histology and clinical pathology in rodents form the core of non-clinical safety assessments, the majority of which are deployed during lead optimization. These measurements are of high quality, but they are time-consuming and resource-intensive. Innovative toxicology biomarkers can be used to improve our efficiency at prioritizing compounds for development by predicting chronic toxicities from shorter duration *in vivo* studies, and by driving the development of *in vitro* screens. A key challenge in reaching these objectives is identifying panels of predictive toxicology biomarkers.

In this chapter we demonstrated the use of toxicogenomics to identify a transcriptional biomarker of oval cell-mediated bile duct hyperplasia. Once identified, the specificity and sensitivity of the lead candidate biomarker, DMBT1, was evaluated in livers of rats treated with more than 30 different compounds comprising hepatotoxicities that ranged from BDH and hepatocyte proliferation, to phospholipidosis, hepatocellular vacuolation, apoptosis, and inflammation. Since its identification, DMBT1 has been used successfully as an early indicator of oval-cell mediated BDH in preclinical toxicology studies *in vivo*, and as a molecular endpoint to screen compounds for their ability to induce BDH *in vitro*. These successes are evidence that biomarkers such as DMBT1, combined with additional toxicology biomarkers being discovered using the strategies described in this chapter, as well as other methods, are tools that will increase the efficiency of the drug discovery process, through improved methods of drug candidate identification and development.

Acknowledgements

The authors thank Ibrahim Kadura, Baohui Li, Tom Baker, and George Searfoss for their intellectual and experimental contributions to the work presented here.

References

van Adelsberg J, Edwards JC, Takito J, Kiss B, al-Awqati Q. An induced extracellular matrix protein reverses the polarity of band 3 in intercalated epithelial cells. *Cell* 1994; 76:1053-1061.

Al-Awqati Q., Vijayakumar S, Takito J, Hikita C, Yan L, and Wiederholt T. Phenotypic plasticity and terminal differentiation of the intercalated cell: the hensin pathway. *Exp Nephrol* 2000; 8:66-71.

Alison M, Golding M, Lalani E-N, Nagy P., Thorgeirsson S., and Sarraf C. Wholesale hepatocytic differentiation in the rat from ductular oval cells, the progeny of biliary stem cells. *J Hepatol* 1997; 26:343-352.

Bisgaard HC, Holmskov U, Santoni-Rugiu E, Nagy P, Nielsen O, Ott P, Hage E, Dalhoff K, Rasmussen LJ, and Tugstrup N. Heterogeneity of ductular reactions in adult rat and human liver revealed by novel expression of deleted in malignant brain tumor 1. *Am J Path* 2002; 161:1187-1198.

Couchie D, Holic N, Chobert MN, Corlu A, Laperche Y. *In vitro* differentiation of WB-F344 rat liver epithelial cells into the biliary lineage. *Differentiation* 2002; 69:209-15.

Dabeva MD, Shafritz DA. Activation, proliferation, and differentiation of progenitor cells into hepatocytes in the D-galactosamine model of liver regeneration. *Am J Pathol* 1993;143:1606-1620.

Desmet VJ, Krstulovic B, and Van Damme B. Histochemical study of rat liver in alpha-naphthylisothiocyanate (ANIT) induced cholestasis. *Am J Pathol* 1968; 52:401-421.

Gall JA, Bhathal PS. Origin and involution of hyperplastic bile ductules following total biliary obstruction. *Liver* 1990; 10:106-115.

Gall JA, Bhathal PS. Isolation and culture of intrahepatic bile ducts and its application in assessing putative inducers of biliary epithelial cell hyperplasia. *Br J Exp Pathol* 1987; 68:501-510.

Germain L, Noel M, Gourdeau H, Marceau N. Promotion of growth and differentiation of rat ductular oval cells in primary culture. *Cancer Res* 1988; 48:368-78.

Hikita C, Vijayakumar S, Takito J, Erdjument-Bromage H, Tempst P, Al-Awqati Q. Induction of terminal differentiation in epithelial cells requires polymerization of hensin by galectin 3. *J Cell Biol* 2000; 151:1235-1246.

Kadura I, Baker TK, Li B, Searfoss G, Watson DE. DMBT1 is a biomarker of bile duct hyperplasia. *Toxicol Sciences*. In Review.

Kossor DC, Meunier PC, Dulik DM, Leonard TB, Goldstein RS. Bile duct obstruction is not a prerequisite for type I biliary epithelial cell hyperplasia. *Toxicol Appl Pharmacol* 1998; 152:327-338.

Kiguchi K, Carbajal S, Chan K, Beltran L, Ruffino L, Shen J, Matsumoto T, Yoshimi N, DiGiovanni J. Constitutive expression of ErbB-2 in gallbladder epithelium results in development of adenocarcinoma. *Cancer Res* 2001; 61:6971-6976.

Li X-J and Snyder SH. Molecular cloning of ebnerin, a von Ebner's gland protein associated with taste buds. *J Biol Chem* 1995; 270:17674-17679.

Lijinsky W, Reuber MD, and Blackwell BN. Liver tumors induced in rats by oral administration of the antihistaminic methapyrilene hydrochloride. *Science* 1980; 209:817-9.

Lopez M, Mazzanti L. Experimental investigation on alphanaphthylisothio-cyanate as a hyperplastic agent of the biliary ducts in the rat. *J Pathol Bacteriol* 1955; 69:243-250.

Ma JF, Takito J, Vijayakumar S, Peehl DM, Olsson CA, Al-Awqati Q. Prostatic expression of hensin, a protein implicated in epithelial terminal differentiation. *Prostate* 2001; 49:9-18.

Mollenhauer J, Deichmann M, Helmke B, Muller H, Kollender G, Holmskov U, Ligtenberg T, Krebs I, Wiemann S, Bantel-Schaal U, Madsen J, Bikker F, Klauck SM, Otto HF, Moldenhauer G, Poustka A. Frequent downregulation of DMBT1 and galectin-3 in epithelial skin cancer. *Int J Cancer* 2003; 105:149-157.

Montag AG, Oka T, Baek KH, Choi CS, Jay G, Agarwal K. Tumors in hepatobiliary tract and pancreatic islet tissues of transgenic mice harboring gastrin simian virus 40 large tumor antigen fusion gene. *Proc Natl Acad Sci* 1993; 90:6696-6700.

NDA 20-702. Pharmacology review of NDA for Atorvastatin (Lipitor™), pp.23, 27, 36, 39. October 28, 1996.

Park DY, Suh KS. Transforming growth factor-beta1 protein, proliferation and apoptosis of oval cells in acetylaminofluorene-induced rat liver regeneration. *J Korean Med Sci* 1999; 14:531-8.

Qin AL, Zhou XQ, Zhang W, Yu H, Xie Q. Characterization and enrichment of hepatic progenitor cells in adult rat liver. *World J Gastroenterol* 2004; 10:1480-1486.

Richards WG, Yoder BK, Isfort RJ, Detilleux PG, Foster C, Neilsen N, Woychik RP, Wilkinson JE. Oval cell proliferation associated with the murine insertional mutation TgN737Rpw. *Am J Pathol* 1996; 149:1919-1930.

Rorig KJ, Ruben Z, Anderson SN. Structural determinants of cationic amphiphilic amines which induce clear cytoplasmic vacuoles in cultured cells. *Proc Soc Exp Biol Med* 1987; 184:165-171.

Ryan TP, Watson DE, Berridge BR. Toxicology biomarkers in drug developement. *Pharmaceutical Discovery* 2028 (2004).

Sasaki K, Sato K, Akiyama Y, Yanagihara K, Oka M, Yamaguchi K. Peptidomics-based approach reveals the secretion of the 29-residue COOH-terminal fragment of the putative tumor suppressor protein DMBT1 from pancreatic adenocarcinoma cell lines. *Cancer Res* 2002; 62:4894-4898.

Schulz BL, Oxley D, Packer NH, Karlsson NG. Identification of two highly sialylated human tear-fluid DMBT1 isoforms: the major high-molecular-mass glycoproteins in human tears. *Biochem J* 2002; 366:511-520.

Smith GS, Hall RL, Walker RM. Applied clinical pathology in preclinical toxicology testing. *Handbook of Toxicologi Pathology, Second Edition, Vol.1* 2002; Academic Press.

Suzuki A, Zheng Yw YW, Kaneko S, Onodera M, Fukao K, Nakauchi H, Taniguchi H. Clonal identification and characterization of self-renewing pluripotent stem cells in the developing liver. *J Cell Biol* 2002;156:173-184.

Takito J, Hikita C, and Al-Awqati Q. Hensin, a new collecting duct protein involved in the *in vitro* plasticity of intercalated cell polarity. *J Clin Invest* 1996; 98:2324-2331.

Takito J, Yan L, Ma J, Hikita C, Vijayakumar S, Warburton D, Al-Awqati Q. Hensin, the polarity reversal protein, is encoded by DMBT1, a gene frequently deleted in malignant gliomas. *Am J Physiol* 1999; 277(2 Pt 2):F277-289.

Yasui O, Miura N, Terada K, Kawarada Y, Koyama K, Sugiyama T. Isolation of oval cells from Long-Evans Cinnamon rats and their transformation into hepatocytes *in vivo* in the rat liver. *Hepatology* 1997; 25:329-34.

Yin L, Sun M, Ilic Z, Leffert HL, Sell S. Derivation, characterization, and phenotypic variation of hepatic progenitor cell lines isolated from adult rats. *Hepatology* 2002; 35:315-324.

13

Predicting Idiosyncratic Drug Reactions

Alastair Cribb, DVM PhD

Professor, Clinical Pharmacology
Canada Research Chair in Comparative Pharmacology and Toxicology

Laboratory of Comparative Pharmacogenetics
Atlantic Veterinary College
University of Prince Edward Island
550 University Ave
Charlottetown, PE C1A 4P3

Table of Contents

Abbreviations

APC ....antigen presenting cells

ER ....endoplasmic reticulum

IDR...idiosyncratic drug reactions

IM-IDR............................immune-mediated idiosyncratic drug reactions

Key Words

Idiosyncratic drug reactions, Adverse drug reactions, Covalent binding, Reactive intermediates, Cytotoxicity, Immune-mediated, Prediction, Lead optimization

Introduction

Idiosyncratic drug reactions (IDR) remain an important cause of late development program failure or drug withdrawal. They represent a significant economic cost and patient burden. Although our understanding of IDR continues to grow, our ability to predict and avoid these reactions remains unacceptably poor. The intent of this chapter is to review approaches that may be used during lead optimization to minimize the likelihood of producing compounds for development that will have a high IDR liability.

Defining Idiosyncratic Drug Reactions

A clear definition and an understanding of how that definition is applied are critical for a rational discussion of prediction of idiosyncratic reactions (see Table 1 for examples of IDR). The definition of idiosyncratic reactions that will form the basis for the following discussion is:

> **An idiosyncratic adverse drug reaction is an uncommon adverse reaction to a drug that is not related to the pharmacological properties of the drug, that occurs at therapeutic doses and/or serum concentrations, and will not occur in the majority of individuals despite increasing the dose to otherwise toxic concentrations.**

The following characteristics are also used to identify adverse drug reactions as idiosyncratic:

- They are dependent on the chemical, not the pharmacological properties of the drug.
- They are highly host-dependent. An idiosyncratic reaction is dependent on a specific interaction between the chemical properties of the drug and the host.
- There is no simple or classical dose-response relationship for the clinical reaction.
- IDR usually occur at frequencies of less than 1/100, and often at frequencies of 1/1000 or 1/10,000. However, rates of up to 50% in specific populations have been reported.
- They can not be predictably reproduced in animals. Idiosyncratic reactions do occur in animals, but they can not be reliably reproduced in an experimental setting with a general laboratory population. If the reaction was reliably produced in pre-clinical studies, the compound would likely not be developed and the reaction would not be identified as being idiosyncratic in humans.
- The mechanism is unknown. This is certainly true for the majority of idiosyncratic reactions. However, an understanding of the mechanism does not preclude a reaction from being defined as idiosyncratic if the primary characteristics of an IDR are observed.

Drug	Predominant Manifestation of Drug Reaction
Sulfonamides	Systemic hypersensitivity syndrome reaction, including dermatopathy, fever, and hepatitis; Stevens-Johnson Syndrome; toxic epidermal necrolysis
Aromatic anticonvulsants	Systemic hypersensitivity syndrome reactions, including dermatopathy, fever, and hepatitis; Stevens-Johnson Syndrome; toxic epidermal necrolysis
Halothane	Hepatitis with systemic signs Malignant hyperthermia
Tienilic acid	Hepatitis
Abacavir	Fever, dermatopathy, malaise, gastrointestinal disturbances
Dihydralazine	Hepatitis
Diclofenac	Hepatitis
Ibufenac	Hepatitis

Table 1. Examples of well-recognized idiosyncratic drug reactions

The clinical presentation of idiosyncratic reactions and the target organ can be highly variable. Common target organs include the skin, liver, kidney, and hematological system. Patients may present with one or more target organs affected. Some drugs target primarily one organ system (e.g. clozapine and agranulocytosis; halothane and hepatitis) while others target multiple organs and have multiple clinical presentations.

Idiosyncratic drug reactions commonly present with signs consistent with an immune-mediated pathogenesis, including delayed onset (usually from 1 to 6 weeks after start of therapy), fever, eosinophilia, dermatopathy and multi-organ toxicity. A more rapid onset of clinical signs is often observed on re-challenge, also consistent with an immune-mediated reaction. Terms such as the idiosyncratic hypersensitivity syndrome reaction, drug-induced immune-mediated disease, or drug-induced lupus, depending on the particular constellation of clinical signs, are used to describe IDR. Demonstration of antibodies or reactive T-cells recognizing the drug, drug-modified proteins, or autologous proteins are required to truly meet the criteria of immune-mediated disease, but many IDR are assumed to have an immunological basis solely on the basis of clinical signs. Many users of the term "idiosyncratic reaction" intend to refer specifically to the subset of idiosyncratic reactions that have an immunological basis. It is generally the most important group of idiosyncratic reactions from a drug development perspective. The evidence for an immunological basis of idiosyncratic reactions will be discussed in more detail below.

Some authors define the term idiosyncratic drug reaction as a genetically determined abnormal reactivity to a chemical or as a rare toxicity of an unknown mechanism.

These definitions share some similarities with the definition of IDR presented above, but they capture different populations of adverse drug reactions. Genetically determined abnormal reactivity to a chemical captures not only immune-mediate idiosyncratic adverse drug reactions, but also drug reactions such as azathioprine hematotoxicity in thiopurine methytransferase deficient individuals (Evans 2004; Farrell 2002; Lennard *et al.* 1989; Stravitz and Sanyal 2003) and perhexilene hepatotoxicity in CYP2D6 deficient individuals (Farrell 2002; Stravitz and Sanyal 2003). I prefer to use the term *hypersusceptibility* to characterize these reactions.

Hypersusceptibility describes those individuals that are particularly susceptible to dose-dependent toxicities. Individual susceptibility may be determined by genetic factors, but the advers reaction can be produced in more individuals by increasing the dose or serum concentration, and it can be produced in a dose-dependent manner in experimental animals. Environmental exposures and drug interactions can also lead to hypersusceptibility. Additional examples of *hypersusceptibilities* are given in Table 2. While I do not consider these reactions to be idiosyncratic, the prediction of potential hypersusceptible individuals in the population, genetic or environmentally-induced, is an important part of drug development and the presence of hypersusceptibility can certainly lead to uncommon adverse events that can result in drug withdrawal.

Drug	Putatitive Susceptible Population
6-mercaptopurine/ azathioprine	Patients deficient in thiopurine methyltransferase are dramatically susceptible to hematotoxicity
Acetaminophen	Alcoholics demonstrate hypersusceptibility to acetaminophen hepatotoxicity
Perhexiline	CYP2D6 deficient individuals show enhanced susceptibility to hepatotoxicity
Dapsone and other arylamines	Glucose-6-phosphate dehydrogenase deficiency increases susceptibility to methemoglobinemia/hemolytic anemia
Valproic acid	Unknown susceptibility factors for hepatotoxicity. Some consider this to be idiosyncratic toxicity but mild liver damage can be dose-dependently and predictably produced in animal models, and there is little evidence of an immunological component in humans with valproate hepatotoxicity. Classification still debateable.
Terfenadine	Patients taking ketoconazole show hypersusceptibility to prolonged QT-interval as a result of a drug interaction
Phenytoin	Patients homozygous for CYP2C9*3 allele show marked susceptibility to phenytoin pharmacological toxicity

Table 2. Examples of Drug Hypersusceptibility

Idiosyncratic reactions to drugs do occur in animals, often with a similar clinical presentation to humans (Cribb *et al.* 1996). However, it is rare that they can be reliably induced in the typical laboratory animal population. This has been a significant limiting factor in understanding the molecular events involved in idiosyncratic reactions. Any potential animal models appear to be compound specific and there are no general models that are currently useful. Therefore, animal models will not be further discussed in this chapter.

Predicting patients versus predicting compounds

It is important to differentiate between predicting which **patients** will experience idiosyncratic reactions and predicting which **compounds** will be associated with an unacceptably high incidence of idiosyncratic reactions. Lead optimization occurs prior to human exposure and assessment of individual risk is neither required nor, with our current understanding, applicable at this stage of drug development. Understanding individual risk may be important during clinical development and will ultimately help us in our efforts to predict compounds that will be associated with idiosyncratic reactions but is not an integral part of the lead optimization process.

There are many marketed compounds that will cause idiosyncratic reactions but not at an incidence or of a severity that limits their use. While the ultimate goal is to eliminate idiosyncratic reactions associated with new chemical entities, a reduction to a clinically acceptable incidence or severity may serve as an intermediate goal. The only approach currently available is to identify the charac-teristics of compounds with a higher probability versus those with a lower probability of triggering idiosyncratic reactions. These characteristics can then be used to optimize lead compounds.

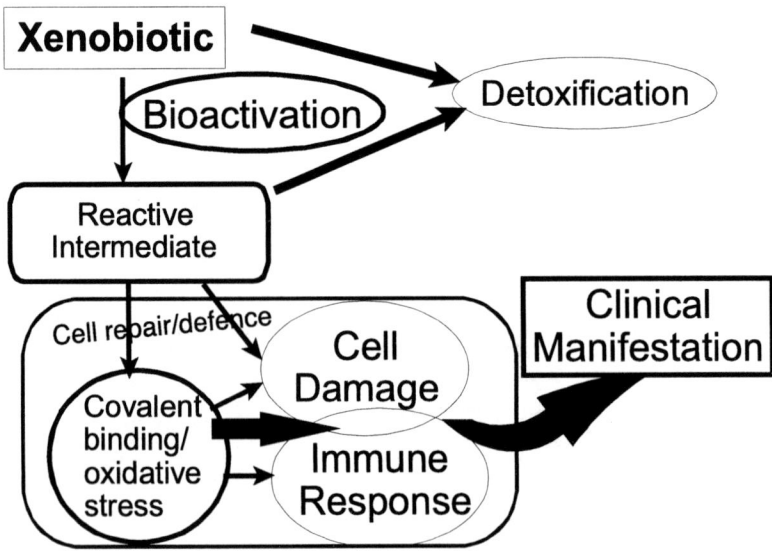

Figure 1. A general paradigm for the pathogenesis of idiosyncratic reactions.

We must have a working concept of the pathogenesis of idiosyncratic reactions if we are to develop a paradigm for optimizing lead compounds to minimize the risk of producing a drug that induces IDR. For the purposes of this chapter, we will focus on idiosyncratic reactions in which the clinical manifestations result from cellular damage to an identified organ or tissue. Although not universally accepted, the majority of experts agree that a pathological immune response underlies the clinical manifestations of the majority of idiosyncratic reactions where cellular or organ damage is an integral part of the pathogenesis. Therefore, this chapter will discuss approaches that may be useful in helping to predict and/or eliminate compounds that may be associated with an unacceptably high frequency of immune-mediated idiosyncratic reactions.

Immunopathogenesis of Immune-Mediated Idiosyncratic Drug Reactions

Our understanding of the pathogenesis of immune-mediated idiosyncratic reactions (IM-IDR) remains incomplete. There have been several recent reviews that address the possible mechanisms of IM-IDR and the reader is referred to these for detailed discussions (Park *et al.* 2001; Pirmohamed *et al.* 2002; Uetrecht 2003; Uetrecht 1999; Williams and Park 2003). Figure 1 presents the general paradigm that will be used to address the pathogenesis and prediction of idiosyncratic reactions.

The initial hypothesis of an immunological basis for idiosyncratic reactions came from the clinical presentation: delayed onset, fever, and the common occurrence of systemic eosinophilia. Histopathological evaluation of idiosyncratic hepatopathies often reveals infiltrating lymphocytes and plasma cells as well as bridging necrosis reminiscent of viral hepatitis. A skin rash is often part of the clinical presentation and histopathological examination reveals lesions consistent with immune-mediated skin disease. Serum sickness-like reactions, including polyarthritis, have also been reported. On re-exposure, there is often, although not always, a shorter period of time to recurrence of clinical signs. This general clinical picture was consistent with an immunological basis, particularly for the systemic hypersensitivity syndrome reactions associated with drugs such as the sulfonamides and aromatic anticonvulsants (Cribb *et al.* 1996; Shear and Spielberg 1988).

Over the last 25 years, a plethora of studies have identified immunological responses in patients experiencing idiosyncratic reactions to drugs (Table 3). In addition to antibodies against the drug or drug-conjugated proteins, antibodies against native cellular and nuclear proteins have been identified. The reader is referred to previous excellent reviews (Pirmohamed *et al.* 2002; Uetrecht 1999). The key conclusions are: 1) there is very strong evidence for activation of the immune response during idiosyncratic reactions; 2) the immune response to a drug can be quite varied, with both antibody and cell-mediated responses being documented; and 3) the nature of the immune response plays a significant role in determining the clinical presentation.

Drug	Antibody Response			Lymphocyte Response
	Drug	Drug-Protein	Protein	
Halothane	+	+	+	ADCC*
Tienilic acid			+	
Sulfonamides	+	+	+	+
Aromatic anticonvulsants			+	+
Amodiaquine	+			
Dihydralazine			+	
Abacavir				+
Procainamide/ hydralazine			ANA antibodies	

Table 3. Examples of immunological responses identified in human patients with idiosyncratic adverse drug reactions. Various types of immunological responses have been identified in subjects experiencing idiosyncratic reactions. Examples of responses that have been identified in multiple patients or by several authors are shown. *Demonstration of antibody directed cell cytotoxicity in in vitro systems, but lymphocyte transformation tests have not been positive.*

Further evidence for an immune response in IDR comes from immunogenetic studies of susceptibility to or severity of idiosyncratic reactions. Specific human major histocompatibility complex (HLA) haplotypes (Andrade *et al.* 2004; Dettling *et al.* 2001; Martin *et al.* 2004; Roujeau *et al.* 1987) and polymorphisms in cytokine or heat shock genes (Aithal *et al.* 2004; Corzo *et al.* 1995; Martin *et al.* 2004; Pirmohamed *et al.* 2001; Yunis *et al.* 1992) have been identified that influence susceptibility or severity to a variety of idiosyncratic toxins. The association is most striking with abacavir (approximately 95% of patients have the at risk genotypes compared to 1% in the control population), however in the majority of cases the association is relatively weak (Mallal *et al.* 2002; Martin *et al.* 2004). Unfortunately, the specific HLA haplotypes or other markers that appear to confer susceptibility are quite variable and appear to be drug specific. Thus, a specific susceptibility genotype that can be used to identify an "at risk" drug-related immunogen characteristic appears unlikely to be consistent across chemically divergent compounds. Nevertheless, the contribution of immunogenetics to individual susceptibility or severity further supports a role for the immune response.

If we accept that an immune response is an important and, in most cases, a required part of the clinical reaction, then we can appreciate that understanding the properties that contribute to a drug acting as an immunogen is necessary to enable us to "dial out" those properties during optimization. It is generally believed that most drug molecules are too small themselves to induce an immune response. The most common underlying hypothesis to explain how a drug can become immunogenic is the **hapten hypothesis** (Park *et al.* 1987). This hypothesis states that drugs must be covalently bound to a macromolecule carrier (usually a protein) to act as an immunogen. This macromolecule is then processed by the immune system such that a new peptide fragment or a peptide fragment containing the covalently bound drug is presented to the immune system and induces an immune response. This raises the question then as to when or how does covalent binding of a drug result in recognition by the immune system and an attendant response. The original hapten hypothesis is based on the traditional self/non-self recognition paradigm: when a drug is covalently bound to a macromolecule, it creates a modified macromolecule that is now recognized by the immune system as non-self, triggering a response. If the peptide fragment presented to the immune system contains the drug, a response directed against the drug or a drug-peptide epitope may be induced. Alternatively, the immune response may be directed against a novel epitope that results from changes in protein confirmation or processing.

An alternative explanation, called the **danger hypothesis**, has been proposed by Matzinger to explain why an immune response occurs against immunogens in some patients and not in others (Matzinger 2002). She has postulated that foreignness alone is insufficient to alone trigger an immune response and that context is more important. An immune response will only occur if a second "danger" signal is presented. Potential danger signals include heat shock proteins or cytokines that may be elevated as a result of cell toxicity or concurrent disease causing cell damage (e.g. viral infections). If true, this may help to explain part of individual susceptibility to idiosyncratic reactions, from either a compound perspective (compounds associated with higher cytototoxicity) or a patient perspective (increased incidence of idiosyncratic reactions in HIV-patients). The reader is referred to recent reviews (Pirmohamed *et al.* 2002; Uetrecht 1999).

A third possibility that does not depend on haptenization by the drug or drug metabolites has been proposed. Picher *et al.* have demonstrated that sensitized lymphocytes can recognize drug molecules non-covalently linked to protein, in an MHC-restricted manner and that, at least *in vitro*, free drug can induce lymphocyte activation in some individuals (Engler *et al.* 2004; Schnyder *et al.* 2000). Whether this "pharmacological induction" occurs *in vivo* or induces a sufficiently strong immune response to cause a clinical reaction is unknown. At the moment, the support for this mechanism is not sufficiently strong to use as a basis for lead optimization.

The difference between the first two hypotheses may be important for understanding individual susceptibility factors, but for the purposes of lead optimization there is little practical difference. Both hypotheses require the formation of covalently bound drug adducts. Cell damage or stress is required to produce the danger signal in the danger hypothesis, while it is often considered an integral part of the hapten hypothesis as well because adducted proteins must be presented to the immune system (Figure 2). The majority of proteins identified as antibody targets (Table 4) are intracellular proteins. For proteins to be

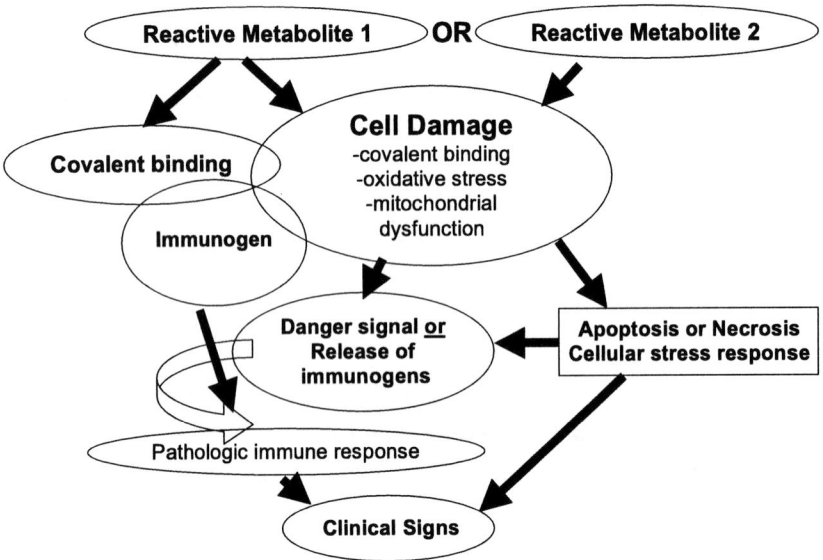

Figure 2. A general scheme for the immunopathogenesis of immune-mediated idiosyn-cratic reactions. The primary difference between the traditional hapten hypothesis and the danger hypothesis is in the nature of stimulation required to trigger an immune response. In both cases, bioactivation to a reactive intermediate and subsequent covalent binding to cellular macromolecules, as well as cell damage or stress, are considered an important and necessary step in the pathogenesis.

processed, they must be taken up or found within antigen presenting cells (APC). One possible mechanism by which modified intracellular proteins can be taken up by an APC is cell damage and death that leads to the release of proteins or engulfment of damaged and dying cells by APC. If protein conjugates are formed in cells that are capable of MHC class I presentation, then intracellular formation of a neo-antigen may lead to processing and presentation for a cell-mediated response. Possible reasons why some individuals may experience a reaction, and others not, include immunogenetic variation, haptenic density, previous sensiti-zation by immunologically-related epitopes, and degree of cell death (and subsequent release of immunogens). For the purposes of lead optimization, these two competing hypotheses may be considered as equivalent.

Once an immune response has occurred, how does the immune system access an intracellular protein? It has now been shown for the majority of proteins identified as immunopathological targets that they are also expressed on the cell surface and that this expression can often be up-regulated. Cell-surface expression presumably allows the immune system to recognize and target cells expressing the antigens.

For anaphylactic IgE-mediated reactions, the antibody response against the drug is generally accepted as being critical. The role of the antibodies directed against the drug in other idiosyncratic rections is less clear. The ability of patch or prick testing to identify patients susceptible to idiosyncratic reactions is highly variable between drugs. Abacavir is a good example of a drug in which patch

Drug	Protein immune targets	
Halothane (and other inhalant anesthetics	CYP2E1 GRP78 GRP94 Protein disulfide isomerase (PDI) others	(Bourdi *et al.* 1996; Gut *et al.* 1993; Knight *et al.* 1994)
Tienilic acid	CYP2C9	(Lecoeur *et al.* 1996)
Sulfonamides	GRP78 PDI 96 kDa protein	(Cribb *et al.* 1997)
Aromatic anticonvulsants	CYP3A-like protein	(Riley *et al.* 1993)
Germander	Epoxide hydrolase	(De Berardinis *et al.* 2000; Loeper *et al.* 2001)
Dihydralazine	CYP1A2	(Bourdi *et al.* 1990)

Table 4. Examples of protein targets identified in immune-mediated idiosyncratic reactions.

testing appears highly effective (Mallal *et al.* 2002), while for many other drugs skin testing is either unreliable or does not produce a positive response. For some drugs, anti-drug antibodies are specific to hypersensitive patients, but for others, anti-drug antibodies have been found in both patients and non-hypersensitive controls (Aithal *et al.* 2004; Clarke *et al.* 1991; Hastings *et al.* 1995). Further, the clinical reaction may continue after the drug is theoretically cleared from the body (Bedard *et al.* 2000), suggesting that the drug-associated antibodies are not the primary cause of the immunopathologic reaction. Animal models exist in which antibodies or an immune response directed against the drug can be induced without associated pathology (Clarke *et al.* 1990; Furst *et al.* 1997; Hastings *et al.* 1995). These observations suggest that, with the exception of IgE-mediated drug allergies, antibodies directed against the drug are more a marker for an immune response than an executioner for the clinical disease.

Antibodies directed against neo-antigens are not associated with pathology unless the drug is also present, suggesting that a drug-induced conformational change is required, that the drug alters the expression or distribution of the protein such that it becomes accessible to the drug, or that the drug must be present to induce a danger signal. *In vitro* studies have shown that antibodies recognizing drug-protein conjugates can mediate antibody-directed cell cytotoxicity *in vitro* and that cytotoxic T cells directed against drug-associated epitopes can lead to cell death (Kretz-Rommel and Boelsterli 1995; Mieli-Vergani *et al.* 1980; Neuberger and Williams 1989; Vergani *et al.* 1980). These studies suggest that cell-mediated immune responses play an important role in the associated pathology.

Our current knowledge of idiosyncratic reactions, then, supports the concept that drug-induced immune responses are involved in the pathogenesis of idiosyncratic reactions. Formation of covalent drug-protein conjugates following bioacti-vation (reactive intermediate formation) is likely a required step in the pathogenesis of IDR. Immune-mediated cytotoxicity is a required end-point for pathology, but early chemical cytotoxicity may play an important role in triggering the immune response. These three characteristics (bioactivation, covalent binding, and cytotoxicity) may then be used in a lead optimization paradigm.

Characteristics of Idiosyncratic Toxins

Reactive intermediate formation

It is generally accepted that formation of one or more reactive intermediates is required before an idiosyncratic reaction can be triggered. Avoidance of "toxicophores" or chemical structures that are likely to undergo bioactivation is a logical initial approach to lead optimization. A number of readily recognizable chemical structures have been associated with idiosyncratic reactions and avoiding these structures will likely reduce the risk of reactive intermediate formation associated with idiosyncratic toxins. The reader is referred to the chapter by John Walsh in this book for a detailed discussion of reactive intermediate formation and toxicophores associated with bioactivation. There is not, however, a direct correlation between the formation of reactive intermediates and occurrence of idiosyncratic reactions. That is, there are many compounds that form reactive intermediates that are either not associated with idiosyncratic reactions or cause a predictable dose dependent toxicity. Formation of free radicals is not generally associated with compounds that cause idiosyncratic reactions, presumably because they are not as commonly associated with covalent binding.

Many methods have been proposed to identify reactive intermediates: covalent binding studies (see below), screening for suicide inhibition of drug metabolizing enzymes, or screening for glutathione conjugates. These approaches do not identify all possible reactive intermediates either because of complex metabolic pathways (i.e. secondary bioactivation of a metabolite) or because of bioactivation by non-cytochrome P450 pathways such as myeloper-oxidase. They do, however, provide a substantive starting point if reactive intermediate formation is a concern from a structural viewpoint.

Eliminating any and all compounds that form or have the potential to form reactive intermediates would be expected to reduce the over-all likelihood of idiosyncratic reactions. However, this approach will also likely result in the loss of potentially useful compounds.

Should we optimize simply to minimize the quantitative formation of reactive intermediates or is there a qualitative difference between reactive intermediates that can be used to aid in lead optimization? A simple quanti-tative assessment of bioactivation is not a good indicator of likelihood of causing idiosyncratic reactions when comparing across groups of structurally unrelated

Compound groups	Risk of idiosyncratic reactions	Extent of bioactivation	Method of assessment
volatile anesthetics	halothane >>enflurane >isoflurane	halothane >>enflurane >isoflurane	Total metabolism; Covalent binding
sulfonamides	slow acetylator >fast acetylator	slow acetylator >fast acetylator	Phenotyping studies; theoretical assessment of metabolism only
procainamide	procainamide >>acetyl-procainamide	procainamide>> acetyl-procainamide	*In vivo* in humans and rats
chloramphenicol series	chloramphenicol>> thiamphenicol	chloramphenicol>> thiamphenicol	Block of metabolic pathway
clozapine	clozapine >>olanzapine	clozapine =olanzapine	% conversion similar but total daily dose of olanzapine much lower

Table 5. Extent of bioactivation/metabolism and risk of idiosyncratic reactions.

compounds. However, there are several examples that suggest quantity remains an influence. First, it is now recognized that idiosyncratic reactions are rarely associated with total daily doses less than 100 mg and practically non-existent at dose less than 10 mg a day (Uetrecht 1999). Within a structurally related series of compounds, there is evidence that reducing turn-over via metabolic pathways associated with bioactivation is associated with a reduced risk of idiosyncratic reactions (Christ *et al.* 1988; Freeman *et al.* 1981; Gardner *et al.* 1998; Gardner *et al.* 1998; Rieder *et al.* 1991; Shear *et al.* 1986). Reduction of metabolic turn-over has been achieved either through chemical modification or through individuals that have genetic polymorphisms that influence the rate of bioactivation directly or indirectly (Table 5). These examples support the concept that within a structurally-related series, a reduction in the total formation of reactive intermediates will reduce the risk of idiosyncratic reactions. There are also examples where there are not large differences in bioactivation rates for compounds with large differences in idiosyncratic reaction rates (clozapine and olanzapine) or where the rate of metabolite turnover measured does not correlate with risk of IDR (ibuprofen and ibufenac) (Bolze *et al.* 2002; Castillo and Smith 1995; Gardner *et al.* 1998). Therefore, we must look at further properties of the compounds and their associated reactive intermediates, specifically there reactivity with cellular proteins and their propensity to cause direct cytotoxicity.

Covalent Binding

Covalent binding appears to be an integral step in the pathogenesis of idiosyncratic reactions, whether you adhere to the traditional hapten hypothesis or to the danger hypothesis. This would suggest that eliminating covalent binding would eliminate idiosyncratic reactions. However, we know that many effective and safe compounds are associated with covalent binding in *in vitro* systems and *in vivo* in animals or humans. Therefore, for covalent binding to be a more useful marker of risk and hence a useful tool in lead optimization, additional characteristics of covalent binding must be considered.

The same arguments that apply to bioactivation to reactive intermediates apply to covalent binding. Compounds that are associated with increased reactive metabolite formation are often also associated with increased covalent binding *in vitro* and *in vivo*. Within a structurally related series, compounds with the lowest covalent binding are likely to have the lowest likelihood of triggering idiosyncratic reactions (Christ *et al.* 1988; Freeman *et al.* 1981; Gardner *et al.* 1998). However, this does not help resolve comparisons across structurally unrelated compounds. It is clear that an absolute level of covalent binding has little relevance to prediction of idiosyncratic reactions. Three properties of covalent binding have therefore received attention: targets of binding, association with cytotoxicity, and *in vivo* binding.

Considerable effort has been devoted to identifying specific targets or patterns of covalent binding that may be linked to idiosyncratic reactions. The majority of protein targets identified to date have been either endoplasmic reticulum proteins or cell surface proteins (Table 6). As discussed in the preceding section on immunopathogenesis, the endoplasmic reticulum (ER) proteins that have been identified as targets of the immune response are also found expressed on the cell surface, albeit not in large quantities. This observation also holds for targets of covalent binding. Most of the work has been performed in animals (usually rats) but some comparisons have been performed with either human hepatocytes or in samples obtained from humans receiving the drug. For several compounds, there have been comparisons of the patterns of covalent bindings based on molecular weights on gel electrophoresis, without attempts to identify specific targets. These studies have not been able to clearly identify any pattern or unique targets associated with idiosyncratic toxins other than a tendency to adduct membrane proteins.

It is instructive to view a few specific examples. Tienilic acid and halothane are two compounds that are associated with idiosyncratic hepatitis with limited systemic signs (e.g. dermatopathy is not a major feature of the reaction). Tienilic acid displays a relatively specific binding to predominantly one target, a cytochrome P450: CYP2C11 in rats and CYP2C9 in humans (Beaune *et al.* 1987; Pons *et al.* 1991). In contrast, halothane binds to a whole range of ER proteins, including CYP2E1 and a number of ER stress proteins (Eliasson and Kenna 1996; Kenna *et al.* 1987; Pumford *et al.* 1997a). Thus, the range from specific binding to wide ranging covalent binding is associated with idiosyncratic reactions, and similar observations have been made regarding compounds that are intrinsically

Compound	Targets	Covalent binding quantitatively/ qualitatively linked to direct cytotoxicity	Method of assessment	
Volatile anesthetics: halothane	ER proteins: GRP78, GRP94, microsomal carboxylesterase, protein disulfide isomerase, 58 kDa PDI-related protein, CYP2E1	No	In vivo rat and human studies In vitro	(Gut *et al.* 1993)
Sulfonamides	ER proteins: GRP78, GRP94, PDI, unidentified P450s Cell surface proteins Unidentified serum protein	No	In vitro only for ER and cell surface proteins; Human in vivo for serum protein	(Cribb *et al.* 1996; Cribb *et al.* 1997; Manchanda *et al.* 2002)
Tienilic acid	CYP2C9/CYP2C11	No	*in vitro/in vivo*	(Lecoeur *et al.* 1994)
Diclofenac	Cell surface ER/nuclear membrane proteins	No	*in vitro/in vivo*	(Aithal *et al.* 2004; Kretz-Rommel and Boelsterli 1994; Wade *et al.* 1997)

Table 6. Examples of targets of covalent binding of idiosyncratic toxins. The following table provides examples of targets of covalent binding of idiosyncratic toxins that have been identified. Many other studies have been performed in which specific targets have not been identified. Examples of covalent binding to cytosolic proteins have been found, but they are less common.

toxic (Pumford *et al.* 1997a). The most consistent feature of the covalent binding of compounds that are associated with idiosyncratic reactions is that covalent binding is heavily weighted towards membrane-associated proteins. The endoplasmic reticulum, nuclear envelope, and cell membrane proteins are the most common targets of idiosyncratic toxins. Non-idiosyncratic toxins also bind to membrane proteins, but there appears to be higher binding to cytosolic proteins (Cohen and Khairallah 1997; Cohen *et al.* 1997; Pumford *et al.* 1997b). Our failure to identify one or more critical targets of covalent binding has three possible explanations. The first is that such common, critical targets do not exist. The second is that scientists as a group have inadvertently studied outlier compounds that do not share critical important targets. The third possibility is that the common, critical targets exist but that we have not been able to identify them because the experimental approaches used have not been sensitive enough or are simply not an appropriate approach. Only further experimentation will resolve this issue.

Another way of looking at covalent binding is to assess its link with cytotoxicity. For compounds that are associated with intrinsic toxicity, there is generally a good correlation between covalent binding and intrinsic toxicity (Gibson *et al.* 1996; Pumford *et al.* 1997a). That is, cytotoxicity is apparent shortly after covalent binding appears and increases in association with total covalent binding. For compounds that are associated with idiosyncratic toxicity, there is generally extensive covalent binding in cells (*in vitro* systems) or in tissues (*in vivo*) at concentrations below that causing overt cellular toxicityl, or the covalent binding is dissociated from cytotoxicity (Kenna *et al.* 1988; Kretz-Rommel and Boelsterli 1993; Naisbitt *et al.* 2002; Reilly *et al.* 2000; Summan and Cribb 2002). For example, *in vitro* studies have shown that covalent binding of sulfamethoxazole can occur without toxicity. In lymphoid cells, surviving cells after exposure to sulfamethoxazole hydroxylamine have extensive covalent adducts (Summan and Cribb 2002). Keratinocytes can bioactive sulfamethoxazole to protein reactive compounds without cytotoxicity and circulating adducts of sulfamethoxazole have been observed in people (Reilly *et al.* 2000). Studies using isolated cells have shown that the concentration of sulfamethoxazole reactive metabolites required to cause covalent binding sufficient to trigger lymphocyte activation through immune recognition are approximately one-tenth the concentration associated with cytotoxicity (Naisbitt *et al.* 2002).

The reactive intermediates responsible for covalent binding and for cytotoxicity are not necessarily the same. Diclofenac is a good example where it has been shown that the covalent binding is primarily related to acylglucuronide formation while cytotoxicity is primarily the result of cytochrome P450-dependent bioactivation (Kretz-Rommel and Boelsterli 1993). Early studies on the molecular basis of liver toxicity from acetaminophen established that it was possible to create compounds that were bioactivated to protein-reactive reactive intermediates, but did not cause cell death (Roberts *et al.* 1990). The partial or complete dissociation between covalent binding and cytotoxicity may allow the accumulation of covalent adducts such that when they are released or a danger signal is received, a relatively strong immunogen exists within the body as haptenic density is important in inducing an immune response against haptens.

In summary, the current data suggest that covalent binding is a risk factor for idiosyncratic reactions particularly when it occurs prior to the onset of intrinsic cellular toxicity. The current data suggest that this property is likely of greater importance than binding to specific cellular targets or the absolute extent of covalent binding in fractionated *in vitro* systems.

Cytotoxicity

All the idiosyncratic toxins examined to date have been shown to be bioactivated to compounds that cause small but measurable cytotoxicity. As was discussed in the previous section, the cytotoxicity occurs at concentrations higher than those that result in covalent binding or may result from a different metabolite than that responsible for the majority of covalent binding. The ability to measure cytotoxicity from idiosyncratic toxins is dependent on the assay system used and the compound involved. For some compounds, toxicity can be demonstrated in isolated human hepatocytes with intact cytochrome P450 systems while in other cases a bioactivation system (e.g. hepatic microsomes or in some cases a peroxidase-based system) must be combined with a sensitive cell type such as lymphocytes (Riley and Leeder 1995; Riley *et al.* 1988; Shear *et al.* 1986). The utility of such systems early in lead optimization is limited, but they may be used in the late phase of lead optimization to assist in further characterization of compounds or in comparisons of compounds. The ability of idiosyncratic toxins to cause cytotoxicity suggests that cell damage or stress is a required part of the pathogenesis, whether through the release of immunogens or the generation of a danger signal.

The weight of evidence therefore suggests that a small and normally clinically insignificant degree of cytotoxicity is a characteristic of idiosyncratic toxins. Compounds that are intrinsically highly cytotoxic or bioactivated to highly cytotoxic intermediates will more likely be associated with intrinsic than idiosyncratic toxicity. If we accept that a low, but measurable, cytotoxic potential exists for idiosyncratic toxins, how can be exploit this information? The degree of cytotoxicity often parallels the over-all extent of bioactivation, so it may move in parallel with bioactivation and covalent binding. Within the few groups of structurally related compounds studied to date, there appears to be a correlation between the frequency of idiosyncratic reactions and the degree of cytotoxicity. The volatile anesthetics are a good example of this. Similarly, it has been observed for olanzepine and clozapine that while metabolic bioactivation is similar, cytotoxicity is lower with olanzepine, as is the frequency of idiosyncratic reactions. *In vitro* studies suggest that clozapine bioactivation can result in cytotoxicity at clinically relevant concentrations, while higher concentrations of olanzepine are required (Gardner *et al.* 1998). These observations suggest that to a certain extent, increased cytotoxicity increases risk but that eventually a compound will become an intrinsically toxic compound. Cytotoxicity is a graded response, so one would predict that some compounds will be in a grey zone. This is indeed that case and there are some compounds, such as diclofenac, where clinical presentation is more consistent with intrinsic toxicity in some patients and idiosyncratic immune-mediated toxicity in others (Boelsterli 2003).

The requirement for an underlying cytotoxic potential may explain the unusual but consistent observation that isolated mononuclear leukocytes from patients are more susceptible to the toxic effects of bioactivation products of drugs associated with idiosyncratic reactions than are controls (Shear and Spielberg 1988; Shear *et al.* 1986). The assay is based on exposure of isolated mononuclear leukocytes from patients and controls to the drugs in the presence of a microsomal bioactivating system to generate reactive metabolites (variously referred to as the MNL toxicity or lymphocyte toxicity assay). Drugs studied include sulfonamides (Rieder *et al.* 1989; Shear *et al.* 1986), cefaclor (Kearns *et al.* 1994), aromatic anticonvulsants (Shear and Spielberg 1988), sorbinil (Shear and Spielberg 1988), and amineptine (Larrey *et al.* 1989). The MNL toxicity assay may be used to characterize and screen compounds in development to help optimize leads but only after idiosyncratic or some other unusual toxicity has been observed. It is not an assay that is appropriate for routine use during lead optimization.

Other Characteristics

The hope remains that array screening will allow us to identify particular patterns of gene activation that will be linked with idiosyncratic reactions. Using proteomics, we may be able to identify critical targets or responses that can be used to guide lead optimization. However, the major limitation is that the animal models that develop the complete idiosyncratic reaction remain limited and not widely applicable, often for practical reasons. It is unclear whether animal models that do not develop the complete clinical profile will ever be predictive. *In vitro* studies with isolated human cells are limited by the lack of cell-to-cell interactions that are likely required for the full manifestation of the response.

Paradigms that may identify highly immunogenic compounds have been proposed. These include the popliteal lymph node assay, co-administration of drugs with Freund's adjuvant as a danger signal, and *in vitro* T-cell priming. However, these assays all have limitations and no assays have been developed or validated to the point that they may be useful in lead optimization.

A Working Paradigm for Lead Optimization: Bioactivation, Covalent Binding, and Cytotoxicity

Many questions remain unanswered regarding idiosyncratic reactions and we do not yet have a clear and consistent marker for compounds that cause idiosyncratic reactions. We can not identify one property of compounds that we can use to eliminate or optimize lead compounds without risking losing valuable compounds. The complete elimination of all idiosyncratic reactions may not be a necessary endpoint. Our goal, however, is to reduce the frequency of idiosyncratic reactions so that the risk associated with a compound is acceptable. Therefore, the current goal for lead optimization is to develop a set of characteristics that identify high risk compounds. The preceding discussion raises several key points that can be used in a step-wise approach in an attempt to minimize the likelihood of compounds causing idiosyncratic reactions.

Step 1 (Figure 3): The available evidence strongly supports the contention that protein reactivity is a necessary characteristic of idiosyncratic toxins. Bioactivation may be required for most compounds, although some compounds (e.g. penicillamine, penicillins) may be inherently reactive. Reactive intermediate

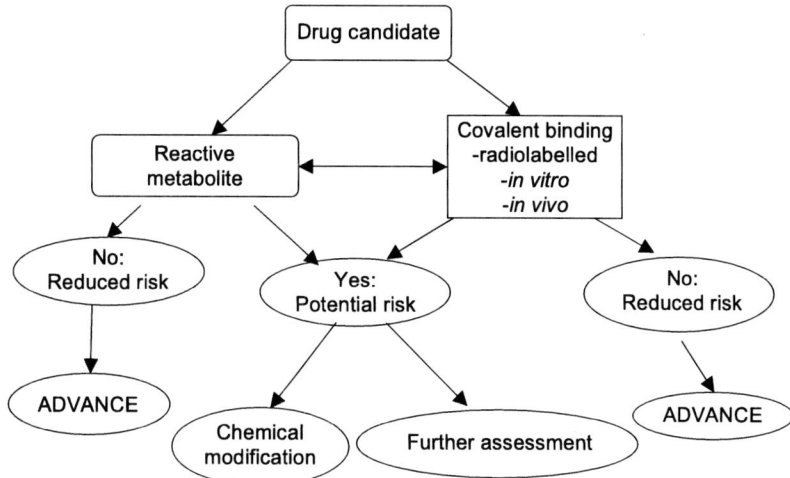

Figure 3. Step 1 in the assessment of risk of a compound being associated with idiosyncratic reactions.

formation increases the risk of idiosyncratic reactions and minimization of bioactivation potential through elimination of toxicophores is a logical first step. Identification of reactive metabolite formation is a useful approach. The methods for identifying reactive intermediate formation have been reviewed elsewhere and they include demonstration of glutathione conjugates, covalent binding, trapping experiments, and suicide inhibition of metabolizing enzymes. None of these methods are fool-proof. Covalent binding studies *in vitro* and/or *in vivo* are a logical part of any pre-screening program and may be included in either Step 1 or Step 2. If bioactivation with or without covalent binding is identified, the

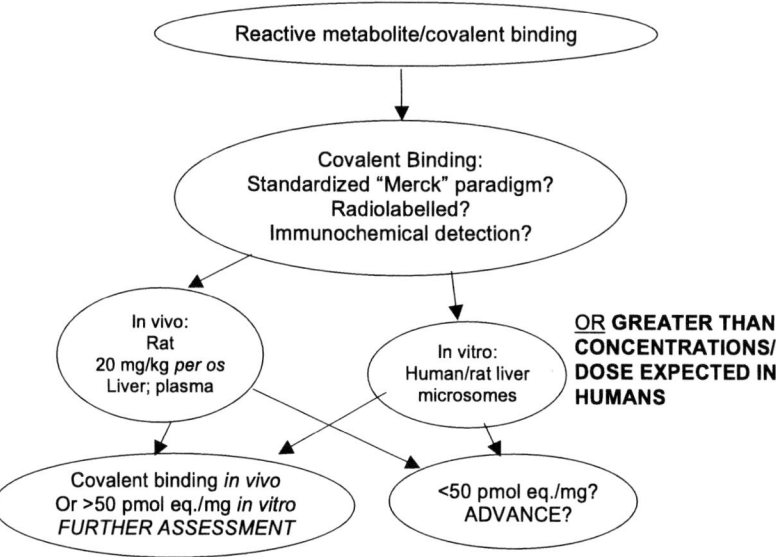

Figure 4. Step 2 in the assessment of risk of a compound being associated with idiosyncratic reactions.

compound may be either modified to remove this property or further characterization to better assess risk undertaken.

Step 2 (Figure 4): Once reactive intermediate formation is identified or predicted, covalent binding *in vitro* (if not previously performed; rat and human systems are both potentially useful) and *in vivo* should be evaluated. *In vivo* studies are generally carried out in rodents. If a series of related compounds is going to be evaluated or re-evaluated, it may be worthwhile to generate antibodies for use in immunochemical detection, otherwise such studies are typically performed with radiolabelled material. There are currently no standardized testing procedures. It has recently been suggested that standard doses of 20 mg/kg *per os* be used for *in vivo* studies and 10 μM for 1 hour be used for *in vitro* studies with human or rat hepatic microsomes (referred to here as "The Merck Paradigm"; (Evans *et al.* 2004)). While these are somewhat arbitrary doses or concentrations, if a bank of data in a standardized format is generated by consistent application of these doses/concentrations, sufficient data may be generated to allow for retrospective analysis. However, it is also recommended that studies be carried out at doses or concentrations that are 5 – 10 times the expected peak plasma concentrations to ensure that nothing is missed. *In vivo* studies should also include standard assessment for cytotoxicity, such as serum liver-related enzyme activities and histopathological analysis. If significant or extensive covalent binding is observed *in vivo* in the absence of evidence of toxicity, then this compound should be considered at an increased risk of being associated with idiosyncratic drug reactions. Not all compounds that are associated with idiosyncratic reactions lead to covalent binding in rodent models when given as the parent compound (e.g. sulfamethoxazole covalent binding is not observed in rodents after administration of the parent, but only after administration of the metabolites (Cribb *et al.* 1996)). In some cases, studies in isolated cells or with synthetic reactive intermediates are required.

The major outstanding question is what constitutes significant covalent binding? The Merck Paradigm suggests 50 pmol/mg protein *in vivo* or *in vitro* as a level of concern. This has not been proposed as a go/no go decision point, but as a level of heightened concern when additional assessment or consideration is required. At the moment, there are insufficient data to support or refute this as a specific level of covalent binding but a review of the literature suggests that is not an inappropriate concentration, provided that doses/concentrations that meet or exceed known or expected human exposures are used.

Step 3 (Figure 5): If covalent binding is observed, particularly *in vivo*, assessment of cytotoxicity can be undertaken. When covalent binding is linked to cytotoxicity in Step 2 or in further investigations in Step 3, then the compound should be treated as an intrinsic toxin and standard assessment of risks and benefits of intrinsic toxins undertaken. If the covalent binding is observed at doses or concentrations below those associated with toxicity *in vivo*, then additional studies *in vitro* may be indicated to determine the cytotoxic potential and its association with covalent binding. While this strays closer to lead selection, this information can be part of the feedback loop for lead optimization.

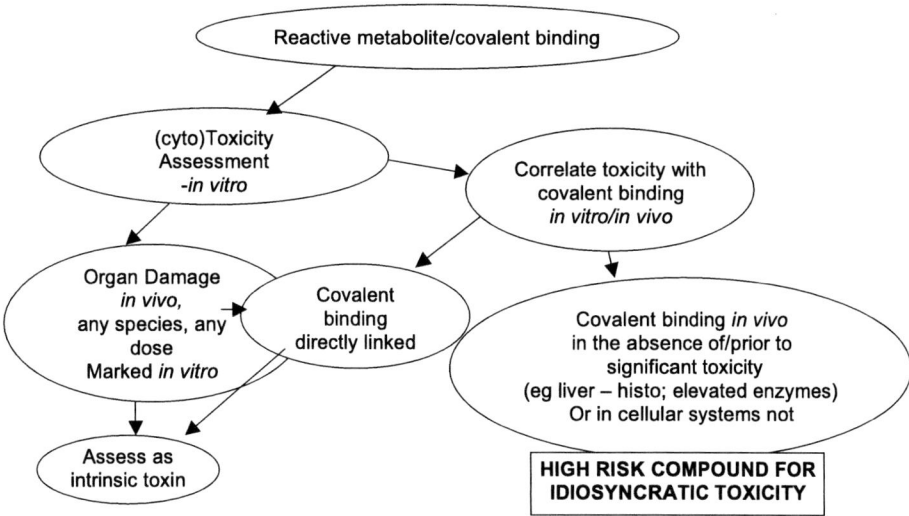

Figure 5. Step 3 in the assessment of risk of a compound being associated with idiosyncratic reactions.

In summary, compounds that undergo bioactivation leading to covalent binding at doses or concentrations below those required to cause cytotoxicity or toxicity *in vivo* are likely at increased risk of causing immune-associated idiosyncratic toxicity in the clinic. Available evidence suggests that within a group of structurally related compounds, increased covalent binding and/or increased cytotoxicity of reactive metabolite increases the risk of idiosyncratic toxicity at some point. Therefore, lead compound structure should be optimized to minimize bioactivation, covalent binding, and cytotoxic potential. Minimizing the total daily dose or duration of therapy further reduces the risk of idiosyncratic reactions. However, dose reduction by increasing affinity for targets must not be undertaken at the expense of drug-like properties.

No decision on lead optimization or selection should be taken without giving consideration to the wealth of caveats or modifying risk factors that surround these decisions:

- What is the potential for chemical modification? If easy without losing other properties, it should be undertaken.
- If bioactivation is associated with additional risks such as cytochrome P450 inhibition/induction, chemical modification is indicated.
- The severity of condition treated may warrant advancement of compounds that have characteristics associated with higher risk of idiosyncratic reactions.
- If alternative therapies with good safety records exist, the risk of idiosyncratic reactions needs to be low.
- If the expected duration of therapy or expected total daily dose is high, than the risk of idiosyncratic reactions is likely higher for compounds with an "at risk" profile.

- The intended target population should also be considered.

Our ability to identify compounds that will be associated with a high incidence of idiosyncratic reactions remains unacceptably limited. Continuing investigations are required to develop suitable animal models to evaluate and modify screening and lead optimization paradigms.

Acknowledgements

The author is the recipient of a Canada Research Chair. The authors own work in idiosyncratic reactions was supported by the Canadian Institutes of Health Research.

References

Aithal, G. P., Ramsay, L., Daly, A. K., Sonchit, N., Leathart, J. B., Alexander, G., Kenna, J. G., Caldwell, J., and Day, C. P. (2004). Hepatic adducts, circulating antibodies, and cytokine polymorphisms in patients with diclofenac hepatotoxicity. *Hepatology* 39, 1430-40.

Andrade, R. J., Lucena, M. I., Alonso, A., Garcia-Cortes, M., Garcia-Ruiz, E., Benitez, R., Fernandez, M. C., Pelaez, G., Romero, M., Corpas, R., Duran, J. A., Jimenez, M., Rodrigo, L., Nogueras, F., Martin-Vivaldi, R., Navarro, J. M., Salmeron, J., de la Cuesta, F. S., and Hidalgo, R. (2004). HLA class II genotype influences the type of liver injury in drug-induced idiosyncratic liver disease. *Hepatology* 39, 1603-12.

Beaune, P., Dansette, P. M., Mansuy, D., Kiffel, L., Finck, M., Amar, C., Leroux, J. P., and Homberg, J. C. (1987). Human anti-endoplasmic reticulum autoantibodies appearing in a drug-induced hepatitis are directed against a human liver cytochrome P-450 that hydroxylates the drug. *Proc Natl Acad Sci USA* 84, 551-5.

Bedard, K., Smith, S., and Cribb, A. (2000). Sequential assessment of an antidrug antibody response in a patient with a systemic delayed-onset sulphonamide hypersensitivity syndrome reaction. *Br J Dermatol* 142, 253-8.

Boelsterli, U. A. (2003). Diclofenac-induced liver injury: a paradigm of idiosyncratic drug toxicity. *Toxicol Appl Pharmacol* 192, 307-22.

Bolze, S., Bromet, N., Gay-Feutry, C., Massiere, F., Boulieu, R., and Hulot, T. (2002). Development of an *in vitro* screening model for the biosynthesis of acyl glucuronide metabolites and the assessment of their reactivity toward human serum albumin. *Drug Metab Dispos* 30, 404-13.

Bourdi, M., Chen, W., Peter, R. M., Martin, J. L., Buters, J. T., Nelson, S. D., and Pohl, L. R. (1996). Human cytochrome P450 2E1 is a major autoantigen associated with halothane hepatitis. *Chem Res Toxicol* 9, 1159-66.

Bourdi, M., Larrey, D., Nataf, J., Bernuau, J., Pessayre, D., Iwasaki, M., Guengerich, F. P., and Beaune, P. H. (1990). Anti-liver endoplasmic reticulum autoantibodies are directed against human cytochrome P-450IA2. A specific marker of dihydralazine-induced hepatitis. *J Clin Invest* 85, 1967-73.

Castillo, M., and Smith, P. C. (1995). Disposition and reactivity of ibuprofen and ibufenac acyl glucuronides *in vivo* in the rhesus monkey and *in vitro* with human serum albumin. *Drug Metab Dispos* 23, 566-72.

Christ, D. D., Satoh, H., Kenna, J. G., and Pohl, L. R. (1988). Potential metabolic basis for enflurane hepatitis and the apparent cross-sensitization between enflurane and halothane. *Drug Metab Dispos* 16, 135-40.

Clarke, J. B., Maggs, J. L., Kitteringham, N. R., and Park, B. K. (1990). Immunogenicity of amodiaquine in the rat. *Int Arch Allergy Appl Immunol* 91, 335-42.

Clarke, J. B., Neftel, K., Kitteringham, N. R., and Park, B. K. (1991). Detection of antidrug IgG antibodies in patients with adverse drug reactions to amodiaquine. *Int Arch Allergy Appl Immunol* 95, 369-75.

Cohen, S. D., and Khairallah, E. A. (1997). Selective protein arylation and acetaminophen-induced hepatotoxicity. *Drug Metab Rev* 29, 59-77.

Cohen, S. D., Pumford, N. R., Khairallah, E. A., Boekelheide, K., Pohl, L. R., Amouzadeh, H. R., and Hinson, J. A. (1997). Selective protein covalent binding and target organ toxicity. *Toxicol Appl Pharmacol* 143, 1-12.

Corzo, D., Yunis, J. J., Salazar, M., Lieberman, J. A., Howard, A., Awdeh, Z., Alper, C. A., and Yunis, E. J. (1995). The major histocompatibility complex region marked by HSP70-1 and HSP70-2 variants is associated with clozapine-induced agranulocytosis in two different ethnic groups. *Blood* 86, 3835-40.

Cribb, A. E., Lee, B. L., Trepanier, L. A., and Spielberg, S. P. (1996). Adverse reactions to sulphonamide and sulphonamide-trimethoprim antimicrobials: clinical syndromes and pathogenesis. *Adverse Drug React Toxicol Rev* 15, 9-50.

Cribb, A. E., Nuss, C. E., Alberts, D. W., Lamphere, D. B., Grant, D. M., Grossman, S. J., and Spielberg, S. P. (1996). Covalent binding of sulfamethoxazole reactive metabolites to human and rat liver subcellular fractions assessed by immunochemical detection. *Chem Res Toxicol* 9, 500-7.

Cribb, A. E., Pohl, L. R., Spielberg, S. P., and Leeder, J. S. (1997). Patients with delayed-onset sulfonamide hypersensitivity reactions have antibodies recognizing endoplasmic reticulum luminal proteins. *J Pharmacol Exp Ther* 282, 1064-71.

De Berardinis, V., Moulis, C., Maurice, M., Beaune, P., Pessayre, D., Pompon, D., and Loeper, J. (2000). Human microsomal epoxide hydrolase is the target of germander-induced autoantibodies on the surface of human hepatocytes. *Mol Pharmacol* 58, 542-51.

Dettling, M., Schaub, R. T., Mueller-Oerlinghausen, B., Roots, I., and Cascorbi, I. (2001). Further evidence of human leukocyte antigen-encoded susceptibility to clozapine-induced agranulocytosis independent of ancestry. *Pharmacogenetics* 11, 135-41.

Eliasson, E., and Kenna, J. G. (1996). Cytochrome P450 2E1 is a cell surface autoantigen in halothane hepatitis. *Mol Pharmacol* 50, 573-82.

Engler, O. B., Strasser, I., Naisbitt, D. J., Cerny, A., and Pichler, W. J. (2004). A chemically inert drug can stimulate T cells *in vitro* by their T cell receptor in non-sensitised individuals. *Toxicology* 197, 47-56.

Evans, D. C., Watt, A. P., Nicoll-Griffith, D. A., and Baillie, T. A. (2004). Drug-protein adducts: an industry perspective on minimizing the potential for drug bioactivation in drug discovery and development. *Chem Res Toxicol* 17, 3-16.

Evans, W. E. (2004). Pharmacogenetics of thiopurine S-methyltransferase and thiopurine therapy. *Ther Drug Monit* 26, 186-91.

Farrell, G. C. (2002). Drugs and steatohepatitis. *Semin Liver Dis* 22, 185-94.

Freeman, R. W., Uetrecht, J. P., Woosley, R. L., Oates, J. A., and Harbison, R. D. (1981). Covalent binding of procainamide *in vitro* and *in vivo* to hepatic protein in mice. *Drug Metab Dispos* 9, 188-92.

Furst, S. M., Luedke, D., Gaw, H. H., Reich, R., and Gandolfi, A. J. (1997). Demonstration of a cellular immune response in halothane-exposed guinea pigs. *Toxicol Appl Pharmacol* 143, 245-55.

Gardner, I., Leeder, J. S., Chin, T., Zahid, N., and Uetrecht, J. P. (1998). A comparison of the covalent binding of clozapine and olanzapine to human neutrophils *in vitro* and *in vivo*. *Mol Pharmacol* 53, 999-1008.

Gardner, I., Zahid, N., MacCrimmon, D., and Uetrecht, J. P. (1998). A comparison of the oxidation of clozapine and olanzapine to reactive metabolites and the toxicity of these metabolites to human leukocytes. *Mol Pharmacol* 53, 991-8.

Gibson, J. D., Pumford, N. R., Samokyszyn, V. M., and Hinson, J. A. (1996). Mechanism of acetaminophen-induced hepatotoxicity: covalent binding versus oxidative stress. *Chem Res Toxicol* 9, 580-5.

Gut, J., Christen, U., and Huwyler, J. (1993). Mechanisms of halothane toxicity: novel insights. *Pharmacol Ther* 58, 133-55.

Hastings, K. L., Thomas, C., Brown, A. P., and Gandolfi, A. J. (1995). Trifluoroacetylation potentiates the humoral immune response to halothane in the guinea pig. *Immunopharmacol Immunotoxicol* 17, 201-13.

Kearns, G. L., Wheeler, J. G., Childress, S. H., and Letzig, L. G. (1994). Serum sickness-like reactions to cefaclor: role of hepatic metabolism and individual susceptibility. *J Pediatr* 125, 805-11.

Kenna, J. G., Neuberger, J., and Williams, R. (1987). Identification by immunoblotting of three halothane-induced liver microsomal polypeptide antigens recognized by antibodies in sera from patients with halothane-associated hepatitis. *J Pharmacol Exp Ther* 242, 733-40.

Kenna, J. G., Neuberger, J., and Williams, R. (1988). Evidence for expression in human liver of halothane-induced neoantigens recognized by antibodies in sera from patients with halothane hepatitis. *Hepatology* 8, 1635-41.

Knight, T. L., Scatchard, K. M., Van Pelt, F. N., and Kenna, J. G. (1994). Sera from patients with halothane hepatitis contain antibodies to halothane-induced liver antigens which are not detectable by immunoblotting. *J Pharmacol Exp Ther* 270, 1325-33.

Kretz-Rommel, A., and Boelsterli, U. A. (1993). Diclofenac covalent protein binding is dependent on acyl glucuronide formation and is inversely related to P450-mediated acute cell injury in cultured rat hepatocytes. *Toxicol Appl Pharmacol* 120, 155-61.

Kretz-Rommel, A., and Boelsterli, U. A. (1994). Selective protein adducts to membrane proteins in cultured rat hepatocytes exposed to diclofenac: radiochemical and immunochemical analysis. *Mol Pharmacol* 45, 237-44.

Kretz-Rommel, A., and Boelsterli, U. A. (1995). Cytotoxic activity of T cells and non-T cells from diclofenac-immunized mice against cultured syngeneic hepatocytes exposed to diclofenac. *Hepatology* 22, 213-22.

Larrey, D., Berson, A., Habersetzer, F., Tinel, M., Castot, A., Babany, G., Letteron, P., Freneaux, E., Loeper, J., and Dansette, P. (1989). Genetic predisposition to drug hepatotoxicity: role in hepatitis caused by amineptine, a tricyclic antidepressant. *Hepatology* 10, 168-73.

Lecoeur, S., Andre, C., and Beaune, P. H. (1996). Tienilic acid-induced autoimmune hepatitis: anti-liver and-kidney microsomal type 2 autoantibodies recognize a three-site conformational epitope on cytochrome P4502C9. *Mol Pharmacol* 50, 326-33.

Lecoeur, S., Bonierbale, E., Challine, D., Gautier, J. C., Valadon, P., Dansette, P. M., Catinot, R., Ballet, F., Mansuy, D., and Beaune, P. H. (1994). Specificity of *in vitro* covalent binding of tienilic acid metabolites to human liver microsomes in relationship to the type of hepatotoxicity: comparison with two directly hepatotoxic drugs. *Chem Res Toxicol* 7, 434-42.

Lennard, L., Van Loon, J. A., and Weinshilboum, R. M. (1989). Pharmacogenetics of acute azathioprine toxicity: relationship to thiopurine methyltransferase genetic polymorphism. *Clin Pharmacol Ther* 46, 149-54.

Loeper, J., De Berardinis, V., Moulis, C., Beaune, P., Pessayre, D., and Pompon, D. (2001). Human epoxide hydrolase is the target of germander autoantibodies on the surface of human hepatocytes: enzymatic implications. *Adv Exp Med Biol* 500, 121-4.

Mallal, S., Nolan, D., Witt, C., Masel, G., Martin, A. M., Moore, C., Sayer, D., Castley, A., Mamotte, C., Maxwell, D., James, I., and Christiansen, F. T. (2002). Association between presence of HLA-B*5701, HLA-DR7, and HLA-DQ3 and hypersensitivity to HIV-1 reverse-transcriptase inhibitor abacavir. *Lancet* 359, 727-32.

Manchanda, T., Hess, D., Dale, L., Ferguson, S. G., and Rieder, M. J. (2002). Haptenation of sulfonamide reactive metabolites to cellular proteins. *Mol Pharmacol* 62, 1011-26.

Martin, A. M., Nolan, D., Gaudieri, S., Almeida, C. A., Nolan, R., James, I., Carvalho, F., Phillips, E., Christiansen, F. T., Purcell, A. W., McCluskey, J., and Mallal, S. (2004). Predisposition to abacavir hypersensitivity conferred by HLA-B*5701 and a haplotypic Hsp70-Hom variant. *Proc Natl Acad Sci USA* 101, 4180-5.

Matzinger, P. (2002). The danger model: a renewed sense of self. *Science* 296, 301-5.

Mieli-Vergani, G., Vergani, D., Tredger, J. M., Eddleston, A. L., Davis, M., and Williams, R. (1980). Lymphocyte cytotoxicity to halothane altered hepatocytes in patients with severe hepatic necrosis following halothane anaesthesia. *J Clin Lab Immunol* 4, 49-51.

Naisbitt, D. J., Farrell, J., Gordon, S. F., Maggs, J. L., Burkhart, C., Pichler, W. J., Pirmohamed, M., and Park, B. K. (2002). Covalent binding of the nitroso metabolite of sulfamethoxazole leads to toxicity and major histocompatibility complex-restricted antigen presentation. *Mol Pharmacol* 62, 628-37.

Neuberger, J., and Williams, R. (1989). Immune mechanisms in tienilic acid associated hepatotoxicity. *Gut* 30, 515-9.

Park, B. K., Coleman, J. W., and Kitteringham, N. R. (1987). Drug disposition and drug hypersensitivity. *Biochem Pharmacol* 36, 581-90.

Park, B. K., Naisbitt, D. J., Gordon, S. F., Kitteringham, N. R., and Pirmohamed, M. (2001). Metabolic activation in drug allergies. *Toxicology* 158, 11-23.

Pirmohamed, M., Lin, K., Chadwick, D., and Park, B. K. (2001). TNFalpha promoter region gene polymorphisms in carbamazepine-hypersensitive patients. *Neurology* 56, 890-6.

Pirmohamed, M., Naisbitt, D. J., Gordon, F., and Park, B. K. (2002). The danger hypothesis--potential role in idiosyncratic drug reactions. *Toxicology* 181-182, 55-63.

Pons, C., Dansette, P. M., Amar, C., Jaouen, M., Wolf, C. R., Gregeois, J., Homberg, J. C., and Mansuy, D. (1991). Detection of human hepatitis anti-liver kidney microsomes (LKM2) autoantibodies on rat liver sections is predominantly due to reactivity with rat liver P-450 IIC11. *J Pharmacol Exp Ther* 259, 1328-34.

Pumford, N. R., Halmes, N. C., and Hinson, J. A. (1997a). Covalent binding of xenobiotics to specific proteins in the liver. *Drug Metab Rev* 29, 39-57.

Pumford, N. R., Halmes, N. C., Martin, B. M., Cook, R. J., Wagner, C., and Hinson, J. A. (1997b). Covalent binding of acetaminophen to N-10-formyltetrahydrofolate dehydrogenase in mice. *J Pharmacol Exp Ther* 280, 501-5.

Reilly, T. P., Lash, L. H., Doll, M. A., Hein, D. W., Woster, P. M., and Svensson, C. K. (2000). A role for bioactivation and covalent binding within epidermal keratinocytes in sulfonamide-induced cutaneous drug reactions. *J Invest Dermatol* 114, 1164-73.

Rieder, M. J., Shear, N. H., Kanee, A., Tang, B. K., and Spielberg, S. P. (1991). Prominence of slow acetylator phenotype among patients with sulfonamide hypersensitivity reactions. *Clin Pharmacol Ther* 49, 13-7.

Rieder, M. J., Uetrecht, J., Shear, N. H., Cannon, M., Miller, M., and Spielberg, S. P. (1989). Diagnosis of sulfonamide hypersensitivity reactions by in-vitro "rechallenge" with hydroxylamine metabolites. *Ann Intern Med* 110, 286-9.

Riley, R. J., and Leeder, J. S. (1995). *In vitro* analysis of metabolic predisposition to drug hypersensitivity reactions. *Clin Exp Immunol* 99, 1-6.

Riley, R. J., Maggs, J. L., Lambert, C., Kitteringham, N. R., and Park, B. K. (1988). An *in vitro* study of the microsomal metabolism and cellular toxicity of phenytoin, sorbinil and mianserin. *Br J Clin Pharmacol* 26, 577-88.

Riley, R. J., Smith, G., Wolf, C. R., Cook, V. A., and Leeder, J. S. (1993). Human anti-endoplasmic reticulum autoantibodies produced in aromatic anticonvulsant hypersensitivity reactions recognise rodent CYP3A proteins and a similarly regulated human P450 enzyme(s). *Biochem Biophys Res Commun* 191, 32-40.

Roberts, S. A., Price, V. F., and Jollow, D. J. (1990). Acetaminophen structure-toxicity studies: *in vivo* covalent binding of a nonhepatotoxic analog, 3-hydroxyacetanilide. *Toxicol Appl Pharmacol* 105, 195-208.

Roujeau, J. C., Huynh, T. N., Bracq, C., Guillaume, J. C., Revuz, J., and Touraine, R. (1987). Genetic susceptibility to toxic epidermal necrolysis. *Arch Dermatol* 123, 1171-3.

Schnyder, B., Burkhart, C., Schnyder-Frutig, K., von Greyerz, S., Naisbitt, D. J., Pirmohamed, M., Park, B. K., and Pichler, W. J. (2000). Recognition of sulfamethoxazole and its reactive metabolites by drug-specific CD4+ T cells from allergic individuals. *J Immunol* 164, 6647-54.

Shear, N. H., and Spielberg, S. P. (1988). Anticonvulsant hypersensitivity syndrome. *In vitro* assessment of risk. *J Clin Invest* 82, 1826-32.

Shear, N. H., Spielberg, S. P., Grant, D. M., Tang, B. K., and Kalow, W. (1986). Differences in metabolism of sulfonamides predisposing to idiosyncratic toxicity. *Ann Intern Med* 105, 179-84.

Stravitz, R. T., and Sanyal, A. J. (2003). Drug-induced steatohepatitis. *Clin Liver Dis* 7, 435-51.

Summan, M., and Cribb, A. E. (2002). Novel non-labile covalent binding of sulfamethoxazole reactive metabolites to cultured human lymphoid cells. *Chem Biol Interact* 142, 155-73.

Uetrecht, J. (2003). Screening for the potential of a drug candidate to cause idiosyncratic drug reactions. *Drug Discov Today* 8, 832-7.

Uetrecht, J. P. (1999). New concepts in immunology relevant to idiosyncratic drug reactions: the "danger hypothesis" and innate immune system. *Chem Res Toxicol* 12, 387-95.

Vergani, D., Mieli-Vergani, G., Alberti, A., Neuberger, J., Eddleston, A. L., Davis, M., and Williams, R. (1980). Antibodies to the surface of halothane-altered rabbit hepatocytes in patients with severe halothane-associated hepatitis. *N Engl J Med* 303, 66-71.

Wade, L. T., Kenna, J. G., and Caldwell, J. (1997). Immunochemical identification of mouse hepatic protein adducts derived from the nonsteroidal anti-inflammatory drugs diclofenac, sulindac, and ibuprofen. *Chem Res Toxicol* 10, 546-55.

Williams, D. P., and Park, B. K. (2003). Idiosyncratic toxicity: the role of toxicophores and bioactivation. *Drug Discov Today* 8, 1044-50.

Yunis, J. J., Lieberman, J., and Yunis, E. J. (1992). Major histocompatibility complex associations with clozapine-induced agranulocytosis. The USA experience. *Drug Saf* 7 Suppl 1, 7-9.

14

Elementary Predictive Toxicology for Advanced Applications

Constantine Kreatsoulas[1]
Stephen K. Durham[1]
Laura L. Custer[1] and Greg M. Pearl[1§]

[1]Bristol-Myers Squibb
Princeton, New Jersey 08453

[§]Delaware Valley College
Department of Chemistry
Doylestown, PA 18901

Table of Contents

List of Abbreviations

ADAPT ....Automated Determination of Associations and Patterns Toolkit

CASE......................................Computer Automated Structure Evaluation

CU ....CASE Unit of activity (scaled activity value for models
built in MultiCASE; 0-inactive; 99-highly active)

DEREK......Deductive Estimation Relationships from Existing Knowledge

ES ....Expert System

FN ....False Negative (an assay positive response
assessed to be a negative response)

FP ....False Positive (an assay negative response
assessed to be a positive response)

IVS..Independent Vendor Software

LUMO..Lowest unoccupied molecular orbital

PS.......................Prediction Set (set of compounds a model is naïve to
– neither in the training or validation set)

QSAR......................Quantitative Structure Activity Relationship

SOS.......................................SOS Chromotest for Genotoxicity

TN...........................True Negative (an assay negative response assessed
to be a negative response)

TP ....True Positive (an assay positive response
assessed to be a positive response)

TS ....Training Set (set of compounds used to develop a model)

VS..Validation Set (set of compounds used to
assess the quality of a model)

Key Words

ADME/TOX, Computational Toxicology, Expert System, Genotoxicity, Informatics, Lead Optimization, Mutagenicity, Predictive Toxicology, Quantitative Structure Activity Relationship, Structure Activity Relationship

Introduction

As the pace of pharmaceutical drug discovery quickens and greater numbers of preclinical candidates are identified using combinatorial and other high throughput methods, the demand on safety assessment assays increases. As most *in vitro* toxicology assays are, at best, medium throughput, it is readily apparent that rapid *in silico* assessment protocols must be developed and validated for their use in the early discovery phase. No strangers to the increased demand for accurate safety assessments of candidate compounds and the additional constraints imposed by limited resources, regulatory agencies have long been at the forefront of utilizing and championing computational methods. As regulatory databases of safety information are populated and legacy data incorporated, methods to utilize this data to extract meaningful information must be developed and validated. As this is not intended to be an exhaustive review of all *in silico* tools for toxicology assessment, the reader is referred to a number of recent articles which do an outstanding job of summarizing the algorithms, benefits and shortcomings of many of the commercial packages available (Pearl, Livingston-Carr *et al.* 2001; Greene 2002; Snyder, Pearl *et al.* 2004).

Role of Predictive Toxicology in Drug Discovery

During the development process, there are many competing factors which influence the success of a candidate compound. Physical properties such as lipophilicity, solubility and permeability are closely monitored during the development process and *in vitro* and *in silico* models are continuously developed and refined on a per chemotype basis. Empirical metrics such as Lipinski's rule of five (Lipinski, Lombardo *et al.* 2001) are routinely used in profiling the drug likeness of candidate compounds. As we strive to increase the success rates of compounds both in the pre-clinical and post-NCE, we must be increasingly stringent on the criteria used to determine if a compound will be successful. Safety assessment is one of the most inflexible of these criteria. Treating safety liabilities as simply another property, in this case one to be minimized, has been a paradigm shift in the pharmaceutical industry over the last decade.

What remains, though, is that differing stages of the development process have dissimilar needs for such a design algorithm. Ideally, one would have an assessment protocol in place which would correctly partition all of the harmful from the innocuous compounds in both the training and test/validation sets (TS and VS, respectively). Furthermore, the most usable model is one which can successfully extrapolate beyond either the training or validation sets when encountering novel compounds in a prediction set (PS). This type of model exists only in an idealized context, as neither the data nor our understanding of the biology is usually of sufficient detail to allow us to construct models of such quality. As such, we are often left with three classes of models, those with high overall predicitivity (concordance), high specificity (ability to partition the inactive subset) or high sensitivity (ability to partition the active subset). Most automated algorithms strive to achieve the first goal, usually achieving a high TS concordance, most easily achieved by skewing the model to identify the majority population in the TS. Subjective algorithms, usually involving human intervention and biasing have been used to achieve high sensitivity or specificity, almost always at the expense of concordance.

A simple question arises: why would one want to bias a model toward high sensitivity or specificity? Three issues determine the form of the biasing: a) the predictive ability of the confirmatory assay; b) the stage in the discovery pipeline of the assessment being performed; and, c) the cost of each assay performed compared to the cost of a missed assessment. If the second tier assay has a high specificity, then a simple approach to achieve high overall process concordance is to have a first-tier, *in silico* method which has high sensitivity (the compounds assessed in the confirmatory assay are those in which the *in vitro* assay has the highest predictive ability), as shown in **Figure 1**. As models become more widely used by bench scientists throughout a research organization, the needs of the various research entities using these models are an influencing factor in how to appropriately bias the models. Scientists involved in the final stages of safety assessment (e.g. before an NCE filing) or formulation tend to be more cautious with models that have a minimal rate of false negative assessments. Scientists involved in scaffold development or lead identification, would typically desire a model with as few false positive assessments as possible, so as not to limit the

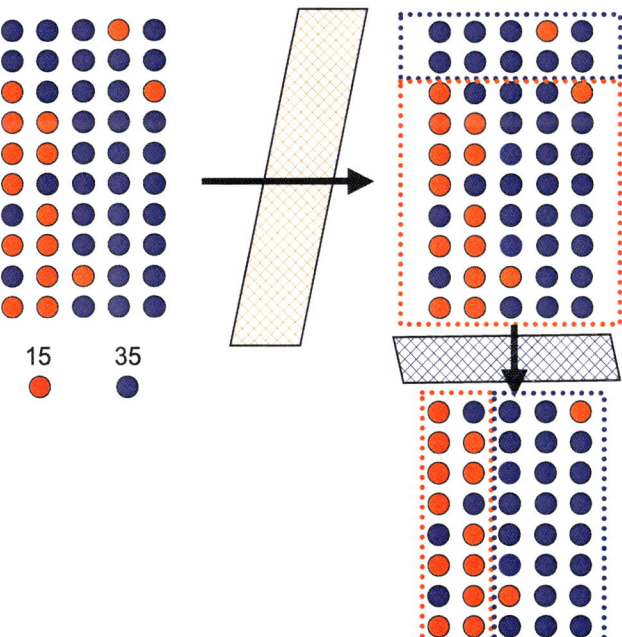

Figure 1. Illustration of a tiered analysis system geared toward correctly partitioning the toxic (red) from the non-toxic in which the first phase has a high sensitivity (93%) and the second phase has high specificity (85%). The overall concordance of this approach is 86%, with an overall sensitivity of 80% and specificity of 89%.

exploration of chemical space. An additional motivation for biasing a model would be if the confirmatory assay were prohibitively expensive or were of low throughput, leading to the need for a model with few false positives.

As an example we will consider carcinogenicity modeling. The assay approved by the Food and Drug Administration (FDA) to evaluate the *in vivo* carcinogenicity of a compound is the two year rodent assay with cohorts of male and female rats. In order to build a model which is not simply an exercise in statistics, a cost-benefit analysis could be conducted as follows: if the cost (either in real dollars or in opportunity cost due to halting a compound's development) of excluding a compound from an assay is higher than the cost of losing a compound in a later stage of development due to carcinogenicity, the model should have high true negative rate. It would be this pool of compounds which would be carried forward and taken into the *in vitro/vivo* assays at a later stage of development.

Tractable Toxicological Endpoints

Our ability to model a liability is not merely dependant on the ability of the modeler or the selection of the optimal algorithm, set of descriptors or subset of data for a given endpoint. More so than with traditional quantitative structure activity models, models in the realm of predictive toxicology must be acutely dependant on endpoints for which they are developed (e.g. models for terato-genicity, in which the phenotype characterized as teratogenic is due to an *unknown* number of biological mechanisms, building a predictive model becomes extremely difficult). Even within an endpoint with a limited number of mechanisms, local models (e.g. the mutagenicity of thiophenes) can often be combined to give a higher overall success rate and interpretability than a single, global model to explain an entire endpoint (e.g. mutagenicity).

Another factor which determines the tractability of a problem is the level of experimental detail available on the biological entities being studied. Modeling of phase I drug metabolism has been greatly impacted by the high resolution x-ray crystal structure of the human cytochrome P450 2C9 and 3A4 enzymes, allowing researchers to carry out high level *ab initio* quantum mechanical calculations in order to predict possible sites of oxidative metabolism upon docking ligands into the active site of the enzyme. As our understanding of this system increases, our ability to predict the inhibition of the enzyme by pharmaceuticals will also increase.

As such, the endpoints which have been successfully modeled are varied; the greatest number of, and most mature, models exist for mutagenicity, rodent carcinogenicity (both genotoxic and non-genotoxic) and occupational toxicities (eye, skin and respiratory irritation/sensitization and lachrymation). As the quantity of high quality, controlled data increases, the predictive ability of the models developed from the data and the insights provided by those models will also increase.

Strengths and Weaknesses of Various Methodologies

There are currently two general approaches used to develop models which assess a compound's potential toxicological liabilities, quantitative structure-activity relationship (QSAR) derived models and expert system (ES) derived knowledge bases. Hybrid approaches which employ QSAR methods to determine the components rules of ES databases have also been developed. Each of these methods has had varying degrees of success in modeling toxicological endpoints. Local models of activity are often best classified by QSAR derived models (e.g. mutagenicity of anilines). Global models of a toxicological endpoint are often best represented by an expert system (e.g. mutagenicity of the world drug index) due to the general nature of the rules (e.g. aromatic compounds with good leaving groups often form DNA adducts). Both of these approaches may also be combined so that several class-specific models create a larger, global model.

QSARs develop an abstract representation of a series of compounds and seek to extract the features (descriptors) which best correlate with an observed activity. Developing a virtual depiction of a molecule is accomplished by the calculation of molecular indices (e.g. counting the number of rotatable bonds, halogens or heavy atoms) and properties (e.g. LUMO energy, polarizability or logP). These *descriptors* are then correlated with the experimental data using multivariate statistical methods (e.g. multiple linear regression, principle component analysis or Shannon entropy methods) to keep only those descriptors with strong resolving power. QSAR models can be used to build structural models of theoretically ideal ligands (such as Comparative Molecular Field Analysis and pharmacophore models) given the current data. In addition, this class of model can give a quantitative estimate as to the likelihood of a novel compound having the activity of interest. It is readily apparent that QSARs benefit most from two things: a) a large pool of high quality data; and, b) a single endpoint assay with few mechanisms of action. As the number of molecules modeled increases, the resolving power of the selected descriptors increases. Likewise, if the assay readout to be modeled is a result of multiple mechanisms, the likelihood of finding simple descriptors with a correlation to activity is low, as the signal from any single mechanism is low. Conversely, QSAR models perform extremely well when assays generate a large volume of data through a single mechanism of action, as most high and medium throughput assays are based on single mechanisms.

Expert systems are built upon a body of knowledge obtained from a specialists and/or literature sources. This information, which can be as varied as "rule of thumb" relationships to experimentally determined relationships (e.g. kinase-substrate pairs) or structure activity data from compounds assayed using the same protocol, is collated, evaluated and then entered into a rules-based system which describes these cause-effect relationships (i.e. *if* **substructure** *is* **aniline** *and* **metabolic activation present** *then* **genotoxic** *else* **nongenotoxic**). Perhaps the best known such relationships in predictive toxicology are the Ashby-Tenant structural alerts for carcinogenicity which have been the basis of numerous expert system databases to identify unwanted activity in compounds. Because each of the rules of an expert system form a component of a decision tree, the collection of rules can be easily combined into modeling global endpoints. Expert systems alone do not provide percent likelihood estimates of an outcome occurring; they merely indicate that it is a possibility (i.e. binary relationship). In order to quantitatively predict an event, predicate logic methods must be applied, as in the DEREK system (discussed below).

The methods described above, QSARs and ESs, can be combined to give greater predictive ability or can each be utilized in the development of the other. A QSAR model can be developed using fragment-based descriptors (e.g. partitioning a molecule at its rotatable bonds) and then these fragments scored for predictive ability. This database of statistically significant fragments can then be used as the expert system. Such methods have been widely utilized by regulatory agencies and are routinely part of the safety assessment process. One such method, the MultiCASE algorithm (Klopman and Macina 1985), will be used extensively in this work to develop novel fragments for the variety of datasets discussed within.

The goal of this paper is not to introduce a novel modeling methodology for toxicology or to present yet another model for a given set of data, but to highlight what can be done with available technologies in order to boost the productivity and predictive accuracy of currently available independent vendor software (IVS) methods. To accomplish this, we will directly compare the performance of these differing methods across a diverse set of chemotypes using a controlled dataset consisting of results from the SOS Chromotest, a gentoxicity screening assay for mutagenicity. Compound libraries for secondary and aromatic amines, thiophenes and polycyclic aromatic compounds have been assayed at Bristol-Myers Squibb. QSAR models for many of these data sets have been developed and published previously and compared to DEREK, Topkat and MultiCASE (He, Jurs *et al.* 2003; Mattioni, Kauffman *et al.* 2003; Mosier, Jurs *et al.* 2003). We have used the MultiCASE algorithm to extract structural fragments with statistical resolving power and will discuss how this new knowledge could be reincorporated into the overall toxicology assessment paradigm to enhance its overall predictive ability.

Methods

Compound Selection

The data employed in this publication have been presented elsewhere and we will give only a description of the methods used to choose compounds and calculate descriptive relationships. All libraries were selected, purchased and assayed at Bristol-Myers Squibb. The compounds comprising these datasets of aromatic amines, thiophenes and polycyclic aromatic compounds were selected based upon their availability from Sigma-Aldrich, in pure form, and their drug-likeness, as profiled using an expanded Lipinski filter. Of the multitude of compounds which could conceivably qualify for this study, the most chemically diverse subset was selected. Chemical diversity was based upon clustering of the

Kier-Hall electrotopological indices (Kier and Hall 1990), molecular weight, and various atom and ring counts. Compound selection was then further enhanced by the selection of specific groups to develop local structure-activity relationships (i.e. *para* versus *ortho* substitution about a ring).

SOS Chromotest Assay

The SOS Chromotest was used in this paper as an alternative method to the widely accepted bacterial-reverse-mutation assay, also known as the Ames test. The SOS test has been used extensively with many different chemical classes. A review of published genotoxicity data between 1982 and 1992 indicated that, for the 1776 compounds evaluated, the SOS Chromotest had 90% concordance with the Ames mutagenicity test (Quillardet and Hofnung 1993). The assay is a simple and rapid test for mutagenicity that requires only a few milligrams of compound. These benefits along with the high Ames test concordance, make the SOS Chromotest a good tool for the purposes in this paper.

The SOS Chromotest assay is a colorimetric assay that measures induction of a lacZ reporter gene in response to DNA damage (Hofnung and Quillardet 1988). The SOS pathway plays a leading role in E. coli response to damage of nuclear material (Sutton, Smith *et al.* 2000). SOS induction is used as an early monitor for DNA damage because this pathway is sensitive to a broad spectrum of genotoxic substances. E.coli were modified with a *lacZ* reporter gene fused to an SOS gene, *sfiA*, with the endogenous *lac* sequence deleted, so all β-galactosidase activity is dependent upon *sfiA* induction. The strain was made more sensitive to genotoxic substances by increasing cell envelope permeability (*rfa* mutation) and by eliminating the excision repair pathway (*uvrA* mutation). In addition, constitutive expression of alkaline phosphatase, an SOS independent gene, was included as a control for cytotoxicity. In response to DNA damage the SOS repair genes are induced resulting in production of ,-galactosidase, the gene product of lacZ. The assay readout is the fold increases in gene induction as determined by measuring β-galactosidase activity using o-nitrophenyl--d-galactopyranoside (ONGP). For taxonomy of activity ranges, both in the presence and absence of S9 activation see **Table 1**.

Data Set	IMax (-S9)		IMax (+S9)	
	Min	Max	Min	Max
Thiophenes	0.88	8.01	0.9	6.08
Polycyclic Aromatic Compounds	0.84	7.29	0.91	9.37
Secondary and Aromatic Amines	0.81	11.66	0.85	10.57

Table 1. Chart of activity ranges for the different data sets discussed in the text. Activity is the fold increase in fluorescence over control.

Computational Assessment Tools – ADAPT

ADAPT is a neural network based QSAR modeling environment (Jurs, Hasan *et al.* 1983). Briefly, relationships are derived using a probabilistic neural network which evolves the optimal descriptor set to partition active from inactive compounds (i.e. mutagens from non-mutagens). The ADAPT software package is a product of the Jurs research group and can be compiled to run on many platforms. Model construction using ADAPT follows several distinct phases: structure geometry optimization and modeling, descriptor generation, training and prediction set formation, objective feature selection, model building and model validation. The exact procedure has been published in the works describing the specific models and will not be discussed here. The ADAPT system has been used to model a variety of toxicologically relevant endpoints.

Computational Assessment Tools – DEREK

DEREK is an expert system created specifically for toxicological endpoints and assessments (Greene, Judson *et al.* 1999). Originally developed and implemented by Schering Agrochemicals, DEREK is currently available on two platforms from two sources. The IRIX instance of DEREK is available from the Lhasa Group at Harvard University (Corey, Long *et al.* 1985). The PC version is available from Lhasa, Ltd. UK (Greene, Judson *et al.* 1999; Judson, Marchant *et al.* 2003) and with an expanded rules base from the IRIX version. As such, it was used for all work presented here (version 5.0 and 6.0). PC DEREK (referred to hereafter as DEREK) covers a broad range of endpoints with its greatest strengths in carcinogenicity, mutagenicity (both genotoxic and non-genotoxic), skin irritation and sensitization. The rules set in DEREK is researched, generated and validated through a collaborative effort involving researchers from academia, industry and the staff of Lhasa. These SARs represented by these rules are encoded as substructures (with the ability to handle exceptions) which are subsequently located in a novel compound. Novel SARs can be incorporated by the user via an ISIS Draw input method.

Computational Assessment Tools – BMS DEREK

"BMS DEREK" is a heavily modified version of DEREK 5.0 for PC. The source code was ported to UNIX with the DEREK engine processing the compounds. BMS DEREK differs from DEREK 5.0 in that it contains thirteen new mutagenicity rules along with six carcinogenicity substructural alerts. The recate-gorized rules were found to give the DEREK higher overall sensitivity with a minimal impact on concordance as evaluated on a BMS validation set.

Computational Assessment Tools – MultiCASE

At its operational core, MultiCASE is a QSAR-derived expert system. The range of activity can be rescaled either automatically by the application or by the user. The descriptors generated are connected structural fragments which are from two to ten non-hydrogen atoms in length (referred to as *biophores*). Once a library of all possible biophores has been constructed, various statistical tests are applied to determine the resolving power of given biophores to correlate to an activity. These biophores are then assigned the average activity of all of the molecules in which they are contained (the CASE algorithm). This procedure is then recursively applied to each biophore to find additional biophores which serve to modify activities (activating and deactivating groups) with their effect being quantified in a manner similar to the above (the "Multi" in MultiCASE). MultiCASE then assesses a compound by giving it a score, calculated as the sum of all biophores present, with additional weight being applied for bioavailability.

Statistical Definitions Used

See Table 2 for definitions of the terms used and the confusion matrix which relates the terms to eachother. The overall agreement between a predcitve method and the experimental data is given by the concordance:

$$Conc = \frac{PA + NA}{PA + PD + ND + NA + PI + NI}$$

The ability of a predictive method to correctly assess the positive compounds is given by the sensitivity of a method:

$$Sens = \frac{PA}{PA + ND + PI}$$

The ability of a predictive method to correctly assess the negative compounds is given by the specificity:

$$Spec = \frac{NA}{PD + NA + NI}$$

The probability of an *in silico* method to correctly assess a compound by random chance is the frequency of success given the known distribution of positive and negative compounds in the data set. It is defined as:

$$Rand = \frac{(PA + ND + PI)^2 + (NA + PD + NI)^2}{(PA + ND + PI + NA + PD + NI)^2}$$

Another method used to evaluate categorical classification models is the κ statistic. In the notation used here, it is defined as:

$$\kappa = \frac{Po - Pe}{(1 - Pe)}$$

with P_o equivalent to the concordance as defined above:

$$Po = \frac{PA + NA}{PA + ND + PI + NA + PD + NI}$$

and P_e as a random weighted by the methods success sensitivity and specificity:

$$Pe = \frac{PA * (PA + ND + PI) + NA * (NA + PD + NI)}{(PA + ND + PI + NA + PD + NI)^2}$$

κ can best be thought of as a concordance adjusted for the random success rate of a model. Models with values for κ above 0.5 are considered to have overall predictive ability when classifying compounds into bins(Agresti 1996).

	Experimental Positives (+/)	Experimental Negatives (-/)
Computational Positives (/ +)	+/+ Pos Agreement (PA)	-/+ Pos Deviation (PD)
Computational Negative (/-)	+/- Neg Deviation (ND)	-/- Neg Agreement (NA)
Computational Indeterminate (/)	Pos Indeterminate (PI)	Neg Indeterminate (NI)

Table 2. Confusion Matrix for calculations in this text

Model Construction

Results from ADAPT models which have been published prior to this work are reported here. Briefly, the compounds were taken into ADAPT after their structures were optimized using CORINA and MOPAC. The data were then partitioned into multiple TS and VS using a bagging algorithm. Multiple models were thus generated and the overall consensus model is the "majority rules" vote of the individual models. This way all compounds were predicted at least once. The DEREK expert system evaluates compounds using substructure-based searches. Standard and BMS modified DEREK were both used to predict the mutagenic activity of all compounds without any specific models being built using this data (the entire data set was treated as the PS). In order to make an equivalent comparison, both the MultiCASE A2I *Salmonella* mutagenicity module and a model trained in an equivalent fashion to the ADAPT models, were used. Briefly, the data were partitioned *exactly* as described in the original ADAPT based models (e.g. identical compound distributions were utilized for the TS and VS). The activities were then scaled automatically in MultiCASE so that the activity range would be between zero (inactive) and 99 (most active) with the active-inactive cutoff at twenty-nine units (corresponding to the experimental cut-off in activity of 1.5 fold activity in the SOS Chromotest assay). Studies varying the cutoff value by ± ten percent showed a minimal impact on the sensitivity and concordance of the resulting models (unpublished data). The models thus generated were then allowed to each vote for the membership of a compound in a given class ("mutagenic" or non-mutagenic").

Results

Tables outlining the various methods' predictive abilities are given (**Tables 3-5**). In all cases, the ADAPT QSAR consensus model (a majority rules voting of several individual models) had the best concordance/κ value, ranging from 95%/0.88 (thiophenes) to 72%/.45 (aromatic and secondary amines). The MultiCASE *Salmonella* mutagenicity module, the A2I database, performed better than random for only the thiophene data set, with a concordance of 65%, but had a low κ value (0.39). In the remaining two data sets, it had the worst overall performance, with a concordance of 24% in the polycyclic aromatic compounds and a concordance of 32% in the aromatic and secondary amines. In two of the three data sets, BMS DEREK had the highest sensitivity, ranging from 100% (thiophenes and aromatic and secondary amines) to 90% (secondary and aromatic amines), but always had a low κ value. The polycyclic aromatic compounds were

	BMS DEREK	DEREK v5.0	DEREK v6.0	MultiCASE (A2I)	ADAPT Consensus	MultiCASE SOS
Concordance	30%	60%	60%	65%	95%	50%
Sensitivity	100%	17%	17%	33%	83%	83%
Specificity	0%	79%	79%	79%	100%	36%
κ	0.2378	0.3135	0.3135	0.3864	0.8816	0.3324

Table 3. Thiophenes. SOS (40+/100-); Random 58% Concordance

	BMS DEREK	DEREK v5.0	DEREK v6.0	MultiCASE (A2I)	ADAPT	MultiCASE SOS
Concordance	37%	58%	55%	24%	81%	77%
Sensitivity	48%	39%	39%	59%	74%	28%
Specificity	35%	62%	58%	17%	84%	87%
κ	0.1520	0.2482	0.2318	0.1228	0.5197	0.4058

Table 4. Polycyclic Aromatic Compounds. SOS (46+/231-); Random 72% Concordance

	BMS DEREK	**DEREK v5.0**	**DEREK v6.0**	**MultiCASE (A2I)**	**ADAPT Consensus**	**MultiCASE SOS**
Concordance	32%	61%	61%	32%	72%	69%
Sensitivity	90%	58%	58%	42%	69%	58%
Specificity	17%	62%	62%	30%	74%	72%
κ	0.2044	0.3341	0.3341	0.1414	0.4452	0.4056

Table 5. Secondary and Aromatic Amines. SOS (69+/265-); Random 67% Concordance.

not classified well by the expert systems approach, chiefly due to the lack of rules for heterocyclic compounds. The high sensitivity reported in the BMS DEREK models is offset by their having amongst the lowest specificity, ranging from 0% (thiophenes) to 35% (polycyclic aromatic compounds). Analysis of the specific performance of the expert system based approaches has been reported elsewhere (He, Jurs *et al.* 2003; Mattioni, Kauffman *et al.* 2003; Mosier, Jurs *et al.* 2003) and will only be touched upon here.

Thiophenes

The mutagenic potential of a thiophene is linked to formation of a stable epoxide. If the epoxide is stabilized at C2, then the likelihood of mutagenicity increases. Likewise, in systems which stabilize the formation of the *S*-oxide, nucleophilic attack at C2 is further stabilized leading to an increased possibility of reactivity with protein and/or DNA. For a more complete discussion of the mutagenicity of thiophenes, see (Mosier, Jurs *et al.* 2003).

The thiophene data set was the smallest of all the data sets, and was thus the only model for which a consensus model was not built (the results given are for a single model in ADAPT and the SOS trained MultiCASE approach). The MultiCASE fragment-based approach derived four biophores, given in **Table 6** and illustrated in **Figure 2**. As is evident from the table, there was very little representation in the PS of any of the biophores derived. Furthermore, while the overall positive accuracy of these biophores is quite high (69%), the biophore corresponding to the primary alcohol was derived from a small sample (N=2) of marginal activity (29 CU, the cutoff between active and inactivity). While the MultiCASE algorithm found this a significant biophore, the author would not utilize this in any further development of structural rules for thiophene (or any other) genotoxicity. Removal of this biophore from the model increases the positive accuracy to 91.7%. These four biophores do successfully select the genotoxic compounds from the PS as is reflected in the very high sensitivity (83%), but do not do an acceptable job of partitioning out the non-genotoxic compounds (36% specificity). This leads to an overall concordance of 50% and a κ of 0.33, worse than random.

KLN Fragment	Average Frequency in TS	Average Activity	Frequency in PS	Positive Accuracy
cH"-S -c >=	14.0	35 CU	4	75%
COH-c =	9.0	35 CU	3	100%
c. =cH -cH =cH - c =c. -	4.0	29 CU	2	100%
OH -CH2-	2.0	29 CU	2	0%

Table 6. Analysis of Statistically Significant Thiophene Fragments (single model). CU is the CASE Unit of activity.

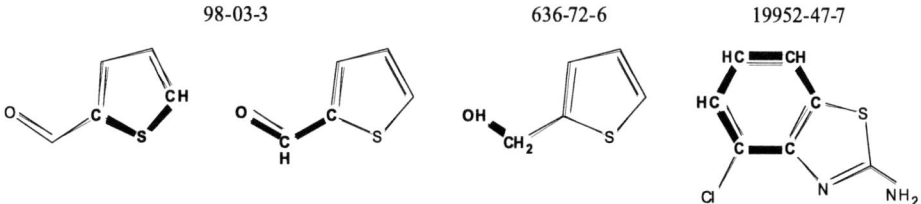

Figure 2. Statistically significant biophores derived from the thiophene dataset highlighted within compounds from the TS in which they are contained. Numbers above the molecules are the CAS identifiers. Atoms represented explicitly in bold are part of the biophore.

Polycyclic Aromatic Compounds

The polycyclic aromatic compounds used in this study were representative of many different classes of polycyclic compounds. Using the bagging approach employed previously in analyzing this data set (He, Jurs *et al.* 2003), three model triplets were generated, each containing an equivalent distribution of active and inactive compounds. The biophores and statistics for the consensus model are presented in **Table 7** and are depicted in **Figure 3**. Of the nine significant fragments, four were found in more than one model and all were based upon at least three molecules in the TS (with a median of 4.7 TS molecules/fragment). The positive accuracy of the MultiCASE derived biophores ranged from a high of 80% (biophore cH =cH –c."-NH -c = contained in molecule 312-73-2 as depicted in **Figure 3**) to a low of 0% (biophore cH =n -c = contained in molecule 1532-84-9 as depicted in **Figure 3**). Unlike the thiophene model above, this consensus model had high specificity (87%), but low sensitivity (28%), failing to identify 33 of the 46 genotoxic compounds in the data set, giving an overall concordance of 77%.

Interestingly, most of the biophores identified by this approach contain a nitrogen atom (see **Table7** and **Figure 3**), either as part of the heterocycle or as a primary amine. Amines can undergo P450 (1A2) activation to form the reactive nitrenium species to yield the ultimate N-hydroxylated form (Colvin, Hatch *et al.*

KLN Fragment	Average Frequency in TS	Average Activity	Models Deriving Fragment	Frequency in PS	Positive Accuracy
NH -c =c -	2.8	35 CU	6	32	69%
NH2-c =cH -c. =	6.3	42 CU	4	26	73%
cH =cH –n =c. -cH =	4.0	27 CU	2	17	24%
n =n -	4.5	33 CU	2	12	50%
cH =c. -c <=cH -	7.0	39 CU	1	10	30%
cH =cH –c-NH -c =	6.0	28 CU	1	5	80%
cH =n -c =	5.0	39 CU	1	5	0%
N -c. =cH -cH =cH -	4.0	30 CU	1	5	60%
cH =cH -c =c. -cH = <3-OH >	3.0	30 CU	1	10	50%

Table 7. Analysis of Statistically Significant Polycyclic Aromatic Fragments (nine models). CU is the CASE Unit of activity.

1998). Polycyclic aromatic amines generally exhibit greater mutagenic potency than other aromatic amines provided that the polycyclic system does not exceed six or more rings in size (Trieff, Biagi *et al.* 1989; Benigni, Passerini *et al.* 1998). The extended aromatic system offers a greater degree of stabilization to the nitrenium ion and may allow for a more efficient activation due to the planarity of the structure (Lai, Woo *et al.* 1996; Benigni, Passerini *et al.* 1998). The aromatic and secondary amines are considered in the following section at length.

Aromatic and Secondary Amines

The aromatic and secondary amines were chosen to be fairly diverse. Using the data subsetting approach employed to develop the ADAPT QSAR models for this in data set (Mattioni, Kauffman *et al.* 2003), nine individual models were generated, each containing an equivalent distribution of active and inactive compounds. The biophores and statistics for the consensus model are presented in **Table 8** and are depicted in **Figure 4**. Of the nine fragments found to be statistically significant, six were derived by more than one model and all were based upon, on average 9.5 TS molecules/fragment, with a minimum of 2.8 TS molecules/fragment. The positive accuracy of these biophores ranged from a high of 80% (biophore cH =cH -c. =c <-cH = represented by molecule 118-44-5 in Figure 4) to 0% (biophore cH =cH -c <=cH -c <= represented by molecule 102-56-7 in Figure 4). The MultiCASE consensus model had the second highest specificity (72%) and concordance (69%) of all of the models reported for this data

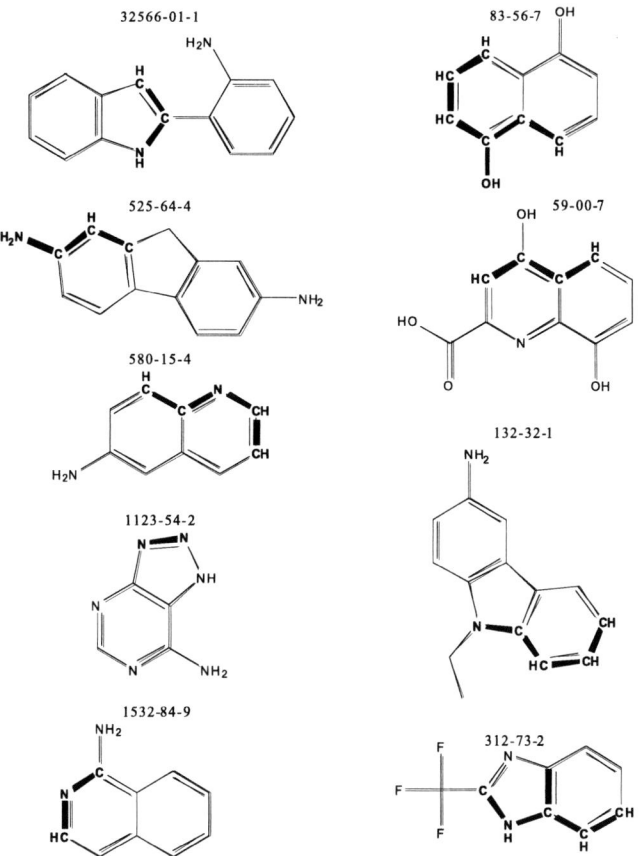

Figure 3. Statistically significant biophores derived from the polycyclic aromatic compounds data set highlighted within compounds from the TS in which they are contained. Numbers above the molecules are the CAS identifiers. Atoms represented explicitly in bold are part of the biophore.

set. The low positive accuracy of the fragments is reflected in the overall sensitivity of the consensus model (58%).

The biophores generated by this fragment based approach are the only ones from three models which show a correlation between overall positive accuracy and activity of the underlying molecules upon which the fragments are based. The Pearson correlation coefficient is 0.79, indicating a statistically significant correlation between these two quantities. In the polycyclic aromatic compounds the overall positive accuracy and activity correlation coefficient is negative and in thiophenes, there is a correlation coefficient of 0.45, indicating an uncorrelated system. The correlation is a product of several features of this data set. The overall population of this set is larger than the other datasets (334 compounds; polycyclic aromatic compounds: 277 compounds; thiophenes: 140 compounds), with a correspondingly larger number of active compounds. This leads to several benefits in model creation. First, as the pool of TS molecules is larger, the number of two to ten atom fragments generated and associated modulating fragments is larger, allowing for a more robust fragment selection process. The

KLN Fragment	Average Frequency in TS	Average Activity	Models Deriving Fragment	Frequency in PS	Positive Accuracy
NH2-c =cH -c. =	12.0	42 CU	6	28	57%
NH2-c =cH -cH =cH -	29.4	31 CU	5	66	42%
S -c <=	8.8	29 CU	4	25	28%
N" -N -	2.8	37 CU	4	5	40%
cH =cH -c. =c <-cH =	6.5	48 CU	2	5	80%
NH2-c =cH -cH =c <-	4.5	30 CU	2	7	14%
cH =c -cH =c. - <2-NH2>	8.0	47 CU	1	9	44%
cH =cH -cH =c -cH =c -	7.0	33 CU	1	8	25%
cH =cH -c <=cH -c <=	7.0	31 CU	1	6	0%

Table 8. Analysis of Statistically Significant Aromatic Amine Fragments (nine models). CU is the CASE Unit of activity.

mean activity of the significant fragments generated is approximately ten percent higher than that of the other data sets, with more fragments having activities in the moderate range (forty to sixty CASE units).

Discussion

The evaluation of independent vendor solutions for prediction of the genotoxic potential of drug-like compounds is presented here. The availability of genotoxicity data from a single lab on several series of congeneric compounds which had been previously assessed by DEREK (a well curated expert system), ADAPT (one of the more advanced neural network based QSAR tool) and MultiCASE (a widely used hybrid QSAR-expert system based modeling tool) made these attractive starting points. We utilized the fragment based approach as implemented in the MultiCASE algorithm to develop a library of genotoxic substructures to analyze these three congeneric series of compounds: thiophenes, polycyclic aromatic compounds and a set of secondary and aromatic amines.

The substructural fragments generated for these data sets were found to vary widely in their predictive ability. For compounds with PS coverage greater than five compounds, the positive accuracy ranged from a high of 80% to a low of 0%). Except for fragments generated from the secondary and aromatic amines, the predictive ability was not correlated with either representation in the PS, the number of training set compounds giving rise to a specific fragment, or the mean activity of the fragment. In the one case with correlation, the number of training

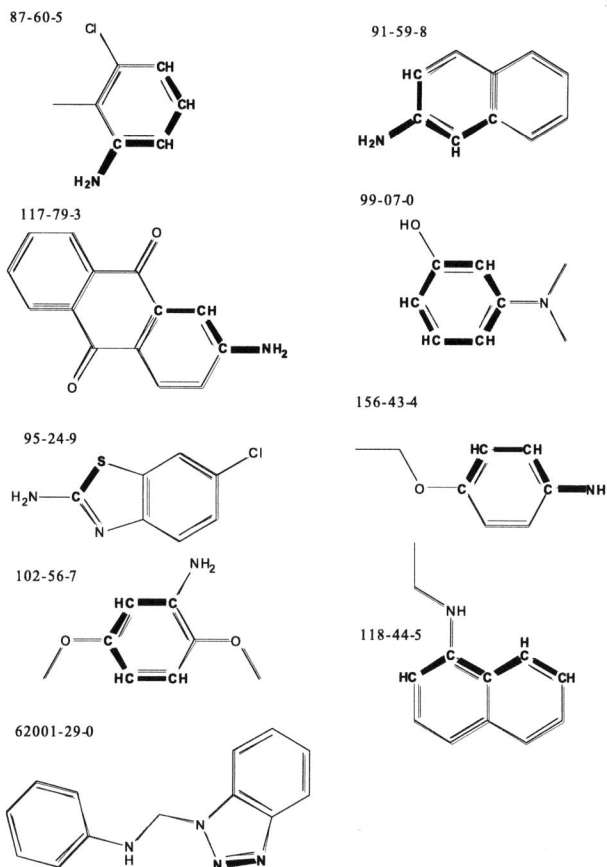

Figure 4. Statistically significant biophores derived from the secondary and aromatic amines dataset highlighted within compounds from the TS in which they are contained. Numbers above the molecules are the CAS identifiers. Atoms represented explicitly in bold are part of the biophore.

set compounds per fragment was found to have significant correlation with activity (correlation coefficient of 0.79).

Developing a QSAR using solely substructural fragments (as is the procedure with MultiCASE) was never as predictive as adding additional QSAR factors, as is evidenced by the difference in predictive ability between ADAPT and MultiCASE as ADAPT uses not only path-based substructural fragments but a variety of additional descriptors. The authors would like to provide a cautionary note to researchers utilizing the power of ensemble based modeling methods (such as many of the ADAPT models presented here, machine-learning algorithms, neural networks and the Random Forest algorithm) in that it is very easy to over-train a model, making it no more than a mapping of the training set. There are over sixty descriptors for the set of 334 compounds in the ADAPT ensemble models for the Secondary and Aromatic Amines. A much simpler model, with nine substructural-fragments as descriptors, developed using MultiCASE has nearly identical predictive ability.

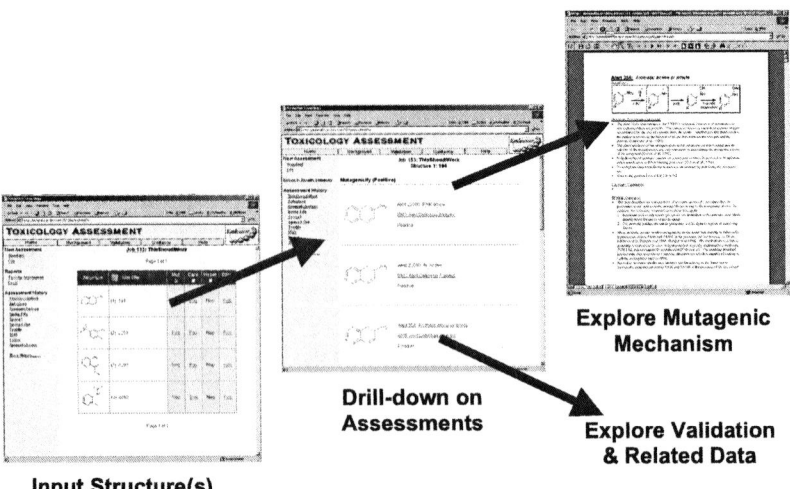

Figure 5. Screenshots of the Toxicology Assessment web portal which has been implemented on the corporate intranet at Bristol-Myers Squibb. It allows the user to import SD formatted files, draw novel structures or reference samples in the corporate database. Once input compounds are run through a battery of safety assessment models and a report is generated. All possibly toxic substructures are hyper-linked to all institutional information regarding this activity.

The system described here was implemented in an internal toxicology assessment web portal at Bristol-Myers Squibb (see **Figure 5**). This system allows any authorized user on a discovery team or in safety assessment to analyze both synthesized and virtual compounds at any phase in the development process, allowing them to prioritize testing in a second tier genotoxicity assay (the SOS Chromotest) or to provide supporting information for other genotoxicity assays (i.e. *in-vitro* micronucleus or bacterial-reverse-mutation assay). Other toxicological endpoints such as hepatotoxicity, non-genotoxic and genotoxic carcinogenicity, environmental toxicity (respiratory, skin and eye irritation and sensitization and lachrymation) can also be added. The ability to query IVS models (such as the standard MultiCASE carcinogenicity and mutagenicity models) as well as internally developed models has been added to the web tool. In addition, this system allows the user to generate reports based on the assessment and provides all supporting documentation, including minireviews on each of the mutagenic endpoints with model statistics and literature references at the users' desktops. While no toxicology model will be as accurate as an *in vitro* model system, if developed with a clear goal in mind *and* used within its scope, models can be used to intelligently triage compounds from the testing queue (thereby increasing the overall capacity of the safety assessment assays). At Bristol-Myers Squibb, using this multi-tiered approach, we have virtually eliminated the mutagenic liability as a cause of attrition during the early development phase.

References

Agresti, A. (1996). An Introduction to Categorical Data Analysis. New York, Chichester, Brisbane, Toronto and Singapore, John Wiley & Sons, Inc.: 246-249.

Benigni, R., L. Passerini, *et al.* (1998). "QSAR models for discriminating between mutagenic and nonmutagenic aromatic and heteroaromatic amines." *Environ Mol Mutagen* 32(1): 75-83.

Colvin, M. E., F. T. Hatch, *et al.* (1998). "Chemical and biological factors affecting mutagen potency." *Mutat Res* 400(1-2): 479-92.

Corey, E. J., A. K. Long, *et al.* (1985). "Computer-assisted analysis in organic synthesis." *Science* 228(4698): 408-18.

Greene, N. (2002). "Computer systems for the prediction of toxicity: an update." *Adv Drug Deliv Rev* 54(3): 417-31.

Greene, N., P. N. Judson, *et al.* (1999). "Knowledge-based expert systems for toxicity and metabolism prediction: DEREK, StAR and METEOR." SAR QSAR *Environ Res* 10(2-3): 299-314.

He, L., P. C. Jurs, *et al.* (2003). "Predicting the genotoxicity of polycyclic aromatic compounds from molecular structure with different classifiers." *Chem Res Toxicol* 16(12): 1567-80.

Hofnung, M. and P. Quillardet (1988). "The SOS Chromotest, a colorimetric assay based on the primary cellular responses to genotoxic agents." *Ann N Y Acad Sci* 534: 817-25.

Judson, P. N., C. A. Marchant, *et al.* (2003). "Using argumentation for absolute reasoning about the potential toxicity of chemicals." *J Chem Inf Comput Sci* 43(5): 1364-70.

Jurs, P. C., M. N. Hasan, *et al.* (1983). "Computer-assisted studies of molecular structure and carcinogenic activity." *Fundam Appl Toxicol* 3(5): 343-9.

Kier, L. B. and L. H. Hall (1990). "An electrotopological-state index for atoms in molecules." *Pharm Res* 7(8): 801-7.

Klopman, G. and O. T. Macina (1985). "Use of the Computer Automated Structure Evaluation program in determining quantitative structure-activity relationships within hallucinogenic phenylalkylamines." *J Theor Biol* 113(4): 637-48.

Lai, D. Y., Y.-t. Woo, *et al.* (1996). "Carcinogenic Potential of Organic Peroxides: Prediction Based on Structure-Activity Relationships (SAR) and Mechanism-Based Short Term Tests." *Journal of Environmental Science and Health, Part C—Environmental Carcinogenesis & Ecotoxicology Reviews.*

Lipinski, C. A., F. Lombardo, *et al.* (2001). "Experimental and computational approaches to estimate solubility and permeability in drug discovery and development settings." *Adv Drug Deliv Rev* 46(1-3): 3-26.

Mattioni, B. E., G. W. Kauffman, *et al.* (2003). "Predicting the genotoxicity of secondary and aromatic amines using data subsetting to generate a model ensemble." *J Chem Inf Comput Sci* 43(3): 949-63.

Mosier, P. D., P. C. Jurs, *et al.* (2003). "Predicting the genotoxicity of thiophene derivatives from molecular structure." *Chem Res Toxicol* 16(6): 721-32.

Pearl, G. M., S. Livingston-Carr, *et al.* (2001). "Integration of computational analysis as a sentinel tool in toxicological assessments." *Curr Top Med Chem* 1(4): 247-55.

Quillardet, P. and M. Hofnung (1993). "The SOS chromotest: a review." *Mutat Res* 297(3): 235-79.

Snyder, R. D., G. S. Pearl, *et al.* (2004). "Assessment of the sensitivity of the computational programs DEREK, TOPKAT, and MCASE in the prediction of the genotoxicity of pharmaceutical molecules." *Environ Mol Mutagen* 43(3): 143-58.

Sutton, M. D., B. T. Smith, *et al.* (2000). "The SOS response: recent insights into umuDC-dependent mutagenesis and DNA damage tolerance." *Annu Rev Genet* 34: 479-497.

Trieff, N. M., G. L. Biagi, *et al.* (1989). "Aromatic amines and acetamides in Salmonella typhimurium TA98 and TA100: a quantitative structure-activity relation study." *Mol Toxicol* 2(1): 53-65.

15

The Application of PK/PD Modeling and Simulations During Lead Optimization

Stuart Friedrich, Ph.D.
Principal Research Scientist
Eli Lilly Canada
Toronto, Ontario, Canada, M1N 2E8

Evelyn Lobo, Ph.D.
Research Scientist
Eli Lilly and Company
Lilly Corporate Center
Indianapolis, IN 46485

Karen Zimmerman
Associate Senior Pharmacologist
Eli Lilly and Company
Lilly Corporate Center
Indianapolis, IN 46285

Anthony Borel, Ph.D.
Principal Research Scientist
Eli Lilly and Company
Lilly Corporate Center
Indianapolis, IN 46285

Carlos O. Garner, Ph.D.
Head, Drug Disposition
Eli Lilly and Company
Lilly Corporate Center
Indianapolis, IN 46285

Table of Contents

Abbreviations

ADME ....Adsorption, distribution, metabolism, and excretion
AUC.....................Area under the plasma concentration versus time curve
BP ....Blood pressure
C_b..Brain concentration
CDER ....Center for Drug Evaluation and Research
C ....Confidence interval
CL...Clearance
CM...Competitor molecule
C_{max} ....Maximal plasma concentration
CSF ....   Critical success factor
C_{ss}..Plasma concentration at steady-state
CV...Coefficient of variation
E_0..Baseline or initial effect
EC_{50}..Concentration where 50% of effect is observed
E_{max} ....Maximal effect
F ....Bioavailability
FDA ....Food and Drug Administration
g...Gram
γ...Hill coefficient
hr...Hour
IND ....Investigational new drug
K_b ....Receptor binding affinity
K_g...Kilogram
K_p...Brain to plasma ratio
LO..Lead optimization
M&S ....Modeling and Simulation
mg...Milligram
min ....Minutes
mL ....Milliliter
mmHg...Millimeter of mercury
MOA...Mechanism of Action
NCE..New Chemical Entity
ng ....Nanogram

PD..Pharmacodynamics
PK..Pharmacokinetics
PK/PD ....Pharmacokinetics/Pharmacodynamics
R&D ....Research and Development
SBA ....Summary Basis of Approval
SE ....Standard error of mean
τ ....Tau (Dosing interval)
μg or mcg ....Microgram
vs...Versus

The Application of PK/PD Modeling and Simulations During Lead Optimization

A quick view of recent periodicals clearly point to the challenges of the pharmaceutical industry as we progress through the first decade of the 21st century – the rising costs of new innovative drugs. Much of the current costs and the continued rising costs of drug prices stem from the high price of drug discovery and development. Many sources have cited studies that estimate the cost of pharmaceutical drug development; all of which conclude the same – pharmaceutical R&D costs increase at a rate much greater than inflation. A study conducted in 1987 (Woltman, 1989) concluded the average cost of the development of a new chemical entity (NCE) to be $108 million. This rate has grown dramatically over the past 15 years to the current estimates of over $800 million (Altshuler *et al.*, 2001; DimAsi *et al.*, 2003). The increase in R&D costs is due mainly to the increased cost of animal testing and conducting clinical trials (Dickson and Gagnon, 2004). The cost of an individual NCE, which is quickly approaching 1 billion dollars, is not the complete source of the large increase in pharmaceutical R&D over the past decade. The development failures of NCEs contribute substantially to this bottom line. One out of every 10 compounds that enter into human testing successfully completes clinical development and is made available to patients. The costs of these failures must be reconciled by the successful marketing of innovative new drugs. The Food and Drug Administration (FDA) recently published a white paper titled "Innovation or Stagnation? – Challenge and Opportunity on the Critical Path to New Medical Products" (FDA, 2004). This paper directly addresses the bottlenecks in the drug discovery and development process. In the agency's view "the applied sciences needed for medical product development have not kept pace with the tremendous advances in the basic sciences... In many cases, developers have no choice but to use the tools and concepts of the last century to assess this centuries candidates."

Pharmacostatistical models (i.e. Population PK models) have routinely been employed to describe drug performance and variability as a function of dose and relevant patient factors. However, the utility of applying these techniques to drug discovery and early clinical development has not yet been fully exploited. In the context of this chapter, pharmacostatistical modeling techniques coupled to simulation methodologies will be discussed as a 21st century tool, which applied in drug discovery and early clinical develop can directly impact the discovery and development cycle and decrease the cost of drug development. The cost savings will be realized by finding the optimal NCE that is drugable and has an increased probability of technical success to reach the patient. The growing interest and application of these tools is appreciated by the FDA and specifically noted as an opportunity to find new medical products. The excerpt below from the recent FDA white paper characterizes their view on these approaches:

The concept of model-based drug development, in which pharmaco-
statistical models of drug efficacy and safety are developed from preclinical

and available clinical data, offers an important approach to improving drug development knowledge management and development decision-making. Model-based drug development involves building mathematical and statistical characterizations of the time course of the disease and drug using available clinical data to design and validate the model. The relationship between drug dose, plasma concentration, biophase concentration (pharmacokinetics), and drug effect or side-effects (pharmacodynamics) is characterized, and relevant patient covariates are included in the model. Systematic application of this concept to drug development has the potential to significantly improve it. FDA scientists use, and are collaborating with others in the refinement of, quantitative clinical trial modeling using simulation software to improve trial design and to predict outcomes. It is likely that more powerful approaches can be built by completing, and then building on, specific predictive models.

Further, the report estimates that a 10% improvement in predicting a NCE failure before clinical trials could save $100 million in development costs per drug.

There are many sources for failure in drug development, including but not limited to pharmacokinetics, animal toxicity, adverse effects in man, lack of efficacy, and commercial factors. The Centre for Medicines Research published data comparing the sources of drug failures for 198 NCEs (Figure 1). These data demonstrate that up to 80% of the compounds evaluated failed due to either lack of efficacy, pharmacokinetics, or animal toxicity (Kennedy, 1997; Kubinyi, 2003). The application of pharmacostatistical models (PK/PD models) along with simulations can afford insight into the probability of drug failure due to these items. This assumes the models are supported with well-designed physiology, pharmacology, toxicology, and pharmacokinetics studies to address the critical questions of drug performance, and this assumes appropriate biological markers (biomarkers) of desired pharmacology and toxicology are available. If part or all of the markers needed to assess drug performance are not available in pre-clinical

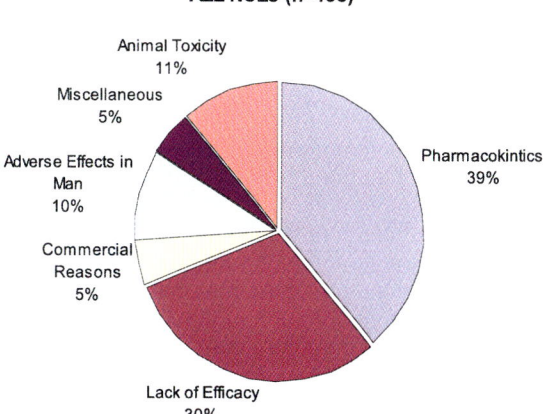

ALL NCEs (n=198)

Figure 1. Reasons for Failure in Drug Development - 198 NCEs in clinical development (Adapted from Kennedy, 1997)

models, the ability of the models to accurately and precisely predict clinical performance will be compromised. This chapter will discuss how to identify value-added opportunities for PK/PD M&S (modeling and simulation), concepts of trial simulations and risk evaluation, and includes two example applications in drug discovery.

Identifying M&S Opportunities

The application of pharmacostatistical modeling using discovery data can be overwhelming with little to no value if the scope of application is not prospectively considered. It is of the utmost importance to understand the issues facing the discovery effort and frame the questions for which M&S will attempt to address. The two most important aspects of PK/PD M&S in drug discovery is "understanding the question" and "how much is enough". There is no value investing weeks developing a robust pharmacostatistical model for a question that needs answered in 3 days. Likewise, there is no value in demonstrating a drug attribute through PK/PD M&S that is not considered an issue for discovery or development. M&S should be judiciously employed to answer key discovery and/or developmental challenges that cannot be answered experimentally in less time with less money.

The ability of PK/PD models to accurately and precisely predict future NCE performance is solely dependent on the knowledge base of the disease target and pharmacology of the chemical class. The discovery areas where models will have the greatest ability to accurately and precisely predict future performance of an NCE are those with "High Prior Knowledge". These include discovery efforts where the target is well described and clinically qualified, such as n^{th} in class molecules or n^{th} in indication targets. For these discovery efforts, the model assumptions are few and the M&S goals are to find the best clinical candidate and to shorten and focus the clinical development. This will be accomplished by leveraging PK/PD models to accurately predict drug dose-concentration-effect relationships, optimize clinical dose and optimize trial design. When prior information is extensive, the M&S opportunity might focus on utilizing that information when making decisions, and thereby avoid conducting experiments or trials that merely confirm existing knowledge.

The second category of M&S opportunity is one of "Intermediate Prior Knowledge". This opportunity will not be inherently as predictive in nature as the previous, but will with iterations improve the discovery and development decisions, and afford a risk-based approach during the development cycle. For example, internal experiences and public information will likely be available to offer prior knowledge, which will add value to the M&S efforts during the development of a novel target for a well-characterized disease. In this scenario, a disease model may exist or be readily developed from prior literature and/or internal laboratory data. This model coupled with simulations can prove insightful when assessing the required drug effect to differentiate drug effects from the disease and its variability. Moreover, the limited existing knowledge base for "Intermediate Prior Knowledge" M&S efforts will afford a robust strategy for development. If the model assumptions are not sufficiently qualified to allow predictive simulations, study simulations may be employed to assess risks, given your assumptions, of specific non-clinical and clinical trial designs. Being able to ask "what if" questions of the models and receive quantitative answers or a domain of answers provides new information on which to base decisions. When the current state of knowledge is further limited, the opportunity could focus on ensuring the study design will perform robustly across assumptions, and that the study can distinguish between assumed "truths."

The third category of M&S opportunities is the "Low Prior Knowledge" category. This opportunity may actually offer very little precise predictive power. However, for novel targets of unmet medical needs, this opportunity may offer the domain for PK/PD M&S to offer the greatest discovery value. In this scenario, M&S allows the discovery scientists to codify their assumptions of the biology and mechanistic pharmacology and determine the optimal experiment to test the scientific hypothesis. For example, if a given biochemical cascade for a selected disease is hypothesized and a xenobiotic blocks or agonizes the biological cascade, a quantitative model of that mechanism will provide the domain of experimental outcomes that must be obtained. Experimental tests that fall outside the predicted domain of outcomes null the hypothesis and challenge the prior knowledge of the mechanism. This quantitative understanding of mechanism during target identification ensures pharmacological relevance during lead optimization, and allows the discovery organization to manage biological risks as they progress their discovery efforts. When little is known, the focus should be on reducing risk by creating an innovative strategy leading to early attrition or early recognition of a blockbuster product – a quick win strategy. In this low-information case, simulations can make the best use of available data and scientific judgment – a point not generally recognized by discovery organizations. Table 1 provides a summary of the three PK/PD M&S opportunities during drug discovery and development based on the amount of information on a compound and the number of assumptions, uncertainty, and the most realistic M&S goals.

Amount of information	Example	Number of Assumptions	Uncertainty in model predictions	Goals
High	Pre-clinical models n^{th} in indication Known M.O.A. n^{th} in class	Few	Low	Shorten and focus development
Intermediate	Mixture	Intermediate	Intermediate	Robust strategy
Low	No pre-clin models Unknown M.O.A. 1st in indication 1st in class	Many	High	Manage risk

Table 1. PK/PD M&S Opportunity Categorization According to the Amount of Prior Information

Where M&S Will Not Add Value

Prior to starting a M&S project it is important to identify the risks and issues not amenable to modeling or where M&S may not be worth the effort. Take the case of a central nervous system disease with no systemic marker of biological activity (i.e. depression). If one were to embark on a proteomics effort to identify central proteins that are affected during the treatment of a xenobiotic designed to stimulate a novel receptor, a bank of proteins may well be identified in brain that indicate pharmacological action and serve as viable discovery biomarkers. However, these protein markers identified in brain tissue are not directly translatable to the clinical setting; thus, their utility in drug discovery is not applicable to the desired species, human. The ability to translate quantitative drug pharmacology to development is precluded, and not an area where PK/PD modeling would be of significant value. Moreover, the establishment of clinical drug pharmacology would only be assumed after the completion of a long and costly disease endpoint trial. PK/PD modeling and simulations have their real value when the pharmacodynamic endpoints (biomarkers or surrogate markers) are translatable from the non-clinical laboratory to the clinic.

How Much is Enough?

M&S is expensive in terms of resources expended and possible opportunities lost. Resource utilization must be justified by value added to the program; a cost/benefit decision. Underestimation of "how much is enough" can occur because an intrinsically complex problem is not adequately vetted. Excessive investment or lost opportunities can occur because: 1) the question was not high enough in value to justify the work; 2) the team does not act on the M&S results; or 3) there was a misunderstanding of the effort required. Although part of this may be related to inexperience of the modeler and the core team, it is also related in part to not developing team consensus on the M&S objectives.

Risks to the M&S Strategy

When considering a M&S project, it is important to identify any major risks that could impact the success of the M&S strategy. The strategy may be at risk from technical difficulties, insufficient information to guide the modeling, incorrect and/or non-testable assumptions, or organizational complexity in the project. Technical difficulties may arise from the complexity of the disease state, subjective or categorical endpoints, bioanalytical limitations, or requirements for establishing a clinical utility index. Attempting to model PK and PD data during lead optimization when PK/PD modeling was not planned prospectively, may leave the analyst with data insufficient to create computational models of value. Modeling and simulation strategies should always be established within a discovery plan; attempting to model data in a post hoc fashion during drug discovery will likely produce imprecise models loaded with unnecessary assumptions. Organizational complexity denotes the need for multiple independent factors or inputs to align in a given time period in order for the M&S strategy to work. Each factor outside of the team's control represents a risk factor. Underestimation of project complexity or resource needs, compression of timelines, "scope creep", external dependencies (milestone payments to development partner), and the need to address multiple experts and "stake holders" may put the M&S effort at risk.

For more extensive M&S projects it is worthwhile to develop a work plan that lists the main steps required to complete the project. The probability of technical success for each of the M&S steps should be addressed in the work plan if there is a good chance that uncontrollable factors (Table 2) might derail the plan. One may encounter a "technical roadblock" that will require changes to the work-plan. To address such problems one might:

- *reduce the scope of the work plan;*
- *simplify the model or make additional assumptions;*
- *compensate for greater uncertainty in the simulation outcome metrics;*
- *re-negotiate resources and timelines.*

The impact of any of these approaches on the simulation outcome metrics should be critically evaluated with the project team.

Risk	Likelihood
Lack of consensus on modeling assumptions; Team acceptance of undesirable findings	Low if team buy-in obtained in advance.
Delays in dataset assembly	High when dealing with multiple studies or archived data.
Modeling effort fails	High when dealing with novel models or multiple, complex simulation outcome metrics.
Model fails qualification	Moderate, particularly when model is empirical or involves substantial linearization.
Original assumptions not justifiedLow	High when there is poor understanding of mechanism of action or efficacy and safety endpoints.

Table 2. Examples of M&S Project Risks

Variability Model Specification

Accounting for hierarchical levels of variability gives the population modeling approach great advantages over naive pooled calculations that do not define, for example, the influence of drug on an individual patient or animal. The variability model then replaces the fixed-point estimate of a parameter for an individual with an estimate of the distribution of that parameter in a population.

Careful thought should be given to defining the population of interest and the nature of the distribution, especially if parametric distributions (normal, lognormal, t distribution, etc) are used. Failure to account properly for variability can lead to misleading predictions. It is important to realize that more data are required to precisely characterize variances than to estimate central tendency. The following types of questions may arise in planning the variance structure:

- If variability is not included, will the underlying physiological process differ substantially between species (i.e. two different non-clinical species or between animals and human)?
- Is an understanding of the variability in a parameter or model and its sources required to answer the question?
- Which model parameters most impact the accuracy of the model outcomes? This question can identify the model parameters in which the model outcomes are most sensitive, and help the discovery team determine which studies are most important to clear decision-making.
- What factors do we believe may affect the magnitude of variability in each animal model and in the patient population? For example, pharmacokinetics may be more precise than pharmaco-dynamics; thus, study power should be focused on the PD endpoints. Baseline variability in human patients may be much greater than in the pre-clinical models. Thus, the time-course and magnitude of the effect must be fully understood prior to clinical development.
- Do the modeled distributions adequately capture the tails of the distribution of observed responses? The tails may drive the simulation outcome metric.

The most popular tools employed to conduct population modeling are restricted to combinations and transformations of normal distributions, although these are not the only sensible possibilities (Linsey *et al.*, 2001). Normal and lognormal distributions are often suitable unless multi-modality occurs, in which case mixture models are useful (Rosner and Muller, 1997). Various other variance models have been proposed within the Markov Chain Monte Carlo framework, which allow greater versatility (Wakefield and Rahman, 2000). When selecting parametric assumptions, the following questions should be considered:

1) **What is the range of the parameter?** For example, drug clearance cannot be negative, so a lognormal distribution is commonly used. Bioavailability is constrained between 0 and 1; thus, a lognormal distribution would not be feasible.

2) **What effect will outliers have?** Normal distributions have light tails so they are sensitive to outliers. In discovery studies that are not appropriately powered to fully model variances, outliers may be an indicator of parameter misspecification or systematic error in an experiment.

Uncertainty Model Specification

Uncertainty models, which are helpful in the "intermediate" and "low prior information" scenarios would generally include major sources of uncertainty, and tactics for assessing each uncertainty component and incorporating it into simulations. Properly accounting for uncertainty will allow the project team to have realistic expectations for the range of plausible outcomes. Conversely, inclusion of excessive uncertainty to mitigate risk of a "wrong answer" will compromise the value of the deliverable.

Uncertainty can be broadly classified as "measurable" or "immeasurable." Any statistic derived from data has measurable uncertainty (under an appropriate model) that can be accounted for in future simulations. For example, simulation from point estimates of fixed and random effects (for example, mean and variance estimates for clearance) does not account for the uncertainty in those point estimates. It is more robust to resample the fixed and random effect estimates from, perhaps, a bootstrapped distribution, and thus account for uncertainty in the estimation process.

It is generally more difficult to account for "immeasurable uncertainty" – uncertainty that cannot be estimated from data and thus requires assumptions that may be wrong. For example, the assumption that relative potency in an animal model scales to humans may be incorrect. Relaxing this assumption and allowing the potency scaling factor to vary from 0.5 to 2.0 based on shared judgment within the project team would be one way to account for this source of immeasurable uncertainty. The area of forecasting has developed many techniques to elicit semi-quantitative information of which fuzzy logic is one of the most natural for combination with quantitative modeling (Nestorov, 2001).

Leveraging Historical Data

Historically, many modeling projects have consisted of developing descriptive models of data from a particular clinical or non-clinical study. For a M&S project, additional data must often be acquired. Ideally, time and concentration data are available. Sometimes, however, AUC or CL, as well as their variability, may be all that's available (as for a competitor's drug) or all that is needed. Patient demographic, drop-out study rates, and/or compliance data or physicochemical and biopharmaceutics information may also be useful. Generally, where one looks is dependent on the development stage of the compound and whether the compound is innovative or a "me-too" compound.

A M&S project is a good opportunity for the analysts to consult with internal colleagues from other disciplines to access the wealth of knowledge available within their organizations. For example, ADME colleagues will have access to PK data from pre-clinical studies. Discovery colleagues can provide PD data and insights into mechanisms of action, which are invaluable in developing mechanistic and predictive models. Toxicologists can provide information critical to modeling margin of safety. Clinical colleagues may provide insight from development of other drugs. In addition to exploiting the expertise of team

Topic	Web Address
Product prescribing information	
PDR	http://www.medecinteractive.com/
CDER	http://www.fda.gov/cder
HPFB	http://www.hc-sc.gc.ca/hpfb-dgpsa/
EMEA	http://www.emea.eu
IDDB	http://www.iddb.com
Pharmacology	
Online Pharmacology Reference Manual TransMed Network	http://www.pharmacology.com/
Clinical Pharmacology Online Gold Standard Multimedia Inc.	http://www.rxrequest.com/cponline/
Martindale's Health Science Guide – 2001 Jim Martindale	http://sun2.lib.uci.edu/HSG/Pharmacy.html
Pharmacokinetic and Pharmaco-dynamic Resources, Oklahoma College of Pharmacy	http://www.boomer.org/pkin/
Demographics & Epidemiology	
Centers for Disease Control and Prevention	http://www.oncolink.upenn.edu/upcc/
OncoLink	http://www.oncolink.upenn.edu/upcc/
The Disease Incidence Model™ Strategic Health Resources	http://www.strathealth.com/dimmain.html
Office of Research and Statistics Health & Demographics Section	http://www.ors.state.sc.us/hd
Disease	
American Heart Association	http://www.americanheart.org/
American Academy of Allergy, Asthma and Immunology	http://www.aaaai.org/
National Fibromyalgia Research Association	http://www.teleport.com/~nfra/
Sjogren's Syndrome Foundation, Inc.	http://www.sjogrens.org/

Table 3. Useful Websites for PK/PD and Clinical Data

members, interest and ownership can be elicited. The following are places to check for available data:

- For n[th] in class or n[th] in indication efforts, existing discovery, pre-clinical and previous clinical studies should be available from internal sources, consultants, or the general scientific literature.
- For compounds prior to first in man, data is available from discovery, pre-clinical and toxicology studies. Predecessor, back-up compounds, or other clinical compounds that have used the same pre-clinical models may also provide relevant data.
- Extensive non-clinical and clinical PD data, and possible models, may be available from compounds with similar modes of action.
- Databases may be available within biology, medical or bioinformatic groups for disease progression or the distribution of important patient factors.

From libraries to the web, there is a wealth of literature data available. An initial search may utilize programs such as Medline, PubMed, and/or Toxline to search books and journal articles for topic of interest. General pharmacology textbooks, for example, Goodman and Gilman's *The Pharmacological Basis of Therapeutics and the Merck Index* or specialized texts such as *Pharmacokinetics and Cancer Chemotherapy* (Workman and Graham 1993) may serve as starting points. Websites (Table 3) may provide a wealth of information (*e.g.* the Summary Basis of Approval for a competitor's compound may be accessed via the FDA/CDER site).

CASE 1. Use of Pharmacokinetic-Pharmacodynamic Modeling to Support the Decision to Terminate a NCE

This example illustrates the use of PK/PD modeling and simulation to support the selection of a NCE for treatment of hypertension. The main objective of the PK/PD support on this project was to evaluate the PK/PD properties of NCEs to aid in the selection of the optimal NCE to take into clinical studies. Following identification of the optimal NCE, PK/PD modeling was used to support the dose selection for Phase 1 clinical studies. The focus of this example is evaluation of a NCE that had PK/PD properties that were found to be less than optimal in comparison to a marketed competitor compound. When the results of the PK/PD evaluation were combined with costs of drug substance and biopharmaceutical properties that would require above-average resources during development of clinical formulations, the project team decided to terminate the NCE and evaluate other molecules.

The PK and PK/PD of the NCE were evaluated based on data collected in rat, dog, and monkey intravenous and oral administration PK studies, a rat hypertension animal model, and data available from the Summary Basis of Approval (SBA) for a competitor molecule. These data were integrated as indicated in Figure 2 to obtain a predicted dose-response for the NCE in clinical hypertension. The main assumptions of these analyses are: 1) the relative efficacy

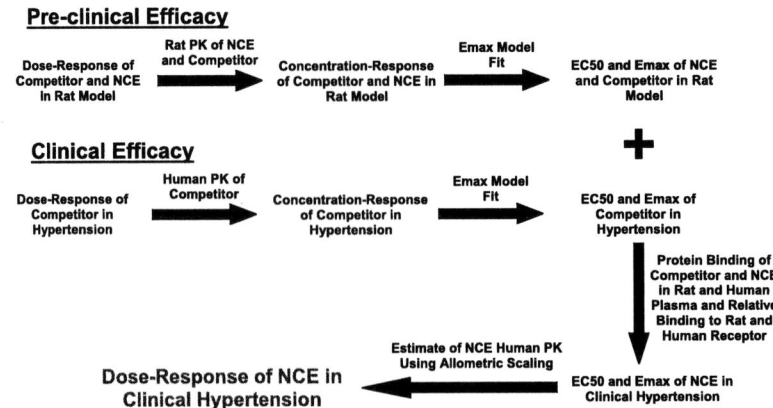

Figure 2. PK/PD Analysis Flowscheme

and potency observed in the rat hypertension model for the competitor and the NCE are predictive of the relative efficacy and potency in humans; and, 2) allometric scaling provides a reasonable estimate of the clearance of the NCE in humans. These assumptions and possible alternative PK/PD methods will be discussed further below.

In the rat hypertension model experiments, animals were administered daily oral doses of either 1, 3, 10, or 30 mg/kg of the NCE, 3, 10, 30, or 100mg/kg of the competitor, or a vehicle control. Hypertension was induced in the animals (undisclosed method) and blood pressures were monitored over a period of 2 weeks. During this time period the vehicle control animals would develop hypertension, and treatment with the competitor or NCE would reduce the development of hypertension. For analysis purposes the blood pressure change on Day 14 relative to baseline in each animal was expressed as a percentage of the average change in blood pressure relative to baseline in the control animals. Therefore, if a treatment produced 100% blood pressure reduction relative to control this would mean that the treatment was able to completely prevent any blood pressure increase during the treatment period. Expressing the blood pressure relative to controls also allowed the results from different experiments to be combined if necessary since the results from each experiment were normalized to control values within each experiment. On the final treatment day each animal would have serial serum samples collected for determination of the exposure in that animal. The individual animal concentration data were analyzed using a population PK approach to determine the exposure of the NCE and the competitor in each animal. Table 4 summarizes the clearance and AUC that were determined from this analysis. As shown, the clearance of the competitor was much greater than that of the NCE, and both compounds also displayed non-linear PK across the dose range studied. Both these observations emphasize the importance of collecting exposure measurements in the same animals that the PD data are collected to improve the accuracy of the subsequent PK/PD analysis. Not shown here but also important for the same reason is the fact that these observations indicated that the PK in the animal model was slightly different than the PK in normal animals, so the use of exposure estimates from separate

Dose (mg/kg)	Competitor Mean AUC (ng*hr/ml)	Competitor Mean Cl (ml/hr/kg)	NCE Mean AUC (ng*hr/ml)	NCE Mean Cl (ml/hr/kg)
1	-	-	1590	630
3	642	4670	5560	540
10	2920	3420	6370	1570
30	5260	5700	20800	1440
100	14500	6870	-	-

Table 4. Mean Plasma Clearance and AUC Determined In Rat Hypertension Pharmacology Model

experiments using normal animals would also have lead to inaccurate PK/PD conclusions.

Figure 3 shows the dose response observed for the competitor and the NCE in the rat hypertension animal model experiments. The individual animal AUC values determined from the PK analysis were converted to average steady-state concentrations (Css) and these were combined with the individual animal blood pressure reduction data. Previous analyses had compared different exposure metrics (Cmax, Css, time above a multiple of binding affinity) and it was found that Css was the most predictive exposure metric. The combined PK/PD dataset was analyzed using an E_{max} model of the form shown in Equation 1. The resulting parameters estimated from this analysis are shown in Table 5. As noted by the calculated parameters, the EC_{50} for the competitor molecule is lower than the NCE; however, the E_{max} for the NCE appears to be much greater than the competitor. Therefore, the results suggest that at higher concentrations the NCE is able to produce superior blood pressure reduction compared to the competitor molecule whereas at low concentrations the blood pressure response of the two molecules would be comparable. Figure 4 and Figure 5 show the observed individual animal data and the model predicted fit. Note that the model predicted fit is shown as a mean and 90% confidence interval. The confidence

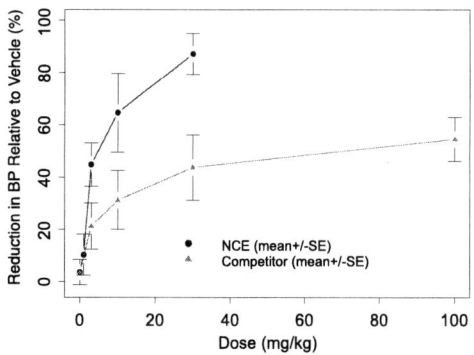

Figure 3. Dose Response of the Competitor Molecule and the NCE in Rat Hypertension Pharmacology Model

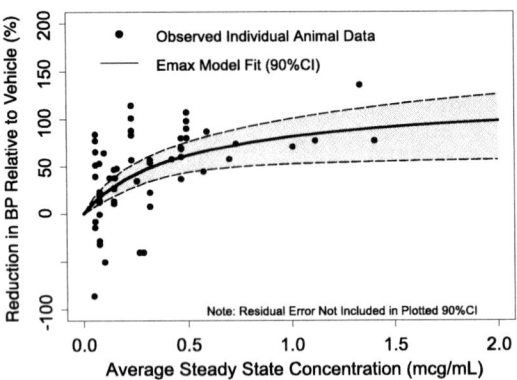

Figure 4. Observed Individual Animal Concentration and Reduction in Blood Pressure and Emax Model Fit for NCE.

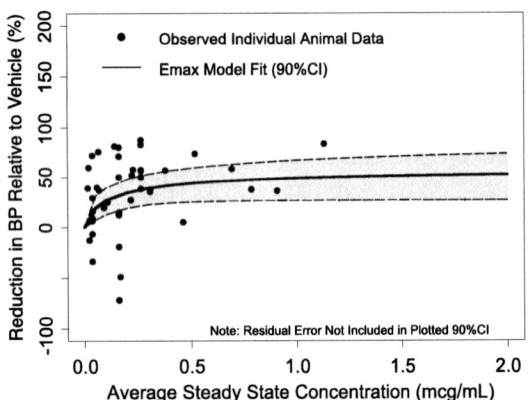

Figure 5. Observed Individual Animal Concentration and Reduction in Blood Pressure and Emax Model Fit for Competitor Molecule.

	Parameter Estimate (mean (90%CI))	
	EC50 (μg/ml)	Emax (% reduction in BP relative to vehicle)
Competitor	0.085 (0.016 – 0.42)	57 (27 – 86)
NCE	0.44 (0.15 – 1.14)	130 (60 – 190)

Table 5. Estimated E_{max} and EC_{50} Values for NCE and Competitor in Rat Hypertension Pharmacology Model

$$Effect = \frac{E_{max} * C_{ss}}{EC_{50} + C_{ss}}$$

Equation 1.

interval represents the uncertainty in the predicted concentration response relationship; i.e. given a certain concentration, we would expect with 90% probability that the true population mean blood pressure reduction is within the model predicted confidence interval. The confidence interval does not include residual error, which is the reason many of the individual animal observations fall outside the model predicted 90% confidence interval.

The SBA for the competitor compound contained information from two dose-response studies in hypertensive patients and PK data from healthy subjects. The PK in healthy subjects was known to be similar to hypertensive patients. The dose response data and PK data were combined to generate a dataset relating average C_{ss} to blood pressure reduction and these data were fit with an E_{max} model. Figure 6 shows the observed concentration response for the competitor and the E_{max} model fit of this data. The estimated (mean (90%CI)) values for E_0, E_{max}, and EC50 from the model fit were 1.64 mmHg (0.63 – 2.6), 8.97 mmHg (4.8 – 13), and 0.43 µg/ml (0.15 – 1.3), respectively.

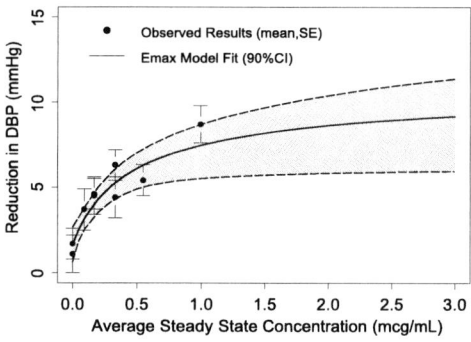

Figure 6. Observed Concentration Response and Emax Model Fit for Competitor in Clinical Hypertension.

The E_{max} parameters for the NCE in clinical hypertension were calculated using an empirical scaling approach by combining the results of the rat hypertension animal model E_{max} parameters and the competitor clinical E_{max} parameters (Equations 2 - 4). The empirical efficacy scaling model basically states that relative potency and maximum efficacy in clinical disease is equal to the relative potency and maximum efficacy in a relevant pre-clinical pharmacology disease animal model. The model equation for EC_{50} also includes additional terms to improve the accuracy and eliminate potential assumptions. Terms are included to account for protein binding of the NCE and competitor, and by adding these terms the model now states that the relative potency of unbound compound in clinical disease is equal to the relative potency of unbound compound in the pre-clinical animal model. Terms are also added to account for the known difference in binding affinity for the NCE and competitor compounds to the human versus pre-clinical species receptors. Not accounting for this binding information would assume that the human/pre-clinical ratio of the binding affinity of the NCE was the same as that for the competitor compound, which in the case of this project was known not to be true. Since each of the terms

$$EC_{50,\ NCE,\ human} = EC_{50,\ Competitor,\ human} \times \left(\dfrac{EC_{50,\ NCE}}{EC_{50,\ Competitor}} \right)_{rat}$$

$$\times \left(\dfrac{fu_{rat}}{fu_{human}} \right)_{NCE} \times \left(\dfrac{fu_{human}}{fu_{rat}} \right)_{Competitor} \quad \left.\begin{array}{l} \text{Adjust for differences} \\ \text{in protein binding} \\ \\ =0.67 \end{array}\right.$$

$$\times \left(\dfrac{Kb_{human}}{Kb_{rat}} \right)_{NCE} \times \left(\dfrac{Kb_{rat}}{Kb_{human}} \right)_{Competitor} \quad \left.\begin{array}{l} \text{Adjust for differences in} \\ \text{binding to receptor} \\ \\ =1.83 \end{array}\right.$$

fu = Fraction Unbound (Plasma Protein Binding)

Equation 2.

$$Emax_{NCE,\ human} = Emax_{Competitor,\ human} \times \left(\dfrac{Emax_{NCE}}{Emax_{Competitor}} \right)_{rat}$$

Equation 3.

$$E_{0,\ NCE,\ clinical} = E_{0,\ Competitor,\ clinical}$$

Equation 4.

in Equation 1 and Equation 2 is represented by a parameter that is described by a distribution of possible values rather than a single value, the resulting predicted EC_{50} and E_{max} values are a distribution of possible values that represent the joint distribution of the values in the equations. The placebo response for the NCE was expected to be the identical to the distribution of placebo responses observed in the competitor compound.

Using the empirical efficacy scaling equations is a powerful approach since it leverages the information of competitor molecules, but also because it implicitly takes into account biological mechanisms that transpire between (or relate) the concentration of drug in plasma to the observed effect, which are not specifically accounted for or may not be known. If this approach were not available due to lack of competitor data, then alternative approaches that require further assumptions would be required. Such alternative approaches would likely include some form of mechanistic modeling that attempted to account for the factors that are implicitly accounted for using the empirical approach, such as drug distribution between plasma and target organs, interaction of molecules with the receptor target, and downstream receptor processes.

The resulting predicted concentration response for the NCE in clinical hypertension generated using the predicted E_0, EC_{50}, E_{max} values is shown in Figure 7 as compared to the observed concentration response data for the marketed dose of the competitor. As indicated by these data, the predicted response at the exposure generated from the marketed dose of the competitor is greater than the predicted most likely (median) response from equal exposure of the NCE. The human clearance of the NCE was estimated using allometric scaling

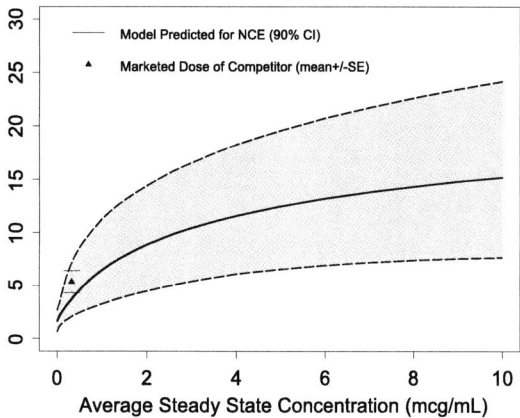

Figure 7. Predicted Concentration Response for the NCE in Clinical Hypertension Relative to Observed Response for the Marketed Dose of the Competitor.

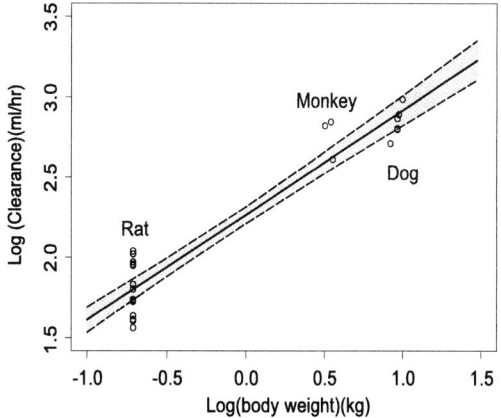

Figure 8. Allometric Model Fit of Observed Intravenous Clearance Versus Body Weight.

of the individual animal clearance values obtained in rat, dog, and monkey studies. In some cases allometric scaling of clearance can be more accurate if differences in the intrinsic clearance between species is accounted for in the allometric equation. However, for this NCE the intrinsic clearance rate based on results from in-vitro microsomal metabolism studies were found to be similar across species, therefore no adjustments to the allometric equation were applied. The observed intravenous clearance versus body weight data and model fit are shown in Figure 8. The estimated allometric coefficient and slope for the intravenous clearance were (mean±SE) 190±13 ml/hr and 0.65±0.041, respectively. These values result in an estimated intravenous clearance for a 70 kg human of (median (90%CI)) 2490 (2100 - 4100) ml/hr. The average fasted bioavailability observed in rats, monkeys, and dogs, was approximately 12% in an non-optimized formulation. For the purposes of estimating doses in humans it was assumed that optimization of the formulation would lead to a bioavailability of 25% in humans, and an uncertainty of 50% (%CV) was applied to this value. Therefore, the estimated human oral clearance was (median (90%CI)): 11700

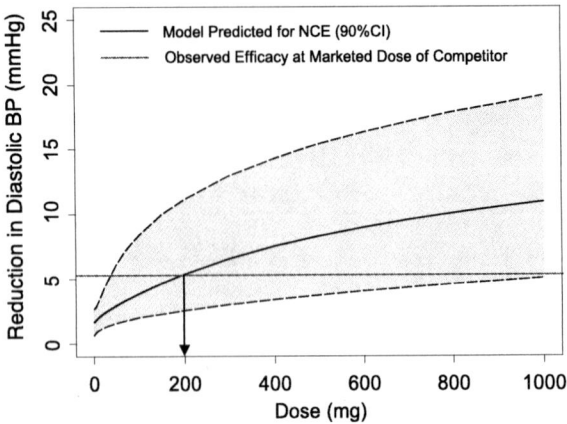

Figure 9. Predicted Dose Response for NCE in Clinical Hypertension Relative to Observed Response for Marketed Dose of Competitor

(4800 – 28600) ml/hr. Combining this estimated oral clearance with the concentration response shown in Figure 7 results in the predicted dose-response for the NCE in clinical hypertension (Figure 9). This analysis suggests that a dose of (median(90%CI)) 200 (40 – 1100) mg would produce the same blood pressure reduction as the marketed dose of the competitor. As expected, there was high uncertainty in the predicted value and this quantified the true current uncertainty in the dose required for efficacy. Therefore, if this NCE were taken into Phase 1 clinical studies, the goal would be to study the PK and tolerability of the NCE across this range of possible efficacious doses to support the design of subsequent efficacy studies. In some cases it may not be possible to study the complete uncertainty range in the efficacy dose, and in this case the modeling results can be used to determine the probability of not achieving the efficacy dose, given our current understanding of the distribution of possible efficacy doses.

During lead optimization, the margin of safety for an NCE is typically calculated using the NOAEL established in early toxicology studies and the exposure required for efficacy in the pre-clinical animal model. The first step in this calculation is to determine what target efficacy in the pre-clinical animal model should be used to determine the corresponding efficacy exposure. The target efficacy can be derived by taking into consideration the efficacy requirement in humans and determining the equivalent efficacy in the pre-clinical animal model. The draft launch label for the project required that a NCE should provide equivalent efficacy as the competitor. The marketed dose of the competitor produces an average predicted reduction in blood pressure of 3.9 mmHg in hypertensive patients relative to placebo. This reduction represents 43% of the theoretical maximum reduction (E_{max} = 8.97 mmHg). Therefore, the equivalent efficacy of the competitor on the pre-clinical efficacy scale is 43% of the maximum efficacy in the rat hypertension animal model (57% reduction in blood pressure relative to vehicle), which equates to approximately a 25% reduction in blood pressure relative to vehicle. The efficacy exposure for the NCE is then calculated by simply determining the exposure required to produce a 25% blood pressure response using the previously determined EC_{50} and E_{max} for the NCE in the rat hypertension model. This calculation results in an average steady state concentration of 0.13 µg/ml or AUC of 3.1 µg·hr/ml. These values were used when estimating the margin of safety of the NCE during pre-clinical evaluation of the molecule.

The PK/PD analysis for this project indicated that the potential dose of NCE required for clinical efficacy was much higher relative to what may have been expected by examining only the dose-response data in the rat hypertension animal model. The high projected dose would result in a higher cost of producing drug substance, making the net present value for the NCE less favorable. In addition, the biopharmaceutical properties of the compound were not optimal, which resulted in difficulties when establishing reasonable margins of safety in toxicology studies, and would result in the requirement for above-average resources during development of clinical formulations. Therefore, as a result of all the above factors the project team decided to terminate further research on the NCE and evaluate other molecules.

CASE 2. Early Projections of Plausible First Human Dose using Pharmacokinetic-Pharmacodynamic Modeling in Lead Optimization for Receptor Antagonist Program

The goal of the modeling and simulation efforts within this example were to develop an integrated human dose projection model to predict the most likely and plausible range of clinical efficacious doses for two brain receptor agonist NCEs (NCE-1 and NCE-2) that is equieffective to a competitor's clinical dose.

The receptor antagonist team was designing and screening compounds to identify a potent and selective receptor antagonist that has pharmacological activity and potency comparable to a competitor's compound. The successful NCE would also need to have acceptable toxicology, ADME, and biopharmaceutic characteristics so that it has a relatively high probability of becoming an effective drug to treat patients. The discovery team needed to accelerate the identification and clinical development of a clinical candidate as the competitor's compound was in Phase III clinical development with a back-up compound in Phase I clinical development.

The team had developed several independent critical success factors (CSFs) based on preclinical data to identify a potent and selective receptor antagonist. The team identified several compounds with higher potency and efficacy in rat models than the competitor compound; however, none of the compounds thus far had passed the bioavailability CSF of greater than 20%. The pharmacokinetic-pharmacodynamic modeling team recommended the use of an integrated model to define a new 'integrated CSF' during lead optimization (LO) to support the discovery of a high quality candidate. The integrated CSF leveraged the PK/PD model outcome, a prediction of human doses equal efficacious as a marketed competitor, cost of manufacturing, and toxicology exposure multiples to select the optimal compound for clinical development. Further, the projected efficacious dose was leveraged to determine manufactured phase 1 dose forms and strengths, to determine the optimal dose range for pre-IND toxicology studies, and guide first in man dose ranging studies.

The integrated model was developed based on the current assumptions and beliefs of the receptor antagonist team about the relationship between certain key properties such as potency, brain:plasma partition coefficient, clearance and systemic bioavailability. The model incorporated the uncertainty in each of the parameters for the NCE and the competitor's compound to generate a distribution of the human equivalent doses. The suitability of the assumptions applied in this specific model are not intrinsic to the concept or use of "Monte-Carlo Simulation of Models under Knowable Uncertainty" but rather reflects the accuracy of capturing the teams current state of knowledge and understanding. The model does not project the expected equi-effective dose range for an individual patient, rather it projects plausible range of NCE clinical doses for the intended population that is equi-effective to the competitors marketed dose.

Several assumptions were made to project the human dose from preclinical pharmacodynamic data and pharmacokinetic data. These include,

- The brain concentration (biophase)– pharmacodynamic relationship determined in rodents was assumed to be identical to that in humans.
- The potency ratio for the NCE and competitor compound was assumed to be similar in rodents and in human (i.e. E_{max} and gamma are identical for NCE and the competitor).
- Equivalent pharmacodynamic effect in rodents would produce equivalent effect in human.
- Average steady state brain concentrations are proportional with clinical effect.
- The brain:plasma concentration ratio (Kp) observed in rodents would be equal to that in humans.
- Human clearance can be allometrically scaled (exponent = 0.75) using two species (rats/dogs).
- Human bioavailabiltiy is equivalent to rat bioavailability.

The following equations can be derived based on the above assumptions. Equation 5 is based on the assumption that if the NCE and the competitor had similar pharmacodynamic effects then they will produce similar pharmacological effects.

Where, E is pharmacodynamic effect; C_b is brain concentration; C_p is average plasma concentration during the dosing interval,τ; γ is hill coefficient; EC is brain concentration producing 50% maximal pharmacodynamic effects; K_p is brain:plasma concentration ratio; CL is systemic clearance in humans; F is bioavailability in humans; NCE is new chemical entity; CM is the competitor molecule.

$$E = \frac{Cb_{NCE}^{\gamma}}{Cb_{NCE}^{\gamma} + EC_{NCE}^{\gamma}} = \frac{Cb_{CM}^{\gamma}}{Cb_{CM}^{\gamma} + EC_{CM}^{\gamma}}$$

Equation 5.

$$Cb = Kp. \, Cp$$

Equation 6.

$$Cp = (Dose/\tau)/ (CL/F)$$

Equation 7.

$$Dose_{NCE} = \frac{Kp_{CM}}{Kp_{NCE}} \bullet \frac{EC_{NCE}}{EC_{CM}} \bullet \frac{CL_{NCE}}{CL_{CM}} \bullet \frac{F_{CM}}{F_{NCE}} \bullet Dose_{CM}$$

Equation 8.

Substituting Equation 6 and Equation 7 in Equation 5, gives the following integrated mathematical model for the NCE efficacious dose in humans (Equation 8).

The objective of the receptor antagonist lead optimization team was to identify an NCE for clinical development through a flow scheme with preclinical pharmacological and a potency profile comparable or better than the leading competitor's market compound. Several previously discussed assumptions were required to develop the PK/PD model using preclinical data. The primary assumption in the development of the PK/PD model was that similar pharmaco-dynamic effects in the rodent species would produce comparable clinical effects. The clinical pharmacokinetics of the competitor compound was not available. Therefore, allometric scaling was applied using rat and dog pharmacokinetic data obtained following intravenous administration of the competitor's compound to predict the average steady-state plasma concentration of competitor's compound in humans following once daily dosing. The brain concentration and plasma concentration at 3 h and 24 h were obtained in the rodent pharmacology model. If rodent and human brain: plasma concentration ratio (K_p) were assumed to be similar, then the average brain concentration following an efficacious dose of the competitor's compound could be estimated. Further, the relationship between receptor occupancy and brain concentrations was determined in rodents. Assuming identical potency in rodents and humans, one could predict the receptor occupancy of the competitor's compounds at the clinically efficacious dose. If similar pharmacodynamics produced identical clinical effects, then an equi-effective dose for the NCE would have receptor occupancy similar to that observed following an efficacious dose o the competitor's drug. The integrated PKPD model as expressed in Equation 8 summarizes the above-mentioned assumptions to project the efficacious dose range of the NCE.

	Kb (nM)	ED50 (mg/kg)	F (rat)	F (non-rodent, dog)	14 day disease effectsa (mg/kg)
CSFs	<14	≤ 2	≥ 20%	≥ 20%	
Competitor	5.4	0.8	10%	26%	1.73
NCE-1	0.6	0.4	10%	100%	0.51
NCE-2	1.6	1.7	17%	27%	1.05

Table 6. Preclinical potency and pharmacological profile of receptor antagonists.[a] CSFs, critical success factors; Kb, binding affinity; ED50, dose producing 50% max PD Effect; F, bioavailability; a = dose producing acceptable disease effect relative to vehicle treated animals.

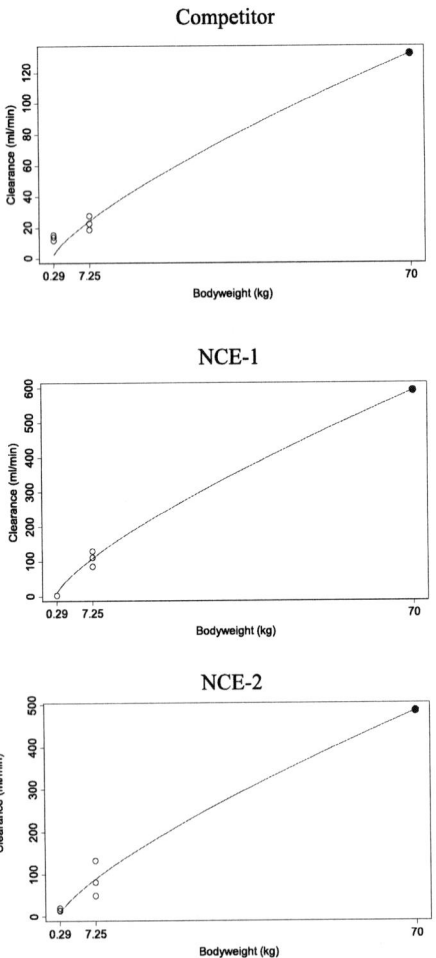

Figure 10. Allometric scaling: Systemic clearance was obtained from the bolus iv data in rats (n=3) and dogs (n=3). Human systemic clearance was estimated using the relationship, CL=aWT 0.75, where CL is the systemic clearance, WT is the body weight. L2589 refers to NCE-1 and L2450 refers to NCE-2. Solid line represents the model predicted clearance. Solid red symbol represents predicted human systemic clearance.

The objective of the modeling and simulation efforts was to incorporate the uncertainty in each of the parameters based on the existing data, uncertainty in the parameters and uncertainty in the current understanding of the relationship between the parameters. The model integrates each of the parameters and their associated uncertainty to generate a distribution of equivalent NCE doses. The model can be modified to accommodate alternative assumptions or to include greater degree of uncertainty in either the parameters or the assumptions. The model does not project the dose range for an individual subject but rather projects the dose range for the population (mean 70 kg subject).

Some of the assumptions required for modeling were related to the availability of the data. For example, the brain:plasma concentration ratios were obtained in Long Evans rats instead of Sprague Dawley rats, therefore it was assumed that Kp was similar in the two strains. Although limited data for the NCEs from receptor occupancy studies in Sprague Dawley and pharmacokinetic studies in Long Evans rats suggested that this assumption may not be true. The brain: plasma concen-

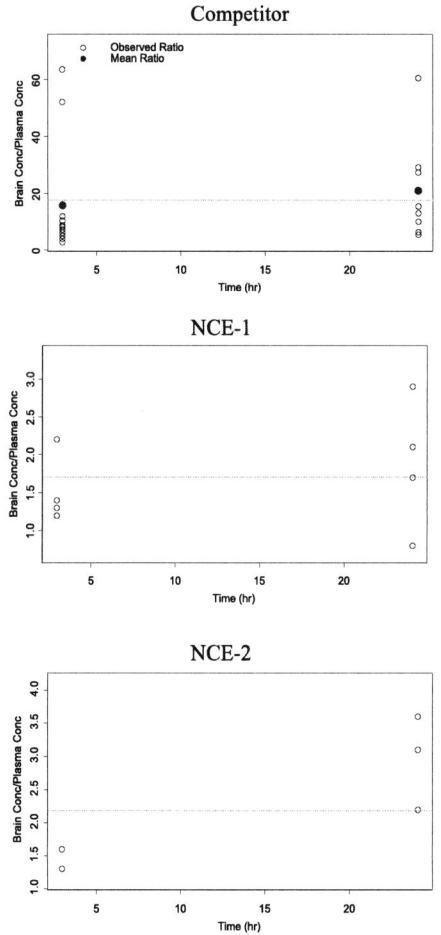

Figure 11. K_p: Brain and plasma concentration data were obtained at 3 h and 24 h following 5, 15, 25 mg/kg dose of the competitor's compound, 2.5 and 5 mg/kg of NCE-1 and 5 mg/kg of NCE-2 in Long Evans rats. Solid blue line represents average K_p values.

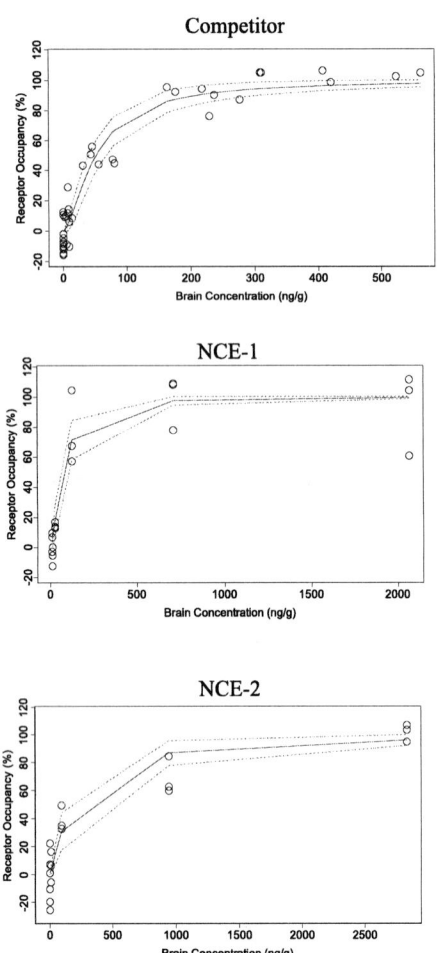

Figure 12. Pharmacodynamic Effects: The pharmacodynamic effect and brain concentration data were obtained following oral administration of the competitor's compound, NCE-1 and NCE-2 at 0.001, 0.01, 0.1, 1, 10 mg/kg. Symbols represent observed data, the solid line represents mean model predictions and the dotted lines refer to the 90% confidence interval.

tration ratio was observed to be more than 5-fold higher in Long Evans rats (K_p =2.2) as compared to Sprague Dawley rats (0.38). The differences in K_p may possibly have been a result of different bioanalytical assays for the two strains; however, this was not confirmed. Similarly, the systemic clearance was assumed to scale with an exponent of 0.75 on the body weight because data was available from only two species. Recent literature on allometric scaling in the literature suggests that true value of the exponent for clearance is likely to be 0.75.

The pharmacodynamic data, brain:plasma concentration data, and pharmacokinetic data were separately fitted to estimate parameters such as EC_{50}, K_p and CL for the competitor's compound and the NCE as shown in Figures 1, 2, 3. The receptor occupancy data for the competitor compound and the NCE were fitted simultaneously with identical γ values as shown in Equation 5. The potency of the

Parameters	Competitor	NCE-1	NCE-2
K_p	17.5 (3.7)	1.7 (0.2)	2.2 (0.4)
CL (ml/min)	132.6 (30.4)	591.4 (46.5)	484.4 (85.4)
EC50 (ng/g)	53 (6.8) 48.3 (7.1)	72.1 (13.3) -	- 197.8 (51.7)
γ		1.6 (0.2)	1.2 (0.1)

Table 7. Mean parameter estimates (standard deviation) following fitting of the PD data, K_p data and pharmacokinetic data.

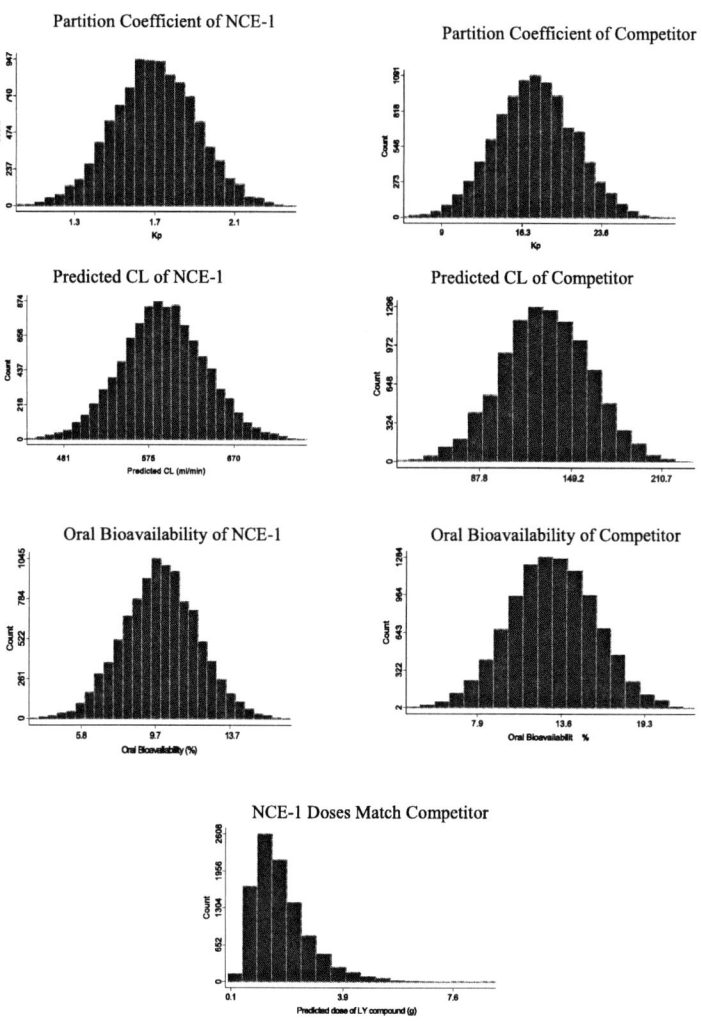

Figure 13. Projected human efficacious dose range for NCE-1 was estimated to be 1.6 g (50th percentile) and ranged from 0.67 to 3.92 g (5th to 95th percentile). Parameter distributions were generated using parameter estimates from fitting the data.

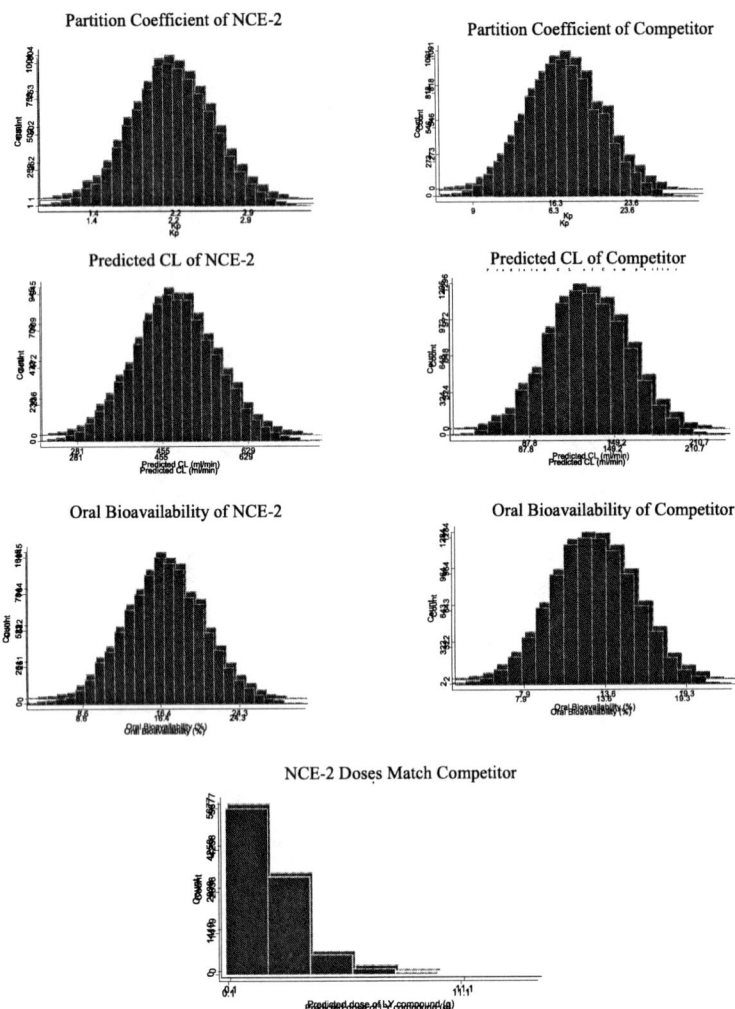

Figure 14. Projected human efficacious dose range for NCE-2 was estimated to be 1.8 g (50th percentile) and ranged from 0.65 to 5.09 g (5th to 95th percentile). Parameter distributions were generated using parameter estimates and standard errors from fitting the data.

NCE (EC_{50} = 72.1 ng/g) was similar to that of the competitor's compound (EC_{50} = 53.0 ng/g), whereas the NCE-2 (EC_{50} = 197.8 ng/g) was nearly 4-fold less potent than the competitor's compound (Table 2).

The brain and plasma concentration data at 3 h and 24 h were also simultaneously fitted assuming time and dose independency in K_p. The K_p for NCE-1 and NCE-2 were similar and nearly 9-fold lower than the competitor's compound (Table 7).

Systemic clearance in each animal was obtained using non-compartmental pharmacokinetic analysis. The systemic clearance for NCE-1 and NCE-2 were higher than the competitor compound. The nominal body weights were 290 g

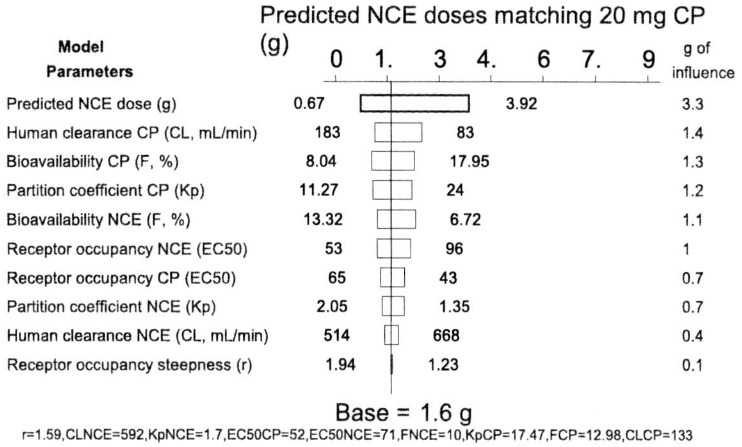

Predicted NCE doses matching 20 mg CP

Model Parameters	(g)	0	1.	3	4.	6	7.	9	g of influence
Predicted NCE dose (g)	0.67				3.92				3.3
Human clearance CP (CL, mL/min)	183			83					1.4
Bioavailability CP (F, %)	8.04			17.95					1.3
Partition coefficient CP (Kp)	11.27			24					1.2
Bioavailability NCE (F, %)	13.32			6.72					1.1
Receptor occupancy NCE (EC50)	53			96					1
Receptor occupancy CP (EC50)	65			43					0.7
Partition coefficient NCE (Kp)	2.05			1.35					0.7
Human clearance NCE (CL, mL/min)	514			668					0.4
Receptor occupancy steepness (r)	1.94			1.23					0.1

Base = 1.6 g
r=1.59,CLNCE=592,KpNCE=1.7,EC50CP=52,EC50NCE=71,FNCE=10,KpCP=17.47,FCP=12.98,CLCP=133

Figure 15. Tornado plot for NCE-1: The impact of uncertainty in the model parameters on the projected dose was evaluated using the tornado plot. The most influential parameters are on the top of the plot. The extent of influence for each parameter is indicated by the width of the bar (5th to 95th percentile). The vertical line represents the most likely dose based on the most likely estimates of the parameters.

Predicted NCE doses matching 20 mg Competitor

Model parameters		0	1.5	3	4.5	6	7.5	9	g of influence
Predicted NCE dose (mg)	0.65				5.09				4.4
Receptor occupancy EC50 (EC50NCE,ng/g)	125			291					1.6
Human clearance CP (CL$_{CP}$, ml/min)	183			83					1.5
Bioavailability NCE (F, %)	24			10.44					1.5
Bioavailability CP (F, %)	8.04			17.95					1.4
Partition coefficient CP (Kp, ml/g)	11.27			24					1.3
Partition coefficient NCE (Kp, ml/g)	2.84			1.53					1.1
Human clearance NCE (CL$_{NCE}$, ml/min)	343			626					1.1
Receptor occupancy CP EC$_{50}$ (EC50,ng/g)	61			38					0.9
Receptor occupancy steepness (r)	1.39			0.93					0.2

Base = 1.8 g
r=1.16,EC50CP=48,CLNCE=485,KpNCE=2.19,KpCP=17.47,FCP=12.98,FNCE=17.01,CLCP=133,EC50NCE=191,DoseNCE=1.8

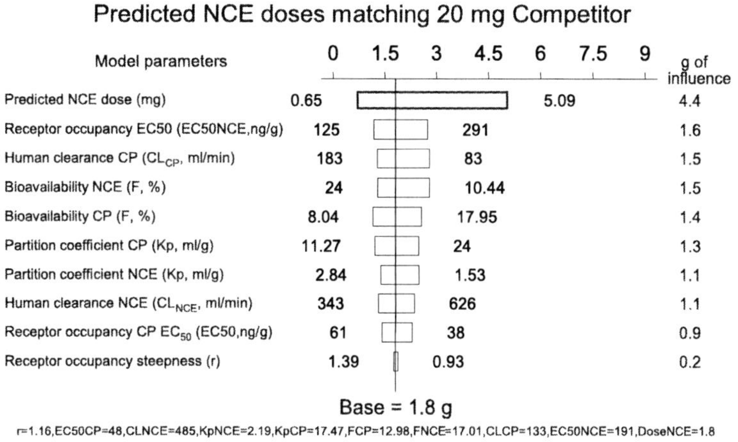

Figure 16. Tornado plot for NCE-2: The impact of uncertainty in the model parameters on the projected dose was evaluated using the tornado plot. The most influential parameters are on the top of the plot. The extent of influence for each parameter is indicated by the width of the bar (5th to 95th percentile). The vertical line represents the most likely dose based on the most likely estimates of the parameters.

and 7.25 kg for rats and dogs, respectively. Table 7 summarizes the estimated mean parameters and the standard deviation/error used for subsequent prediction of human efficacious dose.

The mean estimated parameter and the standard deviation/error were used to generate the probability distribution for the parameter with 10,000 simulations. The distributions for the individual parameters are shown in Figure 13 and Figure

14. The distributions of a human efficacious dose for the NCEs were determined using Equation 8 and the listed parameter distributions. The central tendency of NCE-1 human dose was projected to be 1.6 g and ranged from 0.67 and 3.93 g (5th to 95th percentile). The central tendency of the human dose for NCE-2 of 1.8 g was similar to NCE-1 and ranged from 0.65 and 5.09 g (5th to 95th percentile). Although, the potency for NCE-1 was more than 2-fold the potency of NCE-2 (Table 7), the predicted human doses were nearly equivalent. This is because NCE-2 had higher bioavailability (17% vs 10% for NCE-1), higher Kp value (2.2 vs 1.7 for NCE-1) and lower clearance (484.4 ml/min vs 591.4 ml/min) than NCE-1. All of these parameters compensated for the lower potency of NCE-2 relative to NCE-1 as described in Equation 8.

The influence of the uncertainty in the parameter on the expected human Lilly dose was computed using a sensitivity analysis. Simulations were performed to generate 10,000 sets of parameters from the uncertainty distributions of individual parameters. The dose was predicted from each set of parameters resulting in corresponding 10,000 values of the predicted dose. The relationship between each parameter and the predicted dose was characterized with a regression model. The regression model was used to estimate the dose at the 10th, 50th and 90th quartiles for the parameter to define the influence range. The tornado plots were generated for NCE-1 and NCE-2 to describe the results of the sensitivity analysis (Figure 15 and Figure 16). The most influential parameters are at the top of the plot and are indicated by the width of the bar. The uncertainty in clearance for the competitor's compound was the most influential parameter for NCE-1 whereas the EC_{50} of NCE-2 was the influential parameter for predicting the NCE-2 dose.

References

Altshuler J, Flanagan A, Guy F, Steiner M, and Tollman P. A Revolution in R&D: *How Genomics and Genetics are Transforming the Biopharmaceutical Industry* 2001; Boston Consulting Group, Boston, Massachusetts

Dickson M, and Gagnon J. Key Factors in the Rising Cost of New Drug Discovery and Development. *Nature Rev. in Drug Dis* May 2004; Vol. 3: 417-429

DimAsi J, Hansen RW, and Grabowski HG. The Price of Innovation: New Estimates of Drug Development Costs. *J. Health Econ* 2003; 22: 151-185

FDA, Report. Innovation or Stagnation: Challenge and Opportunity on the Critical Path to New Medicinal Products. http://www.fda.gov/oc/initiatives/criticalpath/whitepaper.html (Accessed June 2004)

Kennedy T. Managing the Drug Discovery/Development Interface. *DDT* 1997; Vol. 2 No 10: 436-444

Kubinyi H. Drug Research: Myths, Hype and Reality. *Nature Reviews in Drug Discovery* 2005; Vol. 2: 665-668

Lindsey JK, Jones B, Jarvis P. Some Statistical Issues in Modeling Pharmacokinetic Data. *Stat Med* 2001; 20(17-18): 2775-2783

Nestorov I. Modeling and Simulation of Variability and Uncertainty in Toxicokinetics and Pharmacokinetics. *Toxicology Letters* 2001; 120(1-3): 411-420

Rosner GL, and. Muller P. Bayesian population pharmacokinetic and pharmacodynamic analyses using mixture models. *Journal of Pharmacokinetics & Biopharmaceutics* 1997; 25(2): 209-33

Wakefield J, Rahman N. The Combination of Population Pharmacokinetic Studies. *Biometrics* 2000; 56(1): 263-270

Woltman, H.R. Reviewing the bidding: R&D costs and profitability of new chemical entities. *J Res Pharm Econ* 1989; v1: 49-65

16

Early Preclinical Evaluation of Brain Exposure in Support of Hit Identification and Lead Optimization

**Thomas J. Raub, Barry S. Lutzke,
Paula K. Andrus[1], Geri A. Sawada,
Brian A. Staton**

Drug Disposition
Lilly Research Laboratories
Eli Lilly and Company
Indianapolis, IN 46285

[1]Retired from Pharmacia Corp., Kalamazoo, MI

Table of Contents

List of Abbreviations

AB ....apical-to-basal direction

ABC ....ATP-binding cassette (gene family)

AIB..aminoisobutyrate

AUC...............................area under the concentration versus time curve

AZT ....azidothymidine (zidovudine)

BA ....basal-to-apical direction

BBB ....blood-brain barrier

BUI..Brain Uptake Index

CBF...cerebral blood flow

CNS ....central nervous systyem

CsA..Cyclosporin A

Cyp..Cytochrome P450

2-DG 2-deoxyglucose

DMSO...dimethylsulfoxide

DXN ....digoxin

FVB..Friends virus B

HPLC ....high-performance liquid chromatography

K_d...dissociation binding constant

K_m...half-maximal saturation constant

LAT...large neutral amino acid transporter

LC/MS/MS............liquid chromatography and tandem mass spectrometry

logBB ....$\log_{10}$ of ratio of brain/plasma concentrations

MBUA...Mouse Brain Uptake Assay

MDCK...Madin-Darby canine kidney

MDR1...human multdrug resistance gene-1

mRNA..messenger ribonucleic acid

P_{app} ....apparent permeability coefficient

PBZ ....phenylbutazone

PCR ....polymerase chain reaction

P-gp ....P-glycoprotein

PS ....permeability-surface area coefficient

Slc ....solute carrier (gene family)

UWL..unstirred water layer

WT ....wild type (parent)

VNB..vinblastine

Introduction

Assessing brain exposure continues to be a central theme for multiple therapeutic areas within the pharmaceutical industry. In addition to optimizing delivery to CNS targets, brain exposure is considered for unwanted CNS access for either on-target activity or for off-target CNS toxicity or adverse events. The biopharmaceutical scientist is challenged to arrive at a rational strategy that is functional within the constraints of limited resources. Common strategies are integrated combinations of *in silico*, *in vitro*, and *in vivo* methods (Caldwell *et al.*, 2001). The appropriate strategy used depends upon the need, i.e., to drive chemistry or to establish a pharmacokinetic-pharmacodynamic relationship. We believe that a rigorous strategy is best so that the best lead series are selected. The intent is to anticipate liabilities of a lead series such that subsequent lead optimization cycle time and clinical attrition rates are ultimately reduced. The rigorous methods should deliver value by aiding synthetic chemistry direction while filtering out difficult templates. We also advocate the use of animal models as early as possible to establish a realistic perspective around the plethora of higher-throughput screening assay data. This application obviously challenges one to increase the capacity of these *in vivo* assays without compromising data quality or wasting vital and limited people resources.

There have been a number of reviews, some relatively dated but still very good, that critique various methods for measuring brain exposure *in vivo* (Fenstermacher *et al.*, 1981; Fenstermacher and Rapoport, 1984; Smith, 1989; Robinson, 1990; Bonate, 1995; Dash and Elmquist, 2003), and the reader is referred to this literature. The reader is also referred to other reviews describing surrogate assays for brain exposure involving *in silico* approaches (Norinder and Haeberlein, 2002; Clark, 2003; Ecker and Noe, 2004), measurements of physico-chemical properties like solvent partition coefficients (van de Waterbeemd *et al.*, 1998; Atkinson *et al.*, 2002), or *in vitro* models of the blood-brain barrier (BBB) (Gumbleton and Audus, 2001; de Boer and Gaillard, 2002; Reichel *et al.*, 2003, Garberg *et al.*, 2004). Although our industry has spent considerable effort seeking singular methods as surrogates for brain exposure assessment, a widely accepted standard approach does not yet exist. It already has been said that "there is no shortcut" to assessing BBB permeability (Pardridge, 2004a). Reliance on any single surrogate method without the appropriate benchmarking to the meaning of the data generated in the context of a pharmacological activity, or an exposure, *in vivo* is a choice of risk. We are advocating the installation of an *in vivo* method to profile hits and leads so that data from parallel *in vitro* profiling assays are interpreted with that context in mind. The different and more common approaches to assessing brain exposure *in vivo* are listed in Table 1.

The appropriate *in vivo* method should be relatively simple to execute and interpret. It should be reasonably rapid, relative to low throughput *in vivo* models, but have an appropriate capacity. Capacity is required not only to support early profiling of the entire portfolio of targets, but also to enable more intense support through optimization of a selected lead series once a limiting issue is identified. The method should be reliable in that the measured data are definitive, accurate

Surrogate Assays	*In silico* prediction
	Brain/plasma ratio, passive diffusion, etc.
	Calculated or measured physical properties
	Partition coefficient, polar surface area, etc.
	In vitro permeability measurement
	Cell monolayer models, PAMPA, etc.
In vivo Assays	CSF concentration
	Brain/plasma ratio
	Single dose intravenous administration
	Pharmacology
	Efficacy
	Ex vivo binding
	Brain Uptake Index
	In situ perfusion
	Microdialysis
	Imaging methods

Table 1. Methods to assess brain exposure.

and repeatable, especially over long periods of time. This requires not only excellent analytical skills, but also demands highly skilled technicians for animal dosing and handling. Even the best analytical chemists cannot deliver sound data from poorly run studies. The method should be compound sparing since the intent is to apply it early in the discovery process when total amounts of compound synthesized are small and the number of assays large. The method should be flexible such that it could be applied in a variety of formats, e.g., alternate dose routes, application of transgenic animals, and utility for collection of multiple tissues or fluids, for answering issue-driven questions. Lastly, the method should be robust with regard to the information provided.

Here is where the differences exist across the industry. The most common methods obtain a central activity in a pharmacology model in the absence of exposure or directly measure total brain and plasma levels at some single time interval following dose route of choice. Central activity can be a measure of exposure, but is not typically robust enough to drive structure-exposure optimization in the absence of understanding rate limiting issues. It is useless in the absence of activity that may or may not reflect delivery especially with a target that is poorly validated. Direct measurement fulfills many of the above criteria, but is also criticized because it only considers total brain levels, and these may not be related to an activity. Another criticism is that it is really a measure of blood-brain partitioning and not a measure of the rate of penetration of a molecule across the BBB (Pardridge, 2004a). Some suggest that CSF levels might be the best surrogate measure of free concentration of compound in brain (Martin, 2004). Yet, this

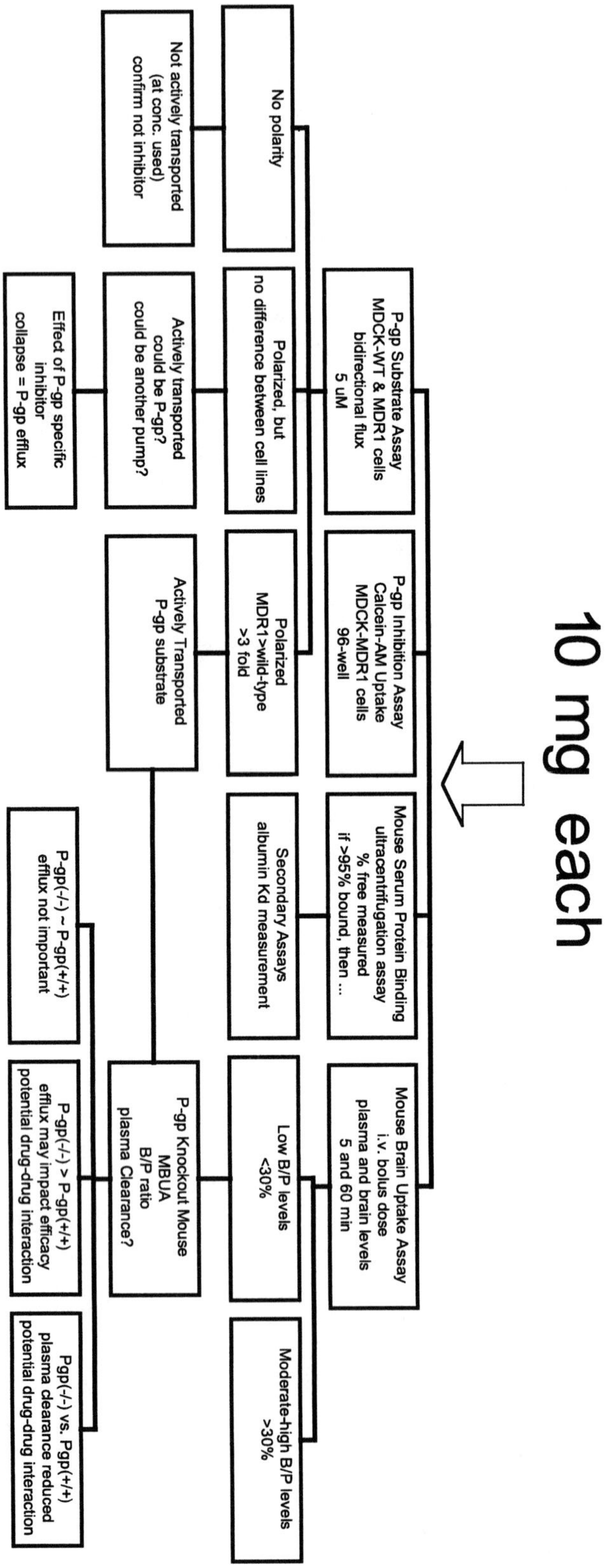

Figure 1. Strategy for the Brain Exposure Assessment.

10 mg each

- No polarity
  - Not actively transported (at conc. used) confirm not inhibitor

- P-gp Substrate Assay MDCK-WT & MDR1 cells bidirectional flux 5 uM
  - Polarized, but no difference between cell lines
    - Actively transported could be P-gp? could be another pump?
      - Effect of P-gp specific inhibitor collapse = P-gp efflux

- P-gp Inhibition Assay Calcein-AM Uptake MDCK-MDR1 cells 96-well
  - Polarized MDR1>wild-type >3 fold
    - Actively Transported P-gp substrate

- Mouse Serum Protein Binding ultracentrifugation assay % free measured if >95% bound, then ....
  - Secondary Assays albumin Kd measurement

- Mouse Brain Uptake Assay i.v. bolus dose plasma and brain levels 5 and 60 min
  - Low B/P levels <30%
    - P-gp Knockout Mouse MBUA B/P ratio plasma Clearance?
      - P-gp(-/-) ~ P-gp(+/+) efflux not important
      - P-gp(-/-) > P-gp(+/+) efflux may impact efficacy potential drug-drug interaction
  - Moderate-high B/P levels >30%
    - Pgp(-/-) vs. Pgp(+/+) plasma clearance reduced potential drug-drug interaction

approach comes with certain assumptions and caveats that complicate interpretation of such data (de Lange and Danhoff, 2002). This debate plays to the intent of the assay and what information is required to match that intent. Since no single approach will likely satisfy all needs, the biopharmaceutical scientist must integrate multiple assays to help drive team decisions.

Our strategy for early pre-clinical assessment of exposure of brain targets to lead compounds uses a combination of *in vitro* and *in vivo* assay screens to provide an array of performance information (Figure 1). The data obtained are total brain and plasma levels, estimates of time-dependent loss from plasma and brain, fraction free in plasma, permeability *in vitro* and *in vivo*, and whether the compound is a substrate for an efflux transport system like P-glycoprotein (P-gp; ABCB1). P-glycoprotein is a multidrug resistance pump that is expressed at the BBB and is responsible for preventing drug molecules from crossing the BBB by actively transporting them back into the blood (Tamai and Tsuji, 2000; Fromm, 2000). Assessing P-gp involvement is unavoidable in understanding brain uptake of new chemical entities. The *in vitro* assays are useful for interpreting the *in vivo* results, for identifying rate-limiting liabilities of scaffolds, and supporting a chemistry strategy during lead optimization that strives to overcome those liabilities. There are two essential *in vitro* assays. One is some measure of permeability that includes P-gp mediated efflux. There are multiple ways to achieve this assessment and we choose to define it in a singular assay using Madin-Darby canine kidney (MDCK) epithelial cells that express the human MDR1 (ABCB1) gene (Polli *et al.*, 2001; Hochman *et al.*, 2002; Schwab *et al.*, 2002). The other *in vitro* assay is a coarse assessment of serum or plasma protein binding since brain uptake can be affected by the free fraction of compound in the blood. Lastly, we use an *in vivo* approach that satisfies many of the desired criteria stated above. We developed a novel, modified version of the traditional single intravenous injection method that provides key information for compounds that often have not yet been dosed into animals. In this chapter we will briefly describe these assays and illustrate through examples how the information generated can be used to support project teams.

Assays of the Brain Exposure Assessment Strategy

In vitro Permeability with P-glycoprotein-mediated Efflux

There are numerous assays for measuring the rate of diffusion of a solute across a cellular barrier. It is beyond the scope of this article to enumerate all of these and the reader is referred to Youdim *et al.* (2003) and the references cited therein. The purists within CNS research prefer to use a cell monolayer comprised of capillary endothelial cells derived from the brain. While such models of the BBB have proven useful and have seen improvements over the last few years, their utility in the pharmaceutical industry for screening has simply not been practical (Terasaki *et al.*, 2003; Pardridge, 2004b; Garberg *et al.*, 2004). This is primarily due

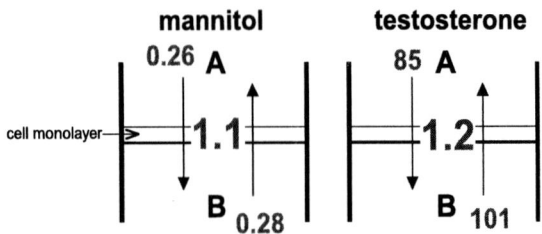

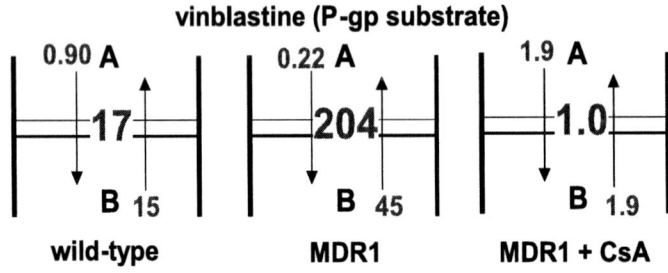

Figure 2. Directional apparent permeability coefficients (P_{app}; in red) for solutes in the MDCK cell model. The dynamic range of passive diffusion is defined by mannitol (paracellular route) and testosterone (transcellular route) in a well-mixed system. Active BA efflux is illustrated by the asymmetry of vinblastine (VNB) permeability. BA/AB P_{app} ratios are shown in blue text. Intrinsic passive diffusion is obtained for VNB by P-glycoprotein inhibition using 5 µM Cyclosporin A (CsA).

to the resource investment in generating these cells and then to their phenotypic deficiencies, relative to the *in vivo* BBB, such as excessive leakiness and differential expression of active transport systems. Consequently, many have compromised and adopted simpler and more robust models such as MDCK cells (Polli *et al.*, 2001; Hochman *et al.*, 2002; Schwab *et al.*, 2002; Garberg *et al.*, 2004). Applications of this assay come in different designs. It is quite robust with an approximate 400-fold range of measured apparent permeability coefficient (P_{app}) values (Figure 2). The basic design is to measure flux in both directions across monolayers of parent versus MDR1-over-expressing cell lines. The cell monolayer separates the system into an upper (A for apical side) and lower (B for basal side) representing the blood and brain compartments, respectively. The parent cell line expresses low levels of canine P-gp whereas the MDR1 cell line over expresses human P-gp. It can be streamlined for increased capacity and throughput by measuring flux over a single time interval and by cassette dosing. If the basal-to-apical (BA) rate is greater than 2.5 fold the apical-to-basal (AB) rate in either cell type, then net efflux by a transporter is indicated. This net efflux should be ablated by pretreatment with an efflux inhibitor (Figure 2). If the ratio of the BA/AB P_{app} ratios from MDR1 versus parent cells is greater than three, validation indicates that this is positive identification of a P-gp substrate (Figure 3). This means that a three-fold increased polarity in MDR1 cells is significant in response

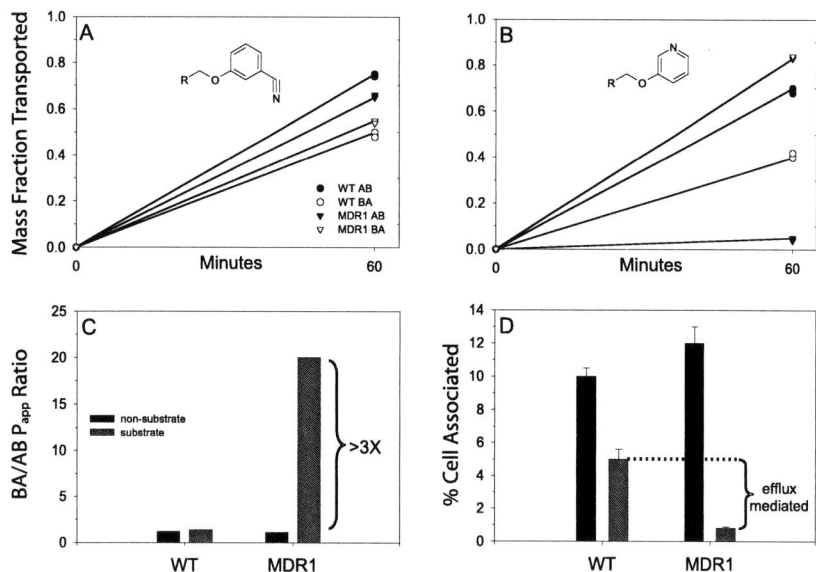

Figure 3. Examples of non-polarized (A) and polarized (B) efflux for two structurally-related compounds tested in the MDCK cell model system. A single time point of 60 min was used in this screen. Slopes are slightly different as plotted because of differences in volume. (C) The magnitude of the BA/AB ratio between the MDR1 and parent or wild-type (WT) cell lines is apparent. (D) Functional efflux of the substrate is confirmed by the reduction in cell-associated compound for MDR1 relative to parent.

Category	AB P_{app}[1]	BA P_{app}[1]	Ratio[2]	% Cell[3]	P-gp Substrate[4]	Comments
1	S	S-M	Invalid	VL	Unknown	Passive diffusion too slow Access to pump limited
2	S	S-M	Invalid	VH	Unknown	Excessive cell partitioning Interpretation invalidated
3	S-M	F	>3	L-H	Yes	Bona fide P-gp substrate
4	S-F	S-F	≤3	L-H	No	No active efflux or false negative

Table 2. Categories describing *in vitro* permeability.
[1]P_{app}, apparent permeability coefficient, x 10^{-6} cm/sec: S, slow ≤ 1; M, moderate 2-9; F, fast ≥ 10. Apical-to-basal (AB) and basal-to-apical (BA) direction,
[2]Ratio of the ratio of BA/AB P_{app} values for MDR1/parent.
[3]The buffer/cell partitioning is expressed as a percent of the total mass added that is recovered in a methanol wash of the cells/filter: VL, very low <1%; L, low 1-4%; M, moderate 5-19%; H, high 20-89%; VH, very high ≥90%.
[4]Binary 'Yes" or 'No'. Unknown when slow passive diffusion may restrict access to the pump (Category 1) or when excessive cell partitioning artificially decreases P_{app} in either direction (Category 2). Category 4 might be a false negative if the compound inhibits P-gp under conditions of this assay, or if passive diffusion is so fast that pump efficiency is decreased.

to over expression of human P-gp. Sometimes a template is quite polarized in the parent cell line so that the MDR1/parent ratio is not robust enough. In these cases or as an alternative design, one can simply run the MDR1 cell line alone in the absence and presence of a P-gp inhibitor.

We also prefer to measure the fraction of compound associated with the cell (and system components) by recovering it with a methanol wash. Achieving mass balance in this way leads to a more accurate P_{app} value and provides additional information about a compound (Sawada *et al.*, 1999; Ho *et al.*, 2000). For example, a reduction in cell associated fraction in the MDR1 versus parent cell line, or in the uninhibited versus inhibited cells, confirms functional P-gp action (Figure 3D). Moreover, the magnitude of that associated cell fraction can be used to categorize chemistry space with one example being a situation where cell partitioning is so extreme (>90%) that P_{app} values are under measured and polarity is nonexistent or meaningless. In such cases, one cannot make an accurate assessment about P-gp interaction. Table 2 demonstrates the potential complexity of this seemingly simple permeability assay. The four categories of behavior were observed within a single program team for a single, albeit complicated, peptidomimetic scaffold. However, each category represents generally defined behavior for many different chemical scaffolds that have been examined over the years.

Four Categories Defining In Vitro Permeability and P-glycoprotein Efflux

Certain compounds are too hydrophilic resulting in membrane-limited diffusion. In this Category 1 scenario, diffusion in both directions is slow or <1 x 10^{-6} cm/sec, and independent of pump (Table 2). BA P_{app} might be slightly faster, but less than 5 fold. Cell partitioning is also very low (<1%). These compounds may be recognized by P-gp, but their access to the pump is rate limited and net efflux is diminished. Category 1 compounds generally have slow brain uptake.

Category 2 compounds act like Category 1 compounds such that permeability is slow in either direction (Table 2). However, the reason this occurs in Category 2 is because cell partitioning is very high (>90%). Cell partitioning is so excessive that compound prefers to remain cell associated rather than desorb from the cell into the aqueous receiver buffer (Sawada *et al.*, 1994; Sawada *et al.*, 1999; Ho *et al.*, 2000). This artificially underestimates the permeability and invalidates an interpretation that lack of polarity is absence of active efflux. These compounds may be transported by P-gp, but the net effect is lost because of the inability of pump to compete with the compound's avidity for the membrane. This could occur by rapid re-partitioning following efflux resulting in a futile cycle. The compound could also be partitioned elsewhere in the cell removing it from access to the pump. Such compounds also have a greater likelihood of inhibiting P-gp activity, and their own transport, because of high concentrations at the pump. Category 2 compounds must be tested *in vivo* to assess their ability to cross the BBB.

Category 3 compounds are *bone fide* P-gp substrates showing the assay defined net efflux (Table 2). AB permeability is typically slow to moderate and increases with reduction in pump expression (parent cell line or inhibited MDR1 cell line). BA permeability is almost always fast and decreases with reduction in pump expression or activity. Cell partitioning is variable, but never very high (>90%), and BA permeability usually decreases as partitioning increases at least above 60%. Category 3 compounds almost always have slow BBB penetration. The exception is when intrinsic passive diffusion is fast enough to reduce the efficiency of pump action. Efficiency of the efflux pump is a product of the rate of passive diffusion, the residence time for that compound at the pump, i.e., within the membrane environment, and the strength of the molecular interaction between compound and pump, e.g, K_m. One begins to see how cell membrane partitioning can complicate measuring a true K_m since local concentrations at the pump can be very high relative to extracellular or even total cellular concentrations (Ferte, 2000; Hochman *et al.*, 2002). Well-partitioned compounds with high K_m values (low affinity) may be efficiently pumped. Partitioning of a substrate into the membrane was suggested to be the rate-limiting step for P-gp interaction (Stein, 1997; Seelig and Landwojtowicz, 2000). The consequences of this are two-fold with regard to chemistry strategy. Instead of altering the K_m to reduce P-gp efflux, one can either increase passive diffusion or reduce cell (membrane) partitioning.

The consequence of reducing P-gp efficiency, or the absence of P-gp-mediated efflux, is a Category 4 compound (Table 2). AB and BA permeability is slow to fast and nearly equal. Again, cell partitioning is variable, but never very high. Such compounds are expected to have rapid BBB penetration if the passive diffusion rate and plasma free fraction are sufficient. It is possible for the MDCK P-gp Substrate Assay to give a false Category 4 if P-gp is inhibited (saturated) at the concentration tested. This is minimized using test concentrations that are ≤ 5 μM, but the likelihood of this occurring is greater when a substrate is highly partitioned in the cell. Consequently, we and others suggest co-running a P-gp inhibition assay such as the Calcein-AM uptake assay (Figure 1; Polli *et al.*, 2001). One can then flag potential cases when inhibition might be occurring, relative to standard P-gp inhibitors, and causing an increase in the AB rate and a decrease in the BA rate.

The permeability of a compound across the cell monolayers involves several activities each of which is multifactorial and determined by overlapping, and sometimes apposed, physicochemical properties. These activities are (1) passive diffusion, (2) cell partitioning, and (3) dose-dependent active transport. Additional activities like poor aqueous solubility and loss to plastic surfaces also have profound effects.

In vitro Plasma Binding

Interpretation of our *in vivo* assay of brain uptake requires some knowledge of plasma or serum protein binding. There are numerous methods to measure the extent of compound binding to plasma proteins and any of these will suffice given an understanding of the limits of the assay. We chose ultracentrifugation as our standard method for assessing plasma protein binding because over a diverse chemistry space this method is the least effected by complications associated with loss due to adsorption. For example, although the ultrafiltration method is much easier to carry out, it is frequently hampered by nonspecific binding of compound to the filter or plastic surfaces. The ultracentrifugation method is not an ideal assay method either since there are times when the % bound result is quite variable and partitioning of compound into lipoproteins can interfere with the collection of the unbound fraction. The ultracentrifugation method appears to be slightly less precise when binding exceeds 80% (data not shown). We compared the relationship of plasma binding for twenty-five radiolabeled compounds *in vivo* to that *in vitro*. *In vivo* binding was measured using mouse plasma that had been collected 5 min after intravenous bolus dose. Thus, all of the complex equilibria are accounted for including any metabolism that occurred in this relatively short time frame and that will have impact because we only measured total radioactivity. *In vitro* binding was done using dilution of a concentrated stock solution in organic solvent into donor plasma and separating free and bound fractions after 30-min equilibration. With a few exceptions, most of the drug molecules were >80% bound *in vivo* and *in vitro*. For seventeen compounds, the two approaches were the same with an average difference in mean values of 2 ± 6%. So, in general, the *in vitro* approach is a reasonable approximation of binding *in vivo*. Exceptions will undoubtedly occur requiring a heightened awareness of this fact when screening certain chemical series. Thus, our measurements are total and free compound to calculate a percent free or bound. The more tightly bound compounds like ibuprofen, diazepam, and imipramine were >90% bound by using the ultracentrifugation method, and this cutoff value is used to consider a reduction in free fraction to have negative impact on brain uptake.

The Calibrated Mouse Brain Uptake Assay

The Mouse Brain Uptake Assay (MBUA) is our *in vivo* measure of the ability of compounds to cross the BBB and distribute to brain (Figure 1). We developed a novel, modified version of a two-compartment single-dose intravenous administration method (Ohno *et al.*, 1978). Rather than determining a plasma AUC_{0-t}, we estimate a permeability-surface area coefficient (PS, $cm^3 \cdot g^{-1} \cdot sec^{-1}$) from a single, 5-min time point. We then calculate an apparent *in vivo* BBB permeability coefficient (BBB P_{app}) assuming a constant published value of surface area (240 cm^2) per gram of brain tissue (Ohno *et al.*, 1978). This assumes that brain concentration (C_{brain}) reflects initial uptake rates where back flux is negligible. Only parent compound is measured by LC/MS/MS. One also assumes that C_{brain} divided by the volume of brain into which solute distributes is much less than the plasma concentration. Thus, when solute partitions favorably into the brain and accumulates there, or as $C_{brain} > C_{plasma}$, the accuracy of the BBB P_{app} decreases. The impact of not maintaining these assumptions was accounted for by using solutes of known brain uptake behavior to calibrate the MBUA. This calibration conducted under defined constant conditions is discussed in subsequent sections.

Summary:				5 min			60 min		
Dose,	mg/kg	2.6							
			Mean	SD	SEM	Mean	SD	SEM	
[Plasma]	nmole/ml		15.2	3.40	1.96	4.93	0.758	0.437	
[Brain]	nmole/g		0.536	0.306	0.177	0.561	0.149	0.086	
% Loss	Plasma					68		5.1	
% Loss	Brain					-5		38	
Brain/Plasma, %			3.7	2.1	1.2	11	1.8	1.0	
% Dose			0.143	0.082	0.047	0.149	0.040	0.023	
P_{app} X 10^{-6} cm/sec			0.52	0.30	0.17				

Dexamethasone

P_{app} X 10^{-6} cm/sec (MDCK)	WT	MDR1		P-gp substrate?		Mannitol leakage % of vehicle control (MDCK-WT)	
Direction: A>B	9.0	3.7					
B>A	22	44					
Ratio	2.4	12		yes		100	

Protein binding	mean % bound ± SEM =	67	2.1		Pgp %I at 5uM	7

Comments	cell partitioning low, 0.6-1.2%

Table 3. Example data output for dexamethasone from the Brain Exposure Assessment. Triplicate mice were used to obtain a mean and standard deviation or standard error mean. Mannitol leakage is the internal control assessing whether the test compound has a negative effect (increased %) on cell monolayer integrity. "Pgp %I at 5 μM" is the % inhibition of P-gp-mediated efflux as measured by Calcein-AM uptake in MDCK-MDR1 cells in the presence of 5 μM test solute, or the concentration used in the permeability assay.

In addition to the 5-min time point that provides an estimate of the rate of brain uptake relative to standard solutes, a 60-min time point provides information on compound pharmacokinetics in brain and plasma. The change in brain and plasma concentration between 5 and 60 min tells us whether compound is lost from the compartment (not a rate) and whether loss from brain is different from loss from plasma. For example, if loss from brain equals loss from plasma, then it usually is consistent with rapid equilibration or fast permeability *in vitro* and *in vivo*. If loss from brain lags behind plasma loss, or remains constant, then this suggests either slow equilibration or tissue partitioning and a potential for accumulation. Differentiating these interpretations can occur from the *in vitro* permeability data.

An example output from the Brain Exposure Assessment for dexamethasone is shown in Table 3. Plasma levels decreased 68% over 1 h, but the brain levels remained constant; however, BBB penetration was limited as shown by the low brain/plasma ratio or slow BBB P_{app} (also see Figure 7). This contributed to an increase in brain/plasma ratio with time, which can be misleading to an interpretation of increase in BBB rate or net exposure. The *in vitro* permeability data confirmed dexamethasone as a P-gp substrate, which then likely contributed to its slow brain uptake. The maintenance of brain levels despite active efflux is not uncommon for P-gp substrates. Loss from brain in this time frame is not always faster in these situations and could have been caused by the compound distributed to locations where pump is unable to remove it efficiently. These data are interpreted within the context of the ever-growing database; we had amassed data for over 300 compounds from 20 different discovery teams and multiple therapeutic areas. We'll briefly describe how some of these assay methods are carried out and then discuss the calibration of the MBUA.

Experimental Methods

Plasma Protein Binding Methods

Heparinized whole blood was centrifuged at 2,000 g for 3 min at room temperature to collect plasma that was assayed for total radioactivity without decolorization or solubilization, or total compound by LC/MS/MS as described below. For *in vivo* binding data, the remaining plasma was used to determine the fraction bound by an ultrafiltration method. A 200-μL aliquot of plasma was separated quickly into bound and unbound radioactivity (filtrate containing molecular weight species of <10 kDa) in a Centrifree® device centrifuged at 2,000 g for 3 min at room temperature. Less than 10% of the total volume or <20 μL was collected as filtrate and 10 μL was assayed for unbound total radioactivity. For *in vitro* binding data, the fraction bound was measured by either the ultrafiltration method described above or an ultracentrifugation method. Radioactive compounds in organic solvent were diluted 1/40 - 1/100 into donor mouse plasma to give a final concentration of solute of 0.25 - 0.50 μCi/mL and a solvent concentration of 1 - 2.5% (v/v). Non-radiolabeled compound in dosing solution at 10 mM was diluted to 10 μM in donor mouse plasma and mixed at 37°C for 30 min. A 75-μL aliquot was removed and frozen immediately at -20°C. Two 1-mL samples of plasma-compound were placed into 11 x 34-mm polycarbonate centrifuge tubes. One tube was stored at 37°C for the duration of the time that the other tube was spun at 100,000 g for 16 h at 37°C in a Beckman TL-100 ultracentrifuge. Each was analyzed as 75-μL aliquots and the post-spin supernatant concentration (free) compared to the total concentration in the non-spun sample. This latter stationary sample was compared to the initially collected sample, stored at -20°C, to account for loss. The centrifugation can be done for 4 h at 150,000 g to shorten the process and also reduce potential for loss caused by instability in plasma.

In vitro Permeability

MDCK cells were maintained at 37°C in humidified 5% CO_2/95% air using Eagle's MEM culture medium supplemented with 10% (v/v) fetal bovine serum, penicillin, and streptomycin. A 1:10 split was done twice per week and cells were plated at 50,000 cells/cm^2 in 6-well Transwell™ filter inserts (4.71 cm^2 surface area). Medium was changed on days 3 and 5 and the cell monolayers used on day 6. Bi-directional flux of compounds was measured across confluent parent MDCK and human P-gp (ABCB1, aka MDR1) expressing MDCK cell monolayers. The cells were obtained from the Netherlands Cancer Institute under a Material Transfer Agreement. Cells were rinsed twice with phosphate-buffered saline (PBS) containing 10 mM Hepes, pH 7.4. Some were pretreated once for 30 min with buffer containing 5 μM Cyclosporin A (CsA) to inhibit P-gp. The upper chamber (A) contained 1.0 mL buffer and the lower chamber (B) contained 2.0 mL buffer. For AB direction, the insert was moved to fresh buffer at regular intervals. For BA direction, the entire upper chamber buffer was replaced at regular intervals. Both methods maintained sink conditions. The system was mixed using a Clay-Adams Nutator® and kept at 37°C in room atmosphere. Solute concentration was determined for the donor and receiver solutions at each time interval. Donor solutions were prepared by dilution of a concentrated stock solution in organic solvent to 5 μM unlabeled compound or 0.25 μCi of radiolabeled compound in buffer. Washed cell monolayers were extracted for 5 min at 37°C with cold methanol to determine the amount of cell-associated compound and to obtain mass balance.

HPLC Analysis of Radiolabeled Vinblastine and Digoxin

Digoxin (DXN) and vinblastine (VNB) were assayed in plasma and brain tissue using HPLC and a Radiomatic C515TR detector with a 500-μL loop. Ultima-Flo M® Scintillation Cocktail was used at a flow rate of 3.0 mL/min. Detection limits were set at 0-18.5 keV for [^{3}H] giving a 7 CPM background and a 35% counting efficiency. UV absorption also was monitored at 250 nm (100-nm bandwidth). The injection volume was 75 μL onto a 15 x 4.6-cm Altima C18 (5-mm) column with guard column. The mobile phase for DXN was 35% (v/v) acetonitrile in 0.5% (w/v) monosodium phosphate, pH 5.5, run at 1 mL/min at 50°C. The mobile phase for VNB was 78% (v/v) methanol in 10 mM monosodium phosphate, pH 7.0, run at 1 mL/min at 25°C. The retention time was 5.7 min for DXN and 5.3 min for VNB. Biosamples were extracted 3:1 (v/w) with acetonitrile. A measured volume of the post-centrifuged supernatant was dried down in 1.5-mL polypropylene microcentrifuge tubes using a Savant SpeedVac Concentrator. These samples were reconstituted using 100-μL mobile phase, mixed, and centrifuged at 3,000 g for 10 min. The supernatants were transferred to 250-μL polypropylene autosampler vials and centrifuged at 500 g for five minutes prior to assay.

In vivo Studies

Dosing

CF-1 female mice were acclimated for one week prior to use at 23 ± 1 g body weight. Non-fasted mice were dosed intravenously by tail vein injection with a 0.3-mL insulin syringe and 28-ga. x ¹/₂" needle (Becton-Dickinson, Franklin Lakes, NJ). Each mouse received 50-μL injectate containing either 150 nmole unlabeled (6.5 μmole/kg) or 2 μCi radiolabeled solute. The most commonly used vehicle was 80:20% (wt/wt) propylene glycol:DMSO. At 5 and 60 min post-injection, the mice were anesthetized and 0.5-1 ml blood was removed using a 1-mL syringe and a 25-ga. X ⁵/₈" needle that had been rinsed with heparin solution.

In some experiments the mice were subjected to transcardiac perfusion after blood draw and prior to tissue removal. A 25-ga. x ⁵⁄₈" needle fixed on a 10-mL syringe was inserted into the right atrium of the heart and 10 mL of 0.9% NaCl were delivered over a ~2-min period. Under these conditions, blanching of lung and liver tissue was observed and fluid exited the nasal passages.

Tissue Sampling

A 200-400 mg portion of the liver was removed from the same lobe. The heart was removed with the lungs and separated. The heart was blotted to remove excess blood. The lungs were blotted onto a paper towel and masticated using forceps to remove residual fluids. The brain was excised by making three cuts through the skull with a pair of scissors. Two cuts were made laterally starting at the base of the skull and ending at the eye socket. One cut was made across the nose bridge connecting the eye sockets. The skull cap was lifted off and the whole brain was removed with forceps or a small spatula. Except for lung, each tissue was divided in two portions and placed into tared scintillation vials to measure wet weight. Brain was divided into each hemisphere; inclusion or exclusion of cerebellum had no net effect on the results.

Sample Processing

Total Radioactivity

Each scintillation vial received 1 mL Solvable® (Packard Instrument Co., Inc., Meriden, CT) and after capping the vials were placed at 50°C overnight or for up to 20 h. After cooling to room temperature, 100 μL of 30% H_2O_2 was added to decolorize the sample and the samples were allowed to stand uncapped for 1-2 h at room temperature. Ultima Gold® scintillation fluid (10 mL) was added, the samples shaken, and the amount of radioactivity (dpm) was measured using a Packard Tri-Carb 2100TR Liquid Scintillation Analyzer with external standard and quench curves.

Unlabeled Solutes Assayed by Liquid Chromatography Methods

Extraction solvent (300 μL 9:1 acetonitrile:tetrahydrofuran) was added to 100-μL thawed, plasma samples and sonicated for 5 sec at a setting of 3 with a Virtis VirSonic 60 sonicator fitted with a micro probe tip. Frozen tissue samples were placed into pre-tared microfuge tubes, weighed and homogenized in an amount of extraction solvent equal to three times the weight of the tissue, for a four fold final dilution. The sonicated extract was spun by centrifuge for 12 min at 4°C at 1,000 g. The supernatants (300 μL) were transferred to 1.5-mL microfuge tubes and dried under nitrogen, using a Pierce Reacti-Therm III heating module. For samples to be analyzed by mass spectrometer, the dried extracts were reconstituted in 150 μL of a mobile phase compatible solvent and injected for HPLC analysis. For samples to be analyzed by ultraviolet or fluorescence detection, the dried extracts were reconstituted in 150 μL of isocratic mobile phase and injected for HPLC analysis.

Data Analysis

For the *in vitro* permeability measurements, the rates for linear appearance of total mass in the receiver solution versus time were calculated as (Ho *et al.*, 2000); units are cm or nm/sec. The starting donor concentration was the total recovered mass. BA/AB P_{app} ratios were calculated for each cell line. If this ratio was >2.5 as defined by outside of experimental error measured using testosterone, then active efflux was suspected. The intrinsic passive P_{app} value was obtained either as the mean of the AB and BA P_{app} values in parent cells, if polarity was absent, or after collapsing the BA/AB ratio toward 1.0 using a P-gp inhibitor. If the MDR1/parent ratio of these BA/AB ratios was >3, then the test solute was identified as a P-gp substrate.

For the *in vivo* studies, all data were expressed as dpm/g tissue or dpm/mL plasma or blood. The brain values were corrected for the plasma volume, or 16 μL/g, as measured independently using the membrane-impermeant inulin. The bioavailability of solute from plasma to tissue was expressed as a ratio or percentage of tissue concentration relative to the plasma concentration assuming equal density (1 mL plasma = 1 g brain). The 5-min data sets for brain were used to estimate a value with units of $cm^{3} \cdot g^{-1} \cdot sec^{-1}$ according to Ohno *et al.* (1978).

Calibrating the Mouse Brain Uptake Assay

Total Water Volumes for Brain, Lung, Heart and Liver

Total water volume (extra- and intracellular) of the four organs was determined by measuring the distribution of tritiated water at 5 min after dosing. All tissues sampled had similar total water volumes on a tissue wet weight basis. Each was between 690 to 820 μL/g with brain having the largest volume. The brain levels of tritiated water represent 1.9 ± 0.2% of the dose. This is within the range of the cardiac output (1.2-2.6%) reported for the rat (Davies and Morris, 1993). Tritiated water also has been used to define the cerebral blood flow (CBF) rate as 0.56 mL/g per minute (Pardridge and Oldendorf, 1975a). Thus, within 5 min approximately 1.1 mL (see below), or ~70% of the total blood volume, has perfused the brain of a mouse. The total water volume for an average CF-1 mouse brain (399 ± 19 mg for a 23 g mouse) of 328 μL or ~82% of the total wet weight. The total water volume for rat brain is reported to be 70-80% (Van Harreveld, 1966; Rapoport, 1976a). In comparison, the total water volumes for average CF-1 mouse lungs (138 ± 20 mg for a 23 g mouse) and heart (116 ± 6 mg for a 23 g mouse) were 100 μL and 88 μL, respectively. Liver cannot be calculated since we only assayed a portion of this organ. The high loss of tritiated water from heart (51%), and especially lung (84%) versus brain (14%) after perfusion implies that extravascular spaces within the tissue are rapidly equilibrated. This was confirmed by the 68 and 88% losses in inulin removed by perfusion.

Total Plasma Volume for Brain and Other Organs

The plasma volume of the brain, liver, lung or heart was determined by measuring the distribution of [^{14}C]inulin at 5 min after dosing. Inulin, with a large mean molecular weight of 5,000 Da, was chosen because it is a membrane impermeant that diffuses slowly across the vascular barrier (Levin et al., 1970). As a result, the distribution of this solute at 5 min should represent the blood or plasma volume within a tissue. As expected, brain with the highly restrictive BBB gave the smallest plasma volume of 16 ± 2 μL/g tissue. Thus, the total plasma volume for an average CF-1 mouse brain (399 ± 19 mg for a 23 g mouse) is 6.4 μL or ~1.6% of the total wet weight. This compared well to the 15 μL/g reported by Blasberg et al. (1983) for the rat brain. In repeat experiments about one year later, the brain plasma volume was again determined twice to be 16 ± 1.1 μL/g and 17 ± 4 μL/g using [^{14}C-methoxy]inulin. It is imperative to use [^{14}C]-labeled inulin, and not [^{3}H] label, because the contaminating free tritium introduces error. Separation of the [^{3}H]inulin by size exclusion chromatography (Bio-Gel P-2) showed that ~4% of the radioactivity had a molecular weight of <500 Da. This resulted in an artificially larger plasma volume and a ~20-fold faster P_{app} value (data not shown).

Transcardiac saline perfusion to remove blood reduced the brain residual plasma volume to 4 ± 2 μL/g tissue. If we assume that all of the inulin is plasma associated, then this gives an average perfusion efficiency of 75 ± 38%. Because the plasma volume was so consistent and the perfusion efficiency was so variable, all subsequent data were corrected for the measured plasma volume in brain *in lieu* of routinely performing saline perfusion. A similar treatment of the data for the other organs is not warranted given that the extraction of tritiated water was much greater. This implies a more rapid equilibration between the vascular and tissue extracellular space in these tissues making the distinction between the two compartments more difficult. This argues that a saline perfusion in certain cases will result in back extraction of compound from non-brain tissue and underestimating total compound concentration within that organ.

Passive Diffusion Across the Blood-Brain Barrier

Brain uptake of most of these ten solutes had been measured in rat using two different methods. The Brain Uptake Index (BUI) has been used often to measure a percent extracted during first-pass through the rat brain following a single injection into the common carotid artery (Oldendorf, 1981). Using their data, we calculated a logBB ($\log_{10}[C_{brain}/C_{plasma}]$) value (Table 4) and compared them to our observed data (Table 5). Figure 4A summarizes this comparison. Reported data using this method were not available for glycerol and ethylene glycol.

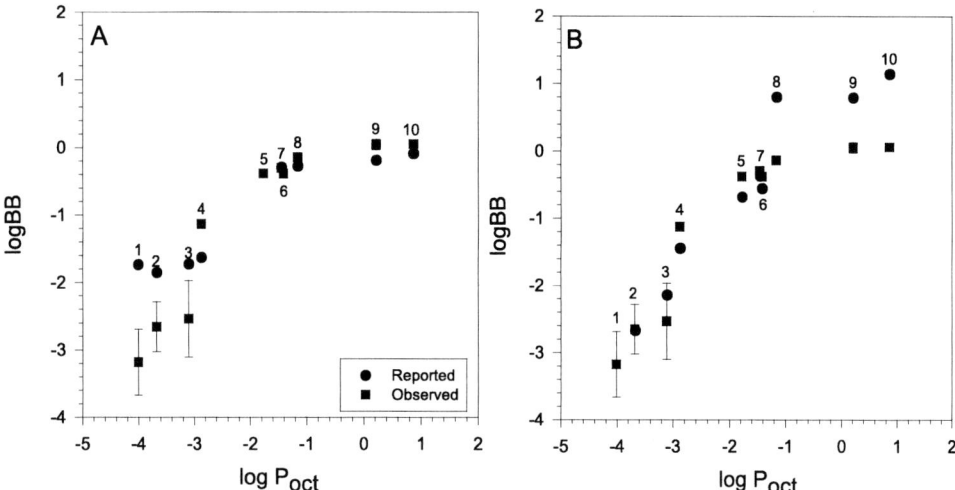

Figure 4. Comparing the performance of the Mouse Brain Uptake Assay to published (reported) values of blood-brain barrier permeability measured using the (A) Brain Uptake Index and (B) In situ perfusion methods. Test solutes are identified in Table 4. P_{oct}, measured octanol/water partition coefficient.

In situ perfusion has been the method of choice for measuring the permeability of molecules across the BBB in rodents (Takasato *et al.*, 1984). Here, solutes are perfused via the carotid artery at a controlled flow rate through a brain hemisphere and a PS value is calculated. Sometimes, the PS value is converted to a P_{app} by assuming that the surface area of the brain capillaries is 240 cm^2/g tissue (Ohno *et al.*, 1978). From these reported data we calculated a logBB value at 5 min (Table 4) and compared them to our observed data (Table 5). Figure 4B summarizes these comparisons. In both published methods, the injectate or perfusate was a physiological buffer lacking blood components; however, since the solutes used are not appreciably plasma protein or red blood cell bound, the effect of blood components on the free concentration in our MBUA design was minimal and slightly indicated only for the most hydrophobic molecules, antipyrine and butanol.

Our modified method is more similar to the BUI method when examining hydrophobic compounds (Figure 4A). This is because an equilibrium between brain and blood has already been reached by 5 min, or within the few minutes used for the BUI, and the logBB reaches a maximum of ~0 or a brain/plasma ratio of ~1.0. Again, we estimate that within 5 min ~70% of the total mouse blood volume has perfused the brain. A hydrophobic compound like antipyrine is lost from the brain with a half life of ~1.5 min (Fenstermacher and Rapoport, 1984). A deviation from linearity when plotting permeability versus log P is much less pronounced in the perfusion method because the short time used assures a sink condition where the rate of flux from blood to brain, or the transfer constant, is unidirectional (Figure 4B). Linear regression analysis of the literature reported data obtained using in situ perfusion gave r^2=0.93 compared to an r^2=0.84 for our observed data. The effect is for our method to underestimate the passive

Table 4. Published brain uptake or penetration values for radiolabeled solutes.

Solute	MW[1]	log P$_{oct}$ [2]	P$_{oct}$	Measured BUI[3]	Calculated logBB[3]	Measured P$_{app}$ [4]	Calculated logBB[4]
1 inulin	5000	≈(-4)	≈0.0001	1.95	-1.71	0.0012	-4.1
2 sucrose	342	-3.67 (-3.16)	0.0002	1.4	-1.85	0.03	-2.67
3 mannitol	180	-3.10 (-2.11)	0.00079	1.9	-1.72	0.1	-2.14
4 urea	60	-2.87 (-1.95)	0.0013	2.4	-1.62	0.5	-1.44
5 glycerol	92	-2.56 (-1.76)	(0.017)	na	—	3	-0.67
6 ethylene glycol	62	-1.40 (na)	0.040	na	—	4	-0.54
7 acetamide	59	-1.44 (-1.17)	0.036	~53	-0.28	6	-0.36
8 water	18	-1.15 (-1.03)	0.071	55	-0.26	90	0.81
9 antipyrine	188	0.23 (0.31)	1.7	68	-0.17	90	0.81
10 butanol	74	0.88 (0.78)	7.6	86	-0.066	200	1.16

[1]MW, molecular weight in Daltons. [2]octanol/water partition coefficient from Leo et al. (1971) or the Pomona Database in parenthesis. [3]BUI or Brain Uptake Index (Oldendorf, 1981; Cornford, 1992) measured as a percent first-pass extraction; logBB is calculated from the BUI; na, not available [4]Apparent permeability coefficient (x 10^{-6} cm/sec) calculated from PS value measured in rat using intravenous methods (Levin et al., 1976; Ohno et al., 1978, Takasato et al., 1978). The capillary surface area is assumed to be constant at 240 cm^2/g brain tissue (Ohno et al., 1978) and the time interval is 5 min; logBB is calculated from the P$_{app}$ assuming a 5 min time interval.

Solute	Plasma Conc.[1] μM (ng/ml)	Brain/Plasma %	logBB	PS[2] X 10^{-6} cm^3·g^{-1}·sec^{-1}	P$_{app}$[3] X 10^{-6} cm/sec	Mean % Lost from Plasma[4]	Mean % Bound In Plasma[5]
1 Inulin	97 (4.9x105)	0.24 ± 0.12	-3.15 ± 0.49	3.3 ± 2.1	0.014 ± 0.009	98	0
2 Sucrose	0.17 (59)	0.29 ± 0.15	-2.63 ± 0.37	9.6 ± 5.1	0.040 ± 0.021	90	nd
3 Mannitol	2.7 (493)	0.31 ± 0.07	-2.51 ± 0.57	15.9 ± 10.6	0.066 ± 0.044	90	0
4 Urea	9.2 (555)	7.9 ± 0.5	-1.10 ± 0.03	262 ± 15	1.1 ± 0.064	53	0
5 Acetamide	1.3 (79)	56 ± 1.1	-0.25 ± 0.01	1,868 ± 37	7.8 ± 0.16	25	0
6 Glycerol	0.42 (39)	44 ± 4.6	-0.35 ± 0.04	1,482 ± 153	6.2 ± 0.64	81	0
7 Ethylene glycol	2.8 (176)	44 ± 4.6	-0.35 ± 0.01	1,482 ± 37	6.2 ± 0.15	40	0
8 Water	nd	78 ± 2.4	-0.11 ± 0.01	2,583 ± 81	10.8 ± 0.34	nd	nd
9 Antipyrine	1.7 (320)	82 ± 6.7	0.09 ± 0.09	2,731 ± 222	17.2 ± 3.10	40	23
10 Butanol	6.9 (510)	124 ± 10	0.09 ± 0.03	4,120 ± 320	17.2 ± 1.33	68	12

Table 5. Summary of results from the Mouse Brain Uptake Assay. Mean and standard deviation of N=3 mice. Brain concentration corrected for volume of plasma (16 μL/g brain tissue). [1]At 5 min post-IV dose. [2]Permeability x Surface Area value per gram of brain tissue. [3]Apparent permeability coefficient for flux across the blood-brain barrier is 'P' in PS solved for a capillary surface area of 240 cm^2/g brain tissue (Ohno et al., 1978). [4]Decrease in plasma radioactivity from 5 to 60 min; mean value of N=3. [5]Fraction (x 100) of solute bound to plasma proteins; mean value of N=3.

permeability of hydrophobic solutes; however, this outcome is of minimal impact because we already establish that the solute measured crosses the BBB readily and is only limited by CBF rate. Our modified method is identical to the perfusion method with regard to the accuracy of measuring hydrophilic solutes that cross the BBB very slowly. In contrast, the BUI method tends to overestimate the permeability of these solutes (Figure 4A). The perfusion method is claimed to be 100 times more sensitive than the BUI method (Cornford *et al.*, 1982; Takasato *et al.*, 1984). A brain/plasma ratio at 60 min will be more complicated by back flux, and metabolism unless the parent molecule is quantified chromatographically.

In addition to logBB, which is identical to the brain/plasma ratio (x 100 to give percent), brain uptake of these solutes can be interpreted as a kinetic measurement of permeability. Ohno *et al.* (1978) described a simplification of the single intravenous bolus administration method that estimates the unidirectional transfer constant, or k_i, as an initial rate (Fenstermacher and Rapoport, 1984). We assert here that an even simpler intravenous method can approximate either a PS, or a P_{app} value calculated from the PS value assuming a surface area of 240 cm²/g tissue, by using a 5-min brain/plasma ratio. The P_{app} value is especially important for comparing these *in vivo* results to the P_{app} values measured *in vitro* (Table 6).

The variability of these assay measurements is shown within experiments with triplicate mice per experiment (Table 6). The mice were likely littermates, which could reduce inter-animal variability. Poorly permeating solutes (inulin, sucrose, mannitol) with low brain levels display the most variability at 50% in measuring a mean value. Variability in the mean is typically 2-10% for the more BBB permeable solutes. The consistency of a measured mean value between

Solute	P_{app} x 10^{-6} cm/sec	
	In vivo BBB[1]	In vitro MDR1-MDCK[2]
Inulin	0.014 ± 0.009	0.017 ± 0.002
Sucrose	0.040 ± 0.021	0.15 ± 0.07
Mannitol	0.066 ± 0.044	0.058 ± 0.005
Urea	1.1 ± 0.064	4.4 ± 0.32
Acetamide	7.8 ± 0.16	15 ± 0.2
Glycerol	6.2 ± 0.64	0.44 ± 0.08
Ethylene glycol	6.2 ± 0.15	10 ± 0.6
Water	11 ± 0.34	264 ± 4
Antipyrine	17 ± 3.1	107 ± 1
Butanol	17 ± 1.3	300 ± 7
Testosterone	17 ± 2.5	113 ± 1
2-DG	13 ± 0.50	0.72 ± 0.03
αAIB	1.7 ± 0.061	1.2 ± 0.06
Warfarin	0.87 ± 0.05	17 ± 2.1

Table 6. Apparent permeability coefficients (P_{app}) for solutes *in vivo* and in the MDCK-MDR1 cell monolayer model. [1]Calculated from the 5-min data. [2]apical-to-basal direction only

experiments run on different days was obtained for the highly permeable solute antipyrine where values ranged from 82% to 124%, but with standard deviations of 7-22% these values were relatively consistent. Three other solutes (urea, glycerol, warfarin) were repeated about one year after the initial studies and these mean values were essentially identical or within 20% of each other.

Solute Distribution Volume

A 20% by weight distribution of mannitol in brain at 60 min is an indicator of the extracellular space. If we assume that metabolism is negligible, then mannitol had by this time diffused across the BBB and equilibrated with the water space between the brain parenchymal cells. The rat brain extracellular space is reported to be 10-25% by weight (Van Harreveld, 1966; Woodward *et al.*, 1967) and 17-20% for rabbit, cat, dog, and monkey (Levin *et al.*, 1970), so our data are in good agreement. Distribution of urea, which is smaller in size than mannitol and slightly more hydrophobic, is greater yet at 54% and by 60 min has likely begun to equilibrate with the brain parenchyma intracellular space. However, because we were only monitoring total radioactivity, the contribution by contaminants must be taken into account. In a separate experiment, we used a stock solution of urea that was 32% degraded to unknown products as determined by thin-layer chromatography ($CHCl_3$: methanol: water, 7:5:1) (data not shown). In this case, the 5-min brain distribution was 56% (versus 11% for the newly purchased radiolabel) at 5 min. Thus, it could be argued that by 60 min urea is slightly metabolized in the mouse. Distribution into non-brain tissues was not affected.

Some metabolism of glycerol likely occurred since the 60-min brain levels were very high and distribution in liver was exaggerated (Table 5 and Figure 5). Formation of a metabolite also was consistent with an increase in red blood cell partitioning (K_p) from 0.69 at 5 min to 1.37 at 60 min (data not shown).

Cerebral Blood Flow-Limited Brain Uptake

The limits on brain uptake that are imposed by CBF rate were characterized using five, hydrophobic compounds. Water, antipyrine, and butanol gave a BBB P_{app} maximum of $\sim 10 \times 10^{-6}$ cm/sec (Figure 5). This was equivalent to a brain/plasma ratio of ~ 1.0. The BBB P_{app} plateau is caused by the rapid equilibrium reached between rate in and rate out. Diazepam was used since it has been declared a tracer for CBF with 100% extraction upon first pass (Keller and Waser, 1984). It had fast permeability *in vivo* and *in vitro* under the mixed conditions used showing that the rate-limiting step for transcellular flux is passive diffusion across the unstirred water layer (UWL) (Tables 7 and 8) (Adson *et al.*, 1995; Ho *et al.*, 2000). Diazepam also showed modest accumulation within cells and demonstrated an avidity for brain tissue as defined by its brain/plasma ratio of >1.0. Testosterone is another uncharged, hydrophobic molecule that is used as an indicator solute *in vitro* for passive diffusion across the UWL (Ho *et al.*, 2000). Its' *in vivo* BBB P_{app} was ideally CBF controlled (Figure 5).

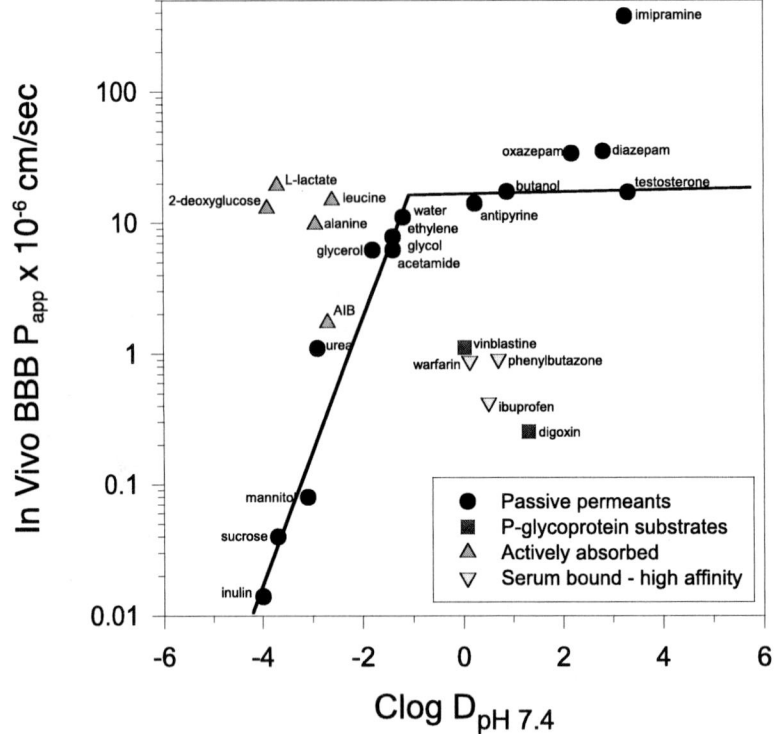

Figure 5. Blood-brain barrier permeability of calibrating solutes measured according to the Mouse Brain Uptake Assay. Mean of three mice. The solid line marks performance of passive permeants. The apparent permeability coefficient (P_{app}) is calculated from the 5-min brain/plasma ratio as described. The measured octanol-buffer (pH 7.4) partition coefficient was used when available or a log D was calculated using PALLAS version 3 software.

Collectively, these compounds define a region of general behavior that we referred to as "blood-flow limited" (Figure 6). The anticonvulsant phenytoin is a simple, hydrophobic compound for which conflicting data exist regarding its interaction with P-gp (Schinkel *et al.*, 1996; Porschka and Loscher, 2001). In our study it behaved *in vivo* as an ideal CBF-controlled solute (Table 7 and Figure 7). Since these are equivalent to water, it was assumed that these molecules reach a distribution volume throughout the brain parenchyma that includes intra- and extracellular space. All gave mean brain levels that were ~0.70-1.4% by weight of the dose.

Performance of Solutes
that are Actively Transported into Brain

Active transport of nutrients from blood-to-brain was measured using the radiolabeled, non-metabolized substrates 2-deoxy-D-glucose (2-DG) and α-aminoisobutyric acid (AIB). 2-DG is transported via the glucose transporter and AIB by the large neutral amino acid (Slc7a5; LAT1) transport system (Pardridge

Compound	Time, min	Plasma, dpm x 10³/mL mean ± sd	Brain, dpm x 10³/g mean ± sd	B/P Ratio[1] mean ± sd	BBB P_{app}[4] x 10⁻⁶ cm/sec mean ± sd
L-Alanine	5	158 ± 14.1	109 ± 7.5	0.67 ± 0.06	9.6 ± 0.8
AZT	5	214 ± 28.9	7.9 ± 2.4	0.032 ± 0.004	0.50 ± 0.09
Caffeine	5	222 ± 11.0	196 ± 36.9	0.80 ± 0.006	8.1 ± 1.2
Cimetidine	5	135 ± 14.2	5.2 ± 1.3	0.034 ± 0.007	0.54 ± 0.14
Diazepam	5	63.6 ± 6.1	199 ± 15.1	3.2 ± 0.04	43 ± 1.1
L-Dopa	5	167 ± 37.8	44.8 ± 2.3	0.30 ± 0.05	3.9 ± 0.8
L-Lactic Acid	5	87.3 ± 10.1	116 ± 7.4	1.4 ± 0.13	19 ± 2.4
L-Leucine	5	101 ± 14.3	105 ± 14.8	1.0 ± 0.15	14 ± 1.9
L-Nicotine	5	25.7 ± 3.7	11.3 ± 1.7	0.51 ± 0.05	6.2 ± 1.4
Phenytoin	5	100 ± 14.6	108 ± 22.7	1.0 ± 0.2	15 ± 2.0
Warfarin	5	305 ± 7.4	19.0 ± 0.80	0.063 ± 0.004	0.87 ± 0.05
Digoxin	5	327 ± 3.7	5.8 ± 3.3	0.018 ± 0.010	0.20 ± 0.10
	60	120 ± 12.9	4.8 ± 0.86	0.040 ± 0.007	
Vinblastine	5	55.1 ± 5.7	4.4 ± 0.9	0.080 ± 0.016	1.1 ± 0.1
	60	7.6 ± 1.2	2.0 ± 0.5	0.26 ± 0.06	
PNU-87201	5	152 ± 19.9	149 ± 19.5	0.98 ± 0.13	9.0 ± 0.6
	60	192 ± 21.1	9.5 ± 4.8	0.049 ± 0.025	
PNU-90152	5	130 ± 54.9	4.5 ± 0.7	0.035 ± 0.005	0.48 ± 0.07
	60	79.3 ± 15.3	2.2 ± 0.8	0.028 ± 0.011	
PNU-101017	5	33.0 ± 12.8	3.8 ± 2.2	0.12 ± 0.07	1.5 ± 0.6
	60	4.4 ± 2.0	1.2 ± 0.5	0.27 ± 0.12	

Table 7. Brain uptake of radiolabeled compounds that are actively and passively absorbed across the blood-brain barrier.
[1]Ratio of the brain/plasma concentrations   [2]Fraction (x 100) of concentration lost from plasma or brain between 5 and 60 min   [4]Apparent permeability coefficient (P_{app}) across the blood-brain barrier (BBB)

and Oldendorf, 1975a; Pardridge and Oldendorf, 1975b; Smith *et al.*, 1987). The 7.5-fold and 5.5-fold increase in C_{brain}/C_{plasma} for 2-DG and AIB, respectively, at 60 min over 5 min is indicative of continued accumulation by active transport despite clearance from the plasma. Their performance at 5 min was plotted relative to solutes of similar hydrophobicity (Figure 5). Solutes with these characteristics diffuse very slowly across the BBB so a transport system is required. Thus, 2-DG is accumulated to levels equivalent to the more hydrophobic solutes antipyrine and butanol and limited by CBF. In contrast, AIB has not yet equilibrated with the brain tissue at 5 min implying a slower transport rate at the dose give. Additional studies with other actively absorbed solutes (leucine, alanine, L-Dopa, lactate) gave similar results (Figures 5 and 7).

Compound	Cell Line	AB P$_{app}$[1]	BA P$_{app}$	BA/AB Ratio	MDR1/WT Ratio	% Cell[2]
Diazepam	Parent	162 ± 18	171 ± 2	1.1	1.0	3.1
	MDR1	153 ± 1	169 ± 2	1.1		3.9
Ibuprofen	Parent	67 ± 4.6	85 ± 0.1	1.3	1.0	0.4
	MDR1	64 ± 3	82 ± 5	1.3		0.5
Imipramine	Parent	62 ± 0.4	73 ± 9.8	1.2	1.3	20
	MDR1	63 ± 8.3	102 ± 3	1.6		19
Oxazepam	Parent	102 ± 2	116 ± 6	1.1	1.0	4.2
	MDR1	98 ± 3.8	118 ± 8	1.2		4.5
Phenylbutazone	Parent	30 ± 1.7	31 ± 0.7	1.0	1.0	0.8
	MDR1	30 ± 0.7	32 ± 1.2	1.1		0.8
Testosterone	Parent	155 ± 7	130 ± 3	1.5	1.0	2.7
	MDR1	147 ± 8	208 ± 2	1.4		2.4
Digoxin	Parent	1.6 ± 0.07	5.8 ± 0.44	3.5	55	0.5
	MDR1	0.10 ± 0.01	19 ± 1.3	192		0.4
Vinblastine	Parent	1.4 ± 0.15	14 ± 1.2	10	38	23
	MDR1	0.076 ± 0.014	29 ± 3.0	376		3.3
Warfarin	Parent	51 ± 1.8	36 ± 3.5	0.7	3.7	0.9
	MDR1	17 ± 2.1	44 ± 1.1	2.6		0.6
PNU-87201	Parent	66 ± 1.8	93 ± 3.8	1.4	1.0	12
	MDR1	62 ± 3.5	94 ± 3.5	1.5		7.0
PNU-90152	Parent	22 ± 1.3	59 ± 2.8	2.6	26	5.4
	MDR1	1.1 ± 0.01	78 ± 5.1	67		0.6
PNU-101017	Parent	17 ± 0.4	50 ± 1.5	3.0	38	13
	MDR1	0.94 ± 0.1	108 ± 5	115		1.2

Table 8. *In vitro* permeabilities for compounds. Mass recoveries were 90-115%.
[1]Apparent permeability coefficient (P$_{app}$) in units of x 10^{-6} cm/sec in forward (AB) and backward (BA) directions [2]Fraction (x 100) of original total mass that was recovered and associated with the cells following methanol extraction

Effect of Plasma Protein Binding on Brain Uptake

Six structurally unique solutes of diverse physical-chemical character were examined because of their different interactions with serum proteins. It is well known that binding can lead to a reduction in free fraction that can reduce the amount of compound that is capable of crossing the BBB on first pass (Tanaka and Mizojiri, 1999). Nevertheless, this simple concept has been plagued with controversy stemming from the observations that brain uptake often exceeds that

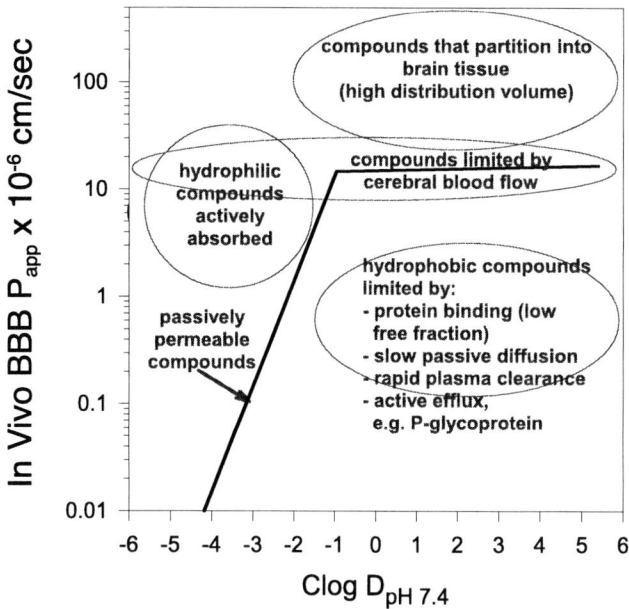

Figure 6. The categorical regions of mechanistic interpretation derived from the behavior of assorted calibrating solutes (see Figure 5) as described in the text. Compounds that diffuse across the blood-brain barrier (BBB) passively are shown by the solid black line. This behavior reaches a maximum where the brain/plasma ratio is ~1 because the rate of efflux equals the rate of influx. This region is limited only by the cerebral blood-flow rate. Compounds that exceed this maximum P_{app} are binding or partitioning into the brain tissue, or rarely within the capillaries themselves. Compounds that are too hydrophilic to diffuse passively and rapidly across the BBB can be actively transported via many different kinds of transport systems. Compounds that are hydrophobic enough to diffuse passively and rapidly across the BBB are often limited by one or a combination of other factors: serum protein binding, poor diffusion within the parenchyma, rapid systemic clearance, or active efflux.

predicted based upon the free fraction that is measured *in vitro*. This led to the free intermediate hypothesis requiring an unknown mechanism for enhanced dissociation *in vivo* (Pardridge, 1981; Pardridge and Landaw, 1984). However, lesser-known data using nonalbuminemic rats with ~5,000 fold lower serum albumin concentrations refute this hypothesis (Dubey *et al.*, 1989; Mendel *et al.*, 1989). It is likely that a non-equilibrium situation exists at the BBB and the partition coefficient of unbound and uncharged compound can favor brain uptake, thus shifting equilibrium away from the plasma protein as occurs in the liver (Weisiger, 1986; Schwab and Goresky, 1996).

Diazepam binds to serum albumin at Site IIIa with a dissociation binding constant (K_d) of 7.7 μM (Epps *et al.*, 1995). This translates to ~99% binding in whole serum with an assumed albumin concentration of 650 μM (Koeplinger *et al.*, 1994). We measured 84% and 91% bound using two different methods. Likewise, brain uptake at 5 min was not apparently limited by the reduction in free fraction

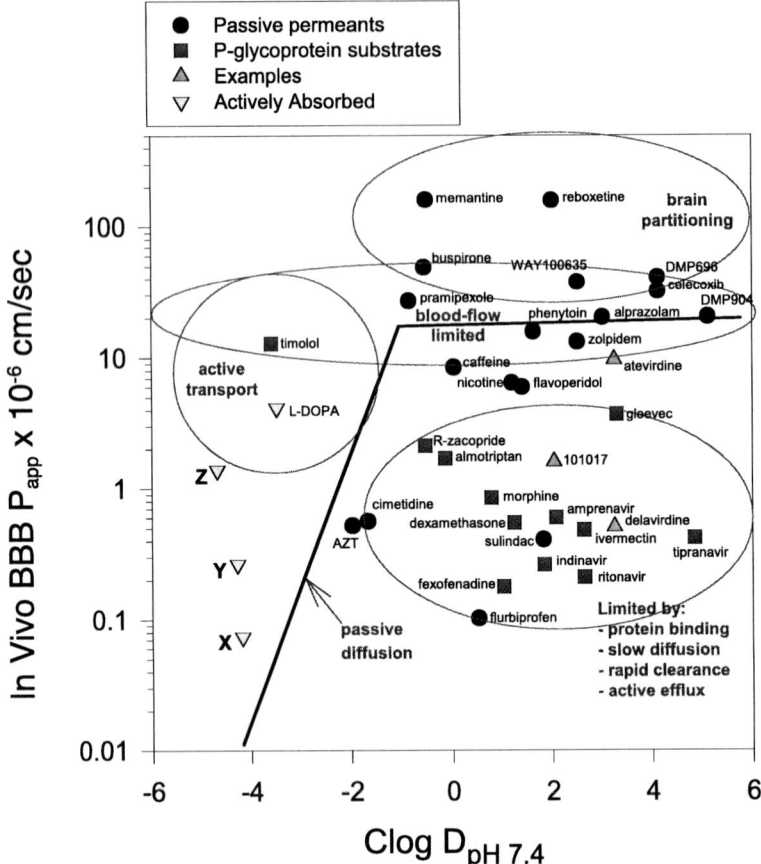

Figure 7. Performance of assorted compounds in the Mouse Brain Uptake Assay. Over 300 compounds have been tested in the full Brain Exposure Assessment over a period of approximately four years. Compounds X, Y and Z are L-arginine-like analogs with increasing affinity for the basic amino acid transporter at the blood-brain barrier.

because of the rapid permeability of the unbound species (Figure 5). Thus, blood-to-brain partitioning was favored in this case. Oxazepam is closely related structurally to diazepam, but is more hydrophilic with the addition of two H-bond donating groups. It was reported that this difference contributes to ~3-fold slower BBB permeability as measured by first-pass extraction in the absence of serum (Jones *et al.*, 1986). The *in vitro* P_{app} measured in our study suggests that although oxazepam is slightly slower than diazepam it is still very fast or UWL limited (Table 8). Oxazepam also has a lower affinity for Site IIIa with a K_d of 28 μM that should translate to a 3-4 fold greater free fraction in whole serum than for diazepam (Epps *et al.*, 1995). This increase in free fraction should offset the slower intrinsic permeability whereby oxazepam and diazepam perform similarly *in vivo* with regard to brain uptake (Figure 5). Arendt *et al.* (1987) reported rat brain/plasma ratios of ~3.3-3.5 for these two, CBF-controlled solutes.

In contrast to these examples, warfarin and the anionic anti-inflammatory drugs and analgesics, ibuprofen and phenylbutazone (PBZ), showed a markedly restricted brain uptake (Figure 5). Warfarin is a weak acid (pK_a = 5.1) at physiological pH and, hence, has a markedly lower log D (0.12) relative to its log P of 2.4. All three compounds gave P_{app} values *in vitro* that exceeded membrane-limited rates; therefore, slow brain uptake was not caused by slow passive diffusion of the negatively charged species at physiological pH (Table 8). These drugs are all tightly bound to serum albumin and, consequently, have very low free concentrations of <0.5% in plasma. Warfarin and PBZ bind to Site IIa with K_d values of 3.4 μM and 1.9 μM, respectively; ibuprofen binds to Site IIIa with a K_d of 2.7 μM (Epps *et al.*, 1995). The high-affinity binding and low free fractions for these three drugs translates to restricted brain uptake as well as low distribution volumes in the mice. The low systemic, distribution volume was suggested by the high plasma concentrations measured at 5 min at this constant, equimolar dose. Both ibuprofen and PBZ gave plasma concentrations that were markedly greater than 4-5 μM whereas most other compounds with unrestricted distribution volumes, or those that can distribute rapidly into tissues, had 5-min plasma concentrations of <2.5 μM.

At the other end of the spectrum is the tricyclic dibenzazepine antidepressant imipramine. Imipramine is a very hydrophobic molecule that is also ~95% bound in serum (Jusko and Gretch, 1976). We measured 93% using ultracentrifugation and *in vitro* methods. However, it binds most tightly to α_1-acid glycoprotein (Riant *et al.*, 1988). Also, despite the apparent serum binding and low free fraction, imipramine shows very rapid brain uptake (Figure 5). In this case, imipramine has a much greater avidity for brain tissue than for the serum proteins as shown by the brain/plasma ratio of 27. This rapid uptake and high distribution volume, despite the degree of binding, has been reported by others (Riant *et al.*, 1988; Sakane *et al.*, 1991). The *in vivo* BBB P_{app} value is in this case unrealistic since brain uptake must be limited by CBF, but tissue binding is dominant. Collectively imipramine, oxazepam, and diazepam define a region of general behavior that we refer to as "brain partitioning" (Figure 6). Because the 5-min plasma concentrations for imipramine were <1 μM, this suggests that the distribution volume is large. This interpretation is consistent with the fast vitro permeability and, in this case, with the excessive partitioning of imipramine with the MDCK cells (Table 8). However, cellular partitioning *in vitro* is not always indicative of brain partitioning (Sawada *et al.*, 1999).

Effect of Vehicle and Vehicle Volume (Aqueous Only) on Blood-Brain Barrier, Brain Plasma Volume, and Brain Blood Flow

In anticipation of using this assay for continued characterization of diverse chemical structures with a wide range of aqueous solubilities, we examined the impact of the solvent or vehicle on blood-brain barrier performance under these assay conditions. Only solutions were dosed. Propylene glycol and DMSO were tested because of their universal use in preclinical testing, their generally good success at solubilizing compounds, and greater LD_{50} values compared to other solvents like ethanol, dimethylformamide, dimethylacetamide, or Tween-20 (Bartsch *et al.*, 1976). Polyethylene glycol 400 also had a higher LD_{50} and is often used for solubilizing compounds, but it was not tested. Propylene glycol and DMSO were compared to unbuffered saline (0.9% NaCl USP, Aqualite®, Abbott Labs, North Chicago, IL) and acidified saline (0.01 N HCl, pH 2.1). A constant injection volume of 50 μL was used per mouse (2 mL/kg) to maintain the vehicle concentrations at ~0.33 x LD_{50}. Mannitol levels in brain versus plasma were used as an indication of a change in plasma volume and/or passive leakage. Antipyrine levels in brain versus plasma were used as an indication of a change in blood flow. Significant changes related to vehicle type were not observed. Brief reactions by the mice to all vehicles, except the saline, were observed immediately after injection, and marked hemolysis occurs with propylene glycol, but none were observed to adversely affect the results. Precipitation of solute during intravenous administration was observed rarely with particularly insoluble compounds. Telltale signs of this occurrence were higher plasma levels at 60 min versus 5 min.

The effect of the injection volume also was examined, but only for saline and its effect on mannitol permeability (BBB integrity and/or plasma volume). The idea was to determine if large injection volumes could compromise BBB integrity through an increase in blood pressure. Pressures of >160-190 mm Hg are reported to damage the BBB (Rapoport, 1976b; Hardebo and Nilsson, 1981). Such volumes could be used in future applications to increase the dose. Volumes from 50 to 200 μL were tested spanning from 3 to 12% of the total blood volume (76 mL/kg) of this size mouse. Neither propylene glycol, the most commonly used vehicle in this assay, nor DMSO were tested because volumes greater than 50 μL would have exceeded the 0.33 x LD_{50} level. There was no effect of these injection volumes of saline on BBB integrity. Studies using up to 300 μL injections of 5% Solutol® (polyethylene glycol 660 12-hydroxystearate; BASF Corp.) in water, 50 μL of 25% Solutol, or 50 μL of Cremophor EL® (polyoxol castor oil; BASF in ethanol (65:35) showed no adverse effects on BBB integrity or blood volume (unpublished results); however, some of these vehicles can effect BBB transporter activities and should be tested prior to use in screening a chemical series. This can be done by measuring brain uptake of radiolabeled digoxin.

Integrated Use of Transport System Knockout Mice

The BBB can prevent CNS candidates from accessing their target sites within the brain, thus determining their apparent activity *in vivo*. P-glycoprotein is a drug efflux pump expressed at the BBB that is a well-known physiological barrier to brain exposure, limiting efficacy, of compounds that are also P-gp substrates (Tamai and Tsuji, 2000; Fromm, 2000). The advent of mdr1a/b knockout mice conclusively showed that P-gp expression at the BBB is a significant barrier to CNS delivery of compounds that happen to be recognized by this efflux pump (Schinkel *et al.*, 1994). Consequently, this required us to have a means to determine when P-gp might be a limiting factor in BBB permeability. Deletion of the mdr1a gene that encodes for the drug efflux P-gp transporter in Friends virus

B (FVB) mice results in a loss of BBB selectivity for P-gp substrates as demonstrated by an elevation in their brain levels. Because the murine equivalent of the human ABCB1 involves two genes, mdr1a (Abcb1a) and mdr1b (Abcb1b), double knockout mice, or mdr1a/b(-/-), were also made (Schinkel *et al.*, 1997). These genes are distributed in tissues differently. mdr1b is expressed mostly in steroid-producing tissues like adrenals, ovary, and gravid uterus. mdr1a is reportedly the relevant drug efflux pump in the brain, as well as the intestine, testis, and placenta (Schinkel *et al.*, 1995).

Use of the mdr1a(-/-) or mdr1a/b(-/-) mice has facilitated a further understanding of the impact that P-gp has on pharmacokinetics, pharmacody-namics, and toxicity of compounds that are P-gp substrates. The first example was the 100-fold increased sensitivity of mdr1a(-/-) mice to the neurotoxin ivermectin (Schinkel *et al.*, 1994). A subpopulation of CF-1 outbred mice was described with a spontaneous recessive mutation in the mdr1a gene resulting in the absence of mdr1a in all tissues (Lankas *et al.*, 1997; Umbenhauer *et al.*, 1997). This mutation follows a normal Mendelian inheritance pattern. Like the FVB transgenic knockouts, these mice also showed altered pharmacokinetics and distribution of P-gp substrates including a large increase in brain exposure (Kwei *et al.*, 1999). Their primary advantage over the FVB transgenic mdr1a(-/-) and mdr1a/b(-/-) mice is their much lower cost. The mdr1a(-/-) mice are an essential tool for delineating the mechanistic role that P-gp plays *in vivo* after the *in vitro* assays have identified a compound as a P-gp substrate. This information confers confidence in a decision to ignore or address P-gp as a key issue within the program team.

Phenotype of P-glycoprotein-deficient Mice

The mdr1a(-/-), mdr1b(-/-), and mdr1a/b(-/-) mice are reported to develop normally and to be viable and fertile with few profound phenotypic effects attributed to loss of P-gp expression (Schinkel *et al.*, 1997). The physiological function of P-gp remains speculative (Schinkel, 1997). Aside from the obvious changes in cellular barrier properties due to the absence of P-gp-mediated efflux, only one other system effect has been reported, and the details of this are only now becoming understood. Panwala *et al.* (1998) reported that some FVB mdr1a/b(-/-) mice develop severe, spontaneous intestinal inflammation when maintained under specific pathogen-free animal facility conditions. This was proposed to be a model for human Inflammatory Bowel Disease. Later, it was reported that mdr1a appears to influence the development of intestinal intraepithelial lymphocyte subpopulations; thus, its absence results in an imbalance of T cell subsets, but not total number of T cells or T cell function (Eisenbraun and Miller, 1999; Eisenbraun *et al.*, 2000). P-glycoprotein is not apparently involved in presentation of antigenic peptides (Russ *et al.*, 1998).

Another interesting function was recently reported, but its significance remains to be determined. Mice deficient in the npc1 gene are a model for Niemann-Pick type C disease, which is a progressive neurological disease hallmarked by aberrant cholesterol storage in the liver. These mice also happen to be sterile due to lack of implantation (Erickson *et al.*, 2002). Using the proposed link between cholesterol homeostasis and P-gp, the npc1(-/-) mice were crossed with the mdr1a(-/-), but this had only one curious effect that did not alter disease progression; the female double knockouts became fertile. Although the reason is unknown, P-gp is thought to be involved in transport of numerous hormones including those involved in reproduction (Schinkel, 1997).

We use the CF-1 subpopulation of mdr1a(-/-) mice that are spontaneously deficient in P-gp (Lankas *et al.*, 1997; Umbenhauer *et al.*, 1997). Pippert and Umbenhauer (2001) showed that this P-gp deficiency is caused by a truncation of the mRNA due to a deleted exon 23. The deletion occurred because of aberrant splicing caused by the insertion of 8.35 kb of DNA from murine leukemia virus. One concern of single gene knockout is that collateral biochemical pathways also are altered to compensate for the loss. It had been reported that mdr1b gene expression was increased in the livers of FVB mdr1a(-/-) mice, thus raising concerns that studies extrapolating hepatic events related to P-gp, like bile elimination, could be misleading (Schinkel *et al.*, 1994). Differential expression of the rodent mdr1 isotypes in brain remains controversial. There are conflicting results that mdr1b mRNA is not expressed in mouse or rat brain (Croop *et al.*, 1989; Schinkel *et al.*, 1995; Kwan *et al.*, 2003). Kwan *et al.* (2003) showed using quantitative PCR that mdr1b mRNA is expressed in hippocampus of rat brain, but not in other brain regions. P-gp also is expressed by non-endothelial cells within the brain parenchyma (Lee and Bendayan, 2004). Uhr *et al.* (2002) suggested that mdr1b expression by parenchymal cells in mice contributes to the pharmacology of endogenous steroid hormones; however, pharmacologic evidence is lacking. The implications of this hypothesis are two fold. First, P-gp may modulate substrate activity through altered distribution volume within the brain in addition to limiting access to the brain while crossing the BBB. This had been proposed by Golden and Pardridge (2000). Second, use of the mdr1a(-/-) mouse model may miss the putative effects of mdr1b P-gp in CNS. In other words, intracerebral expression of mdr1b P-gp in the mdr1a(-/-) mice could still potentially impact target exposure.

Moreover, mdr1b P-gp expression (and mdr2) in the livers of CF-1 mdr1a(-/-) mice appears to be normal (Umbenhauer *et al.*, 1997; Pippert and Umbenhauer, 2001). Expression of efflux transporters from other gene families has not yet been explored exhaustively. There are no changes in expression of cftr (Abcc7), mrp1 (Abcc1), oct1 (Slc22a1), spgp (Abcb11), or mdr2 (Abcb2) in mdr1a/b(-/-) mice (Schinkel *et al.*, 1997).

Another potential difference in P-gp knockout mice relative to normal mice is expression levels of Cytochrome P450 (Cyp) enzymes. Schuetz *et al.* (2000) reported that the mdr1a gene dose was inversely proportional to Cyp3A protein expression in the liver. However, this conclusion was made with substantial heterogeneity among the genotypes and oddly was dependent upon environmental factors as determined by the location in which the mice were housed. Perloff *et al.* (1999) determined that Cyp3A levels in FVB mdr1a/b(-/-) mice were unaffected. Likewise, Kwei *et al.* (1999) showed that CF-1 mdr1a(-/-) mice had unchanged levels of Cyp3A and Cyp2B compared to heterozygous mice. This latter study did detect slight 1.3-2 fold increases in NADPH-cytochrome C reductase and glutathione s-transferase activities in mdr1a(-/-) female mice only. Thus, the CF-1 mdr1a(-/-) mouse appears to be a valuable model with few, if any, cautionary drawbacks identified so far.

Validation of mdr1a(-/-) and mdr1a(+/+) mice in the Mouse Brain Uptake Assay: Passive Diffusion and Active Uptake

We first established that these two subpopulations of mice behaved similarly to normal mice with regard to BBB integrity and general activity. Four solutes (inulin, urea, glycerol, antipyrine) that cross the BBB passively and with different rates due to their different hydrophobicities were tested and the results compared to data obtained in wild-type mice (data not shown). The results were the same in all three, mouse populations indicating that overexpression and absence of P-gp has no effect on the physical integrity of the BBB. The studies with the four passive diffusants included four other tissues: liver, heart, and lung. Tissue distribution was examined at 5 min as a function of plasma concentration. All solutes behaved equivocally in the mdr1a(-/-) and mdr1a(+/+) mice relative to heterozygous mice.

Brain uptake of 2-DG also was unchanged implying that physiological function, with respect to glucose transport, was unaffected by P-gp expression. The 2-DG and antipyrine data indicate that CBF was unaffected by P-gp expression. Degnais *et al.* (2000) reported similar conclusions using in situ brain perfusion of glucose, diazepam, and sucrose or inulin. In a different study, Degnais *et al.* (2001) showed that gender had no effect on the outcome of such brain uptake studies. Caution is recommended, however, when considering gender differences as related to P-gp transport. For example, a recent paper suggested that the often-described higher hepatic elimination in females might be attributed to lower P-gp expression in the livers of females (Meibohm *et al.*, 2002).

Examples of Interpreting the Data from the Brain Exposure Assessment

The Cardiac Glycoside Digoxin

Digoxin (DXN) is a well-known P-gp substrate with clinical ramifications of drug-drug interactions involving P-gp inhibition (Koren *et al.*, 1998). The MDCK-MDR1 AB P_{app} was 0.10 x 10^{-6} cm/sec with very low cell partitioning and the MDR1/WT BA/AB P_{app} ratio was 55 (Table 8). This confirmed DXN as a P-gp substrate. Thus, the *in vitro* P_{app} for MDCK-MDR1 is similar to the *in vivo* BBB P_{app} of 0.20 x 10^{-6} cm/sec (Table 7). However, inhibition of P-gp efflux *in vitro* using CsA only increased the P_{app} to 3.0 x 10^{-6} cm/sec. These data show that although P-gp contributes to slow BBB permeability, slow passive diffusion likely contributes to slow brain uptake (Figure 5). Low free fraction also may play a role since DXN plasma binding results indicated that it is 91% bound.

The relative contribution of P-gp alone was demonstrated by repeating these experiments in P-gp knockout or mdr1a(-/-) mice. Digoxin was dosed at 3.9 mg/kg giving plasma concentrations of 4.2 ng/mL (5.4 nM) at 5 min. Plasma clearance was decreased in the mdr1a(-/-) mice, since the percent change in plasma concentration from 5 to 60 min was 76% for the mdr1a(+/+) and only 27% for the mdr1a(-/-) mice (Figure 8A). The clearance in the mdr1a(+/+) was slightly faster than the 63% measured in heterogygous mice. Consequently, the ratio of plasma concentrations in mdr1a(-/-) versus mdr1a(+/+) increased with time from 0.66 to 2.0 and 2.4 for 5, 60 and 120 min, respectively. These data exemplify a rare situation where P-gp efflux contributes to the systemic clearance of a P-gp substrate. Using a physiologically-based pharmacokinetics model, Kawahara *et al.* (1999) reported a 2.8-fold decrease in total clearance of DXN in mdr1a(-/-)versus mdr1a(+/+) mice. This is likely attributed to a decrease in P-gp-mediated excretion of DXN across the intestinal mucosa, rather than to a decrease in biliary or renal elimination (Schinkel *et al.*, 1997; van Asperen *et al.*, 1996; Kawahara *et al.*, 1999).

Brain levels of DXN in the mdr1a(-/-) mice continued to increase with time (Figure 8B). Similar results were reported elsewhere using the FVB mouse strain (Mayer *et al.*, 1996; Schinkel *et al.*, 1995; Schinkel *et al.*, 1997). Removal of P-gp

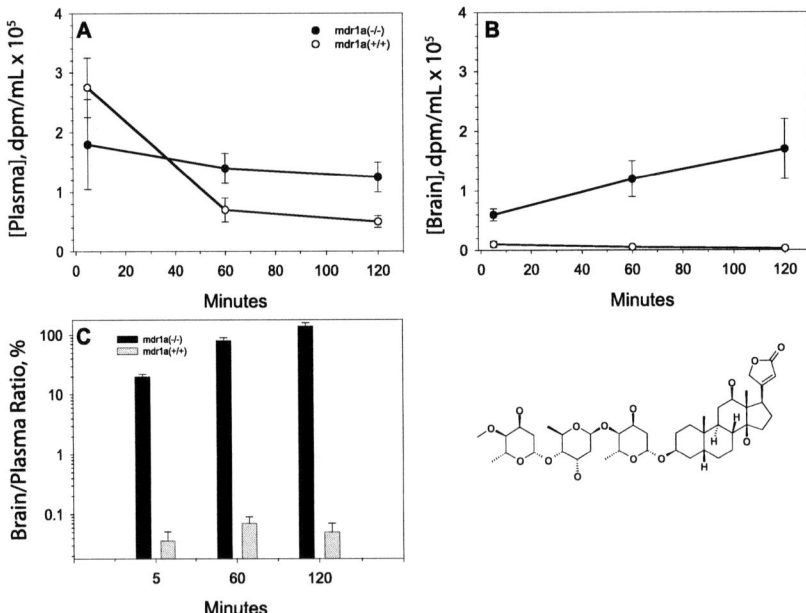

Figure 8. Digoxin (chemical structure shown) levels in plasma (A) and brain (B) at times after intravenous dosing mdr1a(-/-) (•) and mdr1a(+/+) (○) mice. (C) Ratio of concentrations of brain to plasma (x100 to give %) in mdr1a(-/-) (black) and mdr1a(+/+) (gray) mice. Values (mean ± standard deviation; N=3) were measured using HPLC and radiodetection.

increased BBB permeability of DXN 16 fold, but BBB penetration was still only ~25% of CBF-limited uptake (Table 3). Figure 9 illustrates the relative change in brain uptake as defined previously using calibration standards of defined behavior. Thus, brain uptake of DXN via passive diffusion was still slow as indicated by the P_{app} of 2.8×10^{-6} cm/sec in the mdr1a(-/-) mice and in the absence of active efflux and slower systemic loss, brain levels continued to increase with time. This *in vivo* P_{app} value is similar to the intrinsic P_{app} value of 3.0×10^{-6} cm/sec that was obtained using MDCK-MDR1 cells in the presence of the P-gp inhibitor CsA (Table 9). The intrinsic P_{app} value is the passive diffusion of the solute in the absence of active transport. Thus, there is good correlation between the *in vivo* and *in vitro* results in the presence and absence of P-gp. The ratio of relative brain uptake (e.g., brain/plasma ratio) in mdr1a(-/-) versus mdr1a(+/+) increased from 21 to 91 and 117 at 5, 60 and 120 min, respectively (Figure 8C).

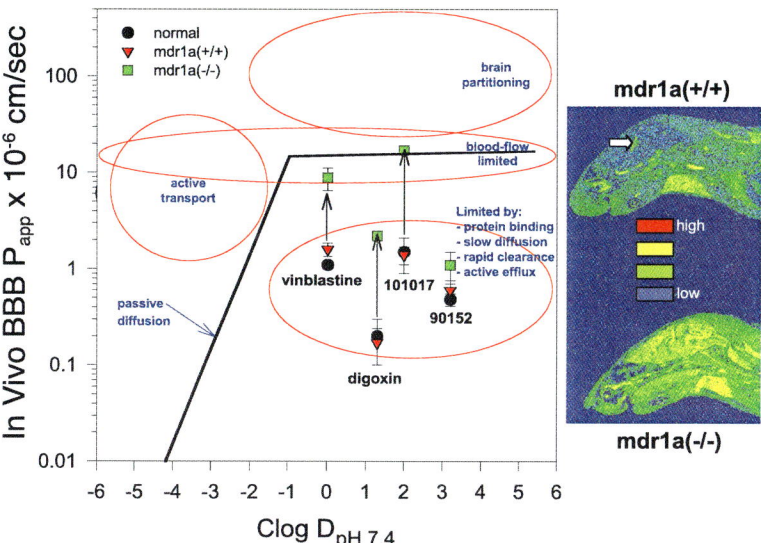

Figure 9. Performance of four P-glycoprotein substrates in heterozygous (•), wild-type (▼) and P-glycoprotein-deficient (■) CF-1 mice. Mean (± standard deviation; N=3) blood-brain barrier (BBB) apparent permeability coefficients (P_{app}) are plotted as a function of the calculated octanol-water partition coefficient at pH 7.4. The solid line represents the behavior of solutes that cross the BBB via passive diffusion as defined in Figure 5. Distribution of a tritiated P-gp substrate in the head region of mice is shown 1 hour after intravenous dose. Compound is excluded from brain in the mdr1a(+/+) mice except for discrete regions (arrow) representing choroid plexus. Images are autoradiograms of cryosections exposed to film that were color digitized to enhance radioactive distribution. Image is courtesy of Margarette Schuette and Ben Amore, legacy Pharmacia Corp.

In vitro – In vivo **Relationship**

It should be counter-intuitive to expect that the MDCK cell assay results will be directly related to the permeability coefficient calculated from the MBUA. This is because the *in vivo* BBB permeability is not only determined by passive diffusion, but also active efflux, systemic clearance, and blood component binding (serum proteins and RBC partitioning). Two papers address the ability of the *in vitro* permeability assays to predict *in vivo* performance. The Merck group showed

Compound	MDCK Cell Line	P_{app}[1] x 10^{-6} cm/sec	% Cell[2]
Vinblastine	WT	3.0 ± 0.2	40
	MDR1	1.9 ± 0.1	36
Digoxin	WT	3.1 ± 0.2	0.6
	MDR1	3.0 ± 0.2	0.8
PNU-87201	WT	83 ± 4	7.9
	MDR1	80 ± 3	8.6
PNU-90152	WT	39 ± 1.7	6.4
	MDR1	24 ± 1.8	6.9
PNU-101017	WT	30 ± 1.3	17
	MDR1	17 ± 1.2	7.2

Table 9. *In vitro* intrinsic passive permeability as measured in the presence of Cyclosporin A to inhibit P-glycoprotein-mediated efflux. [1]Mean value for both directions in the presence of 5 μM Cyclosporin A when the BA ratio is <2.5. [2]Mean fraction (x 100) cell associated after flux in either direction.

for a select group of compounds that polarized flux (BA/AB ratio) across P-gp expressing porcine LLC-PK1 cells correlated well to either brain/plasma concentration ratios at 30 minutes or ratios of the area under the brain concentration versus time curves (AUC_{brain}) from 0 to 60 min for mdr1a(-/-)/(+/+) CF-1 mice (Yamazaki *et al.*, 2001; Hochman *et al.*, 2002). Their data suggested that for certain compounds, mouse P-gp was a better predictor (<3 fold) than human P-gp of performance in mouse. These are the only published data implying that there may be species differences in binding affinities for some substrates. In a slightly different approach with equally promising conclusions, the Sugiyama group compared *in vitro* flux ratios using the same cells (sans the mouse P-gp) to a ratio of the brain/plasma ratios in the mdr1a/b(-/-)/normal FVB mice (Adachi *et al.*, 2001). When we plot our data for ten compounds the same way as described in Adachi *et al.* (2001), the relationship is not so obvious (Figure 10). There was no difference whether the 5-min or 60-min in-vivo data were used. Four of the compounds, including vinblastine and PNU-90152 (see below), were appreciably serum bound, so the *in vivo* ratios were underestimated. Correction for the unbound fraction grossly over exaggerated the results. Thus, for compounds with slow diffusion and low serum binding, there is good *in vitro-in vivo* correlation.

The Antitumor Agent Vinblastine

The Vinca alkaloid anticancer compound vinblastine (VNB) had a MDR1 AB P_{app} of 0.076×10^{-6} cm/sec and the MDR1/WT ratio was 38 confirming it as a P-gp substrate (Table 8). The intrinsic AB P_{app} of 1.9×10^{-6} cm/sec is more similar to the *in vivo* BBB P_{app} of $1.6 \pm 0.25 \times 10^{-6}$ cm/sec (Figure 5). Grieg *et al.* (1990) first reported that VNB was less permeable than expected based upon its hydrophobicity. VNB was ~2-fold slower in our MBUA in the presence of whole blood than reported by Grieg *et al.* (1990) in the absence of blood, and we determined VNB to be 95-99% bound in plasma. Thus, BBB permeability is partly limited by serum

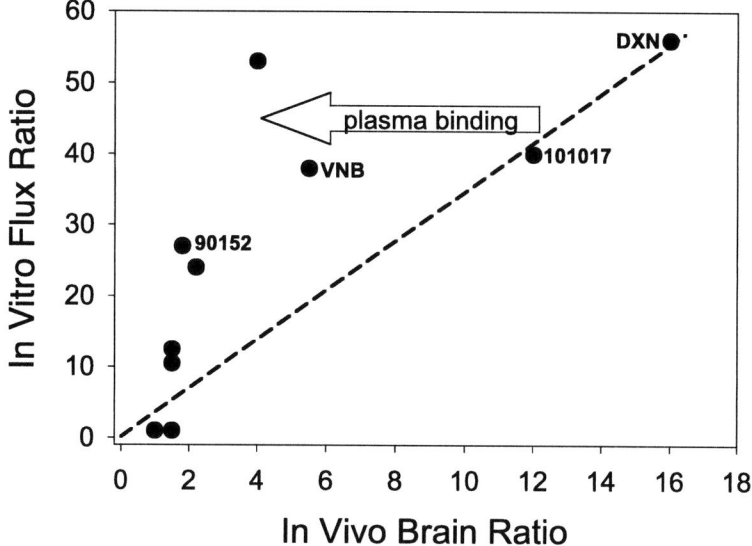

Figure 10. *In vitro-in vivo* correlation according to Adachi et al. (2001). "*In vivo* Brain Ratio" is the ratio of the brain/plasma ratios for mdr1a(-/-) to mdr1a(+/+) mice at 5-min post-intravenous dose. "*In vitro* Flux Ratio" is the BA/AB ratio of the MDCK-MDR1 to MDCK-parent cells. DXN, digoxin; VNB, vinblastine. The dotted line is an arbitrary reference line.

binding and slow passive diffusion, but P-gp efflux is likely the major limiting factor.

Again, the relative contribution of P-gp alone was demonstrated by repeating these experiments in P-gp knockout or mdr1a(-/-) mice. Vinblastine was dosed at 11 mg/kg giving plasma concentrations of 4.8 ng/mL (5.9 nM) at 5 min. Within 5 min, only 38-40% of the total radioactivity in the plasma was parent compound indicating rapid metabolism occurred. Without this correction, the most noticeable effect was an overestimation of brain levels (not statistically different, however) at the longest (120 min) time point (data not shown). Plasma loss of parent compound was 88% over 1 h in the mdr1a(-/-) and 89% in the mdr1a(+/+) mice. The ratio of plasma concentrations in mdr1a(-/-) vs. mdr1a(+/+) was constant at 0.73 to 0.84 and 1.1 for 5, 60 and 120 min, respectively. These data show that systemic clearance of VNB is not dominated by a P-gp efflux mechanism as was DXN clearance. This contrasts the increase in half-life caused by loss of Pgp and reported by van Asperen *et al.* (1996). This difference is explained by the importance of the terminal phase of plasma clearance, which we did not collect data for; the van Asperen *et al.* (1996) study showed no difference in initial clearance profiles.

Unlike DXN, brain levels of VNB in the mdr1a(-/-) mice remained constant or decreased slightly with time. Removal of P-gp increased BBB permeability of VNB 5.4 fold which is ~80% of CBF (Figure 9). Thus, brain uptake of VNB via passive diffusion is fast as indicated by the P_{app} of 8.8×10^{-6} cm/sec in the mdr1a(-/-) mice and this value is faster than the intrinsic P_{app} value of 1.9×10^{-6} cm/sec that was obtained using MDCK-MDR1 cells in the presence of the P-gp inhibitor CsA (Table 9). This could be explained because of favored partitioning into brain tissue, which is consistent with brain/plasma ratios that continued to increase from 0.63 to 5.8 with time. Cell partitioning in MDCK cells also was high or ~38% when P-gp was inhibited. BBB permeability of VNB in the absence of P-gp is partly limited by serum binding confirming that P-gp efflux is the major limiting factor to brain uptake.

Such data have proven helpful in anticipating and identifying compounds as P-gp substrates on many Discovery Program teams. The prevalence of this efflux pump activity across a wide diversity of therapeutic areas and chemical structures is amazing! The significance of these findings must be placed into context of the observed or expected *in vivo* pharmacologic and/or toxicologic activity. It also is still a challenge to interpret these data relative to similar rate limiting parameters in humans.

Comparing Two, Structurally Related HIV-1 Reverse Transcriptase Inhibitors

Atevirdine (PNU-87201) and delavirdine (PNU-90152) are very similar structurally, but had different behaviors *in vitro* and *in vivo* (Figure 11). Both were highly plasma bound at 96-98%. PNU-87201 had fast AB P_{app} in the MDCK-MDR1 without P-gp efflux (Table 8); thus, rapid brain penetration was observed despite the high plasma binding (Figure 7). In contrast, *in vitro* permeability of PNU-90152 was markedly slower in the MDCK-MDR1 with a MDR1/WT ratio of 26 confirming it is a P-gp substrate (Table 8). Accordingly, brain penetration was very slow with a BBB P_{app} of 0.48×10^{-6} cm/sec (Figure 7), or 19-fold slower than atevirdine. Thus, substitution of the ether for a sulfonamide conferred P-gp-mediated transport efficiency. A similar example distinguishes two structurally-related neurokinin-1 receptor antagonists where a terminal methylated sulfonamide confers P-gp recognition (Smith *et al.*, 2001).

When the relative contribution of P-gp on PNU-90152 brain uptake was assessed by repeating these experiments in mdr1a(-/-) mice, the dominant impact of transport was not as obvious (Figure 9). mdr1a(+/+) mice and mdr1a(-/-) mice were dosed at 0.85 mg/kg to give equivocal plasma concentrations at 5 min of 230-270 ng/mL (500-600 nM). Brain levels were elevated in mdr1a(-/-) mice and decreased with time in both strains in proportion to loss from plasma, but removal

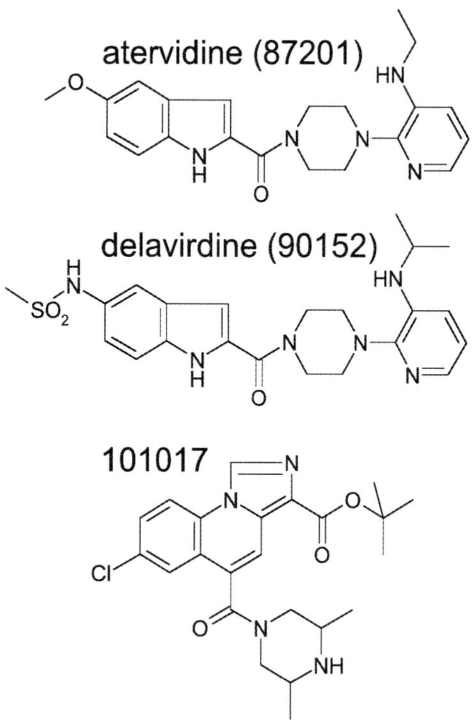

Figure 11. Chemical structures for two HIV reverse transcriptase inhibitors, atervidine (PNU-87201) and delavirdine (PNU-90152), and a GABAA receptor partial agonist (PNU-101017) developed by Pharmacia Corp. See text for explanation of performance in the Brain Exposure Assessment.

of P-gp only increased BBB permeability 1.8 fold (Figure 9). Brain uptake via passive diffusion was slow as indicated by the BBB P_{app} of 1.1 x 10^{-6} cm/sec in the mdr1a(-/-) mice (Table 7) and this value was much slower than the intrinsic P_{app} value obtained using MDCK-MDR1 cells in the presence of the P-gp inhibitor CsA (Table 9). Limited brain uptake is attributed to the marked reduction in free plasma concentration caused by plasma protein binding and P-gp only slightly enhances that rate-limited scenario.

A Saturating P-glycoprotein Substrate

The GABAA receptor partial agonist PNU-101017 was shown to be a P-gp substrate *in vitro* (Table 8). Not surprisingly, brain penetration was slow (Table 7; Figure 7). Performance in mdr1a(+/+) mice and mdr1a(-/-) mice, confirmed that P-gp efflux was the rate-limiting step to brain exposure (Figure 9). Removal of P-gp increased BBB permeability 12 fold restoring brain uptake to a CBF-limited situation commensurate with its intrinsic passive diffusion (Table 9). The data also show that the blood-brain equilibration is unaffected despite this compound being 94% plasma bound (Figure 9). The ideal behavior of PNU-101017 allowed for dose-dependent increase in BBB P_{app}. This reflects the ability of PNU-101017 to

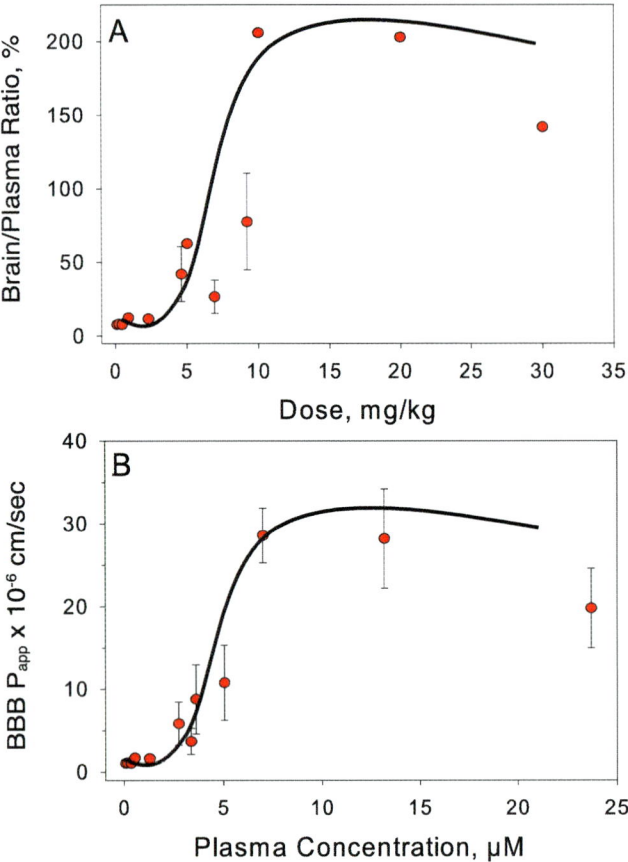

Figure 12. Saturation of P-glycoprotein at the blood-brain barrier by PNU-101017, a GABA receptor partial agonist (A) Brain/plasma ratio increases with increase in intravenous dose reaching a maximum ratio at 10 mg/kg. (B) The same relationship is seen for BBB P_{app} as total plasma levels increase. Mice were visibly stressed at the 30 mg/kg dose.

saturate the P-gp pump *in vivo* resulting in the ~3 fold increase in brain exposure between an intravenous dose of 7.5-10 mg/kg, or a total plasma concentration of 3-4 μM (Figure 12). This has implications for low dose scenarios, particularly imaging ligands administered at very low doses, or in manifestation of CNS toxicity at higher doses.

Applications of the Brain Exposure Assessment to Drug Discovery Issues

Comparing Across and Within Chemical Series

There are two basic uses of this strategy in supporting projects. One is to compare the performance of representative compounds from multiple scaffolds. Each scaffold often will demonstrate a unique pattern when plotted as defined in

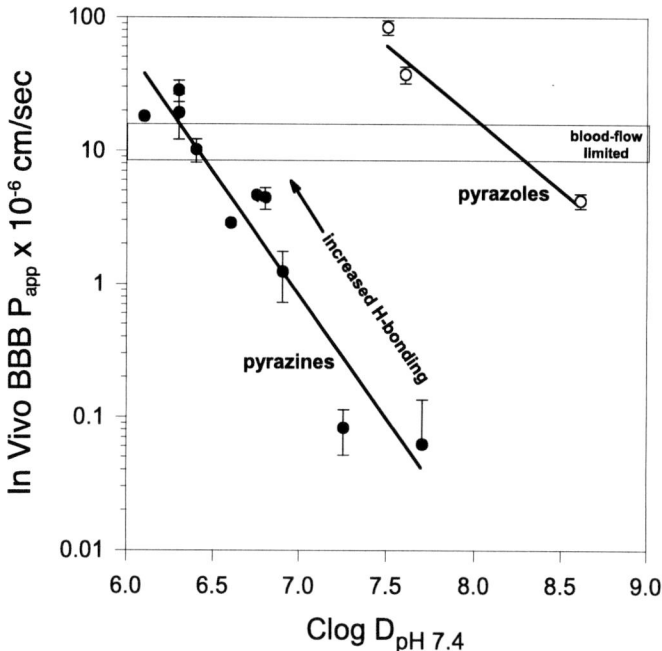

Figure 13. Example application of the Mouse Brain Uptake Assay demonstrating how relative performance within and across scaffolds can be helpful. Brain uptake of the highly-hydrophobic pyrazine series was inversely related to hydrophobicity (ClogD). Addition of one or more H-bonding groups, e.g., ethers, hydroxyls, improved brain uptake by increasing aqueous solubility and decreasing plasma protein binding.

Figure 6. Such clustering is expected since overall physicochemical attributes should be similar. Of course, deviation of individual compounds from the rest of the group is a telltale sign of a structural effect on one or more of the parameters that contribute to brain uptake. This represents the other basic use where the effects of chemistry within a scaffold can be explored to look for intended changes positively or negatively. One example of this use is shown in Figure 13. Here two chemical scaffolds, pyrazoles and pyrazines, show different performances. The earliest tested pyrazines gave very slow brain uptake. This was in part the result of poor aqueous solubility as brain levels continued to increase between 5 and 60 min indicating precipitation upon injection (data not shown). Note that these scaffolds are very lipophilic with unrealistically high, calculated log P values. As a consequence, the *in vitro* permeability assay results were invalid due to excessive buffer/cell partitioning (data not shown). Pharmacological activity of the pyrazines as measured by an ex vivo binding method was lacking or poor. Both brain uptake and *in vivo* activity of the pyrazines improved as simple substitutions with weak hydrogen bonding groups, e.g., ethers, were made (Figure 13).

Optimizing Active Blood-Brain Barrier Absorption

The MBUA is sensitive enough to distinguish chemistry for a scaffold that crosses the BBB by active transport. Figure 7 shows the 5-minute brain uptake rates for three analogs (X, Y, Z) structurally related to L-arginine. Passive diffusion of these compounds in the MDCK permeability assay was very slow at $\leq 1 \times 10^{-6}$ cm/sec. Each has a different apparent affinity for the basic amino acid System y^+ transport system (Slc7a family) expressed at the BBB (Stolle *et al.*, 1993). The apparent affinities were measured using an *in vitro* screen with a non-brain cell type and compound dose-dependently inhibited the initial uptake of radiolabeled arginine. Thus, compound X had the weakest affinity with an IC_{50} of >5 mM and showed the slowest brain uptake. Compounds Y and Z showed incrementally improved brain uptake with an increase in transporter affinity as predicted by their IC_{50} values of 580 μM and 291 μM, respectively.

Switching of Rate Limiting Factors During Lead Optimization

A similar application involved lead optimization of kynurenine-like analogs to increase brain exposure for improved pharmacological activity (Figure 14). Compounds A and B are amino acid in character so that their ability to cross the BBB is dependent upon active transport. Both compounds were actively transported *in vitro* by LAT1 (Slc7a5) (Table 10). The k_{exp} and C_{max} values for phenylalanine and kynurenine uptake kinetics were similar between MDCK parent cells and primary cultures of bovine brain microvessel endothelial cells (Table 10). However, their relative affinities for LAT1 were weak and thought to be insufficient to compete with endogenous substrates for the BBB LAT1. This was evident from the slow brain uptake as measured at 5 min (Figure 14). Accordingly, compound B gave a slow P_{app} value in the MDCK assay (Table 11). One way to increase brain levels of these amino acid analogs was to improve passive diffusion using a prodrug. Compound C, the methylester of Compound A, had fifty fold faster passive permeability *in vitro* and markedly improved brain uptake (Figure 14). The prodrug approach was abandoned due to instability following oral dosing. Thus, the α-amino group was removed to improve passive permeability and a subsequent loss in dependence upon active transport to cross the BBB (Table 10). While these compounds (D and E) showed fifty fold increases in passive diffusion *in vitro*, they also were bound to serum albumin with much greater affinity (Table 11). This resulted in markedly greater plasma concentrations of total compound because the distribution volume decreased. The drastic decrease in free compound as a result of the high-affinity binding (K_d <10 μM) to serum albumin limited brain uptake despite the increase in passive diffusion. Total brain levels within 5 min were >70% of the free concentration in plasma demonstrating the rapid equilibration of plasma free compound with brain. Even continuous infusion over four hours was insufficient to increase brain levels substantially (results not shown). Correction of the apparent P_{app} value, calculated using the total plasma concentration, for the free plasma fraction showed that brain uptake of compound E was CBF limited as expected for a small molecule with such fast passive diffusion (Figure 14). Although removal of the carboxylic acid as in compound G resulted in loss of target activity, it did improve brain uptake/exposure markedly (Figure 14). Compound G had rapid passive diffusion,

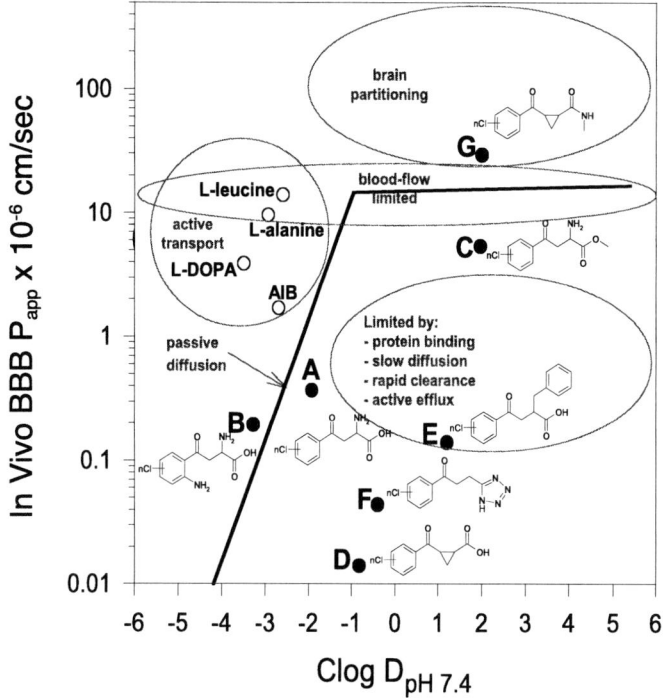

Figure 14. Example application of the Mouse Brain Uptake Assay defining structural-related shifts in rate-limiting steps to brain uptake of a series of kynurenine analogs. Compounds A and B are amino acids with very slow passive diffusion and poor affinity for Lat1 (see Tables 10-11). Compound C is the methylester prodrug of compound A. Compounds D-F are acid analogs lacking the α-amino group so that Lat1 recognition is lost and passive diffusion increases ~50 fold. Compounds D-F are bound to albumin with high affinity. Compound G is the methylamide analog of compound D where affinity for albumin was markedly decreased (Table 11).

but also was bound to albumin with much less affinity (Table 11). It also was substantially more lipophilic as shown by the measured, octanol/pH 7.4 partition coefficient. So, despite lower total plasma concentrations, compound G had brain levels that were much greater than free plasma concentration (Table 11). Thus, sufficiently potent inhibitors within this chemistry space with adequate exposure were never achieved to demonstrate dose-relevant pharmacological activity *in vivo*.

P-glycoprotein-Mediated Active Efflux

This *in vitro-in vivo* approach is useful for discerning when chemistry results in recognition by active efflux transporter systems expressed at the BBB. Figure 15 shows fragments of three scaffolds with identical R and R' groups that were active against the same target. All clustered with similar behavior in the MBUA where brain uptake is rapid. Simple addition of a hydroxyl group to one of these scaffolds resulted in a 25-fold decrease in brain uptake (Figure 15). The

Inhibitors	MDCK Cells		BBME Cells	
	K_i, μM	V_i, pmole $\cdot$ $mg^{-1} \cdot min^{-1}$	K_i, μM	V_i, pmole $\cdot$ $mg^{-1} \cdot min^{-1}$
L-Phe	5.0 ± 0.1	45	1.8 ± 0.1	15
L-Ala	3950 ± 190	53 ± 3	4700 ± 800	23
DL-Kyn	49 ± 3	46	382 ± 106	13
L-Dopa	26 ± 1	66		
Compound A[1] (S)	129 ± 22	50		
Compound A (R)	659 ± 130	54 ± 2	775 ± 103	24
Compound B (S)	83 ± 8	53 ± 1	135 ± 17	24
Compound D	855 ± 127	52		

Table 10. Inhibition of $[^{14}C]$L-Phenylalanine uptake by parent MDCK and bovine brain microvessel endothelial (BBME) cells. [1]See generic structures for, A, B, and D in Figure 14. R- and S- isomers are shown where appropriate

Compound	log D pH 7.4	HSA[1] K_d, μM	fb[2]	P_{app},[3] nm/sec	B/P[4] At 5 min	C_{plasma}, nmole/mL		C_{brain}, nmole/g
						Total	Free	
B[5]	-1.6	33	0.94	10	0.025	41	2.3	0.8
D	-0.6	8	0.993	490	0.005	158	1.1	0.8
G	2.0	23	0.90	1360	2.1	10	1.1	22

Table 11. *In vitro* and *in vivo* data for kynurenine-like analogs. [1]Dissociation binding constant for fatty-acid free human serum albumin measured using tryptophan fluorescence quenching (Epps et al., 1999). [2]Fraction bound in mouse plasma determined using ultracentrifugation. [3]In vitro apparent permeability coefficient (AB) measured in MDCK parent cell line. [4]Brain/plasma ratio at 5 min measured in Mouse Brain Uptake Assay. Concentrations in plasma and brain are shown. Free concentration calculated based upon the fraction bound. [5]See generic structures for B, D and G in Figure 14.

concomitant *in vitro* permeability assay showed that this analog was hyper-polarized in the MDCK-MDR1 cell line with a MDR1/WT ratio of the BA/AB ratios of 9. This identification as a P-gp substrate, and the asymmetry (5.6 fold) seen in the WT cell line where P-gp (canine) expression is marked reduced, suggested that this analog was efficiently pumped by P-gp *in vitro* and *in vivo*. Performance in the mdr1a(-/-) mice confirmed that P-gp was the rate-limiting factor to slow brain uptake and lower brain exposure of this analog (Figure 15).

Guiding Structure-Permeability Relationships When P-glycoprotein-Mediated Efflux is Rate Limiting

A scaffold whose brain exposure is plagued by P-gp efflux can be monitored using the *in vitro* and *in vivo* assays to identify structural moieties that confer or diminish efficient P-gp-mediated transport. The *in vitro* assay is a first-tier

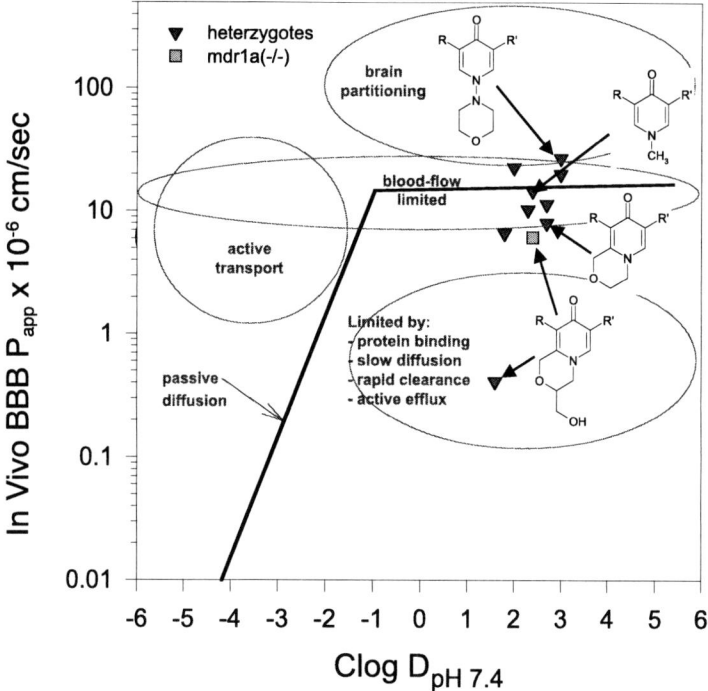

Figure 15. Example application of the Mouse Brain Uptake Assay illustrating how simple structural modifications can markedly impact brain uptake. A structurally-related series (R and R' groups are identical) representing progressive lead optimization shows similar blood-flow limited brain uptake except for the hydroxylated analog. The *in vitro* P-gp Substrate Assay confirmed this as a substrate and dosing in the mdr1a(-/-) P-gp-deficient mice restored brain uptake equal to parent compound.

approach whose capacity can be increased using cassette dosing. The parameters within the assay that effect pump efficiency are passive diffusion and buffer/cell partitioning in addition to molecular interaction between pump and substrate. As passive diffusion increases, pump efficiency decreases. Pump efficiency can decrease too when passive diffusion becomes so slow that access of compound to pump is rate limiting. Membrane partitioning can have a positive effect on P-gp-mediated transport such that local concentration at the pump is increased. Consequently, each of these effects must be considered when interpreting the effect associated with chemistry around a scaffold. Experience tells us that it is best to begin by surveying the extremes of chemistry space within the scaffold so that boundaries of behavior are identified. One should not limit the compounds tested to only those with potent activity, so that a chemistry space bias is not imposed. Once the boundaries are identified, testing of analogs should be purposeful with distinct moiety comparisons to probe microdomains of the scaffold. Examples are demonstrated for a scaffold represented in Figure 16. Substitutions around X and Y either had no effect or some impact on buffer/cell partitioning, but P-gp efflux was unaffected. Secondary substitutions on X, especially those with H-bonding capacity to increase activity, tended to decrease passive diffusion and buffer/cell

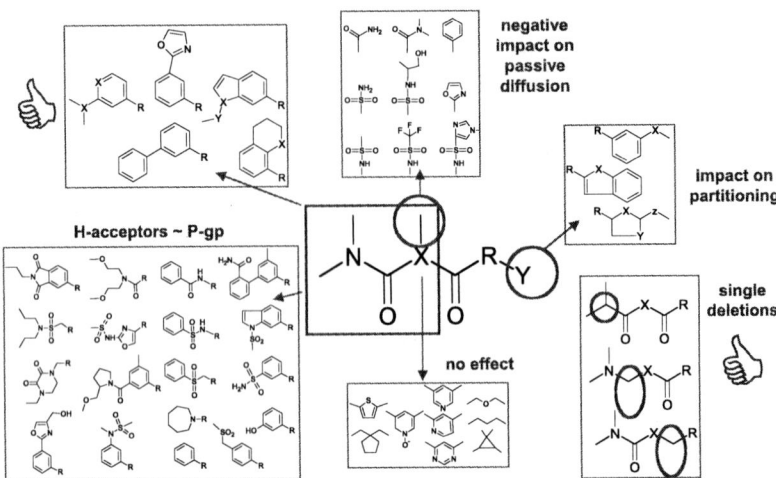

Figure 16. A chemical scaffold can be systematically dissected by iterative testing in the *in vitro* and *in vivo* assays. Single group deletions showed positive effects on lowering P-gp-mediated efflux while increasing brain uptake. This along with other selective moiety substitutions allowed for the identification of a dominant microdomain contributing to apparent P-gp interaction and selection of alternate heterocycles in place of the boxed region.

partitioning, but did not alter net P-gp efflux. Single deletions, as shown here for nitrogens and carbonyls, can be helpful to pinpoint dominating positive effects on P-gp efficiency. It this case, the results implicated a need to pursue different heterocycles where those with fewer H-bonding groups resulted in lowered P-gp-mediated efflux.

As one applies the *in vitro* assay, it is imperative that the results be interpreted relative to *in vivo* performance. In the instance depicted in Figure 16, the rate of brain uptake was limited by P-gp-mediated efflux. This was confirmed by demonstrating rapid brain uptake in mice that are deficient in P-gp. A portion of the compounds that showed lessened P-gp-mediated efflux *in vitro* were tested in the *in vivo* MBUA with the expectation that the moiety changes would result in an increase in rate of brain uptake. In this case, we targeted a BBB P_{app} value of ~4 x 10^{-6} cm/sec, or a brain/plasma ratio of ~0.3 (Figure 17). The range of this series had been profiled by testing compounds that were inactive, but were likely to define the boundaries for behavior of this scaffold. Using the MBUA 5-minute measurement along with 3-in-1 cassette dosing, iterative testing aided chemistry towards the several 2nd generation scaffolds that showed marked improvement in brain uptake (Figure 17). The increased permeability was confirmed to coincide with an increase in distribution volume using concomitant imaging. Selected analogs representing the scaffolds were tritiated, dosed in mice, and total radioactivity imaged using whole-body autoradiography. HPLC-radiodetection also was done to confirm that brain-associated radioactivity was predominantly parent compound. Distribution of compound throughout the parenchyma was important for establishing that increased permeability assured access to the target. In this case, the target was intracellular, which required a preferred larger distribution

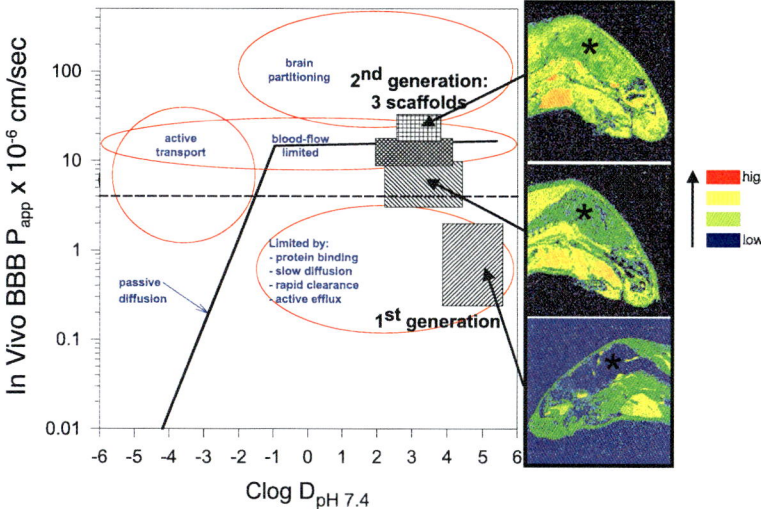

Figure 17. The example in Figure 16 enabled a redirection of chemistry from 1st to 2nd generation compounds with improved brain uptake. Not only was blood-brain barrier permeability increased, but brain distribution volume was, too. This is illustrated in the digitized images of autoradiograms from heads of heterozygous CF-1 mice that were dosed intravenously 30 minutes before with three different, tritiated analogs; one 1st generation compound and two 2nd generation compounds, but from two of three scaffolds. The progressive increase in brain-localized radioactivity (*) is correlated with the Mouse Brain Uptake Assay results.

volume. This exemplifies the value of applying imaging methods earlier in the discovery process.

Final Remarks

The simple, single intravenous dose design of the MBUA is a reliable and sensitive method to accurately estimate the unidirectional rate constant, or apparent permeability coefficient, for a solute to cross the BBB. Calibrating studies used solutes to profile the effects of active uptake, blood-flow rate, serum protein binding, excessive blood-to-brain partitioning, and P-gp active efflux. The MBUA is also flexible so that transgenic and gene-knockout mice, such as the mdr1a-deficient strains, can be directly compared to better understand the role of efflux transport systems in compound distribution. MDCK-MDR1 cells are shown to have a dynamic range and intrinsic characteristics that prove useful as an *in vitro* model of the BBB. Lastly, the MBUA, MDCK-MDR1 cells, and an estimate of plasma binding are key components of the Brain Exposure Assessment strategy to support preclinical development of new compounds. This strategy identifies the rate limiting factors contributing to brain uptake and can be used for iterative optimization of lead series to improve or decrease brain exposure.

Acknowledgements

This work was conducted at the Pharmacia Corporation between 1998-2003 with portions presented at the 2003 V^{th} Cerebral Vascular Biology Conference in Amarillo, Texas. We thank the many people over the years who contributed to the evolution and application of this assay strategy: Jenny Boller, Natalia Borg (Post-doctoral Scientist working with Per Garberg at former Pharmacia-Stockholm), Jeff Day, Kellie Franks, Sandy Kuentzel (retired), Sally Mattern, and Ellen Vera. We thank many former colleagues, who are now scattered about, for discussions. We appreciate Dr. Kathleen M. Hillgren, PhD, for critically reading the manuscript.

References

Adachi Y, Suzuki H, Sugiyama Y (2001) Comparative studies on *in vitro* methods for evaluating *in vivo* function of MDR1 P-glycoprotein. *Pharm. Res.* 18: 1660-1668.

Adson A, Burton PS, Raub TJ, Barsuhn CL, Audus KL, Ho NFH (1995) Passive diffusion of weak organic electrolytes across Caco-2 cell monolayers: uncoupling the contributions of hydrodynamic, transcellular and paracellular barriers. *J. Pharm. Sci.* 84: 1197-1204.

Arendt RM, Greenblatt DJ, Liebisch DC, Luu MD, Paul SM (1987) Determinants of benzodiazepine brain uptake: lipophilicity versus binding affinity. *Psychopharmacology* 93:72-76.

Atkinson F, Cole S, Green C, van de Waterbeemd H (2002) Lipophilicity and other parameters affecting brain penetration. *Curr. Med. Chem.- Central Nerv. Sys. Agents* 2: 229-240.

Bartsch W, Sponer G, Dietmann K, Fuchs G (1976) Acute toxicity of various solvents in the mouse and rat. *Arzneim.-Forsch.* 26(8): 1581-1583.

Blasberg RG, Patlak CS, Fenstermacher JD (1983) Selection of experimental conditions for the accurate determination of blood-brain transfer constants from single-time experiments: a theoretical analysis. *J. Cerebr. Blood Flow Metab.* 3: 215-225.

Bonate PL (1995) Animal models for studying transport across the blood-brain barrier. *J. Neurosci. Methods* 56: 1-15.

Caldwell GW, Ritchie DM, Masucci JA, Hageman W, Yan Z (2001) The new preclinical paradigm: compound optimization in early and late phase drug discovery. *Curr. Topics Med. Chem.* 1: 353-366.

Clark DE (2003) *In silico* prediction of blood-brain barrier permeation. *Drug Discov. Today* 8: 927-933.

Cornford EM, Braun LD, Oldendorf WH, Hill MA (1982) Comparison of lipid mediated blood-brain barrier permeability in the newborn and adult brain. *Am. J. Physiol.* 243: C161-C168.

Croop JM, Raymond M, Haber D, Devault A, Arceci RJ, Gros P, Housman DE (1989) The three mouse multidrug resistance (mdr) genes are expressed in a tissue-specific manner in normal mouse tissues. *Mol. Cell Biol.* 9: 1346-1350.

Dagenais C, Rousselle C, Pollack GM, Scherrmann JM (2000) Development of an in situ mouse brain perfusion model and its application to mdr1a P-glycoprotein-deficient mice. *J. Cereb. Blood Flow Metab.* 20: 381-386.

Dagenais C, Zong J, Ducharme J, Pollack GM (2001) Effect of mdr1a P-glycoprotein gene disruption, gender, and substrate concentration on brain uptake of selected compounds. *Pharm. Res.* 18: 957-963.

Dash AK, Elmquist WF (2003) Separation methods that are capable of revealing blood-brain barrier permeability. *J. Chromatogr. B Analyt Technol Biomed Life Sci.* 797: 241-254.

Davies B, Morris T (1993) Physiological parameters in laboratory animals and humans. *Pharm. Res.* 10: 1093-1095.

de Boer A, Gaillard PJ (2002) *In vitro* models of the blood-brain barrier: when to use which? *Curr. Med. Chem.-Central Nerv. Sys. Agents* 2: 203-209.

de Lange EC, Danhof M (2002) Considerations in the use of cerebrospinal fluid pharmacokinetics to predict brain target concentrations in the clinical setting: implications of the barriers between blood and brain. *Clin. Pharmacokinet.* 41: 691-703.

Dubey RK, McAllister CB, Wilkinson GR (1989) Plasma binding and transport of diazepam across the blood-brain barrier: no evidence for *in vivo* enhanced dissociation. *J. Clin. Invest.* 84:1155-1159.

Ecker GF, Noe CR (2004) *In silico* prediction models for blood-brain barrier permeation. *Curr. Med. Chem.* 11: 1617-1628.

Eisenbraun MD, Miller RA (1999) mdr1a-encoded P-glycoprotein is not required for peripheral T cell proliferation, cytokine release, or cytotoxic effector function in mice. *J. Immunol.* 163: 2621-2627.

Eisenbraun MD, Mosley RL, Teitelbaum DH, Miller RA (2000) Altered development of intestinal intraepithelial lymphocytes in P-glycoprotein-deficient mice. *Dev. Comp. Immunol.* 24: 783-795.

Epps DE, Raub TJ, Kezdy FJ (1995) A general, wide-range spectrofluorometric method for measuring the site-specific affinities of ligands toward human serum albumin. *Anal. Biochem.* 227: 342-350.

Epps DE, Raub TJ, Caiolfa V, Chiari A, Zamai M (1999) Determination of the affinity of drugs toward serum albumin by measurement of the quenching of the intrinsic tryptophan fluorescence of the protein. *J. Pharm. Pharmacol.* 51: 41-48.

Erickson RP, Kiela M, Devine PJ, Hoyer PB, Heidenreich RA (2002) mdr1a deficiency corrects sterility in Niemann-Pick C1 protein deficient female mice. *Mol. Reprod. Dev.* 62: 167-173.

Fenstermacher JD, Blasberg RG, Patlak CS (1981) Methods for quantifying the transport of drugs across brain barrier systems. *Phamacol. Ther.* 14: 217-248.

Fenstermacher JD, Rapoport SI (1984) Blood-brain barrier, In Handbook of Physiology. Section 2: The Cardiovascular System, Renkin EM, Michel CC, eds. Bethesda, MD: *Am. Physiol. Soc.*, pp. 969-1000.

Ferte J (2000) Analysis of the tangled relationships between P-glycoprotein-mediated multidrug resistance and the lipid phase of the cell membrane. *Eur. J. Biochem.* 267: 277-294.

Fromm MF (2000) P-glycoprotein: a defense mechanism limiting oral bioavailability and CNS accumulation of drugs. *Int. J. Clin. Pharmacol. Therap.* 38: 69-74.

Garberg P, Ball M,Berg N, Cecchelli R, Fenart L, Hurst RD, Lindmark T, Mabondzo A, Nilsson JE, Raub TJ, Stanimirovic D, Terasaki T, Öberg J-O, Österberg T (2004) *In vitro* models for the blood–brain barrier. *Toxicol. In vitro* 19:299-334.

Golden PL, Pardridge WM (2000) Brain microvascular P-glycoprotein and a revised model of multidrug resistance in brain. *Cell. Mol. Neurobiol.* 20: 165-181.

Greig NH, Soncrant TT, Shetty U, Momma S, Smith QR, Rapoport SI (1990) Brain uptake and anticancer activities of vincristine and vinblastine are restricted by their low cerebrovascular permeability and binding to plasma constituents in rat. *Cancer Chemother. Pharmacol.* 26: 263-268.

Gumbleton M, Audus KL (2001) Progress and limitations in the use of *in vitro* cell cultures to serve as a permeability screen for the blood-brain barrier. *J. Pharm. Sci.* 90: 1681-1698.

Hardebo JE, Nilsson B (1981) Opening the blood-brain barrier by acute elevation of intracarotid pressure. *Acta Physiol. Scand.* 111: 43-49.

Ho NFH, Raub TJ, Burton PS, Barsuhn CL, Adson A, Audus KL, Borchardt RT (2000) Quantitative approaches to delineate passive transport mechanisms in cell culture monolayers, In *Transport Processes in Pharmaceutical Systems*, Gordon GL, Lee PI, Topp EM, eds. New York: Marcel Dekker, pp. 219-316.

Hochman JH, Yamazaki M, Ohe T, Lin JH (2002) Evaluation of drug interactions with P-glycoprotein in drug discovery: *in vitro* assessment of the potential for drug-drug interactions with P-glycoprotein. *Curr. Drug Metab.* 3: 257-273.

Jones DR, Hall SD, Branch RA, Jackson EK, Wilkinson GR (1986) Plasma binding and brain uptake of benzodiazepines. In *Protein Binding and Drug Transport, Vol. 20*, Symposia Medica Hoechst, Tillement, J-P, Lindenlaub, E, eds. FK Schattauer-Verlag: Stuttgart, pp. 311-324.

Jusko WJ, Gretch M (1976) Plasma and tissue protein binding of drugs in pharmacokinetics. *Drug Metab. Rev.* 5:43-140.

Kawahara M, Sakata A, Miyashita T, Tamai I, Tsuji A (1999) Physiologically based pharmacokinetics of digoxin in mdr1a knockout mice. *J. Pharm. Sci.* 88: 1281-1287.

Keller F, Waser PG (1984) Brain pharmacokinetics of centrally acting drugs, a quantitative autoradiographic study. *Arch. Int. Pharmacodyn. Ther.* 267: 200-212.

Koeplinger KA, Raub TJ, Padbury GE, Zhao Z (1999) Equilibrium distribution of HIV antiviral drugs into human peripheral blood mononuclear cells (PBMC) is controlled by free drug concentration in the extracellular medium. *J. Pharm. Biomed. Anal.* 19: 399-411.

Koren G, Woodland C, Ito S (1998) Toxic digoxin-drug interactions: the major role of renal P-glycoprotein. *Vet. Hum. Toxicol.* 40: 45-46.

Kwan P, Sills GJ, Butler E, Gant TW, Brodie MJ (2003) Differential expression of multidrug resistance genes in naive rat brain. *Neurosci. Lett.* 339: 33-36.

Kwei GY, Alvaro RF, Chen Q, Jenkins HJ, Hop CEAC, Keohane CA, Ly VT, Strauss JR, Wang RW, Wang Z, Pippert TR, Umbenhauer DR. (1999) Disposition of ivermectin and cyclosporin A in CF-1 mice deficient in mdr1a P-glycoprotein. *Drug Metab. Dispos.* 27: 581-587.

Lankas GR, Cartwright ME, Umbenhauer D (1997) P-glycoprotein deficiency in a subpopulation of CF-1 mice enhances avermectin-induced neurotoxicity. *Toxicol. Appl. Pharmacol.* 143: 357-365.

Lee G, Bendayan R (2004) Functional expression and localization of P-glycoprotein in the central nervous system: relevance to the pathogenesis and treatment of neurological disorders. *Pharm. Res.* 21: 1313-1330.

Leo A, Hansch C, Elkins D (1971) Partition coefficients and their uses. *Chem. Revs.* 71: 525-615.

Levin VA, Fenstermacher JD, Patlak CS (1970) Sucrose and inulin space measurements of cerebral cortex in four mammalian species. *Am. J. Physiol.* 219: 1528-1533.

Martin I (2004) Prediction of blood-brain barrier penetration: are we missing the point? *Drug Discov. Today* 9: 161-162.

Mayer U, Wagenaar E, Beijnen JH, Smit JW, Meijer DK, van Asperen J, Borst P, Schinkel AH (1996) Substantial excretion of digoxin via the intestinal mucosa and prevention of long-term digoxin accumulation in the brain by the mdr 1a P-glycoprotein. *Br. J. Pharmacol.* 119: 1038-1044.

Meibohm B, Beierle I, Derendorf H (2002) How important are gender differences in pharmacokinetics? *Clin. Pharmacokinet.* 41: 329-342.

Mendel CM, Cavalieri RR, Gavin LA, Pettersson T, Inoue M (1989) Thyroxine transport and distribution in nagase analbuminemic rats. *J. Clin. Invest.* 83: 143-148.

Norinder U, Haeberlein M (2002) Computational approaches to the prediction of the blood-brain distribution. *Adv. Drug Deliv. Rev.* 54: 291-313.

Ohno K, Pettigrew KD, Rapoport SI (1978) Lower limits of cerebrovascular permeability to nonelectrolytes in the conscious rat. *Am. J. Physiol.* 235(3): H299-H307.

Oldendorf (1981) Clearance of radiolabeled substances by brain after arterial injection using a diffusable internal standard. *Res. Methods Neurochem.* 5: 91-112.

Panwala CM, Jones JC, Viney JL (1998) A novel model of inflammatory bowel disease: mice deficient for the multiple drug resistance gene, mdr1a, spontaneously develop colitis. *J. Immunol.* 161: 5733-5744.

Pardridge WM, Oldendorf WH (1975a) Kinetics of blood-brain barrier transport of hexoses. *Biochim. Biophys. Acta* 382: 377-392.

Pardridge WM, Oldendorf WH (1975b) Kinetic analysis of blood-brain barrier transport of amino acids. *Biochim. Biophys. Acta* 401: 128-136.

Pardridge WM (1981) Transport of protein-bound hormones into tissues *in vivo*. *Endocrine Revs.* 2:103-123.

Pardridge WM, Landaw EM (1984) Tracer kinetic model of blood-brain barrier transport of plasma protein-bound ligands. *J. Clin. Invest.* 74:745-752.

Pardridge WM (2004a) Log(BB), PS products and *in silico* models of drug brain penetration. *Drug Discov. Today* 9: 392-393.

Pardridge WM (2004b) Holy grails and *in vitro* blood-brain barrier models. *Drug Discov. Today* 9: 258.

Perloff MD, von Moltke LL, Cotreau MM, Greenblatt DJ (1999) Unchanged cytochrome P450 3A (CYP3A) expression and metabolism of midazolam, triazolam and dexamethasone in mdr(-/-) mouse liver microsomes. *Biochm. Pharmacol.* 57: 1227-1232.

Pippert TR, Umbenhauer DR (2001) The subpopulation of CF-1 mice deficient in P-glycoprotein contains a murine retroviral insertion in the mdr1a gene. *J. Biochem. Mol. Toxicol.* 15: 83-89.

Polli JW, Wring SA, Humphreys JE, Huang L, Morgan JB, Webster LO, Serabjit-Singh CS (2001) Rational use of *in vitro* P-glycoprotein assays in drug discovery. *J. Pharmacol. Exp. Ther.* 299: 620-628.

Porschka H, Loscher W (2001) *In vivo* evidence for P-glycoprotein-mediated transport of phentoin at the blood-brain barrier of rats. *Epilepsia* 42: 1231-1240.

Rapoport SI (1976a) *Blood-Brain Barrier in Physiology and Medicine.* New York: Raven Press.

Rapoport SI (1976b) Opening of the blood-brain barrier by acute hypertension. *Exp. Neurol.* 52: 467-479.

Reichel A, Begley DJ, Abbott NJ (2003) An overview of *in vitro* techniques for blood-brain barrier studies. *Methods Mol. Med.* 89: 307-324.

Riant P, Urien S, Albengres E, *et al.* (1988) Effects of the binding of imipramine to erythrocytes and plasma proteins on its transport through the rat blood-brain barrier. *J. Neurochem.* 51:421-425.

Robinson PJ (1990) Measurement of blood-brain barrier permeability. *Clin. Exp. Pharmacol. Physiol.* 17: 829-840.

Russ G, Ramachandra M, Hrycyna CA, Gottesman MM, Pastan I, Bennink JR, Yewdell JW (1998) P-glycoprotein plays an insignificant role in the presentation of antigenic peptides to CD8+ T cells. *Cancer Res.* 58: 4688-4693.

Sakane T, Nakatsu M, Tamamoto A, Hashida M, Sezaki H, Yamashita S, Nadai T (1991) Assessment of drug disposition in the perfused rat brain by statistical moment analysis. *Pharm. Res.* 8: 683-689.

Sawada GA, Ho NFH, Williams LR, Barsuhn CL, Raub TJ (1994) Transcellular permeability of chlorpromazine demonstrating the roles of protein binding and membrane partitioning. *Pharm. Res.* 11: 665-673.

Sawada GA, Barsuhn CL, Lutzke BS, Houghton ME, Padbury GE, Ho NFH, Raub TJ (1999) Increased lipophilicity and subsequent cell partitioning decrease passive transcellular diffusion of novel, highly-lipophilic antioxidants. *J. Pharm. Exper. Therap.* 288:1317-1326.

Schinkel AH, Smit JJM, van Tellingen O, Beijnen JH, Wagenaar E, van Deemter L, Mol CAAM, van der Valk MA, Robanus-Maandag EC, te Riele HPJ, Berns AJM, Borst P (1994) Disruption of the mouse mdr1a P-glycoprotein gene leads to a deficiency in the blood-brain barrier and to increased sensitivity to drugs. *Cell* 77: 491-502.

Schinkel AH, Wagenaar E, van Deemter L, Mol CA, Borst P (1995) Absence of the mdr1a P-glycoprotein in mice affects tissue distribution and pharmacokinetics of dexamethasone, digoxin, and cyclosporin A. *J. Clin. Invest.* 96: 1698-1705.

Schinkel AH, Wagenaar E, Mol CA, van Deemter L (1996) P-glycoprotein in the blood brain barrier of mice influences the brain penetration and pharmacological activity of many drugs. *J. Clin. Invest.* 97: 2517-2524.

Schinkel AH (1997) The physiological function of drug-transporting P-glycoproteins. *Semin. Cancer Biol.* 8: 161-170.

Schinkel AH, Mayer U, Wagenaar E, Mol CA, van Deemter L, Smit JJ, van der Valk MA, Voordouw AC, Spits H, van Tellingen O, Zijlmans JM, Fibbe WE, Borst P (1997) Normal viability and altered pharmacokinetics in mice lacking mdr1-type (drug-transporting) P-glycoproteins. *Proc. Natl. Acad. Sci. USA* 94: 4028-4033.

Schuetz EG, Umbenhauer DR, Yasuda K, Brimer C, Nguyen L, Relling MV, Schuetz JD, Schinkel AH (2000) Altered expression of hepatic cytochromes P-450 in mice deficient in one or more mdr1 genes. *Mol. Pharmacol.* 57: 188-197.

Schwab D, Fischer H, Tabatabaei A, Poli S, Huwyler J (2003) Comparison of *in vitro* P-glycoprotein screening assays: recommendations for their use in drug discovery. *J. Med. Chem.* 46: 1716-1725.

Schwab AJ, Goresky CA (1996) Hepatic uptake of protein-bound ligands: effect of an unstirred Disse space. *Am. J. Physiol.* 270 (Gastointest. Liver Physiol. 33): G869-G880.

Seelig A, Landwojtowicz E (2000) Structure-activity relationship of P-glycoprotein substrates and modifiers. *Eur. J. Pharm. Sci.* 12: 31-40.

Smith BJ, Doran AC, Mclean A, Tingley III FD, O'Neill BT, Kajiji SM (2001) P-glycoprotein efflux at the blood-brain barrier mediates differences in brain disposition and pharmacodynamics between two structurally related neuoroknin-1 receptor antagonists. *J. Pharmacol. Exper. Therap.* 298: 1252-1259.

Smith QR, Momma S, Aoyagi M, Rapoport SI (1987) Kinetics of neutral amino acid transport across the blood-brain barrier. *J. Neurochem.* 49: 1651-1658.

Smith QR (1989) Quantitation of blood-brain barrier permeability. In *Implications of the blood-brain barrier and its manipulation*, Neuwelt EA, ed. New York: Plenum Press, Vol. 1, pp. 85-118.

Stein WD (1997) Kinetics of the multidrug transporter (P-glycoprotein) and its reversal. *Physiol. Rev.* 77:545-590.

Stolle J, Wadhwani KC, Smith QR (1993) Identification of the cationic acid transporter (System y+) of the rat blood-brain barrier. *J. Neurochem.* 60: 1956-1959.

Takasato Y, Rapoport SI, Smith QR (1984) An in situ brain perfusion technique to study cerebrovascular transport in the rat. *Am. J. Physiol.* 247: H484-H493.

Tamai I, Tsuji A (2000) Transporter-mediated permeation of drugs across the blood-brain barrier. *J. Pharm. Sci.* 89: 1371-1388.

Tanaka H, Mizojiri K (1999) Drug-protein binding and blood-brain barrier permeability. *J. Pharm. Exper. Therap.* 288: 912-918.

Terasaki T, Ohtsuki S, Hori S, Takanaga H, Nakashima E, Hosoya K (2003) New approaches to *in vitro* models of blood-brain barrier drug transport. *Drug Discov. Today* 8:944-954.

Uhr M, Holsboer F, Muller MB (2002) Penetration of endogenous steroid hormones corticosterone, cortisol, aldosterone and progesterone into the brain is enhanced in mice deficient for both mdr1a and mdr1b P-glycoproteins. *J. Neuroendocrinol.* 14: 753-759.

Umbenhauer DR, Lankas GR, Pippert TR, Wise LD, Cartwright ME, Hall SJ, Beare CM (1997) Identification of a P-glycoprotein-deficient subpopulation in the CF-1 mouse strain using a restriction fragment length polymorphism. *Toxicol. Appl. Pharmacol.* 146: 88-94.

van Asperen J, Schinkel AH, Beijnen JH, Nooijen WJ, Borst P, van Tellingen O (1996) Altered pharmacokinetics of vinblastine in Mdr1a P-glycoprotein-deficient mice. *J. Natl. Cancer Inst.* 88: 994-999.

van de Waterbeemd H, Camenisch G, Folkers G, Chretien JR, Raevsky OA (1998) Estimation of blood-brain barrier crossing of drugs using molecular size and shape, and H-bonding descriptors. *J. Drug Target.* 6: 151-65.

Van Harreveld A (1966) *Brain Tissue Electrolytes*. London: Butterworths Inc.

Weisiger RA (1986) Non-equilibrium drug binding and hepatic drug removal. In *Protein Binding and Drug Transport, Vol. 20, Symposia Medica Hoechst*, Tillement, J-P, Lindenlaub, E, eds. FK Schattauer-Verlag: Stuttgart, pp. 293-310.

Woodward DL, Reed DJ, Woodbury DM (1967) Extracellular space of rat cerebral cortex. *Am. J. Physiol.* 212: 367-370.

Yamazaki M, Neway WE, Ohe T, Chen I, Rowe JF, Hochman JH, Chiba M, Lin JH (2001) *In vitro* substrate identification studies for p-glycoprotein-mediated transport: species difference and predictability of *in vivo* results. *J. Pharmacol. Exp. Ther.* 296: 723-735.

Youdim KA, Avdeef A, Abbott NJ (2003) *In vitro* trans-monolayer permeability calculations: often forgotten assumptions. *Drug Discov. Today* 8: 997-1003.

17

Optimizing Biomarker Development for Clinical Studies at the Lead Optimization Stage of Drug Development

Geoffrey S Ginsburg[1,2]
Julie Lekstrom-Himes[2]
William Trepicchio[2]

[1]Center for Genomic Medicine
Institute for Genome Sciences And Policy
Duke University, Durham, NC 22708

[2]Millennium Pharmaceuticals, Inc.
Cambridge, MA 02139

Table of Contents

List of Abbreviations

BMWG..Biomarker Working Group
PK...Pharmacokinetics
MR...Magnetic Resonance
DME...Drug Metabolizing Enzyme
ADR...Adverse Drug Reaction
PD ....Pharmacodynamic

Keywords

Biomarkers, Proof of concept, Proof of mechanism, Efficacy, Toxicity, Pharmacogenomics, Pharmacogenetics, Pharmacokinetics, Drug metabolizing enzyme.

Defining the sequence of the human genome has brought with it a wealth of potential drug targets of uncertain biology. For pharmaceutical firms to reduce the risk of drug failure after long, expensive clinical development programs, accurate information is required about the biological effects of the compounds being tested. Therefore, there is a strong need for biomarkers that can assist in unraveling the complex biology of these novel drug targets and their use during the drug development process is no longer optional.

In the past, industry had the luxury of extensive literature on targets, many of which were validated across multiple species. In some cases, human data provided strong biochemical evidence and at times even revealed genetic variation that confirmed the target's application to a particular disease. Today, as the industry attempts to develop drugs that interact with "unprecedented" targets – proteins that both lack precedented biology and/or the precedence of a drug interacting with the target (or its pathway) having been approved – key questions need to be addressed along the critical path to approval:

- Does the compound directly interact with the target *in vivo*?
- Are there measurable cellular effects of the drug-target interaction?
- Can downstream actions of the drug be measured in the pathway or mechanism of interest?
- Is there modulation of biological attributes of the disease (directly or indirectly associated with the target mechanism)?
- Is the metabolic fate of the drug perturbed by variation in enzymes or transporters that affect its biodistribution, thereby affecting its efficacy and/or toxicity?
- Is there variation in the target or pathway constituents that could result in altered efficacy and potentially render some patient populations more or less likely to benefit from its action?

Today, the economics of drug development rely upon the accurate and timely answers to these questions. Biomarkers guide these critical decisions; however the reliability of the answer delivered is dependent upon the validity of the assay. Moreover, exquisite planning long before the first-in-man milestone must be in place to ensure the proper co-execution of biomarker related research and application concordant with the clinical development plan.

Interaction of a Compound With a Target *In Vivo*

The simplest of the pharmacodynamic assays, measuring the degree of target interaction with a compound, provides the key elements defining the relationship between dose, drug levels, and target inhibition. The precision of understanding this relationship, however, is governed by the variability of the measurement (including its reproducibility across subjects and time and its repeatability as an assay) and the linearity of the dose-pharmacodynamic measurement. The value of this type of assay is that it measures (and confirms) that the drug indeed interacts with the target and the dose response relationship for that interaction can be determined with precision. Indeed, specificity for the target can be evaluated by comparing this relationship to a series of homologues or potential competitors for the compound in question. However, this type of assay does not reveal the minimally effective dose nor the compound's hypothesized mechanism of action relevant to disease modulation. Additional biomarker development is necessary to address these issues.

Measurable Cellular Effects Downstream of the Drug Target interaction

Cellular effects of compounds interacting with a target can be explored using biomarkers derived from key pathway constituents, usually downstream of the drug target. Depending upon the target, assays may measure subsequent changes in receptor expression, signal transduction elements of the pathway, or gene transcription levels. These assays provide strong confirmatory evidence that the compound-target interaction is biologically meaningful and provides biological plausibility for the hypothetical effects on disease activity. A consequence, however, of using these downstream markers is the inherent "amplification" of the signal delivered from the compound-target interaction that results in significant inter-subject and intra-subject variability to the measurement. Often, the measurements gathered from these assays are qualitative or semi-quantitative at best and hence fail to provide a true dose-response relationship. Further, the readouts from these assays are still too distal from the disease to know for sure whether the compound will actually work in modulating disease biology. Nevertheless, these assays provide critical information regarding the effects of target inhibition or antagonism on the pertinent downstream pathways and provide additional information about the compound's mechanism of action. In cases where the assay robustness and variability allow for quantitative assessment of dose-response relationships, these parameters may provide a more accurate prediction of the compound doses needed to alter disease processes, above and beyond those doses predicted by the compound-target interaction alone. We have observed cases in which this measure can provide a distinctly different dose-response relationship compared to measures of ligand binding to a receptor. Thus log order differences and errors in the minimally effective dose may be realized without the downstream components.

Modulation of Biological Attributes of the Disease by a Drug

In our view the most desirable measure of drug effect is on a measure that brings to bear the integrated biology of the system. In drug development programs for the chemokine receptors, for example, we have utilized a skin based mononuclear cell recruitment assay to examine the impact chemokine receptor antagonists have on leukocyte trafficking (Gerard and Rollins, 2001 and Gladue *et al.*, 2004). This is a key mechanism underlying the inflammatory response in diseases such as rheumatoid arthritis (Loetscher and Moser, 2002), multiple sclerosis (Sindern, 2004), and respiratory inflammation (Sabroe, *et al.*, 2002), and inflammatory bowel disease (Papadakis, 2004), and perhaps atherosclerotic vascular disease (Sheikine and Hansson, 2004).

Modeled after the studies of Lee *et al.*, (2000) we have developed a protocol that utilizes low does of purified human chemokines in intradermal injections. We have used these assays to provide a mechanistically precise means of assessing chemokine receptor blockade in modulating cell recruitment in our chemokine receptor antagonist early phase studies. These assays permit correlation of dose, receptor saturation by the compound, and functional blockade of the mechanistic activity that is the foundation of the disease hypothesis, namely chemotaxis. The advantages of these studies include the information provided for dose selection as well as their applicability to Phase I healthy volunteer subjects. The disadvantages are that they are expensive and require assay development and validation prior to use in Phase II. Furthermore, as these studies are conducted using an accessible tissue, rather than the site of disease, they do not provide the same type of information as would a disease surrogate such as synovial tissue in rheumatoid arthritis or Gadolinium enhanced MR imaging in multiple sclerosis. Hence, while these types of biologically integrated pharmacodynamic assays provide "proof of mechanism", they do not provide disease-specific "proof of concept". They are, however, valuable for dose selection and enhancing the confidence associated with the overall development program.

Drug Efficacy and/or Toxicity May be Determined by Variation in Enzymes or Transporters that Affect Its Biodistribution, Serum and Tissue Levels

Pharmacogenetic studies offer one way to investigate the mechanism underlying variability in drug response (Weinshilboum, 2003). This may result in improved understanding of pharmacokinetic (PK) data and adverse drug reactions (ADRs), rational drug dosing, and predictive markers of response & toxicity. A plethora of literature exists today on common variants in drug metabolizing enzymes that mediate potentially adverse reactions on the one hand and that may also limit efficacy on the other (Weinshilboum, 2003). We believe that a comprehensive examination of gene variant-pharmakokinetic/pharmacodymanic relationships are essential for optimizing drug development.

Our recommendations for DNA sample collections for the purposes of pharmacogenetic analyses are as follows:

- In Phase I studies: DNA samples should be collected from all subjects for potential genotyping of DME and transporter genes and correlation to pharmacokinetic data.
- For Phase II and later trials: DNA should be collected any time PK analysis is conducted, even if PK outliers were not observed in

earlier trials, for potential genotyping of DME and transporter genes.

- For Phase II and later trials: DNA should be collected for genotyping of DME and transporter genes if prior trials suggest a correlation of genotype to PK or toxicity phenotype.

The execution of a pharmacogenetics project is a collaborative effort between Pre-Clinical and Clinical Research. A pre-Clinical research team identifies the enzymes involved in the biotransformation of a compound under development, and Clinical teams will incorporate pharmacogenetics into the clinical protocols.

Variation in the Target or Pathway Constituents and Altered Efficacy in Patient Populations

In contrast to pharmacogenetics which is focused on association between single genes (drug metabolizing enzymes and transporters) and drug response variability (e.g., CYP2C9 and Warfarin; TPMT and thioguanines) (Weinshilboum, 2003), pharmacogenomics is the study of how multiple genes underlie drug response variability (e.g., transcriptional or proteomic signatures). Such signatures may predict which patients will respond or fail treatment or suffer an ADR. Pharmacogenomic studies may move second line therapy to front line, may allow selection of patients for re-treatment with relapse, for maintenance therapy, or for patients with alternative indications to receive therapy.

Executing Robust Biomarker Development in Clinical Programs: Concept of a Biomarker Working Group

The complexity of biomarker integration into clinical development requires new disciplines in drug development. We have developed an operational model that employs a new entity: the Biomarker Working Group (BMWG) (William Trepicchio, Millennium Pharmaceuticals, Inc., personal communication, 2004) that is responsible for the discovery, translation, and development of biomarkers that support the clinical development and approval process of a drug. Below, is a summary of some of the key operational features of this group and its role in the preclinical, early and later stages of clinical development.

The BMWG is a cross functional team that is assembled early in the drug discovery process. Its mission is to assess the biomarker needs for all phases of development and establish a biomarker plan that is consistent with the needs and timelines of the clinical development plan. The BMWG also identifies the functional areas responsible for carrying out details of the plan. Team members of the BMWG include representatives from discovery, drug safety and metabolism, and the clinical research groups. Representatives from the regulatory and commercial organizations become part of this team as needed or as the compound gets closer to the clinic. A clinician-scientist well versed in translational research leads the BMWG.

The BMWG in Preclinical Development

1. In preclinical development, the BMWG determines the extent to which an understanding of the mechanism of action of the compound on the target and the target pathway as well as a thorough understanding of the pathophysiology of the target and pathway in relationship to the disease indication is essential for biomarker planning. This information is important for several reasons. First, it is critical for development of pharmacodynamic, efficacy and disease biomarkers. Secondly, in conjunction with future clinical outcome data, it can assist in second generation compound development. Thirdly, it will be an essential component of regulatory filings. Fourthly, clinical research can use this information in communications with clinical investigators to generate enthusiasm and support of clinical trials. Lastly, the commercial organization can provide this information to prescribing physicians, patients and patient advocacy groups. The discovery organization through either internal efforts or in collaboration with outside collaborators may establish a series of *in vitro* cell culture experiments and *in vivo* animal studies to thoroughly evaluate the mechanism of action of the compound and the link of the target and pathway to disease pathophysiology.

2. The BMWG may examine genetic variation in the target and/or pathway constituents and conduct preclinical studies with mutated constructs to confirm whether the variants are functional. If so, a cross sectional epidemiologic study in patients (or existing patient registry) may likely be required to assess the frequency and distribution mutations in a broader patient population and determine whether the variation may be sufficient to consider it as a prognostic marker of disease (Lekstrom-Himes, *et al.*, 2004). These studies need to be designed well in advance of first-in-man.

3. The BMWG must also develop a PD marker and assay that will be required to determine the optimal dose and schedule selection for this compound. As discussed above, for drugs that have never previously been developed to a target it is important to determine mechanistically that the compound is binding and inhibiting the target as would be anticipated from *in vitro* and *in vivo* preclinical studies. Issues such as intra and inter-patient variability must be assessed. The BMWG may conduct a "Phase 0" study in humans to assess the clinical feasibility of this type of marker prior to its use in Phase I.

4. It is often desirable to have markers of efficacy that could be used to stratify patients during later clinical trials and increase the power of the studies. This would allow smaller clinical studies to

be performed. The BMWG oversees studies to define the candidate markers for drug sensitivity and resistance *in vitro* using dynamic mRNA, protein, or metabolite assays. These resulting signatures may be incorporated into Phase II study plans to validate them with patient outcome data. If successful, the validated marker set may be used in planned Phase III studies as a post hoc stratification endpoint. We cannot overemphasize the importance of planning and executing these studies in a timely fashion such that the data will be available at the initiation of Phase III.

5. Representatives from the drug safety and metabolism groups on the BMWG provide information from *in vitro* and *in vivo* studies on the mechanism of absorption, distribution, metabolism, and excretion (ADME) of the compound. These data are used to develop plans for assaying cytochrome p450 and transporter gene variation in the Phase I/II programs. Information obtained from these studies is used to help explain PK variability if it is observed. It may also be used to insure that at least some patients containing slow or fast metabolizing phenotypes are enrolled in the Phase I studies. If PK variability is extensive and correlates to slow or rapid metabolizing genotypes future experiments should be planned whereby such patients are prospectively excluded, prospectively included if the genotype is rare, or stratified.

The BMWG in Early Development

1. The PD assay described above is incorporated into early Phase I/II studies to assist in dose and schedule selection and validate the mechanism of action. The BMWG oversees the development of a bioassay and must establish the assay performance criteria and identifies an appropriate lab to conduct the clinical assays. Once the data is obtained it is evaluated for performance and accuracy and transferred to the Clinical Pharmacology group for associations with the PK data to model future dose and schedule selection.

2. The BMWG oversees the plan for incorporation of pharmaco-genetic markers for ADME phenotypes into the Phase I/II study design. Coordination of these studies with an outside laboratory may be required in many instances for GLP genotyping studies. The data generated is then associated with PK data to look for correlations to slow or rapid metabolizer phenotypes.

3. Tissue or blood sample collections from patients enrolled in the Phase I/II studies may be critically important for both genotyping and early signals of efficacy. Efficacy variants that are validated from the preclinical findings and may be used to stratify patients

in a pivotal Phase III study. Samples from the Phase II study may also be highly valuable for future drug development purposes of a second generation compound. The BMWG must incorporate biological specimen collection into the plans for early clinical development with the appropriate informed consent issues addressed. Although recruitment may be slowed in some cases, the information to be gained from these studies is may be critical for the future success of the clinical development program.

The BMWG and Late Clinical Development

1. If an efficacy biomarker will be used to select patients for a clinical trial, a test will likely be required to be co-developed along with the drug. A diagnostic partner will need to be identified early for co-development of the test with the compound to insure that the diagnostic test will be ready at the same time as the approved drug. The BMWG must assess the assay requirements and develop the appropriate business and regulatory strategy to assure the timely and coordinated delivery of the diagnostic and therapeutic for approval.

2. If a marker or marker set will be used as a surrogate of a clinically defined endpoint, the BMWG must identify and oversee the performance of the assays required under GLP conditions. The data must be evaluated for accuracy and statistically rigor for its use as a secondary surrogate clinical endpoint. Involvement of regulatory affairs in the BMWG would be appropriate for such an instance.

3. Any observed toxicity or ADR might be related to genetic variation in select DME genes. Therefore as indicated above, the BMWG strategy in early and late stage clinical development includes collection of DNA from all patients to genotype polymorphism analysis in predetermined genes identified in Phase I/II. This information can be used in regulatory updates, in second generation compound development and as a publication to provide the commercial organization with a plausible mechanistic explanation for this ADR.

Summary

The development of appropriate markers and assays to determine dose in Phase I, proof of mechanism, proof of concept in Phase I/II and optimal design of Phase II and Phase III studies requires a complex nexus of basic and clinical research that must be highly coordinated and integrated with the clinical, commercial, and regulatory plans for approval and marketing of the drug. As the industry faces the challenge of a paucity of biological or clinical validation of

420

Chapter 17: Optimizing Biomarker Development for Clinical Studies
at the Lead Optimization Stage of Drug Development

selected drug targets, the use of biomarkers has become as critical to the drug development process as the molecule itself. The BMWG is an innovative solution to the cross functional requirements for biomarker discovery and development.

References

Sindern E. Role of Chemokines and Their Receptors in the Pathogenesis of Multiple Sclerosis. *Front Biosci* 2004 Jan 1; 9:457-463

Papadakis KA. Chemokines in Inflammatory Bowel Disease. *Curr Allergy Asthma Rep.* 2004 Jan; 4(1):83-89

Weinshilboum R. Inheritance and Drug Response. *N Engl J Med* 2003, Feb 6; 348(6):529-537

Sheikine Y, and Hansson GK. Chemokines and Atherosclerosis. *Ann Med* 2004; 36(2):98-118

Loetscher P, and Moser B. Homing Chemokines in Rheumatoid Arthritis. *Arthritis Res* 2002; 4(4):233-236

Gerard C, and Rollins BJ. Chemokines and Disease. *Nat Immunol.* 2001 Feb; 2(2):108-115

Gladue RP, Zwillich SH, Clucas AT, and Brown MF. CCR1 Antagonists for the Treatment of Autoimmune Diseases. *Curr Opin Investig Drugs* 2004 May; 5(5):499-504

Lee SC, Brummet ME, Shahabuddin S, Woodworth TG, Georas SN, Leiferman KM, Gilman SC, Stellato C, Gladue RP, and Schleimer RP, et. al. Cutaneous Injection of Human Subjects with Macrophage Inflammatory Protein-1· Induces Significant Recruitment of Neutrophils and Monocytes. *Journal of Immunology*, 2000, 164:3392-3401

Sabroe I, Lloyd CM, Whyte MK, Dower SK, Williams TJ, and Pease JE. Chemokines, Innate and Adaptive Immunity, and Respiratory Disease. *Eur Respir J.* 2002 Feb; 19(2):350-355

Personal Communication:

Trepiccho William, Millennium Pharmaceuticals, Inc., Personal Communication, 2004.

Symposia:

Lekstrom-Himes J, Shadick N, Meyer J, Lillie J, Chun M, Gutierrez-Ramos JC, Weinblatt M, Weiner H, Khoury S, and Ginsburg GS. Therapeutic Response Biomarkers for Use in Proof of Concept Clinical Trials: Discovery and Validation of Biomarkers Sets Using Large Patient Registries. Keystone Symposia, Biomarkers in Drug Development, Santa Fe, NM, January 2004.

422

Chapter 17: Optimizing Biomarker Development for Clinical Studies
at the Lead Optimization Stage of Drug Development

18

The Relevance of Transporters
in Determining Drug Disposition

Hartmut Glaeser, Ph.D. and Richard B. Kim, M.D.

Division of Clinical Pharmacology
Vanderbilt University School of Medicine
Nashville, TN

Table of Contents

Keywords

Transporters, multidrug resistance, P-glycoprotein, uptake, efflux, pharmacokinetics, organic anion transporting polypeptide, organic anion transport, bile acid, drug disposition

Introduction

Membrane transporters represent an important class of proteins responsible for regulating cellular and physiological solute and fluid balance. With the sequencing of the human genome, it has been estimated that approximately 500 to 1,200 genes code for transport proteins (Venter *et al.*, 2001). In terms of xenobiotic disposition, a smaller fraction of these transporters are currently known to significantly interact with drugs. In particular, transporters that are localized at key gateway tissues within the body such as the intestine (Tsuji and Tamai, 1996; Suzuki and Sugiyama, 2000b), liver (Keppler and Konig, 2000; Suzuki and Sugiyama, 2000a), kidney (Inui *et al.*, 2000; Dresser *et al.*, 2001), placenta (Ganapathy *et al.*, 2000), and brain (Tamai and Tsuji, 2000; Gao and Meier, 2001) are critical modulators of drug absorption, tissue distribution and elimination and have been the subject of recent reviews.

It has now been established that genetic polymorphisms in drug metabolizing enzymes such as the cytochrome P450s (CYP) and the phase II enzyme, thiopurine methyltransferase, are frequently the basis of major interindividual variability in response and adverse reactions to some drugs (Evans and Relling, 1999). Similar to such enzymes, emerging evidence also support the notion that drug transporters are similarly affected and that presence or absence of polymorphisms may be dependent on race or ethnicity. However, determination of the *in vivo* relevance of a specific transporter has been hampered by the presence of multiple transporters within a given tissue with overlapping substrate specificities and a lack of transporter-specific *in vivo* probe substrate drugs.

In this chapter, we review key transporters known to be or of potential importance to the drug disposition process (Table 1). For more information on a comprehensive list of transporters, readers are directed to visit the Internet web page www.med.rug.nl/mdl/tab3.htm. Included in the present compilation are the members of the organic anion transporting polypeptides (OATPs), organic anion transporters (OATs) and bile salt transporters thought to be importantly involved in the cellular uptake of endogenous compounds and drugs. In addition, transporters which mediate the cellular efflux of drugs, such as multidrug resistance proteins (MDRs), and multidrug resistance-related proteins (MRPs) will also be discussed. The molecular, biochemical and physiological aspects of each transporter will be presented.

Uptake transporter

OATPs (organic anion transporting polypeptides)

The human OATPs (organic anion transporting polypeptides) are a superfamily of uptake transporters which are expressed in various tissues and mediate the transport of many amphipathic endogenous and exogenous molecules. The gene symbol is prefixed by SLCO whereas the encoded protein is named OATP (Table 1). The OATPs are divided in families and subfamilies based

Table 1. Human and rat OATP transporters; nomenclature, tissue distribution and substrates.

Transporter			Tissue Distribution	Substrates
	New			
	Gene Symbol	Protein Name		
Human				
OATP-A	SLCO1A2	OATP1A2	Brain, Intestine, Kidney	D-penicillamine enkephalin (DPDPE), deltorphin, fexofenadine, bile acids, BQ123, CRC220
OATP-B	SLCO2B1	OATP2B1	Liver, Kidney, Intestine, Lung, Placenta	Estrone-3-sulfate, bromosulfophthalein, pravastatin
OATP-C	SLCO1B1	OATP1B1	Liver	Bile acids, conjugated steroids (dehydroepiandrosterone sulfate, estradiol-17β-glucuronide, estrone-3-sulfate, eicosanoids (PGE2, TXB2, LTC4, LTE4), thyroid hormones (T4, T3), unconjugated bilirubin (controversial), rifampin, cerivastatin, pravastatin, rosuvastatin
OATP-8	SLCO1B3	OATP1B3	Liver	Dehydroepiandrosterone sulfate, estrone-3-sulfate, bromosulfophthalein, cholecystokinin-8, digoxin, D-penicillamine enkephalin (DPDPE), rifampin
Rat				
Oatp1	Slco1a1	Oatp1a1	Liver, brain (choroid plexus) kidney	Enalapril, temocaprilat, ochratoxin A, BQ-123, CRC 220, bromosulfophthalein, estradiol-17β-glucuronide, ouabain, aldosterone, estrone-3-sulfate, cortisol, APD-ajmalinium, fexofenadine
Oatp2	Slco1a4	Oatp1a4	Liver, brain (capillary endothelial cells)	Pravastatin, BQ-123, thyroid hormones (T4, T3), digoxin, ouabain, estradiol, estrone-3-sulfate, estradiol-17β-glucuronide, fexofenadine
Oatp4	Slco1b2	Oatp1b2	liver	Taurocholate, Cholecystokinin, dehydroepiandrosterone sulfate, stradiol-17β-glucuronide, estrone-3-sulfate, LTC4, BQ-123, DPDPE

on their amino acid similarity (Hagenbuch and Meier, 2004). The OATPs transport their substrates using a sodium-independent mechanism (Jacquemin *et al.*, 1994; Kullak-Ublick *et al.*, 1995; Noe *et al.*, 1997; Walters *et al.*, 2000). The underlying mechanism seems to be an anion exchange coupled with the cellular uptake of organic compounds. For example, the efflux of bicarbonate, GSH (glutathione) and/or GSH-conjugates is thought to mediate the uptake of organic substrates (Shi *et al.*, 1995; Satlin *et al.*, 1997)-(Li *et al.*, 1998; Li *et al.*, 2000).

Oatp1a1 is the first member of this family, originally cloned from rat liver (Jacquemin *et al.*, 1994). Subsequently, additional members were discovered in humans and rodents. One of the best characterized human OATPs is OATP1A2. Originally termed OATP1 or OATP-A, OATP1A2 was cloned from a liver cDNA library; however it is highly expressed in the brain (Kullak-Ublick *et al.*, 1995) as well as kidney (Alcorn *et al.*, 2002), certain colon cancer cells and HepG2 cells (Kullak-Ublick *et al.*, 1997; Tamai *et al.*, 2000; Lee *et al.*, 2001). In the brain, OATP1A2 is expressed in the capillary endothelial cells (Gao *et al.*, 2000), suggesting that OATP1A2 may play an important physiological function at the level of the blood brain barrier. Indeed opioid receptor agonists such as [D-penicillamine 2,5]enkephalin (DPDPE) and deltrophin II (Gao *et al.*, 2000) are substrates of OATP1A2. Given this transporter mediates cellular drug uptake, it is likely OATP1A2 may be a key determinant governing the extent of CNS penetration of many CNS-active drugs into the brain. In addition, OATP1A2 transports a broad spectrum of compounds which includes bile salts (Kullak-Ublick *et al.*, 1995), steroid conjugates (Bossuyt *et al.*, 1996; Kullak-Ublick *et al.*, 1998), anionic dyes such as bromosulfpthalein (BSP) (Kullak-Ublick *et al.*, 1995), the thyroid hormones T3, T4 (Kullak-Ublick *et al.*, 2001), bulky organic cations (Bossuyt *et al.*, 1996; van Montfoort *et al.*, 1999), and drugs such the antihistamine fexofenadine (Cvetkovic *et al.*, 1999), the endothelin receptor antagonist BQ-123 (Reichel *et al.*, 1999), and the thrombin inhibitor CRC-220 (Eckhardt *et al.*, 1996). Furthermore, OATP1A2 is expressed in the kidney (Kullak-Ublick *et al.*, 1995), where it could play an important role in the reabsorption of organic anion compounds and drugs.

Another widely studied member of this family is OATP1B1 (previously referred to as OATP2, OATP-C, and LST1) cloned from human liver (Fig. 1), and expressed on the basolateral membrane domain of the hepatocyte. It is postulated that the expression is restricted to the liver (Abe *et al.*, 1999; Hsiang *et al.*, 1999; Konig *et al.*, 2000a; Tamai *et al.*, 2000). This suggests a key role for this transporter in the hepatic uptake mediated clearance of amphipathic organic compounds. However, a recent study suggested that OATP1B1 may be also expressed on the apical membrane of enterocytes in the human small intestine (Glaeser *et al.*, 2004). Polarity of expression in the intestine and liver would suggest OATP1B1 facilitates the absorption of orally administered compounds, which would then be efficiently taken up into liver. However, *in vivo* functional importance of OATP1B1 role has yet to be clarified. Like OATP1A2, OATP1B1 exhibits a similar extent of substrate specificity. The spectrum of its substrates includes bile salts, conjugated and unconjugated bilirubin, BSP, steroid conjugates, thyroid hormones T3, T4,

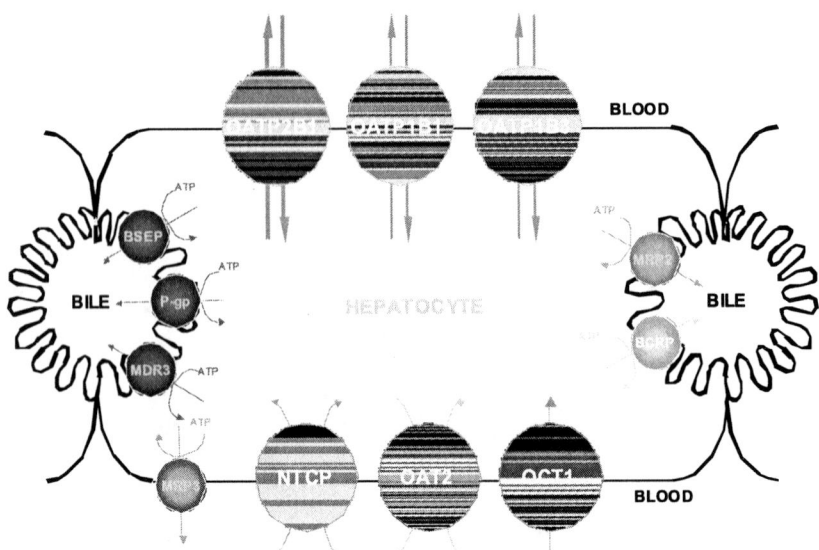

Figure 1. Schematic diagram depicting drug transporters and their subcellular localization in the human hepatocyte.

eicosanoids, cyclic peptides and drugs such benzylpenicillin, methotrexate (MTX), and the HMG-CoA reductase inhibitors pravastatin, rosuvastatin, and cerivastatin (Hagenbuch and Meier, 2003).

OATP1B3, the second member of the human OATP1B was also cloned from human liver (Konig *et al.*, 2000b; Abe *et al.*, 2001). Expression of OATP1B3 has been localized to the basolateral membrane domain of hepatocytes (Konig *et al.*, 2000b; Abe *et al.*, 2001). Interestingly, it has also been detected in certain cancer cell lines and tissues (Abe *et al.*, 2001).

The compounds transported by OATP1B3 include bile salts, monoglucuronosyl-bilirubin, BSP, steroid conjugates, T3, T4 leukotriene C4, linear and cyclic peptides and drugs such digoxin, MTX and rifampin (for review see (Hagenbuch and Meier, 2003)). OATP1B3 has a significant overlap in substrates with OATP1B1. However, OATP1B3 has been shown to transport also oligopeptide hormones such as cholecystokinin 8 (Ismair *et al.*, 2001) and the cardiac glycoside digoxin (Kullak-Ublick *et al.*, 2001).

OATP1C1 is the only human OATP1C member characterized to date. OATP1C1 mRNA was detected in brain and testis (Pizzagalli *et al.*, 2002). In comparison to OATP1A2, 1B1 and 1B3, OATP1C1 it shows a limited substrate specificity (Pizzagalli *et al.*, 2002). T4 is a substrate with high affinity while BSP, estradiol-17β-glucuronide, estrone-3-sulfate and T3 appeared to be transported with limited affinity. The physiological importance of OATP1C1 has to be clarified it may play an important role in the delivery of T4 to the brain and testis.

OATP2A1 was originally cloned from a human kidney cDNA library (Lu *et al.*, 1996) but its mRNA is ubiquitously expressed. Functional studies demonstrated that prostaglandins and thromboxane B2 are substrates of OATP2A1. The OATP

2B subfamily contains only one member, OATP2B1. It is expressed in multiple tissues including spleen, placenta, lung, kidney, heart, ovary, small intestine, and brain. Liver however, has been shown to have the highest expressed level of this transporter (Tamai *et al.*, 2000; Kullak-Ublick *et al.*, 2001; St-Pierre *et al.*, 2002). Similar to OATP1B1 and OATP1B3, OATP2B1 is localized to the basolateral membrane domain hepatocytes (Kullak-Ublick *et al.*, 2001). Substrates for OATP2B1 identified so far include BSP, estrone-3-sulfate and dehydroepiandrosterone-sulfate (DHEAS) (Tamai *et al.*, 2000; Kullak-Ublick *et al.*, 2001).

OATP3A1 and 4A1 represent two additional human OATP members. OATP3A1 was first isolated from human kidney but mRNA expression analysis revealed that it is ubiquitously expressed and detectable in several cancer cell lines (Tamai *et al.*, 2000). Substrate specificity appears to be limited. So far, only estrone-3-sulfate, PGE_2 and benzylpenicilline have been identified (Tamai *et al.*, 2000). OATP4A1 was also originally cloned from human kidney and brain, but noted to be ubiquitously expressed with highest levels in liver, heart, placenta and pancreas. *In vitro* transport studies showed that taurocholate, T3, T4 (Fujiwara *et al.*, 2001) as well as steroid conjugates, PGE_2, and benzylpenicilline are substrates of OATP4A1 (Tamai *et al.*, 2000). Other human OATP members include OATP4C1, 5A1, 6A1. More studies are needed to define the role of these proteins to drug disposition.

Taken together, there have been remarkable recent advances in our knowledge of OATP transporters in terms of their tissue-dependent expression and substrate specificity. There is little doubt OATP transporters will prove to be critical to the delivery of drugs to their target tissues.

Organic anion transporter (OAT)

The OATs (organic anion transporters) belong to a family of transporter proteins which are mainly responsible for the uptake of organic anions from the blood to renal tubule cells. The OATs have been implicated in the renal elimination of endogenous compounds, drugs and their metabolites. The first member (Oat1) was cloned from murine kidney (Lopez-Nieto and Nigam, 1996; Lopez-Nieto *et al.*, 1997; Sekine *et al.*, 1997; Sweet *et al.*, 1997) followed by the subsequent identification of a human ortholog (OAT1) (Hosoyamada *et al.*, 1999; Lu *et al.*, 1999; Race *et al.*, 1999; Bahn *et al.*, 2000). OAT1 is expressed on the basolateral membrane of the proximal tubule cells (Sekine *et al.*, 1997; Hosoyamada *et al.*, 1999). Para-aminohippuric acid (PAH) is a prototypical substrate for OAT1 (Lu *et al.*, 1999; Race *et al.*, 1999). The transport mechanism of OAT1 is known to be indirectly sodium-dependent and involves a tertiary transport process to move organic anions across the basolateral membrane into the proximal tubule cells. A Na^+-K^+-ATPase located on the basolateral membrane pumps Na^+ from intracellular to extracellular space to maintain a Na^+ gradient. The higher extracellular Na^+ concentration then drives the Na^+-dicarboxylate cotransporter which mediates the uptake of dicarboxylates such α-ketoglutarate into the cell to maintain a gradient. OAT1 utilizes this α-ketoglutarate (α-KG) gradient to move organic anionic substrates into the cells in exchange for α-ketoglutarate efflux to the extracellular compartment. Functional studies have revealed that rat Oat1 transports a broad spectrum of substrates, including endogenous organic anions, such as prostaglandins, cyclic nucleotides, folates (Sekine *et al.*, 1997) as well as xenobiotics, such as β-lactam antibiotics (Jariyawat *et al.*, 1999), NSAIDs (Apiwattanakul *et al.*, 1999) and many antiviral drugs (Cihlar *et al.*, 1999; Wada *et al.*, 2000). Human OAT1 also transports adefovir, cidofovir, zidovudine (AZT), acylclovir and ganciclovir (Cihlar *et al.*, 1999; Ho *et al.*, 2000) (Takeda *et al.*, 2002). Four splice variants (OAT1-1, OAT1-2, OAT1-3, OAT1-4) of human OAT1 have been identified. It has been reported that OAT1-1 and OAT1-2 are similar in terms of their functionality (Hosoyamada *et al.*, 1999). OAT1-3 and OAT1-4 are not functionally active due an absence of the putative transmembrane-spanning domains 11 and 12 (Bahn *et al.*, 2000). Molecular modeling techniques and *in situ* microperfusion of rat tubule demonstrated that the interactions between the substrate and the carrier require primarily negatively-charged and hydrophobic region (Fritzsch *et al.*, 1989).

Since the cloning of OAT1, several additional members including, OAT2, OAT3 and OAT4 have been identified. Human OAT2 and rat Oat2 are also expressed in the kidney but the expression levels are much greater in the liver (Sekine *et al.*, 1998; Sun *et al.*, 2001). In contrast to OAT1, rat Oat2 does not use an α-ketoglutarate gradient as the driving force to transport its substrates (Sekine *et al.*, 1998). There are also differences in the membrane localization between rat Oat2 and human OAT2. Human OAT2 is expressed on the basolateral membrane of the proximal tubule cells (Enomoto *et al.*, 2002) whereas the rat ortholog, Oat2 is expressed on the apical membrane of tubule cells (Kojima *et al.*, 2002). Some of the substrates, such as cephalosporin antibiotics, MTX, NSAIDS (e.g. diclofenac, ibuprofen, ketoprofen) are shared by human OAT2 and rat Oat2 (Morita *et al.*, 2001; Khamdang *et al.*, 2002).

The expression of human OAT3 seems to be exclusive to the kidney on the basolateral membrane of the proximal tubule cells (Cha *et al.*, 2001; Sun *et al.*, 2001) while rat Oat3 mRNA is most abundantly expressed in liver and to lesser extent in kidney and brain (Kusuhara *et al.*, 1999).

Similar to OAT1, OAT3 also utilizes a Na^+/α-KG exchange system to transport the substrates into the cell (Sweet *et al.*, 2003). The affinity of PAH to OAT3 is much lower compared to OAT1 (20-fold), but OAT3 exhibits a high affinity to hormone conjugates such as estrone sulfate, dihydroepiandrosterone (DHEA) sulfate and estradiol-17β-D-glucuronide (E_2-17βG) (Cha *et al.*, 2001) (Kusuhara *et al.*, 1999). Interestingly, the antihistaminic cimetidine is also a substrate of OAT3.

Human OAT4 mRNA is highly expressed in the kidney and to some extent in the placenta (Cha *et al.*, 2001; Sun *et al.*, 2001). In contrast to the other OATs, human OAT4 is expressed on the apical membrane of the tubule cells (Babu *et al.*, 2002). Similar to OAT2, the transport mechanism of OAT4 is unknown. OAT4 transports PAH with a low affinity (Cha *et al.*, 2000) but efficiently transports ochratoxin A, steroid sulfates, AZT, MTX.

A better understanding of substrates and/or inhibitor of OATs may prove to be useful avoiding drug-induced nephrotoxicity (e.g. MTX and NSAID).

Bile salt transporter

The enterohepatic circulation of bile acids is an important pathway for the regulation of the cholestrol and bile acid homoestasis as well as for the absorption of cholesterol, dietary lipids and lipid-soluble vitamins. This pathway allows bile acids to be extracted from blood by hepatocytes and secreted into the bile against a very steep concentration gradient. After the secretion of bile acids into the small intestine, bile salts are mainly reabsorbed in the ileum to the portal blood circulation which transports them back to the liver. This efficient enterohepatic recirculation of bile acids minimizes de novo bile acid synthesis.

In the portal circulation, extraction of the mostly albumin-bound bile acids into liver is mediated by the sodium-dependent Na^+-taurocholate cotransporting polypeptide (NTCP), which has been isolated from rat, mouse and human liver (Hagenbuch and Meier, 1994). NTCP is exclusively expressed on the basolateral side of hepatocytes (Ananthanarayanan *et al.*, 1994; Stieger *et al.*, 1994; Kullak-Ublick *et al.*, 1997). Human NTCP and rat Ntcp mediate the sodium-coupled uptake of taurocholate and other bile salts with the same stoichiometry (Na^+:bile salt= 2:1 in isolated hepatocytes (Hagenbuch and Meier, 1996; Weinman, 1997; Kullak-Ublick *et al.*, 2000). The Na^+-gradient across the basolateral membrane is maintained by a Na^+/K^+-ATPase (Kullak-Ublick *et al.*, 2000; Meier and Stieger, 2002). A parallel decrease of rat Ntcp expression and Na^+-taurocholate cotransport was shown in primary rat hepatocytes (Liang *et al.*, 1993; Rippin *et al.*, 2001) and during an *in situ* regeneration of rat liver (Green *et al.*, 1997). In addition, the Na^+-dependent taurocholate uptake in *Xenopus laevis* oocytes was reduced by 95% after the inhibition of NTCP with antisense oligonucleotides (Hagenbuch *et al.*, 1996). All these studies demonstrated that the Na^+-dependent bile salt uptake system is the major transport system in rat hepatocytes. Rat Ntcp also transports glycocholate, taurochenodeoxycholate, tauroursodeoxycholate whereas the highest transport activity was observed for glycine- and taurine-conjugated dihydroxy and trihydroxy bile salts (Meier *et al.*, 1997; Kullak-Ublick *et al.*, 2000; Meier and Stieger, 2002). Ntcp can transport a limited number of non-bile acid compound such as estrone-3-sulfate, BSP, DHEA-sulfate, thyroid hormones and the drug conjugate chlorambucil-taurocholate (Kullak-Ublick *et al.*, 1997; Meier *et al.*, 1997; Kullak-Ublick *et al.*, 2000; Suzuki and Sugiyama, 2000a; Meier and Stieger, 2002). The functional properties of human NTCP are very similar to rat Ntcp, although human NTCP shows a higher affinity for taurocholate than the rat and mouse orthologs (Hagenbuch and Meier, 1994). Furthermore, a recent study showed that polymorphisms found only in African Americans and Chinese caused a markedly reduced activity of taurocholate and cholate transport, indicating there might be ethnic differences in the efficiency in the enterohepatic circulation of bile salts (Ho *et al.*, 2004).

In the intestine, the reabsorption of bile salts is mediated by ASBT (apical sodium bile salt transporter). ASBT has been cloned from hamster, human, rat, rabbit and mouse ileum (Wong *et al.*, 1994; Shneider *et al.*, 1995; Wong *et al.*, 1995; Kramer *et al.*, 1999; Saeki *et al.*, 1999). In rats, expression of Asbt has been shown to be localized on the apical membrane of ileal enterocytes, renal proximal tubule cells and cholangiocytes (Shneider *et al.*, 1995; Lazaridis *et al.*, 1997). Similar to NTCP, ASBT transports the substrates with a Na^+ -bile salt stoichiometry of 2:1 (Weinman *et al.*, 1998). The substrates of ASBT include conjugated and unconjugated bile salts whereas the highest affinity was demonstrated for conjugated dihydroxy bile salts (Oelkers *et al.*, 1997). In contrast to NTCP, which also transports some non-bile salts, the substrate specificity of ASBT appears to be restricted to bile salts. Mutations in the human ASBT result in marked malabsorption of bile salts, indicating that ASBT is the key bile salt reabsorption system in the intestine (Wong *et al.*, 1995; Oelkers *et al.*, 1997).

In addition to ASBT, a second sodium-independent bile salt uptake system has been identified in rat jejunum (Abe *et al.*, 1998; Walters *et al.*, 2000). Similar to other OATPs (Oatp1a1, Oatp1a4), Oatp3 transports amphipathic anions including bile salts (Walters *et al.*, 2000; Cattori *et al.*, 2001). The functional relevance of Oatp3 is not fully understood. Recent findings suggested an expression of human OATP1A2 and OATP1B1 in the human small intestine (Glaeser *et al.*, 2004).

Taken together, bile salt transporters are important for the extraction of albumin-bound bile salts from the blood into hepatocytes and for the reabsorption of bile salts from the intestine. Not surprisingly, the ileal bile acid transporters have been investigated as therapeutic targets for altering cholesterol/bile acid synthesis.

Efflux transporters

P-glycoprotein

P-glycoprotein (ABCB1) was first discovered in certain drug resistant tumor cells (Juliano and Ling, 1976; Gottesman *et al.*, 1996). P-glycoprotein is encoded by the *MDR1* gene and is responsible for a part of the multi-drug resistance during chemotherapy. The hydrolysis of ATP drives the efflux of many chemotherapeutic agents out of the tumor cells, leading to decreased intracellular drug concentration thereby resulting in the multi-drug resistance phenotype. This phenomenon has been particularly evident for anthracyclines, vinca-alkaloides, etoposide and paclitaxel (Schinkel, 1997). In addition to tumor cells, P-glycoprotein is also expressed in various tissues such as liver (canalicular membrane), intestinal mucosa (apical membrane of enterocytes), brain (luminal membrane of endothelial cells in brain capillaries), pancreas (apical membrane of secretorial duct), placenta (microvilli of the syncytiotrophoblast), testis (luminal membrane of endothelial cells and lymphocytes (Thiebaut *et al.*, 1987; Cordon-

Cardo *et al.*, 1989; Cordon-Cardo *et al.*, 1990; Klimecki *et al.*, 1994; MacFarland *et al.*, 1994). The importance of P-glycoprotein for the drug elimination and disposition has been well demonstrated using *mdr1* knockout mice (Schinkel *et al.*, 1995; Schinkel *et al.*, 1997). After intravenous and oral administration of digoxin, a P-glycoprotein substrate, *mdr1* knockout mice showed higher concentrations of digoxin in plasma (2 to 4 –fold) and brain (30 to 50-fold) than control mice (Mayer *et al.*, 1996; Schinkel *et al.*, 1997). Furthermore, after intravenous administration of digoxin, a direct intestinal excretion of the drug was observed in control mice, but this is greatly reduced in *mdr1* knockout mice (Mayer *et al.*, 1996). Recent data indicate that the direct secretion of digoxin from the systemic circulation into the intestine after intravenous administration also occurs in humans and this process can be blocked by an intraluminal administration of the P-glycoprotein inhibitor quinidine (Drescher *et al.*, 2003). The impact of P-glycoprotein on the bioavailability has been also demonstrated for HIV protease inhibitors such as indinavir, nelfinavir and saquinavir using *mdr1* knockout mice. The bioavailability of these drugs is greatly increased in *mdr1* knockout mice in comparison to control mice (Kim *et al.*, 1998). Moreover, P-glycoprotein can also limit the tissue penetration of drugs. It has been shown that P-glycoprotein has an impact on the brain entry of digoxin, quinidine, HIV protease inhibitors and loperamide (Kim *et al.*, 1998; Schinkel *et al.*, 1996; Fromm *et al.*, 1999). For example, the antidiarrheal drug, loperamide is a potent opiate, which does not show central nervous system effects under normal conditions. However, when the P-glycoprotein inhibitor quinidine was administered to healthy volunteers, respiratory depression was observed (Sadeque *et al.*, 2000). Such studies illustrate the importance of P-glycoprotein for the CNS entry of certain drugs and that inhibition of P-glycoprotein at the level of the blood-brain barrier can lead to unexpected central side effects of substrate drugs. In addition, P-glycoprotein appears to limit the entry of xenobiotics in other blood-tissue barrier sites, including the testis (Choo *et al.*, 2000) and fetus (placenta) (Lankas *et al.*, 1998). P-glycoprotein has a very broad substrate specificity and transports many structurally unrelated drugs. These compounds mostly have an amphipathic and hydrophobic properties. P-glycoprotein substrates include anticancer drugs, cardiac drugs, HIV protease inhibitors, immunosupressants, antibiotics, β-adrenoceptor blockers and antihistamines (for review see reference (Fromm, 2002)).

Multi Drug Resistance Protein 2 (MRP2)

MRP2 (multidrug resistance protein 2) is one member of the subfamily C of the ABC transporter superfamily, encoded by the *ABCC2* gene. In the past, MRP2 was also known as cMOAT (multispecific organic anion transporter). MPR2 was first cloned from the rat liver (Büchler *et al.*, 1996; Ito *et al.*, 1997; Paulusma *et al.*, 1997). MRP2 is responsible for the unidirectional transport of endogenous and exogenous glutathione, glucuronide and sulfate conjugates of lipophilic compounds as well as some unconjugated lipophilic compounds (Konig *et al.*, 1999b). Similar to P-glycoprotein, MRP2 is expressed on the canalicular membrane of the hepatocytes (Fig.1), apical membrane of renal tubule cells and enterocytes in humans (Schaub *et al.*, 1999; Tsujii *et al.*, 1999; Fromm *et al.*, 2000). The knowledge on the physiological and pathophysiological role of MRP2 was discovered with various Mrp2-deficient animals models such as the TR- rat, GY rat and the EHBR rat (Paulusma and Oude Elferink, 1997). These animals showed significantly reduced transport capacity for bilirubin glucuronides and leucotriene C_4 from the hepatocyte into bile duct due to mutations in *Mrp2* which lead to an absence of Mrp2 expression in the bile canaliculi (Huber *et al.*, 1987; Guhlmann *et al.*, 1995). Moreover, these Mrp2-deficient animals and animals hyperbilirubinemic via bile duct ligation showed increased expression levels of MRP3 on the basolateral membrane of the hepatocytes (Hirohashi *et al.*, 1999). A higher expression of MRP3 has been also detected in patients with Dubin-Johnson syndrome and in patients with primary biliary cirrhosis (Konig *et al.*, 1999a). In these clinical cases, MRP3 transports the MRP2 substrates such as bilirubin glucuronides into blood and decreases the intracellular concentration of these metabolites thus protecting the hepatocytes from toxic concentrations of bilirubin conjugates. A variety of different mutations in the *ABCC2* gene are known to be responsible for the Dubin-Johnson syndrome (for review see reference (Tirona and Kim, 2002)). These mutations lead to missense mutations, nonsense mutations and incorrect splicing. Patients with this syndrome detectable MRP2 when assessed using immunohistochemistry (Kartenbeck *et al.*, 1996; Paulusma *et al.*, 1997; Tsujii *et al.*, 1999). In addition, divalent bile salts with two negative charges such as sulfated tauro- or glycolithocholate are substrates of MRP2, but not monovalent bile salts (Keppler *et al.*, 1999; Keppler and Konig, 2000). Beside the physiological substrates such as glucuronides and glutathiones and sulfates, various drugs or drug metabolites have been identified for MRP2. For example, grepafloxacin, pravastatin, cefodizime, methotrexate and irinotecan are substrates for MRP2 (Sathirakul *et al.*, 1994; Chu *et al.*, 1997; Yamazaki *et al.*, 1997; Sasabe *et al.*, 1998; Hooijberg *et al.*, 1999). Temocaprilat (the active metabolite of temocapril) and SN-38 (the active metabolite of irinotecan), grepafloxacin glucuronide, SN-38 glucuronide, are examples of metabolites and metabolite glucuronides which are transported by MRP2 (Chu *et al.*, 1997; Ishizuka *et al.*, 1997; Sasabe *et al.*, 1998).

Other members of the MRP subfamily

In addition to MRP2, additional members of the multidrug resistance protein subfamily such as, MRP1, MRP3, MRP4, MRP5, MRP6, MRP7, MRP8 and MRP9 have been identified and characterized. MRP1 was first cloned from a doxorubicin-selected multidrug resistant lung cancer cell line which did not overexpress P-glycoprotein (Mirski *et al.*, 1987; Cole *et al.*, 1991; Cole *et al.*, 1992). The gene encoding for MPR1 is *ABCC1*. MRP1 is ubiquitously expressed although its expressions levels differ in various tissues. For example, MRP1 is expressed in relatively high levels in lung, testis, kidney, peripheral blood mononuclear cells and colon (Cole *et al.*, 1992; Flens *et al.*, 1996; Wijnholds *et al.*, 2000), indicating that MRP1 might play a key role in the protection of such tissues against xenobiotics. In polarized cells such as hepatocytes, blood endothelial cells, proximal tubule cells, enterocytes, MRP1 localizes to the basolateral membrane. MRP1 can transport anthracyclines, vinca alkaloids, epipodophyllotoxins, campthothecins and methotrexate (Cole *et al.*, 1994; Zaman *et al.*, 1994; Breuninger *et al.*, 1995; Chen *et al.*, 1999). Other chemotherapeutic drugs transported by MRP1 include irinotecan, the conjugated and unconjugated of SN-38, the active metabolite of irinotecan as well as the antiandrogen flutamide and its metabolite hydroxyflutamide (Chu *et al.*, 1999; Grzywacz *et al.*, 2003). Moreover, the protease inhibitors ritonavir and saquinavir were also identified as MRP1 substrates (Olson *et al.*, 2002; Williams *et al.*, 2002). In addition to xenobiotic substrates, MRP1 can transport of many endogenous compounds such as GSH conjugated cysteinyl leukotriene (LTC$_4$), E$_2$17βG and the sulfated bile salt sulfatolithocholate (Jedlitschky *et al.*, 1994; Leier *et al.*, 1994; Muller *et al.*, 1994; Jedlitschky *et al.*, 1996; Loe *et al.*, 1996a; Loe *et al.*, 1996b). MRP1 also transports endogenous glutathione conjugates and oxidized glutathione (GSSG), suggesting a potential role for this transporter in decreasing the intracellular concentration of such reactive metabolites (Ishikawa, 1992; Haimeur *et al.*, 2004). In contrast to P-glycoprotein, the MRP1-mediated transport has been shown to involve additional mechanism(s) other than the hydrolysis of ATP. Indeed, the inhibitory potency of vincristine, doxorubicin and verapamil appeared to be significantly enhanced by the addition of GSH (Loe *et al.*, 1996a; Loe *et al.*, 1996b; Loe *et al.*, 1998; Loe *et al.*, 2000). The role of GSH in MRP1-mediated transport appears to be complex and the precise mechanistic details have not yet been elucidated.

MRP3, encoded by the *ABCC3* gene, is expressed in small intestine, liver, pancreas, placenta, colon, kidney and adrenal cortex (Belinsky *et al.*, 1998; Hirohashi *et al.*, 1998; Kiuchi *et al.*, 1998; St-Pierre *et al.*, 2000; Soroka *et al.*, 2001; Scheffer *et al.*, 2002). In polarized cells, MRP3 appear to localize to the basolateral membrane (Kool *et al.*, 1999; Rost *et al.*, 2002; Scheffer *et al.*, 2002). In contrast to MPR1 and MRP2, MRP3 is known to contribute in part to the resistance against etoposide and tenoposide (Kool *et al.*, 1999; Zeng *et al.*, 1999; Zelcer *et al.*, 2001). An important observation about MRP3 is the induction of its expression in hepatocytes under cholestatic conditions (Konig *et al.*, 1999a; Donner and Keppler, 2001). Since it is known that MRP3 transports bile acids such as glycocholate and taurocholate, MRP3 may function to extrude toxic bile acids and bilirubin metabolites from the hepatocytes (Hirohashi *et al.*, 2000; Zeng *et al.*, 2000). Because MRP3 is expressed on the basolateral membrane of the enterocytes and capable of transporting bile salts, MRP3 may also act as a basolateral bile salt export pump in the small intestine. However, the physiological functions and relevance of MRP3 in the small intestine to the enterohepatic recirculation of bile salts remains to be clarified.

MRP4 (*ABCC4*), MRP5 (*ABCC5*) and MRP8 (*ABCC11*) are notable for their ability to transport nucleotide analogs. MRP4 and MRP5 are able to transport cGMP and cAMP, suggesting a potential role for these proteins in nucleotide and cyclic nucleotide homeostasis (Jedlitschky *et al.*, 2000; Chen *et al.*, 2001; van Aubel *et al.*, 2002). For MRP8, the extent of its substrate specificity has not been described in detail, but the ability of MRP8 to transport cyclic nucleotides has been shown in transfected cells (Guo *et al.*, 2003). In addition, it has been shown that MRP4 is also able to transport the antiviral drugs armementarium, 9-(2-phosphonylmethoxyethyl)-adenine (PMEA) and azidothymidine and the chemotherapeutic agent methotrexate (Schuetz *et al.*, 1999; Lee *et al.*, 2000; Chen *et al.*, 2002). MRP4 expression has been detected in various tissues including prostate, lung, adrenals, ovary, testis, pancreas, small intestine and liver (Lee *et al.*, 1998). Interestingly, in the prostate, MRP4 is expressed on the basolateral membrane, whereas MRP4 is expressed on the apical membrane of proximal tubule cells in the kidney (Lee *et al.*, 2000; van Aubel *et al.*, 2002). Like MRP1, MRP5 is ubiquitously expressed with high expression in skeletal muscle, heart and brain (Kool *et al.*, 1997; Belinsky *et al.*, 1998; McAleer *et al.*, 1999; Suzuki *et al.*, 2000; Hirrlinger *et al.*, 2002). Interestingly, the transport activity of MRP5 has been shown to be inhibited by sildenafil (Viagra™) (Jedlitschky *et al.*, 2000). Currently, there are discrepancies about the tissue distribution for MRP8 (Tammur *et al.*, 2001; Wang *et al.*, 2001a; Yabuuchi *et al.*, 2001; Bera *et al.*, 2002).

MRP6 (*ABCC6*) has been associated with pseudoxanthoma elasticum (PXE). Specifically, inherited mutations in MRP6 leads to this rare connective disease whose predominant pathological findings are dystrophic elastin fibers in the skin, retina and large blood vessels resulting in the clinical manifestations of baggy skin, loss of vision and calcification of large blood vessels (Bergen *et al.*, 2000; Le Saux *et al.*, 2000; Ringpfeil *et al.*, 2000). MRP6 protein is abundantly expressed in the kidney and liver on the basolateral membrane of hepatocytes and proximal tubule cells, respectively, but not expressed in many other tissues including those affected in PXE patients (skin, retina) (Scheffer *et al.*, 2002). These findings suggest the possibility that PXE might be caused by the absence of substances which are normally secreted from liver or kidney into the blood, required for the maintenance of normal skin connective tissue function. However, there are other findings which also show expression of MRP6 mRNA in tissues such as skin, blood vessels, and retina (Bergen *et al.*, 2000). *In vitro* studies report that MRP6 is able to transport lipophilic anions such as LTC4, N-ethylmaleimide-glutathione and BQ123 (Belinsky *et al.*, 2002; Ilias *et al.*, 2002). In MRP6 transfected cells, it has been demonstrated that MRP6 is able to confer low levels of resistance against etoposide, teniposide, anthracyclines and cisplatin.

MRP7 (*ABCC10*) and MRP9 (*ABCC12*) are the less characterized members of the MRP subfamily. *In vitro* experiments showed that MRP7 can transport $E_2 17\beta G$ and to lesser extent LTC_4, but no other typical MRP substrates (Chen *et al.*, 2003). Little is known regarding expression pattern of MRP7 and MRP9. Whether these transporters are important for the drug disposition needs to be clarified in future studies.

Breast Cancer Resistance Protein (BCRP)

The breast cancer resistance protein (BCRP) was first cloned from mitoxantrone- and anthracycline-resistant breast tumor cells and colon tumor cells (Doyle *et al.*, 1998). Other names for this protein are MXR or ABCP. This protein is encoded by the *ABCG2* the gene. BCRP is also an ABC-transporter driven by hydrolysis of ATP. BCRP has been speculated to be active as a homo- and/or heterodimer. A BCRP related drug resistance has been observed for the topoisomerase inhibitors, camptothecin and dolocarbazol (Brangi *et al.*, 1999; Maliepaard *et al.*, 1999). BCRP can also contribute in part to methotrexate resistance since BCRP is shown to transport methotrexate and its polyglutamates (Volk and Schneider, 2003). BCRP is expressed in normal tissues, e.g. the syncytiotrophoblast of the placenta, canalicular membrane of hepatocytes, apical membrane of enterocytes and endothelial cells of blood vessels (Maliepaard *et al.*, 2001). The importance of BCRP for the drug disposition has been demonstrated for the cytostatic drug, topotecan (Jonker *et al.*, 2000), in that the bioavailability of topotecan and as well as the drug concentrations in the fetus were increased after oral administration of a BCRP inhibitor. In addition, biliary secretion and the plasma clearance of topotecan were decreased when the BCRP inhibitor was administered. Furthermore, the development of bcrp knock-out mice have allowed the investigation of the physiological function of bcrp (Jonker *et al.*, 2002; Zhou *et al.*, 2002). Of note, bcrp knock-out mice, were found to develop phototoxic skin lesions upon exposure to light and chlorophyll-rich diet (Jonker *et al.*, 2002). The accumulation of the chlorophyll metabolite, pheophorbide was found to be responsible for such lesions, indicating that BCRP could have an influence on the disposition of porphyrines and their metabolites. A recent *in vitro* study revealed that the tyrosine kinase inhibitors imatinib, gefitinib and EKI-785 showed a high-affinity interaction with BCRP, indicating that BCRP expression or activity may contribute to the variable pharmacokinetics and/or pharmacody-namics of these drugs and possibly contribute to tyrosine kinase inhibitor resistance (Ozvegy-Laczka *et al.*, 2004).

Bile salt export pump (BSEP)

The canalicular bile salt export pump (BSEP) was first cloned from pig liver as a partial cDNA, followed by full-length cDNA cloning from rat and mouse liver. It has also been referred to as sister of P-glycoprotein (Spgp) (Gerloff *et al.*, 1998; Green *et al.*, 2000; Noe *et al.*, 2001). The gene encoding for this protein is *ABCB11*. BSEP is expressed on the canalicular membrane of the hepatocytes (Fig. 1), (Meier and Stieger, 2002). Transport studies using overexpressing baculovirus-infected Sf9 insect cells revealed that Bsep transports various bile salts in an ATP-dependent manner. These studies also showed that Bsep transports bile salts with different affinity (in the following rank order according to the K_m values, taurochenodeoxycholate > taurocholate > tauroursodeoxycholate > glycocholate), (Byrne *et al.*, 2002; Noe *et al.*, 2002). Moreover, mutations in the human *BSEP* gene lead to a disease known as progressive familial intrahepatic cholestasis type 2 (PFIC2). This is an inherited progressive liver disease charac-terized by high serum bile salt concentrations in conjunction with low γ-glutamyltransferase serum levels (Strautnieks *et al.*, 1998). In such patients,

BSEP protein is not expressed on the canalicular membrane, resulting in decreased of biliary bile salt concentrations to less than 1% of normal concentrations (Jansen *et al.*, 1999). These findings, along with the results from the *in vitro* transport studies, indicate that BSEP is the major if not the only bile salt export pump in the human hepatocytes. The bile salt excretion by BSEP into the bile represents an important step in the enterohepatic circulation of bile salts. Interestingly, targeted inactivation of Bsep in mice results in nonprogressive but persistent intrahepatic cholestasis, due to the de novo formation and biliary excretion of muricholic acid and a novel tetra-hydroxylated bile salt in mice (Wang *et al.*, 2001b). In these mice, a minimal reduction of bile flow and bile salt excretion (to 30%) was observed, indicating that an additional bile salt transporter system(s) in the hepatocytes may exist. Bsep is highly conserved during vertebrate evolution. This was suggested by the cloning of a Bsep ortholog from the liver of the small skate, Raja erinacea, a 200 million-year-old marine vertebrate (Ballatori *et al.*, 2000; Cai *et al.*, 2001).

Clinical Relevance

Drug-Drug interactions

Drug-drug interactions are common problems in clinical practice especially for illnesses which require multiple medications to be coadministered. We now know that inhibition of drug transporters often contribute the extent of interactions seen with some drugs. For example, coadministration of the antiarrhythmic quinidine with digoxin leads to increased digoxin plasma concentration, thus increasing the risk of digoxin toxicity (Doering, 1979). The underlying mechanism of this interaction is the inhibition of P-glycoprotein by quinidine, which leads to the increased absorption and decreased elimination of digoxin (Fromm *et al.*, 1999). Since digoxin is not subject to significant metabolism in humans, drug interactions involving digoxin are likely due to inhibition of drug transport, specifically P-glycoprotein. Conversely, induction of P-glycoprotein, for example by rifampin or St John's wort, decreases the digoxin plasma levels, which in turn can lead to decreased efficacy of this drug. Indeed, in a study of healthy volunteer subjects, coadministration of digoxin (either orally or intravenously) with rifampin (600mg/d for 10 days) had significant reduction on the AUC of digoxin (Greiner *et al.*, 1999). Moreover, similar findings have been observed with other P-glycoprotein substrates during St John's wort therapy. Specifically, the AUCs of the antihistaminic fexofenadine and the β-adrenoceptorblocker talinolol were substantially decreased (Dresser *et al.*, 2003; Schwarz *et al.*, 2002).

Another interesting topic is the influence of dietary constituents on the pharmacokinetics of drugs. For example, it is well known that grapefruit juice can inhibit intestinal CYP3A4 and increase the bioavailability of many drugs prototypical CYP3A4 substrate drugs such as felodipine, sildenafil and erythromycin. However, coadministration of fexofenadine and grapefruit juice led to a decreased AUC for fexofenadine (Dresser *et al.*, 2002). Since fexofenadine is transported by P-glycoprotein and OATPs, these results indicate that this drug interaction might be related to an inhibition of intestinal OATP transporters (Cvetkovic *et al.*, 1999). These examples illustrate transporter-mediated drug interactions may be important, but heretofore under-appreciated mechanism to responsible for certain drug-drug interactions. Indeed, consideration of drug transporters earlier in the drug development process has the potential to result in drugs with more predictable disposition profiles, and less likely to show unexpected drug-drug interactions.

Drug Transporter Pharmacogenetics

At present, P-glycoprotein is one of the best genetically characterized human transporters. Various mutations the *MDR1* gene have been identified by systematic screening for SNPs (single nucleotide polymorphisms) in this transporter (Hoffmeyer *et al.*, 2000; Marzolini *et al.*, 2004). One of the most commonly investigated SNP is the silent (synonymous) polymorphism in exon 26 (C3435T). However, the overall influence of polymorphisms on P-glycoprotein is still controversial (Marzolini *et al.*, 2004).

Another example for transporter pharmacogenetics is OATP1B1. *In vitro* functional studies have shown that certain OATP1B1 variants had altered transport activity for $E_2 17\beta D$ (Tirona *et al.*, 2001). Studies in humans suggest that indeed, these variants may have and impact in the disposition of a model OATP1B1 substrate, pravastatin (Nishizato *et al.*, 2003).

Clearly drug transporter pharmacogenetics is an emerging field with important implications for drug development. Indeed, similar to how our understanding of SNPs in CYP enzymes have led to the development of drugs which do not depend on a single enzyme pathway known to have polymorphism associated loss of function, data relating to functional SNPs in transporters should be taken into account when considering not only bioavailability related issues, but also for their role in altering target organ drug concentrations.

Summary

It is now becoming clear that rational drug development needs to incorporate drug transporters earlier in the discovery/development process. Multiplicity of transporters in different and sometimes restricted tissue compartments may result in unexpected oral bioavailability or organ toxicity for some drugs. Furthermore, in addition to understanding the biology of transporters, systematic in-silico models based on actual transport data will be needed to better predict the structure activity relationship of a novel compound, especially if one hopes to predict the pharmacokinetic profiles in humans. Moreover, the role of genetic polymorphisms in drug transporters and dietary constituents on transporters will also need careful consideration.

Acknowledgements

Supported by USPHS grants GM54724 and GM31304

References

Abe T, Kakyo M, Sakagami H, Tokui T, Nishio T, Tanemoto M, Nomura H, Hebert SC, Matsuno S, Kondo H *et al*. Molecular Characterization and Tissue Distribution of a New Organic Anion Transporter Subtype (Oatp3) That Transports Thyroid Hormones and Taurocholate and Comparison with oatp2. *J Biol Chem*, 1998; 273:22395-22401

Abe T, Kakyo M, Tokui T, Nakagomi R, Nishio T, Nakai D, Nomura H, Unno M, Suzuki M, Naitoh T *et al*. Identification of a Novel Gene Family Encoding Human Liver-Specific Organic Anion Transporter LST-1. *J Biol Chem*, 1999; 274:17159-17163

Abe T, Unno M, Onogawa T, Tokui T, Kondo TN, Nakagomi R, Adachi H, Fujiwara K, Okabe M, Suzuki T *et al*. LST-2, a Human Liver-Specific Organic Anion Transporter, Determines Methotrexate Sensitivity in Gastrointestinal Cancers. *Gastroenterology*, 2001; 120:1689-1699

Alcorn J, Lu X, Moscow JA, and McNamara PJ. Transporter Gene Expression in Lactating and Nonlactating Human Mammary Epithelial Cells Using Real-Time Reverse Transcription-Polymerase Chain Reaction. *J Pharmacol Exp Ther*, 2002; 303:487-496

Ananthanarayanan M, Ng OC, Boyer JL, and Suchy FJ. Characterization of Cloned Rat Liver Na(+)-Bile Acid Cotransporter Using Peptide and Fusion Protein Antibodies. *Am J Physiol*, 1994; 267:G637-643

Apiwattanakul N, Sekine T, Chairoungdua A, Kanai Y, Nakajima N, Sophasan S, and Endou H. Transport Properties of Nonsteroidal Anti-Inflammatory Drugs by Organic Anion Transporter 1 Expressed in Xenopus Laevis Oocytes. *Mol Pharmacol*, 1999; 55:847-854

Babu E, Takeda M, Narikawa S, Kobayashi Y, Enomoto A, Tojo A, Cha SH, Sekine T, Sakthisekaran D, and Endou H. Role of Human Organic Anion Transporter 4 in the Transport of Ochratoxin A. *Biochim Biophys Acta*, 2002; 1590:64-75

Bahn A, Prawitt D, Buttler D, Reid G, Enklaar T, Wolff NA, Ebbinghaus C, Hillemann A, Schulten HJ, Gunawan B *et al*. Genomic Structure and *in Vivo* Expression of the Human Organic Anion Transporter 1 (hOAT1) Gene. *Biochem Biophys Res Commun*, 2000; 275:623-630

Ballatori N, Rebbeor JF, Connolly GC, Seward DJ, Lenth BE, Henson JH, Sundaram P, and Boyer JL. Bile Salt Excretion in Skate Liver Is Mediated by a Functional Analog of Bsep/Spgp, the Bile Salt Export Pump. *Am J Physiol Gastrointest Liver Physiol*, 2000; 278:G57-63

Belinsky MG, Bain LJ, Balsara BB, Testa JR, and Kruh GD. Characterization of MOAT-C and MOAT-D, New Members of the MRP/cMOAT Subfamily of Transporter Proteins. *J Natl Cancer Inst*, 1998; 90:1735-1741

Belinsky MG, Chen ZS, Shchaveleva I, Zeng H, and Kruh GD. Characterization of the Drug Resistance and Transport Properties of Multidrug Resistance Protein 6 (MRP6, ABCC6). *Cancer Res*, 2002; 62:6172-6177

Bera TK, Iavarone C, Kumar V, Lee S, Lee B, and Pastan I. MRP9, an Unusual Truncated Member of the ABC Transporter Superfamily, Is Highly Expressed in Breast Cancer. *Proc Natl Acad Sci USA*, 2002; 99:6997-7002

Bergen AA, Plomp AS, Schuurman EJ, Terry S, Breuning M, Dauwerse H, Swart J, Kool M, van Soest S, Baas F *et al*. Mutations in ABCC6 Cause Pseudoxanthoma Elasticum. *Nat Genet*, 2000; 25:228-231

Bossuyt X, Muller M and Meier PJ. Multispecific Amphipathic Substrate Transport by an Organic Anion Transporter of Human Liver. *J Hepatol*, 1996; 25:733-738

Brangi M, Litman T, Ciotti M, Nishiyama K, Kohlhagen G, Takimoto C, Robey R, Pommier Y, Fojo T, and Bates SE. Camptothecin Resistance: Role of the ATP-Binding Cassette (ABC), Mitoxantrone-Resistance Half-Transporter (MXR), and Potential for Glucuronidation in MXR-Expressing Cells. *Cancer Res*, 1999; 59:5938-5946

Breuninger LM, Paul S, Gaughan K, Miki T, Chan A, Aaronson SA, and Kruh GD. Expression of Multidrug Resistance-Associated Protein in NIH/3T3 Cells Confers Multidrug Resistance Associated with Increased Drug Efflux and Altered Intracellular Drug Distribution. *Cancer Res*, 1995; 55:5342-5347

Büchler M, Konig J, Brom M, Kartenbeck J, Spring H, Horie T, and Keppler D. cDNA Cloning of the Hepatocyte Canalicular Isoform of the Multidrug Resistance Protein, cMrp, Reveals a Novel Conjugate Export Pump Deficient in Hyperbilirubinemic Mutant Rats. *J Biol Chem*, 1996; 271:15091-15098

Byrne JA, Strautnieks SS, Mieli-Vergani G, Higgins CF, Linton KJ, and Thompson RJ. The Human Bile Salt Export Pump: Characterization of Substrate Specificity and Identification of Inhibitors. *Gastroenterology*, 2002; 123:1649-1658

Cai SY, Wang L, Ballatori N, and Boyer JL. Bile Salt Export Pump Is Highly Conserved During Vertebrate Evolution and Its Expression Is Inhibited by PFIC Type II Mutations. *Am J Physiol Gastrointest Liver Physiol*, 2001; 281:G316-322

Cattori V, van Montfoort JE, Stieger B, Landmann L, Meijer DK, Winterhalter KH, Meier PJ, and Hagenbuch B. Localization of Organic Anion Transporting Polypeptide 4 (Oatp4) in Rat Liver and Comparison of Its Substrate Specificity with Oatp1, Oatp2 and Oatp3. *Pflugers Arch*, 2001; 443:188-195

Cha SH, Sekine T, Fukushima JI, Kanai Y, Kobayashi Y, Goya T, and Endou H. Identification and Characterization of Human Organic Anion Transporter 3 Expressing Predominantly in the Kidney. *Mol Pharmacol*, 2001; 59:1277-1286

Cha SH, Sekine T, Kusuhara H, Yu E, Kim JY, Kim DK, Sugiyama Y, Kanai Y, and Endou H. Molecular Cloning and Characterization of Multispecific Organic Anion Transporter 4 Expressed in the Placenta. *J Biol Chem*, 2000; 275:4507-4512

Chen ZS, Lee K and Kruh GD. Transport of Cyclic Nucleotides and Estradiol 17-Beta-D-Glucuronide by Multidrug Resistance Protein 4. Resistance to 6-Mercaptopurine and 6-Thioguanine. *J Biol Chem*, 2001; 276:33747-33754

Chen ZS, Lee K, Walther S, Raftogianis RB, Kuwano M, Zeng H, and Kruh GD. Analysis of Methotrexate and Folate Transport by Multidrug Resistance Protein 4 (ABCC4): MRP4 Is a Component of the Methotrexate Efflux System. *Cancer Res*, 2002; 62:3144-3150

Chen ZS, Robey RW, Belinsky MG, Shchaveleva I, Ren XQ, Sugimoto Y, Ross DD, Bates SE, and Kruh GD. Transport of Methotrexate, Methotrexate Polyglutamates, and 17beta-Estradiol 17-(Beta-D-Glucuronide) by ABCG2: Effects of Acquired Mutations at R482 on Methotrexate Transport. *Cancer Res*, 2003; 63:4048-4054

Chen ZS, Kawabe T, Ono M, Aoki S, Sumizawa T, Furukawa T, Uchiumi T, Wada M, Kuwano M, and Akiyama SI. Effect of Multidrug Resistance-Reversing Agents on Transporting Activity of Human Canalicular Multispecific Organic Anion Transporter. *Mol Pharmacol*, 1999; 56:1219-1228

Choo EF, Leake B, Wandel C, Imamura H, Wood AJ, Wilkinson GR, and Kim RB. Pharmacological Inhibition of P-Glycoprotein Transport Enhances the Distribution of HIV-1 Protease Inhibitors into Brain and Testes. *Drug Metab Dispos*, 2000; 28:655-660

Chu XY, Kato Y and Sugiyama Y. Multiplicity of Biliary Excretion Mechanisms for Irinotecan, CPT-11, and Its Metabolites in Rats. *Cancer Res*, 1997; 57:1934-1938

Chu XY, Suzuki H, Ueda K, Kato Y, Akiyama S, and Sugiyama Y. Active Efflux of CPT-11 and Its Metabolites in Human KB-derived Cell Lines. *J Pharmacol Exp Ther*, 1999; 288:735-741

Cihlar T, Lin DC, Pritchard JB, Fuller MD, Mendel DB, and Sweet DH. The Antiviral Nucleotide Analogs Cidofovir and Adefovir Are Novel Substrates for Human and Rat Renal Organic Anion Transporter 1. *Mol Pharmacol*, 1999; 56:570-580

Cole SP, Chanda ER, Dicke FP, Gerlach JH, and Mirski SE. Non-P-Glycoprotein-Mediated Multidrug Resistance in a Small Cell Lung Cancer Cell Line: Evidence for Decreased Susceptibility to Drug-Induced DNA Damage and Reduced Levels of Topoisomerase II. *Cancer Res*, 1991; 51:3345-3352

Cole SP, Sparks KE, Fraser K, Loe DW, Grant CE, Wilson GM, and Deeley RG. Pharmacological Characterization of Multidrug Resistant MRP-Transfected Human Tumor Cells. *Cancer Res*, 1994; 54:5902-5910

Cole SP, Bhardwaj G, Gerlach JH, Mackie JE, Grant CE, Almquist KC, Stewart AJ, Kurz EU, Duncan AM, and Deeley RG. Overexpression of a Transporter Gene in a Multidrug-Resistant Human Lung Cancer Cell Line. *Science*, 1992; 258:1650-1654

Cordon-Cardo C, O'Brien JP, Boccia J, Casals D, Bertino JR, and Melamed MR. Expression of the Multidrug Resistance Gene Product (P-Glycoprotein) in Human Normal and Tumor Tissues. *J Histochem Cytochem*, 1990; 38:1277-1287

Cordon-Cardo C, O'Brien JP, Casals D, Rittman-Grauer L, Biedler JL, Melamed MR, and Bertino JR. Multidrug-Resistance Gene (P-Glycoprotein) Is Expressed by Endothelial Cells at Blood-Brain Barrier Sites. *Proc Natl Acad Sci USA*, 1989; 86:695-698

Cvetkovic M, Leake B, Fromm MF, Wilkinson GR, and Kim RB. OATP and P-Glycoprotein Transporters Mediate the Cellular Uptake and Excretion of Fexofenadine. *Drug Metab Dispos*, 1999; 27:866-871

Doering W. Quinidine-Digoxin Interaction: Pharmacokinetics, Underlying Mechanism and Clinical Implications. *N Engl J Med*, 1979; 301:400-404

Donner MG and Keppler D. Up-Regulation of Basolateral Multidrug Resistance Protein 3 (Mrp3) in Cholestatic Rat Liver. *Hepatology*, 2001; 34:351-359

Doyle LA, Yang W, Abruzzo LV, Krogmann T, Gao Y, Rishi AK, and Ross DD. A Multidrug Resistance Transporter from Human MCF-7 Breast Cancer Cells. *Proc Natl Acad Sci USA*, 1998; 95:15665-15670

Drescher S, Glaeser H, Murdter T, Hitzl M, Eichelbaum M, and Fromm MF. P-Glycoprotein-Mediated Intestinal and Biliary Digoxin Transport in Humans. *Clin Pharmacol Ther*, 2003; 73:223-231

Dresser GK, Schwarz UI, Wilkinson GR, and Kim RB. Coordinate Induction of Both Cytochrome P4503A and *MDR1* by St John's Wort in Healthy Subjects. *Clin Pharmacol Ther*, 2003; 73:41-50

Dresser GK, Bailey DG, Leake BF, Schwarz UI, Dawson PA, Freeman DJ, and Kim RB. Fruit Juices Inhibit Organic Anion Transporting Polypeptide-Mediated Drug Uptake to Decrease the Oral Availability of Fexofenadine. *Clin Pharmacol Ther*, 2002; 71:11-20

Dresser MJ, Leabman MK and Giacomini KM. Transporters Involved in the Elimination of Drugs in the Kidney: Organic Anion Transporters and Organic Cation Transporters. *J Pharm Sci*, 2001; 90:397-421

Eckhardt U, Horz JA, Petzinger E, Stuber W, Reers M, Dickneite G, Daniel H, Wagener M, Hagenbuch B, Stieger B *et al*. The Peptide-Based Thrombin Inhibitor CRC 220 Is a New Substrate of the Basolateral Rat Liver Organic Anion-Transporting Polypeptide. *Hepatology*, 1996; 24:380-384

Enomoto A, Takeda M, Shimoda M, Narikawa S, Kobayashi Y, Yamamoto T, Sekine T, Cha SH, Niwa T, and Endou H. Interaction of Human Organic Anion Transporters 2 and 4 with Organic Anion Transport Inhibitors. *J Pharmacol Exp Ther*, 2002; 301:797-802

Evans WE and Relling MV. Pharmacogenomics: Translating Functional Genomics into Rational Therapeutics. *Science*, 1999; 286:487-491

Flens MJ, Zaman GJ, van der Valk P, Izquierdo MA, Schroeijers AB, Scheffer GL, van der Groep P, de Haas M, Meijer CJ, and Scheper RJ. Tissue Distribution of the Multidrug Resistance Protein. *Am J Pathol*, 1996; 148:1237-1247

Fritzsch G, Rumrich G and Ullrich KJ. Anion Transport through the Contraluminal Cell Membrane of Renal Proximal Tubule. The Influence of Hydrophobicity and Molecular Charge Distribution on the Inhibitory Activity of Organic Anions. *Biochim Biophys Acta*, 1989; 978:249-256

Fromm MF. The Influence of *MDR1* Polymorphisms on P-Glycoprotein Expression and Function in Humans. *Adv Drug Deliv Rev*, 2002; 54:1295-1310

Fromm MF, Kim RB, Stein CM, Wilkinson GR, and Roden DM. Inhibition of P-Glycoprotein-Mediated Drug Transport: A Unifying Mechanism to Explain the Interaction between Digoxin and Quinidine. *Circulation*, 1999; 99:552-557

Fromm MF, Kauffmann HM, Fritz P, Burk O, Kroemer HK, Warzok RW, Eichelbaum M, Siegmund W, and Schrenk D. The Effect of Rifampin Treatment on Intestinal Expression of Human MRP Transporters. *Am J Pathol*, 2000; 157:1575-1580

Fujiwara K, Adachi H, Nishio T, Unno M, Tokui T, Okabe M, Onogawa T, Suzuki T, Asano N, Tanemoto M *et al*. Identification of Thyroid Hormone Transporters in Humans: Different Molecules Are Involved in a Tissue-Specific Manner. *Endocrinology*, 2001; 142:2005-2012

Ganapathy V, Prasad PD, Ganapathy ME, and Leibach FH. Placental Transporters Relevant to Drug Distribution across the Maternal-Fetal Interface. *J Pharmacol Exp Ther*, 2000; 294:413-420

Gao B and Meier PJ. Organic Anion Transport across the Choroid Plexus. *Microsc Res Tech*, 2001; 52:60-64

Gao B, Hagenbuch B, Kullak-Ublick GA, Benke D, Aguzzi A, and Meier PJ. Organic Anion-Transporting Polypeptides Mediate Transport of Opioid Peptides across Blood-Brain Barrier. *J Pharmacol Exp Ther*, 2000; 294:73-79

Gerloff T, Stieger B, Hagenbuch B, Madon J, Landmann L, Roth J, Hofmann AF, and Meier PJ. The Sister of P-Glycoprotein Represents the Canalicular Bile Salt Export Pump of Mammalian Liver. *J Biol Chem*, 1998; 273:10046-10050

Glaeser H, Bailey DG, Lee W, Dresser GK, Gregor JC, McGrath JS, Jolicoeur E, Roberts R, Smith LH, and Kim RB. Membrane-Associated Expression of Organic Transporting Polypeptides-A and -C in Human Small Intestine. 7TH International ISSX Meeting. Vancouver, Canada, August 29-September 2, 2004.

Gottesman MM, Ambudkar SV, Cornwell MM, Pastan I, and Germann UA. Multidrug Resistance Transporter. In: Schultz SG. *Molecular Biology of Membrane Transport Disorders*. New York, NY: Plenum Press; 1996: 243-257

Green RM, Hoda F and Ward KL. Molecular Cloning and Characterization of the Murine Bile Salt Export Pump. *Gene*, 2000; 241:117-123

Green RM, Gollan JL, Hagenbuch B, Meier PJ, and Beier DR. Regulation of Hepatocyte Bile Salt Transporters During Hepatic Regeneration. *Am J Physiol*, 1997; 273:G621-627

Greiner B, Eichelbaum M, Fritz P, Kreichgauer HP, von Richter O, Zundler J, and Kroemer HK. The Role of Intestinal P-Glycoprotein in the Interaction of Digoxin and Rifampin. *J Clin Invest*, 1999; 104:147-153

Grzywacz MJ, Yang JM and Hait WN. Effect of the Multidrug Resistance Protein on the Transport of the Antiandrogen Flutamide. *Cancer Res*, 2003; 63:2492-2498

Guhlmann A, Krauss K, Oberdorfer F, Siegel T, Scheuber PH, Muller J, Csuk-Glanzer B, Ziegler S, Ostertag H, and Keppler D. Noninvasive Assessment of Hepatobiliary and Renal Elimination of Cysteinyl Leukotrienes by Positron Emission Tomography. *Hepatology*, 1995; 21:1568-1575

Guo Y, Kotova E, Chen ZS, Lee K, Hopper-Borge E, Belinsky MG, and Kruh GD. MRP8, ATP-Binding Cassette C11 (ABCC11), Is a Cyclic Nucleotide Efflux Pump and a Resistance Factor for Fluoropyrimidines 2',3'-Dideoxycytidine and 9'-(2'-Phosphonylmethoxyethyl)Adenine. *J Biol Chem*, 2003; 278:29509-29514

Hagenbuch B and Meier PJ. Molecular Cloning, Chromosomal Localization, and Functional Characterization of a Human Liver Na+/Bile Acid Cotransporter. *J Clin Invest*, 1994; 93:1326-1331

Hagenbuch B and Meier PJ. Sinusoidal (Basolateral) Bile Salt Uptake Systems of Hepatocytes. *Semin Liver Dis*, 1996; 16:129-136

Hagenbuch B and Meier PJ. The Superfamily of Organic Anion Transporting Polypeptides. *Biochim Biophys Acta*, 2003; 1609:1-18

Hagenbuch B and Meier PJ. Organic Anion Transporting Polypeptides of the OATP/ SLC21 Family: Phylogenetic Classification as OATP/ SLCO Superfamily, New Nomenclature and Molecular/Functional Properties. *Pflugers Arch*, 2004; 447:653-665

Hagenbuch B, Scharschmidt BF and Meier PJ. Effect of Antisense Oligonucleotides on the Expression of Hepatocellular Bile Acid and Organic Anion Uptake Systems in Xenopus Laevis Oocytes. *Biochem J*, 1996; 316 (Pt 3):901-904

Haimeur A, Conseil G, Deeley RG, and Cole SP. The MRP-Related and BCRP/ABCG2 Multidrug Resistance Proteins: Biology, Substrate Specificity and Regulation. *Curr Drug Metab*, 2004; 5:21-53

Hirohashi T, Suzuki H and Sugiyama Y. Characterization of the Transport Properties of Cloned Rat Multidrug Resistance-Associated Protein 3 (MRP3). *J Biol Chem*, 1999; 274:15181-15185

Hirohashi T, Suzuki H, Takikawa H, and Sugiyama Y. ATP-Dependent Transport of Bile Salts by Rat Multidrug Resistance-Associated Protein 3 (Mrp3). *J Biol Chem*, 2000; 275:2905-2910

Hirohashi T, Suzuki H, Ito K, Ogawa K, Kume K, Shimizu T, and Sugiyama Y. Hepatic Expression of Multidrug Resistance-Associated Protein-Like Proteins Maintained in Eisai Hyperbilirubinemic Rats. *Mol Pharmacol*, 1998; 53:1068-1075

Hirrlinger J, Konig J and Dringen R. Expression of mRNAs of Multidrug Resistance Proteins (Mrps) in Cultured Rat Astrocytes, Oligodendrocytes, Microglial Cells and Neurones. *J Neurochem*, 2002; 82:716-719

Ho ES, Lin DC, Mendel DB, and Cihlar T. Cytotoxicity of Antiviral Nucleotides Adefovir and Cidofovir Is Induced by the Expression of Human Renal Organic Anion Transporter 1. *J Am Soc Nephrol*, 2000; 11:383-393

Ho RH, Leake BF, Roberts RL, Lee W, and Kim RB. Ethnicity-Dependent Polymorphism in Na+-Taurocholate Cotransporting Polypeptide (SLC10A1) Reveals a Domain Critical for Bile Acid Substrate Recognition. *J Biol Chem*, 2004; 279:7213-7222

Hoffmeyer S, Burke O, von Richter O, Arnold HP, Brockmoller J, Johne A, Cascorbi L, Gerloff T, Roots I, Eichelbaum M, *et al.* Functional polymorphisms of the human multidrug resistancee gene: multiple sequence variations and correlation of one allele with P-glycoprotein expression and activity *in vivo*. *Proc Natl Acad Sci U S A*, 2000; 97:3473-3478.

Hooijberg JH, Broxterman HJ, Kool M, Assaraf YG, Peters GJ, Noordhuis P, Scheper RJ, Borst P, Pinedo HM, and Jansen G. Antifolate Resistance Mediated by the Multidrug Resistance Proteins MRP1 and MRP2. *Cancer Res*, 1999; 59:2532-2535

Hosoyamada M, Sekine T, Kanai Y, and Endou H. Molecular Cloning and Functional Expression of a Multispecific Organic Anion Transporter from Human Kidney. *Am J Physiol*, 1999; 276:F122-128

Hsiang B, Zhu Y, Wang Z, Wu Y, Sasseville V, Yang WP, and Kirchgessner TG. A Novel Human Hepatic Organic Anion Transporting Polypeptide (OATP2). Identification of a Liver-Specific Human Organic Anion Transporting Polypeptide and Identification of Rat and Human Hydroxymethylglutaryl-CoA Reductase Inhibitor Transporters. *J Biol Chem*, 1999; 274:37161-37168

Huber M, Guhlmann A, Jansen PL, and Keppler D. Hereditary Defect of Hepatobiliary Cysteinyl Leukotriene Elimination in Mutant Rats with Defective Hepatic Anion Excretion. *Hepatology*, 1987; 7:224-228

Ilias A, Urban Z, Seidl TL, Le Saux O, Sinko E, Boyd CD, Sarkadi B, and Varadi A. Loss of ATP-Dependent Transport Activity in Pseudoxanthoma Elasticum-Associated Mutants of Human ABCC6 (MRP6). *J Biol Chem*, 2002; 277:16860-16867

Inui KI, Masuda S and Saito H. Cellular and Molecular Aspects of Drug Transport in the Kidney. *Kidney Int*, 2000; 58:944-958

Ishikawa T. The ATP-Dependent Glutathione S-Conjugate Export Pump. *Trends Biochem Sci*, 1992; 17:463-468

Ishizuka H, Konno K, Naganuma H, Sasahara K, Kawahara Y, Niinuma K, Suzuki H, and Sugiyama Y. Temocaprilat, a Novel Angiotensin-Converting Enzyme Inhibitor, Is Excreted in Bile Via an ATP-Dependent Active Transporter (cMOAT) That Is Deficient in Eisai Hyperbilirubinemic Mutant Rats (EHBR). *J Pharmacol Exp Ther*, 1997; 280:1304-1311

Ismair MG, Stieger B, Cattori V, Hagenbuch B, Fried M, Meier PJ, and Kullak-Ublick GA. Hepatic Uptake of Cholecystokinin Octapeptide by Organic Anion-Transporting Polypeptides OATP4 and Oatp8 of Rat and Human Liver. *Gastroenterology*, 2001; 121:1185-1190

Ito K, Suzuki H, Hirohashi T, Kume K, Shimizu T, and Sugiyama Y. Molecular Cloning of Canalicular Multispecific Organic Anion Transporter Defective in EHBR. *Am J Physiol*, 1997; 272:G16-22

Jacquemin E, Hagenbuch B, Stieger B, Wolkoff AW, and Meier PJ. Expression Cloning of a Rat Liver Na(+)-Independent Organic Anion Transporter. *Proc Natl Acad Sci USA*, 1994; 91:133-137

Jansen PL, Strautnieks SS, Jacquemin E, Hadchouel M, Sokal EM, Hooiveld GJ, Koning JH, De Jager-Krikken A, Kuipers F, Stellaard F *et al.* Hepatocanalicular Bile Salt Export Pump Deficiency in Patients with Progressive Familial Intrahepatic Cholestasis. *Gastroenterology*, 1999; 117:1370-1379

Jariyawat S, Sekine T, Takeda M, Apiwattanakul N, Kanai Y, Sophasan S, and Endou H. The Interaction and Transport of Beta-Lactam Antibiotics with the Cloned Rat Renal Organic Anion Transporter 1. *J Pharmacol Exp Ther*, 1999; 290:672-677

Jedlitschky G, Burchell B and Keppler D. The Multidrug Resistance Protein 5 Functions as an ATP-Dependent Export Pump for Cyclic Nucleotides. *J Biol Chem*, 2000; 275:30069-30074

Jedlitschky G, Leier I, Buchholz U, Center M, and Keppler D. ATP-Dependent Transport of Glutathione S-Conjugates by the Multidrug Resistance-Associated Protein. *Cancer Res*, 1994; 54:4833-4836

Jedlitschky G, Leier I, Buchholz U, Barnouin K, Kurz G, and Keppler D. Transport of Glutathione, Glucuronate, and Sulfate Conjugates by the MRP Gene-Encoded Conjugate Export Pump. *Cancer Res*, 1996; 56:988-994

Jonker JW, Smit JW, Brinkhuis RF, Maliepaard M, Beijnen JH, Schellens JH, and Schinkel AH. Role of Breast Cancer Resistance Protein in the Bioavailability and Fetal Penetration of Topotecan. *J Natl Cancer Inst*, 2000; 92:1651-1656

Jonker JW, Buitelaar M, Wagenaar E, Van Der Valk MA, Scheffer GL, Scheper RJ, Plosch T, Kuipers F, Elferink RP, Rosing H *et al*. The Breast Cancer Resistance Protein Protects against a Major Chlorophyll-Derived Dietary Phototoxin and Protoporphyria. *Proc Natl Acad Sci USA*, 2002; 99:15649-15654

Juliano RL and Ling V. A Surface Glycoprotein Modulating Drug Permeability in Chinese Hamster Ovary Cell Mutants. *Biochim Biophys Acta*, 1976; 455:152-162

Kartenbeck J, Leuschner U, Mayer R, and Keppler D. Absence of the Canalicular Isoform of the MRP Gene-Encoded Conjugate Export Pump from the Hepatocytes in Dubin-Johnson Syndrome. *Hepatology*, 1996; 23:1061-1066

Keppler D and Konig J. Hepatic Secretion of Conjugated Drugs and Endogenous Substances. *Semin Liver Dis*, 2000; 20:265-272

Keppler D, Cui Y, Konig J, Leier I, and Nies A. Export Pumps for Anionic Conjugates Encoded by MRP Genes. *Adv Enzyme Regul*, 1999; 39:237-246

Khamdang S, Takeda M, Noshiro R, Narikawa S, Enomoto A, Anzai N, Piyachaturawat P, and Endou H. Interactions of Human Organic Anion Transporters and Human Organic Cation Transporters with Nonsteroidal Anti-Inflammatory Drugs. *J Pharmacol Exp Ther*, 2002; 303:534-539

Kim RB, Fromm MF, Wandel C, Leake B, Wood AJ, Roden DM, and Wilkinson GR. The Drug Transporter P-Glycoprotein Limits Oral Absorption and Brain Entry of HIV-1 Protease Inhibitors. *J Clin Invest*, 1998; 101:289-294

Kiuchi Y, Suzuki H, Hirohashi T, Tyson CA, and Sugiyama Y. cDNA Cloning and Inducible Expression of Human Multidrug Resistance Associated Protein 3 (MRP3). *FEBS Lett*, 1998; 433:149-152

Klimecki WT, Futscher BW, Grogan TM, and Dalton WS. P-Glycoprotein Expression and Function in Circulating Blood Cells from Normal Volunteers. *Blood*, 1994; 83:2451-2458

Kojima R, Sekine T, Kawachi M, Cha SH, Suzuki Y, and Endou H. Immunolocalization of Multispecific Organic Anion Transporters, OAT1, OAT2, and OAT3, in Rat Kidney. *J Am Soc Nephrol*, 2002; 13:848-857

Konig J, Rost D, Cui Y, and Keppler D. Characterization of the Human Multidrug Resistance Protein Isoform MRP3 Localized to the Basolateral Hepatocyte Membrane. *Hepatology*, 1999a; 29:1156-1163

Konig J, Cui Y, Nies AT, and Keppler D. A Novel Human Organic Anion Transporting Polypeptide Localized to the Basolateral Hepatocyte Membrane. *Am J Physiol Gastrointest Liver Physiol*, 2000a; 278:G156-164

Konig J, Cui Y, Nies AT, and Keppler D. Localization and Genomic Organization of a New Hepatocellular Organic Anion Transporting Polypeptide. *J Biol Chem*, 2000b; 275:23161-23168

Konig J, Nies AT, Cui Y, Leier I, and Keppler D. Conjugate Export Pumps of the Multidrug Resistance Protein (MRP) Family: Localization, Substrate Specificity, and MRP2-Mediated Drug Resistance. *Biochim Biophys Acta*, 1999b; 1461:377-394

Kool M, de Haas M, Scheffer GL, Scheper RJ, van Eijk MJ, Juijn JA, Baas F, and Borst P. Analysis of Expression of cMOAT (MRP2), MRP3, MRP4, and MRP5, Homologues of the Multidrug Resistance-Associated Protein Gene (MRP1), in Human Cancer Cell Lines. *Cancer Res*, 1997; 57:3537-3547

Kool M, van der Linden M, de Haas M, Scheffer GL, de Vree JM, Smith AJ, Jansen G, Peters GJ, Ponne N, Scheper RJ *et al*. MRP3, an Organic Anion Transporter Able to Transport Anti-Cancer Drugs. *Proc Natl Acad Sci USA*, 1999; 96:6914-6919

Kramer W, Stengelin S, Baringhaus KH, Enhsen A, Heuer H, Becker W, Corsiero D, Girbig F, Noll R, and Weyland C. Substrate Specificity of the Ileal and the Hepatic Na(+)/Bile Acid Cotransporters of the Rabbit. I. Transport Studies with Membrane Vesicles and Cell Lines Expressing the Cloned Transporters. *J Lipid Res*, 1999; 40:1604-1617

Kullak-Ublick GA, Stieger B, Hagenbuch B, and Meier PJ. Hepatic Transport of Bile Salts. *Semin Liver Dis*, 2000; 20:273-292

Kullak-Ublick GA, Hagenbuch B, Stieger B, Schteingart CD, Hofmann AF, Wolkoff AW, and Meier PJ. Molecular and Functional Characterization of an Organic Anion Transporting Polypeptide Cloned from Human Liver. *Gastroenterology*, 1995; 109:1274-1282

Kullak-Ublick GA, Fisch T, Oswald M, Hagenbuch B, Meier PJ, Beuers U, and Paumgartner G. Dehydroepiandrosterone Sulfate (DHEAS): Identification of a Carrier Protein in Human Liver and Brain. *FEBS Lett*, 1998; 424:173-176

Kullak-Ublick GA, Ismair MG, Stieger B, Landmann L, Huber R, Pizzagalli F, Fattinger K, Meier PJ, and Hagenbuch B. Organic Anion-Transporting Polypeptide B (OATP-B) and Its Functional Comparison with Three Other OATPs of Human Liver. *Gastroenterology*, 2001; 120:525-533

Kullak-Ublick GA, Glasa J, Boker C, Oswald M, Grutzner U, Hagenbuch B, Stieger B, Meier PJ, Beuers U, Kramer W *et al.* Chlorambucil-Taurocholate Is Transported by Bile Acid Carriers Expressed in Human Hepatocellular Carcinomas. *Gastroenterology*, 1997; 113:1295-1305

Kusuhara H, Sekine T, Utsunomiya-Tate N, Tsuda M, Kojima R, Cha SH, Sugiyama Y, Kanai Y, and Endou H. Molecular Cloning and Characterization of a New Multispecific Organic Anion Transporter from Rat Brain. *J Biol Chem*, 1999; 274:13675-13680

Lankas GR, Wise LD, Cartwright ME, Pippert T, and Umbenhauer DR. Placental P-Glycoprotein Deficiency Enhances Susceptibility to Chemically Induced Birth Defects in Mice. *Reprod Toxicol*, 1998; 12:457-463

Lazaridis KN, Pham L, Tietz P, Marinelli RA, deGroen PC, Levine S, Dawson PA, and LaRusso NF. Rat Cholangiocytes Absorb Bile Acids at Their Apical Domain Via the Ileal Sodium-Dependent Bile Acid Transporter. *J Clin Invest*, 1997; 100:2714-2721

Le Saux O, Urban Z, Tschuch C, Csiszar K, Bacchelli B, Quaglino D, Pasquali-Ronchetti I, Pope FM, Richards A, Terry S *et al.* Mutations in a Gene Encoding an ABC Transporter Cause Pseudoxanthoma Elasticum. *Nat Genet*, 2000; 25:223-227

Lee K, Klein-Szanto AJ and Kruh GD. Analysis of the MRP4 Drug Resistance Profile in Transfected Nih3t3 Cells. *J Natl Cancer Inst*, 2000; 92:1934-1940

Lee K, Belinsky MG, Bell DW, Testa JR, and Kruh GD. Isolation of MOAT-B, a Widely Expressed Multidrug Resistance-Associated Protein/Canalicular Multispecific Organic Anion Transporter-Related Transporter. *Cancer Res*, 1998; 58:2741-2747

Lee TK, Hammond CL and Ballatori N. Intracellular Glutathione Regulates Taurocholate Transport in HepG2 Cells. *Toxicol Appl Pharmacol*, 2001; 174:207-215

Leier I, Jedlitschky G, Buchholz U, Cole SP, Deeley RG, and Keppler D. The MRP Gene Encodes an ATP-Dependent Export Pump for Leukotriene C4 and Structurally Related Conjugates. *J Biol Chem*, 1994; 269:27807-27810

Li L, Meier PJ and Ballatori N. Oatp2 Mediates Bidirectional Organic Solute Transport: A Role for Intracellular Glutathione. *Mol Pharmacol*, 2000; 58:335-340

Li L, Lee TK, Meier PJ, and Ballatori N. Identification of Glutathione as a Driving Force and Leukotriene C4 as a Substrate for Oatp1, the Hepatic Sinusoidal Organic Solute Transporter. *J Biol Chem*, 1998; 273:16184-16191

Liang D, Hagenbuch B, Stieger B, and Meier PJ. Parallel Decrease of Na(+)-Taurocholate Cotransport and Its Encoding mRNA in Primary Cultures of Rat Hepatocytes. *Hepatology*, 1993; 18:1162-1166

Loe DW, Deeley RG and Cole SP. Characterization of Vincristine Transport by the M(R) 190,000 Multidrug Resistance Protein (MRP): Evidence for Cotransport with Reduced Glutathione. *Cancer Res*, 1998; 58:5130-5136

Loe DW, Deeley RG and Cole SP. Verapamil Stimulates Glutathione Transport by the 190-Kda Multidrug Resistance Protein 1 (MRP1). *J Pharmacol Exp Ther*, 2000; 293:530-538

Loe DW, Almquist KC, Cole SP, and Deeley RG. ATP-Dependent 17 Beta-Estradiol 17-(Beta-D-Glucuronide) Transport by Multidrug Resistance Protein (MRP). Inhibition by Cholestatic Steroids. *J Biol Chem*, 1996a; 271:9683-9689

Loe DW, Almquist KC, Deeley RG, and Cole SP. Multidrug Resistance Protein (MRP)-Mediated Transport of Leukotriene C4 and Chemotherapeutic Agents in Membrane Vesicles. Demonstration of Glutathione-Dependent Vincristine Transport. *J Biol Chem*, 1996b; 271:9675-9682

Lopez-Nieto CE and Nigam SK. Selective Amplification of Protein-Coding Regions of Large Sets of Genes Using Statistically Designed Primer Sets. *Nat Biotechnol*, 1996; 14:857-861

Lopez-Nieto CE, You G, Bush KT, Barros EJ, Beier DR, and Nigam SK. Molecular Cloning and Characterization of NKT, a Gene Product Related to the Organic Cation Transporter Family That Is Almost Exclusively Expressed in the Kidney. *J Biol Chem*, 1997; 272:6471-6478

Lu R, Chan BS and Schuster VL. Cloning of the Human Kidney PAH Transporter: Narrow Substrate Specificity and Regulation by Protein Kinase C. *Am J Physiol*, 1999; 276:F295-303

Lu R, Kanai N, Bao Y, and Schuster VL. Cloning, *in Vitro* Expression, and Tissue Distribution of a Human Prostaglandin Transporter cDNA(hPGT). *J Clin Invest*, 1996; 98:1142-1149

MacFarland A, Abramovich DR, Ewen SW, and Pearson CK. Stage-Specific Distribution of P-Glycoprotein in First-Trimester and Full-Term Human Placenta. *Histochem J*, 1994; 26:417-423

Maliepaard M, van Gastelen MA, de Jong LA, Pluim D, van Waardenburg RC, Ruevekamp-Helmers MC, Floot BG, and Schellens JH. Overexpression of the BCRP/MXR/ABCP Gene in a Topotecan-Selected Ovarian Tumor Cell Line. *Cancer Res*, 1999; 59:4559-4563

Marzolini C, Paus E, Buclin T, and Kim RB. 2004. Polymorphisms in human MDR1 (P-glycoprotein): recent advances and clinical relevance. *Clin Pharmacol Ther*, 2004; 75:13-33.

Maliepaard M, Scheffer GL, Faneyte IF, van Gastelen MA, Pijnenborg AC, Schinkel AH, van De Vijver MJ, Scheper RJ, and Schellens JH. Subcellular Localization and Distribution of the Breast Cancer Resistance Protein Transporter in Normal Human Tissues. *Cancer Res*, 2001; 61:3458-3464

Mayer U, Wagenaar E, Beijnen JH, Smit JW, Meijer DK, van Asperen J, Borst P, and Schinkel AH. Substantial Excretion of Digoxin Via the Intestinal Mucosa and Prevention of Long-Term Digoxin Accumulation in the Brain by the mdr 1a P-Glycoprotein. *Br J Pharmacol*, 1996; 119:1038-1044

McAleer MA, Breen MA, White NL, and Matthews N. pABC11 (Also Known as MOAT-C and MRP5), a Member of the ABC Family of Proteins, Has Anion Transporter Activity but Does Not Confer Multidrug Resistance When Overexpressed in Human Embryonic Kidney 293 Cells. *J Biol Chem*, 1999; 274:23541-23548

Meier PJ and Stieger B. Bile Salt Transporters. *Annu Rev Physiol*, 2002; 64:635-661

Meier PJ, Eckhardt U, Schroeder A, Hagenbuch B, and Stieger B. Substrate Specificity of Sinusoidal Bile Acid and Organic Anion Uptake Systems in Rat and Human Liver. *Hepatology*, 1997; 26:1667-1677

Mirski SE, Gerlach JH and Cole SP. Multidrug Resistance in a Human Small Cell Lung Cancer Cell Line Selected in Adriamycin. *Cancer Res*, 1987; 47:2594-2598

Morita N, Kusuhara H, Sekine T, Endou H, and Sugiyama Y. Functional Characterization of Rat Organic Anion Transporter 2 in LLC-PK1 Cells. *J Pharmacol Exp Ther*, 2001; 298:1179-1184

Muller M, Meijer C, Zaman GJ, Borst P, Scheper RJ, Mulder NH, de Vries EG, and Jansen PL. Overexpression of the Gene Encoding the Multidrug Resistance-Associated Protein Results in Increased ATP-Dependent Glutathione S-Conjugate Transport. *Proc Natl Acad Sci USA*, 1994; 91:13033-13037

Nishizato Y, Ieiri I, Suzuki H, Kimura M, Kawabata K, Hirota T, Takane H, Irie S, Kusuhara H, Urasaki Y *et al.* Polymorphisms of OATP-C (SLC21A6) and OAT3 (SLC22A8) Genes: Consequences for Pravastatin Pharmacokinetics. *Clin Pharmacol Ther*, 2003; 73:554-565

Noe B, Hagenbuch B, Stieger B, and Meier PJ. Isolation of a Multispecific Organic Anion and Cardiac Glycoside Transporter from Rat Brain. *Proc Natl Acad Sci USA*, 1997; 94:10346-10350

Noe J, Stieger B and Meier PJ. Functional Expression of the Canalicular Bile Salt Export Pump of Human Liver. *Gastroenterology*, 2002; 123:1659-1666

Noe J, Hagenbuch B, Meier PJ, and St-Pierre MV. Characterization of the Mouse Bile Salt Export Pump Overexpressed in the Baculovirus System. *Hepatology*, 2001; 33:1223-1231

Oelkers P, Kirby LC, Heubi JE, and Dawson PA. Primary Bile Acid Malabsorption Caused by Mutations in the Ileal Sodium-Dependent Bile Acid Transporter Gene (Slc10a2). *J Clin Invest*, 1997; 99:1880-1887

Olson DP, Scadden DT, D'Aquila RT, and De Pasquale MP. The Protease Inhibitor Ritonavir Inhibits the Functional Activity of the Multidrug Resistance Related-Protein 1 (MRP-1). *Aids*, 2002; 16:1743-1747

Ozvegy-Laczka C, Hegedus T, Varady G, Ujhelly O, Schuetz JD, Varadi A, Keri G, Orfi L, Nemet K, and Sarkadi B. High-Affinity Interaction of Tyrosine Kinase Inhibitors with the ABCG2 Multidrug Transporter. *Mol Pharmacol*, 2004; 65:1485-1495

Paulusma CC and Oude Elferink RP. The Canalicular Multispecific Organic Anion Transporter and Conjugated Hyperbilirubinemia in Rat and Man. *J Mol Med*, 1997; 75:420-428

Paulusma CC, Kool M, Bosma PJ, Scheffer GL, ter Borg F, Scheper RJ, Tytgat GN, Borst P, Baas F, and Oude Elferink RP. A Mutation in the Human Canalicular Multispecific Organic Anion Transporter Gene Causes the Dubin-Johnson Syndrome. *Hepatology*, 1997; 25:1539-1542

Pizzagalli F, Hagenbuch B, Stieger B, Klenk U, Folkers G, and Meier PJ. Identification of a Novel Human Organic Anion Transporting Polypeptide as a High Affinity Thyroxine Transporter. *Mol Endocrinol*, 2002; 16:2283-2296

Race JE, Grassl SM, Williams WJ, and Holtzman EJ. Molecular Cloning and Characterization of Two Novel Human Renal Organic Anion Transporters (hOAT1 and hOAT3). *Biochem Biophys Res Commun*, 1999; 255:508-514

Reichel C, Gao B, Van Montfoort J, Cattori V, Rahner C, Hagenbuch B, Stieger B, Kamisako T, and Meier PJ. Localization and Function of the Organic Anion-Transporting Polypeptide Oatp2 in Rat Liver. *Gastroenterology*, 1999; 117:688-695

Ringpfeil F, Lebwohl MG, Christiano AM, and Uitto J. Pseudoxanthoma Elasticum: Mutations in the MRP6 Gene Encoding a Transmembrane ATP-Binding Cassette (ABC) Transporter. *Proc Natl Acad Sci USA*, 2000; 97:6001-6006

Rippin SJ, Hagenbuch B, Meier PJ, and Stieger B. Cholestatic Expression Pattern of Sinusoidal and Canalicular Organic Anion Transport Systems in Primary Cultured Rat Hepatocytes. *Hepatology*, 2001; 33:776-782

Rost D, Mahner S, Sugiyama Y, and Stremmel W. Expression and Localization of the Multidrug Resistance-Associated Protein 3 in Rat Small and Large Intestine. *Am J Physiol Gastrointest Liver Physiol*, 2002; 282:G720-726

Sadeque AJ, Wandel C, He H, Shah S, and Wood AJ. Increased Drug Delivery to the Brain by P-Glycoprotein Inhibition. *Clin Pharmacol Ther*, 2000; 68:231-237

Saeki T, Matoba K, Furukawa H, Kirifuji K, Kanamoto R, and Iwami K. Characterization, cDNA Cloning, and Functional Expression of Mouse Ileal Sodium-Dependent Bile Acid Transporter. *J Biochem (Tokyo)*, 1999; 125:846-851

Sasabe H, Tsuji A and Sugiyama Y. Carrier-Mediated Mechanism for the Biliary Excretion of the Quinolone Antibiotic Grepafloxacin and Its Glucuronide in Rats. *J Pharmacol Exp Ther*, 1998; 284:1033-1039

Sathirakul K, Suzuki H, Yamada T, Hanano M, and Sugiyama Y. Multiple Transport Systems for Organic Anions across the Bile Canalicular Membrane. *J Pharmacol Exp Ther*, 1994; 268:65-73

Satlin LM, Amin V and Wolkoff AW. Organic Anion Transporting Polypeptide Mediates Organic Anion/Hco3- Exchange. *J Biol Chem*, 1997; 272:26340-26345

Schaub TP, Kartenbeck J, Konig J, Spring H, Dorsam J, Staehler G, Storkel S, Thon WF, and Keppler D. Expression of the MRP2 Gene-Encoded Conjugate Export Pump in Human Kidney Proximal Tubules and in Renal Cell Carcinoma. *J Am Soc Nephrol*, 1999; 10:1159-1169

Scheffer GL, Hu X, Pijnenborg AC, Wijnholds J, Bergen AA, and Scheper RJ. MRP6 (ABCC6) Detection in Normal Human Tissues and Tumors. *Lab Invest*, 2002; 82:515-518

Schinkel AH. The Physiological Function of Drug-Transporting P-Glycoproteins. *Semin Cancer Biol*, 1997; 8:161-170

Schinkel AH, Wagenaar E, Mol CA, and van Deemter L. P-Glycoprotein in the Blood-Brain Barrier of Mice Influences the Brain Penetration and Pharmacological Activity of Many Drugs. *J Clin Invest*, 1996; 97:2517-2524

Schinkel AH, Wagenaar E, van Deemter L, Mol CA, and Borst P. Absence of the *Mdr1*a P-Glycoprotein in Mice Affects Tissue Distribution and Pharmacokinetics of Dexamethasone, Digoxin, and Cyclosporin A. *J Clin Invest*, 1995; 96:1698-1705

Schinkel AH, Mayer U, Wagenaar E, Mol CA, van Deemter L, Smit JJ, van der Valk MA, Voordouw AC, Spits H, van Tellingen O *et al*. Normal Viability and Altered Pharmacokinetics in Mice Lacking *Mdr1*-Type (Drug-Transporting) P-Glycoproteins. *Proc Natl Acad Sci USA*, 1997; 94:4028-4033

Schuetz JD, Connelly MC, Sun D, Paibir SG, Flynn PM, Srinivas RV, Kumar A, and Fridland A. MRP4: A Previously Unidentified Factor in Resistance to Nucleoside-Based Antiviral Drugs. *Nat Med*, 1999; 5:1048-1051

Schwarz UI, Hanso H, Dresser GK, Kim RB, Fromm MF, Oertel R, Miehlke S, and Kirch W. St Johns's Wort Reduces Oral Bioavailability of Talinolol in Healthy Volunteers. Annual Meeting of the American Society for Clinical Pharmacology and Therapeutics. Atlanta, GA, March 24-27, 2002.

Sekine T, Watanabe N, Hosoyamada M, Kanai Y, and Endou H. Expression Cloning and Characterization of a Novel Multispecific Organic Anion Transporter. *J Biol Chem*, 1997; 272:18526-18529

Sekine T, Cha SH, Tsuda M, Apiwattanakul N, Nakajima N, Kanai Y, and Endou H. Identification of Multispecific Organic Anion Transporter 2 Expressed Predominantly in the Liver. *FEBS Lett*, 1998; 429:179-182

Shi X, Bai S, Ford AC, Burk RD, Jacquemin E, Hagenbuch B, Meier PJ, and Wolkoff AW. Stable Inducible Expression of a Functional Rat Liver Organic Anion Transport Protein in Hela Cells. *J Biol Chem*, 1995; 270:25591-25595

Shneider BL, Dawson PA, Christie DM, Hardikar W, Wong MH, and Suchy FJ. Cloning and Molecular Characterization of the Ontogeny of a Rat Ileal Sodium-Dependent Bile Acid Transporter. *J Clin Invest*, 1995; 95:745-754

Soroka CJ, Lee JM, Azzaroli F, and Boyer JL. Cellular Localization and up-Regulation of Multidrug Resistance-Associated Protein 3 in Hepatocytes and Cholangiocytes During Obstructive Cholestasis in Rat Liver. *Hepatology*, 2001; 33:783-791

Stieger B, Hagenbuch B, Landmann L, Hochli M, Schroeder A, and Meier PJ. *In Situ* Localization of the Hepatocytic Na+/Taurocholate Cotransporting Polypeptide in Rat Liver. *Gastroenterology*, 1994; 107:1781-1787

St-Pierre MV, Hagenbuch B, Ugele B, Meier PJ, and Stallmach T. Characterization of an Organic Anion-Transporting Polypeptide (OATP-B) in Human Placenta. *J Clin Endocrinol Metab*, 2002; 87:1856-1863

St-Pierre MV, Serrano MA, Macias RI, Dubs U, Hoechli M, Lauper U, Meier PJ, and Marin JJ. Expression of Members of the Multidrug Resistance Protein Family in Human Term Placenta. *Am J Physiol Regul Integr Comp Physiol*, 2000; 279:R1495-1503

Strautnieks SS, Bull LN, Knisely AS, Kocoshis SA, Dahl N, Arnell H, Sokal E, Dahan K, Childs S, Ling V *et al*. A Gene Encoding a Liver-Specific ABC Transporter Is Mutated in Progressive Familial Intrahepatic Cholestasis. *Nat Genet*, 1998; 20:233-238

Sun W, Wu RR, van Poelje PD, and Erion MD. Isolation of a Family of Organic Anion Transporters from Human Liver and Kidney. *Biochem Biophys Res Commun*, 2001; 283:417-422

Suzuki H and Sugiyama Y. Transport of Drugs across the Hepatic Sinusoidal Membrane: Sinusoidal Drug Influx and Efflux in the Liver. *Semin Liver Dis*, 2000a; 20:251-263

Suzuki H and Sugiyama Y. Role of Metabolic Enzymes and Efflux Transporters in the Absorption of Drugs from the Small Intestine. *Eur J Pharm Sci*, 2000b; 12:3-12

Suzuki T, Sasaki H, Kuh HJ, Agui M, Tatsumi Y, Tanabe S, Terada M, Saijo N, and Nishio K. Detailed Structural Analysis on Both Human MRP5 and Mouse Mrp5 Transcripts. *Gene*, 2000; 242:167-173

Sweet DH, Wolff NA and Pritchard JB. Expression Cloning and Characterization of ROAT1. The Basolateral Organic Anion Transporter in Rat Kidney. *J Biol Chem*, 1997; 272:30088-30095

Sweet DH, Chan LM, Walden R, Yang XP, Miller DS, and Pritchard JB. Organic Anion Transporter 3 (Slc22a8) Is a Dicarboxylate Exchanger Indirectly Coupled to the Na+ Gradient. *Am J Physiol Renal Physiol*, 2003; 284:F763-769

Takeda M, Khamdang S, Narikawa S, Kimura H, Hosoyamada M, Cha SH, Sekine T, and Endou H. Characterization of Methotrexate Transport and Its Drug Interactions with Human Organic Anion Transporters. *J Pharmacol Exp Ther*, 2002; 302:666-671

Tamai I and Tsuji A. Transporter-Mediated Permeation of Drugs across the Blood-Brain Barrier. *J Pharm Sci*, 2000; 89:1371-1388

Tamai I, Nezu J, Uchino H, Sai Y, Oku A, Shimane M, and Tsuji A. Molecular Identification and Characterization of Novel Members of the Human Organic Anion Transporter (OATP) Family. *Biochem Biophys Res Commun*, 2000; 273:251-260

Tammur J, Prades C, Arnould I, Rzhetsky A, Hutchinson A, Adachi M, Schuetz JD, Swoboda KJ, Ptacek LJ, Rosier M *et al*. Two New Genes from the Human ATP-Binding Cassette Transporter Superfamily, ABCC11 and ABCC12, Tandemly Duplicated on Chromosome 16q12. *Gene*, 2001; 273:89-96

Thiebaut F, Tsuruo T, Hamada H, Gottesman MM, Pastan I, and Willingham MC. Cellular Localization of the Multidrug-Resistance Gene Product P-Glycoprotein in Normal Human Tissues. *Proc Natl Acad Sci USA*, 1987; 84:7735-7738

Tirona RG and Kim RB. Pharmacogenomics of Drug Transporters. In: Licinio J and Wong M-L. *Pharmacogenomics the Search for Individualized Therapies*. Weinheim, Germany: WILEY-VCH Verlag GmbH; 2002: 179-213

Tirona RG, Leake BF, Merino G, and Kim RB. Polymorphisms in OATP-C: Identification of Multiple Allelic Variants Associated with Altered Transport Activity among European- and African-Americans. *J Biol Chem*, 2001; 276:35669-35675

Tsuji A and Tamai I. Carrier-Mediated Intestinal Transport of Drugs. *Pharm Res*, 1996; 13:963-977

Tsujii H, Konig J, Rost D, Stockel B, Leuschner U, and Keppler D. Exon-Intron Organization of the Human Multidrug-Resistance Protein 2 (MRP2) Gene Mutated in Dubin-Johnson Syndrome. *Gastroenterology*, 1999; 117:653-660

van Aubel RA, Smeets PH, Peters JG, Bindels RJ, and Russel FG. The MRP4/ABCC4 Gene Encodes a Novel Apical Organic Anion Transporter in Human Kidney Proximal Tubules: Putative Efflux Pump for Urinary cAMP and cGMP. *J Am Soc Nephrol*, 2002; 13:595-603

van Montfoort JE, Hagenbuch B, Fattinger KE, Muller M, Groothuis GM, Meijer DK, and Meier PJ. Polyspecific Organic Anion Transporting Polypeptides Mediate Hepatic Uptake of Amphipathic Type II Organic Cations. *J Pharmacol Exp Ther*, 1999; 291:147-152

Venter JC, Adams MD, Myers EW, Li PW, Mural RJ, Sutton GG, Smith HO, Yandell M, Evans CA, Holt RA *et al*. The Sequence of the Human Genome. *Science*, 2001; 291:1304-1351

Volk EL and Schneider E. Wild-Type Breast Cancer Resistance Protein (BCRP/ABCG2) Is a Methotrexate Polyglutamate Transporter. *Cancer Res*, 2003; 63:5538-5543

Wada S, Tsuda M, Sekine T, Cha SH, Kimura M, Kanai Y, and Endou H. Rat Multispecific Organic Anion Transporter 1 (rOAT1) Transports Zidovudine, Acyclovir, and Other Antiviral Nucleoside Analogs. *J Pharmacol Exp Ther*, 2000; 294:844-849

Walters HC, Craddock AL, Fusegawa H, Willingham MC, and Dawson PA. Expression, Transport Properties, and Chromosomal Location of Organic Anion Transporter Subtype 3. *Am J Physiol Gastrointest Liver Physiol*, 2000; 279:G1188-1200

Wang J, Near S, Young K, Connelly PW, and Hegele RA. ABCC6 Gene Polymorphism Associated with Variation in Plasma Lipoproteins. *J Hum Genet*, 2001a; 46:699-705

Wang R, Salem M, Yousef IM, Tuchweber B, Lam P, Childs SJ, Helgason CD, Ackerley C, Phillips MJ, and Ling V. Targeted Inactivation of Sister of P-Glycoprotein Gene (spgp) in Mice Results in Nonprogressive but Persistent Intrahepatic Cholestasis. *Proc Natl Acad Sci USA*, 2001b; 98:2011-2016

Weinman SA. Electrogenicity of Na(+)-Coupled Bile Acid Transporters. *Yale J Biol Med*, 1997; 70:331-340

Weinman SA, Carruth MW and Dawson PA. Bile Acid Uptake Via the Human Apical Sodium-Bile Acid Cotransporter Is Electrogenic. *J Biol Chem*, 1998; 273:34691-34695

Wijnholds J, deLange EC, Scheffer GL, van den Berg DJ, Mol CA, van der Valk M, Schinkel AH, Scheper RJ, Breimer DD, and Borst P. Multidrug Resistance Protein 1 Protects the Choroid Plexus Epithelium and Contributes to the Blood-Cerebrospinal Fluid Barrier. *J Clin Invest*, 2000; 105:279-285

Williams GC, Liu A, Knipp G, and Sinko PJ. Direct Evidence That Saquinavir Is Transported by Multidrug Resistance-Associated Protein (MRP1) and Canalicular Multispecific Organic Anion Transporter (MRP2). *Antimicrob Agents Chemother*, 2002; 46:3456-3462

Wong MH, Oelkers P and Dawson PA. Identification of a Mutation in the Ileal Sodium-Dependent Bile Acid Transporter Gene That Abolishes Transport Activity. *J Biol Chem*, 1995; 270:27228-27234

Wong MH, Oelkers P, Craddock AL, and Dawson PA. Expression Cloning and Characterization of the Hamster Ileal Sodium-Dependent Bile Acid Transporter. *J Biol Chem*, 1994; 269:1340-1347

Yabuuchi H, Shimizu H, Takayanagi S, and Ishikawa T. Multiple Splicing Variants of Two New Human ATP-Binding Cassette Transporters, ABCC11 and ABCC12. *Biochem Biophys Res Commun*, 2001; 288:933-939

Yamazaki M, Akiyama S, Ni'inuma K, Nishigaki R, and Sugiyama Y. Biliary Excretion of Pravastatin in Rats: Contribution of the Excretion Pathway Mediated by Canalicular Multispecific Organic Anion Transporter. *Drug Metab Dispos*, 1997; 25:1123-1129

Zaman GJ, Flens MJ, van Leusden MR, de Haas M, Mulder HS, Lankelma J, Pinedo HM, Scheper RJ, Baas F, Broxterman HJ *et al*. The Human Multidrug Resistance-Associated Protein MRP Is a Plasma Membrane Drug-Efflux Pump. *Proc Natl Acad Sci USA*, 1994; 91:8822-8826

Zelcer N, Saeki T, Reid G, Beijnen JH, and Borst P. Characterization of Drug Transport by the Human Multidrug Resistance Protein 3 (ABCC3). *J Biol Chem*, 2001; 276:46400-46407

Zeng H, Bain LJ, Belinsky MG, and Kruh GD. Expression of Multidrug Resistance Protein-3 (Multispecific Organic Anion Transporter-D) in Human Embryonic Kidney 293 Cells Confers Resistance to Anticancer Agents. *Cancer Res*, 1999; 59:5964-5967

Zeng H, Liu G, Rea PA, and Kruh GD. Transport of Amphipathic Anions by Human Multidrug Resistance Protein 3. *Cancer Res*, 2000; 60:4779-4784

Zhou S, Morris JJ, Barnes Y, Lan L, Schuetz JD, and Sorrentino BP. Bcrp1 Gene Expression Is Required for Normal Numbers of Side Population Stem Cells in Mice, and Confers Relative Protection to Mitoxantrone in Hematopoietic Cells *in Vivo. Proc Natl Acad Sci USA*, 2002; 99:12339-12344

Index

Page numbers followed by f or t indicate figures or tables, respectively.

A

B

D

E

F

N

O

P